Brief Lives

Brief Lives

TWENTIETH-CENTURY PEN PORTRAITS FROM *THE DICTIONARY OF NATIONAL BIOGRAPHY*

Selected by
COLIN MATTHEW

Oxford New York
OXFORD UNIVERSITY PRESS
1997

Oxford University Press, Great Clarendon Street, Oxford OX2 6DP

Oxford New York
Athens Auckland Bangkok Bogota Bombay Buenos Aires
Calcutta Cape Town Dar es Salaam Delhi Florence Hong Kong Istanbul
Karachi Kuala Lumpur Madras Madrid Melbourne Mexico City
Nairobi Paris Singapore Taipei Tokyo Toronto Warsaw

and associated companies in
Berlin Ibadan

Oxford is a trade mark of Oxford University Press

First published 1997

British Library Cataloguing in Publication Data
Data available

Library of Congress Cataloging in Publication Data
Data available
ISBN 0–19–860087–9

1 3 5 7 9 10 8 6 4 2

Typeset by Interactive Sciences Ltd, Gloucester
Printed in Great Britain
on acid-free paper by
Bookcraft (Bath) Ltd
Midsomer Norton, Somerset

Brief Lives

Selections from the twentieth-century DNB

The *Dictionary of National Biography* contains the great and the good, the bad and the exotic. This selection of 150 articles contains examples of each. It does not set out to give a systematic representation either of the contents of the *DNB* or of the character of the British public life which its twentieth-century *Supplements* predominantly record. Rather, it is a personal selection of interesting articles on interesting people, which presents in one volume something of the flavour of the way the British have written about their recently dead contemporaries. Perhaps surprisingly, this is the first-ever published selection of articles from the *DNB*.

For the most part, I have chosen articles on people who died after the Second World War and before 1990 (the end-date of the most recent of the *DNB*'s *Supplements*). The earliest birthdate is that of Harry Lauder (born 1870), closely followed by Bertrand Russell (born 1872) and Winston Churchill (born 1874), and the latest birthdates are those of John Winston Lennon (1940) and Jacqueline du Pré (1945); among the latest deathdates are those of Roald Dahl and Leonard Hutton (both died 1990). I have included articles on monarchs, politicians, clergymen, business people, entertainers, musicians, artists, authors, sportsmen and women, and academics and scientists, criminals and spies. There are two monarchs (Edward VIII and George VI), three prime ministers (Churchill, Attlee, and Macmillan), and five husband-and-wife couples with an article on each spouse (Laurence Olivier and Vivien Leigh, Jennie Lee and Aneurin Bevan, Bertrand and Dora Russell, Leonard and Virginia Woolf, Edward VIII and the Duchess of Windsor).

All these articles were written not long after the subject's death, usually by a colleague or a friend. The articles are often piquant in catching the subject's reputation when he or she was still a contemporary rather than an historial figure. They have the advantage of the author's often intimate knowledge of the subject, and the disadvantage that such personal familiarity sometimes encourages considerable reticence. 'Personal knowledge' and 'Private information' have always been frequent sources of information for such articles.

Supplements to the *DNB* began at the start of the twentieth century, to continue the first A–Z series (whose title was 'from the Earliest Times to 1900'). For most of the century a supplement covered a decade; recently they have covered five-year periods. The first supplement was edited by Sidney Lee, who, with Leslie Stephen, had been co-editor for the original series. The editors for the volumes from which this selection has been made were: L. G. Wickham Legg, E. T. Williams, Helen M. Palmer, C. S. Nicholls, Lord Blake, and Sir Keith Thomas.

Unlike some other national biographical dictionaries, the *DNB* has encouraged individualism on the part of its contributors. Its articles give one person's view of another. The articles always have the same opening format, but after that their character (and length) varies. Even the opening format is less straightforward than it seems at first glance: Clement Attlee, it is said, used to enjoy pondering what he felt was the *DNB*'s idiosyncratic use of the descriptions 'statesman' and 'politician'. Articles in the *DNB* yield many such pleasures: it is a work to ponder and to browse in. I hope this brief selection from its recent articles will be a convenient companion for those who already know it and a stimulating introduction for those who do not.

COLIN MATTHEW

May 1997

Contents

Contents

Contents

Contents

Contents

ABRAHAMS Harold Maurice

(1899–1978)

Athlete, sports administrator, and civil servant, was born at 30 Rutland Road, Bedford, 15 December 1899, the youngest in the family of two daughters and four sons of Isaac Klonimus of Vladislavovi in Russian-occupied Poland and his wife, Esther Isaacs, of Merthyr Tydfil. Klonimus (1850–1921), who proclaimed himself a Lithuanian Jew, escaped to Britain and by 1880 had changed his name to Abrahams, in recognition of his father Abraham Klonimus (born 1810).

Though Isaac Abrahams never mastered the script (and barely the speech) of his host country, he set up the Bedfordshire Loan Company in 1885 and was naturalized in 1902. In the county town in addition to money lending he dealt as a certificated pedlar in jewellery, gold, and silver plate. Despite their tempestuous marriage Esther and he raised four remarkable sons. Adolphe, the eldest, after gaining firsts at Emmanuel College, Cambridge, became a consultant physician at Westminster Hospital and was knighted in 1939. 'Solly', later Sir Sidney Solomon Abrahams, who competed for Britain at both the Olympic celebrations at Athens (1906) and Stockholm (1912), was sworn of the Privy Council after serving as chief justice of Tanganyika and Ceylon (Sri Lanka). The third son Lionel became senior partner of his firm of solicitors and was coroner for Huntingdonshire.

Harold Abrahams was sent to Bedford School, briefly to St Paul's, and afterwards to Repton where he won the public schools' 100 yards and long-jump championships in 1918. His imagination had been fired in the summer of 1908 when he watched his brother compete in the fourth Olympic Games at the White City stadium, London. He served briefly as a second lieutenant in 1919 and then went up to Gonville and Caius College, Cambridge, to read law. If the road to popularity at university lies in never inculcating a sense of inferiority into one's contemporaries, Abrahams stood little chance of being popular. Athletically he swept all before him with three wins in the freshman's sports at Fenners and was immediately selected for the sixth Olympic Games in Antwerp. He won a unique eight victories at the 100 yards, 440 yards, and long jump in the annual Oxford versus Cambridge sports. His election to the Hawks Club was opposed due to a contribution to *The Times*, which the committee regarded as immodest. *Chariots of Fire*, a highly successful film on the life of Abrahams, stressed an anti-Semitic undertone of his time at Cambridge. Though he did not live to see the film, Abrahams, on his own testimony, would certainly have regarded such a portrayal as over-fanciful.

Before the next Olympic Games in 1924, which was to be held in the Stade de Colombes in Paris, he trained assiduously with his north-country coach Sam Mussabini, a French Arab. For nine months they worked on the theory of perfecting the start, on arm action, control of the stride pattern, and a then-unique 'drop' finish of the torso on to the tape. At the 1924 Amateur Athletic Association championship Abrahams won the 100 yards in 9.9 seconds but was still a fifth of a second outside the British record set the previous year by the great Scottish rugby and athletic hero and 440-yards champion, Eric Liddell. In Paris the twenty-three eliminating heats to bring the seventy-five starters down to twelve semi-finalists were to be staged on Sunday 6 July and Liddell, a strong Sabbatarian, felt impelled to confine himself to the 200 and 400 metres in which he took the bronze medal in the shorter event and the gold medal for 400 metres in a time which gave him the metric world record. Abrahams equalled the Olympic record in the 100 metres in the second round with 10.6 seconds and next day, despite being badly 'left' in a poor start in the semi-final, came through (again in 10.6 seconds) to beat by inches the world record holder Charles Paddock from the USA. Abrahams later said that the next three-and-three-quarter hours were the worst in his life because now he knew he could win. At 7.05 p.m. he came out with the four Americans, Paddock, Scholz, Murchison, and Bowman and the Oxford Rhodes scholar Arthur (later Lord) Porritt, from New Zealand.

Abrahams was drawn in lane four and got a perfect start. He showed fractionally ahead at half-way and dropped on to the tape two feet clear of Scholz with Porritt beating Bowman for third. His winning time of 10.52 seconds would under present rules be returned as 10.5 but was rounded up to 10.6. Abrahams thus set three Olympic record-equalling performances in the space of twenty-six hours. In Paris there were no flag-raising victory ceremonies. His gold medal, sadly later stolen, was sent to him by post. In May 1925, now a barrister, Abrahams severely injured a leg when attempting to improve on his English native long-jump record of 24 feet $2\frac{3}{4}$ inches (7.38 metres), which survived for more than thirty years.

His athletic career ended, he applied his analytical mind to the bar (to which he had been called—Inner Temple—in 1924), where he practised until 1940. He also engaged in athletic administration and journalism with the *Sunday Times* (1925–67), and was a consummate radio broadcaster with the BBC for fifty years (1924–74). Against the stolid petty opposition of senior office-holders in various governing bodies, often athletes *manqués*, he managed by sheer force of personality and with very few allies to raise athletics from a minor to a major national sport. His innovative mind and drafting ability enabled him to rewrite the AAA rules of competition which themselves transformed the rules of the International Amateur Athletic Federation. He was possessed of a fresh resonant voice while his clear diction and wide vocabulary were models for any English-speaker.

He served as honorary treasurer (1948–68) and chairman (1948–75) of the British Amateur Athletic Board. In November 1976 he was elected president of the AAA. He was an unrivalled compiler of athletics statistics and was founder-president of both the world and British associations in this field. His *Oxford versus Cambridge 1827–1930* (compiled with J. Bruce-Kerr, 1931), which listed all the 7,489 blues, must have resulted in the exposure of many self-appointed ones in the bars and clubs of the world. During World War II he was with the Ministry of Economic Warfare (1939–44) and with the new Ministry of Town and Country Planning until 1963. He was secretary of the National Parks Commission (1950–63). He was appointed CBE in 1957.

In 1936 Abrahams married Sybil Marjorie, daughter of Claude Pilington Evers, assistant master at Rugby School. She was a singer and producer of light opera and died suddenly in 1963. They had an adopted daughter and an adopted son. Abrahams died 14 January 1978 at Chase Farm Hospital, Enfield.

[Private information; personal knowledge.]

Norris McWhirter

published 1986

ALEXANDER Harold Rupert Leofric George (1891–1969)

First Earl Alexander of Tunis

Field-marshal, was born in London 10 December 1891, the third son of James Alexander, fourth Earl of Caledon, and his wife, Lady Elizabeth Graham-Toler, daughter of the third Earl of Norbury. His youth was spent at the family estate, Caledon Castle, in the county Tyrone. His father, who had served briefly in the Life Guards but was better known as an adventurous deep-water yachtsman, died when Alexander was six; his mother, eccentric and imperious, held aloof from her children; but their four sons were perfectly happy in their own company. It was in Northern Ireland that Alexander developed both the athletic and the aesthetic sides of his character; he trained himself as a runner and enjoyed all the usual country sports, but he also taught himself to carve in wood and stone and began what was to prove one of the main passions of his life, painting. After reading Reynolds's *Discourses on Art* he decided that the thing he wanted most in the world was to be president of the Royal Academy. At Harrow he worked well enough to rise smoothly up the school. His games were cricket, athletics, rackets, rugger, boxing, fencing, and gymnastics and he won distinction at all of them; he is best remembered as nearly saving the game for Harrow in what *Wisden* called the most extraordinary cricket match ever played, at Lord's in 1910. He also won a school prize for drawing.

He went on to the Royal Military College, Sandhurst, and was commissioned in the Irish Guards in 1911. Although he was pleased at the idea of spending a few years in a Guards battalion, he intended to retire before long and make a living as an artist. These plans were upset by the outbreak of war in 1914. Alexander's battalion went to France in August and he served there continuously until early 1919, being in action throughout except when recovering from wounds or on courses. He was twice wounded, awarded the MC (1915), and appointed to the DSO (1916). Promotion was rapid. A lieutenant when he arrived, he became a captain in February 1915, a major, one of the youngest in the army, eight months later, with the acting command of the 1st battalion of his own regiment, and a lieutenant-colonel, commanding the 2nd battalion, in October 1917. During the retreat from Arras in March 1918 he was acting brigadier-general in command of the 4th Guards brigade.

The war was a turning-point in Alexander's character and career. He had painted in the trenches, and he continued to paint throughout his life, reaching at times a standard only just short of the professional; but in the course of the war he had come to realize the fascination of the profession of arms, and had proved to himself, and demonstrated to others, that he was outstandingly competent at it. His reputation stood very high for courage but also for a cheerful imperturbability in all circumstances. For four years he lived the life of a regimental officer, without any staff service; he later criticized senior commanders of that war for never seeking personal experience of the conditions of the fighting troops.

Not wishing to go back to barracks or to the army of occupation in Germany, he applied in 1919 for an appointment to one of the many military missions in Eastern Europe. He was first posted as a member of the Allied Relief Commission in Poland under (Sir) Stephen Tallents and later went with Tallents to Latvia which was in danger of falling either to Russia or to Germany. The Allies had no troops in the Baltic and only a small naval detachment under Sir Walter Cowan. Tallents placed the *Landwehr*, composed of Baltic Germans, under Alexander's command. At the age of twenty-seven he found himself at the head of a brigade-sized formation with mainly German officers. He was good at languages and had taught himself German and Russian; his authority derived from his charm and sincerity and his obvious professionalism. He kept his men steady and resistant to the attractions of the German expeditionary force under von der Goltz and led them to victory in the campaign which drove the Red Army from Latvia.

Alexander retained all his life a keen interest in Russia. During the war of 1914–18 he designed a new uniform cap for himself with a high visor and flat peak, on the model of one he had seen a Russian officer wearing. He always wore the Order of St Anne with swords which Yudenitch awarded him in 1919; when he met Rokossovsky in 1945 the Russian general muttered to him in an aside that he had once had it too. In the second war, like Churchill, he admired Stalin and was enthusiastic about the Soviet Army.

After the Soviet Union recognized the independence of Latvia in 1920 Alexander returned to England to become second-in-command of his regiment. In 1922 he was given command and took it to Constantinople as part of the army of occupation. In 1923, after the treaty of Lausanne, the regiment went to Gibraltar and thence in 1924 to England. In 1926–7 he was at the Staff College. He was very senior in rank, a full colonel, but for the duration of the course he was temporarily reduced to the rank of major. After commanding the regiment and regimental district of the Irish Guards (1928–30), he attended the Imperial Defence College. This was followed by the only two staff appointments in his career, as GSO 2 at the War Office (1931–2) and as GSO 1 at Northern Command (1932–4). He was already widely regarded as likely to make the outstanding fighting commander of a future war; the other name mentioned, from the Indian Army, was that of (Sir) Claude Auchinleck.

In 1934 Alexander was appointed to command the Nowshera brigade on the North-West Frontier, one of the most coveted in India. Auchinleck commanded the next brigade, in Peshawar. Alexander surprised and delighted his Indian troops by learning Urdu as rapidly and fluently as he had Russian and German. Next year he commanded the brigade in the Loc Agra campaign (called after a small village north of the Malakand pass) against invading tribesmen; and not long after, under Auchinleck's command as the senior brigadier, in the Mohmand campaign. Both operations were successful; roads were built, large regions pacified; Alexander was appointed CSI (1936). It was noted not only that he had mastered the difficult techniques of fighting in mountainous country but also that he was always to be seen with the foremost troops. This was both a revulsion from the behaviour he had condemned in his senior commanders in

France and a natural result of his personal courage; it remained to the end a characteristic of his style of leadership.

His promotion to major-general in 1937, at the age of forty-five, made him the youngest general in the British Army; in 1938 he was given command of the 1st division at Aldershot. In 1939 he took the division to France as one of the two in I Corps under Sir John Dill. In the retreat to Dunkirk his division only once fought a serious if brief battle, when he successfully defended the Scheldt for two days, throwing back all German penetrations; for the rest of the time he was obliged to fall back to conform to the movement of other divisions. It was Dunkirk which first brought his name prominently before the public notice. I Corps was to form the final rearguard and Lord Gort superseded the corps commander and put Alexander in command. His orders were definite: to withdraw all the British troops who could be saved. A different interpretation of the military necessities of the moment was held by the French commander, Admiral Abrial, and Alexander confessed that to carry out his orders while leaving the French still fighting made him feel that he 'had never been in such a terrible situation'. During the three days in which he commanded, 20,000 British and 98,000 French were evacuated: Alexander left on the last motor launch in which he toured the beaches to see that there were no British troops remaining.

On his return to England he was confirmed in command of I Corps which was responsible for the defence of the east coast from Scarborough to the Wash. Promoted lieutenant-general, in December 1940 he succeeded Auchinleck at Southern Command. He showed himself an admirable trainer of troops and was the first to introduce the realistic 'battle-schools' which became so prominent a feature of military life from 1940 to 1944. He was also put in command of a nominal 'Force 110' which was to be used for amphibious operations; he and his staff planned a number which never came off, such as the invasion of the Canaries and of Sicily.

In February 1942 Alexander was suddenly informed that he was to take command of the army in Burma where the situation was already desperate. The key battle had been lost before Alexander arrived; the Japanese were across the Sittang river, in a position to encircle and capture Rangoon. It was by the greatest good fortune, and the oversight of a Japanese divisional commander in leaving open one narrow escape route, that Alexander himself and the bulk of his forces were able to escape from Rangoon which, in obedience to ill-considered orders from Sir A. P. (later Earl) Wavell, he had tried to hold almost beyond the last reasonable moment. After its fall Burma had no future military value except as a glacis for the defence of India. Alexander decided that the only success he could snatch from the jaws of unmitigated defeat was to rescue the army under his command by withdrawing it to India. It was a campaign of which he always spoke with compunction and distaste, except for his admiration for General (later Viscount) Slim. Left entirely without guidance after the fall of Rangoon—not that the guidance he had received previously had been of any value—Alexander did the best he could. As a further sign of the gifts he was to display as an Allied commander, it should be recorded that he got on the best of terms not only with Chiang Kai Chek but also with General J. W. Stilwell.

It might be thought that two defeats in succession would have meant the end to Alexander's hopes of high command. Churchill had shown no mercy to Gort or Wavell and was to show none to Auchinleck. But as he wrote in *The Hinge of Fate* (1951), in sending Alexander to Burma 'never have I taken the responsibility for sending a general on a more forlorn hope'. He had formed so high an appreciation of Alexander's ability that he immediately confirmed his designation as commander-in-chief of the First Army which was to invade North Africa, under Eisenhower's command, in November 1942 when the Allies for the first time seized the strategic initiative. But before that could take effect, Churchill felt impelled in early August to visit Egypt. Auchinleck was more impressive in the field than in conversation in his caravan; Churchill decided to replace him with Alexander. It is ironical that one of the main reasons why Auchinleck was replaced was that he declared himself unable to take the offensive until September: Churchill was to accept from Alexander, with but little remonstrance, a postponement until late October.

Alexander took over as commander-in-chief, Middle East, on 15 August 1942. For the first time he found himself in a position which was not only not desperate but full of promise. He had a numerical superiority, and at last equality of equipment, against an army fighting at the end of a long and precarious line of communication with its bases and debilitated by sickness. General Gott, who was to have been his army commander, was killed; but he was replaced immediately by General Montgomery (later Viscount Montgomery of Alamein) who had been one of Alexander's corps commanders in Southern Command and whose capacities as a trainer and inspirer of men were well known to him. He had a sound defensive position, strongly manned, and plans had been prepared for the expected enemy assault; they were based on a partial refusal of the left flank while holding the strong position of Alam Halfa, fortified and prepared by Auchinleck, to block an advance on Alexandria. Reinforcements in men and tanks continued to arrive. Nevertheless there was a problem of morale, since the Eighth Army had been fighting in retreat since May and had lost one position after another; it was natural for the troops to wonder whether they might not find themselves retreating once more. The first step towards victory in Egypt was when Alexander made it known, as soon as he assumed command, that there was to be no further retreat; the decisive battle was to be fought on the Alamein line.

The defensive battle of Alam Halfa and the offensive battle of Alamein were, as Alexander always insisted, Montgomery's victories. He had always had the gift of delegating and no one was more generous in acknowledging the merits of his subordinates. There is reason for argument whether, after the failure of the first plan at Alamein, *Lightfoot*, part of the credit for *Supercharge*, the modified version, should go to suggestions from Alexander. In truth the two generals, the commander-in-chief and the army commander, were aptly suited to their respective roles and played them well. The successful campaign in Egypt, won at almost the lowest point in the Allied fortunes, marked the beginning of a period in which British and Allied armies knew scarcely anything but success.

The invasion of North Africa in November meant that after two months a British Army, the First, with a French and an American corps, was fighting in northern and central Tunisia against a mixed German-Italian army and meanwhile the German-Italian Armoured Army of Africa, defeated at Alamein, was withdrawing towards southern Tunisia pursued by the Eighth Army. It was evident that a headquarters was required to command and co-ordinate the two Allied armies. Alexander was summoned to the Casablanca conference of January 1943. He made a great impression on President Roosevelt, General Marshall, and the United States chiefs of staff; his reputation at home had never been higher. The conference decided to appoint him deputy commander-in-chief to General Eisenhower with command over all the forces actually fighting the enemy. He set up a very small headquarters, called the 18th Army Group from the numbers of the two British armies which made up the bulk of his command; this was originally located in the town of Constantine, but as soon as he could Alexander moved out into the field and operated from a tented camp, moved frequently.

The Tunisian campaign provides a convincing proof of Alexander's capacity as a strategist. It also demonstrates his great gift of inspiring and elevating the morale of the troops he commanded, as well as his skill in welding together the efforts of different nationalities. At the beginning he faced a difficult task. The southern flank of his western front had been driven in by a bold enemy thrust which threatened to come in upon the communications of the whole deployment. Alexander was on the spot, even before the date at which he was officially to assume command (20 February 1943); he was seen directing the siting of gun positions at the approaches to the Kasserine pass. This was a flash of his old style but it was not long before he took a firm grip on higher things and reorganized the whole direction of the campaign. He sorted out the confusion into which the First Army had been thrown by the rapid vicissitudes of the past, brought into play the ponderous but skilful thrust of the Eighth Army, and directed the efforts of both in the final victory of Tunis. In this last battle in Africa he employed an elaborate and successful plan of deception, based on an accurate knowledge of enemy dispositions and intentions, and broke through their strong defensive front with a powerful and well-concealed offensive blow. In two days all was over. A quarter of a million enemy were captured. On 13 May he was able to make his historic signal to the prime minister: 'Sir, it is my duty to report that the Tunisian campaign is over. All enemy resistance has ceased. We are masters of the North African shores.'

Sicily was the next objective on which the Casablanca conference had decided. The forces commanded by Alexander, as commander-in-chief 15th Army Group, consisted of the United States Seventh and British Eighth armies. The principal interest in the campaign lies in the immense size of the amphibious effort required, larger in the assault phase even than for the invasion of Normandy, and in the elaborate planning which preceded it. It fell to Alexander to decide on the final form of the plan, a concentrated assault on the south-eastern corner of the island, rather than, as originally proposed by the planning staff, two separate attacks in the south-east and the north-west. In this decision he was vindicated, mainly because of his correct assessment of the new possibilities of beach maintenance produced by recently acquired amphibious equipment. In the course of the first few days, however, he made one of his few strategic errors in yielding to Montgomery's insistence that the Eighth Army could finish off the campaign by itself if the United States Seventh Army were kept out of its way; admittedly Alexander was deceived by inaccurate reports of the progress that the Eighth Army was making. As a result the reduction of the island took rather longer than expected and a high proportion of the German defenders managed to withdraw into Calabria. Nevertheless, the capture of Sicily in thirty-eight days was not only a notable strategic gain but also brought encouraging confirmation of the validity of the methods of amphibious warfare of which so much was expected in the next year's invasion of France.

That invasion was the principal factor affecting the last two years of Alexander's career as a commander in the field, during which he was engaged on the mainland of Italy. His troops were now no longer the spearhead of the Allied military effort in Europe. He was required to give up, for the benefit of the western front, many divisions of his best troops on three occasions and his task was defined as to eliminate Italy from the war and to contain the maximum number of German divisions. The first part of this directive was rapidly achieved. In his second task also, which from September 1943 onwards represented the sole object of the campaign, he was strikingly successful. So far from diverting troops from Italy to the decisive front, the Germans continuously reinforced it, not only robbing the Russian front but even sending divisions from the west. To obtain this success, however, in a terrain always favouring the defence, Alexander was obliged to maintain the offensive and to compensate for the lack of superior force by using all the arts of generalship.

'The campaign in Italy was a great holding attack', Alexander states in his dispatch. As is the nature of holding attacks, it was directed against a secondary theatre. Nevertheless it gave scope for daring strategic planning in spite of the odds and of the forbidding and mountainous nature of the ground. The initial assault at Salerno, simultaneous with the announcement of the Italian surrender, was a good example; a force of only three divisions, all that could be carried in the landing craft allotted to the theatre, was thrown on shore at the extreme limit of air cover. The landing at Anzio was a masterpiece of deception which caught the enemy off balance and forced him to send reinforcements to Italy. It made a vital contribution to the offensive of May and June 1944 in which the Germans were driven north of Rome, with disproportionately heavy losses in men and equipment. For this offensive Alexander made a secret redeployment of his two armies and mounted a most ingenious plan of deception; his opponent, Field-Marshal Kesselring, was unable to react in time, for all that his defensive positions were strong both by nature and artificially. The capture of Rome just before the landing in Normandy was a fillip to Allied morale. A more important result from the point of view of Allied grand strategy was that this crushing defeat obliged the Germans to reinforce Italy with eight fresh divisions, some taken from their western garrisons; a month later, in contrast, Alexander was ordered to surrender seven of his divisions for the campaign in France. The final battle, in April 1945, was another example of Alexander's skill in deployment and in deception; by 2 May he had routed the most coherent enemy group of armies still resisting; all Italy had been overrun and a million Germans had laid down their arms in the first big surrender of the war.

The Italian campaign showed Alexander at the height of his powers. These included besides the skill of a strategist a thorough grasp of the principles of administration. As an Allied commander he was supreme; there were no instances of friction anywhere in his command in spite of its varied composition, including at one time or another troops from Britain, the United States, India, Canada, New Zealand, South Africa, France, Poland, Italy, Brazil, and Greece. For the greater part of the campaign, as commander-in-chief of 15th Army Group, later renamed Allied Armies in Italy, he acted as an independent commander, since it had been agreed that the commander-in-chief, Mediterranean, Sir Maitland (later Lord) Wilson, should concern himself primarily with the general maintenance of the Italian campaign and with the security of the other areas of the command.

On 12 December 1944 Alexander succeeded Wilson. He was appointed to the rank of field-marshal to date from 4 June 1944, on which day the Allied armies entered Rome. But for all his high rank and heavy responsibilities he remembered his criticism of the commanders in the war of 1914–18. He always spent more time with the forward troops than in his headquarters. His popularity was immense, and his strategic planning benefited because he knew what the war was like at the point that counted.

After the war it was expected by some that Alexander would become chief of the imperial general staff. But W. L. Mackenzie King invited him to be governor-general of Canada, and Churchill pressed him to accept. His sense of duty was reinforced by a strong attraction to the idea of serving Canada. His extended tenure of office ran from 1946 to 1952. He was the last British governor-general and his popularity was as great as that of any of his predecessors. He was comparatively young and brought a young family with him; he toured the whole country, played games, skied, and painted. To his dignity as the representative of the King in Canada and his reputation as a war leader he added an informal friendliness and charm. While in Canada he produced his official dispatches on his campaigns published in the *London Gazette*; they have been described by his biographer as 'among the great state papers of our military history'.

In January 1952 Churchill visited Ottawa and offered Alexander the post of minister of defence in his Government. When a friend remonstrated he replied: 'Of course I accepted. It's my duty.' To another friend he said, 'I simply can't refuse Winston.' As he entered on his first political post in that frame of mind it is not surprising that he did not much enjoy his period of office. He was not temperamentally suited to political life and in any case he had few real powers to exercise. Churchill continued to behave as though it was he who was the minister of defence and Alexander his spokesman in the Lords. Nevertheless, Alexander had the assets of his great personal popularity, his charm, and the fact that he numbered so many personal friends among foreign statesmen and military men, especially in the United States, and especially after the election of President Eisenhower. He made no particular mark as minister of defence because he preferred to rely on discreet persuasion and guidance; but he led a good team and suffered no diminution of his reputation. After two and a half years he resigned at his own request, in the autumn of 1954.

In the last fifteen years of his life he accepted a number of directorates. He was most active as director of Alcan and also served on the boards of Barclay's Bank and Phoenix Assurance. He travelled extensively on business for Alcan. He continued to paint and devoted more and more time to it. In 1960 he was persuaded by the *Sunday Times* to allow his memoirs to be ghosted. They were edited by John North and published in 1962, but were not very favourably received because of the curiously disorganized and anecdotal form. His motive in agreeing to publication was the desire to see that justice was done to the armies in Italy; for himself he preferred to be judged on the basis of his dispatches. For the rest he devoted himself to his garden and to reunions with old comrades. He died suddenly after a heart attack on 16 July 1969, in hospital in Slough. His funeral service was held in St. George's Chapel, Windsor, and he was buried in the churchyard of Ridge, near Tyttenhanger, his family's Hertfordshire home. The headstone of his grave bears at the top the single word ALEX, the name by which he was known to his friends and his soldiers.

He married in 1931 Lady Margaret Diana Bingham (died 1977), younger daughter of the fifth earl of Lucan; she was appointed GBE in 1954. They had two sons, one daughter, and an adopted daughter. He was succeeded by his elder son, Shane William Desmond (born 1935).

Alexander was created a viscount in 1946 and an earl in 1952 on his return from Canada. He was appointed CB (1938), KCB and GCB (1942), GCMG on his appointment to Canada, and in the same year (1946) KG. He was sworn of the Privy Council in 1952 and also of the Canadian Privy Council. In 1959 he was admitted to the Order of Merit. He was colonel of the Irish Guards from 1946 to his death, constable of the Tower of London from 1960 to 1965. From 1957 to 1965 he was lieutenant of the county of London, and for a further year of Greater London. He was chancellor and then grand master of the Order of St. Michael and St. George, an elder brother of Trinity House, and in 1955 president of the MCC. He was a freeman of the City of London and of many other cities. His numerous foreign decorations included the grand cross of the Legion of Honour and the Legion of Merit and Distinguished Service Medal of the United States.

Alexander was 5 feet 10 inches tall, slim, muscular, and handsome. His features were regular in the style which when he was young was regarded as typical of the army officer; he wore a trim Guardsman's moustache all his life. He dressed with careful and unaffected elegance on all occasions; his Russian-style cap was only the precursor of a number of variations on uniform regulations whereas in plain clothes he favoured neatness, fashion, and the avoidance of the elaborate.

There are two portraits of him at the National Portrait Gallery, by

Edward Seago (a close personal friend) and by Maurice Codner; and two at the Imperial War Museum, by R. G. Eves and Harry Carr. The Irish Guards have two, by John Gilroy and Richard Jack; another version of the Gilroy portrait is in McGill University, Montreal. White's Club has a portrait by Sir Oswald Birley. The National Portrait Gallery has a sculptured bust by Donald Gilbert. A bronze bust by Oscar Nemon, in the Old Radcliffe Observatory at Oxford, was unveiled by Queen Elizabeth the Queen Mother in 1973 to mark the endowment of a chair of cardio-vascular medicine at the university in Alexander's memory. In the possession of the family is a bronze bust by Anthony Gray.

[Nigel Nicolson, *Alex*, 1973; dispatches in *London Gazette*, 5 and 12 February 1948, 12 June 1950; I. S. O. Playfair and C. J. C. Molony, and others, (Official) *History of the Second World War. The Mediterranean and Middle East*, vol. iv, 1966, and C. J. C. Molony and others, vol. v, 1973; personal knowledge.]

DAVID HUNT

published 1981

ASHLEY Laura

(1925–1985)

Dress designer, interior decorator, and entrepreneur, was born 7 September 1925 at Dowlais, near Merthyr Tydfil, south Wales, the eldest of the four children (two daughters and two sons) of Stanley Lewis Mountney, a civil servant, of Raleigh Avenue, Wallington, Surrey, and his wife, Margaret Elizabeth Davis. She was educated at Elmwood School, Croydon, and at the Aberdare Secretarial School, before becoming a secretary in the City of London at the age of sixteen. In the latter years of World War II she served in the WRNS. After the war she worked at the London headquarters of the Women's Institute.

During the war she had met Bernard Albert, son of Albert Ashley, grocer. In 1949 they were married; they had two sons and two daughters. In the early 1950s Laura designed tea towels which Bernard printed on a printing machine he had designed and developed in an attic in Pimlico. This was followed by the opening of a small mill in Kent to produce a greater range of products but a disastrous flood brought this particular phase of enterprise to an end. In the early 1960s Laura persuaded Bernard that they should seek to develop in her native Wales and the two, with their three eldest children, explored mid-Wales and fell in love with it. They determined to start afresh in Montgomeryshire and in 1963 began in a small way at Machynlleth. Soon afterwards they moved to the old railway station at the village of Carno, which became the headquarters of the large international empire of Laura Ashley plc. They developed in an area that had virtually no industrial background, recruiting their work force from women whose sewing and cutting experience was entirely domestic and men whose knowledge of machines was largely confined to those of the farmyard. But what was initially lacking in skill was more than made up for by wholehearted enthusiasm, ingenuity, and co-operation.

The Ashleys regarded their work-force as an extension of the family and their friendly, concerned approach ensured great loyalty and support; the factories worked a four-and-a-half day week only as Laura believed that people on repetitive tasks, in particular, should have time for leisure and their families. The area was suffering rural depopulation, which government grants aimed to stem. The Ashleys took full advantage of this financial support. Jobs were provided at all levels—from the factory floor to the boardroom—in what was once regarded as a remote if beautiful area. Retail subsidiaries of the company later sold from the Ashleys' shops in four continents.

The Ashleys had complementary personalities and talents and were each other's greatest critics. Bernard, a man of immense energy, drive, and flair was also a skilled engineer, designer, and printer. Restless and volatile by temperament, he found in the outwardly calm and composed Laura the ideal rudder to direct his energies. He was knighted in 1987. Laura was essentially a 'revivalist' in her approach, drawing her inspiration from nature and ideas of the past. She was never a designer in the formal sense: rather, she would frequently describe a design for other people to implement, or she would produce an old design, the result of her many researches, and would demonstrate how to change it slightly or modify its colouring. She had her own design philosophy which resulted in a projected lifestyle which had a profound influence on the attitudes of her time. Her childhood recollections of periods of time spent with relations living close to the Welsh rural scene bordering the area of Dowlais influenced her greatly. She believed that most people yearned for a more natural lifestyle than had come to be accepted in modern industrial and urban society. In her clothes, furnishings, and interior decorations she put forward a style which was simpler, kindlier, and more romantic than her contemporaries projected. She revived many of the discarded designs of the eighteenth and nineteenth centuries.

Laura Ashley was an active partner in an enterprise which contradicted the trends of the times. When the mini skirt was in full flower she advocated the maxi skirt, which she considered infinitely more attractive. In an age when designers were emphasizing the more savage and tough side of human nature, she pointed to its pretty, peaceful, and generous side. Personally she was nearly always dressed in a skirt and blouse.

Although there were aspects of a large international company, with its annual turnover of £130 million, which Laura Ashley did not relish, the resourcefulness and realism of her business attitude must not be underestimated. The Ashleys moved abroad to develop the business in Europe. They lived in a French château in Picardy and had a town house in Brussels. Essentially Laura Ashley was a very private person with a profound belief in Christian values and the family as the bases of civilized life. She died 17 September 1985 in hospital in Coventry, following head injuries sustained in a fall down the stairs of her daughter's Cotswolds house.

[Iain Gale and Susan Irvine, *Laura Ashley Style*, 1987; private information; personal knowledge.]

EMLYN HOOSON

published 1990

ASHTON Sir Frederick William Mallandaine (1904–1988)

Dancer, and founder and choreographer, with (Dame) Ninette de Valois, of the Royal Ballet, was born 17 September 1904 in Guayaquil, Ecuador, the youngest of four sons of George Ashton, a minor diplomat working for a cable company, and his wife, Georgiana Fulcher, who came from a Suffolk family. Later there was a much-loved younger sister, Edith. The family moved to Peru, where Ashton attended the Dominican School in Lima. In 1917 he was taken to see a performance by Anna Pavlova—'she injected me with her poison'—and resolved to make dancing his life. In 1919 he was sent to England, to Dover College, which he hated, and to spend holidays in London with family friends. With them he saw Isadora Duncan and many dance companies, including that of Sergei Diaghilev in his disastrous production of *The Sleeping Princess* in 1921.

In 1922, aged eighteen, he began dance lessons with Léonide Massine and, later, with (Dame) Marie Rambert. Lacking height, he was nevertheless slim and elegant with a long, large-featured face and melancholy eyes, which would be effective in his future stage career. His dancing talent was not great, and his 'passionate laziness' was noted by Rambert, but this perceptive woman already sensed choreographic talent in the young man. The suicide of Ashton's father in South America brought his impoverished mother to England to join her son. They shared a series of inadequate lodgings while Ashton attended Pavlova's London performances and the last seasons of Diaghilev's Ballets Russes. At one of these he met the Russian designer, Sophie Fedorovitch, who would become his lifelong friend and collaborator.

Rambert, with her group of pupils, gave Ashton an enviable springboard as a budding choreographer; her generous encouragement launched his future career. He composed solos, *pas de deux*, and short ballets for revues, musical shows, the Camargo Society, and the Ballet Club, which later became the Ballet Rambert. His first work of importance was *A Tragedy of Fashion* in 1926 for the revue, *Riverside Nights*. In the thirty years which followed, Ashton choreographed many of his best ballets: *Façade* for the Camargo Society (1931); *Les Rendezvous*, Vic-Wells Ballet for Ninette de Valois (1933); an American interlude to arrange dances for the Virgil Thomson/Gertrude Stein opera, *Four Saints in Three Acts* (1934); and *Le Baiser de la Fée* at Sadler's Wells in 1935, which inaugurated his long partnership with (Dame) Margot Fonteyn. Leaving Rambert for the larger stage of de Valois' company, his most successful works were *Apparitions* and *Nocturne* (1936), *Les Patineurs* and *A Wedding Bouquet* (1937), *Horoscope* (1938), and *Dante Sonata* and *The Wise Virgins* (1940–1).

Ashton served with RAF intelligence during World War II, but was given leave in 1943 to choreograph a new ballet, *The Quest*, with a score by (Sir) William Walton. After the war, with the Sadler's Wells company resident at the reopened Royal Opera House, Covent Garden, Ashton choreographed the ballet considered by many his most perfect—César Franck's *Symphonic Variations* (1946). He ventured into opera production in 1947, at Covent Garden and Glyndebourne, and in 1948 choreographed two short works, *Scènes de Ballet* and *Don Juan*, and Sergei Prokofiev's *Cinderella*, the first three-act British ballet. In 1949 and 1950 ballets in Paris and New York were less successful. In 1951 Ashton also choreographed his first film, *The Tales of Hoffmann*, and this was followed in 1952 by *The Story of Three Loves*. At Covent Garden his highly successful ballet *Daphnis and Chloë* was performed in 1951, to be followed in 1952 by Léo Delibes' three-act *Sylvia*.

Ashton's entire life was lived in the ballet world. From 1953 until the late 1970s he continued to invent and produce work of varying shades and character. Among his notable achievements were *Homage to the Queen* (1953); *Romeo and Juliet* for the Royal Danish Ballet (1955); *Ondine* (1958); *La Fille Mal Gardée* (1960); *Marguerite and Armand* (1963); *The Dream* (1964); *Enigma Variations* (1968); and *A Month in the Country* (1976). He may have reached his largest public with the charming dances for the 1970 film, *Tales of Beatrix Potter*, in which he appeared as Mrs Tiggywinkle. He was both principal choreographer (1933–70) and director (1963–70) of the Royal Ballet.

Ashton was a lyrical choreographer, considered by many to be peerless in this field, though his approach to choreography was idiosyncratic. He seemed to plan little in advance, to arrive for first rehearsals without original ideas, and to use music suggested, occasionally even chosen, by friends. He would ask dancers to invent steps to musical phrases, sometimes selecting ones he liked and discarding others, sometimes discarding everything and commanding new inventions. In this unorthodox manner many of his best-known ballets were built; the original cast of dancers in each production took a considerable part in its creation, the resulting choreography reflecting their particular talents and style. Margot Fonteyn, for whom he made the majority of his ballets, brought into every Ashton role her love of floating, aerial movements while carried by her partner.

Ashton was homosexual and had several enduring relationships during his long life. Over the years he lived in charming, comfortable apartments and small houses in London and in a large country house at Eye in Suffolk, with ten acres, a lake, and a terraced room filled with his collection of Wemyss pottery, vividly displayed in well-lit glass cabinets. He was a supreme socialite, loving gossip and good living, which caused a certain florid portliness in his later years. His sense of humour was delightful and he was an amusing, often witty, companion. He adored everything connected with royalty and became a particular friend of his near contemporary, the queen mother. He was much honoured, receiving the CBE (1950), a knighthood (1962), CH (1970), and the OM (1977). He was given the freedom of the City of London (1981) and the Legion of Honour (1960). He had honorary degrees from Durham (1962), East Anglia (1967), London (1970), Hull (1971), and Oxford (1976). He died 18 August 1988 at his house in Eye.

[Z. Dominic and J. S. Gilbert, *Frederick Ashton, a Choreographer and his Ballets*, 1977; David Vaughan, *Frederick Ashton*, 1977; personal knowledge.]

Moira Shearer

published 1996

ATTLEE Clement Richard

(1883–1967)

First Earl Attlee

Statesman, was born in London 3 January 1883, the fourth son and seventh child of Henry Attlee, a leading solicitor in the City, and his wife, Ellen, daughter of T. S. Watson, secretary of the Art Union of London. The Attlee family had lived near Dorking for generations as farmers, millers, and merchants, but by the middle of the nineteenth century were in the main solid and prosperous members of the professional class.

The Attlee house was in Putney; a country house in Essex was added in 1896. Attlee always said that his was 'a typical family of the professional class brought up in the atmosphere of Victorian England'. He was taught at home until he was nine, acquiring an abiding love of literature from his mother. Other teaching was done by a succession of governesses engaged for his sisters, one of whom had previously had (Sir) Winston Churchill in her charge. A preparatory school at Northam Place, Potters Bar, was then followed by Haileybury College. His record at both was undistinguished. When he left Haileybury he was still immature and painfully shy, having made a mark only as an outstandingly good cadet.

He went up to University College, Oxford, in 1901 and spent three happy years there. He emerged with a deep love of literature and history (he obtained second class honours in modern history in 1904), a half blue for billiards, the sole game for which he had skill, and a lasting affection for his college and Oxford. Otherwise he was as conventional in general outlook and as Conservative in politics as he had been at Haileybury. He had already begun to eat dinners at the Inner Temple and was called to the bar in 1905.

In October 1905 Attlee's life took what proved to be a decisive turn when he paid his first visit to Haileybury House, a boy's club in Stepney, supported by his old school. He soon began to help regularly in the club and took a commission in its cadet corps. In 1907 he agreed to become manager of the club and went to live there. His home was in the East End for the next fourteen years.

By the end of 1907 he was a socialist, converted by his experience of life in Stepney and his reading of the works of John Ruskin, William Morris, Sidney and Beatrice Webb, and other apostles of socialism. In 1908 he joined the tiny Stepney branch of the Independent Labour Party. There was nothing unusual in such a conversion to socialism. Two of his brothers and several of his friends took the same path. What marked out Attlee was that he abandoned any idea of a regular career which might be combined with political agitation and social work on the side. His father's death in 1908 assured him of an income of £400 a year. It enabled him to abandon the law and was enough for his spartan tastes. He took a succession of ill-paid jobs connected with social work or politics: lecture secretary of the Webbs' campaign for the minority report of the Poor Law Commission, secretary of Toynbee Hall, lecturer at Ruskin College, Oxford, in 1911, and official explainer of the National Insurance Act of that year. At the instigation of Sidney Webb (later Lord Passfield), he became a lecturer in social administration at the London School of Economics in 1913. The other candidate was E. Hugh (later Lord) Dalton.

He thus had plenty of time for social work and socialist propaganda. As secretary of the Stepney branch of the ILP he was active in Labour's London organization and, his early shyness conquered, became an experienced, if not very effective, street-corner orator. By 1914, without any abandonment of his old friends and connections, his roots were deep in the East End and the growing Labour movement.

He had not, however, given up his voluntary commission in the cadets and within a few weeks of the outbreak of war, at the age of thirty-one, was a lieutenant in the 6th South Lancashire Regiment. He went with his battalion to Gallipoli and had two spells there, the second ending with command of the rearguard at the evacuation of Suvla Bay. He was in Mesopotamia in 1916, where he was badly wounded by a British shell and invalided home. After recovery he served with the Tank Corps for a year and was promoted to major in 1917. By the summer of 1918 he was back with the South Lancashires in France. During the advance to Lille he was injured and sent home, celebrating the armistice in hospital.

Attlee was unusual among the coming Labour leaders in having served as an active officer throughout the war. For many years he was most commonly known as 'Major Attlee', his vaguely military bearing and appearance, and the clipped anachronisms of his conversation, setting him somewhat apart from his contemporaries in the Labour Party. The war also gave rise to a keen interest in the theory of warfare; he was, for example, convinced that Churchill's strategic conception at Gallipoli had been sound.

Attlee returned to the London School of Economics and to political activity in the East End immediately after demobilization. In 1919 he was co-opted by Stepney Borough Council as mayor. Apart from the routine work of the Council his main concern was the high level of unemployment in Stepney. He helped to form an association of the Labour mayors of London boroughs and became its first chairman, leading a deputation to 10 Downing Street to appeal to Lloyd George for stronger measures to deal with unemployment in London.

Attlee continued, as an alderman, to be active in the affairs of Stepney until 1927. But marriage in 1922, the purchase of a house in an Essex suburb, and election as an MP brought to an end the years of absorption in the life of the East End. His main role became that of representing Stepney on many of the organizations set up to co-ordinate the work of the London borough councils; for some years he served as vice-president of the Municipal Electricity Authorities of Greater London.

When he was elected to the House of Commons in 1922 Attlee gave up his post at the London School of Economics and became, in effect, a full-time politician. His constituency, Limehouse, was one of the few safe Labour seats outside the mining districts. It was a fitting reward for all that he had done in the East End since 1907. Elsewhere, he was virtually unknown. Platform oratory was the route to reputation in the Labour Party and he had little talent for it.

He did, however, have some long-run advantages over the other middle-class and professional men who became Labour MPs in the elections of 1922 and 1923. His experience of working-class life was both extensive and firsthand and he had started at the bottom of the Labour movement. He had already begun to show, too, unusual effectiveness at the hard slog of committee work. His views were well to the left of his party's official policy. He was a member of a small 'ginger group' in the ILP in company with A. Fenner (later Lord) Brockway and R. Clifford Allen (later Lord Allen of Hurtwood), and also attracted by the guild socialism advocated by G. D. H. Cole.

Ramsay MacDonald was elected leader of the Labour Party after the election of 1922 and invited Attlee to be one of his parliamentary private secretaries. But the Parliament was short-lived. Stanley Baldwin (later Earl Baldwin of Bewdley) decided to seek a mandate for tariff reform and went to the country at the end of 1923. The upshot was a minority Labour Government which held office for ten uneasy months. Attlee served as under-secretary of state for war, under Stephen Walsh, a post which he found congenial.

Back in opposition, Attlee's contribution was largely confined to putting his party's case on the Electricity Bill (1926) and a Rating and Valuation Bill (1925) which was one of Neville Chamberlain's key reforms as minister of health. Attlee's growing reputation for competence at the detailed work of committees must have played some part in MacDonald's invitation in 1927 to serve as one of the two Labour members on a statutory commission for India, chaired by Sir John (later Viscount) Simon. For the next two years Attlee devoted himself to the political problems of India. The commission met considerable obstruction on its two visits to India and its report in 1930 was rejected by the leaders of the Congress and denigrated by their supporters in the Labour Party. Attlee himself always defended the commission's proposals for an extension of self-government in the provinces as going as far as was realistic at the time. Certainly his service on the Simon commission gave him a valuable insight into the problems of India.

After the election of 1929 MacDonald broke a promise that serving on the Simon commission would not affect Attlee's chance of a post in the event of Labour coming to power. His opportunity did not come until the spring of 1930 when Sir Oswald Mosley resigned from the chancellorship of the Duchy of Lancaster. Attlee succeeded him but with a considerably reduced brief. He assisted Addison with his Agricultural Marketing Bill, one of the Government's few parliamentary successes, and wrote a major memorandum on 'The Problems of British Industry' which, although it went unheeded by the Cabinet, was the first indication of his ability to analyse a problem and distil a course of action. In March 1931 Attlee was transferred to the Post Office which had gone to seed under Sir G. E. P. Murray, who had ruled it with an autocratic hand since 1914. Attlee set to with a will and inaugurated a number of reforms, the benefits of which largely accrued to Sir H. Kingsley Wood in the succeeding Government.

He was on holiday with his family in August 1931 when he was summoned to Downing Street and told, with the other non-Cabinet ministers, that the Labour Government was at an end and that MacDonald was forming a coalition Government. Attlee was never in any doubt about his own course of action in spite of his past association with MacDonald and a growing reputation for being not only middle-class but also middle-of-the-road. He had become increasingly disillusioned with MacDonald since joining the Government but the reasons for his staying with the Labour Party lay deeper, in the strength of his personal beliefs and his roots in the movement. He never changed his view that MacDonald had perpetrated 'the greatest betrayal in the political history of the country'.

Attlee survived the landslide of the 1931 election but with a majority at Limehouse of only 551. Labour, including the rump of the ILP, was reduced to 52 members. George Lansbury, the sole survivor of those who had sat in Cabinet, was elected leader of the parliamentary party and Attlee became his deputy. Sir R. Stafford Cripps completed a triumvirate; although solicitor-general in the Labour Government he had been in the Commons for little more than a year. The team of three worked harmoniously. Cripps provided the driving force and for a time Attlee was considerably influenced by him. But as Cripps moved further to the left, neither his views nor his crusade against Transport House were to Attlee's liking. Attlee was the last man to wish to split the Labour Party and his own ideas about policy were becoming increasingly balanced and eclectic. He expressed them in *The Will and the Way to Socialism* published shortly before the election of 1935.

The years from 1931 to 1935 were the making of Attlee. He was no longer confined to occasional parliamentary speeches on specialist topics but, as deputy leader, was called upon to cover the whole range of debate. In 1932 he filled more columns of *Hansard* than any other member and led the party for several months in 1934 when Lansbury fell ill. His own parliamentary style was steadily developing. His speeches lacked flourish to the point of being laconic but they were thorough and spiced with an occasional waspish sting. But none of this was enough to suggest that he was a potential leader of the party.

Lansbury resigned the leadership after his defeat at the Brighton conference in October 1935, a bare three weeks before the start of the election campaign. The parliamentary party had little choice but to appoint Attlee as leader. The *Manchester Guardian* reflected universal opinion; it observed, 'This is hardly more than an interim appointment'. Attlee worked hard in the campaign but made little personal impact on the electorate and the result, 154 seats to Labour, was a disappointment. In the contest for the leadership that followed the election the loyalty of his old colleagues, particularly the miners, from the previous Parliament and his reputation for rectitude were enough to ensure the defeat of Herbert Morrison (later Lord Morrison of Lambeth) and Arthur Greenwood, his rivals for the leadership. Even his modesty helped, for his approach to the tasks of leadership was the antithesis of the style which MacDonald had made suspect.

There was a full testing of Attlee in the years that followed. Few leaders have had a more difficult baptism. The Labour Party struggled to cope with its own divisions in the face of Hitler's challenge to the country's security and the seeming impregnability of the 'national' Government. Attlee largely concentrated on his role in Parliament. He recognized that he had no talent for the more flamboyant arts of leadership in opposition and that the constitution of the Labour Party provided little scope for the imposition of his views on others. In so far as he gave a lead it was, as he said, 'from slightly left of centre'.

With political passions running high his gift, as Dalton noted, was that he 'lowered the temperature'. This low-key approach was denounced as colourless and uninspiring by the militants of both Left and Right in the party. Nor did it make Attlee appear to the electorate at large as being of the stuff of which prime ministers are made. But if he did not inspire the Labour Party, he did nothing to divide it and it was this preservation of Labour's fragile unity which made it possible to seize the opportunity of 1940.

Attlee's approach stemmed from his deep understanding of the Labour Party as a loose alliance of divergent views and interests. He was fortunate in one respect. The shock of 1931 and the depth of the economic depression combined to remove most of the ambiguities that had characterized the party's domestic programme in the MacDonald era. By 1935 the Labour Party was firmly pledged to policies of socialist planning and public ownership. This measure of agreement was, however, obscured by a more fundamental debate, stirred by the political and economic crisis of the thirties, in which the defenders of parliamentary democracy came under increasingly heavy Marxist fire.

Attlee put his own views in *The Labour Party in Perspective* which he was invited to write for the Left Book Club in 1937. His intention, he wrote in the introduction, was 'to show the Labour Party in its historical setting as an expression in place and time of the urge for socialism, to show it as a characteristic example of British methods and as an outcome of British political instincts'. This belief in parliamentary institutions and the traditional ways of government was also exemplified in his support for Stanley Baldwin, for whom he had a lasting admiration, during the abdication crisis. They found themselves of one mind on the issue. Nor did Attlee doubt that he was expressing the views of the ordinary supporters of the Labour Party although not, as he noted later, 'of a few of the intelligentsia who can be trusted to take the wrong view on any subject'.

But as Germany grew more menacing, domestic questions gave way to the problem of how the challenge was to be met. Chamberlain, who became prime minister in May 1937, quickly dispelled the hesitations of the Baldwin Government by a forceful combination of policies of positive appeasement and moderate rearmament. The Labour Party found it difficult to make a coherent response. It had previously paid little attention to foreign policy. The split in World War I had been healed with the slogan, 'No more war' and the pull of the pacifists remained powerful. In May 1935 Attlee stated views to which the majority of Labour Party members would have subscribed: 'We stand for Collective Security through the League of Nations. We reject the use of force as an instrument of policy. We stand for the reduction of armaments and pooled security . . . Our policy is not one of seeking security through rearmament but through disarmament.' These policies of disarmament and collective security, tinged with pacifism, were slowly abandoned under the pressure of events. The occupation of the Rhineland, the Spanish civil war, and the Anschluss added substance to the arguments which Ernest Bevin and Dalton, in particular, had been advancing since Hitler's early days in power. Attlee himself denounced Chamberlain with vigour. When (Sir) Anthony Eden (later the Earl of Avon) resigned from the Foreign Office in February 1938 Attlee argued that the Government's policy was one of 'abject surrender to the dictators'. He attacked the Munich agreement as 'a tremendous victory for Herr Hitler' and pressed Chamberlain hard in the summer of 1939 to come to terms with the Soviet Union.

The key issue, however, was rearmament. In July 1937 the Parliamentary Labour Party finally decided to abandon its traditional vote against the defence estimates and to confine itself to abstention. Attlee voted against the change. It was not until after Munich that he began to accept the case for rearmament and when Chamberlain announced the introduction of conscription for military service in April 1939 Attlee attacked the measure as useless and divisive.

The Labour Party was so divided in its views that Attlee, as leader, was in a difficult position. Urged on by Bevin, the leaders of the unions were able to ensure, after 1937, that the official line was in support of rearmament. But the main movement of opinion among the rank and file was sharply to the left and looked to the Soviet Union for salvation. The middle path followed by Attlee sprang as much from conviction as from his conception of his role as leader. The conclusions that he had arrived at after World War I were not readily discarded and his hostility to Chamberlain and his policies ran deep. In later years Attlee came close to admitting that the Labour Party had been in blinkers. His own comment on the vote against conscription is perhaps the best epitaph: 'Well, it probably wasn't awfully wise.'

Attlee was ill when war broke out. Two operations for prostate trouble kept him out of action for several months and Arthur Greenwood took over the leadership. It was not until the fiasco of the Norwegian campaign in April 1940 that the opportunity arose to topple Chamberlain.

After the debate on 7 and 8 May 1940 it was evident that he could not carry on without Labour support. When Attlee and Greenwood saw Chamberlain on 9 May, Attlee said that he would put two questions to the Labour National Executive Committee: (1) Are you prepared to serve under Chamberlain? (2) Are you prepared to serve under someone else? He telephoned the replies on the following afternoon: 'The answer to the first question is, no. To the second question, yes.' Chamberlain resigned within the hour. Churchill was summoned to the Palace and during the night he and Attlee agreed on the distribution of posts in a coalition government.

Attlee served in the War Cabinet as lord privy seal until February 1942. He then became secretary for the Dominions and, from September 1943, lord president of the Council. He was also deputy prime minister, at first *de facto*, but, from February 1942, with the formal title. At the highest level the war was run by the War Cabinet and two subsidiary bodies; military matters were dealt with by the Defence Committee, civil by the Lord President's Committee. Attlee alone served on all three bodies and did so for the life of the Government. But although he played his part on the Defence Committee, his main responsibility lay on the civil side where, by 1944, he was very much the committee workhorse of the coalition. Most of the key committees were chaired by him and by the end of the war he had earned a high reputation for the efficient and business-like dispatch of business.

The day-to-day care of Government business in the House of Commons also fell mainly on Attlee and as deputy prime minister he took the chair at the War Cabinet and the Defence Committee when Churchill was absent from the country, as he increasingly was during the last two years of the war. These arrangements rested on a confidence and trust that lay at the heart of the coalition's high degree of harmony. Attlee's loyalty to Churchill never wavered for an instant, even in the dark days of 1941 and 1942.

From his central position in the machinery of government, Attlee was called upon to preside over much of the discussion of social reform that not only made the coalition one of the most considerable of all reforming governments but led to a consensus of view between the two parties and laid the framework for much of the work of Attlee's own administration. The war was fought on the home front with the weapons of economic control and social amelioration advocated by the Labour Party and it was evident by the end of 1943 that peace would bring further reforms: the implementation of the report of the committee on social insurance and allied services chaired by Sir W. H. (later Lord) Beveridge, the establishment of a National Health Service, and the carrying out of economic policies aimed at full employment.

Attlee was well suited by temperament and experience to soothe such strains as these great changes brought to the coalition. In backing proposals for reform he eschewed the socialist arguments and socialist labels which would have antagonized his Tory colleagues. The case was put in terms of national unity and what was needed to win the war. But it was not easy for Attlee to avoid offending Tories without outraging many of his own supporters who wished Labour to use its leverage in the coalition for more socialist purposes. Attlee's reply was that 'we cannot dictate to others the acceptance of our Socialist programme', but this realism was usually tempered with emphasis on how much had been gained by participation: 'The acceptance', as he said at West Hartlepool in January 1944, 'of so much of what our party has preached in the last thirty years.'

Attlee's wider responsibilities included the chairmanship of the committee on India and of committees dealing with the details of the post-war settlement in Europe. He opposed the Morgenthau plan to destroy Germany's industrial capacity although convinced of the need to enforce fundamental changes in its economic and social structure. He found himself very much in sympathy with Eden on more general questions and they combined on occasion to restrain Churchill, particularly when they thought him too influenced by Roosevelt. But the disagreements were minor and the bipartisan policy of the post-war years was forged during the coalition. No member of the Government was more hostile to Stalin than Attlee and he fully agreed with Churchill that long-term American participation in the peace settlement and the maintenance of the British Commonwealth were essential to counter the Russians and ensure stability.

Attlee's record during the war earned him little public reputation compared, for example, with Bevin and Morrison whose departments covered much of the home front. Within Whitehall, however, his standing grew as a chairman and conciliator of unusual quality. Churchill and he made an effective combination, of leader and chairman, which echoed that of Lloyd George and Bonar Law in the previous war. It also became increasingly clear that Attlee could not be lightly crossed; he could be devastating in his criticisms and his judgement, if sparsely offered, lacked neither crispness nor authority. It was an appreciation of these qualities, as he had seen them emerge during the war, that led Bevin to compare Attlee with Campbell-Bannerman as possessing 'that gift of character which enabled him to hold a team of clever men together'.

One of his Tory colleagues in the War Cabinet said subsequently that he could not remember Attlee 'ever making a point which I felt came from him as leader of the Labour Party' as distinct from his pressing for improvements in the lot of the working class and for effective preparation for the post-war period. It was this non-partisan approach to the coalition which led Aneurin Bevan to accuse Attlee of bringing 'to the fierce struggle of politics the tepid enthusiasm of a lazy summer afternoon at a cricket match'. Attlee's own view was that his biggest achievement had been 'to take a party intact into a coalition, to keep it intact for five years and to bring it out intact'.

In May 1945 Attlee accompanied Eden to the foundation conference of the United Nations in San Francisco. The prospect of a general election forced them to return early, but, on his way back, Attlee was able to meet Truman and found to his pleasure that they 'talked the same language'.

Churchill and Attlee would have preferred to continue the coalition until Japan had been defeated but opinion in both parties, especially on the Labour side, was in favour of a quick end. Churchill formed a caretaker Government and a general election followed immediately.

During the campaign Attlee established himself for the first time in the public eye. His broadcast in reply to Churchill's 'Gestapo' speech was a model of effective restraint and his campaign, for which he was driven about by his wife in their small family car, was in telling contrast to his opponent's almost regal style. He also emerged with credit from the one testing episode of the campaign, an attempt by Churchill and Beaverbrook to take advantage of some tiresome interventions by Harold Laski, the chairman of the Labour Party's National Executive Committee.

The result of the election, much to Attlee's surprise, was a Labour landslide with a majority over the Tories of 170. But he did not become prime minister without some exchanges in which, in Emanuel (later Lord) Shinwell's words, 'the brotherly love advocated by the movement was conspicuous by its absence'. Bevin's unwavering support ensured the defeat of a challenge by Morrison for the leadership and Attlee proceeded to form a strong and experienced Government. His first task, once the principal posts had been filled, was to return to the Potsdam conference with the new foreign secretary, Ernest Bevin.

Conservatives feared and socialists hoped that the election of 1945 presaged fundamental changes. The Labour Party's manifesto had declared, 'The Labour Party is a Socialist Party. Its ultimate aim is the establishment of the Socialist Commonwealth of Great Britain.' Attlee's own horizon was more restricted: to the implementation of the manifesto's specific proposals and the tackling of the problems which the post-war period would bring, particularly in economic policy and foreign affairs. During the war he and all his leading colleagues had participated in a gigantic exercise in planning and economic control so that, to a considerable extent, the election of 1945 signified not change but continuity. Nor, in spite of the dismay of defeat, did the Conservative Party lag far behind Labour. It was by 1945 already well on the way to embracing both the managed economy and the Welfare State. If Attlee presided over a revolution, therefore, it was, as he himself stressed, an extraordinarily quiet and peaceful revolution which had begun well before 1945 and was to lead more to consensus between the parties than to conflict.

The leading figures in the Government, Bevin, Morrison, Cripps, Dalton, and Bevan, formed an exceptionally able but difficult team, managed by Attlee with great skill. He was at his best when he could delegate substantial control of major areas of policy to ministers in whom he had complete confidence, as with Bevin at the Foreign Office and Cripps at the Treasury, and so be free to concentrate his own efforts on one or two key political problems and the general tasks of co-ordination and management. 'If you have a good dog, don't bark yourself' was a favourite Attlee proverb.

The backing of Bevin was proof against all intrigues but Attlee's authority over his principal colleagues and his more general mastery of the Cabinet sprang from his own qualities. He was a good judge of men and adept at managing them, rarely allowing his judgement to be clouded by personal prejudice. His integrity was accepted as being beyond question.

From the beginning Attlee succeeded in enforcing his own style on the working of his Government. He put high value on the bureaucratic virtues of formality, order, and regularity and in structure and method the Government conformed to them to an unusual degree. His own strong preference was for working through paper. Even at the highest level the circulation of boxes was the medium by which the work of the Attlee Government was mainly done. There was little of the informal and speculative discussion typical of Churchill's methods. The same puritanical concentration on the matter in hand characterized Attlee's running of the Cabinet and its committees. As he later remarked, 'I was always for getting on with the job.' Some indulgence was shown to senior ministers but short shrift was usually dealt out to anyone who had failed to master his brief or who attempted to read it. In summing up Attlee was invariably precise and succinct. Otherwise he said little and rarely took a vote. His aim was to make the Cabinet and its committees efficient machines for the dispatch of well-prepared business and to cut to the minimum their tendency to become talking shops.

The main defect of such methods was that Attlee remained remote from his party and the general public, and even from ministers who were not privy to the inner circle. The impression that he gave of a Victorian headmaster keeping his school under strict control was compounded by an inability to participate in the complimentary small-talk of politics, a consequence doubtless of his innate shyness. His considerable kindliness was invariably expressed by letter.

'The little man', as Bevin affectionately called him, had few of the attributes normally looked for in a political leader but this was of little significance while Bevin was attempting to forge a Western alliance or Cripps was embarking on his austere crusade. But when ill health compelled them to resign and Morrison proved a palpable failure at the Foreign Office, it was beyond Attlee's power to fill the gap. The Labour Party respected him to an unsurpassed degree but could not rise to him. Nor had he the gift, possessed by Bevin and Cripps, of rallying those outside the ranks of his own party even though his lack of partisan spite and devotion to the broad national interest came to be increasingly recognized. But as a catalyst among politicians engaged in the business of government Attlee has few rivals.

In domestic politics the first eighteen months or so of his office were almost untarnished honeymoon. The Opposition showed few signs of recovery and major legislation poured from Parliament at an unprecedented rate. Attlee was determined to push ahead and by the end of 1946, an *annus mirabilis*, acts had been passed nationalizing the Bank of England, the coal industry, civil aviation, and Cable and Wireless; there had also been a National Insurance Act, a New Towns Act, a Trade Disputes Act, an Act for the establishment of a National Health Service, and a host of minor measures. The legislation remains as a permanent memorial. It was passed in a period of optimism in politics and cheap money in the economy. The Japanese war ended with unexpected speed, taxation was cut, demobilization went smoothly with none of the unemployment that had been feared, and industry was turning over to peacetime production with remarkably little friction. The Welfare State was in an advanced state of construction and the nation was still proud of its rationing system and its sense of social discipline.

At this stage there was little public consciousness that there would be tight physical constraints on what could be done. J. M. (later lord) Keynes, for example, wrote to Dalton about the latter's National Land Fund to say that he should have 'acquired for the nation all the coastline round the island at one stroke'. It was a time when anything seemed possible.

Attlee did not share this euphoria. He was shocked by the sudden ending of Lend-Lease in August 1945 and, while adamant that there was no alternative but to accept the terms on which the American loan was subsequently made, knew that the most severe difficulties would be likely to arise from the requirement to make sterling convertible within a year of the commencement of the loan.

In foreign affairs events at first appeared to match the fears that Churchill and Attlee had shared in the last months of the war. Stalin cemented his hold on Eastern Europe and was obstructive in Germany. Large Communist parties in France and Italy awaited his bidding. It was, however, the uncertainty engendered by American policy which most disturbed the Government.

Attlee did not doubt Truman's own goodwill but the negotiation of the loan and the passing of the McMahon Act by Congress in 1946 were jolting experiences and the American reaction to Russia seemed ambivalent and at times naïve. Relations between the two countries were further strained by Bevin's policy in Palestine, fully backed by Attlee, which American opinion thought pro-Arab and anti-Zionist.

A transformation of American policy began with the arrival of General Marshall at the State Department in January 1947. The Truman Doctrine which secured aid to Greece and Turkey, previously British responsibilities, was declared in March. A year later the Marshall Plan was launched and followed in 1949 by the setting up of the North Atlantic Treaty Organization. Together they ensured the economic recovery and political security of Western Europe. If the main influence bringing about the change was the effect of Stalin's obduracy on American opinion, the patient persuasion of Bevin and Attlee should not be discounted. In a relationship which Attlee called 'the closest of my political life' they were of one mind on the necessity of involving the United States in the defence of Western Europe.

Attlee's own most important contribution, and one with which his name will always be associated, was, however, the granting of independence to India. He acted in effect as his own secretary of state and all the major decisions bear his unmistakable stamp. He began with the intention of modifying the plan which Cripps had proposed to the Indians in 1942 but the failure of the Cabinet mission in 1946 convinced him of the need to take full account of the strength of the Muslim League and its determination to establish Pakistan. Viscount (later Earl) Wavell, who had been viceroy since 1943, was dismissed and replaced by Attlee's personal choice, Lord Louis Mountbatten, who was charged with the negotiation of independence within a time limit. The new viceroy arrived in India in March 1947 and acted with great speed and decisiveness. On the day of the declaration of Indian independence he wrote to Attlee, 'The man who made it possible was you yourself. Without your original guidance and your unwavering support nothing could have been accomplished out here.'

Attlee was also mainly responsible for the decision that Britain should manufacture her own atomic bomb. Concern at the narrowness with which American officials were interpreting the Quebec agreement for the exchange of atomic information led him to fly to Washington in November 1945. His discussions with Truman were cordial but the President was in the event unable to deliver even the little that he offered. The *coup de grâce* was delivered by Congress a few months later with the passage of the McMahon Bill. Attlee had no hesitation in deciding that Britain should make her own bomb: 'It had become essential. We had to hold up our position *vis-à-vis* the Americans. We couldn't allow ourselves to be wholly in their hands, and their position wasn't awfully clear always.' He also insisted on the maximum of secrecy. All but a few members of the Cabinet were kept in the dark, questions in Parliament discouraged, and large sums concealed in the estimates. 'The project', as Attlee put it, 'was never hampered by lack of money.'

The Government ran into its first major trouble early in 1947 when fuel supplies broke down in savage weather. For a time two and a half million men were out of work. During the following months the Cabinet was further shaken by a dispute over the nationalization of iron and steel and by an economic crisis. The nationalization of iron and steel was the only major item of the 1945 programme on which there had been no progress. Morrison, whose responsibilities included the co-ordination of economic policy, had always been lukewarm. With some encouragement from Attlee, he succeeded in negotiating an agreement with the leaders of the industry which fell well short of nationalization. But the compromise ran into trouble in the Cabinet, with Bevin, Cripps, and Dalton in opposition, and raised a storm in the party. Although Attlee took care to leave the running to Morrison, it was evident that he had made an error of judgement.

A growing exchange crisis came to a head in July when sterling became freely convertible, under the terms of the American loan. The Cabinet dithered for five weeks before suspending convertibility. His critics were confirmed in their view that Attlee, never at his best in discussions about finance, was losing his grip.

Foremost among these critics was Cripps who had some success in persuading one or two of his leading colleagues that Bevin should replace Attlee, with the latter taking the Exchequer. The attempt was doomed from the start by Bevin's response: 'What has the little man ever done to me?' But Cripps persisted. Although deserted by his fellow conspirators he went to see Attlee on 9 September. The interview began with Cripps suggesting that Attlee should give way to Bevin. It ended with Cripps agreeing to take on the new post of minister for economic affairs. Whatever the summer might have disclosed of Attlee's failings, his touch with men had not deserted him.

Dalton was compelled to resign in November as a consequence of a few indiscreet words to a journalist immediately before his budget speech. He was succeeded at the Exchequer by Cripps who thus came to dominate economic affairs and, to Attlee's immense relief, soon brought authority and purpose to domestic policy. Cripps's policies were hard and austere. Rations were, for a time, lower than they had been in the war. The housing programme was cut and the building of hospitals and roads brought almost to a halt. The bombed wastes at the centre of cities became even more derelict. But the aim was clear: to bring the balance of payments into equilibrium and, in particular, to solve the problem of the dollar shortage while maintaining the benefits which the Government had earlier secured for the working class.

Attlee was content to leave the lead to Bevin and Cripps. In foreign affairs, the early work began to bear fruit. The Organization for European Economic Co-operation was set up and the Marshall Plan implemented in 1948, so providing the underpinning for Cripps's policies. The Russian challenge at Berlin was successfully met by the Anglo-American airlift and the North Atlantic Treaty Organization was established in 1949. But the growing movement in favour of a federal Western Europe was met by Bevin with a mixture of hostility and scepticism. Attlee was of the same mind. As he later wrote, 'Britain has never regarded itself as just a European power. Her interests are world-wide. She is the heart of a great Commonwealth and tends to look outwards from Europe.'

By the end of 1949, ten years of continuous office had taken its toll of the leading members of Attlee's Government. They had all suffered bouts of serious illness and Bevin and Cripps were soon to be forced to resign. It was also evident that the Government had little to offer by way of new ideas and policies once it had exhausted the capital of the 1945 manifesto. Cripps had successfully completed the transition from a war economy by marrying Keynesian techniques of budgetary manipulation to the system of rationing and controls inherited from the Churchill coalition but it could scarcely be argued that this was more than a temporary solution to the problem of how the economy should be run.

The inevitable consequence was an intensification of the ancient dispute between the left and right wings of the Labour Party. Attlee offered no lead, took no initiative. He increasingly concentrated his energies on contriving to achieve agreement in Cabinet and became even less disposed than before to contemplate crossing his bridges before he came to them.

Nevertheless, Attlee and his colleagues approached the general election in February 1950 with some confidence in spite of having been forced to devalue sterling in the previous autumn. No other industrial country in Europe had made a comparable recovery, the promises of 1945 had been broadly kept, and the working class, in particular, had much to be grateful for. The result was a disappointment, a majority of ten for Labour. Attlee, who had represented Limehouse since 1922, stood at West Walthamstow. He remained in office although no one expected that his Government would last more than a few weeks. In the event it survived for twenty difficult months. Few governments have achieved so little, been so battered by external circumstances, or suffered so much from internal disharmony. The Korean war, which began in June 1950 and brought in its train a massive rearmament programme, inflation, and a disruption of the balance of payments, was the main catalyst of disaster. Much of the ground that had been so painfully gained during the previous three years was lost. When Attlee's Government was defeated at the polls in October 1951, it ended as it had begun, running a war economy.

The strain on Attlee was considerable. The two mainstays of his Cabinet were forced to resign after long periods of ill health, Cripps in October 1950 and Bevin in March 1951. But he enjoyed something of a Roman triumph in December 1950 when, with Bevin too ill to fly, he decided suddenly to go to Washington because of a general worry that the Americans were intending to extend the Korean war and a particular fear, based on a misunderstanding, that Truman was contemplating the use of the atomic bomb. Morrison, who took Bevin's place, was a disaster at the Foreign Office; 'the worst appointment I ever made', was Attlee's conclusion. He was of necessity drawn into direct intervention in the conduct of foreign policy and it was largely due to his steadying hand that there was such a muted response to Musaddeq's expropriation of the Anglo-Iranian Oil Company.

Hugh Gaitskell succeeded Cripps at the Exchequer. There was no doubt about his competence but his promotion roused the resentment of Bevan who stood high in the party and had done well as minister of health. Attlee thought highly of Bevan's talents but had always found him difficult, in respect both of temperament and opinions, and had usually tried to deal with him through an intermediary. What he now had to face was not just personal animosity between the two men but a conflict between the standard bearers of the right and left wings of the party.

Matters came to a head with the preparation of the budget in April 1951. Gaitskell was determined to impose charges for a number of services which had previously been provided free in the National Health Service. Attlee was in hospital with a duodenal ulcer and Morrison, his deputy, made little attempt to confine the resulting conflict. When Attlee returned to duty, the breach was beyond repair. Bevan, (Sir) Harold Wilson, and John Freeman had already resigned and were soon leading a wide-ranging attack on the Government's policies.

A spurious unity was patched up for the election in October but the Labour Party entered it with considerable handicaps. Attlee was its sole leader with a reputation that still counted with the electorate and he campaigned with his wife in what had become his familiar style. He lost and Churchill took office but the total Labour vote was greater than that of the Conservatives and indeed the highest achieved by any party in any election.

The size of the vote was a remarkable indication of the loyalty which the Attlee Government aroused in its supporters. Labour's straightforward mixture of social concern and sensible pragmatism, exemplified by Attlee's own views, may not have been socialist enough to satisfy the Left or been a reliable pointer to the party's future but it satisfied its supporters. The main legacies of the Attlee Government were that it ensured the country's safety and initiated policies of welfare, full employment, and the budgetary control of the economy to such effect that Governments for the next twenty years had no alternative but to attempt to follow in its wake.

Attlee remained leader of the party for four more years. But they were years of frustration and anticlimax. In the House of Commons he continued to speak at a high level of statesmanship, particularly in support of the bipartisan policies in defence and foreign affairs of which he and Bevin had been the principal architects. But it was as leader of the Labour Party that he was judged and for much of this period the leadership was virtually in commission. The broad consensus of the 1940s had disappeared and divisions of opinion had inexorably hardened into faction. Attlee, bereft of the authority of a prime minister, found it hard to cope with the dissensions of Opposition and failed to regain his old touch with back-benchers and the rank and file of the party.

His aim, as it had been before 1939, was to hold the party together. Although unwilling to make any policy concessions to the left wing, he consistently opposed the hounding of Bevan and its other leaders which was enthusiastically led by Arthur Deakin, Bevin's successor at the Transport and General Workers' Union. But passions were too high and the division of opinion too deep for there to be a chance of more than a passing reconciliation. Attlee increasingly withdrew into silence and the anonymity of committee membership. As one of his colleagues put it, 'At the National Executive, he doodled where he should have led'.

The election of May 1955 was a dull affair. The result was a comfortable Conservative victory and it was evident that Attlee's retirement could not be long delayed. The candidates for the succession were Morrison, Bevan, and Gaitskell and by the autumn they were all in the field. But Attlee held on. The consequence, and almost certainly the intention, was that the prize went to Gaitskell. Attlee announced his retirement in a brief and unheralded speech at a regular meeting of the Parliamentary Labour Party on 7 December 1955. The Queen conferred an earldom on him; he had already been admitted to the Order of Merit in 1951.

Attlee was sworn of the privy council in 1935, was made CH in 1945, and KG in 1956. He became an honorary bencher (Inner Temple) in 1946 and FRS in 1947. He was awarded honorary degrees by many universities, and was made an honorary fellow of University College, Oxford (1942), Queen Mary College, London (1948), and LSE (1958).

Attlee's retirement was happy and busy. He travelled widely and wrote and lectured about politics with a frankness that surprised many of his former colleagues. His own stock rose as his virtues of integrity, fairness, and coolness in adversity came to be more widely appreciated. Even his habitual restraint and understatement, which had so often offended his supporters by making him appear remote and almost disinterested, appealed to a generation over-fed on political hyperbole.

Attlee is the leading example in modern times of a politician who achieves high office against all expectations, only then to reveal unsuspected talents. Before 1940 it was assumed that he held a short lease on the leadership of the Labour Party. Many of his colleagues still thought him unfitted for the premiership in 1945. Five years later there would have been little disagreement with Bevin's reported verdict, 'By God, he's the only man who could have kept us together'. Attlee's contribution doubtless lacked the ideas, stimulation, and flair, which are usually thought of as the stuff of leadership. He could act decisively, as he did with India, but he was in general content to wait until opinion had formed before he moved out to express it.

The qualities that made him indispensable and gained him the respect and loyalty of his colleagues were his sense of justice, his imperturbability in a crisis, his skill at the business of administration, and, above all, his adroitness in choosing and managing men. In the main, these are qualities not for opposition, but for office. They enabled Attlee to play a significant part during the war of 1939–45 and then to harness men of inherently greater ability and imagination into a team which effectively laid the foundations of post-war politics both at home and abroad.

Attlee was a solitary man but only in the sense that he had no political cronies. 'It's very dangerous', he said, 'to be the centre of a small circle.' His gregariousness was expressed in other ways. He liked formal dinners and kept in close touch with the ramified Attlee family. The fortunes of his old friends of school, university, and army were followed in *The Times*; his daily recreation was then to solve the crossword. But his wife, to whom he remained devoted until her death in 1964, and his family, provided all the ordinary company and relaxation that he needed.

He married in 1922 Violet Helen, daughter of H. E. Millar, of Hampstead. They had three daughters and a son, Martin Richard (born 1927), who succeeded his father in the earldom. Attlee died in Westminster Hospital 8 October 1967.

There are portraits of Attlee by Flora Lion (1941); Rodrigo Moynihan (1948) in the Oxford and Cambridge Universities Club; G. Harcourt (1946) in the National Portrait Gallery; Cowan Dobson (1956); Lawrence Gowing (1963); and Derek Fowler, at Haileybury. There is also a bronze presentation medallion (1953), a bronze head by David McFall (1965) in the National Portrait Gallery, and a statue by Ivor Roberts-Jones in the lobby of the House of Commons (1979).

[Attlee's own writings, principally *As It Happened*, 1954; Kenneth Harris, a biography of Attlee in draft; Francis Williams, *A Prime Minister Remembers*, 1961; *The Times*, 9 October 1964; personal knowledge.]

MAURICE SHOCK

published 1981

AUDEN Wystan Hugh

(1907–1973)

Poet, essayist, teacher, and collaborator in writing plays and libretti, was born in York 21 February 1907, the third and youngest son (there were no daughters) of Dr George Augustus Auden and his wife, Constance Rosalie Bucknell. In 1908 Dr Auden was appointed school medical officer of the city of Birmingham, to which the Auden family then moved. Dr Auden was a classicist in Greek and Latin and also had a strong interest in psychology. His wife, who had been trained as a hospital nurse, was a high Anglican, and was musical. Auden was brought up in a home where there were books on scientific subjects, English literature, and Nordic sagas. It may have been important to his own emotional development that his father was away from home (in the Royal Army Medical Corps) from 1914 to 1918. All his life the mother figure was dominant for him.

Clergymen, schoolmasters, and antiquarians were among Auden's forebears. From childhood onward he was interested in limestone landscape, superannuated mining machinery, and place names. Late in life he said that if ever there were to be a school for poets courses in geology should be obligatory. Stimulated perhaps by the Nordic sound of his surname and his Anglo-Saxon Christian name, Auden cherished the belief that he was of Icelandic origin, and made several trips to Iceland; after one of these he published, in collaboration with Louis MacNeice, who had accompanied him, *Letters from Iceland* (1937).

He was educated first at St. Edmunds, a preparatory school at Hindhead in Surrey, where a fellow schoolboy was Christopher Isherwood—who became his lifelong friend, collaborator in writing plays, and, intermittently, lover; then at Gresham's School, Holt, a self-consciously 'modern' school where the emphasis of the teaching was on science (though Gresham's was also distinguished in music and drama); and, finally, at Christ Church, Oxford. His tutor there was Nevill Coghill, to whom, early on, he confided that it was his intention to become not just a poet but a great poet.

The decisive influence on Auden's poetry when he was at Oxford was *The Waste Land* of T. S. Eliot. He also derived from Eliot's early critical essays the view that the poet should be a kind of scientist of language who made, with detached objectivity, poems which were verbal artefacts rather than vehicles for expressing the poet's personality and feelings. Yet his early poems contain images of barriers, impassable frontiers, broken bridges, which seem to express his feelings of personal isolation, but in impersonal guise.

After leaving Oxford with a third class in English literature in 1928, Auden went, in August of the same year, for a year to Berlin. There he met John Layard, an ex-patient of the American psychologist and guru Homer Lane, who interested him in Homer Lane's teaching. This aimed at liberating the forces of the unconscious in the individual without applying moral censorship to whatever behaviour resulted from such release. The healing power of uninhibited love became a theme of the poetry of Auden's Berlin period.

In 1929 the allowance which his parents had given him at Oxford ceased and Auden was obliged to return to England to earn his living. For a year he did this by private tutoring in London. In 1930 he embarked on a five years' period of school-mastering; first at Larchfield Academy in Helensburgh; and then, from autumn 1932, three years at the Downs School, Colwall. Known to his pupils as Uncle Wiz, Auden's performance as a schoolmaster was later described by one of his pupils as a non-stop firework display; but through his psychological knowledge, his empathy for the very young, and his self-discipline as a writer he was a wise educator, both of the boys and his colleagues.

His first book, privately printed by Stephen Spender in an edition of about forty-five copies, was *Poems* (1928). There followed (published by Faber) *Poems* (1930), *The Orators* (1932), and numerous articles and reviews. Periodicals, pre-eminent among which were *New Verse* and the anthologies *New Signatures* and *New Country*, usually incorporating in their titles the epithet 'new', seemed to spring up in response to a new movement in poetry presumably associated with Auden. The names most often cited together with his were Cecil Day-Lewis, Stephen Spender, and (a year or two later) Louis MacNeice.

That brilliant though obscure *tour de force, The Orators*—a medley of prose and verse—through wit, strangeness, surrealist effects, beautiful poetry, and uninhibited high spirits, communicated its excitement to a whole generation of Auden's young English contemporaries, often public schoolboys, who discovered in it exhilarating answers to the question posed in its first section: 'What do you think about England, this country of ours where nobody is well?'

Because of Fascism's increasing threat to individual liberty, Auden's poetry began to reflect his growing awareness that the individual was largely conditioned by the society in which he lived and that he had to defend his freedom against Fascism. In his private ideology he now added Marxism to Freudian psychoanalysis (he was later to add Christianity to both). He became involved in work and causes which were anti-Fascist. In mid-1935 he gave up schoolmastering and went to London. He joined the GPO Film Unit, where he worked with his friend the painter (Sir) William Coldstream and the producer John Grierson. In collaboration with Christopher Isherwood he wrote for the Group Theatre *The Dog Beneath the Skin* (1935) and *The Ascent of F6* (1936).

On 15 June 1935, at the instigation of Isherwood, he married Erika, daughter of Thomas Mann, who was a potential victim of Nazi persecution—and whom, before the marriage, he had never met—in order to provide her with a British passport. This particular union was never consummated.

In 1937 he visited Spain, having volunteered to drive an ambulance for the Republican side, a visit which resulted in his most politically committed poem: 'Spain' (1937). From January to July 1938 Isherwood and he travelled together to China and produced jointly *Journey to a War* (1939), a book which certainly showed that their political sympathies lay with the invaded and occupied Chinese. Its sonnet sequence about the war contains some of Auden's greatest poetry. They returned from China by way of America, a detour which changed their lives: for it was now that they decided that America was the country where they would take up residence.

The poetry Auden wrote when he was an undergraduate might be said to be well within the tradition of the modern movement; in it there were influences of James Joyce, Gertrude Stein, and T. S. Eliot, as well as of Anglo-Saxon and Norse sagas. But the poetry he wrote during the thirties was a departure from symbolist and imagist purism. He renounced *vers libre* and the search for new forms and wrote with virtuosity in a wide variety of traditional forms. He unabashedly introduced into poetry many elements of journalism and declared that poetry, to be interesting, had to contain news. When he wrote, during his visit to Iceland, the dazzling 'Letter to Lord Byron', it was the newsy, gossipy and satiric aspects of *Don Juan* that appealed to him in Byron, not the romantic.

On 18 January 1939 Auden and Isherwood left England for New York, having every intention of taking up residence in America and becoming American citizens, though, at the time, they did not tell their friends of this decision. After the outbreak of war in September of that year they were much criticized in the English press for not returning to England. On various occasions Auden produced reasons for his leaving England and it seems clear that the England which he had loved in his childhood and youth—an England of private values and pleasures and Edenic landscape—had in his mind ceased to exist. Moreover a result of his involvement with anti-Fascist politics and the public activities connected with them, was that he found himself regarded as leader of a movement called 'the Thirties'. This role, though flattering to him, was false to his vocation. Had he remained in England, he would have almost inevitably found himself becoming the public poetic voice of wartime England, which would have been alien to his gift.

America also meant for him Chester Kallman, a young poet whom he first met in New York in the spring of 1939 and in whom, within a matter of weeks of meeting him, he saw his destiny. In the relationship with Kallman lay his future and nothing would ever alter this. He thought of the relationship as a marriage, to which he was wholly committed. Kallman was in fact congenitally incapable of being faithful within a partnership and this brought Auden (and perhaps Kallman too) much agony.

Paradoxical as it may seem it was in America that Auden was able to reinvent the conditions necessary to his vocation, as the poet with a private voice who could 'undo the folded lie' and as teacher. After a brief spell at St. Mark's School in Massachusetts he taught undergraduate and graduate students at a whole series of universities and colleges (among them Michigan, Swarthmore, Bennington, Barnard, and Virginia). At the end of the war (April to August 1945), with the rank equivalent to major, he was one of a team of researchers into the effects of the bombing of German cities on their inhabitants (the morale division of the US Strategic Bombing Survey). He regarded New York as his home in America and would describe himself not as an American but a New Yorker. It might be said that after 1939 his true homeland was an island called Auden since he owed to New York the opportunity it offered him of being alone.

But after the end of the war he resumed, at least in part, his European life. He rented a house on the island of Ischia to which he went every spring and summer from 1949 to 1957. With the proceeds of an Italian literary prize in 1958 he bought a house in the village of Kirchstetten, near Vienna. His delight in possessing this modest home was such that on first arriving there from New York, he would sometimes stand in the garden with his eyes filled with tears of gratitude.

It is widely held, especially in England, that Auden's poetry declined after his arrival in America. Admittedly the poems written after 1938 rarely communicate the exuberance and restless vitality of some of the earlier work. In *The Double Man* (1941), *The Age of Anxiety* (1947), *The Sea and the Mirror* (1944), *Nones* (1951), and *The Shield of Achilles* (1955) the poet seems to have withdrawn into deeper levels of his consciousness, where he is much preoccupied with working out a system of religious ideas which will enclose and illuminate lived and observed experience. He now rejected utterly the idea that poetry could exercise the slightest influence on politics. Nevertheless, Auden's greatest poems are surely those of the American period, precisely because they transform into the terms of his theology and in his unique language so much of the surrounding life of our time. Moreover, several poems—notably, the title poem of *The Shield of Achilles* volume and 'In Praise of Limestone'—equal, if they do not surpass, the greatest poems of the thirties period. In America Auden also wrote highly individual and imaginative essays and lectures—themselves sometimes a kind of prose poetry—contained in *The Enchafèd Flood* (1950) (based on the 1949 Page-Barbour lecture at the University of Virginia), *The Dyer's Hand* (1962), and *Forewords and Afterwords* (1972).

Auden's collaboration with Chester Kallman in writing the libretto —*The Rake's Progress* (1951)—for Igor Stravinsky's music celebrated for him the fusion of their loves through their gifts: as did also their work together on libretti for operas by Hans Werner Henze and Nicolas Nabokov.

In 1956 Auden was elected professor of poetry at Oxford University. In his inaugural lecture, *Making, Knowing and Judging* (1956), he discussed autobiographically his experience of writing poetry. As poetry professor, Auden would go every morning to the Cadena café in Cornmarket in Oxford and make himself available for consultation and advice to whatever undergraduate poets chose to discuss their work with him. The advice he was most willing to give was about technique.

Probably his life did begin to take a downward curve in the 1960s. In October 1964 he spent six months in Berlin under an 'artists-in-residence' programme there, sponsored by the Ford Foundation. But he did not get on well with those German writers he met—who knew little about him—and he was not happy.

In the early 1970s he lobbied privately to have himself given rooms in Christ Church, his old Oxford college, on terms similar to those granted to E. M. Forster by King's College, Cambridge. In 1972 he was granted residence in a 'grace and favour' cottage in the grounds of Christ Church. That he ever wished for such an arrangement, and that he persisted in it when difficulties arose, are symptoms of loss of self-confidence. His isolation in his New York apartment had begun to have terrors for him. He had visions of falling dead there and his body not being discovered for a week. The return to Oxford was also an attempt to return to his origins by one whose view of his own life was perhaps cyclical. Through no-one's fault, the arrangement did not work out well. Industrialized, tourist-trodden, hooting and hustling modern Oxford did not correspond to

Auden's memory of Peck Quad where, as an undergraduate, he had rooms and met his friends. The Students (fellows) of Christ Church, when they found that he was repetitive at high table and often drunk, did not extend to him the amused and admiring tolerance which he had enjoyed in New York. Auden was not in Oxford but Vienna when on 29 September 1973, after a very successful reading of his poems, he died in a hotel bedroom. He was buried in his much loved Kirchstetten on 4 October of that year.

Friends, English and American, whom Auden had known for a long time, formed a kind of constellation of smiled-at presences in his mind, an accompaniment throughout his life. That he had quarrelled with one of them—Benjamin (later Lord) Britten—was a source of grief to him. Despite his magnanimity and his many acts of generosity, there was a streak of inconsiderateness for others in his behaviour. This was one reason why he never found anyone to live with him. He was obsessively punctual and complained loudly if a meal, or a visitor, was five minutes late. He imposed his idiosyncrasies on others as a regime. These minor faults, which created an isolation for him, were outweighed by greater virtues. He had a sense that being a bachelor did not absolve him from family responsibility.

When he was young he was excessively funny, often in an outrageous way, and he remained greatly amusing all his life. His funniness consisted partly in his playing so uncompromisingly his own uniqueness, expressed already in his dress—the crumpled suit and the carpet slippers which he wore in later life—and even in his face, with its skin which, smooth in youth, became in age like crinkled parchment.

He was grateful for his own success and considered himself happy, though to friends it seemed that in old age he was an illustration of whatever is meant by the term 'broken-hearted'. Probably the happiest period of his life was when, a colleague among colleagues, he taught at the Downs School: as that superb poem of undiluted happiness beginning with the line 'Out on the lawn I lie in bed' would seem to testify.

Many people have found it difficult to take his religion seriously because, in irreligious company, he was inclined to 'camp it up' with references to 'Miss God' etc. But in fact theology provided the culmination of his intellectual life-explaining system; and, in the simplest way, in his benign attitude to others, his forgiveness of those who sinned against him, and the centrality of his feeling of love he was Christian and, in a quite old-fashioned sense, a Christian gentleman.

A portrait of him by (Sir) William Coldstream (1937) is in the Humanities Centre, Houston, Texas; there is a pencil drawing by Don Bachardy (1957) in the National Portrait Gallery; in private hands there are three drawings done by David Hockney (1968). There are also sketches by Maurice Field (1932–5) when he was at the Downs School, Colwall, and a page of sketches done by the Viennese artist Anton Schumich at the reading Auden gave in Vienna on the night of his death.

[Humphrey Carpenter, *W. H. Auden: a Biography*, 1981; Edward Mendelson, *Early Auden*, 1981; Stephen Spender (ed.), *W. H. Auden, a Tribute*, 1975; private information; personal knowledge.]

Stephen Spender

published 1986

AYER Sir Alfred Jules (1910–1989)

Philosopher, was born 29 October 1910 at Neville Court, Abbey Road, north-west London, the only child of Jules Louis Cyprien Ayer, financier, later in the timber trade, who came from a Swiss Calvinist family, and his Jewish wife, Reine Citroën, who came from the Citroën car family and ultimately from Holland. He had no religious upbringing, and his childhood years, which he described as lonely, were spent in London. At the age of seven he was sent to Ascham, at Eastbourne, and from there went on, first to Eton as a scholar, and then, with an open scholarship in classics, to Christ Church, Oxford. Choosing not to read classical honour moderations, he obtained in 1932 a first in *literae humaniores*, which, so out of sympathy was he with the prevailing tone of Oxford philosophy, he owed entirely to his marks in ancient history.

On the advice of his tutor, Gilbert Ryle, who had already introduced him to the ideas of Bertrand (third Earl) Russell and Ludwig Wittgenstein—and to the latter personally—Ayer spent the winter of 1932–3 in Vienna, attending Moritz Schlick's lectures and the meetings of the Vienna Circle, and then returned to a lectureship at Christ Church, to which he had been elected while still an undergraduate, and which he held until 1939.

In 1936 Ayer published his most famous book, *Language, Truth and Logic*, written at the age at which (as he liked to recall) David Hume had written his *Treatise of Human Nature* (1739). It was his version of Viennese logical positivism, though he also saw it as a recasting of the traditional theses of British empiricism into linguistic terms. The book is full of passionate iconoclasm, expressed in a fine cadenced prose. Its central thesis is the verification principle, which divided all statements into the verifiable or the unverifiable. Verifiable statements were either reducible to observation statements (everyday beliefs, science) or transformable by means of definitions into tautologies (logic, mathematics), and only they were meaningful. Unverifiable statements (metaphysics, ethics, religion) were literally nonsense. Difficulties found in formulating the principle were treated as comparatively insubstantial, though, when the book was reissued in 1946, the new thirty-six-page introduction, itself a model of philosophical frankness, gave them much greater weight.

Ayer's ideas scandalized established philosophy, not least through their self-assurance, and they infiltrated pre-war Oxford mainly through a discussion group of younger dons that met in (Sir) Isaiah Berlin's rooms in All Souls College. The young J. L. Austin was an early convert, but only briefly, and was then, for over twenty-five years, Ayer's relentless critic. The more open-minded of the older philosophers, such as William Kneale and H. H. Price, regarded Ayer's impact on Oxford philosophy as salutary.

Ayer's next book, *The Foundations of Empirical Knowledge*, philosophically his most refined work, supplemented the earlier attempt to set the limits of human knowledge with an account, based on sense-data, of how we attain this knowledge. The book appeared in 1940, by which time Ayer was in the army. He was commissioned in the Welsh Guards, but mostly served in the Special Operations Executive. He ended the war as a captain, attached to the British embassy in Paris.

In 1945 Ayer went to Wadham College, Oxford, as philosophy tutor, a post to which he had been appointed in 1944, but in 1946 he obtained the Grote chair of the philosophy of mind and logic at University College London. Here Ayer's charismatic powers as a teacher, enhanced by his swiftness in discussion, and his broad and growing fame as the author of *Language, Truth and Logic*, came into their own, and he converted a run-down department into the rival of Oxford and Cambridge. This was the happiest period of his career. In 1956 he published *The Problem of Knowledge*, in which, abandoning reductionism, he justified our everyday beliefs by their power to explain our sense-experience. This line of argument was developed in such later works as *The Origins of Pragmatism* (1968) and *Russell and Moore* (1971), in which the history of philosophy was deftly blended with philosophical argument, and *The Central Questions of Philosophy* (1973), which aimed at updating Russell's *The Problems of Philosophy* (1912).

In 1959 Ayer had accepted the Wykeham chair of logic at Oxford, which was held at New College, partly to continue his polemic with Austin, who died the following year. Ayer always held that philosophy, to be worth while, must aim at generality: Austin saw no reason to believe this. Though perhaps no longer at the epicentre of debate, Ayer fought with immense skill and undiminished speed and agility against such developments as ordinary-language philosophy, Wittgensteinianism, and the new essentialism. He liked philosophy to be high-spirited as well as serious. He remained a great and generous teacher, and a prolific writer, with twenty-six publications before his death and one after. He shone at international conferences. He retired in 1978 and was a fellow of Wolfson College, Oxford, from 1978 to 1983.

Like his friend and hero, Bertrand Russell, Ayer did not treat philosophy as a cloistered enterprise. In the postwar years he reached a wide audience through the BBC *Brains Trust*, and later was active against anti-homosexual legislation.

'Freddie', as he was known, was highly gregarious, elegant, and an animated conversationalist. He was short, with large, dark brown eyes, and a sudden smile which irradiated his fine, slightly simian features. He spoke very fast, and to the accompaniment of quick, fluent gestures. His friends included writers, painters, politicians, and journalists. He hated religion, and followed competitive sport, particularly football, avidly. He loved the company of women, and was much loved in turn. Vanity was in his nature, but he combined this with great charm and total loyalty to his friends.

Ayer was made FBA in 1952, and a foreign honorary member of the American Academy of Arts and Sciences in 1963: he was knighted in 1970, and became a chevalier of the Legion of Honour in 1977. He received honorary degrees from Brussels (1962), East Anglia (1972), London (1978), Trent in Canada (1980), Bard in the USA (1983), and Durham (1986). He became an honorary fellow of New College (1980).

Ayer was married four times: first, in 1932 to (Grace Isabel) Renée, daughter of Colonel Thomas Orde-Lees, explorer, of the Royal Marines; there was one son and one daughter. The marriage was dissolved in 1941 and in 1960 he married Alberta Constance ('Dee'), former wife of Alfred Wells, American diplomat, and daughter of John Chapman, business executive, from the local newspaper-owning family in Providence, Rhode Island: they had one son. The marriage was dissolved in 1983 and in the same year he married Vanessa Mary Addison, former wife of Nigel Lawson MP (later Baron Lawson of Blaby), and daughter of Felix Salmon, businessman. She died in 1985 and in 1989 he remarried Alberta Ayer, who survived him. Ayer also had a daughter with Sheilah Graham, the Hollywood columnist (see Wendy W. Fairey, *One of the Family*, 1993). When Ayer died in University College Hospital, London, 27 June 1989, the event received much publicity in the press, serious and popular, and it was seen as bringing to an end a long line of outspoken arbiters of liberal or secular opinion.

[A. J. Ayer, *Part of My Life*, 1977, and *More of My Life*, 1984; A. Phillips Griffiths (ed.), *A. J. Ayer, Memorial Essays*, 1992; information from friends; personal knowledge.]

RICHARD WOLLHEIM

published 1996

BAIRD John Logie

(1888–1946)

Television pioneer, was born at Helensburgh, Dumbartonshire, 13 August 1888, the youngest of the four children of the Revd John Baird, minister of the West Parish church, by his wife, Jessie Morrison Inglis, who came of a shipbuilding family in Glasgow. He took an electrical engineering course at the Royal Technical College, Glasgow, and afterwards went to Glasgow University, where he was in his final B.Sc. year when the war of 1914–18 interrupted his studies. Rejected as unfit for the forces, Baird served as superintendent engineer of the Clyde Valley Electrical Power Company, but at the end of hostilities he had to give up engineering owing to ill health. He then set up in business, marketing successively a patent sock, jam, honey, and soap, but each business venture, whether in Glasgow, the West Indies, or in London, although otherwise successful, was ended by the ill health which was to dog him throughout life.

Following a complete physical and nervous breakdown, he retired to Hastings, Sussex, in 1922. Here he turned to his early love of research and decided to concentrate upon television which had been the dream of scientists for fifty years. Baird occupied an attic at 8 Queen's Arcade, and, having very little capital, assembled his crude, makeshift apparatus on a wash-stand. The base of his motor was a tea-chest, a biscuit tin housed the projection lamp, scanning discs were cut from cardboard, and fourpenny cycle lenses were utilized. Scrap-wood, darning needles, string, and sealing-wax held the apparatus together. In 1924 at Hastings he transmitted the flickering image of a Maltese cross over a distance of feet; in that year he brought his crazy apparatus to London, where he occupied two attic rooms at 22 Frith Street, Soho, and struggled alone under the twin handicaps of ill health and poverty. Success came at last, and on 26 January 1926 Baird gave the world's first demonstration of true television in his attic before about fifty scientists. The London County Council blue plaque commemorates this event; the apparatus used is now in the Science Museum, South Kensington.

Later in the same year Baird demonstrated 'Noctovision', or seeing-in-darkness by use of infra-red rays. In 1927 he demonstrated television over 438 miles of telephone line between London and Glasgow. In that year the Baird Television Development Company, Ltd., was formed, the Television Society was founded, and Baird was elected a fellow of this and of the Physical Society. In 1928 came his world's first transatlantic television transmission between London and New York and the world's first transmission to a ship in mid-Atlantic. The same year he gave the world's first demonstrations of television in natural colour, and also stereoscopic television. An experimental television service on the Baird system was inaugurated by the British Broadcasting Corporation in 1929, but sound and vision were sent alternately until 1930 when both were broadcast simultaneously; it was not until 1932 that the Corporation took over responsibility for the programmes which up to then had been provided by Baird's company.

In 1930 Baird showed big-screen television in the London Coliseum programme and afterwards sent his big-screen to Berlin, Paris, and Stockholm. In 1931 he televised the Derby from Epsom and in 1932 he gave the world's first demonstration of ultra-short-wave transmission. In 1937 he was the first British subject to receive the gold medal of the International Faculty of Science and in the same year he was elected an honorary fellow of the Royal Society of Edinburgh. In spite of his physical and financial handicaps Baird was the first exponent of every development associated with television. Following the report of a committee of inquiry in January 1935, a rival all-electronic television system, working on 405 lines to Baird's 240, was tried out by the British Broadcasting Corporation side by side with Baird's system, and in 1937 the latter was dropped. Baird continued his colour, stereoscopic, and big-screen experimental work until he died at Bexhill, Sussex, 14 June 1946.

Baird married in 1931 Margaret, daughter of the late Henry Albu, diamond merchant, of Johannesburg, who had come to London to study music and was known as a concert pianist. They had one son and one daughter. A portrait of Baird by James Kerr-Lawson is in the engineering section of Glasgow University, and a pencil drawing by the same artist is in the Scottish National Portrait Gallery; a bust by Donald Gilbert, which was shown at the Royal Academy exhibition in 1943, became the property of the sculptor's mother.

[R. F. Tiltman, *Baird of Television*, 1933; Maurice Gorham, *Broadcasting and Television since 1900*, 1952; personal knowledge.]

R. F. Tiltman

published 1959

BALCON Sir Michael Elias (1896–1977)

Film producer, was born in Birmingham 19 May 1896, the youngest of three sons among the five children of Louis Balcon, prospector in South Africa, who later went to America before returning to England and becoming a salesman, and his wife, Laura Greenberg. He grew up in a family which he described as 'respectable but impoverished'. His Jewish father, who had connections in South Africa, was something of a wanderer, often leaving the mother to run the family, sometimes with the help of her eldest son. Michael was educated at the George Dixon Grammar School, Birmingham; he left in 1913. In 1914 he tried to join up, but was rejected because of a flaw in his left eye, and throughout the war he worked for the Dunlop Rubber Company.

When peace came he joined Victor Saville (later a well-known director and producer) in forming a modest film distribution company. Presently with a joint capital of £200 the two of them set off for London; raised financial backing from figures in the industry; imported an American star; and produced a melodrama, *Woman to Woman* (1922). It was a success, but a second venture was a failure. Not discomfited, Balcon managed to found a film company which was to become famous, Gainsborough Pictures. Also in 1924 he married a girl from Johannesburg, South Africa, Aileen Freda, daughter of Beatrice Leatherman. She was appointed MBE in 1946. The marriage lasted in happiness to the end of his life. There were two children: a son, Jonathan, and a daughter, the actress Jill Balcon, who was to marry the poet laureate, Cecil Day-Lewis.

The first Gainsborough films were made at Islington in what was a converted power house. With the business help of Reginald Baker, his accountant and lifelong friend, Balcon bought the studios. There followed a series of silent films which included *Blighty* (1927) and two pieces with Ivor Novello, *The Rat* (1925) and *The Lodger* (1926), which was directed by (Sir) Alfred Hitchcock.

Balcon welcomed the advent of sound. Despite his conviction that the British screen must not be dominated by America, he was obliged for technical reasons to go to Hollywood for the production of his *Journey's End* (1930). But a year later he was in charge of production not only at Islington but also at the Gaumont-British Picture Corporation.

Years of intense activity followed. The films were not world-beaters, but they were made with a serious care for the standing of the British cinema: *The Constant Nymph* (1933); *The Good Companions* (1932) with Jessie Matthews; Conrad Veidt was brought from Germany to play in *Rome Express* (1932) and *Jew Süss* (1934); Walter Huston starred in *Rhodes of Africa* (1936). Balcon had seen the work of Alfred Hitchcock as a beginner; now he saw the blossoming of a giant talent in *The Man Who Knew Too Much* (1934) and *The Thirty-Nine Steps* (1935). And he has the credit of having backed Robert J. Flaherty's *Man of Aran* (1932).

In 1936 his work at Gaumont-British ended, and he was invited to take charge of Metro-Goldwyn-Mayer's production in Britain. The first film was *A Yank at Oxford* (1938). He disapproved of the script, and with his strong feeling about a national British cinema he was unhappy with his position. The association ended, leaving him free to pursue his true work; and, resuming his partnership with Reginald Baker, he began working, quite modestly, at Ealing Studios. By 1938 he was in charge of production. He was to make the name of Ealing internationally famous.

War was imminent: Balcon recognized the need for a documentary approach, and, joined in 1940 by the celebrated documentary director Alberto Cavalcanti, he was responsible for a series of notable war films: *The Foreman Went to France* (1941), *San Demetrio, London* (1943); *Next of Kin* (1942); and Cavalcanti's own *Went the Day Well?* (1942). After the war the serious mood continued in *The Cruel Sea* (1952), and the problems of readjustment were tackled in such films as *The Divided Heart* (1954). As early as 1945 Ealing produced a brilliant exercise in the ghostly *Dead of Night*. And Balcon was ready to explore new territory; films were made in Australia, among them *The Overlanders* (1946).

But probably the greatest achievement was in the field of comedy, *Passport to Pimlico* (1949), *Whisky Galore* (1948), *The Lavender Hill Mob* (1951), and the special triumphs of (Sir) Alec Guinness—*Kind Hearts and Coronets* (1949), *The Man in the White Suit* (1951), and *The Ladykillers* (1955). Even the Americans were won over, and in the 1950s one could see New Yorkers queueing to see Ealing comedy. And there were other notable films: *It Always Rains on Sunday* (1947), *The Blue Lamp* (1949), *Mandy* (1952), and *Scott of the Antarctic* (1948).

Balcon was knighted in 1948. Eleven years later Ealing closed. But he was still ceaselessly active. He was chairman of British Lion and of the adventurous Bryanston Company, and his name is associated with such films as *Saturday Night and Sunday Morning* (1960) and *Tom Jones* (1963). Meanwhile he became a director of Border Television. The output was huge, varied, and distinguished; truly he was among the creators of the British cinema. Quick to appreciate talent, he collected at Ealing a band of remarkable directors; the young Pen Tennyson (killed in the war), Sandy Mackendrick, Robert Hamer, Charles Frend, Harry Watt, Charles Crichton. Of a shy but sometimes explosive temperament, in private life he was a man of great charm, and his house on the Kent–Sussex borders, secluded in gardens and farmland, was a place of genial family hospitality.

Balcon was a fellow of the British Film Academy, a governor of the British Film Institute, an honorary fellow of the British Kinematograph Society, a senior fellow of the Royal College of Art, and was awarded an honorary D.Litt. from Birmingham (1967) and Sussex (1975). He died at his home at Upper Parrock, Hartfield, Sussex, 17 October 1977.

[Michael Balcon, *A Lifetime of Films*, 1969; personal knowledge.]

Dilys Powell

published 1986

BEATON Sir Cecil Walter Hardy

(1904–1980)

Photographer, artist, writer, and designer of scenery and costumes, was born at 21 Langland Gardens, Hampstead, London, 14 January 1904, the eldest in the family of two sons and two daughters of Ernest Walter Hardy Beaton, a London timber merchant, and his wife, Esther ('Etty') Sisson, of Temple Sowerby, Cumberland. After Harrow, he went up to St. John's College, Cambridge, in 1922 to read history and architecture, and though he never graduated, he took an active part in the theatrical life of the university. His first love was the theatre but his first success was in photography, a medium that had absorbed him from his earliest days. His sisters became his first models and assistants. He designed their costumes, entered them into fancy dress competitions, and photographed them. A childhood heroine was Lily Elsie. Coming down from Cambridge in 1925, he spent some unhappy months working in the Holborn office of a friend of his father's. He worked hard to escape from this and by his industry and imagination he began to establish a name as a photographer. When at the end of 1926 he suddenly found himself friends with (Sir) Osbert and

(Dame) Edith Sitwell, and the 'Bright Young Things', he found a world thirsting for his talents. His rise to fame thereafter was nothing less than meteoric. His ingenious photographic portraits of the Sitwells led to his employment with *Vogue* as photographer, caricaturist, and illustrator, both in New York and London. In 1927 and 1930 he held one-man exhibitions at the Cooling Gallery, Bond Street, for both of which Osbert Sitwell wrote the introduction. He produced his first book, *The Book of Beauty* (1930).

In the 1930s he worked on two revues of (Sir) Charles Cochran—*Streamline* (1934) and *Follow the Sun* (1936)—and continued to photograph in London and New York, though as he noted 'At no stage of my photographic career could I ever have believed that photography could be my life's work'. It was in 1930 also that he rented Ashcombe, a derelict country house in the Wiltshire Downs, which he converted into an idyllic home and where he entertained friends such as Rex Whistler, Augustus John, and Edith Olivier. In 1937 he was chosen to photograph the wedding of the Duke of Windsor in France. Beaton's career was progressing well until a disagreement with *Vogue* brought his contract with the magazine to an abrupt end in 1938. For some years he was unable to work in America, but his career was saved by two things. First, Queen Elizabeth invited him to photograph her at Buckingham Palace, and secondly war was declared. Beaton found that he was able to make an important contribution as a war photographer. He travelled throughout England for the Ministry of Information and later journeyed to the Middle East and Far East. Any glossy magazine image his previous work may have had now disappeared and by his courage, industry, and wholly professional approach, he earned the respect of the three Services. Six books emerged from these years. One of his most famous pictures was of a bombed-out child in hospital. This photograph became the front cover of *Life* magazine in September 1940 and was said, more than any other picture, to have influenced American feeling concerning the war.

In the years that followed stage, film, ballet, and opera work gave him more opportunities. In 1945 he designed *Lady Windermere's Fan*, with an opulence of style that held an immediate appeal for post-war Britain. The following year he took the part of Cecil Graham in the American production. In 1948 he did the costumes for the films *An Ideal Husband* and *Anna Karenina*. Other noted productions on which he worked were *The School for Scandal* (1949), *Quadrille* for (Sir) Noël Coward (London 1952, New York 1954), *Turandot* (New York 1961 and London 1963), and *La Traviata* (New York 1966). His greatest stage success was of course the designing of costumes for *My Fair Lady* in 1956, a success he repeated when he spent a year in Hollywood in 1963 working on the film version of the play. For his costume design and art direction he won two Oscars. (He had been awarded his first Oscar for the film *Gigi* in 1958.) During this time and in fact for a period of thirty years from 1944 to 1974, he was preoccupied with the writing of his play, *The Gainsborough Girls*, staged at Brighton in 1951 and in a revised version in 1959. Unfortunately this floundered on both occasions.

Beaton also made a considerable contribution to the world of fashion. His best book is certainly his personal survey of fifty years of changing fashion, *The Glass of Fashion* (1954), and he amassed a collection of the dresses he most admired at the Victoria and Albert Museum, some of which were exhibited in 1971. He was a dedicated diarist from 1922 to 1980 and six volumes were published in his lifetime. These and his photographs combine to give a unique portrait of the age in which he lived. In 1968 his career was crowned with an important exhibition of his photographs at the National Portrait Gallery. In 1950 he was awarded the Legion of Honour. He was created CBE in 1957 and knighted in 1972. Two years later he suffered a bad stroke but gradually learned to paint, write, and photograph with his left hand. He died at his second Wiltshire home, Reddish House, Broadchalke, 18 January 1980.

Beaton was a man of immense style and sartorial elegance, forever fascinated by new ideas and attitudes. He possessed an extraordinary visual sense and an eye which in a flash took in every minor detail around him. His conversation was witty and penetrating, and while he enjoyed the company of glittering society, above all he valued and sought out talents and individuality. He suffered from the accusation that much of his work was light or trivial, but his industry alone and the wide range of his achievements makes this an unfair assessment. He was not granted much personal happiness, but relished his work, his garden, and his friends. He was unmarried.

There is a portrait of Beaton by Christian Bérard in the National Portrait Gallery.

[*The Times* and *Daily Telegraph*, 19 January 1980; Cecil Beaton, *Photobiography*, 1951; R. Buckle (ed.), *Self Portrait with Friends, the Selected Diaries of C. Beaton 1926–1974*, 1979; 6 vols. of *Diaries*, 1961, 1965, 1972, 1973, 1976, and 1978; Charles Spencer, *Cecil Beaton Stage and Film Designs*, 1975; Hugo Vickers, *Cecil Beaton*, 1985; private information; personal knowledge.]

HUGO VICKERS

published 1986

BEECHAM Sir Thomas

(1879–1961)

second baronet

Conductor, was born 29 April 1879 at St Helens, Lancashire, the elder son and second child of (Sir) Joseph Beecham, chemist, of St Helens and later Huyton, and Josephine Burnett. His family background was that of the very prosperous business started by his grandfather, Thomas Beecham, a famous name in the world of digestive pills, which were sold at first personally by their inventor, and later marketed and advertised in vast quantities. There was good personal rapport between Beecham and his grandfather, better than that between him and his father.

At an early age Beecham showed two personal gifts—a good memory for words, and a passion for music. He was taught the piano from the age of six. He was also interested in sport, and despite his short stature, played football and cricket for Rossall School, Lancashire, which he attended from 1892 to 1897 and where he was a house-captain. He later went for eighteen months to Wadham College, Oxford (1897/8), where he practised the piano, played football, and indulged in bouts of foreign travel to hear his favourite operas. It soon became obvious that music was to be his chosen life's work. He was given, at twenty, and obviously by family influence, the opportunity to conduct his first professional orchestra—the Hallé, upon a visit to St Helens, who were faced with an empty podium because Dr Hans Richter, who had been asked to conduct, had other engagements. Previously Beecham had learnt something about conducting with his own St Helens Orchestral Society—which he had founded two years previously—and seemed to find no difficulty in leading the Hallé orchestra through an almost unrehearsed performance, a capacity he was to demonstrate superbly with a succession of orchestras over the next sixty years.

Having left Oxford without taking a degree, Beecham went to live in London in 1900, where he studied musical composition with Charles Wood, Frederic Austin, and other teachers. In 1902, aged twenty-two, Beecham joined, as one of its conductors, a small London touring opera company directed by Kelson Trueman, and soon had committed its repertory to memory. In 1903 he married Utica ('Utie') Celestia, daughter of Charles Stuart Welles, of New York, an American diplomat, at a time of serious discord in his own family. There were two sons of his marriage. It was a short-lived union of which he rarely spoke in later years, although the separation which soon followed seemed sad rather than bitter. They were divorced in 1943 and Utica, Lady Beecham, died in 1977.

An injury to his wrist in 1904 destroyed Beecham's ambition to be a concert pianist. Most of that year he spent travelling on the Continent with his wife, attending performances and collecting musical scores. In December 1905 he gave his first public orchestral concert in London, with players of the Queen's Hall orchestra. Press notices were poor, and Beecham himself far from satisfied. In 1906, helped by the clarinettist Charles Draper, he founded the New Symphony Orchestra, which expanded to sixty-five players in 1907, all of whom were carefully selected. This time Beecham's arresting style triumphed, and it was obvious that Britain had an important young conductor. It was at this stage that he met Frederick Delius, whose music was to be such an important part of Beecham's work. In 1908 he presented several works by his new friend, with whom he went to Norway on holiday. In 1910, backed by his father, whose friendship he had now regained, Beecham mounted the first of his many Covent Garden opera seasons, a mammoth affair with thirty-four works represented, many of them very grand in scale and quite unknown in Britain. There were works by Richard Strauss (*Elektra* and *Feuersnot*); Wagner (*Tristan and Isolde*); Debussy (*L'Enfant Prodigue*); four of the less familiar Mozart operas; and many works by lesser composers. This did not prevent—indeed it inevitably produced—very heavy financial losses; but it could well be taken as a pattern for many of Beecham's finest achievements in the years which followed. In 1911 he presented Diaghilev's Russian Ballet with Nijinsky and in 1913 he introduced Chaliapin in a season of Russian opera, as well as giving the first London performance of Richard Strauss's *Der Rosenkavalier*. The tragic international events which followed in 1914 cut short Beecham's operatic activities, but he remained indefatigable in his fight to keep music going, and sustained both the Hallé Society and the London Symphony Orchestra with financial and artistic help. His greatest achievement at this time was the touring of his opera company, working in theatres large and small up and down the country, performing more than thirty different operas, including such works as *The Boatswain's Mate* by (Dame) Ethel Smyth and Isidore de Lara's *Naïl*, all at prices so low as to put them within reach of everyone. In 1916 Beecham succeeded to his father's baronetcy, having been knighted earlier in the same year. A final financially disastrous Covent Garden season in 1920 left him fighting to stave off bankruptcy, and until 1923 he was almost absent from the musical scene. From then until 1929 his life seems to have been a gradual climb back to the pinnacle he had achieved so early. In that year he presented the first Delius Festival in London, which was attended by the now blind and paralysed composer, who for the first time began to receive the public appreciation he deserved.

In 1932, after heated negotiations, lasting some years, with the BBC and the London Symphony Orchestra for the foundation of a full-time permanent symphony orchestra in London, Beecham founded, with the assistance of Courtaulds, the excellent London Philharmonic Orchestra, which still exists (1979). With them he was to present many excellent concert and opera seasons until 1939, when war once again changed the London scene. In 1934 Delius died and the Delius Trust, planned by Beecham, took over the task of presenting his music on records and in concert-halls. In 1936 Beecham took his orchestra to Nazi Germany, and had the audacity to include in his party his secretary Berta Geissmar, the expatriate German who travelled safely and openly with him. Two occasions are remembered from this tour—the evening when Beecham refused to precede Adolf Hitler into the concert-hall, thus avoiding having to salute the arrival of the Führer, and the concert at Ludwigshaven, in the concert-hall of BASF, manufacturers of recording equipment, which marked the first recording ever made on tape of any orchestra. From 1939 to 1944 Beecham travelled constantly abroad, in the USA and Australia, and his reputation as a wit and a raconteur grew as rapidly as his stature as a conductor.

Upon his return to London in 1944, and after trials and arguments with both the London Philharmonic Orchestra and what was soon to be the Philharmonia under Walter Legge's direction, in 1946 he formed the Royal Philharmonic Orchestra, which was to be his last orchestra and the one with which he was to be longest in association. In 1946 he gave an important series of concerts in the second Delius Festival; and in 1947, in the presence of the eighty-three-year-old composer, a Richard Strauss Festival.

In 1950 he presented his orchestra in a lengthy tour of North America—an enterprise which somehow supported itself without government help and with Beecham's own generous donation of his services to balance a precarious budget. In the years which followed, Beecham busied himself with almost every possible aspect of orchestral and operatic activity at the very highest level. His recordings were among the finest produced anywhere. He conducted extensively in Britain, America, and Paris. He was made a Companion of Honour in 1957, an event which was clouded for him by the death of his second wife, Betty, daughter of Daniel Morgan Humby, a surgeon, of London. She was a pianist who was formerly the wife of the Revd H. C. Thomas, of London, and they had been married in 1943, after Beecham terminated his long association with Lady Cunard. Beecham's publications included an early autobiography, *A Mingled Chime* (1944), which described his life only until 1924, and should have been augmented by a later volume; and a biography of Frederick Delius (1958). In 1956 he gave the Romanes lecture at Oxford.

In 1959 he married his personal secretary, Shirley Hudson, who was with him in the United States in 1960, when illness forced him to return to London, where he died 8 March 1961. He was succeeded in the baronetcy by his elder son, Adrian Welles Beecham, born in 1904.

Beecham was often a harsh taskmaster and could sometimes be inconsiderate to those working for him. Punctuality was not among his most noticeable virtues. Nevertheless, such peccadilloes were easily overlooked in view of his effervescent enthusiasm which communicated itself to musicians and public alike. Orchestral players will long remember him as not only a great conductor, but a witty and stimulating person who could inspire them to produce their best and showed obvious pleasure in what he heard. He was a man of wide reading, which informed and enlivened his conversation, and he was renowned for his wit. Sometimes his interpretations of the music he conducted were controversial—for example, it was felt that he failed to bring out the heroic nature in some passages by Beethoven. But he succeeded in giving a freshness of outlook to performances and often astonished the public by his vitality, his flamboyance of manner, and his deep musical understanding. His own favourite composer was Mozart.

In appearance Beecham, although invariably an impressive figure, changed considerably over the years. In youth he was, judging from the many photographs and cartoons of the time, slim, elegant, dark-haired, and something of a dandy. The famous story of his summer evening walk along Piccadilly when he is said to have hailed a cab, thrown in his redundant overcoat, and said 'Follow me' as he continued his stroll is probably exaggerated, but contains a germ of the truth about the 'Beech' of the time. By his fifties he had already become a more sturdy character, but by no means rotund; now white-haired and with his famous 'goatee' beard jutting formidably (especially if he were arguing or directing a more dramatic musical work), he took on a more pinkish hue and a somewhat more benign aspect in moments of repose. With the passing years the figure became stouter, but Beecham was never anything like a fat man, and to the very end he presented an impressive pair of shoulders to orchestras the world over. Sitting down at this time he seemed gigantic; it was when he stood that he was revealed as a very short man—his legs were surprisingly short, belying every other physical aspect of this remarkable man. One feature remained constant through the years—the large and lustrous eyes, at once the agents of fear and confidence in the hearts of the players who faced him, and possibly the most important tool in his conducting equipment.

Apart from photographs and cartoons, portraits of Beecham seem to be few and rarely successful. Simon Elwes painted a portrait in 1951, but it is generally regarded as not a good likeness. In the Royal Festival Hall there is an excellent if somewhat skeletal bust in bronze which catches the mercurial conductor very much in action with a typical sideways cut-off which was extremely characteristic of his technique. There is a portrait of Beecham in oils by Gordon Thomas Stuart (1953) and a drawing by Guy Passet (1950), both in the possession of Alan Denson. One of six bronze bust casts by David Wynne (1957) is at the National Portrait Gallery, and others are at the Festival Hall, Bristol, and Aberdeen. Several caricatures were drawn by Edmund Dulac. There is also a portrait by Dorothy E. F. Cowen (1952). Sketches made at the Queen's Hall, London, during the Delius Festival of 1929, by Ernest Procter, are in the National Portrait Gallery, and the Royal Philharmonic Orchestra has a sculpture by Muriel Liddle (1979).

[Charles Reid, *Thomas Beecham*, 1961; Neville Cardus, *Sir Thomas Beecham*, 1961; Humphrey Proctor-Gregg, *Beecham Remembered*, 1976; Ethel Smyth, *Beecham and Pharaoh*, 1935; Sir Thomas Beecham, *A Mingled Chime, Leaves from an Autobiography*, 1944; Harold Atkins and Archie Newman, *Beecham Stories: Anecdotes, Sayings and Impressions*, 1978; Alan Jefferson, *Sir Thomas Beecham: A Centenary Tribute*, 1979; personal knowledge.]

JACK BRYMER

published 1981

BETJEMAN Sir John

(1906–1984)

Poet, writer on architecture, and broadcaster, was born 28 August 1906 at 52 Parliament Hill Mansions, north London, the only child of Ernest Betjemann, a furniture manufacturer, and his wife, Mabel Bessie Dawson. The family name, of Dutch or German origin, can be traced back to an immigration in the late eighteenth century. The poet adopted his style of it about the age of twenty-one.

He attended the Dragon School, Oxford, and Marlborough College and was active at both in school theatricals and in various forms of writing. He entered Magdalen College, Oxford, in 1925 but was rusticated three years later after failing in divinity. To his father's deep disappointment he declined to enter the family business, becoming successively a preparatory school master (at Thorpe House School, Gerrard's Cross, and at Heddon Court, Cockfosters, Hertfordshire), assistant editor of the *Architectural Review* in 1930, and film critic of the London *Evening Standard* in 1933.

Shortly after his marriage that year he moved to a farmhouse in Uffington, in the Vale of White Horse, Berkshire, where his wife was able to keep horses.

His first two collections of poems, *Mount Zion* (1931) and *Continual Dew* (1937), showed a poet already fully formed, with the impeccable ear, delight in skill, and assured mastery of a wide range of tones and themes that so distinguished all his subsequent work in verse. In these early volumes, as later, Betjeman moved with perfect assurance from light pieces, *vers de société*, satirical sketches of muscular padres or philistine businessmen (as in the famously ferocious tirade 'Slough') to sombre reflections on the impermanence of all human things. In a remarkable variety of metres and manners the poems make an equally clear-cut impression on the reader, never drifting into obscurity and never once tainted with the modernism then fashionable. Here too he gave glimpses of the world of gas-lit Victorian churches and railway stations, of grim provincial cities and leafy suburbs that he was to make his own, not forgetting the grimmer contemporary developments, shopping arcades, and bogus Tudor bars, that he saw effacing it and strove to resist.

These concerns are reflected in his publication of 1933, *Ghastly Good Taste*, subtitled 'a depressing story of the rise and fall of English architecture', which attracted more immediate attention than either of his first books of poems. In it he attacked not only modern or modernistic trends but also the other extreme of unthinking antiquarianism, nor had he any time for the safely conventional. While still at school he had become interested in Victorian architecture, thoroughly unmodish as it was at the time. His writings on the subject over the years led to a revival in appreciation of the buildings of that era and paved the way for the eventual founding of the successful Victorian Society. Further afield, he showed among other things his fondness for provincial architecture in his contributions to the Shell series of English county guides, of which the most notable is that on Cornwall, another enthusiasm acquired in boyhood. He had joined the publicity department of Shell in the mid-1930s.

Betjeman's poetical career had begun to flourish with the appearance in 1940 of *Old Lights for New Chancels* and continued with *New Bats in Old Belfries* (1945) and *A Few Late Chrysanthemums* (1954). Many of the poems in these three volumes became classics of their time, including 'Pot Pourri from a Surrey Garden', 'A Subaltern's Love-song' and 'How to Get On in Society'. His *Collected Poems* came out in 1958 and went through many impressions. *Summoned by Bells* is dated 1960, a blank-verse poem of some 2,000 lines that gives an account of his early life up to schoolmastering days with characteristic animation, humour, sadness, and abundance of detail.

Both these volumes were widely successful, the first edition of the *Collected Poems* selling over 100,000 copies. Betjeman's poetry has continued to enjoy a popularity unknown in this country since the days of Rudyard Kipling and A. E. Housman. No doubt it was poems like the three mentioned above and the more obviously quaint period pieces that made an immediate appeal. Nor should one underestimate the sheer relief and delight to be felt at the appearance of a poetry of contemporary date that was easy to follow and yielded the almost forgotten pleasures of rhyme and metre expertly handled. Nevertheless it may not be instantly obvious how so strongly personal a poet, one given moreover to evoking characters and places that might seem outside general interest, should have proved so welcome. He is full of nasty jolts for the squeamish too.

The answer must lie in the closeness of the concerns of Betjeman's poetry to the ordinary day-to-day experience of his readers, something else that had been far to seek in the work of his contemporaries. For all the delight in the past, it is the past as seen from and against the present; for all the cherished eccentricities—as such hardly repugnant to British taste anyway—the subject is ourselves and our own world. The point was well made by Philip Larkin, the friend and admirer who best understood his work: 'He offers us something we cannot find in any other writer—a gaiety, a sense of the ridiculous, an affection for human beings and how and where they live, a vivid and vivacious portrait of mid-twentieth-century English social life' (Philip Larkin, 'It Could Only Happen in England', 1971, in *Required Writing*, 1983, pp. 204–18).

In World War II Betjeman volunteered for the RAF but was rejected and joined the films division of the Ministry of Information. He then became UK press attaché in Dublin (1941–3) to Sir John Maffey (later Lord Rugby) and subsequently worked in P branch (a secret department) in the Admiralty, Bath. In 1945 he moved to Farnborough and in 1951 to Wantage where his wife opened a tea shop, King Alfred's Kitchen. By the mid-1950s his main income came from book reviewing, broadcasting, and his poems. He pursued a highly successful career as a broadcaster, and with the help of the image he projected through television, engaging, diffident, exuberant, often launched on some architectural or decorative enthusiasm, he became a celebrated and much-loved figure in national life. He used this position to further zealously the defence of many buildings threatened with demolition. He was able to save many of these, from St Pancras station to Sweeting's fish restaurant in the City of London, though the Euston Arch was lost despite his vigorous campaign. Appropriately, it was at St Pancras, naming a British Rail locomotive after himself, that he was to make his last public appearance on 24 June 1983.

In later years Betjeman continued his work in poetry, publishing *High and Low* in 1966 and *A Nip in the Air* in 1974. The contents of these two volumes reveal no loss of energy; indeed, poems like 'On Leaving Wantage 1972' embody a melancholy, even a tragic, power he had never surpassed. All the same, apart from the ebulliently satirical 'Executive', almost none of them have achieved much individual popularity. They were incorporated entire in the fourth edition of the *Collected Poems* in 1979. Those in *Uncollected Poems* (1982) were such as the poet was content should remain in that state and are unlikely to gain him many new readers, though lovers of his work would not be without any of them.

No account of Betjeman's life could fail to stress his devoted adherence to the Anglican Church, not only for the sake of its buildings, its liturgy, and its worshippers but for its faith. Expressions of doubt and the fear of old age and death are strong and memorable in his poetry, but 'Church of England thoughts' are pervasive too, and one of its chief attractions, seldom given proper weight, has been the sense of an undemonstrative but deep Christian belief of a kind able to contain the harsh, ugly, absurd realities of present-day existence.

John Betjeman was a sociable man, one who loved company and valued it the more for being also a shy man. Although he was renowned for his youthful gregariousness and was endlessly affable with all manner of people, his was a life rich in intimacy. Latterly he was partial to small gatherings and old friends and a sufficiency of wine. His expression in repose was timid, perhaps not altogether at ease, and even at the best of times it was possible to surprise on his face a look of great dejection. But all this was blown away in an instant by laughter of a totality that warmed all who knew him. His presence, like his work in verse and prose, was full of the enjoyment he felt and gave.

He was chosen as poet laureate to universal acclaim in 1972. He received many distinctions besides, being awarded the Duff Cooper memorial prize, the Foyle poetry prize, and in 1960 the Queen's medal for poetry. In that year too he was appointed CBE, in 1968 he was elected a Companion of Literature by the Royal Society of Literature, and in 1969 he was knighted. He was an honorary fellow of his old college, Magdalen (1975), and also of Keble College, Oxford (1972). He had honorary degrees from Oxford, Reading, Birmingham, Exeter, City University, Liverpool, Hull, and Trinity College, Dublin. He was also honorary ARIBA.

In 1933 he married Penelope Valentine Hester, only daughter of Field-Marshal Sir Philip Walhouse Chetwode, first Baron Chetwode, OM, commander-in-chief in India at the time. In latter years they were amicably separated and Betjeman was cared for by his friend Lady Elizabeth Cavendish, sister of the Duke of Devonshire. Lady Betjeman, a writer of travel books (as Penelope Chetwode) and a devotee of Indian culture, died in 1986. There were a son and a daughter of the marriage. From the mid-1970s Betjeman had suffered increasingly from the onset of Parkinson's disease and he died at Treen, his home in Trebetherick, Cornwall, 19 May 1984. He is buried in nearby St Enodoc churchyard.

[*The Times*, 21 May 1984; Bevis Hillier, *John Betjeman: a Life in Pictures*, 1984, and *Young Betjeman*, 1988; personal knowledge.]

KINGSLEY AMIS

published 1990

BEVAN Aneurin

(1897–1960)

Politician, was born 15 November 1897 in Tredegar, Monmouthshire, the sixth of the ten children, seven of whom survived, of David Bevan and his wife, Phoebe, daughter of John Prothero, blacksmith. David Bevan was a miner, a Baptist, a regular reader of Blatchford's *Clarion*, a lover of music and of books: a gentle, romantic man who had more cultural influence on his son than the elementary school in which Bevan was a rebellious pupil and acquired little but the ability to read. A stammer which he later persevered to overcome probably had some part in his hatred of school; his immense desire for knowledge had hardly developed when at thirteen he left; thereafter he had to educate himself. The Workmen's Library was well stocked with 'the orthodox economists and philosophers, and the Marxist source books'. But it was not in Nye Bevan's undisciplined temperament to become a Communist. Until the failure of the general strike of 1926 he believed that industrial action would bring the workers to the promised land of which he dreamed as he roamed the Welsh mountains, disputed with his friends, or declaimed the poetry which he loved.

Meantime Bevan had gone into the pits. He became an expert collier and almost equally expert at making trouble for his employers: by 1916 he was chairman of his lodge. He was exempt from military service on account of an eye disease and became well known in Tredegar and beyond for his opposition to what he considered a capitalist war. In 1919 the South Wales Miners' Federation sent him to the Central Labour College in London for two years which were probably not quite the waste of time he thought them: his horizons widened and his debating skill improved.

Bevan returned in 1921 to Tredegar and his conflict with the owners who had resumed control of the mines after the war, despite the Sankey recommendation of nationalization. It was not perhaps surprising that Bevan could find no work. His meagre unemployment benefit was stopped when his sister began to earn, and when his father fell ill with the chest disease which was to kill him he received no sickness benefit until his son fought the case. Bevan's enforced familiarity with the intricacies of sickness and unemployment benefit was at the disposal of all who cared to consult him. To keep his position in the mining industry he worked for some months as a checkweighman until the pit closed down and he was once more on the dole. Then in 1926 he became disputes agent for his lodge at a salary of £5 a week. In the long conflict with the owners in that year he showed himself an efficient organizer of relief; made fighting speeches at special national conferences of the Miners' Federation in July and October; yet a month later opposed Arthur Horner by recommending negotiation before the drift back to work should bring about the disintegration of the Federation.

In the following year the local guardians who were deemed to have been too generous with poor relief were replaced by commissioners: 'a new race of robbers' whom Bevan never forgot or forgave. He realized now that power to redress the miseries of the unemployed in the South Wales coalfield must come through political action. Already a member since 1922 of the Tredegar urban district council, in 1928 he was elected to the Monmouthshire county council and in 1929 was returned to Parliament as Labour member for Ebbw Vale, a seat which he retained until his death. For all his turbulence, his highly independent outlook, his criticism of his own leaders, Bevan remained to the last convinced that only through Parliament and the Labour Party could he achieve his aims.

Throughout the early thirties unemployment was a major issue on which Bevan had plenty to say and he soon became known in Parliament as an attacking speaker of considerable if erratic brilliance, marred by a vituperative inability to keep his temper. He was prominent in opposing non-intervention in the Spanish civil war, and as foreign affairs became of increasing concern found himself allied with Sir Stafford Cripps whom he supported in his unity campaign of 1937 and as a founder of and regular contributor to *Tribune*, which he was himself to edit in 1942–5. Early in 1939 he was expelled from the Labour Party for supporting Cripps in his Popular Front campaign, but he was readmitted in December.

The outbreak of war meanwhile had brought Bevan new fields of discontent. His opposition to the Government throughout the war earned him notoriety and suspicion and Churchill's description of him as 'a squalid nuisance' probably reflected the opinion of the man in the street. Yet his complaints had some basis: Churchill, he maintained, was conducting a one-man government; furthermore, was no strategist. Bevan pressed for an early second front; and later mistrusted the 'Big Three' conferences as ignoring the claims of lesser countries and preventing the post-war development of a western Europe strong enough to stand between the opposing American and Soviet powers. He came into conflict with Ernest Bevin over his treatment of the coalmining industry, and in 1944 was nearly expelled again from the Labour Party for his violent opposition to a regulation imposing penalties for incitement to unofficial strike action in essential industries: 'the disfranchisement of the individual'. He was asked for, and gave, a written assurance that he would abide by standing orders. At the Labour Party conference of December 1944 he was elected for the first time to the national executive; and in the Labour Government of the following year C. R. (later Earl) Attlee made him minister of health and housing. He was then sworn of the Privy Council.

The National Health Service Act of 1946 provided free medical and dental care for all who cared to avail themselves of it and in the event ninety-five per cent of the nation did. The scheme derived from a number of sources but Bevan included such daring ideas as the nationalization of the hospitals, to be run by regional boards, and the abolition of the sale of general practices. The service was to be financed from general taxation. There followed two years of negotiation with the doctors before the scheme came into effect in 1948. The battle was fought on the grand scale. Yet Bevan displayed more patience and flexibility than were usually at his command in bringing to a successful outcome a cause which was very dear to his heart and was certainly his finest achievement. He was ably assisted by his permanent secretary, Sir William Douglas. With the minister of national insurance Bevan was also responsible for the National Assistance Act of 1948 which completed the break-up of the Poor Law and introduced a comprehensive scheme of assistance and welfare services. Housing he tackled with schemes for the repair of war damage, for prefabricated houses, and for large subsidies to local authorities to enable them to provide houses to rent to people in the lower income groups.

For all his achievement, Bevan was still an uncertain asset to his party. He was apt to get carried away by his own rhetoric: his 'lower than vermin' onslaught on the Tories in July 1948 did him more harm than it did the Tories who were estimated by Harold Laski, no friend of Bevan, to have gained some two million votes thereby. It was seized upon by the British press, still smarting from Bevan's attack upon it as 'the most prostituted in the world'. With his own Government Bevan was increasingly out of sympathy, mainly over armaments expenditure and Ernest Bevin's policy of alliance with the United States and the containment of Russia. It was unfortunate that Cripps, to whom Bevan was much attached and who could exercise a moderating influence upon him, fell ill and resigned in October 1950. In January 1951 Bevan moved to the Ministry of Labour, only to resign in April when he came into conflict with Hugh Gaitskell over the latter's proposal to introduce certain charges into the health service. Harold Wilson and John Freeman also resigned: the armament programme, it was thought, would impoverish the country. In the election of constituency members to the national executive in October Bevan headed the poll, with Mrs Barbara Castle second and two other supporters gaining places: a shift of opinion within the Labour Party noted perhaps by the electorate which returned the Conservatives to power at the general election later in the month.

For the remainder of his life Bevan was in opposition. *In Place of Fear* (1952), his only book, set out his belief in democratic socialism 'based on the conviction that free men can use free institutions to solve the social and economic problems of the day, if they are given a chance to do so'. He deplored American foreign policy and discounted Russia's military aims. For a time it seemed that Bevan would bring about a split in his own party by the growth of the 'Bevanite' group within it. At the Labour Party conference of 1952 six Bevanites were elected to the national executive with Bevan again at the head of the poll. But at a subsequent meeting of the parliamentary Labour Party in October Attlee successfully moved a resolution calling for the abandonment of all unofficial groups within the party. The Bevanites protestingly complied, but the philosophy of 'Bevanism' remained. At the ensuing annual elections of the parliamentary party Bevan unsuccessfully challenged Herbert Morrison (later Lord Morrison of Lambeth) for the deputy leadership; but he was elected to the shadow Cabinet. This position he resigned in April 1954 when he attacked Attlee's approval of S.E.A.T.O. In the summer he went with Attlee in a Labour Party delegation to Russia and Red China. But in March 1955 he was again defying his leader in the House: this time over the use of nuclear weapons in the event of hostilities, even if not used by the aggressor. The party whip was withdrawn and his expulsion from the Labour Party sought, but again Bevan gave an assurance of conformity. Once again a general election was in sight and again Labour lost. When Attlee resigned in December, Bevan unsuccessfully challenged Gaitskell for the leadership, although he outstripped Morrison; then he stood for the deputy leadership, only to be defeated by James Griffiths. But in October 1956, by a narrow majority over George Brown, he attained the post of party treasurer which he had failed to wrest from Gaitskell in the two preceding years.

In Gaitskell's shadow Cabinet Bevan was entrusted with first colonial, then foreign, affairs: an attempt to close the ranks in which Bevan saw that he must co-operate if Labour were to return to power, even if he regarded Gaitskell as 'a desiccated calculating machine'. On colonial problems, Malta, Cyprus, Kenya, and during the Suez crisis, Bevan spoke with skill and moderation for the Opposition. Although he urged the banning, by agreement with Russia and America, of nuclear and hydrogen bomb tests, at the party conference of 1957 he helped to defeat a motion demanding that Britain should make a unilateral renunciation of such bombs, saying that it would send a British foreign secretary naked into the conference chamber. His standing within his party became more secure and in October 1959 he was elected unopposed as deputy leader of the parliamentary party; he continued as party treasurer. His speeches had become persuasive rather than aggressive, but were delivered with all the old felicity which, despite the hatred and fear he could engender, had made him generally considered the best speaker, after Churchill, to be heard in the House. If a touch of melancholy was to be detected now, it might be attributed to the trend of international affairs and to the decline of his own physical powers. After some months of illness he died at his home at Chesham, Buckinghamshire, 6 July 1960.

With Bevan's passing some of the colour and much of the passion went out of politics. He fought vehemently, with deadly invective, but with gaiety and wit as well, for his beliefs. Not everybody shared them, least of all within his own party where he was strongly opposed by the trade-unionists. He was essentially an original—complex, baffling, and infuriating, especially when he gave way to indolence or showed a tendency to disappear at times of crisis; but the sincerity and stature of the man were not in doubt. If on occasions he could be a menace to, he also vitalized, the Labour Party and enlarged and influenced its thinking. He was sustained throughout by Jennie Lee, herself a staunch left-wing member of the Labour Party, later to hold office, whom he married in 1934; they had no children. Art, literature, and music, as well as politics, contributed to the richness of the domestic life which they enjoyed, for preference in the country. Bevan always hated London and indeed would personally have fitted better into a more exotic background than the British, although politically he would have been unlikely to survive. A large man whose thatch of black hair silvered elegantly early, he was immensely alive, exercising a personal magnetism which made it difficult even for those who most detested his views to resist his charm. The very large congregation which attended the memorial service in Westminster Abbey was a tribute to the affection and respect in which he had come to be held.

[Aneurin Bevan, *In Place of Fear*, 1952; Jennie Lee, *This Great Journey*, 1963; Michael Foot, *Aneurin Bevan*, vol. i, 1897–1945, 1962; Vincent Brome, *Aneurin Bevan*, 1953; Mark M. Krug, *Aneurin Bevan: Cautious Rebel*, 1961; Francis Williams (with Earl Attlee), *A Prime Minister Remembers*, 1961; *The Times*, 7 July 1960; private information.]

HELEN M. PALMER

published 1971

BLUNT Anthony Frederick

(1907–1983)

Art historian and communist spy, was born in Bournemouth, Hampshire, 26 September 1907, the third and youngest son (there were no daughters) of the Revd Arthur Stanley Vaughan Blunt and his wife, Hilda Violet, daughter of Henry Master of the Madras Civil Service. His father was a kinsman of the poet, anti-imperialist, and libertine, Wilfrid Scawen Blunt, his mother a friend of the future Queen Mary; both these connections were to have a curious significance for Blunt's future career. After a childhood acquiring a lasting enthusiasm for French art and architecture while his father was chaplain of the British embassy in Paris, he went to Marlborough College; his artistic interests were further stimulated by his eldest brother, Wilfrid, a future art master. Going up to Trinity College, Cambridge, on a scholarship, Blunt graduated there with a second in part i of the mathematical tripos (1927) and a first in both parts (1928 and 1930) of the modern languages tripos (French and German). In 1932 he was elected a fellow of the college on the strength of a dissertation on artistic theory in Italy and France during the Renaissance and seventeenth century. By now he was already writing for the *Cambridge Review* and within a year was contributing articles and reviews on modern art to the *Spectator* and *Listener*. At first he championed the modern movement, which for him was a product of the School of Paris, but later, influenced by the Marxism which he had first espoused in 1934, he just as fiercely, if temporarily, attacked modernism as irrelevant to the contemporary political struggle.

While still an undergraduate he was invited to join the Apostles. The values of this exclusive Cambridge society between the wars (derived in part from the teaching of the philosopher, G. E. Moore) have been summed up as the cult of the intellect for its own sake, belief in freedom of thought and expression irrespective of the conclusions to which this freedom might lead, and the denial of all moral restraints other than loyalty to friends. An influential minority of the society's members were, moreover, like Blunt himself, homosexual, and, at a time when homosexual acts were still illegal in Britain, he seems to have relished the resulting atmosphere of secrecy and intrigue. Where he stood out from most of his contemporaries was in his phenomenal intellectual energy, powers of concentration, and capacity for self-discipline—qualities he retained into old age. Endowed with charm, vitality, and good looks, he lived an active social life and also travelled widely during the 1930s on the Continent. In 1936–7 he resigned his Cambridge fellowship, joined the staff of the Warburg Institute, lectured on baroque art at the Courtauld Institute, and allowed himself to be drawn into working for the Russian secret intelligence service by the charming, scandalous Guy Burgess. Much ink has since been spilt over the identity of the individual who recruited spies for the Russians at Cambridge in the 1930s, but in Blunt's case his fondness for Burgess, to whom he remained devoted until the latter's death in Moscow in 1963, is probably sufficient explanation. His decision seems to have been at once emotional and cold-blooded. There is no doubt of his hatred of Fascism at the time but whether he was ever a convinced communist is far from clear. Yet his sense of professional dedication would have made him as capable a spy as he was an art historian.

After a futile spell in France in the Field Security Police, he joined the British counter-intelligence service, MI5, in 1940 and remained with it in London throughout World War II. He is known to have given his Soviet controllers every detail of the service's organization and the names of all its personnel and he presumably also gave away any military secrets to which he had access. How much damage he actually did to the British war effort is hard to say; it may have been rather slight. But there was a real danger that the information he supplied might have been leaked to the Germans, so causing the deaths of Allied agents in occupied Europe, or, alternatively, used by the Russians in preparing policies hostile to the British and Americans. At the end of the war in 1945, Blunt left MI5 and thereafter had no more secrets to impart, though he remained in touch with Burgess until the latter's defection to Moscow in 1951 and he continued occasionally to see another of the Cambridge spies, H. A. R. ('Kim') Philby. In May 1951 Philby told Blunt that the security authorities were planning to arrest Donald Maclean. When Blunt passed on the warning both Maclean and Burgess were able to escape to Moscow.

All this went on concurrently with the development of Blunt's career as an art historian. Already before the war he saw that the refugee scholars at the Warburg Institute had brought with them from Hamburg both an intellectual rigour and a soundly-based historical method that were new to the study of the art of the past in Britain. In 1937–9 he published scholarly articles in the Warburg *Journal* on such diverse topics as 'The Hypnerotomachia Poliphili in 17th-century France' and 'Blake's *Ancient of Days*' and began his great work on the seventeenth-century French painter, Nicolas Poussin, characteristically with an article showing that Poussin's 'Notes on Painting' were not original but were largely copied from obscure ancient and Renaissance literary sources. Blunt also helped to establish friendly relations between the Warburg and Courtauld Institutes, becoming deputy director of the latter in 1939. In 1940 most of his fellowship dissertation was published as *Artistic Theory in Italy 1450–1600*; written with his customary lucidity and stylistic grace, it remains a useful introduction to its subject. During the war he wrote further articles in periodicals and a book on the French architect, François Mansart (1941); in 1945 he published a catalogue of the French drawings in the royal collection at Windsor Castle.

In the same year, 1945, to the puzzlement of his friends, who knew of his political sympathies though not of his activities as a spy, he accepted appointment as surveyor of the King's (after 1952 the Queen's) Pictures. One of his motives in taking the job may well have been to deflect suspicion away from himself in the event that any of his fellow conspirators was caught—for who in authority, he would have calculated, would think of doubting the loyalty of a senior royal servant? On the other hand, his activity, soon after appointment, in helping to rescue on behalf of George VI from a castle in Germany what are now said to be compromising letters from the Duke of Windsor quite possibly had no sinister implications so far as Blunt was concerned. At all events, he gave every sign of enjoying the post of surveyor, which he retained until 1972. While the day-to-day work was left to his deputy and eventual successor, (Sir) Oliver Millar, Blunt took the major decisions, including that of opening the Queen's Gallery, Buckingham Palace, in 1962. (For his services he was appointed CVO in 1947 and KCVO in 1956.) In 1947 he had become director of the Courtauld Institute of Art and professor of the history of art in the University of London. Thenceforth the Institute was to be his home (he had a flat at the top of the building, designed by Robert Adam, in Portman Square) and the centre of his life. In almost every sense he was a superb director. He had a natural authority, an infectious enthusiasm for his subject, and a winning way with students and younger colleagues. Teaching more by example than by precept, he inspired those around him to give of their best, and it was under him that the Courtauld, whose staff and student numbers more than doubled during his time, earned the position, which it had had in theory since its foundation in 1931, of being the principal centre for the training of art historians in Britain.

The first phase of his scholarly career was crowned by a masterly survey in the Pelican History of Art series, *Art and Architecture in France 1500–1700* (1953). Lucid, penetrating, and comprehensive, this is still the best study of its subject and is perhaps Blunt's single most successful book. The next dozen years were spent mainly working on Poussin, an artist for whose intellectual power, self-discipline, and personal reticence he had a natural sympathy. His erudite monograph on Poussin, based on a thorough study of the artist's ideas and including a catalogue of the paintings, appeared in 1966–7. Afterwards Blunt turned his attention as a scholar chiefly to Italian baroque architecture, on which he also wrote several books. He retired from the Courtauld and the university in 1974, covered with British and French academic honours, including honorary D.Litts. of Bristol (1961), Durham (1963), and Oxford (1971), and the Legion of Honour (1958).

Yet all this time he was at risk of exposure as a former spy. For many years he successfully resisted interrogation by the security services but in 1964, after the FBI had found a witness prepared to testify that Blunt had tried to recruit him during the 1930s, he made a secret confession in return for a promise of immunity from prosecution. In the later 1970s the pressure mounted again, as a result of investigations by independent writers on espionage relying on information leaked by former security officers. On 15 November 1979, the prime minister confirmed in the House of Commons that Blunt had been an agent of, and talent spotter for, Russian intelligence before and during World War II, although she added that there was insufficient evidence on which criminal charges could be brought. His knighthood was annulled, as was the honorary fellowship he had held at Trinity College since 1967, and immediately the press, radio, and television began a campaign of vilification. There was also much discussion by intellectuals in the serious press not only of Blunt but of the whole phenomenon of the Cambridge spies who had put belief in communism above loyalty to country in the 1930s and 1940s.

Undoubtedly some of the agitation was motivated by class hatred, and it is a striking fact that both Blunt's own actions and the treatment of him not only by the public but also by officials were pervaded at every turn by the class divisions in British society. More immediately, his career can perhaps best be explained by the fatal conjunction in him of his own outstanding gifts and his desire to be at once part of the establishment and against it; or, as an acquaintance put it, 'The trouble with Anthony was that he wanted both to run with the hare and hunt with the hounds.' He died of a heart attack, in the London flat to which he had retired near the Courtauld, 26 March 1983. He was unmarried.

[E. K. Waterhouse, introduction to *Essays in Renaissance and Baroque Art presented to Anthony Blunt*, 1967; Anthony Blunt, essay in *Studio International*, 1972; Andrew Boyle, *The Climate of Treason*, 1979; Barrie Penrose and Simon Freeman, *Conspiracy of Silence*, 1966; Peter Wright, *Spycatcher*, 1987; John Costello, *Mask of Treachery*, 1988; personal knowledge.]

MICHAEL KITSON

published 1990

BLYTON Enid Mary

(1897–1968)

Writer for children, was born 11 August 1897 at Lordship Lane, East Dulwich, London, the eldest child in a family of one girl and two boys of Thomas Carey Blyton, a businessman of modest means, formerly of Sheffield and then of London, and his wife, Theresa Mary Harrison. He was ambitious for her to be a concert pianist and she studied hard for many years, taking her LRAM at an early age. But after he had left the family house to live with another woman—an event that must have psychologically affected Enid who was then thirteen and loved him deeply—she gradually dropped her studies and took to writing poems and stories. Educated at St Christopher's School for Girls (1907–15), where she became head girl in 1913, she subsequently spent some months studying music, and in 1916 she began to train as a teacher at Ipswich, where she studied the Froebel and Montessori methods for teaching the young—a training that influenced her writing techniques in later years. Having completed the course by December 1918, in 1919 she went to teach at Bickley Park School in Kent and the following year became nursery governess in Surbiton to a family of four young boys and the children of neighbours.

In the last decade of her life, she often claimed to have papered her bedroom with rejection slips from magazine and book publishers but her surviving diaries of those formative writing years tell a story of early and ever-growing success. At the age of fourteen she had published a poem in one of the children's papers of Arthur Mee, and in March 1917 *Nash's Magazine* published one of her poems. In 1921 and 1922 various short stories and poems appeared in the *Saturday Westminster Review*, the *Bystander*, the *Londoner*, *Passing Show*, and other magazines of the period. Her first book, *Child Whispers*, a collection of poems, was published in 1922 and in the next year she earned well over £300 from her published work. In 1924 the total exceeded £500 and in 1925 over £1,200—a substantial income for any contemporary author. By then she had given up her teaching work.

In 1924 she married Major Hugh Alexander Pollock, DSO, the son of an antique bookseller in Ayr. After a distinguished army career in the war of 1914–18, in 1923 Pollock had become editor of the book department at Newnes, the magazine and book publishers. Pollock had been married before, but his wife had left him during the war. He submitted Enid's books to his employers and also arranged for her to write and edit *Sunny Stories*, a new weekly publication with which she was to be associated for nearly a quarter of a century. They had two daughters, Gillian, born in 1931, and Imogen, born in 1937. But by the outbreak of war in 1939 the relationship was already under strain and Hugh Pollock's later absences on military duties increased the pressures. In 1942 they were divorced and six months later, in 1943, Enid married a middle-aged London surgeon, Kenneth Fraser Darrell Waters (died 1967). The second marriage was a happy and harmonious one. Darrell Waters, whose first marriage had been childless, looked on Enid's daughters as his own; their names were eventually changed to Darrell Waters by deed poll.

By the mid 1930s, Enid Blyton had got into the prolific stride which she maintained for a further thirty years. In 1935 she published six different titles and in 1940 eleven titles and two under the pseudonym 'Mary Pollock' emerged from her facile pen: or rather, from her portable typewriter. She had the habit of typing on a sunny veranda at her home, Green Hedges, in Beaconsfield, Buckinghamshire, with a portable typewriter on her knees and a shawl around her shoulders. Ten thousand words a day was a good cruising speed and she was known to complete a full-length book for children between a Monday and a Friday of the same week. So vast was her output that her books were rumoured to be created by a team of ghostwriters. The rumours were baseless. With the help of her immense energy, years of practice, and a vast if quiet self-confidence, she would tell close friends that she could sit down with the typewriter on her knees, think of a compelling opening sentence, and then go off into a trance-like state while the story flowed from her imagination through her nimble fingers on to the page. When this became public knowledge, unkind critics maintained that the resulting story read as though the author had indeed been in a trance at the time of writing.

Because of paper-rationing during the war of 1939–45, Enid Blyton's output was too prolific to be confined to one publisher. By the early fifties, she had close on forty British publishers. At the end of her active writing career around 1965, she had published over four hundred different titles, many of which had also appeared in translation in about twenty different languages or dialects—from Afrikaans to Swahili, as she was proud to claim. The English-speaking sales alone (1977) were in excess of two hundred million copies and, nearly ten years after her death, were increasing at the rate of about five million copies per year. She was the first major children's author to appear in paperback editions and in 1977 over one hundred of her individual titles were continually in print. She deliberately wrote, in the language of every age-group, for children from five to fifteen, so that those who discovered her works when very young would remain faithful for the next decade.

She became a well-known author in the 1940s with her *Famous Five* and *Secret Seven* stories, and her *Adventure* series, but in 1949 she became a major public figure with the creation of Little Noddy. One day she called on a publisher and was shown some original line and colour drawings depicting puppet figures by a Dutch artist named Harmsen van der Beek. At once she began to weave names, stories, and a continuing background for the characters depicted—Little Noddy, Big Ears, Mr Plod the policeman, and the other characters of Toyland Village. Noddy and his friends were not only immensely successful in book form—the sales ran into several million copies—but manufacturers rushed to produce Noddy dolls, Noddy toothpaste, Noddy pyjamas, and Noddy drawings on cereal packets. There was a very popular 'Noddy in Toyland' pantomime for children each Christmas and fifty-two Noddy puppet films shown weekly on commercial television.

Such a huge popular success was bound to create an adverse reaction in certain quarters. Literary articles were published which criticized the moral qualities inherent in Enid Blyton's work. Some librarians banned her works from public libraries on the grounds that the simple prose style and black-and-white moralizing in the plots deterred young children from reading books with more subtle literary values. The simple and incontrovertible answer was that the children themselves *wanted* to read her books and continued to do so in ever-increasing numbers.

Although she produced several hundred thousand words every year, conducted an immense correspondence by postcard with her many young fans, edited and wrote the *Enid Blyton Magazine*, actively supported charities for children, and ran the domestic household at Green Hedges, up to the last fifteen years of her life Enid Blyton did not use the services of a literary agent for her voluminous and intricate publishing affairs. She dealt with a variety of British and foreign publishers and with her incisive business mind always drove a good bargain. She would never accept an advance payment on account of royalties but insisted that the minimum printing of each book should be twenty-five thousand copies. She also insisted on having complete control over the choice of artist for the dust-jacket and illustrations: the publisher who erred once in presenting indifferent art-work to her never did so twice.

As a famous writer who for many years enjoyed an annual income of well over £100,000, Enid Blyton was quiet and unostentatious in her private life. She shunned publicity and often wrote to literary editors asking them not to review her books but to devote the space to up-and-coming authors. Once her legal advisers took action because of a humorous remark about her in 1952 on the *Take it From Here* radio programme on the BBC. She saw life in simple, unshaded terms and sensed from her early teaching days that young children prefer certainty and the familiar in their reading tastes. Her monument remains on the shelves of bookshops and libraries.

In her prime, Enid Blyton was a woman of striking appearance—somewhat above average in height, with dark, curly hair and eloquent dark eyes, a longish nose, and ruddy complexion. She was handsome in a Spanish gypsy style rather than conventionally pretty and, although she was not well versed in social small talk, she would light up and become the focus of any conversation that settled on her favourite topics—children, her books for and about them, and the publishers who helped to introduce the former to the latter. She died in a Hampstead nursing home, 28 November 1968. There is a portrait in oils by Derek Houston, which is in the possession of the family.

[Barbara Stoney, *Enid Blyton*, 1974; Enid Blyton, *The Story of My Life*, 1952; personal knowledge.]

George Greenfield

published 1981

BRITTAIN Vera Mary

(1893–1970)

Writer, pacifist, and feminist, was born at Newcastle under Lyme 29 December 1893, the only daughter of Thomas Arthur Brittain, paper manufacturer, and his wife, Edith Mary Bervon. Her only surviving brother, Edward, less than two years her junior, a cherished companion, was killed in action in 1918. Vera Brittain grew up in Macclesfield and then in Buxton in Derbyshire, amidst provincial restrictions against which she increasingly chafed. Her intellectual powers were stimulated by her brother and his Uppingham friends and at St Monica's, Kingswood, a school which afforded unusual scope for extra-curricular reading and discussion. When she left, she was already set on one of the paths which she followed to the end of her days, the cause of feminism.

That her awakened mind should seek deeper and more disciplined experience would never have occurred to her kind but conventional parents had not chance brought to their Buxton home a distinguished university extension lecturer in the person of (Sir) John Marriott. With his encouragement, she won an open exhibition to Somerville College and went up to Oxford in 1914. There followed the nightmare years of war. University life became insupportable and she enrolled as a VAD, among the young women who were not trained nurses, but who worked and suffered side by side with them. She served in France and Malta as well as London. In the carnage of trench warfare one by one her gifted fiancé, Roland Leighton (brother of the artist Clare Leighton), their closest friends, and finally her beloved brother were killed or died of wounds.

Post-war Oxford (where she obtained a second in history in 1921) brought frustrations but it enabled her to establish a friendship of remarkable quality with a fellow student from Yorkshire, Winifred Holtby, author of *South Riding*, whose untimely death in 1935 led Vera Brittain to commemorate her in *Testament of Friendship* (1940). Meanwhile, another Oxford graduate had noticed the talented young woman who was beginning to make her way in her chosen career as a lecturer and writer. (Sir) George Catlin (died 1979), of New College, became professor of politics at Cornell University in 1924 at the age of twenty-eight. In 1925 he and Vera Brittain were married at St James's, Spanish Place. She herself never embraced the Roman Catholic faith, although Roland Leighton, her husband, and her daughter did so.

Marriage posed for Vera Brittain in its sharpest form the dilemma of home and career. She had no doubt that, for her, a career as writer and speaker was essential. Transatlantic correspondence on this necessity preceded marriage. One winter at Cornell convinced her that she could not work there. There followed a long period of what she termed 'semi-detached marriage', with Catlin going each winter to Cornell and later to other universities, while she and their son and daughter remained at home. Despite much physical separation, the bond of affection remained strong and when, in her last years, her strength began to fail, nothing could have exceeded the devotion with which her husband tended her.

It was in 1933 that the book which brought her fame was published. *Testament of Youth* spoke with the most moving eloquence for a whole generation. There had been other war books and much war poetry. But this autobiographical narrative, based on diaries and the letters of a group of exceptionally intelligent, sensitive, and articulate young people, was the first book of note to view the horror and heartbreak of war through the eyes of a woman: 'The world was mad and we were all victims . . .' The book's controlled poignancy brought immediate and overwhelming response: Vera Brittain awoke to find herself famous. The impression made on the post-war generation as well as on her contemporaries was intense.

She wrote the book to release her deeply felt obligations to the dead, but also with the conviction that, for those who had survived, nothing mattered so much as to persuade the world of the criminal futility of war. Already a socialist, in 1936 she joined the Peace Pledge Union of Canon Dick Sheppard and spoke widely at pacifist meetings. During the war of 1939–45 her courageous denunciation of the saturation bombing of Germany brought much public criticism in the United States as well as Britain.

As a publicist for feminist and pacifist causes, Vera Brittain achieved a fair measure of success. As a novelist, she lacked the humour and skill in characterization of her friend Winifred Holtby. The special interest of a further autobiographical instalment, *Testament of Experience* (1957), lies in the references to her children, especially her daughter who, as Mrs Shirley Williams, was destined to become a leading Labour politician and Cabinet minister, thus fulfilling both her mother's feminist aspirations and her father's unrealized personal political ambitions.

In youth, Vera Brittain's slight figure and 'large, melting dark eyes' were clearly very attractive, although she frequently lamented her lack of stature and 'immature appearance' as handicaps on public platforms. She took a lively interest in clothes. Always reticent and a little formal, within her own circle she could arouse intense devotion. She received an honorary D.Litt. from Mills College, California, in 1946. She died in London 29 March 1970. A drawing and a portrait by Sir William Rothenstein are in the possession of her daughter.

[Vera Brittain, *Testament of Youth*, 1933, and *Testament of Experience*, 1957; private papers; personal knowledge.]

Eirene White

published 1981

BROCKWAY (Archibald) Fenner

(1888–1988)

Baron Brockway

Socialist campaigner and parliamentarian, was born 1 November 1888 in Calcutta, the only son and eldest of three children of the Revd William George Brockway, London Missionary Society missionary, and his wife, Frances Elizabeth, daughter of William Abbey. His mother died when he was fourteen. Educated at the School for the Sons of Missionaries at Blackheath (subsequently Eltham College), he became a journalist. He moved from Liberalism to the Independent Labour party and by 1912 was editor of the ILP newspaper, the *Labour Leader.* Still in his twenties, he worked closely with leading figures on the British left.

He played a heroic role in the ILP's opposition to the war of 1914–18, as a journalist, and then through the No-Conscription Fellowship as an opponent of military conscription. On four occasions he was sentenced to gaol—the last time in July 1917 to two years' hard labour. When released in April 1919, he had served a total of twenty-eight months, the last eight in solitary confinement. His war record increased his status in several sections of the Labour movement and in the election of 1929 he was returned as the Labour member for East Leyton. In 1919 he became editor of *India* and joint secretary of the British committee of the Indian National Congress. From 1926 to 1929 he was editor of the *New Leader,* the renamed organ of the ILP, of which he had become organizing secretary in 1922.

Brockway's continuing involvement in the ILP section of the wider Labour party made him an increasingly controversial figure. From 1926 the ILP moved to the left under the leadership of James Maxton, and called for 'socialism in our time', a radicalization backed enthusiastically by Brockway. With the 1929 Labour government proving helpless in the face of rocketing unemployment, Brockway was prominent amongst a small group of ILP rebel members. This small section of left-wingers refused to accept the party's disciplinary guidelines, and were denied endorsement for the 1931 election. Like most Labour MPs, Brockway lost his seat. The dispute over discipline was symbolic of a much more fundamental division over policy. In July 1932, with Brockway in the chair, the ILP voted to disaffiliate from the Labour party.

There followed the most radical period of Brockway's career as he sought to articulate a socialism distinct from the pragmatism of Labour and the Stalinism of the Communist party. But the ILP's membership dwindled, and it was squeezed between its rivals. The Spanish civil war modified his pacifism and deepened his suspicion of the Communist party. In 1937 he visited Spain and observed the repression of the ILP's Spanish equivalent by the Communist party. During the war of 1939–45, he felt cross-pressured between his distaste for militarism and his thorough antipathy to fascism. In wartime by-elections he argued for socialism as a means of ending the war. After Labour's 1945 electoral success, he decided that the ILP offered no distinctive way forward and rejoined the Labour party. From 1942 to 1947 he was chairman of the British Centre for Colonial Freedom and in 1945 he helped establish the Congress of Peoples against Imperialism.

In February 1950 he returned to the Commons as the member for Eton and Slough. He remained firmly on the left, participating in the faction centred around Aneurin Bevan, but his radicalism was always tempered by a concern not to reproduce what he had come to see as the disastrous split of 1932. His strong anti-militarism was expressed in his involvement with the Campaign for Nuclear Disarmament. His principal fame came from his championing of anti-colonial movements. His interest in Indian independence had been long-standing and from 1950 he began to visit Africa regularly. Some called him the member for Africa and he knew several of the first generation post-independence African leaders. From 1954 he was chairman of the Movement for Colonial Freedom. His anti-colonialism was reflected in a thorough opposition to racism in Britain. In nine successive sessions he introduced Bills into the Commons aimed at outlawing discrimination. Ironically, when the 1964 Labour government embarked on such legislation, Brockway had just lost his parliamentary seat. The margin was eleven votes and some commentators ascribed his defeat to the race issue. Despite misgivings, he accepted a life peerage (1964) and campaigned for his causes within the traditionalism of the upper house. His radicalism remained vibrant in his new environment. Brockway was a prolific writer, of books, pamphlets, and articles. These included four volumes of autobiography and major studies of two ILP contemporaries, Fred Jowett (*Socialism over Sixty Years*, 1946) and Alfred Salter (*Bermondsey Story*, 1949).

In 1914 he married Lilla, daughter of the Revd William Harvey-Smith. They had four daughters, two of whom predeceased him (1941 and 1974). As Brockway acknowledged later, the marriage was not a success and he had several, often short-lived, affairs in the interwar years. After a divorce in 1945, in 1946 he married Edith Violet, daughter of Archibald Herbert King, electrician; they had one son. Both his wives shared many of his political views.

Many found Brockway to be highly principled and warmly sympathetic. His style inherited something of his missionary background and his socialist politics owed much to a broader tradition of English radicalism. Not an intellectual, he was yet an independent thinker. Born in the age of Gladstone, he died in the age of Thatcher 28 April 1988, at Watford General Hospital, Hertfordshire.

[*Guardian*, 29 April 1988; *The Times*, 30 April 1988; *Independent*, 2 May 1988; Fenner Brockway, *Inside the Left*, 1942, *Outside the Right*, 1963, *Towards Tomorrow*, 1977, and *98 Not Out*, 1986; personal knowledge.]

DAVID HOWELL

published 1996

BUCHAN John

(1875–1940)

First Baron Tweedsmuir

Author, and governor-general of Canada, born at Perth 26 August 1875, came of mainly Border lowland stock, being the eldest child in the family of four sons and one surviving daughter (the novelist 'O. Douglas') of John Buchan, minister of the Free Church of Scotland, by his wife, Helen, daughter of John Masterton, farmer, at Broughton Green, Peeblesshire. Buchan's father, who had been brought up in the atmosphere of the Disruption, served congregations at Kirkcaldy and at John Knox's church, in the Gorbals district of Glasgow, and the impression made by these rather different places can be easily traced in his son's writings. Perhaps an even greater influence on Buchan was wielded by his mother, a woman sentimental yet shrewd, contemplative but alert, able to hold her own in any company, who lived to see her son surrounded by the pomp of Holyrood and the splendour of Ottawa. In 1895, after attendance at Hutcheson's Boys' Grammar School at Glasgow and at lectures at Glasgow University, he was awarded a scholarship at Brasenose College, Oxford, and thenceforth his life was bound up with England, South Africa, and Canada. Nevertheless, Scotland always 'haunted him like a passion', and he never lost the impress of his home and native land; he remained throughout his life a Christian who said his prayers, read his Bible, and knew the *Pilgrim's Progress* almost by heart.

At Oxford, Buchan won in 1897 the Stanhope historical essay prize on the subject of 'Sir Walter Raleigh' and in 1898 the Newdigate prize for English verse with the 'Pilgrim Fathers' as its theme. He was president of the Union in 1899 and was awarded a first class in *literae humaniores* that same year. Having one or two books already to his credit, he was commissioned by his college to write its history for the Robinson series of 'College Histories'. It appeared in 1898 while he was yet an undergraduate, and called forth severe criticism from antiquarian reviewers unaccustomed to so unconventional a style of historical writing. Disappointed of a prize fellowship, Buchan went to London, where he widened the large circle of his friends and was called to the bar by the Middle Temple in 1901, earning his living by journalism, and reading with J. A. Hamilton (later Lord Sumner) and (Sir) Sidney Rowlatt. But his legal career was cut short when, after his call to the bar, Lord Milner summoned him to South Africa as one of his assistant private secretaries.

Although Buchan spent only two years (1901–1903) in South Africa, the appointment was the most important step in his career. He gained enormously from daily association with Milner and from his modest tasks in the resettlement of the country, where his warm human desire to make friends with the Boers and bury the hatchet gave him horizon and a sense of size, and his imperialism, cleansed of vulgar jingoism, became elevated above the patronizing 'trust' conception into an association of free peoples in loyalty to a common throne. So Pieter Pienaar, resourceful and true, becomes one of the heroes of his adventure novels. Indeed he was eager for a career in Egypt under Lord Cromer when his work in South Africa was over. For the second time and again for the good he was disappointed. Yet it may be affirmed with confidence that, without apprenticeship in Africa, there would have been no governor-generalship of Canada, for Buchan had there learned to think as statesmen think.

In 1903 Buchan returned to the bar in London, 'devilling' for Rowlatt and 'noting' for Sir R. B. (later Viscount) Finlay who, while assessing his mind as not exact enough for supremacy at the bar, admired his abilities and character. He wrote 'opinions', one, for instance, on the legality of Chinese labour (after the liberal victory of 1906) in which his seniors were Arthur Cohen, Finlay, and Rufus Isaacs (later Marquess of Reading). But this episode was a backwater. In 1907 T. A. Nelson the publisher, a friend from Oxford days, invited him to join the firm as 'literary adviser' and as a limited partner. He was to reside in London and superintend the issue of, *inter alia*, the sevenpenny edition of *The Best Literature*. He accepted and was in his element. He could never have mortified the flesh as he describes Milner doing, nor could he have given himself body and soul to the bar. His admirable, but ephemeral, *Law relating to the Taxation of Foreign Income* (1905), written at the instance of R. B. (later Viscount) Haldane, remains as his testament to the Middle Temple, which elected him a bencher in 1935. He was also engaged to be married to one of that world which had fascinated him since his Oxford days by its ease and grace. With her he enjoyed unclouded happiness for thirty-three years. Being free from drudgery he could, as a man of letters, give scope to the dominating activity of his life. Hitherto his books, some written before he ever came to Oxford (*Sir Quixote of the Moors*, 1895, *Scholar Gipsies*, 1896, *Grey Weather*, 1899, *The Half-Hearted*, 1900, and *The Watcher by the Threshold*, 1902), had contained the freshness of youth and were charming harbingers of even better to come. These had been followed by the African books, *The African Colony* (1903) and *A Lodge in the Wilderness* (1906), more interesting perhaps as autobiography than as literature, while *Prester John* (1910) begins the long series of his books of adventure. Except for the Stanhope essay, *Sir Walter Raleigh* in dramatic form (1911) is the first sign of his turn towards history, and then, after two more adventure stories, came *The Marquis of Montrose* (1913), now out of print and not included in his collected works. This was Buchan's first serious attempt at writing history and a good deal of it was history, and very good history, the most impressive feature being the power which he exhibited of describing marches and battles and their wild natural settings. But zeal for his idolized 'discovery' (although the tragedy of the 'great Marquess' had pointed many a moral and adorned many a tale) led him to commit so many elementary blunders, all of which invariably told in favour of Montrose and against Argyle and the Estates, tinged with a certain 'acerbity' and an air of omniscience, that he was severely taken to task by D. H. Fleming in a review printed in *The British Weekly* of 12 February 1914. No reply was or could be made. *Montrose* (1928) is the sequel: the blemishes complained of are gone, but whether we have the final Marquess 'in his faults and failings, in his virtues and valour' (Hay Fleming) is open to question among those for whom historic truth is all in all, and brilliant writing no more than decoration.

The outbreak of war in 1914 found Buchan, on the eve of his thirty-ninth birthday, seriously ill for the first time since his childhood, when at the age of five he had fallen out of a carriage and a wheel passing over the side of his skull had left its mark for life. He had then lain for a year in bed and had to learn once more how to walk. He grew to be about 5 feet 8 inches in height, lean, sinewy, well knit, and active as a chamois. A daring and expert cragsman, he had sampled many rock climbs in Skye and Austria, and he had literally climbed into the Alpine Club. He was a keen fisherman but an indifferent shot, and his riding was purely utilitarian, preferring as he did Shanks's mare, a nimble, sure steed which never tired. Games, accomplishments, and parlour tricks were outside his activities.

Compelled to keep his bed, Buchan wrote. He made a start with his well-known *History of the Great War*, which occupied twenty-four volumes of the 'Nelson Library' series; but he also wrote *The Thirty-Nine Steps* (1915) which fairly stormed the reading world with its combination of excitement and sensation, written as only a master of English can write. He was well enough by 1915 to be on the staff of *The Times* on the western front, and by 1916 he had joined the army as a major in the Intelligence Corps and enjoyed confidential innominate duties at general headquarters at Montreuil-sur-Mer, which brought him into personal touch with another Borderer by extraction, Sir Douglas Haig, whom he admired as a great man and soldier. Summoned to London in 1917, he made such a personal success of the new Department of Information that it became a ministry with Buchan as subordinate director until the armistice. With renewed successes his pen consoled him for irritating drudgery and unreasonable people: *Greenmantle* (1916) and *Mr. Standfast* (1919) completed the trilogy on the war opened by *The Thirty-Nine Steps*. In *Poems, Scots and English* (1917) some of the poems are topical of the front, but the book is at once a monument of detachment from ugly actuality and a source of regret that he did not write more verse. Buchan loved poetry and had it in his bones.

Private life resulted in settlement at Elsfield Manor, near Oxford, purchased in 1919 after deliberation of several years. That 'ivory tower' was so unlike Buchan's native land that nostalgia was not aroused, and in this phase of his life there was a copious output of books. *The History of the South African Forces in France* and the memoir of *Francis and Riversdale Grenfell* (1920) were the aftermath of the war, together with the *History of the Great War* which was revised, compressed, and republished in 1921–1922 and the complete regimental *History of the Royal Scots Fusiliers* (1925), a valuable tribute to the memory of his youngest brother, Alastair, killed in 1917.

The excellence of the tribute to the Grenfells may have led to his life of *Lord Minto* (1924) which proved to be the forerunner of the historical biographies, on which he undoubtedly intended that his future fame should rest. By an interesting chance it familiarized him with a stage on which, as a successor to Minto, he was destined to play his part. Meantime novel after novel poured from his pen. *Huntingtower* (1922) opened a new series based on Glasgow memories and the scout movement, with a coy candidature of Peeblesshire. *Midwinter* (1923) was a historical novel linking Elsfield with Samuel Johnson just as Elsfield and Henry VIII were drawn together in *The Blanket of the Dark* (1931). *Witch Wood* (1927) links Tweeddale with Montrose and Philiphaugh and is a by-product of the preparation for *Montrose*. But the majority were the yarns (as he called them) spun easily for his own and an eager public's enjoyment.

It is remarkable that he went on writing in the last phase of his life, when he was a public man. The almost inspired literary criticism of his *Sir Walter Scott* (1932) and the sympathetic understanding of the spiritual side of the Protector in *Oliver Cromwell* (1934) show Buchan at his best. At a by-election in 1927 he was elected conservative member of parliament for the Scottish Universities, and held the seat until his elevation to the peerage in 1935. He fitted the constituency like a glove. He loved the House of Commons and the House listened to him. Moreover he had achieved fame in America chiefly as a historian and a novelist. He was a member of the Pilgrim Trust and in that capacity he did good service to Oxford City and Oxford University. And then, in 1933 and 1934 the elder of St Columba's church at Oxford was appointed lord high commissioner to the General Assembly of the Church of Scotland. In that illustrious office, eloquent of the history of the struggles between church and state since the Reformation, Buchan was supremely happy both in his manner and in his utterances, as befitted the joint author (with Sir George Adam Smith) of the masterly little treatise *The Kirk in Scotland, 1560–1929* (1930). And it was again Ramsay MacDonald who in 1935 advised the appointment of Buchan to the governor-generalship of Canada, the supreme opportunity of Buchan's life, to show of what mettle he was made.

That Lord Tweedsmuir (the appropriate title conferred upon Buchan) had qualities which fitted him in no common degree for the office was shown by *The King's Grace: 1910–1935* (1935). The auspices, save in the matter of his health, were good. He was a Scot, a Presbyterian, and his wife was descended from the two noble houses of Grosvenor and Stuart-Wortley, and in her ancestry she could count more statesmen than most people. His vigour was undiminished and in 1937 *Augustus* brought to a close his studies in ancient history and the humanities.

As governor-general Tweedsmuir had to face the change in the position of the representative of the crown made by the Statute of Westminster (1931). He therefore requited a warm welcome with unwearied devotion to duty on ceremonial occasions, courts, reviews, the delivery of addresses and lectures, not only in English but in French, for he took a special interest in Lower Canada and the French-Canadian culture. Moreover, he was discreet and tactful, and he possessed charm in both its forms, sympathy with the interlocutor or audience, and sympathy of bearing. He was made a Red Indian chief. The author of *The Last Secrets* (1923) never neglected a chance of exploration and he travelled to visit all sorts and conditions of men throughout the Dominion.

But Tweedsmuir overtaxed his strength, and the anxiety inseparable from the visit of the King and Queen in 1939 strained it in spite of the excellence of the arrangements. Any chance of a needed rest was lost by the outbreak of war in September. His death, which took place at Montreal 11 February 1940, was followed by a spontaneous outburst of sorrow from all quarters of the free world. It was felt in Canada that his public services in voicing the spirit of Canadian loyalty, in promoting recruiting, and showing a gallant front had, as Cardinal Villeneuve said, been a factor in cementing national unity in Canada. Nor was his influence confined to Canada. Since 1937 at least he had been on terms of real friendship with President Roosevelt, and, with Lord Lothian at Washington, another member of Milner's South African 'kindergarten', he played his part in maintaining relations with the United States on the right plane.

Tweedsmuir married in 1907 Susan Charlotte, elder daughter of Captain Norman de l'Aigle Grosvenor, third son of the first Lord Ebury, and had three sons and one daughter. He was succeeded as second baron by his eldest son, John Norman Stuart (born 1911). His honours, public and academic, came freely. He was sworn of the Privy Council in 1937, and was appointed CH in 1932, GCMG in 1935, and GCVO in 1939. He was elected chancellor of Edinburgh University in 1937 and an honorary fellow of Brasenose College in 1934, and he received honorary degrees from three of the four Scottish universities, and from Oxford, Harvard, Yale, and most of the Canadian universities.

A portrait of Lord Tweedsmuir, by Sholto Johnstone-Douglas (1900), is in the possession of Mr J. W. Buchan, Bank House, Peebles, who also owns a bust by T. J. Clapperton. A posthumous portrait, by Alphonse Jongers, was presented to Lady Tweedsmuir by the women of Canada.

[*Manchester Guardian*, 12 February 1940; *The Times*, 12 and 15 February 1940; John Buchan, *A Lost Lady of Old Years*, 1899, and *Memory Hold-the-Door*, 1940; Hon. A. C. Murray, *Master and Brother*, 1945; Anna Buchan (O. Douglas), *Ann and her Mother*, 1922; *Unforgettable: Unforgotten* (1945); *John Buchan*, by his wife and friends, 1947; personal knowledge.]

S. A. Gillon

published 1949

BURGESS Guy Francis de Moncy

(1911–1963)

Soviet spy, was born 16 April 1911 in Devonport, Devon, the elder son (there were no daughters) of Commander Malcolm Kingsford de Moncy

Burgess, lieutenant in the Royal Navy, and his wife Evelyn Mary, daughter of William Gillman, gentleman. Burgess's father died in 1924, and his mother later married John Retallack Bassett, a retired lieutenant-colonel. Burgess was educated at Eton. He went on to the Royal Naval College, Dartmouth, for two years before poor eyesight ended plans for a naval career, and he returned to Eton. In 1930 he won an open scholarship to read modern history at Trinity College, Cambridge, and he gained a first in part i of the modern history tripos (1932), and an *aegrotat* in part ii (1933).

At Cambridge he was renowned for his brilliance and charm, and his exuberance, but he also soon became notorious for his homosexuality and drunkenness, and his dirty and dishevelled appearance. Malcolm Muggeridge later said that Burgess 'gave me a feeling of being morally afflicted in some way', and described him as the 'sick toast of a sick society'. Anthony Blunt sponsored his entry into the exclusive intellectual secret society, the Apostles. Burgess joined the Communist party, organized strikes among college servants, and joined hunger marches. It is not clear whether he was recruited as a Soviet agent at Cambridge or during his trip to Moscow in the summer of 1934. Hoping to become a history don, he embarked on research into the 'bourgeois revolution' of the seventeenth century in 1933, but the appearance of Basil Willey's *The Seventeenth Century Background* (1934) robbed him of his topic, and he left Cambridge.

At this point he announced his disillusionment with Marxism, and began to express right-wing views. As secretary to Captain 'Jack' Macnamara, a Conservative MP and member of the Anglo-German Fellowship, from 1935 to 1936, he made several visits to Germany. Burgess joined the BBC in October 1936 as a producer in the talks department, and later became producer of 'The Week in Westminster'.

In December 1938 Burgess was offered a job in Section D of SIS (Secret Intelligence Service), set up to investigate sabotage and propaganda in the event of war. It was he who managed to get H. A. R. ('Kim') Philby his first job in intelligence, in 1940. When Section D was absorbed into the newly formed SOE (Special Operations Executive) in 1940, Burgess was not given a job, and he returned to the BBC in 1941, responsible for propaganda to occupied Europe and liaison with the SIS and SOE.

In the summer of 1944 Burgess got a temporary job in the press department of the Foreign Office. In 1947 he became private secretary to Hector McNeil, minister of state at the Foreign Office, and despite his drunkenness and unreliable behaviour he not only survived but was promoted. Later in 1947 he spent three months in the Information Research Department, which was formed to launch a propaganda counter-offensive against

Russia. During his time with the IRD he provided the Russians with useful details of its staff and operations. Following a period in the Far Eastern department of the Foreign Office, from November 1948, he was posted to Washington in August 1950 as a second secretary with special responsibility for Far Eastern affairs, just after the beginning of the Korean war. He clashed with his superior and was moved to a different section, and after a series of complaints about his behaviour he was sent back to England at the request of the ambassador at the beginning of May 1951.

Burgess defected to Moscow with Donald Maclean on 25 May 1951. Maclean, a Cambridge contemporary of Burgess, fellow Apostle, and fellow communist, had recently been made head of the American department at the Foreign Office. But investigations into the leaking of sensitive material from Washington had narrowed down to Maclean as chief suspect, and it seems that Burgess was detailed, probably by Philby, who was still in Washington, to warn him and organize his escape, although it does not seem to have been intended that Burgess should go too. He was not under suspicion at the time, although he was about to be dismissed for his indiscretions and outrageous behaviour. Later, Burgess was to tell friends that he had only intended to accompany Maclean as far as Prague before returning to London. Philby remained bitter towards Burgess, whose defection had thrown suspicion on him and ultimately led to his unmasking. The whereabouts of Burgess and Maclean were not revealed until February 1956, when they held a press conference in Moscow.

Once in the USSR, Burgess and Maclean spent six months in the provincial town of Kuybyshev before being allowed to settle in Moscow. Burgess was lonely and bored, missed his bohemian life in Soho, never attempted to learn Russian, and never became a Russian citizen. He did have a job in the Foreign Literature Publishing House, but he sought out any visitors from London, eager for gossip, and frequently talked about returning. Burgess was memorably portrayed by Alan Bates in Alan Bennett's television play *An Englishman Abroad* (1983).

Burgess died unmarried of a heart attack in Moscow 30 August 1963. His ashes were returned to England and buried in the churchyard in West Meon, Hampshire.

[*The Times*, 2 September 1963; B. Penrose and S. Freeman, *Conspiracy of Silence: the Secret Life of Anthony Blunt*, 1986; Robert Cecil, *A Divided Life: a Biography of Donald Maclean*, 1988; Philip Knightley, *Philby: the Life and Views of the K.G.B. Masterspy*, 1988; Anthony Glees, *The Secrets of the Service. British Intelligence and Communist Subversion 1939–51*, 1987.]

Anne Baker

published 1993

BUTLER Richard Austen

(1902–1982)

Baron Butler of Saffron Walden

Politician, was born at Attock Serai in the Punjab, India, 9 December 1902, the eldest of a family of two sons and two daughters of (Sir) Montagu Sherard Dawes Butler and his wife, Anne Gertrude Smith. His father, who had passed top into the Indian Civil Service, was a member of a remarkable academic dynasty (since 1794) of Cambridge dons, which included a master of Trinity, two headmasters of Harrow, and one of Haileybury. He later became governor of the Central Provinces and, finally, of the Isle of Man. His mother, warm, sympathetic, and encouraging, and to whom Butler was always devoted, was one of ten talented children of George Smith, CIE, a Scottish teacher, journalist, and editor in India. She was the sister of Sir George Adam Smith.

When Butler was six, he fell from his pony and broke his right arm in three places, an injury which was aggravated by a hot-water-bottle burn. The arm never fully recovered, and successful games playing was thus ruled out though he became a keen shot. Returning to be educated in England, Butler attended the Wick preparatory school at Hove. Having rebelled against going to Harrow because of a surfeit of Butlers there and having failed a scholarship for Eton, Butler (by now known as 'Rab' as his father had intended) went to Marlborough. After a final year learning modern languages which were better taught than the classics he had earlier endured, Butler went to France to improve his French with the Diplomatic Service in mind. He won an exhibition to Pembroke College, Cambridge—the money was needed—which after a first class in the modern and medieval languages tripos (1923) was converted into a scholarship. He became secretary of the Union as a Conservative. An unsuccessful love affair and a mainly nervous collapse did not stop him becoming president of the Union (1924). In his fourth year Butler gained a first in history (1925) and a fellowship at Corpus Christi College.

While an undergraduate he had met Sydney Elizabeth Courtauld, a capable, strong-minded girl, who became his wife in April 1926. Her father, Samuel Courtauld, an industrialist, settled £5,000 a year on Butler for life tax free. This financial independence enabled him to decide on a parliamentary career, though his father told him that strong personal executive decisions were not his forte and he should aim for the speakership. While the honeymooners went round the world, the Courtauld family secured for them a fairly safe seat, Saffron Walden in Essex, and on their return Butler was duly selected without the complication of competing candidates. He had a comfortable victory in the general election of 1929 and held the seat until his retirement in 1965. Before the election he had become private secretary to Sir Samuel Hoare (later Viscount Templewood), and he soon became known to the party hierarchy. His first notable public act was a sharp exchange in *The Times* with Harold Macmillan (later the Earl of Stockton), who was advised to seek 'a pastime more suited for his talents' than politics.

In the national government in 1931 Hoare became India secretary and Butler his parliamentary private secretary. At the second Round Table conference, Butler was deeply impressed by M. K. Gandhi, the current hate figure of many Conservatives and of his father. After a tour of India, Butler became Hoare's under-secretary in September 1932. His support of constitutional reform and knowledge of the Indian scene made him a natural choice, even though he had been in Parliament only three and a half years and was easily the youngest member of the government. India was the issue on which (Sir) Winston Churchill was challenging Stanley Baldwin (later Earl Baldwin of Bewdley), and in the Commons Butler compared himself to 'the miserable animal', a bait 'in the form of a bullock or calf tied to a tree awaiting the arrival of the Lord of the Forest'. Yet he was never devoured by Churchill and proved himself Hoare's able lieutenant in defending the India Bill during the fierce two-and-a-half-year war waged against it by the Conservative right wing.

The Butlers had since 1928 lived in the constituency first at Broxted and then at Stansted Hall, Halstead, where their three sons and a daughter were largely brought up, and where in 1935 Baldwin came for the weekend and Churchill was invited. They also had a flat in Wood Street, London, until they moved to 3 Smith Square in 1938. They entertained generously in both London and the country.

Neville Chamberlain's accession to the premiership in May 1937 brought Butler a welcome release from the India Office but not a department of his own. However, his stint as parliamentary secretary at the Ministry of Labour gave him a useful acquaintance with the depressed areas and with mass unemployment. After nine months he went to the Foreign Office as under-secretary of state in February 1938. With the foreign secretary, the first Earl of Halifax, in the House of Lords he was once again prominent—in the long run, indeed, too prominent. The policy of appeasement cut across the Conservative Party much more deeply than India or unemployment, and, when Churchill took over, Butler was on the wrong side of the divide. Appeasement was held against him in a way it was not against those more minor supporters of the Munich agreement, Lord Dunglass (later Lord Home of the Hirsel) and Quintin Hogg (later Lord Hailsham of St Marylebone).

Butler was an enthusiastic Chamberlainite and like Chamberlain regarded Munich not as a means of buying time but as a way of settling differences with Adolf Hitler. He was disposed, however, to interpret Benito Mussolini's invasion of Albania as a general threat to the Balkans, until Chamberlain told him not to be silly and to go home to bed. Butler remained an appeaser down to the outbreak of war, opposing the Polish alliance signed on 25 August 1939 because it would have 'a bad psychological effect on Hitler'. After Chamberlain's fall he, together with Alec Dunglass and two friends, drank to 'the King over the water' and described Churchill as 'the greatest political adventurer of modern times'.

Despite his conspicuous identification with the *ancien régime*, Butler survived Churchill's reconstruction of the government in May 1940. 'I wish you to go on', Churchill told him, 'with your delicate manner of answering parliamentary questions without giving anything away'; the prime minister also expressed appreciation of having been asked to 'Butler's private residence'. The Foreign Office was now a backwater, whose calm was only disturbed by Butler's imprudent conversation about peace with the Swedish minister in June 1940, which Churchill thought might indicate a lukewarm attitude to the war if not defeatism. Bombed out of both Smith Square and his father-in-law's house, Butler went for a time to stay in Belgrave Square with (Sir) Henry Channon, his parliamentary private secretary since 1938.

Butler remained at the Foreign Office against his wishes when Sir Anthony Eden (later the Earl of Avon), whom he did not admire, succeeded Halifax in December 1940. But in July 1941 after nine years as an under-secretary he became president of the Board of Education. Even further removed from the war than the Foreign Office, education was nevertheless a political minefield and had seen no major reform since 1902. Ignoring Churchill's warnings not to stir up either party politics or religious controversy, Butler decided on comprehensive reform. Although in the end he had to exclude the public schools, every child was given the right to free secondary education and, to make that right a reality for the poor, provision was made for the expansion of both nursery and further education and for the raising of the school leaving age. All Butler's formidable diplomatic and political skills were needed to secure the agreement of the churches and the acquiescence of Churchill. The 1944 Education Act was Butler's greatest legislative achievement and was deservedly called after him.

Butler became chairman of the Conservative Party's post-war problems central committee in 1941, and in November 1943 he joined the government's reconstruction committee. The only leading Conservative clear-sighted enough to oppose an early election, he became minister of labour in Churchill's 'caretaker' government in May 1945. After the electoral defeat in July—Butler's own majority fell to 1,158—Churchill made him chairman both of the Conservative Research Department and of the high-powered industrial policy committee. From these two positions Butler exerted the major influence in reshaping Conservative policy, and, even more than Macmillan, was chiefly responsible for the civilized conservatism of the post-war party. In 1947 the industrial policy committee produced the *Industrial Charter*, which, Butler later wrote, was 'an assurance, that in the interests of efficiency, full employment, and social security, modern Conservatism would maintain strong central guidance over the operation of the economy'. Mass unemployment was to be a thing of the past; as Butler put it, those who advocated 'creating pools of unemployment should be thrown into them and made to swim'. The right wing regarded Butler's efforts as 'pink socialism', a recurring charge under various names in his later career. He himself believed that, without the rejection of unemployment and the acceptance of the Welfare State, the spectre of the thirties would not be exorcized and the Conservative Party would remain in opposition.

Contrary to the general expectation and his own, Butler became chancellor of the Exchequer in October 1951 and inherited the usual economic crisis. He tackled it by import controls and the resurrection of monetary policy. The cabinet rejected, however, his plan for a floating exchange rate, a decision which Butler both then and later regarded as a fundamental mistake. Butler's first two budgets were popular and successful, expansion and the promotion of enterprise being his general themes, and such was his standing that in September 1952 in the absence of both Churchill and Eden he was left in charge of the government. The same happened for a longer period in the summer of 1953 when, with Eden ill in Boston, Churchill was felled by a stroke. The gravity of Churchill's illness, concealed by his entourage, was known to Butler; this was perhaps the first occasion on which he could have become prime minister had he striven for the job. He had no such thoughts and ran the government well. Since Marlborough, painting had been Butler's chief hobby; after the war he occasionally painted with Churchill, once being commanded by him to 'take the mountains', while his leader would 'take the sea'. Butler thought their paintings were of about the same standard.

At the Treasury Butler, who was one of the two best post-war chancellors, had two special difficulties. Sir Walter Monckton (later Viscount

Monckton of Brenchley) had been made minister of labour by Churchill to conciliate the unions, and conciliation entailed conceding excessive wage claims, sometimes in concert with the prime minister and without consulting the chancellor. The second was the Conservatives' pledge to build 300,000 houses a year, which Macmillan, the minister of housing, never allowed the chancellor or the cabinet to forget. In consequence, too many of the nation's resources went into the housing drive. In 1954 Butler's third budget was, as he said, a 'carry-on affair' with few changes, but later in the year he predicted the doubling of the country's standard of living within twenty-five years.

In December 1954 his wife died after a long and painful illness. His grief and the loss of her influence as well as the effects of three gruelling years affected Butler's political judgement. His troubles were in any event growing: inflation and balance of payments difficulties necessitated a 'stop', and in February 1955 Butler raised the bank rate and brought back hire-purchase restrictions. Nevertheless he produced an electioneering budget, taking *6d.* off income tax. That was his first mistake. After the election Eden invited him to give up the Treasury, but Butler refused, which was his second mistake. A run on the pound compelled an autumn budget whose unimaginativeness underlined the errors of its predecessor—his third mistake. In December 1955 Eden decided to replace Butler with Macmillan, who showed by his stipulated terms that he was determined also to replace Butler as Eden's heir apparent. Butler consented to become merely lord privy seal and leader of the House—his fourth and biggest mistake. He needed a change, but ministerial power in British politics rests with the big departments and for Butler to allow himself to be left without a department was a gratuitous act of unilateral disarmament.

Though Macmillan was to the left of him on economics, there was no issue on which Butler was, in the eyes of the Conservative Party, seen to be right wing. Many Conservatives saw him as a 'Butskellite'. Hence he was always more popular in the country than in his own party. His appearance was not charismatic, with his damaged arm, his sad, irregular features, and his clothes, described by Channon as 'truly tragic'. But behind it there was a Rolls-Royce mind and a sharp sardonic wit which he enjoyed exerting at the expense of his colleagues. He was the master of many types of ambiguity—'my determination is to support the prime minister in all his difficulties' or 'there is no one whose farewell dinner I would rather have attended'—and occasionally the cause of ambiguity in others. His famous saying that Eden was 'the best prime minister we have' was put to him as a question to which he rashly assented. Butler had a strong vein of innocence, rare in sophisticated politicians. He was also abnormally good-natured and inspired great affection.

Butler was ill when President Nasser of Egypt nationalized the Suez Canal Company in 1956 and was in no danger of being infected by the collective reaction. He missed the first cabinet meeting at which the fatal route to Port Said was mapped and he was not included in the Egypt committee that Eden set up, though he occasionally attended it. His freedom from departmental responsibilities would for once have been an advantage, but cool, detached advice was not what Eden wanted. Over Suez Butler's predicament was acute. Far too intelligent to accept Eden's likening of Nasser to Mussolini, he had nevertheless an 'appeasing' past to live down. Believing that party and public opinion required action of some sort, Butler also believed that Britain should act in accordance with international law.

Hence Butler was in a similar position to John Foster Dulles, the American secretary of state, and was driven to similar deviousness: as the international position altered, different expedients had to be produced to prevent Eden launching an attack on Egypt. But what was permissible in Dulles, trying to divert an ally from folly, looked less so in the cabinet's nominal number two seeking to restrain his leader, sick and unbalanced though Eden was. Butler would probably have done better to state his position unequivocally or to keep quiet or to resign; doubts were not enough. Even so, if he had succeeded, as his phrase went, in keeping Eden 'in a political strait-jacket' he would have done the prime minister and the country a great service. But by October Butler had run out of strait-jackets, and he used the wrong tactics for defeating the Anglo-French-Israeli plan. Instead of joining with Monckton in direct opposition to a grubby conspiracy which was bound to fail, Butler implausibly advocated an open attack on Egypt by the three countries which would have been scarcely less disastrous. After the UN had voted for an emergency force and an Israeli-Egyptian cease-fire seemed imminent, Butler tried to prevent the Anglo-French invasion as it was by then redundant; and when two days later Eden told the cabinet that a cease-fire was essential, Butler like Macmillan strongly supported him.

Butler's deviousness over Suez was honesty itself compared with the duplicity of Eden and some colleagues; and he was more consistent than Macmillan whose fire-eating bellicosity first drove Eden on towards destruction and who then suddenly demanded peace. Yet Butler ended up by pleasing virtually no one, and his varying indiscretions to different back-bench groups gave the impression that he was not playing the game. Others were playing a deeper one.

Eden's retreat to the West Indies to recuperate left Butler to do the salvage work at the head of a weak and divided government. Butler was at his best but gained no credit for limiting damage that he had not caused.

Instead he incurred odium for unpopular though necessary decisions, made at Macmillan's insistence, over Britain's unconditional withdrawal from Egypt. In consequence, when Eden finally resigned in January 1957, Butler had no chance of succeeding him. The cabinet voted overwhelmingly for Macmillan, and back-bench soundings gave a similar result. Churchill, too, recommended Macmillan. Eden gave no advice to the Queen: he disliked both men although he preferred Butler. Butler took his defeat well. Macmillan refused him the Foreign Office, and Butler did not insist, accepting the Home Office while remaining leader of the House. At least he now had a department. He also, as under Churchill and Eden, had the government to run from time to time. When Macmillan in 1958 went on his Commonwealth tour after settling his 'little local difficulties' over the resignation of his entire Treasury team in January, Butler was left, as he said, 'to hold the baby'. As usual he held it well, and this time was popular. As home secretary he was a reformer, which was less popular.

After the October 1959 election Butler became chairman of the Conservative Party in addition to being home secretary and leader of the House. Other than demonstrating that there was almost no limit to his capacity for transacting public business—at which he was indeed the unrivalled master—there was little point in Butler's new job. It was in any case scarcely compatible with his existing ones. His leadership of the House entailed trying to get on with the opposition in the Commons, while his chairmanship of the party entailed attacking the opposition in the country. Further, as home secretary, Butler was intent on penal reform, while many of his party faithful were intent on the return of flogging. However Butler was always adept at squaring circles, and he squared those three. Much more important to him than the acquisition of offices was his wedding, in the presence of the couple's ten children, in October 1959 to a relative by marriage of his late wife, Mollie, widow of Augustine Courtauld, polar explorer, and daughter of Frank Douglas Montgomerie, of Castle Hedingham, Essex. The marriage was strikingly happy and gave Butler renewed strength. He was an outstanding home secretary, making few mistakes in handling a notoriously tricky department and initiating much useful legislation. He beat the flogging lobby and passed a major Criminal Justice Act; he reformed the laws of gambling, public houses, prostitution, and charities; and also passed in 1962 the Bill to curb immigration which had been prepared by Churchill's government and successively deferred.

In October 1961 Butler lost two of his offices, retaining only the Home Office, and was made overseer of the common market negotiations which in practice meant little. In March 1962 Macmillan, tired of the squabbling between the Colonial and Commonwealth Offices, formed a new central

Africa department and persuaded Butler to take charge of it. This was a real job, if a thankless one; characteristically, Butler merely added it to his other one. But in the cabinet massacre of July 1962 he lost the Home Office and was left with his central African responsibilities with the honorific title of 'first secretary of state' plus the intimation that he would be serving as deputy prime minister. Macmillan was thus able both to heap burdens on to the good-natured Butler and to strip him of them again almost at will. For nearly all his long parliamentary career Butler had been a minister: this gave him a unique experience of administration but made him too addicted to Whitehall ever to think of withdrawing. He had, too, the character and quality of a great public servant.

Macmillan weakened his government by banishing Butler from the home front. Yet the government gained in Africa. At the Victoria Falls conference in July 1963 Butler achieved the seemingly impossible feat of an orderly dissolution of the Central African Federation without conceding full independence to Southern Rhodesia.

Butler made no attempt to take advantage of Macmillan's considerable troubles in the first half of 1963, and the prime minister's revived fortunes had persuaded him to fight the next election, when his prostate operation altered that decision. Butler was yet again asked to deputize. Yet Macmillan was determined to prevent Butler succeeding him and played an unprecedented part in choosing his own successor. At first he supported Hailsham and then switched to Home. Even more important, he devised a procedure under which he kept control of events. In acquiescing, the leading cabinet ministers, Butler above all, were markedly trusting or negligent. And after fudged consultations with cabinet ministers by the lord chancellor, Lord Dilhorne, who produced an idiosyncratic reading of the results, and with MPs by the whips, some of whom knew the answer they wanted and went on till they got it, and after some apparent refining of the figures by the chief whip, Sir Martin (later Lord) Redmayne, Macmillan adjudged Home the winner.

This decision was leaked on 12 October 1963, the day before Macmillan was to see the Queen. That evening a meeting of cabinet ministers at Enoch Powell's house telephoned Butler urging him to fight. Hailsham did the same very strongly. Butler's response was merely to ask the lord chancellor the next morning to call a meeting of all the leading candidates. Home felt like withdrawing, but was dissuaded by Macmillan who ignored the opposition to his 'compromise' choice and did not change his intended advice to the Queen. Shortly afterwards Home was on his way to the palace where he was asked to see if he could form a government. Even then Butler could have prevailed: both Hailsham and Reginald Maudling had agreed to serve under him, he had much cabinet support, and his wife was urging him on. But his heart was not in the fight, and after reserving his position he became foreign secretary on 20 October. Perhaps, as his father had long ago told him, he could not take strong personal executive decisions. Perhaps, like his old chief in 1940, Halifax, he did not really want the job. More likely he was inhibited by fears of splitting the party; and Home had been a friend since their Chamberlain days. Whatever the truth, his forbearance did not help the Conservatives. The supporters of both Butler and Hailsham thought their man would win the election of 16 October 1964, and both were probably right. Home just lost it. In his farewell message to the party conference, Macmillan hailed the coming into existence of 'the party of our dreams', which accepted a 'pragmatic and sensible compromise between the extremes of collectivism and individualism'; at the very same time he was blocking the man who was at least as responsible as himself for the existence of such a party, thus ensuring that the dream was short-lived. The 1964 election was crucial. A Conservative victory would have consolidated such a party and probably produced a Labour realignment. Defeat led to the later polarization of the parties and an abandonment of Macmillan's 'compromise'.

The rest, politically, was for Butler anticlimax. The job he had wanted in 1957 and 1960 no longer presented much of a challenge. He ran the Foreign Office easily, but had no opportunity or inclination to do anything of note. Had the Conservatives won the election, he would not have been reappointed. Butler was given no part in the election preparations and only a bit part in the election itself, though he gave one rather unfortunate interview. After the election he lost his chairmanship of the Conservative Research Department. Home offered him an earldom which he refused; in 1965 the new prime minister, Harold Wilson (later Lord Wilson of Rievaulx), offered him the mastership of Trinity College, Cambridge, which he accepted. He then accepted a life peerage in 1965 and took his seat on the cross-benches. Butler was the first non-Trinity man to become master for 250 years, and his appointment was at first not wholly welcome in the college. Nevertheless he and his wife were pre-eminently successful there, and in 1972 91 out of 118 fellows present voted for the maximum extension of Butler's term of office. In 1971 he published his autobiography. Lively, wise, and relatively accurate, *The Art of the Possible* was a strong contrast to the multi-volume efforts of Eden and Macmillan and was one of the very few political autobiographies to enhance its author's reputation. This was followed in 1977 by *The Conservatives*, a history of the party, which Butler edited and introduced. In the same year he retired from Trinity.

His son, Adam, was a member of the 1979 Conservative government, but Butler like Macmillan had no great liking for the new Conservative regime. In February 1980 he defeated in the Lords the government's proposal to allow local authorities to charge for school transport, which he saw as a breach of the 1944 Act's promise to provide free secondary education for all. Butler's portrait was painted by Margaret Foreman for the National Portrait Gallery, where he was last seen in public. He finished *The Art of Memory* (1982) which was little more than a footnote to its predecessor and was published after his death. He died 8 March 1982 at his home in Great Yeldham, Halstead, Essex.

Butler was sworn of the Privy Council in 1939, and was appointed CH in 1954 and KG in 1971. He was awarded honorary degrees by thirteen universities (including Oxford and Cambridge, both in 1962), and elected an honorary fellow of Pembroke College, Cambridge, in 1941, Corpus Christi College, Cambridge, in 1952, and St Antony's College, Oxford, in 1957. He was rector of Glasgow University (1956–9), high steward, Cambridge University (1958–66), chancellor of Sheffield University (1960–78), chancellor of Essex University from 1962, and high steward, City of Cambridge, from 1963. He was president of the Modern Language Association and of the National Association of Mental Health from 1946, and of the Royal Society of Literature from 1951. He was given the freedom of Saffron Walden in 1954.

[R. A. Butler, *The Art of the Possible*, 1971, and *The Art of Memory*, 1982 (autobiographies); Anthony Howard, *Rab*, 1987; Molly Butler, *August and Rab*, 1987; Robert Rhodes James (ed.), *Chips, The Diaries of Sir Henry Channon*, 1967; John R. Colville, *The Fringes of Power*, 1985; private information; personal knowledge.]

IAN GILMOUR

published 1990

CARDUS Sir (John Frederick) Neville

(1889–1975)

Writer and critic, was born possibly 2 April 1889 at 2 Summer Place, Rusholme, Manchester, the home of his maternal grandparents. His maternal grandfather was a retired policeman. His unmarried mother, Ada Cardus, died in 1954, and on his marriage certificate he gave the name of his father (whom he never knew) as the late Frederick Cardus, Civil Service clerk. In his *Autobiography* (1947) Cardus disclosed that his real father was 'one of the first violins in an orchestra' who vanished from his mother's life almost as soon as he casually entered it. His mother and his aunt he described as having joined 'the oldest of professions'. Even Cardus's year of birth is uncertain. Although he gave it in *Who's Who* as 2 April 1889, on his marriage certificate of 17 June 1921 he gave his age then as thirty-one. Cardus was equally evasive about his childhood and education at a board school, but Summer Place in Rusholme was not the slum that his book implies. He educated himself by reading and had various menial jobs. His first connection with journalism was in a printer's works, where he had to boil the type in a pan to clean it after it was removed from the page-formes. Later he sold chocolates in the Manchester theatre where the repertory company of Annie Horniman later performed. There his lifelong relish of the music hall began. In 1901 he first entered Lancashire's county cricket ground at Old Trafford, where he saw A. C. MacLaren hit a boundary before rain stopped play. But it was enough to start another passion; thereafter he went there often and watched the cricketers of the 'Golden Age'.

In 1904 Cardus was a clerk in a marine insurance agency, where his employers were indulgent towards his frequent absences in the reference library or at Old Trafford. He began to read the music criticism of Ernest Newman and the dramatic criticism, in the *Manchester Guardian*, of C. E. Montague, James Agate, and Allan Monkhouse, and he also began to write in imitation of them. This was Manchester's cultural heyday, when Hans Richter and Adolf Brodsky guided its musical life. Cardus went to the Free Trade Hall on the night of 3 December 1908 when the First Symphony of Sir Edward Elgar had its first performance, and he educated himself in opera during the regular visits of the touring companies.

In 1912 he became assistant cricket coach at Shrewsbury School, where the headmaster was Cyril Alington. Cardus acted as his secretary from 1914. He volunteered for the army but was rejected because of his short sight. Returning to Manchester in 1916, Cardus was for three months Manchester music critic of the Socialist newspaper *Daily Citizen*. Unemployed and unfit for the army, he wrote to C. P. Scott, editor of the *Manchester Guardian*, seeking any kind of work on the paper. Scott took him on as a secretary, then decided he did not need one. But three months later, in 1917, he appointed Cardus to the reporting staff at 30 shillings (£1.50) a week. Soon the initials 'N.C.' appeared at the end of music-hall notices, but he made his real mark on the paper in the summer of 1919, after an illness, when the kindly news editor sent him to recuperate by reporting the opening of Lancashire's first post-war cricket season. Soon he was writing about cricket not merely as a reporter, but as an essayist, an observer of character. His prose was allusive, studded with poetical quotations and musical analogies. A game had not been written about in this way before. He adopted the pseudonym 'Cricketer', and before long was one of the *Guardian*'s chief attractions to readers. Other writers on cricket have displayed more strategic knowledge of the game; none has captured its spirit and atmosphere as perceptively and humorously. He created a Dickensian gallery of characters, as he admitted, and the characters themselves played up to him. In 1922 Grant Richards published Cardus's *A Cricketer's Book*. There followed *Days in the Sun* (1924), *The Summer Game* (1929), *Good Days* (1934), and *Australian Summer* (1937).

In spite of cricket, Cardus still hankered after the arts. His interest in music being known to Scott, in 1920 he became assistant to the paper's chief critic, Samuel Langford, succeeding him in 1927. Unlike some critics, Cardus did not isolate himself from the artists upon whom he passed judgement, for he enjoyed their company as much as their performances. Thus he became the friend of Sir Thomas Beecham, Kathleen Ferrier, Sir John Barbirolli, Artur Schnabel, and Claudio Arrau. In his writings on music, as on cricket, Cardus was more interested in aesthetics than technicalities, in emotional rather than intellectual response. Newman described him as a 'sensitized plate', and he did not demur. Cardus inherited Langford's championship of the music of Gustav Mahler. His essay on Mahler in *Ten Composers* (1945, revised as *A Composers' Eleven*, 1958), made as many converts to the music as Bruno Walter's 1936 recording of *Das Lied von der Erde*. It is Cardus at his best, whereas his analytical study of the first five symphonies (*Gustav Mahler: his Mind and his Music*, 1965) was not a success and was significantly not followed by a planned second volume.

In January 1940 Cardus arrived in Australia where he wrote on music for the *Sydney Morning Herald* and gave many broadcasts. He returned to Britain in June 1947, writing on cricket for the *Sunday Times* while expecting to succeed the long-lived Newman as music critic. In 1951 he returned to the *Manchester Guardian* as its chief London music critic and occasional cricket contributor. He continued in this role to the end of his life although he felt increasingly out of sympathy with the paper after it loosened its Manchester ties. Even if he now visited his native city ever more rarely, his spiritual home remained Scott's *Guardian* in Cross Street. He was happiest in his late years holding court behind the Warner Stand at Lord's—he was a wonderful raconteur—or in the Garrick Club. He returned to Australia for brief visits in 1948, 1949, and 1954. After he had reached his mid-seventies, many honours came to him—the CBE in 1964, a knighthood in 1967, Austria's decoration of honour (1st class) for science and art in 1970, and honorary membership of the Royal Manchester College of Music (1968)—his sole Manchester honour—and of the Royal Academy of Music in 1972. But he valued highest the presidency of Lancashire County Cricket Club in 1970–1, seventy years after he had seen MacLaren's drive for four. His last book of essays, *Full Score*, was published in 1970.

In 1921 Cardus married Edith Honorine Watton (died 1968), a schoolmistress, daughter of John Thomas Sissons King, schoolmaster; there were no children. Edith was active with one of Manchester's most enterprising amateur stage companies, the Unnamed Society. Cardus died in London 28 February 1975.

[Neville Cardus, *Autobiography*, 1947, and *Second Innings*, 1950; Robin Daniels, *Conversations with Cardus*, 1976; Christopher Brookes, *His Own Man* (biography), 1985; *Daily Telegraph*, *Guardian*, and *The Times*, 1 March 1975; private information; personal knowledge.]

MICHAEL KENNEDY

published 1986

CECIL Lord (Edward Christian) David (Gascoyne-)

(1902–1986)

Man of letters, was born 9 April 1902 at 24 Grafton Street, London W1, the fourth and last child and the second son of James Edward Hubert Gascoyne-Cecil, fourth Marquess of Salisbury, politician, and his wife, Lady (Cicely) Alice Gore, second daughter of the fifth Earl of Arran, descended on her mother's side from the Melbourne family. A delicate child, he was much at home and benefited in this from the company of his brilliant aunts and uncles, notorious for their eccentricities, wit, and zeal. Between 1915 and 1919 he was at Eton, where the confidence fostered by this remarkable family carried him through an unfamiliar and in some ways uncongenial atmosphere. His experience of Oxford—he entered Christ Church in 1920—was different. He loved the life and the place. His exceptionally quick, associative mind served him well in his final examinations where he took a first class in modern history (1924). Though he failed to win an All Souls fellowship, he was elected to a fellowship at Wadham in 1924 to teach mainly history. At the same time, with characteristic independence, he was writing a life of the poet William Cowper, *The Stricken Deer*, his first and one of his best books, which was published in 1929 and won the Hawthornden prize in 1930.

This success led to his decision to resign his fellowship in 1930 and take up the life of a writer in London. There he met and fell in love with Rachel, only daughter of (Sir) (C. O.) Desmond MacCarthy, literary critic, one of the original members of the Bloomsbury group. Their marriage took place in 1932. Virginia Woolf in a wry but affectionate entry in her *Diary* describes 'David and Rachel, arm-in-arm, sleep-walking down the aisle, preceded by a cross which ushered them into a car and so into a happy, long life, I make no doubt' (A. O. Bell (ed.), *The Diary of Virginia Woolf*, vol. iv, 1982, p. 128). She was not to know how accurate her ironic prediction would prove. A remarkable woman in her own right, Rachel MacCarthy was the perfect match for her husband. Of a simpler, more practical nature, she shared his vivacity and his unfailing curiosity about people, literature, and life. Like him, she was instinctively religious and a practising Christian. They were perfectly happy together, drawing their many friends into that happiness, for fifty years.

As he now moved into the country near Cranborne, David Cecil's new life, though congenial, showed him that he missed Oxford, especially the teaching. In 1939 he accepted a fellowship in English at New College and it was here as tutor and, from 1949, as Goldsmiths' professor that he exercised his widest influence and produced much of his best work. He had a genius for teaching, communicating enjoyment, and drawing out the best from others. A brilliant conversationalist, his wit consisted in verbal sharpness and accuracy, together with a peculiarly sympathetic humour that was always adapted to the company and the occasion. He was a celebrated lecturer, but his influence was most felt in tutorials, classes, or small, intimate groups. He and his wife, naturally hospitable, were eager to mix their friends and share them with young unknowns. Without condescension or pretension they spread over a wide circle of acquaintances and pupils the best-known cultural, political, and artistic influences of the mid-twentieth century.

In the 1960s David Cecil began to feel that his particular concern for English literature was under attack in an increasingly professional age. He never avoided, indeed enjoyed, debate, and was confident of his position, but he shared his family's clear-sightedness about the signs of the times. Developments in graduate studies, and the insistence on advanced degrees as a qualification for university teaching, made him feel his way was out of favour. In 1969 he reached retirement age and went happily to Cranborne, where he continued to write and entertain until his wife's death in 1982, and, though less happily, with remarkable resilience and little diminished powers of enjoyment until his own death.

David Cecil's writings, especially his biographies of William Cowper (*The Stricken Deer*, 1929), Lord Melbourne (1955), Jane Austen (1978), and Charles Lamb (1983), are a substantial contribution to the understanding of different kinds of personality and period. As such they had a value beyond the academic, and reached a wide readership. His literary criticism came to be badly underestimated. *Early Victorian Novelists* (1934) was ahead of its time in a subtle analysis and discussion of the structure of *Wuthering Heights*. *Hardy the Novelist* (1943) remains a classic exposition of the work of one of his favourite authors. His best essays, too often written off as *belles-lettres*, are as acute as they are sensitive. But most typical of his imagination is his response to extrovert, worldly figures like Melbourne, or balanced moral observers like Jane Austen, and, on the other hand, to introverted, despondent, but gentle and humorous spirits, like Cowper and Lamb. To their situation he was drawn by a sympathy typical of the depth and complexity of his own nature.

He considered himself, with good reason, the most fortunate of men. Born into one of the first families in the land, gifted with intellectual and imaginative sympathies of a high order, professionally successful, idyllically happy in his marriage and family life, he might well have grown complacent and a figure of envy. But complacency was not in his nature or his background: he was self-critical and self-aware. As for enemies, he had few if any. He was greatly loved because of the unusual sweetness of his temper and his genuine humility. Naturally high-spirited and with some vanity, he felt most strongly an inherited impulse of service and purpose. Himself a devout Christian, what he possessed he wanted to share, and he had been given precisely the gifts to enable this. His appearance was extraordinary and memorable: elegant and at the same time spontaneously gauche, continually in motion from the twirling thumbs to the enthusiastic forward lurch. His voice, too, was rapid, stuttering, and spasmodic, with Edwardian pronunciation. David Cecil was one of the most influential cultural figures of his age.

He was appointed CH in 1949 and C.Lit. in 1972. He had honorary doctorates from London, Leeds, Liverpool, St Andrews, and Glasgow universities. He died at Cranborne 1 January 1986.

[W. W. Robson (ed.), *Essays and Poems Presented to Lord David Cecil*, 1970; Hannah Cranborne (ed.), *David Cecil: a Portrait by his Friends*, privately printed, 1990; family information; personal knowledge.]

RACHEL TRICKETT

published 1996

CHAPLIN Sir Charles Spencer

(1889–1977)

Film actor and director, was born 15 April 1889 in East Street, Walworth, London, the son of Charles Chaplin, variety comedian, and his wife, Hannah ('Lily Harley'), daughter of Charles Hill, cobbler, of county Cork. The birth appears not to have been registered. His father drank and the parents separated a year after Charles was born; however the mother was successful enough as a vaudeville singer to support herself and her two sons (the elder, Sydney, was the result of an early affair which had taken her to South Africa). But her voice failed, engagements dwindled, and the family was reduced to the workhouse. Mental instability followed, and Chaplin has described how as a child, with his brother at sea in the navy, he struggled alone in London to keep alive, employed as newsboy, printer's boy, doctor's boy, and, for a brief disastrous adventure, glass-blower. He had for a time been a member of a team of clog-dancers, the Eight Lancashire Lads; he continued to dream of the stage, and when Sydney, released from the navy, was back in London and able to help him he found employment in the theatre, first in a short-lived play called *Jim*, then as the page-boy in *Sherlock Holmes*, which with H. A. Saintsbury in the title-role toured for three years. Music hall followed; he joined Sydney in the Fred Karno Company. He quickly learned the vaudeville technique which was to serve him so well. Soon he was in America, touring with the second Karno company. In 1913 he received an invitation from Keystone, a company producing short comic films. Doubtful of his future in the world of the cinema, he hesitated, but the offer of $150 per week persuaded him, and at the end of the year he was in Hollywood, working for Mack Sennett.

The story of his beginnings in the cinema is familiar. There was an inauspicious start: then Sennett told him to go and pick out a costume and make-up of his own choice. He selected baggy trousers, outsize shoes, a tight jacket, a hat too small, a moustache, and a cane. With the outfit the idea of the character grew in his mind. There was, of course, no script; he knew only, he was to say, that Mabel Normand (she was a star of silent comedy) was involved with her husband and a lover. He was not allowed to develop the character he had created. The old hands could not accept what they saw as his stage technique. Used to inventing his own comic business, he chafed.

In May 1914 he was allowed to write and direct a one-reel piece. His creative career had begun; and for the next four years, first with Keystone, then with other companies—Essanay, Mutual, First National—he made the series of short silent comedies which were to establish him as the darling of the public. The figure in the baggy pants became the universal Tramp. The titles are indicative: *The New Janitor* (1914), *The Rink* (1916), *The Floorwalker* (1916). Chaplin appeared as various characters; he was the fireman, the roller-skater, the boxer, the pawnbroker, the immigrant, and the patient in the sanatorium. In the earlier pieces he was the scallywag capable of snatching the coin from the blind man's wallet. But the character softened and absorbed sentiment. Pathos was added to laughter.

By the end of 1918 he was extending not only in emotional scope but in length. His ironic joke about the miseries of trench warfare, *Shoulder Arms* (1918), ran for three reels, and in 1920 there came the first of his feature films, *The Kid*, a story with fully developed action. It was followed in 1923 by the four-reel *The Pilgrim*, and Chaplin, now his own master, took a rest. There was a much fêted visit to London, Paris, and Berlin; then he embarked on an experiment in a mood alien from the works which had made him world-famous. Himself appearing for no more than a few moments, and with Edna Purviance from his short comedies cast as the heroine, he directed *A Woman of Paris* (1923), a melodramatic story of a country girl frustrated in love who becomes a notorious Paris beauty; Adolphe Menjou played the insouciant seducer. The playing had a restraint far ahead of the period. But without the expected Chaplin comedy the film was a failure. Withdrawn, it remained a mere title in film history books until the 1980s, when it was revived to a critical acclaim greater than it deserved. Its chief interest is still historical. Fortunately Chaplin returned to the path of his true genius. In 1925 he made *The Gold Rush* with its enchanting visual jokes such as the hand-dance and the meal off a shoe. In 1928 *The Circus* followed.

In 1931 there was *City Lights*, perhaps the culmination of Chaplin's career. In Europe again, he was hailed by the great and the humble; he was admired by G. Bernard Shaw and royalty received him. Police had to restrain crowds gathered to see him. Nevertheless times were changing in the cinema for the screen had found its voice; now Chaplin was faced with the challenge of the 'talkies'. He compromised: *City Lights* had sound, but it was not a 'talkie'; in one hilarious moment he mimicked the hiccups of a man who has swallowed a toy whistle but he did not speak. Five years later he was still compromising; in *Modern Times* (1936) Chaplin contented himself with a nonsense song. And he was committing himself to political opinions; the film, ridiculing the mechanization of factory work, was taken as a defence of unions and the labour movement. Political unpopularity (Chaplin was openly pro-Russian) in the United States was followed by moral attack when he was involved in a painful paternity case. His Hitler satire, *The Great Dictator* (1940), failed to win back his popular esteem. He was losing the sureness of his touch in mingling comedy and sentiment —for example, the fervour of his final speech in *The Great Dictator* seemed hollow. The American public turned against its favourite—who had never renounced his British citizenship.

Chaplin was shedding the Tramp character. In *The Great Dictator*, with Chaplin attempting the role of a political leader, the figure of a barber shared the narrative with a satirized Hitler figure. Seven years later, in

Monsieur Verdoux (1947), he completely abandoned his famous early character; now he was playing a multiple murderer who, comparing his handful of deaths with the massive exterminations of war, becomes the advocate of pacifism. It was a brilliant film; but it was a failure with the public. Chaplin was to make one more film in America, *Limelight* (1952), a sentimental tale of an old music-hall star and the young dancer he befriends. Chaplin's name carried it through, but Buster Keaton, playing a minor role, outshone him. When he left the United States for the European première the American government banned his re-entry and he took up residence in Switzerland. His two last films were made in Britain: *The King in New York* (1957), an attempt, only momentarily successful, to revive his old comedy style, and *A Countess from Hong Kong* (1966), a romantic comedy in which he directed Sophia Loren and Marlon Brando but himself made only brief appearances.

Chaplin was the supreme example of the artist in one sphere of entertainment who was able not only to transfer to a much larger field the talents he had acquired but also to transform the development of the second sphere. Beginning in the British music hall, given a chance in the American cinema, he had insisted that he had something to contribute: insisted against opposition, for his physical comedy—the falls, the run suddenly halted by the limits of the stage—was at first pure vaudeville. But nature had endowed him with a genius for invention. Creator as well as performer, he observed the oddities of human behaviour and enshrined them in a superb gallery of fictions. To the character he had invented in his first days in Hollywood he added social and political satire—and emotional range. He was the born novelist who wrote in visual absurdities. Enormously gifted, he composed music for his films and wrote autobiographical books which stand the test of time. The miseries of his childhood, combined with the triumph of his maturity, gave him the confidence to attack the society which had fostered him, and inevitably he was attacked as a result. His latest work was flawed by sentimentality; and like many comedians he sometimes stretched his gifts beyond their proper limits. But his invention was boundless; and in *Monsieur Verdoux* he showed that his genius went far beyond physical comedy. His finest films were illuminated by passages of a visual brilliance which have never been surpassed. It is possible to argue that his best work is to be found in the short pieces which preceded his feature-length successes: in *Easy Street* (1917), for example, or in the miraculous details of *The Pawnshop* (1916). But however one assesses his genius, he must be recognized as one of the creators of the art of the cinema.

In social encounters Chaplin was an easy and inspiring companion, eager to lavish on chance acquaintance his gifts as raconteur and mimic. In

1962 he received honorary D.Litts. from Oxford and Durham universities and in 1971 he became a commander of the French Legion of Honour. In 1973 he was received back into the American film establishment and given a special Oscar. He was appointed KBE in 1975.

He was married four times: in 1918 to Mildred Harris (died 1944); in 1924 to Lolita McMurry ('Lita Grey'); in 1936 to Marion Levy ('Paulette Goddard'). These three marriages, which were stormy and racked with scandal, ended in divorce (in 1920, 1927, and 1942). Of the first there was a son who lived three days, of the second two sons, and of the third no children. Finally in 1943 he married the daughter of the playwright Eugene O'Neill, Oona, with whom he lived happily for the rest of his life. They had three sons and five daughters, one of whom, Geraldine Chaplin, achieved considerable success as a film actress. Chaplin died 25 December 1977 at his home, Vaud, Vevey, Switzerland. There is a statue by John Doubleday (1981) in Leicester Square.

[Theodore Huff, *Charlie Chaplin*, 1952; Charles Chaplin, *My Autobiography*, 1964, and *My Life in Pictures*, 1974; David Robinson, *Chaplin, his Life and Art*, 1985.]

DILYS POWELL

published 1986

CHICHESTER Sir Francis Charles

(1901–1972)

Airman, sailor, and navigator, was born 17 September 1901 at Shirwell, the younger son (there were later two daughters) of the Revd Charles Chichester, vicar of Shirwell, Devon, seventh son of the eighth baronet, and his wife, Emily Annie, daughter of Samuel Page, of Chitt's Hill, Wood Green, London. He was educated at the infants' school in Barnstaple, at preparatory schools in Ellerslie and Bournemouth, and at Marlborough. He spent an unhappy childhood, left Marlborough at the age of seventeen, and emigrated in December 1919 to New Zealand with only ten sovereigns in his pocket. There he tried a variety of jobs, until as a land agent and property developer he was able to earn a substantial income and to accumulate some capital. In 1923 he married Muriel Eileen, daughter of M. L. Blakiston; they had two sons, the first stillborn, the second, George, who died in 1967. The marriage broke up within three years and in 1929 his first wife died. George was brought up by his New Zealand grandparents until Chichester's second marriage.

Chichester became the hero of the British people and achieved world fame when at the age of sixty-five he sailed solo around the world between August 1966 and May 1967, 29,600 miles in 226 days sailing time. Nearly forty years earlier he had established himself as a record-breaking pilot in small aircraft and his feats as a navigator became well known. Indeed navigation is the link between his exploits in both spheres. He would not have claimed to be either a natural pilot or a natural sailor and it is in the technique of navigation that he made his immediate contribution to the development of aviation and later demonstrated his capabilities at sea.

Together with his partner in the estate agency, Geoffrey Goodwin, he formed an aviation company, and learnt to fly at a New Zealand air force station. Returning after ten years' absence to England he took further flying lessons at Brooklands, bought a plane, a Gipsy I Moth, gained his A licence, made a preliminary tour of Europe, and then in 1929 set off for Australia. After nineteen days' solo flight and a variety of incidents, including twice damaging the plane, he landed at Sydney, New South Wales, to an uproarious welcome from thousands of people, being only the second pilot successfully to accomplish this hazardous operation.

Back in New Zealand Chichester determined to be the first to fly solo from east to west across the Tasman Sea. This necessitated landing on two small islands, roughly equally spaced across the ocean, to refuel. To do so demanded absolutely accurate navigation. His method was to aim off the mark and having reached the selected point, checked by a sun sight, to turn and sweep along the position line until he could see his target. He used a sextant, five-figure logarithmic tables, and a scribbling pad strapped to his knee, all in the very cramped space of a small cockpit. Having fitted floats to his Gipsy I Moth to enable him to land on the island lagoons, he made accurate landfalls at Norfolk Island, where he encountered engine trouble on take off, and Lord Howe Island, where his plane sank and had to be rebuilt, before reaching Jarvis Bay, south of Sydney. By his resourcefulness, skill, and determination he had triumphed. Continuing by stages what he now envisaged as a round-the-world tour later in 1929 he crashed in Japan after hitting telephone wires at Katsuura, seriously injuring himself and writing off his plane. Back in England he married in 1937 Sheila Mary, daughter of Gerald Craven, of Belle Eau Park, Nottinghamshire, the son of Thomas Craven, of Kirklington Hall, Nottinghamshire; they had one son, Giles. After a year in New Zealand together they returned to live permanently in England and Chichester took up a post as a navigation specialist with a firm of instrument makers.

Frustrated during the first years of World War II by the failure of the RAF to make use of his navigational experience, he was eventually appointed navigation officer at the Empire Flying School (1943–5). After the war he established his own publishing firm for maps and guides. He then took up ocean racing, first as a navigator and later, in 1958, with his own boat Gipsy Moth II. In 1958–9 he suffered from lung cancer but recovered and in 1960 with Gipsy Moth III he won the first single-handed transatlantic race. In the same race two years later he knocked nearly seven days off his previous record but came second. Gipsy Moth IV was built to circumnavigate the globe which he successfully accomplished with one stop at Sydney. What had been denied him in the air he had been granted at sea. He failed in his subsequent attempt in Gipsy Moth V to sail four thousand miles in twenty days, from Guinea Bissau across the Atlantic to San Juan del Norte in Nicaragua, but his time of twenty-two days established another record. The fourth single-handed transatlantic race in 1972 proved to be his last. Frail when he started, he became ill and returned to Plymouth. He died there shortly afterwards, 26 August 1972.

Chichester was appointed CBE in 1964 and KBE in 1967, when he reached Sydney half way through his single-handed voyage round the world. The Queen dubbed him with Sir Francis Drake's sword at Greenwich after his return. He received many other honours and awards. He recorded his exploits both in the air and at sea in a number of books, but his personality and his philosophy can best be summed up in his own answer to a question after his tumultuous welcome at Plymouth. Why did he do it? 'Because', he replied, 'it intensifies life.'

[Francis Chichester, *The Lonely Sea and the Sky*, 1964; Anita Leslie, *Francis Chichester*, 1975; personal knowledge.]

EDWARD HEATH

published 1986

CHRISTIE Dame Agatha Mary Clarissa

(1890–1976)

Detective novelist and playwright, was born 15 September 1890 at Torquay, the third and youngest child and second daughter of Frederick Alvah Miller, of independent means, formerly of New York, and his wife, Clarissa ('Clara') Margaret Boehmer. She had no schooling at all, not even a governess. But, once having frustrated her mother's current belief that no child should read until the age of eight, she devoured books voraciously, as well as conducting in her mind an endless school story with a vivid and varied cast. She began to write, too. At eleven there was a poem in a local paper ('When first the electric tram did run'). But the notion of being a writer as such, she says in *An Autobiography* (1977), never entered her head.

Her talents were seen to lie in the direction of music. At sixteen she went to Paris and studied both singing and the piano, hoping for a concert career only to learn that her temperament was too reticent for public performance. Her happy, quiet life in Torquay—it was to be reflected in the values that underlay all her books—was plunged into a more dramatic tempo when, rejecting a suitor with whom she had an unannounced engagement, she fell in love with a young officer, Archibald Christie (died 1962), just about to join the Royal Flying Corps. She married him, at two days' notice, in 1914 during his first leave after war had broken out, and then returned to the Voluntary Aid Detachment nursing she had taken up and the dispensary work that followed.

It was during lulls in the dispensary that she began a detective story. Seeking some point of originality for a sleuth in the Sherlock Holmes tradition she thought of the Belgian refugees in Torquay and Hercule Poirot, retired Belgian policeman evacuated to England, was born, though it was not until 1920 and six unsuccessful trips to publishers that he saw the light of day in *The Mysterious Affair at Styles*, a book that shows little indeed of the prentice hand. Once embarked on a writing career, however, books followed in regular succession until in 1926 she produced *The Murder of Roger Ackroyd* which by its daring reversal of the understood conventions of the genre created a considerable sensation.

It was a sensation that in the same year was echoed in her own life. Her husband, now Colonel Christie, had fallen in love with a friend's secretary, Nancy Neele, and at the same time following the death of her much loved mother she undertook the clearing up of the old family home. The strain was too much. Leaving no explanation, she made her way from Surrey to a Harrogate hotel where she registered under Miss Neele's name. The disappearance of a figure associated with crime and a highly popular form of writing caused an immense furore, and when after nine days she was recognized the newspaper brouhaha left her always suspicious of publicity. She divorced Colonel Christie in 1928. There was one child of the marriage, a daughter.

It was as the result of a visit during an impromptu holiday to the archaeological site at Ur then being excavated by (Sir) C. Leonard Woolley, whose wife was a passionate admirer of *The Murder of Roger Ackroyd*, that she met (Sir) Max Mallowan. They were married in 1930 and for the remainder of her life, except for his period of service in the war of 1939–45, she was closely associated with his work, learning to photograph, clean, and register the hundreds of small finds of a dig, to run a camp and pay the many workmen. She accompanied her husband on his expeditions, and a handful of her novels reflect the archaeological life, notably *Death Comes As the End* (1945), ingeniously set in Ancient Egypt, as well as a slim factual account enlivened with humour, *Come Tell Me How You Live* (1946).

But archaeology did not prevent her producing a book a year, sometimes more, and her best work is to be found in the twenty-five novels she wrote up to the end of the war of 1939–45 with two 'last books' written in the war years and consigned to her solicitor's safe to appear, *coronat finis opus*, as *Curtain: Hercule Poirot's Last Case* in 1975 and as *Sleeping Murder* in 1976, which contained the final appearance of Miss Marple, her equally popular sleuth brought from short stories to the novel in *Murder at the Vicarage* (1930), whose intuition replaced the logicality of Poirot's 'little grey cells'.

These books show her two great gifts, ingenuity of puzzle and unhesitating narrative. The ingenuity is to be found both in basic plot and in beautifully skilful minor misdirection. That basic conjuring trick may be exemplified in the idea for *Evil Under the Sun* (1941) in which a character is presented to the reader as the archetypal misused wife only to be revealed finally as co-conspirator with her supposedly arrogantly straying husband. The minor misdirections—there are scores of them—may be typified as either verbal sleight of hand ('I did all that was necessary', neutrally says the character who has in fact been arranging his alibi) or visual trickery (seeping blood that is nail polish with a real wound self-inflicted later).

The narrative skill is always unobtrusive. It consists primarily in a shunning of all irrelevance, even of the fine phrase, that is almost heroic, coupled with a fine sense of timing (perhaps deriving from her musicality). To these two positive factors must be added, in accounting for the enormous success of the books, some more negative ones. Characters are seldom portrayed in any depth or much described, so that readers as far apart as Nicaragua and Bengal can each see them through their own experience. Nor did she often leave the territory she knew best, upper middle-class English life, limiting but safe. Physical description of all kinds is minimal and as much as possible of the story is told through dialogue, easy everyday talk.

These virtues, and these avoidances of the pitfalls awaiting the ambitious, account too for her success as a playwright, artistic in *Witness for the Prosecution* (1953), financial in *The Mousetrap* (1952). Two other aspects of her work should be mentioned, the six romantic novels she wrote as Mary Westmacott, uneven but personally revealing, and the volume of religious stories for children, *Star over Bethlehem* (1965), which speaks a little of the spiritual commitment that sustained her until her death, wheeled in her invalid-chair from the luncheon table by her husband at their Oxfordshire home, Winterbrook House, Wallingford, 12 January 1976.

So popular did her books become that totalling her sales defied all the efforts of her publishers and literary agent. She was translated into 103 languages. Her film rights were sold for record sums. Her play *The Mousetrap* achieved a run on the London stage exceeding a quarter of a century and far outpacing any other. She was honoured with the CBE in 1956 and appointed DBE in 1971. She was a D.Litt. of the University of Exeter.

[Agatha Christie, *First Lady of Crime* (ed. H. R. F. Keating), 1977, and *An Autobiography*, 1977; Janet Morgan, *Agatha Christie*, 1984.]

H. R. F. KEATING

published 1986

CHURCHILL Sir Winston Leonard Spencer (1874–1965)

Statesman, was born, prematurely, at Blenheim Palace, his grandfather's Oxfordshire seat, 30 November 1874, the elder of the two sons of Lord Randolph Spencer Churchill, third son of the seventh Duke of Marlborough, and his wife, Jennie, daughter of Leonard Jerome, of New York. After a not particularly happy childhood, he was packed off to Harrow where, after a year, he found himself in the army class. Thence, at the third attempt, he passed into Sandhurst, but he passed out twentieth of 130 and was commissioned, 20 February 1895, in the 4th Queen's Own Hussars, a financial strain on his extravagant and recently widowed mother. In October he set off with a fellow subaltern, via New York, to Cuba to survey the rebellion there. He first saw action on his twenty-first birthday and reported it for the *Daily Graphic*. For the rest of his life he was able to keep himself by his journalism, took a siesta in the afternoon, and smoked cigars.

The two young officers were awarded the Spanish Order of the Red Cross, then, after a spell of London life and polo, left with their regiment for India. His mother sent Churchill books which he 'devoured', Gibbon and Macaulay becoming the anvil of an intensely idiosyncratic literary style. 'A few months in South Africa', he told her, 'would earn me the S.A. medal and in all probability the Company's Star. Thence hot-foot to Egypt—to return with two more decorations in a year or two—and beat my sword into an iron despatch box' (Randolph Churchill, *Winston S. Churchill*, companion vol. i, 1967, p. 676).

In August 1897, on returning to Bangalore from leave, he hurried north after arranging to cover the campaign for two newspapers, to join Sir

Bindon Blood for reprisals upon the Pathans on the frontier. Barely a couple of months later he had completed his enthralling *The Story of the Malakand Field Force*, which came out in March 1898, and resumed *Savrola*, his only novel, which was published in 1900.

'It is a pushing age and we must shove with the best', he told his mother (10 January 1898: Randolph Churchill, op. cit., p. 856). Through her influence with the prime minister, he was attached by a reluctant sirdar, the future Lord Kitchener, to the 21st Lancers as they moved on Khartoum. They engaged the Dervishes at Omdurman (2 September 1898), an earlier shoulder injury compelling Churchill to carry a pistol instead of a lance: which may have saved his life in that last cavalry charge of the dying century.

Back in Bangalore he helped the 4th Hussars to win the inter-regimental polo tournament, scoring, despite the strapped shoulder, three of their four goals in the final. Meanwhile he had completed his superb *The River War*, which appeared, nearly a thousand pages long, in the autumn of 1899, by when he had already resigned his commission and had been narrowly defeated in the Oldham by-election in July.

With an arrangement with the *Morning Post*, he set sail 14 October 1899 for South Africa alongside J. B. Atkins of the *Manchester Guardian* who recalled him as 'slim, slightly reddish-haired, pale, lively, frequently plunging along the deck "with neck out-thrust" as Browning fancied Napoleon' (*Incidents and Reflections*, 1947, p. 122). Churchill himself would not have found the comparison incongruous.

He got himself to Durban, thence was swiftly involved in the Boer ambush of an armoured train. He was taken prisoner, but escaped from Pretoria, with a price on his head, and made his way back to Durban, to be carried shoulder-high. He attached himself to the South Africa Light Horse, in which his brother 'Jack' soon joined him, but by June 1900 he was ready for home once more. There he published (1900) a couple of books based on his *Morning Post* dispatches, *London to Ladysmith, via Pretoria* and *Ian Hamilton's March*, and, with his accumulated royalties and the proceeds of lecture tours in England and North America, he had by now accumulated £10,000, which Sir Ernest Cassel, his father's friend, agreed to invest for him.

He was elected Unionist MP for Oldham in the 'khaki' election of October 1900 and had barely been sworn in before he rose, 18 February 1901, from the corner-seat above the gangway which his father had occupied in 1886 after his sensational resignation, to make a maiden speech in which Winston Churchill informed the House that 'If I were a Boer, I hope I should be fighting in the field'.

He was evidently in the wrong party and soon the tariff reform proposals of Joseph Chamberlain, which electrified the political world in May 1903, convinced Churchill of this and of his own free trade credo. By December 1903 the Oldham Unionists had disowned him and in January 1904 he was refused the Conservative whip. At the end of May he crossed the floor and took his seat on the Liberal benches.

Conservatives never forgave him: Tories have always placed a high premium upon loyalty. Joseph Chamberlain, himself a party renegade, misread his Balfour in maintaining that 'Winston is the cleverest of all the young men and the mistake Arthur made was letting him go' (Margot Asquith, *Autobiography*, vol. ii, 1922, p. 134).

For Churchill January 1906 was momentous. Already in office since 15 December 1905 in Campbell-Bannerman's new administration, he issued his election address as Liberal candidate for North-West Manchester, which was followed next day by the publication of the two masterly volumes of his *Lord Randolph Churchill*. 'Few fathers have done less for their sons', his cousin was to aver. 'Few sons have done more for their fathers . . . perhaps the greatest filial tribute in the English language' ((Sir) Shane Leslie, *The End of a Chapter*, 1916, p. 110).

Churchill's exciting election meetings were crowded to the doors; refusing to be 'henpecked' by the suffragettes, he was elected (15 January), whilst, in another part of Manchester, Balfour had lost his seat and the 'Stupid Party' had been routed.

John Burns having preferred to remain at the Local Government Board, Churchill was relieved of his dread of being 'shut up in a soup-kitchen with Mrs Sidney Webb', but to the prime minister's surprise he refused the post of financial secretary to the Treasury, choosing instead to become parliamentary under-secretary for the colonies, his chief Lord Elgin, the former viceroy of India, being in the Lords. In the Colonial Office Churchill discovered (Sir) Edward Marsh as his private secretary and signed him on for life. In his first important state paper (2 January 1906) Churchill persuaded Elgin to abandon the new Transvaal constitution proposed by his predecessor Alfred Lyttelton, in favour of fully responsible government: to make another friend for life in Jan Christian Smuts. But Churchill's vivid brain raced ahead of the Opposition's unforgiving prejudice which rejected the turncoat's eloquent appeal (31 July) to make the new dispensation 'the gift of England'. Chinese labour on the Rand was another stumbling block, even though Churchill had already explained to the House in February that it might not be termed slavery without 'some risk of terminological inexactitude'; and he badly misjudged the mood of the Commons in a carefully prepared speech about Lord Milner. Nor was his relationship with Elgin invariably plain sailing. 'These are my views', one of his exhaustive memoranda concluded; 'but not mine', the colonial secretary subjoined (Sir Austen Chamberlain, *Politics From Inside*, 1936, p. 459).

Churchill was sworn of the Privy Council, 1 May 1907. Intent on seeing for himself more than public funds or criticism might allow, he arranged to write for the *Strand Magazine* to pay for an extended—and voluble—visit to East Africa which inevitably became an official progress. In *My African Journey* (1908), the final text of which he was to complete on his honeymoon, he visualized harnessing the Nile waters and the industrial development of colonial Africa.

From the industrialization of the Empire his soaring imagination and compulsive reading were already turning to social reform at home and a growing emphasis on the minimum wage began to suggest far less reluctance to sup with Mrs Webb. In April 1908, when Asquith succeeded Campbell-Bannerman as Liberal prime minister, he offered Churchill the presidency of the Board of Trade in succession to David Lloyd George who was about to replace Asquith himself at the Exchequer. A by-election was accordingly necessary in the case of the youngest Cabinet minister since 1866 and, to unbridled Tory jubilation, Churchill was narrowly defeated in North-West Manchester. He was, however, promptly re-elected to Parliament, at Dundee, and 'settled down to enjoy the Board of Trade'.

His engagement was announced, 15 August 1908, to Clementine Ogilvy, younger daughter of Lady Blanche Hozier, eldest daughter of the seventh Earl of Airlie and widow since 1907 of Colonel Sir Henry Hozier, secretary of Lloyd's. They were married, 12 September 1908, at St Margaret's, Westminster, with Lord Hugh Cecil (later Lord Quickswood) as best man, the bridegroom busily discussing the political situation with Lloyd George in the vestry during the signing of the register.

The elegant, accomplished, but dowerless twenty-three-year-old bride was to devote the rest of her very able life to helping her extraordinary husband in his career. The extent of her self-sacrifice was revealed after her death, 12 December 1977, in *Clementine Churchill* (1979), by her youngest daughter, Lady Soames. Marriage to a genius can never have been easy. Her invariably sound advice was always cheerfully received but rarely taken. Since 'Clemmie' was primarily interested in Winston and so was Winston, their relationship to each other was always closer than that with their five children. They had four daughters: Diana (1909–63); Sarah (born 1914); Marigold (1918–21); and Mary (born 1922) who grew up beloved by both her parents. They had one son: Randolph (1911–68), the godson of F. E. Smith (later the Earl of Birkenhead), the Tory *sabreur* into whose high-living company Churchill had plunged in the summer of 1907, to forge a steadfast friendship with perhaps the only man he recognized, warily, to be his intellectual superior.

From 1908, whilst both men readily acknowledged allegiance to Asquith's chairmanship over the next seven years, to the exasperated incomprehension of less gifted souls, Churchill with Lloyd George as his senior partner comprised a political alliance from which much of modern Britain stems. Each in his own very different way was a self-made man, the one the grandson of a duke, the other brought up by the village cobbler. Each, like the prime minister, discovered in himself the power to sway the mass meetings then still popular in a sermon-tasting age before the advent of radio. If Lloyd George told people what he sensed they wanted to listen to, Churchill told them what he, Churchill, wanted them to hear. A prodigious amount of preparation preceded his every speech which, because he had once 'dried' in the House (22 April 1904), was always learned by heart after extensive dictation. A sheaf of notes in his right hand, shoulders hunched forward, Churchill exhibited a studied oratory in the grand manner with a highly personal vocabulary and humour, the lisp which the Boers had noted in their prisoner being turned to advantage. Because they were so assiduously rehearsed, his speeches still read well today, whereas Lloyd George's, with a few glowing exceptions, have blown away with the atmosphere which went to create them.

From Lloyd George Churchill 'was to learn the language of Radicalism', the prime minister's daughter came to explain [Lady Violet Bonham Carter (Lady Asquith), *Winston Churchill as I Knew Him*, 1965, p. 161]. 'It was Lloyd George's native tongue', but it was not Churchill's and he spoke it, as it were, in translation. 'Lloyd George was saturated with class-consciousness. Winston accepted class distinction without thought.' Churchill's main preoccupation at this period was the alleviation of distress, whereas Lloyd George purposed to refashion the State itself. Believing, because of his own escapes from death already, that he was to die early like his father, Churchill was 'full of the poor whom he has just discovered. He thinks he is called by providence—to do something for them' (Lucy Masterman, *C. F. G. Masterman*, 1939, p. 97). The study of socialism had been amongst Churchill's manifold activities on his East African journeyings, and on his return he had favoured an unimpressed Asquith with one of his strenuous memoranda on future policy. At the Home Office Herbert (later Viscount) Gladstone was to discover in Churchill the only colleague to go out of his way to support him over the Coal Mines Regulation (Eight Hours) Bill which became law in 1908.

The Board of Trade, with Sir Hubert Llewellyn Smith as the permanent secretary and because of the existence since 1886 of the Labour Department which he had built up there and which was shortly to be joined by George (later Lord) Askwith, was peculiarly geared to undertake the reforms which Churchill had in mind. Throughout his long career he had the knack of galvanizing and enthusing exceptionally able civil servants and deploying the figures with which they furnished him to buttress his most uncommon powers of persuasion.

He made a beginning with 'sweated labour', a problem which the Home Office had neglected. The Trade Boards Act of 1909 concerned in the first instance four trades only, but empowered the Board of Trade to extend their number. And, whilst at the Local Government Board John Burns was failing to tackle unemployment, Churchill brought William Henry (later Lord) Beveridge into the Board of Trade to establish labour exchanges as 'the Intelligence Department' of labour. Then, with Asquith's concurrence, he introduced an insurance Bill against unemployment which Lloyd George himself had been planning to include in his own legislative proposals and which eventually became law as part ii of the National Insurance Act of 1911.

To pay for their welfare programme Lloyd George and Churchill cabal-led to cut back on defence expenditure (in Churchill's case a hereditary posture), and an exasperated prime minister found himself compelled to resort to the formula by which Reginald McKenna, the first lord of the Admiralty, was vouchsafed an immediate four of the eight Dreadnoughts he was seeking to have laid down, the rest to come later. To pay for them as well as social insurance—for old-age pensions were to be non-contributory—Lloyd George came to formulate his 'People's Budget'. In the consequent controversies over the powers of the House of Lords, if Churchill did not resort to Lloyd George's brand of 'Limehouse' demagogy, his own inborn pugnacity, together with a convert's over-reaction, led him into 'teasing goldfish'—and, of course, reinforced Tory hatred of the renegade grandson. Lloyd George even suggested that Churchill was, in fact, 'opposed to pretty nearly every item in the Budget except the "Brat" ' (children's allowances against income tax). Nevertheless, Churchill was chairman of the Budget League and one of the most effective Liberal campaigners. He was rewarded in 1910 by the appointment of home secretary, Gladstone going out to South Africa as governor-general.

Recalling his own imprisonment, Churchill was eager to improve the lot of the prisoner and, with the aid of Sir Evelyn Ruggles-Brise, chairman of the Prison Commission, books and entertainment were introduced into prisons and the sentences of all child prisoners were reviewed. The principal piece of Home Office legislation during Churchill's secretaryship was the Mines Act of 1911 affecting safety in the pits, with a substantial increase in the inspectorate. A Shops Bill to improve the lot of shop assistants did little (because of the shopkeepers' obduracy) to improve conditions, but at least a weekly half-holiday became compulsory. Churchill became president of the Early Closing Association (1911–39).

Much of the home secretary's time came to be occupied by questions of law and order. Churchill was, of course, suspect already as a firebrand, and two episodes in his tenure at the Home Office, the one eternally distorted, the other too much in character, cast doubts especially amongst 'Lib-Labs' about how genuinely naturalized as a Radical this young reformist aristocrat was at bottom. In November 1910 rioting miners on strike at Tonypandy in the Rhondda Valley were dispersed by metropolitan policemen using rolled-up mackintoshes as truncheons, but the soldiery arrived as the riot was ending. For the rest of his life Churchill was branded as having used troops against the miners at Tonypandy whereas in truth, as the relevant general (Sir) Nevil Macready recorded, 'it was entirely due to Mr Churchill's forethought . . . that bloodshed was avoided' (*Annals of an Active Life*, 2 vols., 1924).

Not long after Tonypandy, in January 1911, Churchill rushed from his bath to superintend 'the battle of Sidney Street' in which he was photographed apparently directing troops who were assisting police in the ambush of a gang in a house off the Mile End Road. Arthur Balfour drew acid attention in the House to the incongruity of the home secretary's presence. 'Now Charlie. Don't be croth. It was such fun', Churchill reassured Charles Masterman, his remonstrating parliamentary under-secretary. Churchill lent credence to malicious criticism by his obvious enjoyment of moving bodies of troops about the country for use in emergency—'mistaking a coffee-stall row for the social revolution', John Burns called it—and his flamboyant ever-readiness throughout his life never to mind his own business did little to widen his friendships. 'His future is the most interesting problem of personal speculation in English politics', wrote A. G. Gardiner in the *Daily News*. 'At thirty-four he stands before the country one of the two most arresting figures in politics, his life a crowded drama of action, his courage high, his vision unclouded, his boats burned. . . . But don't forget that the aristocrat is still there—latent and submerged, but there nevertheless. The occasion may arise when the two Churchills will come into sharp conflict' (*Prophets, Priests and Kings*, 2nd edn., 1914, pp. 233–4).

With a major responsibility for national security as home secretary Churchill began to take a close interest in the Committee of Imperial Defence. Returning from being the guest of the Kaiser at the German manœuvres, 'I can only thank God', he remarked, 'that there is a sea between England and that Army.'

The Agadir crisis (July/August 1911) led Churchill to contemplate at length what might happen if it came to war with that army. He foresaw the Germans crossing the Meuse on the twentieth, but the tide of battle turning by the fortieth, day. The Admiralty, he pointed out to Asquith, had no proper plans for an emergency, nor an appropriate staff such as Lord Haldane had created in the War Office.

Whilst they were on a golfing holiday together at Archerfield, on the Firth of Forth, Asquith abruptly invited Churchill to exchange places with McKenna. Churchill became first lord of the Admiralty (25 October 1911), McKenna departing stiffly to the Home Office.

Churchill's immediate task was to impose a staff system upon the navy, most hierarchical of Services, which had survived the reforms of Lord Fisher, first sea lord in 1904–10, without one. Churchill was the last man to concur in a structure which left the war plan in the undisclosed possession not of the first lord of the Admiralty but of the first sea lord. So, Sir Arthur Knyvet Wilson, who had succeeded 'Jacky' Fisher as first sea lord, departed for Norfolk in October 1911. (He was to come back in 1914.) Fisher, not wanting to return to become 'second fiddle', stayed in the wings advising Churchill from the Continent. Since Asquith, on Lloyd George's advice, opposed the promotion of Prince Louis of Battenberg beyond second sea lord at this juncture, Sir Francis Bridgeman arrived from the Home Fleet as first sea lord when Churchill, a month after taking office, announced his Navy Board, 28 November 1911.

Left behind by Churchill's intellectual pace and physical stamina, Bridgeman lasted precisely a year, his dismissal enabling the Opposition to raise a political storm in which Lord Charles Beresford was able to renew his feud with Fisher in the Commons, where the leader of the Opposition was by then Andrew Bonar Law, who distrusted Churchill profoundly despite his own close friendship with Max Aitken (later Lord Beaverbrook), who had been introduced to Churchill by F. E. Smith. Even so, Bonar Law was an early member of 'The Other Club', which Churchill and F. E. Smith had invented to straddle the benches.

On arriving at the Admiralty Churchill had immediately appointed as his naval secretary David (later Earl) Beatty, by far the youngest flag officer in the navy. They had not encountered one another since the eve of Omdurman when the wealthy young sailor had lobbed a bottle of champagne from his gunboat to the impecunious 4th Hussar on the Nile bank.

Churchill and Beatty got along famously, Beatty at once spotting Churchill's proclivity to be utterly engrossed in the immediate. He had now discovered the navy just as three years earlier he had discovered the poor. 'He talks about nothing but the Sea', Beatty told his wife, 27 May 1912, 'and the Navy and the wonderful things he is going to do.' Lloyd George was soon complaining that he could no longer catch Churchill's political attention since he would 'only talk of boilers'. With the powerful support of the Committee of Imperial Defence and the Cabinet, Churchill at once, January 1912, reorganized the Navy Board into an Admiralty War Staff of three divisions, Operations, Intelligence, and Mobilization, under a chief of staff. Churchill evidently wanted this officer to be answerable to himself as first lord of the Admiralty, but, as ever, he was rushing his fences and, with Haldane's support, Prince Louis, as second sea lord, successfully resisted the proposal. In the first instance the Staff was advisory only. Moreover, there were no trained staff officers. Accordingly, a staff course was instituted at the Naval War College, Portsmouth, the cost being met by suppressing the private yachts of the three shore-based commanders-in-chief. Naval tradition stood in the way of the ablest young officers being posted there, since sea service, gunnery, and navigation were the paths to promotion.

'Tug' Wilson had warned Churchill that responsibility uncertainly divided between the first sea lord and a chief of war staff was unlikely to be viable and Prince Louis, when he succeeded Bridgeman in December 1912, evidently held it *infra dig.* for the first sea lord to become chief of staff to a civilian. Not until quite long after war had broken out, and then only after a minor disaster, did the roles of first sea lord and chief of staff become fused. Until then the former remained responsible not only for operations but also for manifold administrative tasks. An additional civil lord was introduced to lessen the burden by transferring Sir Francis Hopwood (later Lord Southborough), whom Churchill had known in the Colonial Office, to take charge especially of contracts. But this only became another point of friction between Bridgeman and Churchill. Although Churchill did not manage to have matters all his own way, at least he had achieved the major change: war plans were no longer locked in the immaculate bosom of the first sea lord, and effective co-ordination with the War Office, via the Committee of Imperial Defence, had at last become feasible. An Expeditionary Force might now be conveyed across the English Channel.

Churchill's task was as speedily as possible to modernize and strengthen the Royal Navy which he soon held to be quintessential to Great Britain, whereas, as he incautiously pointed out in Glasgow (February 1912), Germany's fleet was 'more in the nature of a luxury', an observation not advancing hopes of a 'naval holiday'. He worked incredibly long hours in wielding an intensely busy and often impulsive new broom. He visited every naval dockyard and establishment at home and in the Mediterranean in his first eighteen months in the Admiralty, during which he spent 182 days at sea, often in the Admiralty yacht *Enchantress*. Senior officers were scandalized by what Sir John (later Earl) Jellicoe, the second sea lord, termed his 'meddling', all taking exception especially to his direct dealings with junior officers and even the lower deck in these ceaseless tours of inspection. In July 1912 Rear-Admiral (Sir) Lewis Bayly informed him on the bridge of the *Lion* in Weymouth that 'on any repetition of his inquisitorial methods he would turn him off the ship. Winston took his drubbing very well' (*Inside Asquith's Cabinet*, the diaries of Charles Hobhouse, ed. Edward David, 1977, p. 117). A year later a more serious instance arose when Sir Richard Poore, at the Nore, complained to the second sea lord, whose province was naval discipline, and the second, third, and fourth sea lords threatened resignation (Sir Peter Gretton, *Former Naval Person*, 1968, pp. 89–92).

Anyone who attempted naval reform was likely to find opposition among the more senior officers. The more junior found Churchill's ways exciting and in the lower deck he was popular as the only first lord to pay attention to their pay and punishments or to devise a slender promotion channel for exceptional seamen to reach commissioned rank.

The most revolutionary change lay in the field of *matériel*. It was decided, on Fisher's advice, to build a new fast division of battleships—the Queen Elizabeth class—armed with 15-inch guns and faster because driven by oil instead of coal: which necessitated the acquisition of distant oilfields and of the Anglo-Persian Oil Company and was clearly unpopular with MPs from mining constituencies. Churchill also went out of his way to encourage the Royal Naval Air Service which was experimenting with various types of aircraft, frequently flying himself and taking lessons as a pilot.

War inevitably revealed untackled weaknesses: insufficient attention had been paid to protection of the Fleet's bases from submarine attack; ammunition supply to gun turrets was poorly designed, and so were shells. Churchill had rubbed a lot of people up the wrong way, from the King downwards, by his impulsive, opinionated, and constant interference, and he had strained his relationship with his Cabinet colleagues, especially Lloyd George, because of the cost of his revolutionary changes (F. W. Wiemann in *Lloyd George: Twelve Essays*, ed. A. J. P. Taylor, 1971); yet the German naval attaché could report to Admiral Tirpitz (4 June 1914): 'On the whole the Navy is satisfied with Mr. Churchill, because it recognizes that he has done and accomplished more for them than the majority of his predecessors in office. There is no doubt that there has been friction between Mr. Churchill and the officers at the Admiralty as well as those at sea. That is not surprising with such a stubborn and tyrannical character as Mr. Churchill. The intensive co-operation of all forces for an increase in the power and tactical readiness of the English Navy has under Mr. Churchill's guidance not only not suffered but has experienced rather energetic impulses and inspiration. The English Navy is very much aware of it' (Arthur J. Marder, *From The Dreadnought to Scapa Flow*, vol. i, 1961, pp.

263–4). As Kitchener was to tell Churchill when they parted in May 1915: 'There is one thing, at least, they can never take away from you. When the war began, you had the Fleet ready.'

Engrossed as Churchill was during his four years in the Admiralty in getting the navy expensively readied for war, he could never ignore the obligations of party in a Liberal Cabinet. Nor did he forget—and this was characteristic of him throughout his life—the calls of friendship, as Lloyd George had cause to remember over the Marconi affair (1912–13). He found it needful, too, for party reasons, 'to mingle actively in the Irish controversy'. With typical courage the Churchills, for his wife went with him, had fulfilled a speaking engagement in Belfast in February 1912. Two years later he was involved, once more, as a member of the Cabinet committee from which the 'Curragh incident' emerged. Characteristic ardour led him to overplay his hand both in demanding at Bradford (14 March 1914) to 'put these grave matters to the proof' and in directing the third battle squadron (under the self-same Lewis Bayly) to Lamlash on 19 March, to overawe Belfast: a flamboyant order which Asquith countermanded. In this episode the vindictive distrust of the Opposition, Bonar Law's especially, was intensified by their suspicion of Churchill.

In July 1914 the trial mobilization of the fleets, which had been decided on as less expensive than manœuvres, was in train and, in view of the Austrian ultimatum to Serbia, Prince Louis took the decision to cancel their dispersal. Churchill returned from a family holiday in Cromer to confirm this. When Austria declared war on 30 July, with Asquith's concurrence Churchill ordered the fleets to their battle stations. Unlike some of his Cabinet colleagues, he housed no doubts but was 'geared up and happy' and 'the splendid *condottiere* at the Admiralty' (as Viscount Morley of Blackburn affectionately called him in his *Memorandum on Resignation*, 1928) influenced Lloyd George towards the arbitrament of war. On the evening of 1 August 1914 Churchill 'went straight out like a man going to a well-accustomed job' (Lord Beaverbrook, *Politicians and the War*, 2 vols., 1928 and 1932, vol. i, p. 36).

Churchill's brief popularity from having the fleet ready on the outbreak was dissolved by his intervention in Antwerp in early October 1914. He went there post-haste, at the request of his Cabinet colleagues, and, with complete disregard for his own safety, personally superintended the defence of the city. A week was gained and the Channel ports (Dunkirk, Calais, and Boulogne) saved before the Allied line was stabilized—till March, 1918. But some of the newly formed Naval Division perished or were interned and Churchill, who clearly enjoyed the whole affair, was accused of having neglected his primary duties at the Admiralty for a characteristically impulsive adventure. So enthralled had he been by being in action once more that he offered to take military command, a suggestion which his colleagues, Kitchener apart, treated with incredulous laughter. Not for the first time Asquith came to question Churchill's priorities.

Not long afterwards Churchill was to make the mistake which led to his political downfall. Prejudice having forced the resignation (29 October 1914) of Prince Louis as first sea lord, Churchill, against advice (the King's especially), brought in Fisher to succeed him. Those who knew them both, Beatty, for example, or Admiral R. E. Wemyss (later Lord Wester Wemyss), realized that the arrangement involving such domineering characters, each used to having his own way, fond as they were of each other, would not work; it was only a matter of time before an irreconcilable clash. Moreover, their timetables, like their age-groups (for Fisher was seventy-three and Churchill not yet forty) were too incompatible. Fisher got up early and finished his work in the daytime to be off to bed by 9 p.m., by when Churchill, having slept in the afternoon, was just getting his second wind.

After a series of setbacks and a defeat at Coronel (2 November 1914) the navy badly needed a success. Moreover, the British Expeditionary Force was bogged down in Flanders. Trench warfare evoked Churchill's two most signal contributions. 'Impatient, resourceful and undismayed', as Asquith noted 27 October 1914, Churchill saw clearly that the alternatives were to break through by new methods or to outflank: hence his part in the evolution of the tank by establishing the Admiralty landship committee under (Sir) E. H. W. Tennyson-d'Eyncourt in February 1915; and his initiation of the Dardanelles campaign.

'Are there not other alternatives', he had asked Asquith (29 December 1914) 'than sending out armies to chew barbed wire in Flanders? Further, cannot the power of the Navy be brought more directly to bear upon the enemy?'

His first preoccupation lay in the Baltic and Fisher was enthusiastic about seizing the island of Borkum, to block the German Navy's exit. On the far-off opposite flank, Churchill envisaged opening up the passage to the sea of Marmora where the fleet might turn its guns on Constantinople and help to relieve the hard-pressed Russians. In early January 1915 the Grand Duke Nicholas asked for a demonstration to relieve Turkish pressure in the Caucasus. Fisher was willing to use obsolete pre-Dreadnought battleships unfit for service in the North Sea but Kitchener was reluctant at this stage to provide military support in the Mediterranean. As a result, an exasperated Churchill contemplated forcing the Dardanelles by naval forces alone. Admiral (Sir) S. H. Carden, commanding in the Eastern Mediterranean, replied: 'I do not think that the Dardanelles can be rushed but they might be forced by extended operations.' This was enough for

Churchill, whose ardour was whetted by Fisher's suggestion that the *Queen Elizabeth* should conduct her trials by demolishing the Dardanelles forts.

'The idea caught on at once', reported Maurice (later Lord) Hankey, who was secretary of the War Council. 'The whole atmosphere changed. Fatigue was forgotten. The War Council turned eagerly from the dreary vista of a "slogging match" on the Western Front to brighter prospects, as they seemed, in the Mediterranean. The Navy, in whom everyone had implicit confidence and whose opportunities had so far been few and far between, was to come into the front line. . . . Churchill had secured approval in principle to the naval attack on the Dardanelles on which he had set his heart. Fisher alone, whose silence had not meant consent as was generally assumed, was beginning to brood on the difficulties of his position which were eventually to lead to his resignation' (*The Supreme Command* 1914–1918, vol. i, 1961, pp. 265–7). At the end of January 1915 Asquith saw Churchill and Fisher together before the War Council assembled. 'I am the arbitrator', he told them (28 January 1915), 'I have heard Mr Winston Churchill and I have heard you and now I am going to give my decision. . . . The Dardanelles will go on' (Henry Pelling, *Winston Churchill*, 1977, p. 192).

Should the naval demonstration appear successful, military action would be called for and Kitchener agreed in mid-February that a regular division, the 29th, should be available to stiffen the proposed expeditionary force of Australians and New Zealanders, to whom Churchill added his own favourite Naval Division. Delay compounded delay. Churchill grew tempestuously impatient. The Turkish guns could not be silenced until the mines were swept; the mines could not be swept until the guns were silenced. By mid-March Admiral (Sir) John De Robeck, who had succeeded Carden, paused to co-ordinate his activities with Sir Ian Hamilton, the military commander. There were muddles too about the transports and it was not until 25 April that the military assault began: by then the enemy was ready.

Fisher insisted on the return of the *Queen Elizabeth* to safer waters and by mid-May it was evident that he was in a highly nervous state. Arriving at the Admiralty on Saturday, 15 May, he was met with an overnight draft list from Churchill of the naval vessels they had agreed to send to the Mediterranean, but which now included two submarines which had not been part of the previous day's bargain between them. Unwilling to face Churchill's relentless persuasiveness any longer, Fisher resigned and left the Admiralty. Attempts to get him to withdraw led him to lay down impossible terms for his return. Sir Arthur Wilson, who had been serving with Fisher and Churchill on the War Council, persuaded the other sea lords not to resign with Fisher and showed himself most generously willing to serve as first sea lord under Churchill. Asquith, who was facing an additional crisis over an attack in *The Times* on the shell shortage in France, seized the opportunity to form a coalition. Amongst Bonar Law's conditions for Opposition adherence was that Haldane should leave the Government and Churchill the Admiralty. Dumbfounded, Churchill went on begging to stay on, but on 20 May 1915 Asquith told him in writing: You must take it as settled that you are not to remain at the Admiralty.' Mrs Churchill joined his pleas. 'Winston may in your eyes', she wrote to the prime minister, '& in those with whom he has to work have faults but he has the supreme quality which I venture to say very few of your present or future Cabinet possess—the power, the imagination, the deadliness, to fight Germany' (Roy Jenkins, *Asquith*, 1964, p. 361). On 22 May her husband took his dignified leave of the departmental heads in the Admiralty where Balfour succeeded him. He became chancellor of the Duchy of Lancaster but with continued membership of the War Council, now to be renamed the Dardanelles Committee. 'If he could do things over again, he said without rancour (27 May 1915), he would do just the same with regard to appointing Fisher, as . . . he has done really great organising work' (Lady Cynthia Asquith, *Diaries 1915–18*, 1968, p. 31).

The Dardanelles Commission, which a reluctant Asquith was obliged to set up in September 1916 was eventually in its report of March 1917 to exonerate Churchill from the widely held suspicion that he had wilfully persisted in the enterprise without the concurrence of his naval experts or the co-operation of the War Office and more blame came to be laid at Asquith's door for his failure in timely and effective co-ordination and, by implication, on Kitchener who by this time had perished in the *Hampshire* (June 1916).

Meanwhile Churchill, not knowing quite what to do with himself—'my veins threatened to burst from the fall in pressure'—took refuge in the silent recreation of painting.

His Conservative colleagues vetoed a personal visit to the Dardanelles and when Sir Edward (later Lord) Carson joined the Dardanelles Committee, Churchill's support of Hamilton's continued operations was outweighed. He urged yet another naval attempt to force a way through, but by the end of October 1915 Sir Charles C. Monro replaced Hamilton and recommended evacuation.

Churchill, who had again asked Asquith for a military command on the western front, was not included in the smaller War Committee which replaced the Dardanelles Committee. He now faced no alternative but to resign from a post of 'well-paid inactivity'. On 18 November 1915 Major Churchill crossed to France to rejoin his yeomanry regiment, the Oxfordshire Hussars. After a brief attachment to the reluctant 2nd battalion,

Grenadier Guards, to experience trench warfare, and disappointed, as a result of Asquith's intervention, of his hope of a brigade, he was posted in January 1916 to command the 6th battalion of the Royal Scots Fusiliers in the 9th (Scottish) division and was allowed Sir Archibald Sinclair (later Viscount Thurso) as his second-in-command. Churchill was a fearless and well-liked commanding officer.

Perforce out of touch, Churchill baffled the House of Commons, when on leave in March 1916, by calling for Fisher's recall. Pressed by Beaverbrook to return to politics, Churchill, deprived by seniority when the 6th battalion had to be merged with the 7th because of manpower shortage, took the opportunity to resume his parliamentary and political duties. He returned to England in May 1916.

His family had to be provided for and he began a series of well-paid articles, first for the *Sunday Pictorial*, then for the *London Magazine*.

When Lloyd George formed his Government in December 1916 Churchill was still awaiting his exoneration. The new prime minister, using the two newspaper proprietors, Beaverbrook and Sir George (later Lord) Riddell as intermediaries, tried to propitiate Churchill in his frustrated loneliness. After the second session in May 1917 Lloyd George and Churchill met behind the Speaker's chair and 'he assured me of his determination to have me at his side. From that day, although holding no office, I became to a large extent his colleague. He repeatedly discussed with me every aspect of the war and many of his secret hopes and fears' (Winston S. Churchill, *The World Crisis*, 5 vols., 1923–31, vol. ii, p. 1144). But it was not until July 1917 that Lloyd George felt himself strong enough to ride off organized Conservative opposition to Churchill's reinstatement in high office and, even then, Bonar Law had difficulty with his back-benchers. Only then did a chastened Churchill himself come to appreciate the problem posed by the firm Tory prejudice against him: political alignments made Lloyd George's attitude unavoidably ambivalent. It was a measure of Churchill's stature that, despite the personal unpopularity of his old ministerial ally, the prime minister sought opportunity to risk the reabsorption of his unique energy into the war effort.

Churchill resumed office as minister of munitions (17 July 1917), but was outside the War Cabinet. He swiftly took grip of the sprawling empire in the Hotel Metropole by establishing a Munitions Council of business men already enrolled in the ministry, Lloyd George's 'men of push and go': to be served by a proper secretariat organized by Sir W. Graham Greene and (Sir) James E. Masterton-Smith, whom he had known in the Admiralty. Because he was at last happy again himself, he could assure the prime minister, early in September, that 'this is a very happy Department' (Pelling, op. cit., p. 232). There were frontier incidents with Sir Eric C. Geddes, the new first lord, since the Admiralty retained control of its own supply, and with Lord Derby (seventeenth Earl) at the War Office. A War Priorities Committee was established by the prime minister under J. C. Smuts's chairmanship—it had been at Churchill's suggestion that Lloyd George had taken General Smuts into his Cabinet—and if squabbles over munition workers, leaving certificates, wage rates, and differentials continued to arise, stoppages, because of Churchill's imaginative approach, were rarely serious or extensive. Churchill proved himself a quite exceptional departmental head in successfully imposing coherence upon a vast organization. He kept closely in touch with his French and American counterparts and was at pains as 'a shopman at the orders of the War Cabinet' to serve the needs of his customers. He gradually wore down Sir Douglas (later Earl) Haig's suspicion of him; indeed, the commander-in-chief arranged to put the Château Verchocq in the Pas de Calais at his disposal.

Although Churchill was not a member of the War Cabinet, Lloyd George was increasingly glad to avail himself in private of Churchill's courage and resourcefulness as well as his first-hand reports. When Churchill returned from a visit to his old division in the Third Army when the German March offensive began, Lloyd George and Sir Henry H. Wilson, the new CIGS, dined with the Churchills at 33 Eccleston Square (24 March). Churchill was the prime minister's chosen emissary to Clemenceau (who shared Churchill's love of danger) following the appointment of Foch to the Supreme Command. In August he flew over to Amiens to witness a British tank attack and Haig went out of his way to refer to 'the energy and foresight which you have displayed as Minister of Munitions' (Pelling, op. cit., p. 241).

Mollified by the implied offer of post-war Cabinet membership, Churchill agreed to fight the general election of December 1918 as a Coalition Liberal and was again returned for Dundee. Lloyd George had evidently been impressed by his departmental ability and asked him to move to the War Office (with which he combined responsibility for the Air Ministry) to deal with the frictions arising from demobilization. With Haig's agreement, he scrapped the existing scheme and substituted one based on age, length of service, and wounds, 'to let three men out of four go, and to pay the fourth double to finish the job'. His decisive formula was successful and more than two and a half million men were released, leaving under a million for garrisons abroad whilst the peace treaties were being negotiated.

Whereas Lloyd George was anxious to terminate British aid to the anti-Bolshevik forces in Russia as soon as possible, Churchill, not without some Conservative support, gave the impression of being himself far from averse to much more positive action. Happily (though not in his view), war weariness undermined further crusades and, somewhat ignominiously,

Allied intervention dribbled away leaving Churchill worsted. 'So ends in disaster', wrote Sir Henry Wilson savagely in his diary, March 1920, 'another of Winston's military attempts—Antwerp, Dardanelles, Denikin' (Major-General Sir C. E. Callwell, *Field Marshal Sir Henry Wilson*, vol. ii, 1927, p. 231).

Impressed by the inexpensive intervention of the Royal Air Force in Somaliland, Churchill supported Sir Hugh (later Viscount) Trenchard in his struggle for an independent air force as imperial policeman, particularly in view of the tasks created by the new territories falling under British control in the eastern Mediterranean. Lloyd George seized upon Churchill's suggestion that the Colonial Office should take charge of new territories, with the RAF keeping the peace. At the end of an inconclusive 1920 he sent Churchill to the Colonial Office, from which Milner was retiring, and by 1 March Churchill had brought a new Middle Eastern Department into existence and, to the envy of George Nathaniel Curzon (later Marquess Curzon of Kedleston), a grandiose conference, which T. E. Lawrence was to attend, was arranged at the Semiramis Hotel in Cairo to determine the future, especially of Iraq. 'First, we would repair the injury done to the Arabs and to the House of the Sherifs of Mecca by placing the Emir Feisal upon the throne of Iraq as King, and by entrusting the Emir Abdulla with the government of Trans-Jordania. Secondly, we would remove practically all the troops from Iraq and entrust its defence to the Royal Air Force. Thirdly, we suggested an adjustment of the immediate difficulties between the Jews and Arabs in Palestine which would serve as a foundation for the future' (Churchill, *Great Contemporaries*, 1937, p. 134).

Churchill's economical dispositions lasted longer than many expected and even in Palestine, where Sir Herbert (later Viscount) Samuel, his old, pre-war, Cabinet colleague, was by now the high commissioner, there was a period of comparative quiet. Churchill reasserted the Balfour Declaration in Jerusalem but received Arab delegates to assure them that Great Britain, as 'the greatest Moslem state in the world', cherished Arab friendship.

Whilst he was still at the War Office Churchill had attempted to reassert British control in Ireland but Lloyd George had come to realize that some sort of political settlement was called for. The dominant figures on the Government side in the negotiations with the Sinn Fein representatives were Lloyd George himself and Birkenhead but Churchill's personal rapport with Michael Collins, the leader of the Irish Republican Army, was a significant factor. 'Tell Winston', Collins said, 'we could never have done anything without him.' Fighting continued after a treaty which left the Tories most unhappy and it was General Sir Nevil Macready, commanding in Ireland, whose blind eye enabled the Provisional Government to survive.

At Chanak (15 September 1922), the episode which brought the Government down, Sir Charles Harington was the general whose blind eye saved the Government from head-on collision with Mustapha Kemal in the Dardanelles. Churchill himself had been trying to dissuade a too euphoric prime minister who was increasingly rude to him—theirs was 'the relationship of master and servant', he was to tell Robert (later Lord) Boothby years afterwards (Robert Boothby, *I Fight to Live*, 1947, p. 45)—from over-enthusiastic support of the Greeks, but in the event joined him in a solemn warning to Kemal. Churchill's request, as colonial secretary, for Dominion support unluckily became public; and so was the rebuff (J. G. Darwin, 'The Chanak Crisis', *History*, vol. 65, 1980). The Tories in the coalition had been made to take too much from the Liberals. The Carlton Club meeting ensued, 19 October 1922, and Lloyd George resigned. At the subsequent general election, 15 November 1922, Churchill, himself recovering from acute appendicitis, was beaten into fourth place at Dundee and found himself 'without a seat, without a party, and without an appendix'. He was appointed a Companion of Honour in the resignation honours list, 1922.

By February 1923 serialization of his *World Crisis* began in *The Times*, the whole torrential book (save the *Aftermath* some years later, 1929) appearing by the end of October. It was 'a brilliant autobiography disguised', as Balfour told a friend, 'as a history of the universe', a staggering performance from a man who for most of the time when he was dictating the huge volumes had been still busy in high office. Rhetorical as it inevitably is, for it is an orator's autobiography, there are magnificent passages in it which Churchill himself scarcely ever bettered.

He was by now politically isolated. He fought his last election as a Liberal and free trader in Leicester West, where he was defeated by F. W. (later Lord) Pethick-Lawrence, the Labour candidate (6 December 1923). Repulsed by Asquith's acquiescence in suffering the Labour Party to take minority office in January 1924, Churchill stood as an 'Independent anti-Socialist', with the young Brendan (later Viscount) Bracken among his supporters, in a by-election for the Abbey division of Westminster, only to be defeated by 43 votes in March 1924 by a Conservative.

A lifeline back to the Conservatism of his youth was uncoiled by Sir Archibald Salvidge, his father's old Liverpool henchman. Free trade, the issue on which he had left the party twenty years before, no longer seemed quite the same shibboleth. He swallowed the McKenna duties and a form of imperial preference, which had been dividing him from Stanley Baldwin, in a speech at Liverpool in May 1924, after which he remarked of his wife at supper in the Adelphi: 'She's a Liberal, and always has been. It's all very strange for her. But to me, of course, it's just like coming home' (Stanley Salvidge, *Salvidge of Liverpool*, 1934, p. 275).

He was adopted at Epping in September and a month later was elected as a 'Constitutionalist' by a majority of nearly 10,000 in a high poll. Baldwin, like Lloyd George before him (and both were advised by Thomas Jones), preferred Churchill on the inside looking out rather than sniping from the flank, but there was considerable surprise when, Neville Chamberlain having somewhat unexpectedly chosen to go to the Ministry of Health, the prime minister invited Churchill (8 November 1924) to become chancellor. 'Of the Duchy?' Churchill asked. 'No, the Exchequer', replied Baldwin. Tears came to Churchill's eyes (G. M. Young, *Stanley Baldwin*, 1952, p. 88): 'You have done more for me than Lloyd George ever did' (Thomas Jones, *Whitehall Diary*, ed. Keith Middlemas, vol. i, 1969, p. 303). Lord Randolph's robe, kept for thirty years in tissue paper and camphor by his widow, who had died not long before, lay ready. Birkenhead (with whom Churchill and Beaverbrook dined that night) and (Sir) Austen Chamberlain, the other coalitionists, were also included in Baldwin's encompassing administration in which Churchill himself, in Asquith's phrase, towered like 'a Chimborazo or Everest amongst the sandhills' (H. H. Asquith, *Letters to a Friend*, 1934, p. 123).

Eventually it became fashionable in retrospect to deplore what J. M. (later Lord) Keynes called at the time *The Economic Consequences of Mr. Churchill* (1925) and Churchill's decision in his first, superbly introduced, budget to return to the gold standard: a cautious and reluctant decision, made after taking considerable advice, to return to such orthodoxy as could be had. All his five bravura budgets, each brilliantly stage-managed, were ingenious rather than fundamental in their thinking and could do little to alter the country's changed position in the post-war international economy. With Neville Chamberlain's assistance, he was able to resume both his own pre-war preoccupation with pensions and an even earlier reluctance to concede increases in defence expenditure: an issue which led to brushes with Beatty, by now first sea lord, and William C. (later Viscount) Bridgeman, the first lord of the Admiralty and perhaps Baldwin's closest ally. It also led to the consequent extension of the 'ten years rule' —that war was unlikely for ten years—from a more recent starting-point than 1919 when it had first made its appearance. Income tax was reduced to 4*s*. in the £ by the substitution of indirect taxation, such as the revival of the McKenna duties or duties on silk, real and artificial.

Churchill always went all out for victory; and, having achieved it, showed magnanimity towards the defeated. So it was over the Great War, over the Irish Treaty, and in the general strike of 1926. But if Churchill did not in this particular case want a fight to the finish, his handling of the

British Gazette, which became under his strenuous editorship an anti-strikers broadsheet, served to inflame rather than to inform, since Churchill characteristically refused 'to be impartial between the fire brigade and the fire'. He strove hard, after the strike folded, to find a settlement in the coal industry but, in the main, despite his constructive interventions, when the miners had to return to work, it was on the owners' terms. Churchill chose to close the resultant deficit, £32 million of which was attributable to strikes, by a series of juggling expedients until he 'reached the end of (his) . . . adventitious resources'. In the following year, again in not always easy collaboration with Neville Chamberlain, he introduced his de-rating scheme for industry, which was coupled with Chamberlain's Local Government Act (1929), transferring the powers of the old Poor Law Unions and Boards of Guardians to the counties and boroughs; and he felt able to abolish the tax on tea. Abroad, bad 'dun' as he was—this was what (Sir) P. J. Grigg, then his private secretary, called him (*Prejudice and Judgment*, 1948, p. 208)—he could claim that British war debt repayments to the United States were just about balanced by the receipts from German reparations and other foreign debtors to this country.

In September 1922 he had bought Chartwell manor, an estate of 300 acres near Westerham in Kent and proceeded to rebuild it with the assistance of Philip Tilden, the architect who had redesigned Churt for Lloyd George. Although he continued to play polo—his last game was in Malta in 1927, when he was fifty-two—and his painting was assiduously practised, much of his time when he was not staying with friends was devoted to the development, surrounded by his family, of Chartwell, to which his wife, although she made it delightful, was less devoted than he was, and to working on and dictating his books. In 1928 he told a less assiduous Baldwin that he had spent the whole of August 'building a cottage & dictating a book: 200 bricks and 2,000 words per day' (Pelling, op. cit., p. 335). He lived very well but he worked very hard to live very well. His stamina, his assiduity, his fertility of mind, and his sense of enjoyment were prodigious, his conversation a unique delight.

Totally at odds with Baldwin's mildly liberal policy towards India, Churchill resigned his membership of the Conservative shadow Cabinet (January 1931) and, with minimal support, fought the Government's India Bill clause by clause, to the bitter end. He had never seemed so isolated and he found solace in preparing a huge four-volume (1933–8) life of his ancestor, the first Duke of Marlborough (Maurice Ashley, *Churchill as Historian*, 1968). In the thirties he also published *My Early Life* (1930), his most delightful book, followed by *Thoughts and Adventures* (1932), and the almost unexpectedly perceptive *Great Contemporaries* (1937). His political isolation made it all the harder to recover an attentive audience for a growing series of warnings about the threat of a revived and rearming Germany, about which he made sure that he was remarkably well informed. An extraneous occurrence in December 1936 cast him further into the wilderness when the abdication of King Edward VIII restored Baldwin's popularity, whereas the romantically loyal Churchill for the first time in his life was shouted down in the House of Commons. He had gathered round him a small 'Focus' group which challenged the Government's foreign policy but Neville Chamberlain, who had become prime minister, was determinedly pursuing his own course, deliberately impervious to Churchill's eloquent prophecies.

When the brief popularity of the Munich agreement abated, Churchill's consistency gathered more appreciation outside the Cabinet but it was not until the German invasion of Poland (1 September 1939) that he was reluctantly invited to take office once again. He returned to his room in the Admiralty. 'Winston is back', the Fleet was informed (Arthur Marder, *Winston is back: Churchill at the Admiralty 1939–40*, 1972). There were a few exciting successes: the *Graf Spee* sank itself in the River Plate to avoid capture; and a British ship rescued our prisoners from the *Altmark* in a Norwegian fjord; but in April 1940 an ill-prepared incursion into Norway, from which British forces were forced to withdraw, led to a debate in the House which revealed the strength of the opposition to Chamberlain. It was ironical that Churchill, who was the responsible minister, should emerge victorious. Two days after the debate Hitler's armour invaded France and the Netherlands and the Labour Party demanded a coalition, refusing to serve under Chamberlain, who resigned (10 May 1940). Churchill became prime minister. 'At last I had authority to give directions over the whole scene. I felt as if I were walking with destiny . . .' (*The Second World War*, vol. i, 1948, pp. 526–7).

Churchill's first task was to formulate an administration. He was determined from the outset so to construct it as, by integration under the prime minister, to avoid and render impossible the sort of clash between 'frocks' and 'brass hats' which had bedevilled Lloyd George. 'Winston's concrete contribution to the war effort,' Lord Attlee was to recall in the *Observer* (in 1965), '. . . the setting up of the intragovernmental machine that dealt with the war, was most important. Winston, on becoming prime minister, also became minister of defence. Within the Cabinet he formed a Defence Committee, which, of course, he dominated in his twin capacity as prime minister and minister of defence. The committee had a nucleus of permanent members: myself as deputy chairman, the service ministers, and the three chiefs of staff. Other ministers attended as required. . . . Given Winston's knowledge of military men, his own military experience and flair, his personal dynamism, and the sweeping powers that any prime minister in wartime can have if he chooses to use them, the deadly problem of civilians-versus-generals in wartime was solved. Everybody involved should get some credit for this. But Winston's role has only to be described for its over-riding importance to be clear' (reprinted in *Churchill: a Profile*, ed. Peter Stansky, 1973, pp. 189–90).

'When we heard he was to be Prime Minister,' Sir Ian Jacob explained, '. . . I well remember the misgivings . . . in the War Cabinet Office. We had not the experience or the imagination to realise the difference between a human dynamo when humming on the periphery and when driving at the centre . . . the lack of administrative understanding displayed by Mr Churchill would hardly have been counterbalanced by the other qualities he possessed, if he had not been quickly harnessed to a most effective machine. . . . It was in achieving this that General Ismay made . . . his greatest contribution. . . . He had to jostle the friends and adherents of Churchill who were at first like bees round a honey pot. He had to ensure that the Prime Minister received from the military machine rapid and effective service . . . and . . . in spite of occasional disagreements and temporary estrangements, the Prime Minister and the Chiefs of Staff came increasingly together as parts of a well-designed team. . . . As the Prime Minister's Chief Staff Officer, and as an additional member of the Chiefs of Staff Committee, Ismay took the knocks from above and below . . . to ensure that misunderstandings were smoothed out, and that the often exasperating vagaries of the Prime Minister and the sometimes mulish obstinacy of the Chiefs of Staff did not break up the association' (*Action This Day: Working with Churchill*, ed. Sir John Wheeler-Bennett, 1968, pp. 162 and 164–5).

Churchill gave himself to the task completely. To avoid misunderstandings, everything had to be submitted on paper. He began his long day with a secretary on one side of his bed providing him with the papers and a shorthand writer on the other side taking down the answers or any other observation which might occur to him. Copies of minutes on civil topics went to the secretary of the War Cabinet, Sir Edward (later Lord) Bridges, to be followed up by him and the civil side of the War Cabinet Office. Those on military topics were fielded by Sir Ian Jacob and duly processed.

If Churchill retained as a potential point of friction the private evaluation with which 'the Prof' (F. A. Lindemann, later Viscount Cherwell) and his statistical office supplied him, he shared with the chiefs of staff an incredible flow of information from Bletchley of the enemy's decrypted wireless traffic. Rarely has a wartime organization become so rapidly coherent and never so well informed. This did not mean, however, that, in galvanizing the swiftly adjusted central machinery into a new intensity of activity which was palpable throughout Whitehall, Churchill's own dominant part in it all was impeccably clear-headed and far-sighted, with long- and short-term objectives unwaveringly tuned into strategic coherence. His brain was too active, his interests too all-embracing, his urge to leave unplucked no benefit, covenanted or uncovenanted, too strong, his energy too unremitting, for this to be straightforwardly accomplished. 'Winston was always in a hurry', said Attlee. 'He didn't like to wait for the pot to boil, you know' (Marder, *From the Dreadnought to Scapa Flow,* vol. ii, p. 261). He could and did waste the time of busy experts by harebrained interventions, impatient short cuts, and chimerical projects so that the central machinery operated betimes in a series of judders. Yet within it might be detected—at least in retrospect—a corrective mechanism, Ismay on the military and Bridges on the civilian side as governors, which managed to prevent disaster without subduing the incredible impetus which Churchill's genius elicited.

'What Winston did, in my view, was to keep us all on our toes', wrote Attlee. 'He did very little work in the Cabinet. Churchill's Cabinets, frankly, were not good for business, but they were great fun. He kept us on our toes partly by just being Winston, and partly because he was always throwing out ideas. Some of them were not very good, and some of them were downright dangerous. But they kept coming, and they kept one going, and a lot of them were excellent . . . the best were those that came out of his gift of immediate compassion for people who were suffering. . . . If Winston's greatest virtue was his compassion, his greatest weakness was his impatience. He never understood that a certain time was always bound to elapse between when you ask for something to be done and when it can be effected. He worked people terribly hard, and was inconsiderate. On the whole, he did not vent his impatience on people in bursts of temper or in bullying. But . . . he kept people working impossible hours' (Stansky, op. cit., pp. 191–3). Such was the force of his personality, his charm as well as his purposefulness that none of the 'secret circle' whom he took into his family resented this: there was a war on and this was their dutiful and bewitched contribution.

'He lived well and ate everything', wrote Beaverbrook. 'He exaggerated his drinking habits by his own remarks in praise of wine and brandy' (*Men and Power,* 1956, p. xiv). He could never remember the time when he 'could not order a bottle of champagne for myself and offer another to a friend' (Lady Violet Bonham Carter, op. cit., p. 135). He invariably drank champagne at lunch and dinner followed by brandy. After his afternoon sleep and during the long evening he would sip weak whisky and water. 'None of this affected him in the least and he was as alert and active-minded at 8 a.m. as at midnight or midday. As for his cigars he didn't really smoke them. He never inhaled and simply lit and re-lit until the cigar was half done when he threw it away' (Sir Ian Jacob in *The Listener*, 25 October 1979). 'His use of matches', Beaverbrook noted, 'outstripped his consumption of cigars.' His working day suited himself; a routine which he also maintained throughout his travels. It fell into two: from when he awoke, when a secretary brought him the papers, until he withdrew after luncheon for his afternoon sleep; and from when that sleep ended until the early hours of the following morning. Many night meetings, beginning at 10 or 10.30 p.m., continued until after midnight, after which Churchill conversed with his cronies whilst the Secretariat worked through the night to have ready the minutes for the breakfast tables of all who should receive them.

Having urgently forced the central machinery to his will, he then had to inspire the British people with his own uncomplicated belief in ultimate victory and the recognition that life would be extremely unpleasant before it came. He would offer them nothing but 'blood, toil, tears, and sweat', and the impossibility of surrender. To inspire the French, too, was beyond him but even he was surprised to discover how bad their case was. Five abortive, even dangerous, visits, including an offer of 'union' of the two states, were accompanied by the eventual decision to send to France no more metropolitan fighter aircraft. His aim, if France dropped out of the struggle, was to guarantee that the minimum of gain should accrue to the enemy and the minimum of loss to the British. And he had shown the Americans that he would not desert an ally. At them his eye was cocked from the outset since, unflagging as was his belief in ultimate victory, he was far from certain how to achieve it, but he was quite clear in his own mind that it would not come about without American assistance 'until, in God's good time, the New World, with all its power and might, steps forth to the rescue' (speech in the Commons, 4 June 1940). His first success in the systematic wooing of the Americans away from neutrality was to begin a sustained correspondence with President Roosevelt from a 'Former Naval Person' with a shopping list (15 May 1940) of British needs from what he already envisaged as the arsenal of democracy (*Roosevelt and Churchill: their Secret Wartime Correspondence*, ed. F. L. Loewenheim *et al.*, 1975). American subventions began to be dispatched in June 1940. Political devices such as Lend-Lease kept the flow of munitions going across the Atlantic while America was still neutral, and it never ceased till the war itself ended.

On 3 July 1940 he informed the Russian ambassador cheerfully that his 'general strategy at present is to last out the next three months'. On the same day he personally supervised the plan to seize French warships in

British ports and immobilize those elsewhere, which entailed Admiral Sir James F. Somerville destroying three French battleships which refused an ultimatum at Oran in French North Africa. For the first time Churchill received a warm ovation from the Conservative benches in the House.

On 19 July 1940 Churchill chose Sir Alan Brooke (later Viscount Alanbrooke) to succeed Sir W. Edmund (later Lord) Ironside as C.-in-C. Home Forces, a significantly personal choice of the best man to deal with invasion. Convinced that invasion would not be attempted until the enemy had gained air supremacy over the British Isles, Churchill threw himself characteristically into measures which would defeat that enterprise, supporting to the hilt Lord Beaverbrook's frenetic acceleration of fighter aircraft production and giving urgent attention to such technical countermeasures for which, with Lindemann as interpreter, he could help to ensure priority. Persuaded by a young scientist that the Germans were bombing on a navigational beam, Churchill insisted that it should be 'bent' (R. V. Jones, *Most Secret War*, 1978). And with that unique capacity to combine fierce concentration on the immediate with awareness of the more distant problem, he sent Sir Henry Tizard to Washington armed with the unrestricted gift of every technical secret the British possessed, whilst at the same time he was inaugurating what were to become the airborne divisions and the commandos of the future. He had asked the President in May to send obsolete destroyers to supplement the Royal Navy and eventually achieved an arrangement by which they were exchanged for long leases for American bases in British islands in the West Indies, in Bermuda, and in Newfoundland. The affairs of the British Empire and the United States, he reported contentedly to the Commons, 20 August 1940, 'will have to be somewhat mixed up together'.

Of the Battle of Britain itself, he was, like the rest of his fellow countrymen, an amazed spectator but, unlike them, entirely articulate and able on their behalf to voice their relief with a singularly heartening felicity. 'Never', he recorded, 'has so much been owed by so many to so few.'

By 15 September 1940 he had realized that the threat of the invasion of Britain would ease (indeed, Hitler postponed Operation Sea Lion on 17 September) and Churchill's reaction was typical—to hasten a supply of tanks, which were therefore to his mind no longer needed at home, straight through the Mediterranean to Egypt instead of by safer route via the Cape; also to strengthen the Mediterranean Fleet under Admiral Sir A. B. Cunningham (later Viscount Cunningham of Hyndhope).

General Sir Archibald (later Earl) Wavell, whose vigour Churchill came to doubt, launched an offensive in the Western Desert which culminated in February 1941 in the annihilation of the Italian land forces there. But the German threat to Greece prevented successful exploitation towards Tripoli.

Meanwhile at home the blitz (from September 1940) had been withstood without undue loss of production or morale which Churchill's personal example, as he stumped about amidst the debris, did much to sustain. He had become a legend in his lifetime. Babies were all said to resemble him. Many of the population in the temporarily classless society could produce their own parody of his accents and what he might have said. Moreover, the blitz convinced the Americans that Britain could 'take it', and was worth support. By December 1940 Roosevelt was willing to help to put his neighbour's fire out without haggling over the price of the hose.

Chamberlain's death (9 November 1940), which Churchill himself deeply regretted, for their relations had shown both men at their best (David Dilks, 'The Twilight War and the Fall of France', *Transactions of the Royal Historical Society*, 5th series, vol. xxviii, 1978), nevertheless eased the political situation. Churchill was elected to succeed him as leader of the Conservative Party and his parliamentary majority was now assured. In September Sir John Anderson (later Viscount Waverley) had already succeeded Chamberlain as lord president.

The sudden death of Lord Lothian, the British ambassador in Washington, 12 December 1940, led to other ministerial changes. Lord Halifax was persuaded to succeed him and (Sir) Anthony Eden (later Earl of Avon) replaced Halifax as foreign secretary. Captain David (later Viscount) Margesson, the Conservative whip, succeeded Eden at the War Office.

In January 1941 Harry Hopkins, President Roosevelt's trusted confidant, arrived at Claridge's and Churchill's conquest of him ratified the link with Roosevelt (Robert Sherwood, *The White House Papers of Harry L. Hopkins*, 2 vols., 1948 and 1949).

Eden, accompanied by the CIGS (Sir John Dill), set off for Cairo, Athens, and Ankara to attempt some sort of barrier to German expansion in the Balkans but Yugoslavia swiftly capitulated and the Allied forces sent to Greece had rapidly to withdraw, some to Crete, which was quickly lost, the rest to Egypt.

The decision to support Greece with troops will always remain controversial. No aid had gone to Poland; efforts to buttress France had proved of no avail. Was Greece to be denied succour? Churchill was at pains to allow those on the spot to make the decision which he hoped they would make. It was needful to show Roosevelt that the British meant business. The President's response to what he told Churchill was a 'wholly justified delaying action' in Greece was to dispatch across the Atlantic seventy-four ships bearing further munitions for Egypt.

In May 1941 Churchill easily survived a vote of confidence in the House but, as became his technique, he subsequently conceded some ministerial changes and on 29 June Beaverbrook became minister of supply, responsible for the production of tanks as previously of aircraft.

Fearful that the Germans would leap-frog into Iraq, Churchill asked the Indian Government to send troops to Basra. Sir Claude Auchinleck's rapid response as C.-in-C. India impressed Churchill in sharp contrast to Wavell's lack of immediacy. In early June Wavell had to be prodded into the invasion of Syria, where the regime was still loyal to the Vichy Government. The failure of Operation Battleaxe in the Western Desert, upon which Churchill set much store and which began on 15 June 1941, led to Auchinleck and Wavell being made to change places. When Auchinleck became C.-in-C. Middle East, at the suggestion of Randolph Churchill, who was serving in GHQ Middle East, he was joined in Cairo as minister of state by Captain Oliver Lyttelton (later Viscount Chandos), who had been until then president of the Board of Trade.

Churchill had become convinced that Russia was Hitler's next target and he personally warned Stalin of his suspicion without response. When Russia was invaded (22 June 1941) his reaction was immediate. In a strategic instant, his anti-Bolshevik past went overboard. 'If Hitler invaded Hell,' he had told his secretary the day before, 'I would at least make a favourable reference to the Devil in the House of Commons.' In July an Anglo-Soviet agreement was signed that neither country would make a separate peace with Germany; and two squadrons of Hurricanes were sent to Murmansk to protect the northern shipping route. A supply route via Iran was also opened and in September 1941 an Anglo-American Supply Conference in London allocated to Russia what had previously been destined for Britain.

Throughout this whole period the Battle of the Atlantic was a constant anxiety. American willingness to help was useless unless the help could be delivered successfully. None knew better than Churchill that Britain could not survive if she lost command of the sea. In February 1941, through his intervention, the Western Approaches Command was moved from Plymouth to Liverpool and on 18 March a Battle of the Atlantic Committee was set up with Churchill in the chair. The Canadian and American governments extended the range of their naval activities and the sinkings by U-boats and Focke-Wulfs were brought under control. In May Churchill, remembering Frederick Leathers from when he himself had held a peacetime directorship in the P & O Company in 1930, combined the Ministries of Shipping and Transport, put Leathers in charge of a new Ministry of War Transport and, to avoid his being badgered in the House of Commons, sent him to the Lords as Lord Leathers (8 May). There was grave worry too in May when the *Bismarck*, the new German battleship, moved into the North Atlantic and sank the cruiser *Hood*. On 27 May the *Bismarck*, after an anxious hunt, was sunk in its turn.

Auchinleck was summoned home to explain why he could not resume the attack in the desert before 1 November and 'Pug' Ismay took 'the Auk' aside at Chequers to brief his old Indian Army friend about the prime minister. 'Here is the gist of what I said. Churchill could not be judged by ordinary standards; he was different from anyone we had ever met before, or were ever likely to meet again. As a war leader, he was head and shoulders above anyone that the British or any other nation could produce. He was indispensable and completely irreplaceable. The idea that he was rude, arrogant and self-seeking was entirely wrong. He was none of these things. He was certainly frank in speech and writing, but he expected others to be equally frank with him. . . . He was a child of nature. He venerated tradition, but ridiculed convention. When the occasion demanded, he could be the personification of dignity; when the spirit moved him, he could be a *gamin*. His courage, enthusiasm and industry were boundless, and his loyalty was absolute. No commander who engaged the enemy need ever fear that he would not be supported. His knowledge of military history was encyclopaedic, and his grasp of the broad sweep of strategy unrivalled. At the same time, he did not fully realise the extent to which mechanisation had complicated administrative arrangements and revolutionised the problems of time and space; and he never ceased to cry out against the inordinate "tail" which modern armies required . . . [and] refused to subscribe to the idea that generals were infallible or had any monopoly of the military art. He was not a gambler, but never shrank from taking a calculated risk if the situation so demanded. His whole heart and soul were in the battle, and he was an apostle of the offensive. . . . He made a practice of bombarding commanders with telegrams on every kind of topic, many of which might seem irrelevant and superfluous. I begged Auchinleck not to allow himself to be irritated by these never-ending messages, but to remember that Churchill, as Prime Minister and Minister of Defence, bore the primary responsibility for ensuring that all available resources in shipping, man-power, equipment, oil, and the rest were apportioned between the Home Front and the various theatres of war, in the best interests of the war effort as a whole. Was it not reasonable that he should wish to know exactly how all these resources were being used before deciding on the allotment to be given to this or that theatre? He was not prone to harbouring grievances, and it was a mistake to take lasting umbrage if his criticisms were sometimes unduly harsh or even unjust. . . . The way of life of the politician was very different from that of the soldier' (*The Memoirs of Lord Ismay*, 1960, pp. 269–71).

In August 1941 Churchill and Roosevelt had their long-postponed meeting at Argentia in Placentia Bay off the Newfoundland coast. Churchill arrived in the *Prince of Wales*, the newest battleship, just refitted after the successful sinking of the *Bismarck*. The upshot was the Atlantic Charter, but more important than this statement of principles was the assumption by the American navy of the task of convoying fast merchant ships as far east as Iceland, which Churchill visited on his way back to England.

Whereas it was the cardinal doctrine of the chiefs of staff that the defence of Singapore was more important than that of the Suez Canal, Churchill in his heart of hearts never adhered to this priority. He knew that he could not hope to be strong everywhere. In the Anglo-American staff talks of February and March 1941 the British had hoped that the Americans would commit themselves to the defence of Singapore, but they refused. Advice from the CIGS to reinforce the Far East found Churchill dragging his feet. He believed, mistakenly, that Singapore was capable of all-round defence. 'I ought to have known. My advisers ought to have known, and I ought to have been told and I ought to have asked' (*The Second World War*, vol. iv, p. 43). He sent out Alfred Duff Cooper (later Viscount Norwich) to report and he arranged that the *Prince of Wales* and the *Repulse* should be sent to the Far East, under the command of Sir Tom Phillips, whom he had known as vice-chief of the naval staff and who shared his exaggerated view of the efficacy of battleships. They were to have been accompanied by the aircraft-carrier *Indomitable* but it had run aground and no substitute was forthcoming. Unprotected they proved a purposeless and expensive sacrifice.

On Sunday 7 December Churchill heard on the wireless of the Japanese attack on the American battleships in Pearl Harbor and immediately recognized that this must result in American entry into the war. 'So we had won after all' was his reaction, and that night he slept 'the sleep of the saved and thankful' (*The Second World War*, vol. iii, pp. 539–40). He also realized that what he had been visualizing primarily as a European struggle was now world-wide. Hitler's declaration of war against the United States helped him to keep the Americans to their agreed plan to defeat Germany first despite Pearl Harbor. He set off for the United States with a party of about eighty in the *Duke of York*, working over three clear-headed strategic papers with the staff on the uncomfortable voyage. He argued for American intervention in French North Africa to free the Mediterranean for Allied shipping. He hoped, too, for American troops to relieve the British in Northern Ireland and that American aircraft would begin to bomb Germany from bases in the United Kingdom. The invasion of mainland Europe he did not envisage until 1943. Throughout he was determined that that invasion should not begin until its success was as certain as it could be.

On Boxing Day 1941 he successfully addressed both Houses of Congress noting that had his father been American and his mother British 'instead of the other way round, I might have got here on my own'. On his return to the White House he had what his accompanying physician, Sir Charles Wilson (later Lord Moran), realized had been a slight heart attack.

He accepted Roosevelt's proposal for a united Allied command in the south-west Pacific under Wavell, agreed to the establishment as a consequence of a Combined Chiefs of Staff Committee in Washington (perhaps the most important piece of administrative machinery devised in the war), and left Sir John Dill, who had just been succeeded as CIGS by Brooke, as the senior British representative there.

Before he left Washington he and Roosevelt signed the declaration which led to the creation of the United Nations Organization.

On his return to Britain he found opinion very uneasy not only about the losses of the *Prince of Wales* and the *Repulse* to Japanese aircraft but also because of German success in Cyrenaica. A three-day debate on a vote of confidence at the end of January 1942 resulted in a vote of 464 to 1 in his favour but the news continued to worsen: the Germans recaptured Benghazi and the Japanese took Singapore: 'the worst disaster and largest capitulation in British history'; the German cruisers *Scharnhorst, Gneisenau*, and *Prinz Eugen* passed apparently unscathed through the English Channel from Brest.

Again he decided to reconstruct his ministry. Sir R. Stafford Cripps had returned from his embassy in Moscow and, as the symbol of strong pro-Russian sentiment, was an obvious candidate for office. After some jostling, he became lord privy seal and leader of the House. Attlee was restyled deputy prime minister and also took over the Dominions Office. Beaverbrook set off for the United States and was succeeded by Oliver Lyttelton as minister of production. A surprised Sir James Grigg replaced Margesson as secretary of state for war and was found a seat in the Commons.

In April 1942 Churchill proposed a visit to Roosevelt because he felt that the President was exhibiting too lively an interest in the future of India and that Colonel Louis Johnson, the President's representative in New Delhi ostensibly dealing with war *matériel*, was dipping too intrusive a finger in the Indian political pie. The War Cabinet, which included several members with considerable Indian experience, was not at one in the matter and it was eventually agreed to send Sir Stafford Cripps, a friend of both Nehru and Gandhi, to discuss Dominion status after the war. Churchill seemed determined to stymie whatever Cripps came up with and the mission petered out largely because Churchill preferred it that way; moreover, through American success in the Pacific war, the threat to India receded.

In May 1942 Molotov, the Russian foreign minister, began to press for a 'Second Front' in Europe together with recognition of the Russian frontiers of 1941. Churchill could not agree without repudiating the British guarantee to Poland. He was himself still toying with an assault on Norway (Operation Jupiter) to 'roll the map of Hitler's Europe down from the top'. The chiefs of staff successfully frustrated this proposal and when he went to the United States in mid-June with Brooke and Ismay his plan was to revert to a joint Anglo-American assault on French North Africa. During the visit to the President's family home at Hyde Park, New York State, he agreed with Roosevelt in the strictest privacy on the manufacture of the atomic bomb in the United States instead of in Britain. On 21 June in the White House he received the news that Tobruk (which he had made symbolic of British resistance in North Africa) had capitulated with the loss of 25,000 men taken prisoner. It was a singular tribute to their relationship that Roosevelt immediately proffered help. The Americans sent 300 Sherman tanks together with 100 self-propelled guns: a gift which was to turn the tide in North Africa.

Churchill returned home to learn that a by-election at Maldon had gone against the Government and to face a motion in the House expressing dissatisfaction with the central direction of the war. His critics, headed by a long forgotten figure, Sir John Wardlaw-Milne, produced contradictory remedies and Churchill rode off the last parliamentary criticism of his wartime coalition by 475 votes to 25.

Roosevelt sent Harry Hopkins, General Marshall, and Admiral King to London to discuss future strategy. The British chiefs of staff strongly opposed invasion of Europe in 1942 and Roosevelt agreed 25 July upon an American assault on French North Africa. Churchill then set off with Brooke for Cairo to consider the Middle East Command with Smuts's help. General Sir Harold Alexander (later Earl Alexander of Tunis), Churchill's favourite field commander, was appointed to succeed Auchinleck, Brooke recognizing that he himself should remain as CIGS and, after Churchill's choice to command the Eighth Army—Lt.-Gen. W. H. E. Gott—almost at once was killed, Lt.-Gen. B. L. Montgomery (later Viscount Montgomery of Alamein), Brooke's choice, was summoned from England to take command at El Alamein.

Churchill then flew to Moscow to tell Stalin to his face (12 August 1942) that there could be no Second Front in 1942. He went on to explain, as Averell Harriman told the President, the advantages of attacking the 'underbelly' of a crocodile which he drew for Stalin, in telling him of the proposed Anglo-American assault (Operation Torch) on French North

Africa. The difficult visit seemed to end amicably enough. Churchill promised a Second Front in Europe in 1943. Stalin 'now knew the worst and yet we parted in an atmosphere of goodwill' (Churchill, *The Second World War*, vol. iv, p. 430).

Back in England he instituted a weekly luncheon in 10 Downing Street with the American General Dwight D. Eisenhower, the commander designate for North Africa. Eighth Army attacked on 23 October at El Alamein with the aim of capturing the Martuba airfields in time for air cover to be furnished for the last convoy to reprovision Malta. Churchill now felt confident enough to allow church bells, silent since 1940, to be rung again (15 November 1942). A few days before, he had gone out of his way at the Mansion House to emphasize that he had 'not become the King's First Minister in order to preside over the liquidation of the British Empire'.

With the conquest of North Africa on the strategic horizon it was time to meet with Roosevelt again. Stalin was unable to join them and the President and premier met (January 1943) in a curious atmosphere of picnic on the Moroccan coast at Casablanca. Churchill had been persuaded, at least temporarily, by Brooke that the cross-Channel invasion which he had promised Stalin and which General Marshall continued to demand from the American side, was not feasible in 1943 and Marshall was eventually argued into a reluctant agreement to invade Sicily. The two political leaders attempted also to effect a political settlement of French North Africa by reconciling General de Gaulle with General Giraud and Roosevelt introduced in the final stages of the meeting the concept of 'unconditional surrender', in which Churchill, after consulting the War Cabinet, concurred.

At Casablanca command arrangements were changed and Alexander took over 18 Army Group, under Eisenhower's over-all command, to co-ordinate what were hoped to be the rapid final stages of the North African campaign which lasted, in fact, until mid-May.

By mid-April Churchill had realized that, because of the Pacific war, shortage of shipping and landing-craft would rule out a cross-Channel invasion in 1943. Already he had had to tell Stalin of delays in polishing off North Africa and of the need to interrupt the Arctic convoys in order to mount the invasion of Sicily. The disturbing discoveries at Katyn made for further friction with the Russians.

Churchill felt that he must see Roosevelt once more. Feeling confident that the next stage should be the collapse of Italy, he travelled with the chiefs of staff in the *Queen Mary*, which had become a troop carrier. The American chiefs of staff remained adamant about a cross-Channel attack and it was agreed that General Marshall and the prime minister should go together to Algiers to consult Eisenhower and Alexander about the question of invading Italy. Since Eisenhower would not commit himself until he knew the fate of the invasion of Sicily, which was not due till 10 July, Churchill, who had been joined by Eden, had to face the question of what to tell Stalin. He was dissuaded because of his recent illness—he had had pneumonia in February—from going in person; the news by telegram was ill received.

Churchill had hoped that landing-craft, which had 'all our strategy in the tightest ligature', would not have to be switched too early from the Mediterranean to be available for the cross-Channel invasion (Operation Overlord), so as to imperil the development of the Italian campaign on which he had set his heart. His very eloquence served to make the Americans suspicious of his arguments, some of which were better than others. He was genuinely anxious to bring such pressure on the Germans as might relieve their pressure on the Russians and was successful to the extent that Hitler called off his Kursk offensive on 13 July 1943 to reinforce Italy. The combined chiefs of staff came round to the decision for a direct amphibious landing at Salerno Bay.

In the middle of the excitement over the collapse of Italy Churchill and Roosevelt met in Quebec in mid-August 1943 and sharp disagreements ensued. Churchill's advocacy of the development of the Italian campaign was coupled incongruously with his raising the question of Norway once more, which served to arouse suspicion of his genuine support for a cross-Channel invasion.

The Americans were also anxious to clear the Burma road to sustain China and build up air bases for an assault on Japan. Churchill sought to propitiate them by agreeing to a forward move in Burma under the newly appointed Lord Louis Mountbatten (later Earl Mountbatten of Burma) as supreme commander of a new South-East Asia Command, Churchill's own choice.

After a few days' holiday, Churchill returned as the President's guest to the White House during which visit, in the course of receiving an honorary degree at Harvard, he proposed a common citzenship for Britain and the United States.

Events in Italy led to some diminution of the German pressure on the Eastern Front and, despite his insulting remarks about Arctic convoys, Stalin let it be known that he was willing to have a meeting in Tehran with Roosevelt and Churchill. The president and prime minister conferred beforehand in Cairo where, to Churchill's discomfort, they were joined by Chiang Kai-shek. Churchill failed to get American agreement to keep enough landing-craft in the Mediterranean to allow for not only the capture of Rome but also the seizure of Rhodes and the opening up of supply routes in Yugoslavia for the partisans under Tito. Roosevelt was opposed to an attack on Rhodes unless Turkey first entered the war—Churchill's persistent and unfulfilled hope. On their return to Cairo after meeting with Stalin in Tehran at the end of November, Roosevelt agreed to two supreme commanders being appointed, an American for Overlord, the European invasion (he chose Eisenhower in order to retain Marshall in Washington), and a British general for the Mediterranean, where the bulk of the forces would be British. Churchill chose General Sir Henry Maitland (later Lord) Wilson, who thus became responsible for an abortive Dodecanese expedition under Churchill's pressure.

On 12 December 1943 Churchill flew to Tunis as Eisenhower's guest before a proposed visit to the Italian front, but he fell gravely ill and his wife flew out to join him. His recovery at Marrakesh was aided by the news of the sinking of the *Scharnhorst* while attacking an Arctic convoy, and the American agreement to delay the return of the landing-craft from the Mediterranean in order to mount an amphibious assault on Anzio. Owing to American tardiness to exploit, the result was deeply disappointing to him, and instead of the 'wild cat' Churchill was hoping to hurl ashore, the result was 'a stranded whale'. The main forces, attempting to break out from the south, were held up by ferocious fighting at Monte Cassino. Churchill reassured the House of Commons: 'We must fight the Germans somewhere, unless we are to stand still and watch the Russians. This wearing battle in Italy occupies troops who could not be employed in other greater operations, and it is an effective prelude to them.' Not until mid-May 1944 was Alexander, deprived of troops who had returned to England to prepare for Overlord, able to renew his offensive. Rome was taken on 4 June.

On returning home from Marrakesh in January 1944, Churchill decided at last to give the invasion of Normandy priority in his attention even over the struggle with the U-boats. He instituted a weekly committee, over which he presided, to keep careful watch on how preparations were proceeding—in the production of artificial harbours ('Mulberry'), perhaps his own most personal contribution to the invasion, and the plans for both the airborne drop and the naval bombardment. By March he felt able to tell General Marshall in Washington that he was 'hardening very much on this operation'.

The role of the air forces in the proposed cross-Channel invasion was in dispute and it was Churchill who furnished the working formula in his proposal that they should be co-ordinated by Eisenhower's deputy as supreme allied commander, Sir Arthur (later Lord) Tedder, in consultation with the commanders of Bomber Command and the American Eighth Air Force. By now Churchill, who had allowed considerable independence to Sir Arthur Harris at Bomber Command when he could see no other way to assist Russia than by the bombing of Germany, was less willing to accept its effectiveness and Tedder was able to pursue an interdiction programme aimed to isolate the invasion area from early reinforcement. Churchill, however, had second thoughts when he contemplated the potential casualties which might be inflicted upon the French population. However, in the upshot, Roosevelt refused 'to impose from this distance any restriction on military action by the responsible commanders' and Churchill gave in.

On 15 May the King and the prime minister attended General Montgomery's presentation of his assault plans at St Paul's School in Hammersmith. It was agreed reluctantly between them that neither should have his wish and go to sea on D-day. Churchill had to content himself with having his special train, in which he was accompanied by Smuts and Ernest Bevin, near Eisenhower's headquarters outside Portsmouth, where de Gaulle raised last minute difficulties which led to Churchill's exasperated observation that if forced to choose between France and the United States he would always choose the latter.

Accompanied by Brooke and Smuts, Churchill paid his first visit to Normandy on 12 June, but, as the American effort in France began to bulk larger and the British contribution lessened, his influence (like Montgomery's) diminished notably and, when on 1 September Eisenhower assumed direct command of the land forces, it abated further. He was unable to persuade Eisenhower to reconsider the decision taken at Tehran to reinforce the invasion of France from the Mediterranean by landings on the Riviera, at the expense of the Italian campaign. Having failed in this, he tried at almost the last perverse moment to have the operation switched from the Riviera to Brittany instead. He had to content himself with witnessing, from the destroyer *Kimberley*, the invasion he had attempted to divert.

The dispute over Montgomery's criticism of how the campaign should develop left Churchill out on a limb since Eisenhower did not welcome his interference or his suggested recipe.

In Italy, where the command was predominantly British, Churchill was more welcome. He was also preoccupied with the situation in Greece, where he wished to avoid a Communist *coup* in Athens as the Germans began to withdraw. He agreed with Roosevelt in mid-August that a British force should be sent there. Russian behaviour over the Warsaw rising upset him deeply and he grew more sombre about the post-war world.

In September, accompanied by a large staff in the *Queen Mary*, he went to see Roosevelt again, and he was persuaded to agree to the Morgenthau plan to 'pastoralize' Germany after the war, a decision he quickly repented. He insisted that there should be a substantive British contribution to the Pacific war and Mountbatten was instructed to recapture Burma. It was, however, very evident that Admiral King, the American chief of naval staff, was reluctant to receive the assistance of the Royal Navy.

Meanwhile German resistance in the West was stiffening and the failure of the Arnhem operation presaged a harsh winter. Churchill decided to visit Stalin again to achieve some sort of agreement about Poland and Greece. Roosevelt could not go. Churchill reached a paper agreement with Stalin about spheres of influence taking no account of American views and not really tackling the Polish question. On his return he managed to secure Roosevelt's agreement to American recognition of de Gaulle's Government in France. The path was clear at last for Churchill to visit Paris, where he had a triumphant reception on 11 November 1944.

Greece was not so simple nor was it improved by a press leakage of Churchill's signal to Lt.-Gen. (Sir) R. M. Scobie, the commander of the British force sent to Athens: 'Do not however hesitate to act as if you were in a conquered city where a local rebellion is in progress.' He gained Roosevelt's agreement to the appointment of a regency pending elections and the return of the Greek king, and, with his customary disregard of danger, decided to go with Eden to Athens to settle the situation on the spot. About Damaskinos he inquired, 'This Archbishop, is he a cunning, scheming prelate more interested in temporal power than celestial glory?' and, on being told that he was, decided 'Then, he's our man'.

In replying to Smuts's message for his seventieth birthday (30 November 1944) Churchill admitted that 'it is not so easy as it used to be for me to get things done'. This was not only because he was influencing the Americans increasingly less and the Russians not at all, but also because he himself was tired and, through playing too many away matches, losing his grip over an increasingly irritated Cabinet. Attlee sent him a long letter, 19 January 1945, criticizing his 'method or rather lack of method of dealing with matters requiring Cabinet decisions' and of paying too much attention to the views of his cronies Bracken and Beaverbrook, neither of whom was in the War Cabinet.

The last meeting of the 'Big Three' took place in February in the Crimea. It was a sign of the times that, although Roosevelt agreed to staff talks in Malta *en route*, he did not wish for long discussions with Churchill himself lest they appeared to be 'ganging up' on Stalin. The atmosphere at Yalta was apparently cordial and agreement was reached on the establishment of the United Nations and the occupation of Germany, but the Polish question remained unsolved. Stalin was at this time still trusted by Churchill, who none the less felt that too many concessions were made to him because of American anxiety for Russian participation in the war against Japan.

After a visit to Balaclava (13 February 1945) Churchill flew to Athens, and thence to Egypt before leaving for home again.

He was determined to see for himself the closing stages of the campaign in the West and flew to Venlo (23 March) to watch the Rhine crossing with Montgomery and Eisenhower. He crossed the Rhine himself at Wesel. Eisenhower, who had already told Stalin direct, much to Churchill's annoyance, how he proposed to move into Germany, refused Churchill's advice to forestall the Russians by capturing Berlin first. Since Roosevelt supported Eisenhower, Churchill perforce dropped the matter (5 April).

On 12 April Roosevelt died suddenly and Churchill felt bereft. His first instinct was to go to Washington, but Eden, in any case due to go to the San Francisco conference later in the month, went instead. On 8 May Churchill declared the war in Europe finally at an end. On 12 May he wrote to President Harry S. Truman of his concern at the proposed early withdrawal of American forces from Europe and was reassured by the new President's swift and determined reaction to Yugoslav intransigence over Trieste.

He proposed formally to Attlee the continuation of the wartime coalition until Japan had been defeated. The Labour Party refused and Churchill formally resigned (23 May 1945) and was invited by the King to form what was to be a caretaker government until the election, which was settled for 5 July. On 28 May he took an unashamedly tearful farewell of his wartime senior ministers. It was assumed that the war against Japan might last another eighteen months.

With a contested election in prospect it would have been out of character if Churchill had not reverted to partisanship. His reference to Labour introducing some sort of Gestapo was counter-productive. Churchill and Attlee fought very different campaigns, Churchill inevitably on the grand scale, Attlee in an old car driven, none too well, by his wife. Churchill and Attlee met again at Potsdam, as had been agreed, and were told by the Americans of the successful experiment with an atomic bomb in New Mexico. There was no argument about using such a bomb against Japan. The three Englishmen, Churchill, Eden, and Attlee, returned to England on 25 July and next day it was clear that Churchill had been heavily defeated in the election. The Labour Party won a total of 393 seats whereas Churchill's supporters barely exceeded 200. Churchill at once visited the Palace to submit his resignation and advised the King to send for Attlee. He was offered the garter but felt, as did Eden, who was also offered it, that the moment was inappropriate.

'God knows where we should be without him', Brooke told himself (4 December 1941), 'but God knows where we shall go with him' (Arthur Bryant, *The Turn of the Tide*, 1957). Brooke was not alone in both the realization and the conjecture. It had rested with the chiefs of staff, with Brooke himself, as their eventual chairman, and with Ismay, to frustrate and divert the minister of defence when he was for striking out everywhere and anywhere and to be prepared to argue with him till far into the night without forfeiting the urgency which Churchill brought to every matter, good, bad, or indifferent.

The availability from Bletchley of information about the enemy compounded his impatience and made life intolerable for Wavell, then Auchinleck in the Middle East, wore out Pound, then Dill in Whitehall. There was scarcely an admiral but had been threatened with dismissal in his time (Stephen Roskill, *Churchill and the Admirals*, 1977). Unable to perceive how best he might help Russia, save by expensive and most hazardous convoys of munitions, Churchill was perforce committed, though with reluctant and increasingly disillusioned wrestling about its effectiveness, to strategic bombing until it was possible to hazard a Continental invasion.

Home affairs he had in the main to leave to others though not without bombarding them with queries and injunctions, 'Action this Day', which reflected an underlying recognition of the importance of domestic morale, particularly over rationing, and of achieving a proper balance between civilian and military needs, especially in the allocation of shipping. There were as a result only two backbench revolts, by the Tories against Ernest Bevin's catering wages Act in February 1943 and shortly afterwards by Labour supporters against the Government's apparently tepid attitude to the Beveridge Report. In March 1944 the Government lost a Labour amendment (which concerned the pay of women teachers) on its Education Bill (Paul Addison in *British Prime Ministers*, ed. J. P. Mackintosh, vol. ii, 1978, p. 25). Churchill compelled the House to reverse itself but on the whole he relied on Anderson and Attlee to cope with the Home Front for him and sensed that the size of Ernest Bevin warranted the minimum of his intrusion where manpower was concerned. Bevin for his part backed him to the hilt (Alan Bullock, *Bevin*, vol. ii, 1967, p. 108). Moreover, the prime minister came increasingly to spend less time in England.

As the war developed, he moved from his initial task of keeping Britain at war to trying to direct a war in which his country was to play a diminishing part. Up to September 1944 his was the most powerful voice. The last (the sixth) volume of his war memoirs exhibits his saddened recognition that his influence in Allied counsels had gone over the crest and that his voice was no longer as effective. He had come to confide in Smuts instead of Roosevelt, who was no longer listening. For five years the architect of the 'Grand Alliance' had done most to hold it together. The huge and welcome responsibility of war leadership did not abate the fertility of his monologue, the range of his interests and vocabulary, or his willingness to interfere in anything which crossed his path or stimulated his abundant fancy. Never readily persuaded, he became, thanks to his position at the top, less persuadable than ever before and the vastness of the work-load he set himself meant that he was ever liable to emphasize matters less important to busy chiefs of staff than they seemed to him. The chiefs of staff who with Ismay survived the war were men of considerable physical resilience and extraordinary technical competence in their own professions; Cunningham, who had succeeded Pound as first sea lord, in October 1943, was impervious to Churchill's spell. Brooke, Portal, and Cunningham had to be prepared to return to arguments on issues which the three of them had hoped were regarded as settled when the whim of their political master swung his searchlight once again in that direction. It was claimed at the war's end that on no matter of real import did Churchill eventually overrule them: some decisions were in any case overtaken by events. He could be petulant and unfair to individuals, and he could side-track decisions he was reluctant to take, but in the big things—'matters of great moment', as he would call them—he and the chiefs of staff, after some wrestling, had usually achieved an eventual concurrence.

Churchill took some time to adjust himself to the leadership of the Opposition. Much of the parliamentary battle he left to others and he devoted much of his time to the production of his very personal *The Second World War*. The theme running through his public speeches was the need for European unity in a cold war. He set the tone at Fulton, Missouri (March 1946), and at Zurich (September 1946). Again and again he harked back to the notion of 'summit' talks between the Americans, the British, and the Russians, which the Americans, more conscious than he appeared to be of the change in British power, were reluctant to undertake.

He returned to office in 1951 with a majority of seventeen. He resumed his old post of minister of defence for a while but the load proved too much. Earl Alexander of Tunis was brought back from Canada, where he was happily governor-general, to take over the defence portfolio, but this scarcely proved an apt appointment. Ismay was brought back from retirement to become Commonwealth secretary and an experiment with three 'overlord' ministers—Lords Woolton, Leathers, and Cherwell—did not last long, since political responsibilities remained with the individual departments over which they were supervisory. Eden, of course, resumed as foreign secretary, and other wartime ministers came back to new offices: R. A. Butler (later Lord Butler of Saffron Walden) as chancellor of the Exchequer, Oliver Lyttelton as colonial secretary, and Harold Macmillan to deal with housing. Sir Walter Monckton (later Lord Monckton of Brenchley) was brought in to charm the trade unions into inactivity.

If Churchill was still vigorous in Cabinet he showed less willingness to interfere and less zeal in furthering business. Colleagues in the European movement came to feel that Churchill's hankering after a 'special' relationship with the United States caused him to drag his feet with regard to Europe. He himself realized that he was no longer the man he had been. He was increasingly deaf. 'In the midst of the war', he said, 'I could always see how to do it. Today's problems are elusive and intangible' (*Memoirs of Lord Chandos*, 1962, p. 343).

In April 1953 he accepted the garter, which he had refused at the end of the war, and was able to wear it at the coronation in June. He suffered a stroke on 23 June but forced himself to complete his four-volumed *A History of the English-Speaking Peoples* (1956–8), which he had begun before the war. In December he attended a meeting with President Eisenhower in Bermuda which postponed the sort of summit which he had been advocating for so long. A minor Cabinet reshuffle preceded his eightieth birthday and it became clear that he could not fight another election as prime minister. On 4 April 1955 he gave a dinner party for the Queen and the Duke of Edinburgh at 10 Downing Street and next day made his formal resignation at the Palace. He toyed with becoming Duke of London but was dissuaded by his son who had no wish to go to the Lords. Eden, who had waited so long, was summoned to succeed him. Churchill was returned for the Woodford division at yet another election (26 May 1955). When Eden's health gave way after Suez Churchill was amongst those whom the Queen consulted about his successor. He recommended Harold Macmillan, who like himself had fought in World War I. He visited the House of Commons for the last time on 27 July 1964 and celebrated his ninetieth birthday later in the year. On 24 January 1965 he died at his home at 28 Hyde Park Gate. After the lying-in-state at Westminster Hall the funeral service was at St Paul's Cathedral in the presence of the Queen. The final journey was by train to a station near Blenheim Palace. He was buried beside his parents in the nearby Bladon churchyard.

Chancellor of Bristol University from 1929, Churchill held honorary degrees from more than twenty universities, was an honorary freeman of more than fifty cities, and was an honorary fellow of many learned societies. He was lord warden of the Cinque Ports from 1941 and was admitted to the Order of Merit in 1946. In 1953 he won the Nobel prize for literature. He was decorated by General de Gaulle with the Cross of Liberation in 1958 and was proclaimed an honorary citizen of the United States 9 April 1963. An honour which he relished particularly was honorary Royal Academician Extraordinary (1948), and his speeches at the annual banquet were one of its features. But he was most at ease in Zion at the Harrow songs which he tried to attend every year. Churchill College, Cambridge, was founded in 1960 as a memorial, and in 1964 Churchill became its first honorary fellow. In 1965 the Winston Churchill Memorial Trust was established to provide for 100 travel scholarships a year.

'Half-American but all British', Winston Churchill may have changed parties, or his rig, or his head-gear, readily enough, but he scarcely changed his basic concepts. 'If anyone wishes to discover his views on the large and lasting issues of our time, he need only set himself to discover what Churchill has said or written on the subject at any period in his long and exceptionally articulate public life, in particular during the years before the First World War: [Churchill] . . . knows with an unshakeable certainty what he considers to be big, handsome, noble, and worthy of pursuit by someone in high station, and what, on the contrary, he abhors as being dim, grey, thin, likely to lower or destroy the play of colour and movement in the universe . . . Churchill is one of the diminishing number of those who genuinely believe in a specific world order' (Sir Isaiah Berlin, *Personal Impressions*, 1980, p. 7).

This most extraordinary human being, with a lifetime in politics, seemed to have an intuitive comprehension of what might irk the ordinary man whose way of life was so conspicuously different from his own. Beneath his torrential impatience there lay an almost unexpected core of compassion. From the magniloquence peeped an impish sense of humour. Abreast as he was of modern inventions and devices, nevertheless he was impelled by an old-fashioned patriotism nourished by a sense of history and an awareness that he himself was one and not the least distinguished of a line of historical figures.

'Churchill on top of the wave', Beaverbrook once wrote, 'has in him the stuff of which tyrants are made' (*Politicians and the War*, vol. ii, p. 82). But he had been brought up or had brought himself up to oppose tyranny wherever he might discern it: as the duty of an Englishman; tyranny was for foreigners. Overbearing in counsel, often intolerably difficult to persuade, nevertheless he elected to be surrounded by men of great ability who could stand up to him and speak frankly—'we are not here to exchange compliments'. 'All I wanted', he would maintain, 'was compliance with my wishes after reasonable discussion.' Incapable of sustained rancour and too open-hearted to stoop to intrigue, in the long run, at the end of the argument, he had succeeded for the main part of the war in enforcing his own grand strategy twice over: at the time; then, in six majestic volumes, how it should come to be remembered. The 'central sanity of his character', the constraints imposed by having to operate within an ill-assorted alliance, and the quality of those with whom he came to work as a war leader—all these stood in the path of tyranny. Above all, he was most happily married to someone who did not fear him in the least and could never have been a tyrant's wife.

Of the many portraits of Churchill, the National Portrait Gallery holds those by Walter Sickert (1927), Juliet Pannett (1964), and Bernard Hailstone (1965). Oscar Nemon sculpted Churchill frequently. Examples of his work are the 1946 bronze head, the 1955 study of Churchill seated (commissioned by the Guildhall), the bust in Churchill College, Cambridge, and the 1968 bust in the Conservative Central Office. Nemon also sculpted Churchill and his wife 'in informal mood' (1978, Blenheim Palace), and provided the House of Commons with the Churchill statue (1969). Many museums have a copy of the bronze head by (Sir) Jacob Epstein (1946). The portrait by (Sir) William Orpen (1916), a copy of which (by John Leigh Pemberton) is at Churchill College, is a good depiction of Churchill as a young Cabinet minister. A portrait by Graham Sutherland, a gift to Churchill on his eightieth birthday by both Houses of Parliament, is believed to have been destroyed.

[See F. B. Woods, *A Bibliography of the Works of Sir Winston Churchill* (1963, 2nd revised edn. 1975). The official life was begun by Churchill's son, Randolph, and then continued, more ably and most exhaustively, by Martin Gilbert (5 volumes, with companion volumes of documents 1966–76). Robert Rhodes James, *Churchill, a Study in Failure, 1900–1939* (1970), is useful as is his *Gallipoli* (1965). The most comprehensive biography in a single volume is Henry Pelling, *Winston Churchill* (1974), to which this notice is greatly indebted. Chester Wilmot's *The Struggle for Europe* (1952) appeared before Churchill's own final volumes v and vi came out. The admirable *Grand Strategy* volumes of the official war history are most helpful, especially Michael Howard's volume iv (1972). John Ehrman, author of volumes v and vi (1956) also compared 'Lloyd George and Churchill as War Ministers' in *Transactions of the Royal Historical Society*, 5th series, vol. ii, 1961. See also Ronald Lewin, *Churchill as Warlord* (1973) and his *Ultra Goes to War* (1978). There is a perceptive essay on the Statistical Office by Sir Donald MacDougall in *Policy and Politics*, edited by David Butler and A. H. Halsey (1978). Elisabeth Barker, *Churchill and Eden at War* (1978) is helpful. A distasteful book by Churchill's physician, Lord Moran—*Churchill, the Struggle for Survival, 1940–65* (1966)—provoked members of Churchill's personal staff to write an attractive collection of essays entitled *Action this Day: Working with Churchill*, edited by Sir John Wheeler-Bennett (1968). See also Sir George Mallaby, *From my Level* (1965); Sir David Hunt, *On the Spot* (1975); Sir John Colville (a contributor to *Action this Day*), *Footprints in Time* (1976). Other relevant publications are cited in the text above.]

E. T. WILLIAMS

published 1981

CLARK Kenneth Mackenzie

(1903–1983)

Baron Clark

Patron and interpreter of the arts, was born in London 13 July 1903, the only child of Kenneth Mackenzie Clark, and his wife, (Margaret) Alice, daughter of James McArthur, of Manchester and formerly of Paisley, a cousin of her husband's on his mother's side. The father was a wealthy Scottish industrialist, sportsman, gambler, and ultimately alcoholic. The wealth derived from the well-known family textile firm, Clark of Paisley, and was to provide his son with a buoyancy throughout his career that was an essential factor in the maintenance of his independence. The Clarks lived at Sudbourne Hall, Suffolk, and Ardnamurchan, Argyllshire.

Kenneth Clark was educated at Winchester and won a scholarship to Trinity College, Oxford, where he gained a second class in modern history in 1925. A first class had been expected, but his interests had already turned conclusively to the study of art. An inborn sensitivity of response (sometimes described in almost mystical terms) to works of art, together with an insatiable appetite for them, allied to an acute, fastidious, and articulate intelligence, had developed from childhood on. He was a workmanlike draughtsman himself, and read widely and voraciously.

His introduction to the severer disciplines of close scholarship and analytic connoisseurship were provided at Oxford by Charles F. Bell amongst the superb drawings and prints of the Ashmolean Museum. In autumn 1925 Bell introduced Clark to the renowned art historian, Bernhard Berenson, at the latter's house, I Tatti, on the hills above Florence. Berenson gave him lunch and afterwards forthwith asked Clark to come to assist him in the revision of his great corpus of Florentine drawings.

There followed two years of concentrated practice and refinement of judgement of works of art together with Berenson in the library at I Tatti and in the great collections of Italy. He was however also discovering, in the course of completing his first full-length book, *The Gothic Revival* (the rather unexpected subject suggested by Bell, published in 1928), the controlled exhilaration of prose composition, an art which (he was to observe later) was to yield him as much pleasure in life as anything he ever did.

In 1929 he was offered the enviable task of cataloguing the rich hoard of Leonardo da Vinci drawings at Windsor Castle, and he also acted as joint organizer of an exhibition, which later became legendary, of Italian painting at the Royal Academy, involving masterpieces never seen before (or since) out of Italy. In 1931 his career took a decisive turn when he accepted

Bell's former post, as keeper of the department of fine art at the Ashmolean, and became a full-time professional museum man. Less than three years later, in 1933, at the unprecedently early age of thirty-one, he was appointed director of the National Gallery in London (1934–45), and shortly afterwards became also surveyor of the King's Pictures (1934–44).

In 1927 he had married Elizabeth Winifred ('Jane'), daughter of Robert Macgregor Martin, a businessman, of Dublin, and his wife, Emily Dickson, a medical doctor. Between 1934 and 1939, lodged in an almost palatial house in Portland Place, with his wife as president of the Incorporated Society of London Fashion Designers and a leading hostess, the Clarks in joint alliance became stars of London high society, intelligentsia, and fashion, from Mayfair to Windsor. This was a period he later dubbed 'the Great Clark Boom'.

In the National Gallery he made a considerable contribution. Acquisitions during his directorship included such masterpieces as Rubens's 'Watering Place', Constable's 'Hadleigh Castle', Rembrandt's 'Saskia as Flora', Ingres's 'Mme Moitessier', and Poussin's 'Golden Calf'. He established a scientific department, and a carefully supervised programme of picture cleaning. In the art of administration however his touch failed with his senior staff, whom he alienated. Major crises occurred in 1937, culminating when, against the united advice of his professional staff, he persuaded the trustees to acquire four small minor Venetian School paintings and labelled them as Giorgiones. The virulent subsequent controversy became public scandal, and contributed to a lingering mistrust of his integrity, especially amongst some fellow art historians, that was perhaps never quite dispelled. On the other hand, he fought off the reappointment of Lord Duveen as trustee, believing that a dealer's interests were irreconcilable with those of a trustee and that, although Duveen's natural charm and indeed generosity were compelling, they were about matched by his natural duplicity.

In 1939, at the outbreak of war, Clark was responsible for the evacuation of virtually the entire collection from London, ultimately into a cavern in the slate quarries of north Wales. In the emptied Gallery, he organized with Dame J. Myra Hess the very popular and morale-raising lunchtime music recitals that continued despite the blitz, and then a scheme by which he brought back one masterpiece each month for display. He also found time to serve in the Ministry of Information, first as director of the film division and then as controller, home publicity. Perpetually frustrated however by Ministry bureaucracy, he resigned in 1941.

He was meanwhile establishing himself in the activity in which his greatest talents were to find their most congenial and successful employment. His catalogue of the Windsor Leonardo drawings (1935) still holds an honourable place in the Leonardo literature, but was to be his last exercise in what he came to term 'plodding scholarship'. His monograph, *Leonardo da Vinci . . . His Development as an Artist* (1939) established itself at once as the best general introduction in English, and was widely acclaimed. In 1946, following the successful return of the collections to the National Gallery, he resigned as director, to devote himself to his now paramount interest in writing. Between 1946 and 1950 he was Slade professor of fine art at Oxford, developing an already highly accomplished lecturing technique. For a more popular audience, he became known as a broadcaster in such programmes as 'The Brains Trust'. In the drab post-war years of austerity, a new public avid for the arts was emerging.

He had bought works of art for himself since his schooldays, but his very generous and imaginative activity as collector-patron was especially fruitful. Several artists, struggling in the 1930s and kept afloat by Clark, later became national and international figures, most notably Henry Moore, who like Graham Sutherland and John Piper were to become life-long friends. In 1939–40 Clark had been involved with the setting up of the Council for the Encouragement of Music and the Arts (CEMA). This, the first step towards state support for the living arts, subsequently became the Arts Council. As the Council's third chairman (1953–60), Clark underwent a frustrating experience. He felt little more than a figurehead, and his own commitment to the validity of state support of individual creative artists was ambivalent. His last appointment as a public administrator, as the first chairman of the Independent Television Authority (1954–7), was more rewarding. The concept of commercial television, in rivalry with the BBC, was controversial, and so too was Clark's appointment, though his claim that he was subsequently booed at the Athenaeum is disputed. The prime task was to ensure the quality, balance, and political impartiality achieved by the licensed programme contractors. Almost at once Clark had to fight off an attempt by the government to use the new channels for its advantage. Clark was not averse to an injection of 'vulgar vitality', but managed to preserve a news service under the direct control of the Authority rather than of the contractors. Though not reappointed in 1957, he had exercised a constructive and beneficent influence on the development of the British version of the most powerful instrument of mass communication yet known to mankind.

His finest books, mostly allied to lecture series, were now behind him: *Piero della Francesca* (1951); *The Nude* (1956, from the Mellon lectures in Washington, 1953); and *Rembrandt and the Italian Renaissance* (1966, from the Wrightsman lectures in New York). He was now to emerge as an outstanding writer and performer for television. In 1966 the programme series *Civilisation* was mooted with the BBC and finally broadcast in 1969. Its success in English-speaking countries, and beyond, was spectacular and unparalleled; he became as celebrated as a film star, known to a wider audience personally than even John Ruskin had been a century before. Ruskin had been the greatest single influence on his mind since his school-days, and he aspired to being Ruskin's heir in spreading the gospel of art, though with little of Ruskin's social, political, and moral involvement. The style too was very different; the prose in which the message was delivered was coolly lucid and elegantly lapidary but never rhapsodic. *Civilisation* was avowedly a very personal, selective interpretation and illustration of the title's grandiose theme. Though in it he ranged widely, with great erudition, in time and space, his conceptions generally were conditioned by Mediterranean values. The areas in the study of art—psychological and philosophical; sociological, iconographical, scientific—that challenged some of his most remarkable contemporaries, were generally not for him, though he acknowledged, for example, the fruitful influence of Felix ('Aby') Warburg. Though he recognized the achievement of Mondrian, and even of Jackson Pollock, he did not respond generally to abstract art, and his primary concern was to arouse response in individual human beings to individual works of art, essentially by accounting for his own response. If he was in a sense old-fashioned, with a sensibility prone (though not in his prose) to tears and visionary flashes, he made art accessible to a whole generation as no other English-speaking writer was able to do.

Despite his proven qualities as a lecturer, that he was able to succeed so well, in the demandingly personal medium of television appearances, was to many unexpected. He proved able to achieve that most difficult balance on screen between the presenter's own presence and the object that he is presenting, never obscuring the object by his own brilliance. Though (in the interests of 'style') there might be 'an occasional sacrifice of the whole truth in the interests of economy', he did not talk down. Yet in more private life, while often charming and entertaining, and imaginatively generous to younger students, for many he remained aloof and arrogant, and finally, even to some amongst his closest friends, elusive behind an impenetrable urbanity. Probably he was most relaxed in self-revelation only with a few gifted women: in the earlier days of his marriage, with his first wife (his loyalty to whom in the later distress of her prolonged decline from health due to alcoholism caused his friends such admiration and such embarrassment), and then with others.

His two autobiographical volumes are elegantly and subtly polished, at times very moving, often very funny, ironical, entertaining and perceptive, if somewhat distanced as if about someone else. There is modesty but little searching self-examination.

He was of medium height, slender, and elegantly tailored, then thickening somewhat in later life and becoming more relaxed in dress. His head was handsomely browed and aquiline, though its carriage was such that in repose his features could too easily (and not necessarily accurately) convey the impression that he was looking down his nose. Portraits include a profile painting by Graham Sutherland, of which two versions (1963–4) are in the National Portrait Gallery.

He was much honoured: KCB, 1938; FBA, 1949; CH, 1959; a life peerage, 1969; OM, 1976. He was chancellor of York University (1969–79), and a trustee of the British Museum. Honorary degrees, fellowships, and distinctions were conferred on him by universities and academies in Britain, America, France, Spain, Italy, Sweden, Austria, and Finland, but the honour he cherished most was his appointment to the Conseil Artistique des Musées Nationaux, Paris.

His first wife died in 1976; they had a son and a twin son and daughter. The elder son, Alan, became a military historian and Conservative politician. In 1977 Clark married Nolwen, former wife of Edward Rice, cattle and sheep farmer, and daughter of Frederic, Comte de Janzé. Clark died in a nursing home in Hythe, Kent, 21 May 1983. At the close of a crowded memorial service in St James's, Piccadilly, most of the congregation were startled to hear that in the last days of his life he had been received into the Roman Catholic Church.

[*The Times*, 23 and 27 May 1983; Kenneth Clark, *Another Part of the Wood*, 1974, and *The Other Half*, 1977 (autobiographies); Meryle Secrest, *Kenneth Clark*, 1984; private information; personal knowledge.]

David Piper

published 1990

COLLINGWOOD Robin George

(1889–1943)

Philosopher and historian, was born at Cartmel Fell, Lancashire, 22 February 1889, the only son of William Gershom Collingwood by his wife, Edith Mary, daughter of Thomas Isaac, corn merchant, of Notting Hill. His mother was an accomplished pianist; his father was a painter and archaeologist who was Ruskin's secretary and biographer and became professor of fine art at University College, Reading. His parents were poor and indifferent to money; even food was not always plentiful: and at first their son was perforce educated at home. He early learnt the frugality which often showed itself in later life as when in travelling he seemed to prefer conditions of maximum discomfort or when he wrote books and lectures on the back of scholarship examination papers. He became deft-fingered, adept at making paper boats or cardboard boxes, and this manual dexterity was in evidence throughout his maturity in, for example, his firm and regular handwriting, his carpentry, and his bookbinding. From his parents he absorbed the love of art which never left him, and he learnt to play the violin and the piano, as well as to draw and paint. But he also received from his father more formal instruction, especially in Greek and Latin, and it is to his father that he refers in the dedication of *Speculum Mentis* (1924) as his 'first and best teacher'.

A friend's generosity enabled his father to send him at thirteen to a preparatory school and a year later to Rugby. More studious, more widely read, more intellectually alert than most boys of his age, he was perhaps out of place at a public school, and his unhappiness there is reflected in his remarks on education in *The New Leviathan* (1942). When he went up to University College, Oxford, with a classical scholarship in 1908, he breathed more congenial air. Here he could drink his fill of learning without shame or constraint; perhaps he drank too deep, for he may have sown the seeds of his later ill health, and it was certainly then that he first made the acquaintance of his life-long enemy, insomnia. When he came to read *literae humaniores*, after obtaining a first class in classical moderations in 1910, he was unwilling to specialize in either the philosophical or the historical side of the school; he mastered both, but then, as always, he gave to philosophy a certain primacy, and it was to a philosophical fellowship that he was elected at Pembroke College in 1912 shortly before his first class in *literae humaniores* was announced.

In the war of 1914–18 Collingwood worked in the intelligence department of the Admiralty. In the autumn of 1918 he vacated his fellowship for a few months on his marriage to Ethel Winifred, third daughter of Robert Chelles Graham, landowner, of Skipness; they had a son and a daughter. From 1921 to 1928 he undertook the philosophical teaching for Lincoln College in addition to his work at Pembroke, and from 1927 to 1935 he was university lecturer in philosophy and Roman history. In 1935 he left Pembroke for Magdalen on his appointment as Waynflete professor of metaphysical philosophy.

During his years at Pembroke Collingwood had acquired international repute as an authority on Roman Britain in virtue of his numerous publications in that field, and his first care was to wind up his historical work by fulfilling his promise to write the first volume of the *Oxford History of England (Roman Britain and the English Settlements*, 1936, with Mr. J. N. L. Myres), and by placing in other hands for publication in the corpus of

Roman inscriptions the drawings which he had made of all the important Roman inscriptions in Britain. This left him free to devote all his energies to preparing for the press a series of volumes on philosophy; but these energies were already seriously impaired. In 1932 he had been granted a term's leave of absence for ill health, but it was not then realized that he had begun to suffer from a process which led in 1938 to the first of a series of strokes which eventually reduced him to helplessness. In 1941 he resigned his chair and eventually retired to Coniston, where he died from pneumonia 9 January 1943. In 1942 his marriage was dissolved on his wife's petition, and in the same year he married Kathleen Frances, daughter of Francis Edgcumbe Edwardes, mathematical master at Fettes and later at Harrow. A daughter was born of his second marriage. He was elected FBA in 1934 and he received the honorary degree of LL D from the university of St Andrews in 1938.

In breadth of interest and knowledge, Collingwood invites comparison, amongst modern philosophers, with Hegel. He was in fact one of the most learned men of his generation, and he had his learning constantly at command. But he also possessed an originality of mind which enabled him in history to pose new questions and in philosophy to take a promising line of his own. In this very strength, however, lay his weakness; he had critical gifts of a high order, but his imagination outranked them. Alike in history and archaeology he sometimes saw more than the evidence warranted and even overlooked what evidence there was; and in philosophy he had visions the validity of which he did not succeed in justifying to others by argument. In later years, ill health clouded his judgement, and the books of his last quinquennium, despite their wealth of fructifying ideas, are marred by febrility and a sense of strain. In history he made it his obligation to strengthen the school of Romano-British studies founded by F. J. Haverfield; his work on Roman inscriptions is a permanent monument to his memory; and his earlier papers on Roman Britain are milestones in the progressive study of the subject. In philosophy, especially in his philosophical masterpiece, *An Essay on Philosophical Method* (1933), he carried forward the tradition of the English idealists by modifying and developing their doctrine through meeting the criticisms levelled against it by his contemporaries, but he also brought about a *rapprochement* between philosophy and history by showing how a modern philosophy must become through and through historical and so orientate itself to history just as the philosophy of the last three centuries had orientated itself to natural science. His whole work gains its individuality from the fact that he was at once a philosophical historian and a historically minded philosopher; in the crucible of his powerful mind history and philosophy were fused.

In his family circle and with a few intimate friends Collingwood was kindly and affectionate. But he was too much concentrated on his original work not to be something of a recluse. He had a fondness for the society of young women, but he had little time for attending discussion clubs or fulfilling social engagements. He gave up the violin before his first marriage; at one time he composed songs and much instrumental music, and even thought of devoting his life to composition, but this too he abandoned before he was thirty; he played the piano or painted a picture occasionally until his health broke down; he was always fond of sailing a yacht, but archaeology, which he described as his hobby, was the only recreation to which he devoted himself with any continuity during his maturity, unless there could be included in that category his work as a delegate of the University Press from 1928 to 1941. All his life he was deeply interested in religion. The influence of Dr Albert Schweitzer early made him a liberal in theology but partly through talks with intimate friends, partly by a study of the scholastics, he gradually worked his way to the more positive and even dogmatic attitude which underlies his *Essay on Metaphysics* (1940). In politics, and in college business, he was on the conservative side for most of his life, but his views turned sharply to the Left when the attitude of the British Government to the European dictatorships seemed to him to be too supine. As a lecturer in Oxford he attracted large audiences of undergraduates; his voice was high-pitched and clear; the spoken word was as polished as his written prose. He wrote remarkable letters to his friends, but he did not wish them to be published, and he directed that no attempt should be made to write his biography. There is a bibliography of his publications in the *Proceedings* of the British Academy, volume xxix, corrected and supplemented in the preface to his *Idea of History* (1946).

[R. G. Collingwood, *An Autobiography*, 1939; R. B. McCallum in *Proceedings* of the British Academy, vol. xxix, 1943, with supplementary notices by T. M. Knox and I. A. Richmond; *Times Literary Supplement*, 16 January 1943; *Oxford Magazine*, 4 February 1943; private information; personal knowledge.]

T. M. Knox

published 1959

COTTON (Thomas) Henry

(1907–1987)

Golfer, was born 26 January 1907 in Holmes Chapel, Cheshire, the second son in the family of two sons and one daughter of George Cotton, industrialist, inventor, and Wesleyan lay preacher, and his second wife, Alice le

Poidevin, a native of Guernsey. His early childhood was spent in Peckham. He and his brother Leslie went to Ivydale Road School, Peckham, and, after their evacuation from London in World War I, to Reigate Grammar School. Thereafter Cotton won a scholarship to Alleyn's School. The war over, George Cotton obtained junior membership for both boys at the Aquarius Golf Club, and both won the club championship before reaching their teens. From the time he left Alleyn's (after irritating the headmaster) to become a golf professional at sixteen, Cotton trod a path of his own. His aloofness lost him popularity with contemporaries, and his strong will brought him into conflict with golf's rulers, but he rarely deviated from his chosen course. His achievements were founded on intense application and self-reliance.

When he entered his profession, the status of golf professional was barely above that of a senior caddy. By personal example Cotton did more than anyone of his time to alter that. He sought the best: silk shirts from Jermyn Street, limousines rather than taxis, and the best restaurants. Though he was to win three British Open Championships and many famous victories, the impact he made on his own profession was his greatest attainment. He was not long content to be the junior of six assistants at Fulwell Golf Club on 12*s.* 6*d.* a week. Within a year he had moved to an assistant's post at Rye. There he made friends with Cyril Tolley, a fine amateur golfer, who assisted his next move. At nineteen, Cotton went to Langley Park, the youngest head professional in the history of British golf.

At this point Cotton perceived that to reach the top in golf he must challenge American supremacy. With the blessing of his club, £300, and a first-class ticket on the *Aquitania*, he joined America's winter season of 1928–9. A year later he was invited to Argentina to teach and play exhibition matches with a fellow professional. There (Maria) Isabel Estanguet Moss booked him for fifty lessons. The daughter of Pedro Estanguet, a wealthy landowner, and his wife Epifania, and married to Enrique Moss, of Argentina's diplomatic service, 'Toots', as she became universally known, was five years Cotton's senior. They formed a close partnership, which transformed both their lives. Eventually, on the annulment in Latvia in June 1939 of her first marriage, they married at a Westminster register office in December 1939. They had no children, although there were two daughters from Isabel's first marriage. Passionately loyal to Cotton's interests, when occasion demanded she became his most trenchant critic.

Cotton won three Open victories (1934 at Royal St George's, 1937 at Carnoustie, and 1948 at Muirfield). After seven years at Langley Park, Cotton had taken a post at Waterloo, a fashionable club near Brussels. But after his first Open win, he was persuaded by the sixth Earl of Rosebery to build up the reputation of Ashridge Golf Club. The outbreak of World War II interrupted a career at the peak of success. Cotton joined the Royal Air Force, and suffered a regime which aggravated his stomach ulcer. Medically discharged, with the rank of flight lieutenant, he raised £70,000 for the Red Cross and other war charities from 130 matches which he organized. He took appointments first at Coombe Hill and then Royal Mid-Surrey. From there he won his last Open in 1948. That was the apogee of a career in which he had dominated tournament golf for some twenty years. He was also captain of the British Ryder Cup team in 1939, 1947, and 1953. Though there were minor wins in 1953 and 1954, writing, teaching, and golf architecture became main outlets. He wrote several books on golf, as well as designing thirteen golf courses in Britain and ten more abroad.

In 1963 Cotton went to Portugal and on the Algarve coast created from a swamp the Penina Golf Course, which became his memorial. He became virtually squire of the place until the Portuguese revolution of April 1974, during which he was expelled. Profoundly depressed by enforced exile, Cotton was rallied by his wife and they moved for a spell to Sotogrande in Spain. After a two-year interlude they returned to Portugal. There, at Christmas 1982 Toots died, ending half a century's close partnership. In 1987 Cotton entered King Edward VII Hospital, and there received intimation of his knighthood. He had been appointed MBE in 1946. During his convalescence he died suddenly in King Edward VII Hospital, London, 22 December 1987, and was buried at Mexilhoeira Grande in Portugal. He was knighted posthumously in the New Year's honours of 1988.

Always an individualist, Cotton taught that golfing excellence demanded infinite pains. He believed in strong hands and could hit a succession of one-handed shots without regripping the club. A severe opponent, he was also an excellent host. Tireless in pursuit of his own goals, he freely shared with a generation of young golfers more insight into the game than any other figure of his time.

[Henry Cotton, *This Game of Golf*, 1948; Peter Dobereiner, *Maestro: the Life of Henry Cotton*, 1992; personal knowledge.]

W. F. Deedes

published 1996

COWARD Sir Noël Peirce

(1899–1973)

Actor, playwright, composer, lyricist, producer, author, occasional poet, and Sunday painter, was born 16 December 1899 at Teddington, Middlesex, the second in the family of three sons (the eldest of whom died at the age of six) of Arthur Sabin Coward (described as a clerk, but whose passion was music) and his wife Violet Agnes, daughter of Henry Gordon Veitch, a captain in the Royal Navy. His grandfather was James Coward, organist and chorister. Both parental backgrounds had a strong influence on the boy and the man. His mother was also musical—the parents met as members of the local church choir—and was an ardent and knowledgeable theatre-goer. Coward was soon to be a chorister himself, but was frustrated by the absence of applause after his solos. His birthday treats were invariably visits to the theatre; and by the time he was 'rushing towards puberty' he could play accurately by ear numbers from the show he had seen that day. His formal education was sporadic, not helped by a quick temper—he left one school after biting the headmistress in the arm; and though he attended the Chapel Royal choir school at Clapham in 1909, he failed surprisingly, but perhaps providentially, to be accepted for the choir. The start of his professional career was less than a year away—27 January 1911—playing Prince Mussel in *The Goldfish* as one of a 'Star Cast of Wonder Children'. (Indeed, they included Michael MacLiammóir and (Dame) Ninette de Valois.) His success led to a number of engagements with (Sir) Charles Hawtrey, from whom he learned much about playing comedy, and—quite as important—gained an insight into the anatomy of writing plays. In 1913 he appeared as an angel in *Hannele* by Hauptmann with the fifteen-year-old Gertrude Lawrence. (And so began a very special personal and professional relationship which lasted until her death in 1952.) Christmas 1913 saw a dream realized when he played Slightly in *Peter Pan* with Pauline Chase.

Throughout 1914–15 there was little work and some anxiety about his health. However the period was not uneventful. Worldly-wise for his years, his sophistication was purely theatrical; but in June 1915 an invitation to visit a Mrs Astley Cooper at Hambleton Hall gave Coward a first exciting view of that undiscovered country of high society, in which he would become increasingly at home, as welcome as he was at ease, and from which, both as writer and actor, he was to develop an important element of his comedy. Also from this period comes that distinctive mark of self-awareness—a new and durable signature, described by Sir John

Betjeman at the Coward memorial service: 'Noël with two dots over the "e", and the firm decided downward stroke of the "l" '. At Christmas 1915 he at last worked again, in *Where the Rainbow Ends;* followed by a tour in the thankless part of Charley in *Charley's Aunt* (1916). After a two-week run in *Light Blues*, singing and dancing with the newly-wed Jack Hulbert and (Dame) Cicely Courtneidge, he had his first solo number in *The Happy Family* (1916), of which one critic wrote: 'He combined the grace of a Russian dancer with the manner of an English schoolboy'. In 1916 he wrote the lyrics and music of his first song; by 1917 he had written three plays. The best of them, *The Rat Trap* (produced in 1924), was described as 'lousy in construction' by American impresario Gilbert Miller. Dialogue is not enough, was Miller's message. Coward took it to heart. Miller was enthusiastic about his acting, however, and engaged him for the juvenile lead in a star-studded production of *The Saving Grace* (1917). Before that he appeared in his first film, *Hearts of the World*, directed by the legendary D. W. Griffith.

In the spring of 1918 began a frustrating nine-month 'engagement' in the army. Though at home with the rigorous discipline of the theatre, and already recognizing the no less demanding self-discipline required of the writer, Coward found that the military equivalent actually made him ill. (Would it have been the same, one wonders, if his call-up had been to the navy?) Although personally little affected by 'the war to end war' Coward shared the hectic relief of his contemporaries that it was over; and was soon considered by press and public as typical of the Bright Young Things, and also paradoxically, of the cynically disillusioned minority as well. The epithet 'brittle' was first applied to him now; it was to haunt him and his reputation to the grave and beyond.

Through his friendship with the tragically short-lived Meggie Albanesi he came to know Lorn Macnaughtan, who as Lorn Loraine became his secretary and 'one of the principal mainstays' of his life until her death forty-six years later. (It was she who first called him 'master'—as a joke.) In 1920 he first appeared in London in a play of his own *I'll Leave It to You*, which, despite good notices, closed in five weeks. Undaunted, he went abroad for the first time, visiting Paris, and going on to Alassio to Mrs Astley Cooper, where he met another lifelong member of his inner circle—Gladys Calthrop, who was to design sets and costumes for a host of his plays. A rapid escape abroad, when his contribution to a production was over (whatever its fate), became hereafter part of the pattern of his life. 'Like a window opening in my head', he called it.

In *The Young Idea* (1922) Coward shamelessly borrowed his brother and sister from the twins in *You Never Can Tell* by George Bernard Shaw. Shaw was not offended, but wrote Coward a most constructive letter, including the advice 'never to see or read my plays. Unless you can get clear away from me you will begin as a back number, and be hopelessly out of it when you are forty'. (In 1941, when Coward had unwittingly breached the currency regulations and received much bad publicity, Shaw was his doughty champion, reminding him that there was no guilt without intention, and telling him to plead 'not guilty' despite his lawyers' advice. He did; and received a minimal fine.) He was composer and part-author of *London Calling* (1923), a revue starring himself and Gertrude Lawrence. As with *The Young Idea* the majority of critics preferred his writing to his performances. The rest would only accept him as a performer in the works of others—a contradiction only explicable by the hostility of both factions to versatility. (Meanwhile in 1921 he had paid his first exciting but impoverished visit to New York, meeting Alfred Lunt—Lynn Fontanne he already knew from London; and also Laurette Taylor and family, whose absent-minded hospitality and parlour games gave him the idea for *Hay Fever*.)

In November 1924 *The Vortex*—his play about drug addiction—put Coward triumphantly and controversially on the map, winning the allegiance of the beau monde led by the Mountbattens; confirming the worst fears of the stuffier elements of society. During its seven-month run—the longest he would ever permit himself—his output included *On With the Dance* (1925), a revue for (Sir) C. B. Cochran, an association which lasted for nine years (to see its Manchester opening Coward left *The Vortex* briefly to his understudy—(Sir) John Gielgud); *Fallen Angels* (1925) with Tallulah Bankhead—another *succès de scandale*; and *Hay Fever* (1925) with (Dame) Marie Tempest, which ran for a year. In September 1925 *The Vortex* took New York by storm, and Coward bought his first Rolls-Royce. *Easy Virtue* (1925) was written and produced while he was there. There were two consequences of this astonishing burst of successful activity, neither surprising. In 1926 he suffered a severe breakdown; and he yielded to the temptation to allow the production of three plays from his bottom drawer. All were failures—the most notorious being *Sirocco* (1927), which starred his great friend Ivor Novello. It was the only time they worked together.

Thanks to Cochran, Coward soon bounced back, with his most successful revue *This Year of Grace* (1928). *Bitter Sweet* (1929) followed—its most famous number 'I'll see you again' being composed in a taxi in a New York traffic jam. Even a Far Eastern holiday was productive. Alone in Shanghai, he had a mental picture of 'Gertie' in a white Molyneux dress in the South of France. Four hours later *Private Lives* had been mapped out; the actual writing took four days. It opened in London in 1930—Laurence (later Lord) Olivier playing a minor role—and was sold out for its three-month season, as it was in New York. Arnold Bennett called Coward 'the Congreve of our day'. 'Thin' and 'brittle' replied the critics. *Cavalcade* (1931) was his most ambitious production, suggested to his ever fertile mind by a photograph of a troop-ship leaving for the Boer war. It gave him the opportunity to proclaim in a brilliant mixture of pageantry and understatement his intense patriotism, coupled with a warning that 'this country of ours which we love so much' was losing its way. His enemies found it obscene that the author of *The Vortex* should treat such a subject. The nation and the English-speaking world responded differently. *Design for Living* (1932) was written in South America to redeem a promise made to the Lunts. It was so successful that he broke his three-month rule and played five in New York, using the mornings to write his first volume of autobiography *Present Indicative* (1937). From a Caribbean cruise with the navy he emerged with the libretto of *Conversation Piece* (1934), his last collaboration with Cochran. 1935 saw the writing of the nine playlets, some with music, which were presented in three programmes as *To-night at 8.30* (1936). *Operette* (1938) broke this long run of success, despite the hit number 'The Stately Homes of England'. Coward spent the summer of 1939 writing *Present Laughter* and *This Happy Breed*, but their production was postponed until 1942 by the outbreak of war, and by Coward's prearranged war job in Paris. This and a proposed intelligence assignment in America came to nothing, due in part, he believed, to the hostility of Lord Beaverbrook. Angry and frustrated, he turned with relief to his own field. The results included his longest running comedy *Blithe Spirit* (1941); his finest film script *In Which We Serve* (1942) about the sinking of Mountbatten's destroyer *Kelly*; and one of his most enduring songs 'London Pride'.

Cole Lesley, who died in 1980, writer of the best biography of Coward, came to work for him in 1936; Graham Payn joined the resident 'family' in 1947, completing with Joyce Carey, Lorn Loraine, and Gladys Calthrop the inner circle, which apart from Lorn Loraine's death in 1967, remained unchanged until his own. But if the domestic background was serene, Coward for the next twenty years was to endure much professional disappointment and disparagement. Between 1946 and 1964 six musicals and two plays fell short of Coward's highest hopes; fortunately *Relative Values* (1951), *Quadrille* (1952), *South Sea Bubble* and *Nude With Violin* (1956), though not his own favourites, were box-office successes.

In 1948, after a disastrous New York revival of *To-night at 8.30*, Coward took Graham Payn, who had starred in it with Gertrude Lawrence, to Jamaica. He fell in love with the island, built a house by the sea called Blue Harbour, and later, on the hill above ('piling Pelléas on Mélisande' he called it) a small retreat—Firefly Hill (where he died, and is buried). Also in 1948 he performed *Present Laughter* (*Joyeux Chagrins* in French) in Paris—a remarkable achievement, which failed dismally. His French was too good, they said, and the humour did not translate.

In 1951 he accepted an engagement which led to lifelong financial security. He appeared singing his own songs in cabaret at London's Café de Paris. Three more sell-out seasons followed; and then one in 1955 at Las Vegas, at 35,000 dollars a week for four weeks. From this in turn came highly lucrative American television and film engagements; and the difficult decision to emigrate, first to Bermuda and later to Switzerland, to mitigate the depredations of the Inland Revenue, and because, intending to perform less in future, 'I might as well do it for double the appreciation and ten times the lolly'. In any case, as Sir Winston Churchill told him, 'An Englishman has an inalienable right to live wherever he chooses'.

In 1953 he had a great success as King Magnus in Shaw's *The Apple Cart*; in 1960 his only novel *Pomp and Circumstance* was predictably more successful in America than Britain.

In 1964 an invitation by Sir Laurence Olivier to direct Dame Edith Evans in *Hay Fever* for the National Theatre marked the beginning of the last sunlit years of Coward's career, demonstrating once again that the British only feel comfortable with talent or genius when their possessors are 'over the hill'. Coward decided to risk his new reputation as 'demonstrably the greatest living English playwright' (Ronald Bryden) by appearing one last time in the West End. The result was *A Song at Twilight* and a double bill *Come Into the Garden, Maud*, and *Shadows of the Evening* (1966). Though seriously weakened by the onset of arterio-sclerosis, and by amoebic dysentery caught in the Seychelles, and for the only time in his life suffering the indignity of occasionally drying up, the season was a triumphant sell-out. There was only one bad notice. 'Good', he said reading it, 'I thought I might be slipping.' Professionally that was the final curtain. What followed was a trip round the world with Cole Lesley and Graham Payn; the seventieth birthday celebrations, culminating in an emotional midnight tribute by his fellow professionals; his long delayed and much deserved knighthood (1970); in America a special Tony award (1970)—his first—for services to the theatre; an honorary D.Litt. from Sussex University (1972); peaceful days in Switzerland and Jamaica with his friends, and finally, without warning, the end in Jamaica 26 March 1973.

How to assess him? His staccato speech, developed, it is said, to penetrate his mother's deafness, became the instrument of both his comedy and of his conversation. A hostile journalist once asked him for what he would be remembered after his death. 'Charm', he replied. T. E. Lawrence called him 'a hasty kind of genius'. In 1930 W. Somerset Maugham predicted that he would be responsible for the manner in which plays would be written for thirty years. He said himself that it was only natural that 'my writing should be appreciated casually, because my personality, performance, music and legend get in the way'. Of his homosexuality Dame

Rebecca West, a close and clear-sighted friend, wrote: 'There was impeccable dignity in his sexual life, which was reticent but untainted by pretence.'

A quintessential professional himself, he could be a scathing and witty critic of the second-rate; but he was outstandingly generous in his praise, never standing on dignity because of his position. He had the capacity to inspire great devotion. Gertrude Lawrence's last letter to him ended: 'It's always you I want to please more than *anyone*'—a sentiment that would be widely echoed among those who knew him.

There are portraits of him by Edward Seago in the Garrick Club and the Phoenix Theatre and by Clemence Dane in the National Portrait Gallery. In 1984 a black memorial stone, with the words 'A talent to amuse', was unveiled in Westminster Abbey.

[*Noël Coward Autobiography*, 1986 (ed. Sheridan Morley); Cole Lesley, *The Life of Noël Coward*, 1976; Charles Castle, *Noël*, 1972; Sheridan Morley, *A Talent to Amuse*, 1969; *Who's Who in the Theatre* (15th edn.) for a comprehensive list of his writings and performances; personal knowledge.]

MICHAEL DENISON

published 1986

CROSLAND (Charles) Anthony (Raven)

(1918–1977)

Politician and writer, was born 29 August 1918 at St Leonard-on-Sea, Sussex, the only son and the second of three children of Joseph Beardsel Crosland, CB, under-secretary, War Office, and his wife, Jessie Raven, lecturer in Old French at Westfield College, University of London. He was educated at Highgate School and, as a classical scholar, at Trinity College, Oxford, where he obtained a second class in classical honour moderations in 1939. His university years were interrupted by World War II, in which he served from 1940 to 1945. He was commissioned in the Royal Welch Fusiliers in 1941, transferred to the Parachute Regiment in 1942, and subsequently served in North Africa, Italy, France, and Austria. His most notable military exploit was to land by parachute on the casino at Cannes, during Operation Anvil in the summer of 1944.

At Oxford he had a notable career, both academically and as an undergraduate politician. He lost interest in classics and turned to philosophy, politics, and economics (primarily economics). After his return to the university in 1946, he secured a first class in PPE in 1946 and was elected a lecturer and later a fellow in economics at Trinity. He held this position from 1947 to 1950, and in 1966 became an honorary fellow. Before the war he was an active and orthodoxly Marxist member of the Labour Club. In the early months of the war, however, he found himself increasingly out of sympathy with its fellow-travelling and neutralist line, and in May 1940 he joined with others to lead the successful breakaway of the Democratic Socialist Club, which was much closer to the national Labour Party position. He was elected treasurer of the Union Society, but was defeated for the presidency. Six years later, however, on his return from the army, he redressed this set-back and secured the higher office.

Crosland was an imposing undergraduate, apparently self-confident, irreverent, and even glamorous, with striking good looks, intellectual assurance, a long camel-hair overcoat and a rakish red sports car. Later, as a young don, he with one or two contemporaries formed something of a cult group, of which the distinguishing characteristic was the unusual combination of hard intellectual endeavour and undisciplined, even rather riotous, relaxation. Crosland was, and remained, a puritan (his family were Plymouth Brethren) shot through with strains of self-indulgence.

In 1950, at the age of thirty-one, he was first elected an MP, for the constituency of South Gloucestershire, which he was able to win for the Labour Party and hold for the next five years because it contained a good deal of Bristol suburb as well as south Cotswold countryside. He gave up his Oxford fellowship a few months later, and never returned to professional academic life, although he remained very much an intellectual in politics. In the House of Commons he had a considerable, although not perhaps a remarkable, success. He was an economic specialist, and a close friend and assistant of Hugh Gaitskell, who for most of that period was shadow chancellor of the Exchequer. In 1952 Crosland married Hilary Anne Sarson, of Newbury, the daughter of Henry Sarson, a member of the vinegar family, but the marriage was short-lived and was finally dissolved in 1957.

Before the 1955 general election the boundaries of South Gloucestershire were redrawn in a way unfavourable to Labour, and Crosland decided to seek another seat. This was a mistaken move, for the one which he found, Southampton, Test, produced a larger Conservative majority than the one he had left. He was not, however, greatly disconcerted by his exclusion from Parliament, for although devoted to politics in a broader sense, he regarded the trappings and life of the House of Commons with some indifference.

He had other things to do. In 1953 he had already published his first book, *Britain's Economic Problem*. This was a lucid but fairly conventional analysis of the country's post-war trading difficulties. By 1955 he was already well into a much more original and substantial work, which he completed in the next year and published in the autumn of 1956. *The Future of Socialism* was well received at the time, but only gradually, over the next decade or so, achieved its position as the most important theoretical treatise to be written from the moderate left of British politics in the twenty-five post-war years. It assumed the triumph of Keynesianism, and with it a future of broadening abundance and the withering of the Marxist class struggle. It disputed the importance of nationalization and challenged the bureaucratic socialism of the Fabian tradition of Sidney and Beatrice Webb: 'Total abstinence and a good filing system are not now the right sign-posts to the socialist Utopia; or at least, if they are, some of us will fall by the wayside.' It was at once libertarian and strongly egalitarian. It saw no conflict which could not be resolved by the flowing tide of continuing economic growth. It was in the mainstream of the optimism, many would now say the complacency, of the English liberal tradition. It influenced a generation.

Political theory having been disposed of with imagination, even if not total prescience, Crosland showed his practical sense by devoting the next two years to acting as secretary (under Gaitskell's chairmanship) to the independent committee of inquiry into the Co-operative Movement and writing a good report. Then he re-entered the House of Commons in 1959 as member for Grimsby, the constituency which he represented for the remaining seventeen and a half years of his life. He was quickly involved in all the Labour Party disputes which followed that lost election, urging Gaitskell on in the argument over 'clause four' (the nationalization clause in the Party's constitution), supporting him against unilateral disarmament, sharply disagreeing with him over his reticence towards Macmillan's initiative for British entry to the European community. Even apart from the European issue, however, he was in no way a client of his leader. He had too strong a personality and too critical a judgement for that. In some ways Gaitskell sought him more than he sought Gaitskell, and he was less thrown by Gaitskell's early death in 1963 than were some others in the circle. In the election to the leadership which followed he supported James Callaghan, who ran a bad third, rather than George Brown (later Lord George-Brown) who was the candidate of the majority of the 'Gaitskellites'.

In 1964 Crosland married again and also entered government for the first time. His second marriage was to Mrs Susan Barnes Catling, daughter of Mark Watson, of Baltimore, Maryland, who subsequently (under the name of Susan Barnes) became a prolific writer of skill and perception; unlike the first marriage, it was a great and continuing success and brought Crosland two step-daughters. His initial government post was minister of state in the newly-created Department of Economic Affairs, but after only three months he filled an unexpectedly early Cabinet vacancy and became secretary of state for education and science. He was admitted to the Privy Council in 1965.

The combination of these events, some close observers felt, produced a considerable change in Crosland's personality. He had a happier and more rounded life, and became more benign. He also became more of a party politician, more stirred by ambition, less the uninhibited and fearless commentator. He was a successful departmental minister, a master of various subjects, but occasionally lacking in decisiveness, always believing that a decision had so carefully and logically to be thought through that he sometimes missed the moment at which to make it. His popular impact was also limited, and, surprising though this may seem in retrospect, he was frequently confused in the public mind with Richard Crossman.

He stayed at education for two and a half years and then became president of the Board of Trade in 1967, hoping that this would lead on to the Exchequer. When the vacancy in the chancellorship occurred a few months later and this did not follow, he was deeply disappointed. His relations with Harold Wilson (later Lord Wilson of Rievaulx) were not close, and in the autumn of 1969 there was some doubt about his survival in the government. But he was too able a man to lose and for the last few months of that government occupied a co-ordinating role over unmerged departments as secretary of state for local government and regional planning.

There followed nearly four years in opposition. He worked hard as a party spokesman, published another book, *Socialism Now*, in 1974 (which, like its 1962 predecessor, *The Conservative Enemy*, was a collection of political essays, but more circumscribed in scope by his housing and local government responsibilities) but surprised and disappointed many of his friends by failing to vote with sixty-eight Labour MPs in favour of Britain's entry to the European community in the decisive division of October 1971; he did not vote against, but abstained. This probably accounted for his poor result in the deputy leadership election of 1972.

In the 1974 Wilson government he was secretary of state for the environment, essentially the same job but with a different name, tighter control over his subordinate ministers, and a more senior position at the Cabinet table than he had occupied in 1969. His experience as an upper middle rank departmental minister was unrivalled. The great offices of state continued to elude him. He responded by being increasingly effective in his department, and by exercising more authority in the Cabinet than in the previous government, while moving consciously away from the right and towards the centre of the party. In March 1976, when Harold Wilson resigned as prime minister, Crosland was determined to contest the succession. He ran fifth of five candidates, securing only seventeen votes. Yet the contest did not damage him. He succeeded to the Foreign Office in the new Callaghan administration with an unimpaired authority, and had he lived might well have been a stronger rival to Michael Foot in 1980 than Denis Healey proved to be.

He was foreign secretary for only ten months. Although he had always tried to think and write in an internationalist context, his experience was insular. He was unacquainted with the intricacies of foreign or defence policy. He was impatient of many of the nuances of the game. He knew foreign sociologists rather than foreign statesmen. Yet, after a hesitant start, he impressed most of his officials and his foreign colleagues by his authority, his wit, and his intellect. His personality, if not his fame, was a match for that of his principle confrère, Henry Kissinger. He was no longer the glamorous *enfant terrible* of his Oxford days, or even the adventurous thinker of *The Future of Socialism*. He was not old, but he had become a little tired in body, heavy and hooded-eyed, yet mordant of phrase, contemptuous of pomposity, and capable of a still dazzling charm.

He was pleased to be foreign secretary, but he still wanted, as ten years before, to be chancellor of the Exchequer, and devoted some of his overtaxed and waning energy to preparing for that job which he was never to hold. This was a last but typical manifestation of the paradox of Anthony Crosland. His intellect was one of the strongest in post-war British politics, and he fortified it by exceptional powers of application. But it was weakened by some uncontrolled demon of discontent, which marred his satisfaction in his own particular roles of excellence. He died at Oxford 19 February 1977, in office and at the age of fifty-eight, six days after a massive cerebral haemorrhage.

[Susan Crosland, *Tony Crosland*, 1982; personal knowledge.]

ROY JENKINS

published 1986

DAHL Roald

(1916–1990)

Writer of children's fiction, was born 13 September 1916 in Llandaff near Cardiff, the youngest in a family of four daughters and two sons of Norwegian parents: Harald Dahl, who had given up farming near Oslo to make a fortune as a ship-broker in Wales, and his wife, Sofie Magdalene, daughter of Olaf Hesselberg, a meteorologist and classical scholar. His sister married the microbiologist (Sir) Ashley Miles.

When Dahl was only three, a beloved older sister and, a few weeks later, his father both died. This was the first in a series of mortal disasters that dogged him, and, he said, gave his work a black savagery. His mother ran the family and gave Dahl a passion for reading. He was a rebel at Llandaff Cathedral School, St Peter's in Weston-super-Mare, and Repton. In his account of his childhood, he revealed the cruel flogging pleasurably inflicted by Repton's headmaster, G. F. Fisher (later Baron Fisher of Lambeth, archbishop of Canterbury).

Resisting the attractions of a university education, at the age of eighteen he joined the Public Schools Exploring Society's expedition to Newfoundland, sponsored by Shell, and then joined Shell in 1934 and was sent to Dar-es-Salaam, Tanganyika. When war broke out in 1939, he drove to Nairobi, Kenya, to volunteer for the Royal Air Force. He served with No. 80 Fighter Squadron in the Western Desert (1940) and was severely wounded when his Hurricane crashed over Libya. He rejoined his squadron to serve in Greece and then Syria (1941). Invalided home to London, he was posted to Washington as assistant air attaché (1942–3), and worked in security (1943–5). He was appointed wing commander in 1943.

While he was in Washington in 1943, C. S. Forester, creator of Captain Hornblower and author of many popular novels, asked Dahl to write an account of his most exciting RAF experience. Forester liked the contribution so much that he sent it to the *Saturday Evening Post*, which published it. Dahl's first book, originally written as a film script for Walt Disney, was *The Gremlins* (1943), which concerned a tribe of imaginary goblins who were blamed by the RAF for everything that went wrong with an aircraft. Dahl claimed, mistakenly, to have invented the name.

His short stories, published in such notice-boards of the genre as the *New Yorker* and *Harper's Magazine*, tiptoed along the tightrope between the macabre and the comic in a manner reminiscent of Saki (H. H. Munro) in that mode. In a typical Dahl plot, a woman murders her husband with a frozen leg of lamb and then feeds it to the investigating detectives, or a rich woman goes on a cruise, leaving her husband to perish in an elevator stuck between two floors in an empty house. When the stories were published as collections, *Someone Like You* (1954) and *Kiss Kiss* (1960), they made Dahl a celebrity, his fame being augmented by their translation to the television screen as *Tales of the Unexpected*, which ran for many years from 1965. They are bizarre examples of the fashionable genre of black comedy.

In 1953 Dahl married the film star Patricia Neal (on the rebound from her long affair with Gary Cooper). She was the daughter of William Burdett Neal, manager of the Southern Coal and Coke Company, of Packard, Kentucky. They had one son and four daughters, but one daughter died of measles in 1962, and their son was brain-damaged at the age of four months, when a cab hit his pram in New York. Dahl started writing children's books for his own children, characteristically because he thought the existing ones were 'bloody awful', and because he said he had run out of ideas for macabre short stories.

James and the Giant Peach (1967) was an instant new planet in the sky of children's books. Dahl also wrote, among others, *Charlie and the Chocolate Factory* (1967, filmed as *Willy Wonka and the Chocolate Factory*, 1971), *Fantastic Mr Fox* (1970), *Charlie and the Great Glass Elevator* (1973), *Danny, the Champion of the World* (1975), *The Enormous Crocodile* (1978), *The Twits* (1980), and *George's Marvellous Medicine* (1981). The books are rude, naughty, and violent, and children loved them, though some librarians and teachers did not. Children think that Dahl is on their side against the interfering and misunderstanding adult world.

While pregnant with their fifth child, Patricia Neal suffered a series of massive strokes, and was helped through her long recovery by Dahl, until she was well enough to resume acting. He then divorced her, in 1953, and in the same year married her best friend and his long-time mistress, Felicity Ann, former wife of Charles Reginald Hugh Crosland, businessman and farmer, and daughter of Alphonsus Liguori d'Abreu, thoracic surgeon, of Birmingham. They lived with the eight children of their previous marriages at Gipsy House, a white Georgian farmhouse in Great Missenden in Buckinghamshire. There Dahl wrote, always in pencil, in a hut in the garden.

Dahl wrote several scripts for films, among them the James Bond adventure, *You Only Live Twice* (1967), and *Chitty Chitty Bang Bang* (1968). He was six feet six inches tall, a chain-smoker, a lover of fine wine, a collector of contemporary painting, and a keen gambler on horses. His public statements were often intemperate, and some of his stories about himself were as tall as he was. But he had a magical touch for the macabre and the surrealist, and for a lord of misrule topsy-turvydom that made him the most popular children's writer of his age. He died 23 November 1990 in the John Radcliffe Hospital, Oxford.

[Barry Farrell, *Pat and Roald*, 1970; Roald Dahl, *Boy*, 1984, *Going Solo*, 1986, and *Ah Sweet Mystery of Life*, 1989 (autobiographies); Jeremy Treglown, *Roald Dahl: a Biography*, 1994; personal knowledge.]

PHILIP HOWARD

published 1996

DIMBLEBY Richard Frederick

(1913–1965)

Journalist and broadcaster, was born at Richmond on Thames 25 May 1913, the elder child and only son of Frederick J. G. Dimbleby, and his wife Gwendoline M. Bolwell, the daughter of a Bath surveyor. Educated at Mill Hill School, in 1931 he went to work in the composing room of the family paper, the *Richmond and Twickenham Times*, then edited by his father, who later became a political adviser to Lloyd George. After gaining experience on the *Bournemouth Echo* and the *Advertisers Weekly*, in 1936 Dimbleby thrust his way with typical determination into the Topical Talks Department of the BBC, becoming one of the Corporation's first news reporters 'at a small empty desk in a small and otherwise empty room about to tackle a job which did not yet exist and about which I knew nothing at all'. But his flair, his sense of purpose, and a decided gift for self-assertion made him a pioneer and then a central figure in the development of reporting and public commentary first in radio and then in television. Experience in the Spanish civil war equipped him for service, in 1939, with the British Expeditionary Force in France as the BBC's first war correspondent. In fact his career was a succession of 'firsts'.

Subsequently Dimbleby covered the campaigns in the Middle East, East Africa, Greece, and the Western Desert. Recalled to London in 1942, he was the first BBC correspondent to fly with Bomber Command (to Berlin in 1943) and he had twenty further missions to his credit. In battle his instinct was to go forward, but a suffocating censorship and the BBC's own muddled policies about war news seemed, too often, to flavour his Mediterranean dispatches with the cosy optimism of rear headquarters. Yet though he was in part a conformist, at heart he was a rebel for the truth and his essential integrity was marked by responsible direction of the BBC's war-reporting team from D-Day onwards and by his own coverage of the final advance into Germany. He was the first reporter into Belsen, on which he filed a classic dispatch. He found time to write a number of books during the war and was always a prolific contributor to newspapers and periodicals.

Television's post-war expansion converted a voice familiar on the radio to one intimate by one's fireside. Remorseless in preparation and in the refinement of his techniques, Dimbleby became the irreplaceable 'anchorman' for elaborate commentaries on televised state occasions and for the burgeoning political programmes like 'Panorama': a figurehead, universally enjoyed, aspersed, respected, and envied. For years his magisterial presence dominated the screen. But he was also an indefatigable contributor to radio, as chairman of 'Twenty Questions' and the peregrinating interviewer of 'Down Your Way', and he busily concerned himself with the conduct of the family paper.

Fortunate in his time and opportunities, Dimbleby exploited them seriously, creatively, and ruthlessly. He had no equal. Where he went first and alone, able competitors have since crowded, and after the collapse of the BBC's monopoly no single personality has reigned over the complete territory of the nation's screens like an emperor. The programmes of complicated ceremonial at which he was adept have lost their compelling novelty in the course of broadcasting's evolution. But though his art's product was perishable, he made an enduring mark. His subject-matter, whether a coronation or a general election, was rarely trivial, and viewers followed him readily to the height of his theme.

In later years he was a man of substance, and looked it: bulky, formidable, wearing a mantle of success as if by right, although, like all good performers, he was dogged by fears of failure. A natural belligerence was enriched by struggle with his BBC superiors over matters of administrative and editorial policy where, particularly during the war, wise heads at Broadcasting House were often more addled than their representatives in the field. But behind the revealed persona, suave, sometimes pompous and overbearing, there was a true vein of compassion and humanity which pervaded his dispatches and often, in private, his actions. His career was sweetened by his sense of humour, and he laughed best at himself.

In 1965 he seemed to reach a peak with his handling of the televised commentary on Churchill's funeral, but on 22 December he died of cancer in St Thomas's Hospital, London. For five years he had successfully concealed his condition, and undertaken the most intensive and exacting treatment, without ceasing to work in the public eye. His fortitude and will-power were exemplary. The memorial service at Westminster Abbey was a national event, and a torrent of public subscriptions funded, in his memory, a fellowship of cancer research at St Thomas's Hospital, London University. His stoicism and the cause of his death evoked a universal sympathy, and there was an important social consequence. Millions for whom cancer had been unmentionable now found that a taboo had been lifted.

In 1937 he married his father's personal assistant, Dilys, the daughter of Arthur A. Thomas, a barrister and member of the London County Council. They had three sons, Jonathan, David, and Nicholas, and a daughter, Sally. Jonathan and David both have successful television careers. Dimbleby was appointed OBE in 1945 and CBE in 1959. In 1965 Sheffield University awarded him an honorary LL D.

[Jonathan Dimbleby, *Richard Dimbleby*, 1975; *Richard Dimbleby, Broadcaster* (ed. Leonard Miall, 1966); Asa Briggs, *The History of Broadcasting in the United Kingdom, vol. iii, The War of Words*, 1970, and *vol. iv, Sound and Vision*, 1979; personal knowledge.]

Ronald Lewin

published 1981

DOWDING Hugh Caswall Tremenheere (1882–1970)

First Baron Dowding

Air chief marshal, was born at Moffat, Dumfriesshire, 24 April 1882, the eldest in a family of three boys and one girl of Arthur John Caswall Dowding, a schoolmaster of Wiltshire stock, and his wife, Maud Caroline, daughter of Major-General Charles William Tremenheere, chief engineer in the Public Works Department in Bombay.

During his early schooldays at St Ninian's, Moffat, he lived at home enjoying the combination of kindly parents who were also the respected headmaster and his wife. He entered Winchester, his father's old school, in 1895, where he spent four not entirely happy years. His lack of facility with the classics led him to join the army class, thence to choose an army career.

By way of the Royal Military Academy, Woolwich, he became a gunner in the Royal Garrison Artillery, following the advice of his family. His subaltern's life in Gibraltar, Ceylon, and Hong Kong was that of a typical young gunner officer. After transfer to a mountain battery in 1904, he spent six years in India, half the time with a native battery. He relished the strenuous, solitary, and often dangerous life on manœuvres in the Himalayan foothills. Subsequently (1912–13), two years at the Staff College, Camberley, coincided with his developing interest in aviation. In his own time he learned to fly at Brooklands, the flying school run by the firm of Vickers, and obtained his Royal Aero Club pilot's certificate No. 711 early in the morning of the same day as he passed out from Camberley, 20 December 1913. He then took a three-month course at the Central Flying School at Upavon, where his flying instructor was (Sir) John Salmond and his assistant commandant H. M. (later Viscount) Trenchard. Dowding returned to the Garrison Artillery in the Isle of Wight as a Royal Flying Corps Reserve officer.

When war was declared in 1914 he was appointed commandant of the RFC Dover camp whence the squadrons left for France. Thereafter he served at home and in France with Nos. 7 and 6 Squadrons, both as observer and pilot and then as flight commander with No. 9 Squadron. He specialized in early experiments in wireless telegraphy. Appointed to command No. 16 Squadron at Merville in 1915, Dowding in many ways found it a testing time. His nickname from Camberley days of 'Stuffy' appeared to younger aircrew to suit his older, more withdrawn, and austere approach to flying duties. His general reputation was not advanced by a brush with Trenchard over a supply of propellers, although Dowding proved that he himself had the better technical knowledge. Promotion followed regularly until by 1917 he was a brigadier-general; however, another brush with Trenchard in 1916, when Dowding commanded the headquarters wing of HQ, Royal Flying Corps, probably denied him field command for the rest of the war.

Becoming, not without difficulty, a permanent officer in the newly created Royal Air Force in 1919, Dowding was group commander at Kenley and then chief of staff at Headquarters, Inland Area. His name became prominent as the organizer of the second and some subsequent Hendon pageants. A posting as chief staff officer to Air Headquarters, Iraq, in 1924 provided further opportunities for active flying. In 1926 he became director of training at the Air Ministry and achieved a much-needed rapport with Trenchard, who was now at the height of power as the chief of air staff. So far did Dowding gain Trenchard's confidence that he was sent in 1929 to Palestine to report on the need for Service reinforcements when an Arab rising seemed imminent. His balanced reports won favour with Trenchard.

After a brief spell in command of the Fighting Area on return from Palestine, Dowding joined the Air Council in 1930 as air member for supply and research. His period of office saw continuous revolutionary changes in the design and construction of aircraft. It saw the development of all-metal monoplanes like the Hurricane and Spitfire, early work on the Stirling and other heavy bombers, and the development of eight-gun armament and especially of radar. Dowding's practical bent, his insistence on experimentation and trials, and his imaginative grasp of aircrew requirements often led him into conflict with colleagues or other holders of received orthodox opinions. Although Dowding was willing to listen to his scientific advisers, it was clear that he formed his own opinions. His title changed to air member for research and development when in 1935 supply became another member's responsibility.

Dowding

It was fitting that Dowding was appointed AOC-in-C of the new Fighter Command in 1936. The fifty-four-year-old widower moved to Stanmore where his sister Hilda was hostess for him. (Dowding had married in 1918 and his wife died suddenly in 1920.) For the next four years in Fighter Command he dedicated himself to preparing the air defences of the United Kingdom. The introduction of efficient land-line communications, operations rooms, improved VHF R/T, and above all the completion of the chain of radar stations round the east and south coasts were his concern. Together with these went the creation of new squadrons of Spitfires and Hurricanes. The announcement that Sir Cyril (later Lord) Newall was to be appointed chief of air staff in 1937 must have been a blow to any hopes Dowding may have had of achieving that office. He bore this just as stoically as he endured the five separate indications between August 1938 and August 1940 of Air Ministry intention to terminate his active service on grounds of age.

Although a massive Luftwaffe attack did not come, Dowding had to fight a constant paper war to resist diversions of his modern fighters from home defence. Single-mindedly, Dowding sought to retain in readiness the number of squadrons he deemed essential to resist the destruction of his force and the invasion of the country. The loss of fighters in Norway was small compared with the fighter reinforcements demanded by the French premier after the German assault on France. In an appearance at his own request at a Cabinet meeting on 15 May, and in his historic letter to the Air Ministry of 16 May 1940, Dowding set out the stark issues of survival or irremediable defeat. On 20 May the War Cabinet decided that no more fighter squadrons should leave the country. Providing fighter cover at long range during the withdrawal from Dunkirk provided successful combat experience for Dowding's men, but at the cost of further losses of aircraft and pilots. At this time a sympathetic working relationship between Dowding and his AOC No. 11 Group in south-east England, Air Vice-Marshal (later Air Chief Marshal Sir) Keith Park was confirmed and deepened in the summer and autumn of 1940. A similar sympathetic accord was established with his colleague, Lieutenant-General (later General) Sir Frederick Pile, GOC-in-C Anti-Aircraft Command.

The Battle of Britain was fought tactically at Group and Sector Operations Room level. But it is to Dowding that praise must go for his over-all mastery of the air weapon. The deployment of his forces, his rotation of squadrons which had been heavily engaged, his constant regard for reserves of aircraft and personnel, indicated skill of a high order. In addition to commanding the struggle by day for air superiority over south-east England, Dowding spent most nights in monitoring the development of airborne radar and other techniques to meet the threat of the night bomber. His complete personal commitment partly explains his failure to control the clash of tactics and personalities which developed between Park and Air Vice-Marshal Leigh-Mallory (AOC No. 12 Group) over the use of squadrons in big wing formation. Dowding was replaced at Fighter Command on 25 November 1940 by the deputy chief of air staff, Air Marshal Sholto Douglas (later Lord Douglas of Kirtleside). Dowding was undoubtedly very tired. He was also a victorious airman and an embarrassingly senior officer.

To many, Dowding's replacement so soon after his victory in Britain's first great air battle appeared ungrateful. Some unusual mark of recognition might have tempered the eventually inevitable decision to appoint a new commander for Fighter Command in its more offensive role. Dowding was persuaded by the prime minister to visit the United States on behalf of the Ministry of Aircraft Production. The trip was not successful. Dowding was inclined to put forward his own views which were not always in accord with those of Britain's permanent representatives there. On his return in June 1941 he was asked to prepare a dispatch on the Battle of Britain. This was ready before October, the date of his retirement as indicated to him by the Air Ministry.

The prime minister expressed 'indignation' when he learned of this intention and virtually commanded Dowding to accept an appointment in the Air Ministry involving the scrutiny of RAF establishments. At the same time he took possession of a book *Twelve Legions of Angels* which Dowding had submitted for clearance. The new appointment was not to Dowding's taste and before long the old arguments with the Air Ministry reappeared. At his own request he eventually retired in July 1942 but his book was suppressed under the wartime regulations until 1946.

In his retirement Dowding devoted himself to a study of spiritualism and theosophy. His nature had always been contemplative and philosophical. He published several books—*Many Mansions* (1943), *Lychgate* (1945), *God's Magic* (1946), and *The Dark Star* (1951). He wrote articles for newspapers and gave lectures on occult subjects. His second marriage in 1951 brought him a wife and companion who shared his beliefs. He gave up shooting and became a vegetarian.

As a young officer Dowding seemed set for an honourable but conventional soldier's life. Aviation opened new possibilities for his devoted spirit and inquiring mind. He became a dedicated airman, rising almost to the top of his profession. His stern sense of duty, added to his well-founded competence in practical flying matters, made him a formidable advocate for views strongly held. No easy compromiser or politician, he often aroused hostility, sometimes unwittingly. His vision was intense but narrow. His high moment was in the Battle of Britain. Few served their country more selflessly and courageously. His life had many bleak and lonely periods but his old age was mellow, surrounded, as he was, by the affection of family and friends. After the war Dowding became a legendary figure to the Battle of Britain pilots and one of his proudest moments was to receive a standing ovation from his so-called 'chicks' at the première of the film *Battle of Britain* in 1969. In his later years as a senior officer Dowding had an erect lean figure. He was dour in aspect with an almost expressionless face. This appearance coupled with his sparing use of speech had a daunting effect on some who met him for the first time. But a twinkle in the eye and a slight pursing of the lips showed his inner kindliness and humour to those of whom he approved. He died at his home in Kent 15 February 1970. His ashes are interred in Westminster Abbey. Dowding was appointed CMG in 1919, CB in 1928, KCB in 1933, GCVO in 1937, and GCB during the Battle of Britain in 1940. In 1943 a barony was conferred on him and he took the style of his old headquarters, Bentley Priory.

His first marriage was in 1918 to Clarice Maud Vancourt, daughter of Captain John Williams of the Indian Army and the widow of an army officer, who had one daughter by her first marriage; in January 1919 she gave birth to a son. She died suddenly in 1920. Dowding's second marriage was in 1951 to Muriel, widow of Pilot Officer Maxwell Whiting, RAF, and daughter of John Albino. Dowding was succeeded by his only child, Wing Commander Derek Hugh Tremenheere Dowding.

There is a pastel drawing (1939) by Sir W. Rothenstein in the Imperial War Museum, a portrait (1942) by Sir W. Russell at Bentley Priory, and one by F. Kenworthy-Browne in the possession of the family. A bronze by David Wynne was exhibited in 1968 at the National Portrait Gallery.

[*The Times*, 16 February 1970; Basil Collier, *Leader of the Few*, 1957; Robert Wright, *Dowding and the Battle of Britain*, 1969; private information.]

E. B. HASLAM

published 1981

DU MAURIER Dame Daphne

(1907–1989)

Novelist, was born 13 May 1907 at 24 Cumberland Terrace, Regent's Park, London, the second of three daughters (there were no sons) of Sir Gerald

Hubert Edward Busson du Maurier, actor-manager, and his wife Muriel, actress, daughter of Harry Beaumont, solicitor. She was educated mainly at home by governesses, of whom one, Maud Waddell, was highly influential, and afterwards spent three terms at a finishing school near Paris.

She began writing stories and poetry in her childhood and was encouraged by her father, with whom she had a very close relationship. He longed for her to emulate her grandfather, George du Maurier, artist and author of three novels, including the best-selling *Trilby* (1894). But the circumstances of her upbringing, with its constant emphasis on pleasure and distraction, called for self-discipline of a kind she did not manage to exert until she was twenty-two, when she finally completed several short stories. The first published story was 'And now to God the Father', which appeared in the *Bystander* (May 1929), a magazine edited by her uncle. It was a cynical view of society as she saw it.

Her ambition then was to write a novel. She settled down to do so in the winter of 1929–30 at Bodinnick-by-Fowey in Cornwall, where her parents had bought Ferryside to be their country home. Here she wrote *The Loving Spirit*, the story of four generations of a Cornish family, which was published to considerable acclaim by Heinemann in February 1931. She immediately wrote second and third novels which confounded expectations by differing radically from her first, but it was her fourth book, *Gerald*, a frank biography of her father, written when he died in 1934, which made the greatest impact. It was published by (Sir) Victor Gollancz, with whom she then began a long and fruitful partnership.

Gollancz recognized that her strengths lay in narrative drive and the evocation of atmosphere. He encouraged her to develop these and the result was *Jamaica Inn* (1936), an instant best seller. At this point in her career she was obliged, as an army wife, to go abroad, to Egypt, with her husband, Major (Sir) Frederick Arthur Montague ('Boy') Browning, the son of Frederick Henry Browning. The latter ran various businesses and also worked for MI5, as well as having a distinguished army career. They had married in 1932 and in 1933 had a daughter, Tessa, who was later to marry the son of the first Viscount Montgomery of Alamein (her second marriage).

This was a deeply unhappy period in Daphne du Maurier's life—she was an untypical army wife, being very anti-social, and she loathed Egypt and was profoundly homesick—but it produced *Rebecca* (1938). This was meant to be a psychological study of jealousy, and was based on her own feelings of jealousy towards a former fiancée of her husband's, Jan Ricardo, but was hailed as a romantic novel in the tradition of *Jane Eyre*. She was astonished by the success of *Rebecca*—hardback copies in Britain alone passed the million mark in 1992—and mystified by the readers' interpretation of the novel. In 1941 she produced *Frenchman's Creek* and in 1943 *Hungry Hill.*

In 1943, while her husband was away fighting in the war, she went to live in Cornwall with her three children, daughters Tessa and Flavia (1937), and son Christian (1940). She took on the lease of Menabilly, a house (owned by the Rashleigh family) with which she had become obsessed. The war years affected her marriage deeply and adversely. She felt estranged from her husband, in spite of her love for him, and wrote a play, *The Years Between* (performed in 1944), about how war affected marriages.

After the war her husband became comptroller of the household and treasurer to Princess Elizabeth, which meant that he lived in London while she stayed in Cornwall, with only weekends shared. This led to tensions which heavily influenced her work. Outwardly charming, witty, and lighthearted, she was struggling inwardly with feelings of rejection and uncertainty about her personal life. In two collections of short stories, *The Apple Tree* (1952) and *The Breaking Point* (1959), she expressed the extent of her confusion and frustration. These stories are of great biographical significance.

Her career flourished, though not precisely in the way she wished. *My Cousin Rachel* appeared in 1951. Her novels translated well into films and *Jamaica Inn* (1939), *Rebecca* (1940), *Frenchman's Creek* (1944), and *Hungry Hill* (1946) were notable successes. Her short story, *The Birds*, became famous in the hands of (Sir) Alfred Hitchcock in 1963. *Rebecca* had made her a popular, worldwide, best-selling author, but she felt her later, more serious, work was not given its due. In *The Scapegoat* (1957) she was writing at a deeper level, but the novel was treated as a romantic thriller. She turned to biography, partly in an attempt to show she could do serious work, though it was also true that she had temporarily lost the creative urge to write fiction. *The Infernal World of Branwell Brontë* (1960) gave her tremendous satisfaction, and was well researched, but did little to alter her image.

In 1965 her husband died. Her grief, together with the distress caused by her fear that her imagination was deserting her, made her depressed. The news that she could not renew her lease on Menabilly again added to her misery but in 1969, the year in which she was appointed DBE, she moved to Kilmarth, the dower house of Menabilly, and wrote *The House on the Strand* (1969), which restored her confidence. Her last novel, *Rule Britannia* (1972), destroyed it again. She was unable to write any more fiction afterwards. In 1977 she wrote a slim volume of autobiography (*Growing Pains*), which she regretted producing. In 1981 she had a nervous breakdown and then a mild coronary. The last eight years of her life were spent mourning her lost talent, without which she felt her days were empty and meaningless.

Daphne du Maurier was in her youth an extremely beautiful woman, of medium height, fine-boned and slender, with thick blonde hair and arresting eyes of a startlingly bright, clear blue. She was a very complex person, well aware, through constant self-analysis, that she acted out her life to an extraordinary degree. Her novels were her fantasies and seemed more real to her than her actual life. She needed them, to give expression to what she called, through her fascination with Jungian theory, her 'no. 2' self. This was a darker, violent self, which she suppressed in a most determined manner. Part of this suppression was sexual: she believed she should have been born a boy and that she had to keep this masculine side of herself hidden, which she did, except while writing, for most of her life. The problem of her life she herself defined as 'a fear of reality'. Only when she was alone, and especially alone in Menabilly, was she able to still this fear.

Her work has been consistently underrated, in spite of critical acknowledgement that *Rebecca* and *The Scapegoat*, at least, are of literary worth. Her influence on the growth of 'women's writing' as a separate division, and on writing for the cinema (eight of her novels and stories were made into successful films), was significant in the 1930s and 1940s, but it is as a popular novelist that her position remains secure, especially among the young. She died at her home in Par, Cornwall, 19 April 1989.

[Margaret Forster, *Daphne du Maurier*, 1993; private information; family papers.]

MARGARET FORSTER

published 1996

DU PRÉ Jacqueline Mary

(1945–1987)

Cellist, was born 26 January 1945 in Oxford, the younger daughter and second of three children of Derek du Pré, financial writer and editor, who became secretary to the Institute of Cost and Works Accountants, and his wife, Iris Greep, who taught piano at the Royal Academy of Music. The family name had twelfth-century origins in Jersey. In 1948 the family went to settle in Purley, a suburb south of London. At four years of age, Jacqueline heard a cello for the first time and wanted to have such an instrument; she was given one for her fifth birthday. Her mother soon recognized that her daughter showed unusual talent; even when singing, neither her intonation nor her rhythms could be faulted. She arranged lessons and jotted down little tunes for her. With such support, coupled with Jacqueline's own outstanding talent and enthusiasm, the girl's early music lessons could not but succeed. After one year the six-year-old Jacqueline began studying at the London Cello School, directed by Herbert Walenn; when seven, she gave her first public performance at a children's concert.

The well-known teacher William Pleeth entered her life when she was ten; she was to stay with him for the next seven years. It was from him, she said later, that she learned to love the big concertos she was to play with unmatched brio, as well as the chamber music for which she always had a particular affection. She had a private tutor for general schooling. When she was eleven Jacqueline du Pré won London's first Suggia gift, an international cello prize, a remarkable result in a competition which set its age limit at twenty-one. From then on her tuition was financially secure, enabling her to study in Paris with Paul Tortelier, who predicted a great future for her. After being awarded all possible prizes at the Guildhall School of Music, London, including the gold medal 'for the outstanding instrumental student of the year', Jacqueline du Pré gave her first recital in March 1961, at the Wigmore Hall in a sonata programme, accompanied by Ernest Lush. This recital brought her to the attention of the public and of professional musicians, and from then on her career was assured.

In her first appearance in a chamber music recital for the National Trust Concert Society, she was joined by Yehudi (later Baron) Menuhin and his sister Hephzibah at Osterley Park. In March 1962 she played with the BBC Symphony Orchestra, at London's South Bank, Sir Edward Elgar's Cello Concerto, which she was to repeat at two Promenade Concerts under Sir Malcolm Sargent and which was to become the work with which her audiences would associate her for years to come. She then launched into a career that was to take her to the Continent and the USA. In 1966 there followed an intense time of study with Mstislav Rostropovich at the Conservatoire of Moscow, from where she wrote to Yehudi Menuhin: 'Over the past two years I have felt extremely lost with my work and generally fatigued by it. Now, under Rostropovich's tuition, I am finding a new freshness in it, and the old desire to go ahead with what I love so deeply is returning.' From this honest declaration it would appear that her meteoric rise to fame had taken its toll. The following year saw her return to London for concerts with the BBC Symphony Orchestra. An extensive tour of the United States and Canada further established the fame which had followed her first visit in 1965. American critics wrote about 'waves of intensity and love', her 'awesome gifts', her 'dazzling technique'. Beyond her cultivated and deeply musical approach to her playing she almost compelled the music to yield its utmost intensity, passion, and emotional abandon and was at one with it.

A first casual meeting with the young Argentinian-born Israeli pianist Daniel Barenboim (only son of Enrique and Aida Barenboim, pianists) turned out to lead not only to a musical partnership which was to become legendary but to Jacqueline adopting his Jewish faith before their marriage on 15 June 1967 in Israel, a country then at war. The following day they were the soloists in a concert with the Israel Philharmonic in Tel Aviv. On the programme were Schumann's Cello Concerto, which Barenboim conducted, and a Mozart Piano Concerto which he played, the conductor being Zubin Mehta. From then on the young Barenboims were involved in three musical careers: his, hers, and theirs. Their knowledge of each other's interpretive ideas was almost uncanny; they thought as one and their performances radiated this complete understanding. Though visual opposites—Jacqueline tall, with long, flowing, blonde hair and lively light-blue eyes, Daniel slim and slightly shorter with dark curly hair and intense brown eyes—they were beautiful to behold as a pair; their exuberance and joy in music-making and their deep respect for composer and score, together with their love of performance, never failed to reach the audience. Their musical partnership, which began at great speed, was to last for just four years, but this short period was filled with recitals, concerts, and recordings, the latter embracing a large catalogue, mainly on the EMI label, with which Jacqueline du Pré had an exclusive agreement. She recorded virtually the entire cello concerto repertoire with the greatest orchestras and conductors of her time, as well as numerous sonatas and other cello pieces with eminent pianists, amongst them Gerald Moore.

When in the autumn of 1973 odd symptoms, which had begun to disturb her playing two years earlier, were diagnosed as signs of the beginning of the crippling illness multiple sclerosis, which allows only brief periods of remission, all happiness and hope for the future were taken away and the musical world was stunned. Jacqueline du Pré took this fatal blow without complaint. With typical spirit she taught, gave master classes, cooked, and, whenever possible, played chamber music with her husband and friends. Her generosity of character and unselfish nature made her an ideal chamber music player. She became a familiar and beloved sight in her wheelchair at many London concerts, and she would ask people to come and play to her. Alexander Goehr wrote his *Romanze* for her (1968).

She was appointed OBE in 1976, was a fellow of the Guildhall School of Music (1975) and the Royal College of Music (1977), and was an honorary fellow of the Royal Academy of Music (1974) and of St Hilda's College, Oxford (1984). She won the gold medal of the Guildhall School of Music and the Queen's prize (both 1960), the City of London midsummer prize

(1975), and the Incorporated Society of Musicians' musician of the year award (1980). She had honorary doctorates from Salford (1978), London (1979), the Open University (1979), Sheffield (1980), Leeds (1982), Durham (1983), and Oxford (1984). She had no children. In her final years she was saddened by her husband's relationship with Helena Bachkirev and the birth of their two children. At times she gave way to depression. She died 19 October 1987 in her flat at Chepstow Villas, and was buried at the Jewish cemetery in Golders Green.

[Carol Easton, *Jacqueline du Pré*, 1989; private information; personal knowledge.]

Yehudi Menuhin

published 1996

EDWARD VIII

(1894–1972)

King of Great Britain, Ireland, and the British Dominions beyond the seas, Emperor of India—the only British sovereign to relinquish the crown voluntarily—was born at White Lodge, Richmond Park, 23 June 1894, the eldest of the family of five sons and one daughter of the then Duke and Duchess of York. With the death of Queen Victoria in 1901 his parents became Prince and Princess of Wales, and in 1910, when Edward VII died, King George V and Queen Mary. As their eldest son Prince Edward was from birth in the direct line of succession, and of the seven names (Edward Albert Christian George Andrew Patrick David) given to him at his baptism four were those of British patron saints. In the family he was always known as David.

Though in most respects pampered by Fate, he was unlucky in the inability of his parents to communicate easily with their children, who consequently suffered from a lack of human warmth and encouragement in early life. Their father, though kind-hearted, was a martinet in his treatment of them, and their mother was deficient in the normal maternal instincts. Nor did the man chosen to be their principal tutor, Henry Peter Hansell, make up for what their parents failed to give, since he too was a rather aloof and limited character.

Edward was an intelligent child, endowed with curiosity and a powerful memory. Though it is unlikely that he would ever have developed as a scholar, his mental gifts deserved imaginative teaching. As it was, he grew up with a poor grounding of knowledge, no taste at all for any books worth the name, and unable even to spell properly. Only as a linguist were his attainments equal to his position, since he learnt French and German in childhood, and later acquired a fluent command of Spanish.

Other valuable qualities belonged to him naturally. Despite his small stature he had exceptional good looks, which never lost their boyish appeal. He had boundless energy and zest, and was full of courage. Above all, he had a spontaneous charm of manner which drew people to him and put them at their ease. His personality would have been remarkable even if he had not been royal; allied to his princely status it was irresistible.

In 1907 he was sent to Osborne, and two years later to Dartmouth. While he was there his father became King, and he himself heir apparent to the throne. On his sixteenth birthday he was created Prince of Wales, and on 13 July 1911 became the first English holder of the title to be formally invested at Caernarvon castle. The ceremony was stage-managed by the constable of the castle, David Lloyd George (later Earl Lloyd-George of Dwyfor) who personally taught him a few words of Welsh to utter when he was presented to the crowd at Queen Eleanor's gate.

The following year he went into residence at Magdalen College, Oxford, but there was little to show for his brief university career. During vacations he paid two visits to Germany and one to Scandinavia. In 1914 he was anyway due to leave Oxford at the end of the academic year, to begin a period of service in the army; but in the event he did so as Britain was entering the most terrible war in her history.

Commissioned in the Grenadier Guards, he asked only to be allowed to fight alongside his contemporaries, but was told that this would not be possible, because of the danger that he might be captured and used as a hostage. Soon, however, he managed to get himself posted to the staff of the British Expeditionary Force's commander in France, and thereafter spent most of the war abroad, attached to various headquarters but essentially serving as a visitor of troops and general morale-raiser. He lived frugally and, though provided with a Daimler, preferred to travel around on a green army bicycle, covering hundreds of miles. His desire always was to be at the scene of action, and he had a narrow escape when visiting front-line positions before the battle of Loos.

Given his enforced role as a non-combatant he could hardly have done more to share the ordeal of other young men of his generation. Yet he was mortified that he could not share it more fully, and genuinely embarrassed when he was awarded the MC. The humility of his attitude enhanced the value of the work he did, which was never forgotten by the countless ordinary soldiers to whom he brought understanding and cheer.

His war service was a crucially formative episode in his own life, vastly broadening his range of human experience and showing how good he was at establishing contact with his fellow-men, whatever their backgrounds. As well as meeting people of all classes from the United Kingdom, he also got to know Allied troops, including Americans, and a variety of British subjects from overseas. While visiting the Middle East in the spring of 1916 he met Australians and New Zealanders evacuated from Gallipoli. At the time of the armistice in 1918 he was with the Canadian Corps in France, and after the armistice was attached to the Australian Corps in Belgium.

Thus he was unconsciously introduced to the next and most fruitful phase of his career, which began with his visits to Newfoundland, Canada, and the United States in the summer and autumn of 1919. Lloyd George, now prime minister, was convinced that 'the appearance of the popular Prince of Wales in far corners of the Empire might do more . . . than half a dozen solemn Imperial Conferences'. So it proved. The Canadian tour was a triumphal success, in Quebec no less than in the English-speaking provinces. Wherever he went the response was overwhelming. In Alberta he bought a ranch for himself—an admirable gesture, though a source of trouble to him later.

His first visit to the United States was equally successful, though briefer and far less extensive. In Washington, he called on the stricken President Wilson, and in New York was given a ticker-tape welcome as he drove to the City Hall to receive the freedom. Yet it was not such important occasions that lingered most persistently in his mind after his return to England, but rather the song 'A Pretty Girl is like a Melody', which he had heard at the Ziegfeld Follies. His endless whistling of this 'damned tune' caused annoyance to his father, and shows that American culture had made an immediate conquest.

In 1920 he visited New Zealand and Australia, travelling there in the battleship *Renown*, by way of the Panama canal, Hawaii, and Fiji. Again, he carried all before him. In 1921–2 he toured India, where nationalists had been disappointed by the modest scope of the Montagu–Chelmsford reforms, and where the Amritsar massacre was still a recent memory. Despite the unfavourable circumstances, he made an excellent impression on such Indians as he was allowed to meet, many of whom were quoted by a British observer as saying: 'If only all you Europeans were like him!' In many places large and friendly crowds turned out to greet him, defying the Congress boycott of his visit.

The same voyage took him to Nepal, Burma, Malaya, Hong Kong, Japan, the Philippines, Borneo, Ceylon, and Egypt. On his return to London after eight months' absence there was a banquet in his honour at Guildhall, at which his health was eloquently proposed by Lloyd George—the last official act of his premiership.

This intensive travelling during the early post-war years was not a flash in the pan, but set the pattern for his subsequent way of life as Prince of Wales. In all but three years until his accession he spent long periods outside Britain. Hardly any part of the Empire, however small or remote, failed to receive at least one visit from him, and he was also welcomed in many foreign countries. Particularly noteworthy were his South American tours in 1925 and 1931, which inspired the greatest enthusiasm in a region traditionally important to Britain, though much neglected by British public figures. (A by-product of the second tour was the Ibero–American Institute of Great Britain, founded under his auspices, which led in turn to the creation of the British Council in 1935.)

At home, too, he was very busy and mobile, giving special attention to ex-servicemen and young people. In a period of mass unemployment and widespread social deprivation there might be little he could do to help the victims, but at least he went out of his way to talk to them, and it was obvious that they had his sympathy.

For all his exertions in the public interest, his life was by no means all work. While touring overseas, no less than in Britain, he would always devote a lot of his time to games and sport, and at the end of the most arduous day he was usually eager to dance into the small hours. His daylight recreations could be dangerous—after repeated spills and fractures he was prevailed upon to give up steeplechasing, only to take to flying instead—but in the long run his late nights were more harmful to him. A tendency to unpunctuality and moodiness was certainly made worse by lack of sleep.

As he moved from youth to middle age the strain of his life began to tell upon a nature that was nervous as well as physically robust; and at the same time, inevitably, he was becoming rather spoilt by the universal adulation to which he was exposed. Above all he seemed increasingly solitary, and without any firm base to his existence.

From 1919 he had his own London establishment at York House, St James's Palace, and in 1929 he obtained from his father the 'grace and favour' use of Fort Belvedere, a small architectural folly near Windsor (originally built for the Duke of Cumberland in the 1750s, but improved by Sir Jeffry Wyatville, in the reign of George IV). 'The Fort' became his favourite residence, where he could entertain a few friends at weekends, and in whose garden he invested much of his own—and his guests'—hard labour. But something vital was missing, as no one knew better than himself.

While his brothers were acquiring wives, the world's most eligible bachelor remained single. His natural craving for domesticity was satisfied only by a succession of affairs with married women. For many years he was very closely attached to Mrs (Freda) Dudley Ward, and his love for her was not fundamentally affected by passing affairs with Lady (Thelma) Furness and others. But through Lady Furness he became acquainted with her friend and fellow-American, Mrs Simpson (died 1986), and within a few years acquaintance had turned into the supreme passion of his life.

Wallis Simpson, daughter of Teakle Wallis Warfield who died when she was a few months old, came from Baltimore, Maryland, where she was brought up as a rather impoverished member of a family with pride of ancestry on both sides. When her first marriage (to Lieutenant Earl Winfield Spencer, of the US Navy, who became an alcoholic) ended in divorce, she married an Anglo-American, Ernest Simpson (who had a shipping business in England), with whom she lived comfortably in London. For a time they were together friends of the Prince, but when it became apparent that he wanted nothing less than to make Wallis his wife, Simpson resigned himself to divorce.

Her attraction, so far as it can be defined, owed much to her vivacity and wit, her sophisticated taste, and her ability to make a house feel like a home. She and the Prince shared a mid-Atlantic outlook—he being a child of Old-World privilege excited by American informality, she an east coast American with a hankering for the Old World and its gracious living. They met, as it were, half-way.

When George V died, on 20 January 1936, Edward came to the throne in the strong hope that he would be able to make Wallis Queen. This may, indeed, have been his principal motive for accepting a charge which he had often said, privately, he would rather be spared. Impatient of ritual and routine, he knew that his temperament would be less well suited to the role of King than to that of Prince of Wales.

There was, indeed, much that needed changing in the royal set-up, and it is possible that Edward VIII might have had some success as a reforming monarch if he had reigned for a fair number of years, with his mind on the job. No judgement can confidently be made either way on the strength of his brief reign, during which he was largely distracted by his anxiety about Wallis and their future. As it was, he merely gave offence to old courtiers and retainers by relatively trifling changes, and caused misgivings in official quarters by his casual attitude to state papers.

The public, however, neither knew nor cared about such matters, and he was a popular King. There was a shock when, in July, a loaded revolver was thrown in front of his horse on Constitution Hill, and relief that he had come to no harm. Later in the year he was cheered lustily in the Mall by the Jarrow hunger marchers at the end of their pilgrimage.

Meanwhile the so-called 'King's matter' was unfolding in a way destined to bring his reign to a swift close. It was only in Britain that his intimacy with Mrs Simpson was a secret. When, during the summer, she accompanied him on a cruise in the Adriatic and eastern Mediterranean, in the private yacht *Nahlin*, full reports appeared in the foreign press, more especially in the United States, with the correct conclusions either stated or implied. The British press remained silent from a sense of loyalty, but it could not be long before the story would break at home. At the end of October the Simpsons' divorce suit was due to come up, and this might well arouse speculation even though it was to be heard in a provincial court.

On 20 October, therefore, the prime minister, Stanley Baldwin (later Earl Baldwin of Bewdley), saw the King by request and raised with him for the first time the question of his relations with Mrs Simpson. At this meeting Baldwin tried to enlist the King's co-operation in persuading her to withdraw her divorce petition, but to no avail. The King would not co-operate, and at the end of the month a decree *nisi* was duly granted.

An interlude followed during which (on 3 November) the King opened Parliament—driving there in a closed car rather than in the traditional open carriage—and inspected the fleet at Portsmouth. But on 16 November there was another meeting with Baldwin, at which the King stated his determination to marry Mrs Simpson, despite the prime minister's advice that the marriage would not receive the country's approval. On 18–19 November he visited the distressed areas of south Wales, where he made the much-quoted remark about the unemployed: 'Something must be done to find them work.' His hearers little knew how soon he would be unemployed himself.

On 25 November he saw Baldwin again, having meanwhile been persuaded by Esmond Harmsworth (later Viscount Rothermere) to suggest that he might marry Mrs Simpson morganatically. This was a disastrous error, since it could be said to carry the admission that she was unfit to be Queen.

It is probable, though unprovable, that majority opinion in Britain and throughout the Empire would have been against the idea of Mrs Simpson as Queen, though whether most people would have maintained their opposition, knowing that the price would be to lose Edward as King, is more doubtful. Ecclesiastical anathemas counted for much less, even then, than those who pronounced them liked to believe, and objections to Mrs Simpson on social grounds were likely to be much stronger in privileged circles than among the people at large. But the idea of a morganatic marriage would almost certainly have been less generally acceptable.

In any case it would have required legislation, and this the government was not prepared to introduce. Moreover, the leader of the opposition, Clement (later Earl) Attlee, told Baldwin that Labour would not approve of Mrs Simpson as Queen, or of a morganatic marriage; and similar, though rather less clear-cut, views were expressed by the dominion prime ministers. When, therefore, the facts were at last given to the British public on 3 December, the crisis was virtually over. If the King had no option but to renounce either Mrs Simpson or the throne, the only possible outcome —granted the man he was—was abdication.

He would have liked to make a broadcast, taking his subjects into his confidence, before reaching a final decision; but when Baldwin told him that this would be unconstitutional and divisive, he at once abandoned the idea. Even (Sir) Winston Churchill's plea that he should stand and fight went unheeded. On 10 December he signed an instrument of abdication, and the following day ceased to be King when he gave his assent to the necessary Bill. That evening he delivered his farewell broadcast from Windsor Castle, containing the celebrated words: 'I have found it impossible to carry the heavy burden of responsibility, and to discharge my duties as King as I would wish to do, without the help and support of the woman I love.'

Later the same night he crossed to France, and the rest of his life was spent in almost permanent exile. It was some months before Mrs Simpson's divorce became absolute, but in June 1937 she and Edward were married, at a chateau in Touraine, by a Church of England parson acting without authority from his bishop. No member of the royal family came to the wedding, which was attended only by a few old friends, including Walter Monckton (later Viscount Monckton of Brenchley), the attorney-general to the Duchy of Cornwall, and a busy go-between during the abdication crisis, and Major E. D. ('Fruity') Metcalfe, who was best man. There were no children of the marriage.

The new King, George VI (formerly Duke of York), had some of the qualities of his father, George V, but hardly any of his elder brother's—a fact of which he was painfully conscious. From the moment of his accession he seems to have been haunted by the fear that the ex-King would overshadow him, and this fear was undoubtedly shared by his wife and other members of his entourage. It was felt to be essential that the ex-King should be kept out of England, out of the limelight, out of popular favour; and self-righteousness came to the aid of self-interest, in the form of a myth that the Prince's abdication and marriage had brought disgrace upon the British monarchy.

Though it is unlikely that George VI was familiar with *The Apple Cart* by G. B. Shaw, he was nevertheless immediately alive to the theoretical danger that his brother might, unless made a royal duke, be tempted to stand for the House of Commons, in the manner of Shaw's King Magnus. The first act of his reign was, therefore, to confer upon Edward the title of Duke of Windsor. But under letters patent issued the following year the title Royal Highness was restricted to him, and expressly denied to his wife and descendants, if any. This studied insult to the Duchess cannot have been solely due to uncertainty about the duration of the marriage, since it was maintained by George VI and his successor throughout the thirty-five years that the Windsors were man and wife (and into the Duchess's widowhood).

As a result relations between the Duke and his family were poisoned, and further bitterness was caused by an indecent wrangle over money. No provision was made for the Duke in the Civil List, but the King eventually agreed that he should receive a net £21,000 a year, which was mainly interest of the sale of Sandringham and Balmoral to royal trustees, at a valuation which favoured the King rather than the Duke. An attempt to make the agreement conditional upon the Duke's willingness to stay abroad at the King's pleasure was only with difficulty resisted. (In addition to the income thus assured, the Duke had capital deriving from Duchy of Cornwall revenue unspent while he was Prince of Wales.)

Between their marriage and World War II the Windsors lived in France, but in October 1937 they paid an ill-advised visit to Germany as guests of the Nazi government. The Duke's declared reason for going was to see how unemployment had been tackled and to study labour relations, but of course the Nazis made the most of the visit for propaganda purposes, as he should have foreseen. At a meeting with Hitler the Duke gave no indication (according to the interpreter) of any sympathy with Nazi ideology, and there is, indeed, virtually no evidence that he had any such sympathy. But he had considerable affection for the German people, with whom he had many links, and above all he had the feeling—overwhelmingly prevalent at the time—that another war would be an unimaginable calamity.

When war came, however, he at once offered to return to Britain without conditions, and at first was offered a choice of two jobs, one of which, that of assistant regional commissioner in Wales, would have enabled him to stay in Britain. But when he accepted it, no doubt unexpectedly, it was promptly withdrawn, and he was then obliged to take the other job, that of liaison officer with the French army (which involved a drop in rank from field-marshal to major-general). He did it well, among other things sending home a remarkably prescient report of French weakness on the Ardennes front. But when France fell in the summer of 1940 he and the Duchess had to escape as best they might.

They made their own way to Madrid, whence the Duke was able to communicate with the British government, now headed by his old friend Winston Churchill. His requests for suitable employment at home, and the barest recognition for the Duchess (not that she should have royal status, but merely that his family should receive her) were turned down, even Churchill having in the circumstances neither time nor inclination to champion the Duke's cause against Buckingham Palace. He then reluctantly accepted the governorship of the Bahamas, and on 1 August sailed from Lisbon, as agreed, despite an elaborate plot engineered by Ribbentrop to keep him in Europe. Though at this time he undoubtedly believed that there would have to be a negotiated peace, he did not despair of his country and had no desire to be a German puppet.

In the Bahamas the Windsors were on the whole a conspicuous success, in a post which was both difficult and unpleasant. The Duke stood up to the 'Bay Street boys' (as the local white oligarchy was called), achieved some economic improvement in the neglected outer islands, and dealt effectively with a serious outbreak of rioting for which he was in no way to blame. In December 1940 he had the first of about a dozen wartime meetings with Franklin D. Roosevelt, at the president's invitation, and the two men got on particularly well. The authorities in London tried very hard to prevent the meeting, and in general did not at all favour visits by the Windsors to the United States, though a few were grudgingly permitted. The Duke's immense popularity there was regarded at home as invidious and embarrassing, rather than as a major potential asset to Britain.

In May 1945 the Windsors left the Bahamas and returned to Europe, no better alternative having been offered to the Duke than the governorship of Bermuda. The rest of his life was spent chiefly in France, where he was treated as an honoured guest. Partly to repair his finances—which had suffered from mismanagement, and more especially from a costly and futile attempt to strike oil on his Canadian ranch—he turned to authorship. With the help of 'ghosts' he wrote his memoirs, which were serialized in *Life* magazine and then published in book form as *A King's Story* (1951). This became a world bestseller, and was later turned into a film. He also published two much slighter books—*Family Album* (1960) and *The Crown and the People 1902–1953* (1953)—and two more were written, though unpublished at the time of his death.

Because of the continued ostracism of the Duchess, his post-war visits to Britain were brief and rare. On 28 May 1972 he died at his house in the Bois de Boulogne, from throat cancer. His body was then flown back to England and lay in state for three days in St George's chapel, Windsor, while 57,000 people came—many over long distances—to pay their respects. On 5 June there was a funeral service in the chapel, and afterwards the Duke was buried in the royal mausoleum at Frogmore. The Duchess was present as the Queen's guest.

Though King for less than a year, Edward VIII will rank as an important figure in the history of the British monarchy. During the dangerous and volatile period which followed World War I, when republicanism was sweeping the world, he and his father succeeded, in their very different ways, in giving new strength to an old tradition. Neither could have succeeded so well without the other, and the contrast between them was of great value to the monarchy.

Edward will also be remembered as a character out of the ordinary. His faults were substantial, and aggravated by the circumstances of his life. His mind, inadequately trained, was incapable of deep reflection and prone to erratic judgement. He could on occasion be selfish, mean, inconsiderate, ungrateful, or even callous. Yet his virtues more than compensated for his faults. He was a brave man, morally as well as physically, and his nature was basically affectionate. He had a marvellous gift for conversing easily with people, and for making charming, unpompous speeches off the cuff. There was about him the indefinable aura known as star quality.

In a sense he was a harbinger of the Americanization of Europe. Superficially, his values were more those of the New World than of the Old. Playing the bagpipes wearing a white kilt or golfing in plus-eights, he seemed more like a Hollywood representation of a Scottish laird or English gentleman than like the genuine article. His anyway slightly Cockney accent became overlaid with American intonations (in his farewell broadcast he referred to the *Dook* of York), and he also acquired a number of American habits long before he was married to an American.

Yet at heart he was more a creature of the Old World than he appeared to be, or probably realized himself. What a Labour MP, Josiah (later Lord) Wedgwood, said at the time of the abdication—that he had given up his royalty to remain a man—was only a half-truth. Though he had, indeed, given up his kingship, he never ceased to be royal. Had it been otherwise, there would have been no problem about the duchess's status. All the same, he surely deserves honour for the chivalrousness of his decision to abdicate, no less than for the perfect constitutional propriety with which it was carried out; and above all for his pioneering work as Prince of Wales.

There are many portraits of Edward, representing almost every phase of his life. Only a selection can be mentioned here. A caricature appeared in *Vanity Fair* on 21 June 1911 (the original is in the National Portrait Gallery). The first full-length portrait in oil was painted by Sir A. S. Cope in 1912, the year after Edward's investiture as Prince of Wales. It is in the Royal Collection, which also contains, from the same period, a sketch (head only) by Sir John Lavery. A charcoal drawing by J. S. Sargent (*circa* 1918) belonged to the Duchess of Windsor. In 1919 H. L. Oakley painted a full-length profile, and in *circa* 1920 R. G. Eves a half-length portrait in uniform. Both of these are in the National Portrait Gallery. A full-length portrait in golfing dress (1928), by Sir William Orpen, hangs in the Royal and Ancient Golf Club, St Andrews; and a full-length portrait in Welsh

Guards uniform (1936) done by W. R. Sickert from photographs, in the Beaverbrook Art Gallery, Fredericton, NB, Canada. A full-length portrait in Garter robes by Sir James Gunn (*circa* 1954) was in the Duchess of Windsor's possession, as were a number of portraits by the French artist A. Drian. Apart from paintings and drawings, there is a bronze statuette by Charles S. Jagger (1922) in the National Museum of Wales at Cardiff, and a marble bust by Charles Hartwell (*circa* 1920–4) belonging to the Corporation of London.

[Hector Bolitho, *Edward VIII*, 1937; Compton Mackenzie, *The Windsor Tapestry*, 1938; Duke of Windsor, *A King's Story*, 1951; Duchess of Windsor, *The Heart Has Its Reasons*, 1956; John W. Wheeler-Bennett, *King George VI*, 1958; Frances Donaldson, *Edward VIII*, 1974; Michael Bloch, *The Duke of Windsor's War*, 1982, and *Operation Willi*, 1984; private information.]

John Grigg

published 1986

ELIOT Thomas Stearns

(1888–1965)

Poet, playwright, critic, editor, and publisher, was born in St Louis, Missouri, 26 September 1888. He was the youngest son in the family of seven children of Henry Ware Eliot, a successful industrialist, and his wife, Charlotte Chauncy Stearns, a woman of literary interests. His mother wrote two books, one a biography (1904) of her father-in-law, William Greenleaf Eliot, who after completing his course at the Harvard Divinity School had gone in 1834 to settle in St Louis. He founded the first Unitarian church in the city, and was also the founder of Washington University there. But for a humility which he transmitted to his grandson, it would have been named Eliot University. Mrs Eliot's second book (privately printed in London in 1926 at her son's behest) was a dramatic poem about Savonarola. A respect for family tradition and a predisposition to intense religious experience may have come to Eliot through her.

His family, as Eliot wrote, 'zealously guarded' its New England connections. He himself, after spending seven years (1898–1903) at Smith Academy (another of his grandfather's foundations) in St Louis, was sent back to Milton Academy in Massachusetts in 1905, and then in 1906 to Harvard University. He completed in three years the four-year course, and received his BA in 1909. He wrote later that in St Louis he had felt himself to be a New Englander, but that in New England he felt himself to be a Southwesterner. He was later to experience, with ambivalent feelings, further deracination.

He planned at this time to become a professor of philosophy, and to that end entered the Harvard Graduate School. In 1910 he took his MA and then went to the Sorbonne for a year. On his return to Harvard he began to write a doctoral dissertation on the philosophy of F. H. Bradley. The conception of 'immediate experience' as a means of transcending appearance and achieving the 'Absolute' had an effect upon Eliot's own thought, but other influences had also begun to make themselves felt. At Harvard his principal teacher was Irving Babbitt, who in a notable book excoriated *Rousseau and Romanticism*. Eliot's anti-romantic tendencies perhaps derived from him. Another intense interest came in 1908 when he was introduced to the poetry of Jules Laforgue, of whom he would say that 'he was the first to teach me how to speak, to teach me the poetic possibilities of my own idiom of speech'. A little later he studied intensively the languages Sanskrit and Pali, and read a good deal in Indic religion, admiring especially its concern with diligently working out a means of transcending individual selfhood. Gradually these interests were to coalesce.

While still an undergraduate Eliot had contributed a few poems to the *Harvard Advocate*, the later ones exercises in Laforguian irony. In 1910 he composed his first mature poem, 'The Love Song of J. Alfred Prufrock'. In 1914, after having assisted in philosophy courses at Harvard, he was awarded a travelling fellowship by the university. He went to study for the summer in Marburg, but the outbreak of war in August obliged him to make his way, in a less leisurely fashion than he had intended, to Oxford. He continued there, at Merton College, under the supervision of Harold Joachim, his study of Bradley's *Appearance and Reality.*

The year 1914–15 proved to be pivotal for Eliot. He came to three interrelated decisions. The first was to give up the appearance of the philosopher for the reality of the poet, though he equivocated a little about this by continuing to write reviews for philosophical journals for some time thereafter. The second was to marry, and the third to settle in England, the war notwithstanding. He was helped to all three decisions by Ezra Pound, whom he met in September 1914. Pound had come to England in 1908 and was convinced (though he changed his mind later) that this was the country most congenial to the literary life. He not only encouraged Eliot to marry and settle, but he succeeded (where Eliot had failed) in having some of Eliot's poems published. The first to appear was 'Prufrock' in *Poetry* (Chicago) for June 1915. This was a bizarre lament for the surrender of deeper impulses to elegant proprieties. The mysterious interstices of this poem, its mixture of colloquialism and elegance, and its memorable ironies were established with great confidence. The portrait of enervation was executed with contradictory energy.

In the same month that 'Prufrock' was published, Eliot married. His wife was Vivien Haigh Haigh-Wood, an Englishwoman with aspirations to be a painter or writer. The marriage proved most unhappy, and unhappiness, fostered by the war, and by what he once described as a lifelong aboulia, became the tenor of much of Eliot's verse. Domestic anxiety may have encouraged him to search out images of ruin and devastation, which joined with the international disasters of the war and the evils of modern industrial society. The witty, humorous side of his nature—well known to his friends—found only sporadic written expression, in the partly satirical cast of his first volumes of verse, in the flamboyant *Sweeney Agonistes* (1932), and, more genially, in *Old Possum's Book of Practical Cats* (1939).

After his marriage Eliot resisted the urgings of his parents that he return with his wife to the safe side of the Atlantic and teach philosophy. They did not cut him off, but, while they wished their son to finish his dissertation, they did not give enough money for full support. To manage at all, Eliot took up schoolteaching. His first position was at High Wycombe Grammar School from September to December 1915, after which he changed to Highgate Junior School and taught until December 1916. During this period he had completed and submitted his dissertation, which was found acceptable, and in April 1916 he was set to return to Harvard for his oral examination. But the ship did not sail and he made no further efforts to secure his doctorate. Teaching did not prove a satisfactory way of life, since it left him no leisure time, and in March 1917 he shifted to a position in the colonial and foreign department at Lloyds Bank in London, and kept at it for eight years, until November 1925. When the United States entered the war he was rejected for active service, on medical grounds, and his subsequent efforts to volunteer for military or naval intelligence were also unsuccessful. After the peace treaty was signed, the bank put him in sole charge of dealing with debts and claims of the bank and Germans. He manœuvred dexterously among the complications.

But his principal work during this period had to be conducted at night: this was the conquest of a position as both poet and critic. As poet he had to create a new style, and as critic to validate it. He wrote many reviews and essays, and, with a sparseness already habitual, a few poems. In 1917 he published *Prufrock and Other Observations*, in 1919 *Poems*, in 1920 *Ara Vos Prec* (which included the two previous volumes). An American edition of his verse to date also appeared in 1920 under the title *Poems*. The same year he collected his prose pieces and published them under the title *The Sacred Wood*.

The combination of careers sapped his strength and kept him on the verge of breakdown. Vivien Eliot's health was also bad, and the drugs which she increasingly required to alleviate her migraine and nervous pains were a new source of tension for her husband. In 1921 Eliot felt ill enough to consult a neurologist, who advised him to take three months' convalescent leave. With the consent of Lloyds Bank, Eliot went in October to Margate and in November, for a psychiatric consultation, to Lausanne. While in Switzerland, where he remained into December, he brought to completion *The Waste Land*, the long poem on which he had been working seriously since late in 1919. The publication in 1971 of the original manuscript of this poem (edited by his second wife, Valerie Eliot), after it had been missing for almost half a century, explained and confirmed Eliot's acknowledgement, in the poem's dedication, of his debt to Ezra Pound. It was Pound who helped him sift the final version from many drafts and false starts.

The Waste Land appeared with considerable fanfare on both sides of the Atlantic late in 1922. Although many readers found it outrageous, it gave Eliot his central position in modern verse. The work brought poetry into the same atmosphere of innovation which characterized music and painting of the time, and as with those arts, its effect was not of tentative but of consolidated experiment. In later life Eliot would speak severely of *The Waste Land* as 'just a piece of rhythmical grumbling', but in fact it broke with traditional structure and prosodic conventions, and if it grumbled, did so for a generation as well as for the poet himself. What appeared to be bits of actuality adventitiously juxtaposed with fragmentary allusions from literature, opera, and popular song, were actually parts of a mosaic with definite outlines. Eliot brought together various kinds of despair, for lost youth, lost love, lost friendship, lost value. Sombre and obscure, the poem also offered some possibilities of renewal (though these were not immediately recognized) in its blend of pagan vegetation rites, Christian resurrection, and exhortations from the *Upanishads*. In spite of many shifts of scene, it was anchored firmly in London, and with all its mustering of past ages, it spoke sharply to its own time.

After *The Waste Land* it was incumbent upon Eliot to choose between immobile lamentation, never his mode, and a new journey of the spirit. His next poems, including 'The Hollow Men' (1925), 'Journey of the Magi' (1927), and 'Ash-Wednesday' (1930) testified that he had found his direction not in Indic religion but in Christianity. The process had been taking place, he said, 'perhaps insensibly, over a long period of time'. The year 1927 was almost as momentous as 1915: he was confirmed in the Church of England and he became a British subject. Soon thereafter, in his preface to a book of essays, *For Lancelot Andrewes* (1928), he characterized himself as 'classical in literature, royalist in politics, and anglo-catholic in religion'. (He would later regret the phrasing, though not the stances.) His politics became steadily more conservative. To the astonishment of admirers of his early work, in which the Church had played a less dignified role (as in 'The Hippopotamus'), Eliot became active in many church activities, participating as church warden, committee member, and lay apologist. His most resolute effort in this field was his book, *The Idea of a Christian Society*, published just after the onset of war in 1939. The ideal of an organic society had been implicit in his work almost from the beginning, though represented chiefly by depiction of its opposite; but the explicitly Christian form of the society was a summation of his later views.

The more lasting and effective expression of his spiritual quest came in *Four Quartets* (1944), a group of four poems which were interrelated but first published separately, *Burnt Norton* (1935), *East Coker* (1940), *The Dry Salvages* (1941), and *Little Gidding* (1942). Written in conversational and lyrical modes, the poems confront the problems of history, art, virtue, and mortality; the search for religious truth is subtly, expertly blended with the search for aesthetic expression, and both are shown to be the poet's intimate, lifelong pursuit. The language is triumphantly varied and modern; the imagery blends dive-bombers and the London underground with almost immemorial symbols of spiritual life. *Little Gidding* concludes with a vision of paradisal completeness for which his early verse, with its satirical portrayal of the infernal aspects of modern life, and his middle verse, instinct with purgatorial pain and hope, seem preparatory.

From 1922 Eliot devoted much of his time to work as editor and publisher. He founded in that year a new quarterly review, the *Criterion*, and became its editor, at first not printing his name so as to avoid complications at Lloyds Bank. The review was primarily literary, but its interests extended to social and political subjects as Eliot expanded the range of his own enquiries. He wished, he said, to create a place for the new attitudes to literature and art, and to make English letters a part of the European cultural community. He published work by the leading writers on the Continent as well as in England and America. A crisis ensued in 1925 when the patron of the *Criterion*, Lady Rothermere, withdrew her support. About the same time Eliot left the bank to become a director in the publishing firm of Faber & Gwyer (later Faber & Faber), and shortly afterwards the firm took over the review. It resumed publication as a monthly until June 1927, and then as a quarterly until January 1939, when the last number appeared. Although its circulation was modest, the *Criterion* had a large following among intellectuals. Besides his work for the review, Eliot took responsibility for his firm's selection of poets, and his taste set a standard; to be published by Eliot's firm was the ultimate guarantee. His own work was translated into many languages, and the latest poet in Arabic, Swahili, or Japanese was more likely to sound like Eliot than like earlier poets in those languages. His eminence became, in fact, a hazard to young poets who felt that their fundamental aesthetic problem was to avoid imitating him.

In the thirties Eliot took up seriously a form which had always attracted him, poetic drama. His first efforts were for a Christian pageant, *The Rock* (Sadler's Wells, 1934), and led the following year to *Murder in the Cathedral*, a play about the martyrdom of Thomas à Becket which was produced in Canterbury Cathedral chapter house. Eliot showed great skill in exploring dramatically the psychology of both martyrdom and political assassination. His later plays dwelt, seemingly, on secular matters, but with various degrees of obliquity explored problems of conscience in profane circumstances. *The Family Reunion* (Westminster Theatre, 1939) deals with sin and expiation; its hero returns to England after an absence of many years and believes himself pursued by the Furies for the putative murder of his wife. This play had a great success in the commercial theatre, as did, ten years later, *The Cocktail Party* produced by Henry Sherek (Edinburgh Festival, 1949), a play about ways of existence and redemption. The last two plays were *The Confidential Clerk* (Edinburgh Festival, 1953), in which the search for parentage by three foundlings—a staple of Greek comedy—becomes an existential search for identity; and *The Elder Statesman* (Edinburgh Festival, 1958), in which the title character has gradually to shed his pretences and come to terms with his real self. All these moral comedies were written in verse, which Eliot increasingly brought as close to prose as possible, on the theory that a more obvious metric would seem unnatural and distracting on the modern stage.

Eliot's dramatic talent was not negligible, but it was limited; his criticism, along with his verse, is more certain to last. In *The Sacred Wood* he enunciated certain cardinal principles. The essay, 'Tradition and the Individual Talent', held that a new work of art alters the arrangement of the 'existing monuments', so that tradition is not to be understood as a fixed entity, but as a changing one. He also made here his famous comparison of the writer to a catalytic agent, who joins the literary tradition to the experience and language of his own time. Against the romantic conception of self-expression, Eliot described the creative process as an escape from personality. The writer, he said in his essay on 'Hamlet', has to find an 'objective correlative' for his emotion. This process had become more difficult since the seventeenth century when, as he argued in 'The Metaphysical Poets' (*Homage to John Dryden*, 1924), there took place 'a dissociation of sensibility', so that poets could no longer feel a thought 'as immediately as the odour of a rose'. A mental disjunctiveness had led to what he sometimes regarded as the 'cultural breakdown' of the twentieth century.

Eliot's essays on these matters, on the Elizabethan dramatists, on Milton and the romantic poets, on Dante and Baudelaire, and on such contemporaries as Joyce, Pound, and Lawrence, became focal points of modern criticism. Many of them, as he said, offered a theoretical basis for his poetic practice. He did not wish this basis to be taken as systematic, and often insisted that particular ideas required expression at particular times, and were polemical rather than dogmatic. As his religious bent became more pronounced, both in his verse and in his life, he strove to see literature as part of a larger spiritual enterprise. His book, *After Strange Gods* (1934), based on lectures he gave at the university of Virginia in 1933, bore the sub-title 'A Primer of Modern Heresy', and tried to pick a path among contemporary writers according to the degree of orthodoxy or heterodoxy he found in them, the former being exalted. The result was a simplification of his position which he regretted and afterwards suppressed. But his other critical volumes, such as *Selected Essays* (1932) (expanded later), *On Poetry and Poets* (1957), and *To Criticize the Critic* (1965), have commanded and kept attention. His later criticism is less confidently assertive than his earlier, which he sometimes repudiates, yet it abounds in untrammelled and precise discriminations.

Eliot's later life became rather stately. In 1932–3 he went back to the United States for the first time to give the Charles Eliot Norton lectures at Harvard. (These were published as *The Use of Poetry and the Use of Criticism*, 1933.) At this time he arranged a permanent separation from his wife, and provided for her support. On his return to London he lived with various friends; his longest stay was with the critic John Hayward, who shared Eliot's flat from 1946 to 1957. His wife died in 1947. The following year Eliot received the Nobel prize for literature, and also the Order of Merit. He was to receive eighteen honorary degrees; he was an honorary fellow of Merton College, Oxford, and of Magdalene College, Cambridge; and he was an officer of the Legion of Honour. With his plays on Broadway and in the West End, his best lines on every lip, his opinions cited on all manner of subjects, he was the man of letters *par excellence* of the English-speaking world. He was also a man of generous spirit and firm friendship.

In 1957 Eliot married (Esmé) Valerie, only daughter of James Fletcher, of Headingley, Leeds, with whom he lived in great contentment for the rest of his life. He died in London 4 January 1965. His ashes were buried in St Michael's church in East Coker, the place from which his ancestors had emigrated to the United States and the scene of the second *Quartet*. A memorial service was held in Westminster Abbey where a stone has been placed to his memory.

In appearance Eliot was tall and a little stooped. His beaked nose encouraged him to describe himself in one poem as an 'aged eagle'. Though even in youth he was an impressive and powerful presence, he had a vein of self-mockery, and was known to play practical jokes. In conversation he spoke with great deftness, and often with fine wit. If seized by an idea, he would follow it to its end, oblivious to others' attempts to interrupt, but he could also be silently attentive. His courtesy, self-abnegation, and kindness in difficult situations were celebrated. In later life his affection for his second wife, to whom he wrote the dedicatory poem of *The Elder Statesman*, was proudly manifest.

There is an early portrait of Eliot by Wyndham Lewis in the National Gallery in Durban, South Africa, and a late one by Sir Gerald Kelly, in the possession of the family. The best photographs are by Edward McKnight Kauffer and by Angus McBean, the latter at the London Library of which Eliot was president from 1952 until his death. The National Portrait Gallery has a bust by Sir Jacob Epstein.

[Introductory matter in Valerie Eliot's edition of the manuscript of *The Waste Land*, 1971; Lyndall Gordon, *Eliot's Early Years*, 1979; private information.]

RICHARD ELLMANN

published 1981

EPSTEIN Sir Jacob

(1880–1959)

Sculptor, was born 10 November 1880 in Hester Street, New York City, in the Jewish quarter near the Bowery, the third son of Max and Mary Salomon Epstein, a well-to-do merchant family of orthodox Jews, immigrants to America as a result of the persecutions and pogroms in Tsarist Russia and Poland. Epstein was interested in drawing as a boy and made many studies of life in the streets around his home, crowded by Russians, Poles, Italians, Greeks, and Chinese. Attracted in time to the practice of sculpture, he learned bronze casting in a foundry and studied modelling at evening classes for professional sculptors' assistants conducted by George Grey Barnard.

He continued to draw and was invited by Hutchins Hapgood to illustrate a book on the life of the East Side of New York, called *The Spirit of the*

Ghetto, which was published in 1902. With the fees from this work he paid for a passage to Paris in search of European influences and the inspirations he had failed to discover in the sculpture of America. He studied the sculpture in the Parisian museums and art galleries; notably the early Greek work, Cycladic carvings, the limestone bust of Akenaton, and also the primitive sculpture at the Trocadero and the Chinese collection at the Musée Cernuschi. He shared a studio with a New York friend, Bernard Gussow, in the rue Belloni behind the Gare Montparnasse. At the Beaux-Arts School he studied modelling from the nude; but he left through the animosity of the French students when he refused to 'fag' for the entrants for the Prix de Rome Concours, and transferred to the Julian Academy where he studied until he left Paris.

In 1905 he moved to London and took a studio in Camden Town. A visit as a steerage passenger to America failed to attract him to stay; he returned to London, settled in a studio in Fulham, and was naturalized in 1911. Meantime he met Francis Dodd, (Sir) Muirhead Bone, Augustus John, and the artists of the New English Art Club circle; and studied at the British Museum: especially the Elgin Marbles and the other Greek sculpture, the Egyptian rooms, and the collections of Polynesian and African art.

Francis Dodd introduced Epstein to Charles Holden, the architect, who invited him to decorate his new British Medical Association building in the Strand. For this commission Epstein carved eighteen over-life-size nude figures symbolizing the stages of human life from birth to death, well proportioned and simple in movement. These very orthodox sculptures became a music-hall joke through a philistine outcry against their nudity, started by a front-page article by an anonymous journalist in the *Evening Standard and St. James's Gazette* 19 June 1908. Correspondence in various journals, also petitions and parliamentary questions followed this essay. The statues were examined by a police officer who noted them as 'rude'. The bishop of Stepney, Cosmo Gordon Lang, later archbishop of Canterbury, climbed the scaffolding to examine them and declared them innocent of any offence. They were also defended in the columns of *The Times*. Nevertheless the sculptor suffered the ordeal of a summons before a committee of the British Medical Association, reminiscent of the appearance of Veronese before the Inquisition in 1573. The officials of the Southern Rhodesian Government who later owned the building procured the mutilation and virtual destruction of the sculptures after twenty-nine years, against the protests of many of London's citizens.

Epstein's sculpture drew further puritan attacks in later years; notably in 1912 over his carving for the tomb of Oscar Wilde in the Père Lachaise

Cemetery in Paris; and also his first figure of Christ in bronze made during the war and exhibited at the Leicester Galleries, London, in 1920 (it was bought by Apsley Cherry-Garrard); and his memorial to W. H. Hudson, which was commissioned by the Royal Society for the Protection of Birds for a site in Hyde Park where it was unveiled by Stanley Baldwin in 1925. Epstein was particularly attacked by Roger Fry, a critic who assailed many contemporary artists; and also by John Galsworthy. His supporters in the different artistic crises were Muirhead Bone, Augustus John, Francis Dodd, and (Sir) Matthew Smith; Walter Sickert resigned from the Royal Academy in 1935 in protest at the Academy's equivocal attitude regarding the Strand statues.

An original member of the London Group, Epstein was rejected as a candidate for membership of the Royal Society of British Sculptors *circa* 1910, when proposed by Havard Thomas; and later by the Royal Academy when proposed by Sir John Lavery. The National Portrait Gallery refused his original casting of his bust of Joseph Conrad (though a slightly damaged casting was later accepted). His Lucifer (1943–5) was refused as a gift by the Fitzwilliam Museum, Cambridge, and also by the Victoria and Albert Museum and the Tate Gallery. Several provincial art galleries requested it and it went to the Birmingham City Art Gallery.

Epstein's stone carving was more difficult for the public to assimilate than his modelled bronzes. Whilst the former were rooted in early or primitive sculpture, his modelling was in the baroque tradition deriving from the Renaissance or was at the earliest from the Byzantine, as with the Madonna and Child (1927).

Epstein's career falls into clearly marked phases. He was drawing and illustrating in New York until 1902 and studied in Paris from 1902 to 1905. His early struggles in London from 1905 to 1912, and his essays in cubism and the Vorticist movement from 1913 to 1915, were followed by a wide acceptance of him as a modeller of portrait bronzes from 1916 to 1929. During the latter period, however, his sitters were usually friends or professional models, and Rima (1925) was his only public commission between 1912 (the Wilde memorial) and 1929 (the London Underground Headquarters' building, again for Charles Holden). In 1938 he received an honorary LL D from Aberdeen. Apart from this, his large stone carvings —Genesis (1931), Sun God (1933), Ecce Homo (1935), Consummatum Est (1937), and Adam (1939)—did not obtain for him the official recognition he desired.

During the war of 1939–45 he had several official war commissions for the Ministry of Information to make portrait bronzes of Service chiefs and also, just after the war, of (Sir) Winston Churchill. Although his next big venture Lazarus (1948) was not well received, it was officially invited to the Battersea Park exhibition for the Festival of Britain (1951); and in 1952 it was bought for New College, Oxford ('one of the happiest issues of my working life'). From this time onwards he received more important official commissions than he could execute for large sculptures in prominent public positions in London and elsewhere; including the Madonna and Child, for the Holy Child Convent, Cavendish Square; Liverpool Giant, for Lewis's of Liverpool; Christ in Majesty, for Llandaff Cathedral; the TUC war memorial; Saint Michael and the Devil, for Coventry Cathedral; and the Bowater House Group.

In 1953 he received an honorary DCL at Oxford and the following year was appointed KBE. The Royal College of Art, in 1954, placed a studio at his disposal in which he worked daily on the figure and bas reliefs for Lewis's building, Liverpool, and on the Christ for Llandaff Cathedral. In his autobiography Epstein expressed regret that he had never been asked to teach by any college.

Epstein possessed a gracious and courteous manner. His conversation was cultivated and, on the subject of art, very learned. He never lost his American accent. Despite his many frustrations and the attacks he had suffered he was of a kindly and compassionate disposition though impatient of anyone lacking humility concerning art. He might well have succeeded as a painter. His picture exhibitions were usually sold out: Paintings of Epping Forest (1933), Flower Paintings (1936 and 1940). As an illustrator he was less successful; neither his series of drawings for *The Old Testament* (1929–31) nor those for Baudelaire's *Fleurs du Mal* (1938) was well received. On 19 August 1959, although he was ill, he worked at his studio at Hyde Park Gate, London, on the Bowater Group, discussed the casting of it with his bronze moulder, and died the same night.

In 1906 Epstein married Margaret Gilmour Dunlop (died 1947), by whom he had one son and one daughter. In 1955 he married Kathleen Esther, daughter of the late Walter Chancellor Garman, surgeon.

The National Portrait Gallery has a bronze of Epstein modelled by himself and drawings by Augustus John and Powys Evans.

[Bernard Van Dieren, *Epstein*, 1920; Jacob Epstein to Arnold Haskell, *The Sculptor Speaks*, 1931; Jacob Epstein, *Let There Be Sculpture*, 1940, and *Autobiography*, 1955; Richard Buckle, *Jacob Epstein, Sculptor*, 1963; *Epstein Drawings*, 1962; *Catalogue* of the Epstein retrospective exhibition at the Tate Gallery, 1952; *Catalogue* of the Epstein memorial exhibition at the Edinburgh Festival, 1961; *Catalogues* of sixteen Epstein exhibitions at the Leicester Galleries, London; private information.]

RICHARD SEDDON

published 1971

EVANS-PRITCHARD Sir Edward Evan

(1902–1973)

Social anthropologist, was born 21 September 1902 at Crowbridge, Sussex, the younger of two sons, the only children of the Revd Thomas John Evans-Pritchard, a Welsh-speaking Church of England clergyman from Caernarvon, and his wife, Dorothea, daughter of John Edwards, of Liverpool. 'Evans' came into the name from his maternal grandmother, daughter of Eyre Dixon Evans JP, merchant of Liverpool. He was educated at Winchester College (1916–21) and Exeter College, Oxford (1921–4), where he took a second class in modern history.

Though Evans-Pritchard never lost the values and sentiments of his upbringing, there was a non-conforming side to him, attracted to the unconventional, the Bohemian, even the raffish. When at Oxford he was a member of the privileged artistic coterie, the Hypocrites Club, and is described at that time by a fellow member, Anthony Powell, the novelist, as 'Evans-Pritchard the anthropologist, grave, withdrawn, somewhat exotic of dress'. In middle and later life, his conviviality, and sometimes mischievous humour, often concealed that deeper reclusiveness, while in dress he became notably careless, though formal enough for formal occasions.

At Exeter College, with anthropologist R. R. Marett as a fellow and later rector, Evans-Pritchard read works on primitive cultures by Sir Edward B. Tylor and Sir James G. Frazer. The immense variety of the forms of social life they described, with all that remained to be discovered, caught his imagination; and—Celt as he was—people who held to their own customs and beliefs, in the face of powerful foreign interference, had his sympathy. In their direction he saw a future that would satisfy both his appetite for adventure and his intellectual curiosity. So it was that he chose an anthropological career, for which he was well endowed by physical stamina, self-reliance, sociability, and a subtle understanding of human relationships.

Since no teacher in Oxford then had experience of anthropological field-research, in 1923 he moved to the London School of Economics, where C. G. Seligman and B. Malinowski were gathering around them young anthropologists with aspirations similar to his own. Malinowski (though Evans-Pritchard came to dislike him personally and sometimes to depreciate his work) set an outstanding example of thorough field-research conducted through the native language. Seligman, who, with his wife B. Z. Seligman, had earlier made surveys in the (then Anglo-Egyptian) Sudan, arranged with the Sudan government for him to undertake more intensive research there. He chose eventually to study the Azande of the southern Sudan among whom he lived on and off between 1926 and 1930. With characteristic industry, in 1927 he gained the Ph.D. of the University of London for a preliminary thesis on them.

His first book, *Witchcraft, Oracles and Magic among the Azande* (1937), a brilliant analysis of Zande mystical belief and practices, implicitly raised general questions of the relationship between faith and reasoning, impressing not only the anthropologists but philosophers (for example, R. G. Collingwood and Michael Polanyi) and social historians (for example, Keith Thomas). In this book Evans-Pritchard already shows two characteristics of his own style of social anthropology; the development of general ideas through detailed ethnography rather than by abstract argument, and unusual insight into the intellectual and moral coherence of apparently disparate social phenomena. As in his other writings, sociological analysis never deprives the reader of a living and sympathetic impression of the people themselves. In later life, he regretted that, in their formalism, some of his successors in the subject were losing this touch, and making of the study of man what the scholastics had made of the study of God.

Between 1930 and 1940 he was a wandering scholar, with part-time lectureships in London and Oxford, and three years (1932–4) as professor of sociology at King Fuad I University in Cairo, where he began to learn Arabic. His field-research continued the while, mostly in the southern Sudan. In 1930 he started twelve months' difficult and interrupted work among the warlike, pastoral Nuer tribes of the Upper Nile swamps, where he arrived shortly after a government punitive expedition; but though, as he wrote, he 'entered [the Nuers'] cattle-camps not only as a stranger but as an enemy', he respected their recalcitrance and eventually gained their confidence. The research produced many articles and three books: *The Nuer, a Description of the Modes of Livelihood and Political Institutions of a Nilotic People* (1940); *Kinship and Marriage among the Nuer* (1951); and *Nuer Religion* (1956). The first provided a model for much subsequent anthropological analysis of political institutions, showing as it did the structural principles of political order among peoples without any centralized authority. *African Political Systems* (1940), a symposium which he co-edited with his friend Meyer Fortes, extended that discussion.

Nuer Religion (unusually, for a social anthropologist, written from an explicitly theistic view-point) again brought him readers among psychologists, theologians, and philosophers, and he was wryly pleased that the meaning of Nuer expressions should add to British philosophical speculations. Evans-Pritchard had become a Roman Catholic in 1944 and, though he was not, as some were led to suppose, a zealous convert, he advocated religious faith, for him an answer to his own inveterate scepticism. This religious stance, and his dismissive attitude to claims then being made for social anthropology as 'a natural science of society', raised controversy, and some polemic, among professional colleagues.

In 1939 Evans-Pritchard married Ioma Gladys, daughter of George Heaton-Nicholls, later South African high commissioner in London; they had three sons and two daughters. He was commissioned in the Sudan Defence Force in 1940, and for some time returned to the Sudan-Ethiopian border to fight against the Italians alongside irregular troops of the Anuak, whom he knew from his brief researches there in 1935 (published as *The Political System of the Anuak of the Anglo-Egyptian Sudan* in 1940). Later he spent some time among the Alawites in Syria, and ended the war as a political officer of the British administration among the Bedouin of Cyrenaica. His book *The Sanusi of Cyrenaica* (1949) shows the effect, on an acute anthropological observer, of close personal involvement in practical affairs. But though he never wished, as he wrote later, 'to become just, I almost said, an intellectual', and had many friends outside intellectual circles, he remained by temperament a scholar and in some measure a contemplative.

He was appointed reader in social anthropology in Cambridge in 1945, and professor of social anthropology in Oxford in 1946. There he built up a large and lively postgraduate school at the Institute of Social Anthropology. His energies, diverted from field-research, were then directed towards promoting and consolidating the position of his subject within the academic world and beyond it, as, for example, in his course of lectures for the BBC, published as *Social Anthropology* (1951). He was president of the Royal Anthropological Institute (1949–51), a founder and first life president of the Association of Social Anthropologists of the British Commonwealth, FBA (1956), foreign honorary member of the American Academy of Arts and Sciences (1958), and honorary fellow of the School of Oriental and African Studies (1963). Among other distinctions were honorary doctorates of the universities of Chicago (1967), Bristol (1969), and Manchester (1969) (in company there with the sculptor Henry Moore, and Lord Sieff, who became a friend). He was knighted in 1971 and became a chevalier of the Legion of Honour in 1972.

Meanwhile he continued to teach and to write prolifically (his bibliography has nearly 400 entries), co-edited the *Oxford Library of African Literature*, promoted the translation of French anthropological classics, and gave numerous foundation lectures. He retired in 1970 and died suddenly 11 September 1973 at his home in Oxford, The Ark, Jack Straw's Lane, where he had continued to bring up his family after his wife's early death in 1959. He never got over that loss, which is commemorated by a junior fellowship in her name at her Oxford college, St Anne's.

Evans-Pritchard's international academic reputation, wide range of friendships, and sharp intelligence, at once pragmatic and intuitive, gave him a central position in his profession, and on his retirement he could not relinquish it. Even in his last few years, when intermittent illness, deafness, and a sometimes factitious, or nostalgic, conservatism, might have reduced his circle of friends or admirers, they remained with him, whether in All Souls College, or gathered regardless of age or status in his favourite Oxford pubs. Disarming though he was, he could make enemies; nevertheless, the many Festschriften and dedications in his honour affectionately acknowledge the debt so many owed to his example, encouragement, and personal generosity.

In ease of manner, literary and artistic taste, and love of the wild and the natural world, Evans-Pritchard preferred to remain in some ways an Edwardian country gentleman; but he had a free, inventive imagination uniquely his own, which undermined—and from within—the bastions of Edwardian prejudice alienating 'modern' from 'primitive' man.

[Personal knowledge.]

R. G. LIENHARDT

published 1986

FEILING Sir Keith Grahame

(1884–1977)

Historian, was born 7 September 1884 at Elms House, Leatherhead, the elder son (there were no daughters) of Ernest Feiling, stock-broker, and his wife, Joan Barbara Hawkins who was a sister of the novelist Anthony Hope (Sir Anthony Hope Hawkins) and a first cousin of Kenneth Grahame. He was educated at Marlborough and Balliol College, Oxford. Starting in 1903 his undergraduate career was one of mounting success culminating in 1906 with a brilliant first class in modern history and a prize fellowship at All Souls College.

These successes pointed him towards an academic career. In 1907 he was appointed lecturer in history at the University of Toronto. In October 1909 he returned to Oxford as lecturer and tutor in modern history at Christ Church with the expectation of a Studentship (i.e. fellowship). In June 1911, his fellowship at All Souls having determined, he was duly elected a Student of Christ Church—a position he was to retain for the next thirty-five years. In December 1912 he married Caroline (died 1978), daughter of Dearman Janson, gentleman, to whom he was devoted for the rest of his life. (They were to have a family of two daughters and a son.) At that time marriage still required a Studentship to be vacated and reappointment to be sought. In Feiling's case reappointment was granted immediately, though not before a small minority of the governing body had voted to postpone it for a year. As a tutor before 1914 Feiling shared with his senior colleague, Arthur Hassall, the care of between thirty and thirty-six pupils. This was more than two tutors could properly sustain even in the somewhat relaxed atmosphere of pre-war Christ Church and at the end of 1913 a third tutor was appointed, (Sir) J. C. Masterman. Feiling wished to apply more positive tutorial methods than had hitherto obtained; Hassall dissented, telling Masterman that undergraduates should be encouraged to depend on themselves and deploring Feiling's 'rather too kind' approach. The war postponed the resolution of this difference.

In December 1914 Feiling was commissioned in the Black Watch. In 1916 he was posted to India, served for a year with his battalion, and then, in 1917, became secretary to the Central Recruiting Board of India. He held this post until early in 1919, being appointed OBE for his services in 1918. He was back at Christ Church for the summer term of 1919 and immediately threw himself into his teaching. Hassall, now in sight of retirement, yielded to his enthusiasm which Masterman shared. Together these two gave a new impetus to the Christ Church history school which, many years later, Masterman generously described as 'the creation of Keith Feiling'. For his part Feiling paid tribute to Masterman's 'system and staff work'. Both were right. Their complementary talents and sympathetic co-operation explain their outstanding success. Between 1921 and 1936, while Feiling was an active tutor, Christ Church historians won thirty-one first classes although it was no part of his teaching to emphasize the importance of the class list. For the first three years after his return Feiling taught some twenty pupils a term. At the same time he examined in the final schools, 1920–2, and served on the faculty board acting as its chairman in 1924–5.

Naturally this burden of teaching and administration interfered with his research; the appointment of a fourth history tutor in 1922 to teach the medieval period provided some easement and for one term that year he was allowed to halve his teaching—but at his own expense. These indulgences enabled him to complete his first big book, *A History of the Tory Party 1640–1714*, which was published in 1924. Three terms of sabbatical leave in 1927–8 led to his *British Foreign Policy 1660–1672*, which appeared in 1930, and in the same year he brought out his *Sketches in 19th Century Biography*, a collection of essays originally written for *The Times* and the *Times Literary Supplement*. These works earned him the degree of D.Litt. in

1932. His research interests were now moving towards the eighteenth century. When in 1931–2 he was appointed Ford's lecturer in English history—he had been a university lecturer since 1928—he took as his subject the 'Tories in Opposition and in Power 1714–1806' and these lectures were the foundation of his book *The Second Tory Party 1714–1832*, published in 1938. He also planned at this time to draw together his wide knowledge in a narrative *History of England*. This great project took twenty years to complete in spite of his giving up all undergraduate teaching in 1936 when Christ Church elected him to a research Studentship. He allowed himself to be diverted between 1932 and 1936 by helping (Sir) Winston Churchill first with his life of Marlborough and then with the first volume of his *History of the English-speaking Peoples*. Then when the war came he nobly returned to a period of teaching and examining between 1940 and 1943. Finally, at the particular request of the Chamberlain family, he turned aside to write *The Life of Neville Chamberlain*. Only when this was published in 1946 was he free to turn back to his projected *History*.

The year 1946 also saw his election to the Chichele chair of modern history which he held until his retirement in 1950 when his *History of England* finally appeared. His short tenure of his chair, to which he had been seen as the natural heir for many years, was the unfortunate result of his predecessor's longevity. In retirement his distinction was acknowledged at home and abroad by his election to an honorary studentship at Christ Church in 1952, by his knighthood in 1958, and by his becoming an honorary member of the Massachusetts Historical Society in 1958. Meanwhile he had continued to work on his life of *Warren Hastings*, first planned in 1946, which was awarded the James Tait Black memorial prize on its appearance in 1954. His last book, a charming collection of biographical essays entitled *In Christ Church Hall*, was published in 1960. He lived in retirement first in London, then in Norfolk, and for his last years in Gloucestershire. When well into his eighties he endured major abdominal surgery which he overcame with characteristic courage. He died in a nursing home in Putney 16 September 1977.

Neat and thoughtful in appearance, kindly and courteous in manner with a slight stammer which reinforced his charm, Keith Feiling has rightly been described as a cultured, well-informed, and liberal-minded man. The dedications of his books indicate his loyalties—to his wife, to his pupils, and to his friend and colleague in caring for those pupils, J. C. Masterman. He was exceptionally perceptive in his judgement of young scholars and in sustaining in their early days those who would later make their mark. As a writer his style was allusive, sometimes congested, but particularly in his essays and his *History* he wrote in a way that was clear, stimulating and, on occasions, moving. As a historian he was, as G. M. Trevelyan wrote of him, 'more interested in religious, political and constitutional issues than in the social and economic'. His outlook was that of a romantic Tory and a patriot. He was English to the core. Although he had founded the Oxford University Conservative Association in 1924 and was accepted as the leading historian of the Tory Party he was not politically partisan. He drew a distinction between Toryism and Conservatism, identifying more with the first than the second. Above all he was optimistic, closing his inaugural lecture in 1947 with Robert E. Lee's moving words 'it is history that teaches us to hope'.

[*The Times*, 19 September 1977; *English Historical Review*, 1925; J. C. Masterman, *On the Chariot Wheel: an Autobiography*, 1975; Lord David Cecil, foreword to *Essays in British History* (ed. H. R. Trevor-Roper), 1964; H. R. Trevor-Roper, address in Christ Church Cathedral, 22 October 1977 (privately printed 1977); Christ Church archives; private information.]

CHARLES STUART

published 1986

FIELDS Dame Gracie

(1898–1979)

Music-hall artiste and film star, was born Grace Stansfield in Rochdale, Lancashire, 9 January 1898, the eldest of four children (three daughters and a son) of Fred Stansfield, engineer, and his wife, Sarah Jane Bamford. Her education, at Rochdale Parish School, was disrupted by her mother's attempts to put her on the stage, and ceased when she was thirteen. It was at this time that she changed her name to Gracie Fields.

Her stage career began with singing competitions, brief appearances at local music halls, and membership of various juvenile troupes, but in 1913, when she was fifteen, she became a member of a touring music-hall company, and began a full-time career as a singer and *comédienne*. In 1916, Archie Pitt, another member of the company, broke away to form a company to perform his own revues, and invited Gracie Fields to be his leading lady. She toured with Pitt for eight years, acquiring a tremendous depth of experience in all aspects of music-hall and revue work. She was naturally versatile, and Pitt worked hard to exploit her many talents—dancing, singing, mimicry, acting, improvisation—and to reinforce in her that dedication to her work and to the show which her mother had instilled in her at an early age. Archie Pitt exercised an almost complete control over Gracie's life, and in 1923 they married—an arrangement of convenience on both sides. Pitt (a stage name) was the son of Morris Selinger. There were no children of the marriage.

In 1924 Pitt's company, which had been touring continuously since 1916, was invited to stage its current revue, 'Mr Tower of London' in the West End. This was the company's first exposure to the London critics, and the production was widely acclaimed. Gracie Fields found that she had become a star, literally overnight.

Her fame spread rapidly—she became known to millions as 'Our Gracie'—and soon she was in demand everywhere. As well as starring in Pitt's revues, she also performed in cabaret after each nightly show, and made records during the day. Pitt guided her career and used her vast earnings to create a lifestyle of luxury and display which Gracie Fields, always a simple Lancashire girl at heart, neither desired nor enjoyed. Their marriage, which had never been a close one, deteriorated further, but although by 1931 separation was imminent, the professional partnership flourished, and Pitt seized the opportunity to launch Gracie Fields into the most recent development in popular entertainment—film-making.

In this new venture Gracie Fields was instantly successful with the film *Sally in our Alley* (which included the famous song). The plots of the early films were weak, and the direction poor, but in spite of this the public flocked to see them. In 1935 Monty Banks (Mario Bianchi), an Italian director, was brought in, the quality of the films improved, and in 1938 Gracie Fields began to make films in Hollywood, with a contract which made her the best paid film star in the world.

In 1939 Gracie Fields underwent major surgery for cancer, and it is a measure of her popularity at this time that prayers were said for her in the churches, and newspapers and radio carried daily bulletins. She made a complete recovery, but the outbreak of war a few months later led to an event in her life which overnight changed public adulation into almost universal condemnation.

In 1938 Gracie had agreed to marry Monty Banks, and in 1940 she followed him into voluntary exile in America (Banks's Italian nationality meant that he ran the risk of internment if he remained in Britain) and, after a divorce from Archie Pitt in 1940 (the year in which he died) they were married there the same year. The popular press immediately accused Gracie Fields of deserting Britain in its moment of need, and of taking her wealth with her. Although the accusations were unfounded, her reputation was tainted for many years: her dedicated work for ENSA throughout the war did little to redeem her in the eyes of the British public.

After the war, Gracie Fields settled at her home in Capri. She was gradually taken back into the favour of the British, and she returned home periodically to record and give concerts. In 1950 Monty Banks died, and in

1952 she married Boris Alperovici (died 1983), a Bessarabian radio engineer living in Capri. With him she at last found real contentment and she led a peaceful life in Capri. She had no children.

Gracie Fields's career cannot be fully appreciated without recognizing that her roots lay in the music hall, where she received her training and formulated her act. When the music halls died, and she progressed to films, records, and variety work, it was the grounding in the music hall which gave her the strength and the ability to project herself, which was the key to her success. The great talent which she undoubtedly had, combined with her excellent training and her dedication to her work meant that, whatever the medium, she could win her audience and allow them to share a memorable experience.

On stage she was exceptionally versatile, her only prop a headscarf, held in her hand during romantic or sentimental songs, but tied over her head for the comic Lancashire songs which had made her famous. Even her voice changed according to the song—her lovely, clear singing voice became in the comic songs coarse and raucous. Her hold over her audience was so great that she could move in a moment from a comic to a religious song, and change laughter into tears. Only Gracie Fields could offer 'The Lord's Prayer' and 'Ave Maria' alongside 'The Biggest Aspidistra' and, 'Walter, Walter, lead me to the Altar'.

In her personal life, Gracie Fields never allowed her success to affect her. She remained open, affectionate, home-loving, generous with both time and money, and with a deep religious faith. She gave thousands of pounds to charity and in 1935 endowed and maintained the Gracie Fields Orphanage at Peacehaven, Sussex. She was also very humble—and touchingly unsure of herself when meeting other stars, almost unable to believe their respect for her.

Gracie Fields was appointed CBE in 1938 and DBE in 1979. In 1937 she received the freedom of Rochdale. She made over 500 records and fifteen films and she appeared in eleven Royal Variety performances. Her portrait, by Sir James Gunn, hangs in Rochdale Art Gallery.

She died in Capri 27 September 1979.

[Gracie Fields, *Sing As We Go* (autobiography), 1960; private information; personal knowledge.]

ELIZABETH POLLITT

published 1986

FISHER Geoffrey Francis

(1887–1972)

Baron Fisher of Lambeth

Archbishop of Canterbury, was born 5 May 1887, the youngest of the ten children (of whom three girls and four boys survived) of the Revd Henry Fisher and his wife, Katherine Richmond. His father was curate and then rector of Higham-on-the-Hill in the county of Leicester for forty years. His grandfather and great-grandfather had been rectors of the parish for similar periods of time, and this long country parson background may well have accounted for Geoffrey's own love of the countryside. He was educated at Marlborough which he entered as a foundation scholar in 1900. During his years there he came under the influence of the headmaster, (Sir) Frank Fletcher, a talented teacher who encouraged his pupils to think for themselves. Fisher did well at school in games and in work. He became senior prefect, a position in which he showed the qualities of courage and firmness which were much in evidence all through his life.

From Marlborough he went to Exeter College, Oxford, on a scholarship in 1906. He became president of the junior common room, captain of boats, and was given his colours for rugby. He attended chapel services regularly and shared in many of the activities connected with them. Of Fisher's deep Christian convictions there seems to have been no doubt at this or indeed at any time in his life. He gained first classes in classical honour moderations (1908), *literae humaniores* (1910), and theology (1911).

After Oxford he was offered a teaching post at Marlborough by Frank Fletcher. He remained there for three years during which time he was ordained. He went to Wells Theological College in the long vacation of 1911, was ordained deacon in 1912, and priest in 1913. The following year he was encouraged to apply for the headmastership of Repton, vacant through the resignation of William Temple, who later became archbishop of Canterbury. He was elected and took up the appointment in June 1914 at the age of twenty-seven. This was a difficult time for any headmaster as it was within weeks of the outbreak of World War I. One problem which Fisher faced immediately was that a number of masters and senior boys had left to join the forces. A fresh timetable had to be drawn up, and this was done very effectively by the new headmaster. Another problem was that of discipline, which had become somewhat lax under the otherwise remarkable headmastership of William Temple. The problem proved to be short-lived, for Fisher was a born disciplinarian who achieved his ends by acting quickly, firmly, and when necessary with severity.

In 1917 Fisher married Rosamond Chevallier, daughter of the Revd Arthur Francis Emilius Forman, a former master at Repton, and granddaughter of S. A. Pears, a former headmaster of the school. She was the ninth of fourteen children, and her marriage to Fisher marked the beginning of a happy, loving, and close-knit family life. There were six sons of the marriage, each of whom achieved distinction in his particular sphere.

Fisher's years as headmaster were successful both from the administrative and pastoral points of view, but he felt that after eighteen years he had been there long enough. He would gladly have moved to a parish in the country, but there were other plans for him. When he was offered the bishopric of Chester, he accepted and was consecrated in York Minster on 21 September 1932. The new bishop succeeded the greatly loved Luke Paget, and their difference in churchmanship proved to be no obstacle to the affection and regard each had for the other. Fisher set about his new work energetically and with a kind of all-embracing good humour. He was from all accounts very popular with clergy and laity alike, though he could be on occasions somewhat dictatorial. Among his chief qualities were his sense of humour, his imperturbability, his resilience, and his astonishing physical stamina. Short and sturdy in build, he seemed to exude energy and strength. For example, he always drove himself to institutions in the diocese, and when the service was over he joined in the festivities in the parish hall with the greatest enthusiasm. He loved meeting people, and it was the informal friendliness of his approach which won their respect and affection wherever he went both at home and abroad. His appointment as bishop of Chester brought him into close contact for the first time with convocation and the church assembly. He enjoyed taking the chair at meetings and was an admirable chairman though, as he said himself, he was apt to talk too much. His predecessor when once asked how he survived the ordeal of taking the chair at meetings of the assembly for the inside of a week three times a year humorously replied 'By prolonged bouts of deliberate inattention'. Fisher was never inattentive. His first big task in the diocese was an Industrial Christian Fellowship Mission. This involved him speaking in the evenings in the slums of Birkenhead. He accepted the unaccustomed task with that genuine humility of spirit which was reflected in so many of his activities. The seven years at Chester were happy ones for both the Fishers. As mother of six growing boys Rosamond Fisher had plenty to do at home but also took her full share in the life of the diocese, becoming president of the Diocesan Mothers' Union and later its central president.

In 1939 Fisher was called upon to succeed Arthur Foley Winnington-Ingram, who had been bishop of London since 1901. He had no wish to leave Chester, but London provided a fresh challenge which he faced with cheerfulness and confidence. There seemed little cause for either for World War II had broken out by the time of Fisher's enthronement in November 1939. Mass evacuation was causing immense problems, and in September 1940 the nightly bombing of London began. The diocese itself had its own problems, chiefly those of church order and ecclesiastical discipline, and because of the war there was also a shortage of clergy, disorganization of parish life, and destruction on a vast scale of churches and other buildings. Yet in the words of Bertram Simpson, suffragan bishop of Kensington and afterwards bishop of Southwark, Fisher 'left London a much more orderly diocese than he found it'. One of his major contributions was the setting up of the metropolitan area reconstruction committee which included all the churches, the Salvation Army, the Quakers, and the Jews, and which dealt directly with the Ministry of Works. He was also chairman of the churches' main war damage committee, which gave invaluable help to the war damage commission. Another important development which began in Fisher's time was the amalgamation of Queen Anne's Bounty with the ecclesiastical commission to form the Church Commissioners for England. A further concern of Fisher's was his association with the Sword of the Spirit movement founded in August 1940 by Cardinal Hinsley, archbishop of Westminster. He became chairman of a joint committee, the aim of which was to promote co-operation between the Roman Catholic and other churches.

In 1944 an event occurred which profoundly affected Fisher's future. William Temple died suddenly and unexpectedly. Fisher knew that his was one of the names that had been mentioned as a possible successor, and he was aware of Temple's hope that he would succeed him. The prospect did not alarm him unduly; he was not easily frightened, but he had no wish to leave London or the people he had learned to love. After some delay, however, the choice was made, and on 2 January 1945 his appointment was announced. Shortly afterwards in a BBC broadcast Henry Montgomery-Campbell, later bishop of London, laid special stress on the new archbishop's pastoral gifts. He predicted that Fisher would still remain at heart the true pastor he had always shown himself to be. And so it was. But he had many other gifts. He was a born organizer; he revelled in administrative details, and it came as no surprise that one of the first tasks to which he set his mind was the revision of the canon law of the church. Unrevised since 1604 there was much clarifying and modernizing to be done. Fisher approached this monumental task with enthusiasm. He once described it as 'the most absorbing and all-embracing' topic of his life.

The archbishop was also deeply involved in the political and social issues of the day. He had important and often controversial things to say on matters as various as the Suez crisis, the law in relation to homosexuality, marriage, discipline, lotteries, and premium bonds (to which he was strongly opposed), and the Wolfenden committee report which dealt with such moral problems as the practice of human artificial insemination.

One of the greatest national events in the years of his archiepiscopate was the coronation of Queen Elizabeth II in Westminster Abbey on 2 June 1953. Fisher was at his best on such an occasion. He conducted the ceremony with dignity and with an almost fatherly concern for the welfare of the young Queen. He succeeded in creating a person-to-person relationship with the monarch which was obvious to those who were present at the service. This was equally true of his relationship with other members of the royal family. He once said on this topic, 'I who am no courtier by nature at all found myself at ease with them.' They were equally at ease with him. It was the same, though the circumstances were very different, in his relationship with successive prime ministers, Sir Winston Churchill, Harold Macmillan (later the Earl of Stockton), Anthony Eden (later the Earl of Avon), Clement (later Earl) Attlee, and other members of the government. He preferred the direct personal approach to people, though he was never afraid to express his views in public debate. So it was with the press, with whom his relations were reputed to be bad. He was quite prepared to criticise the press in public if he thought it was abusing its freedom, but he normally got on very well with individual reporters.

Fisher's relations with the other churches and their leaders were always cordial. He was one of the presidents of the World Council of Churches (1946–54). His own initiative in drawing together the Church of England and the Free Churches will always be associated with the sermon he preached in Cambridge on 3 November 1946. During the course of it he pleaded for a free and unfettered exchange of life in worship and sacrament between the churches; he suggested that as a step towards full communion the Free Churches should 'take episcopacy into their own system'. In a notable passage towards the end he posed the crucial question, 'Cannot we grow to full communion with each other before we start to write a constitution?' The response was immediate. Discussions took place between the Church of England and the Free Churches over the next five years, and in 1958 the Methodist Church declared its 'readiness to proceed to a further stage in the promotion of intercommunion with the Church of England' subject to being given certain assurances. Although the conversations ended in breakdown in 1963, Fisher continued to show a lively interest in this as in all schemes for reunion.

Fisher's archiepiscopate will, however, be remembered chiefly for the number of journeys which he took to various parts of the Anglican communion and beyond. He was by far the most widely travelled archbishop of Canterbury in Anglican history, as, with the advent of the television camera, he was far the best known by sight. Between 1946 and 1960 he visited the United States and Canada several times, and in 1950 he and his wife went to New Zealand and Australia. In 1951 he visited West Africa; in 1955 Central Africa; in 1959 India, Japan, Korea; in 1960 Nigeria for its independence day celebrations, and East Africa. The visits to West, Central, and East Africa had as their chief purpose the inauguration of new provinces. All the new provinces of the Anglican communion which came into existence after World War II, and in addition the jurisdiction of the archbishopric in Jerusalem and the East Asian episcopal conference belong to his archiepiscopate. As Edward Carpenter wrote in his *Cantuar* (1971), 'Wisely, he appreciated the need to divest himself of authority for the African and Asian areas of the Communion, and it is probably here that historians will see his most enduring work.' In 1960, at the age of seventy-three, Fisher embarked on his final journey. In his own words, 'The actual idea came to me all in one flash. I was in my study . . . thinking about one thing and another, and suddenly there came, as a single inspiration, Jerusalem, Istanbul, Rome.'

The grand climax of the tour was the visit to Pope John XXIII. It was the first time an archbishop of Canterbury had visited the Holy See since Thomas Arundel made his journey in 1397. 'We talked', wrote Fisher, 'as two happy people, who had seen a good deal of the world and of life, and of the Churches.' In speaking to the Pope he said: 'We are each now running on parallel courses; we are looking forward, until, in God's good time, our two courses approximate and meet.' After a moment's hesitation the Pope replied: 'You are right.' The courtesy call, which was all Fisher claimed it to have been, was nevertheless a historic occasion, a significant breakthrough, and a triumphant conclusion to the tour. Fisher arrived back in England on 3 December, and on 17 January 1961 the announcement of his resignation came from Downing Street. He was appointed to a life peerage at the same time. He had been sworn of the Privy Council in 1939 and appointed GCVO in 1953. After a number of moves the Fishers went to live in Trent rectory near Sherborne in Dorset. Acting as assistant curate, Fisher ministered on Sundays in Trent and neighbouring churches with obvious content until his death in hospital in Sherborne 15 September 1972. He was buried in the churchyard at Trent.

Fisher received honorary degrees from Cambridge, Princeton, Pennsylvania, and Colombia (all 1946), London (1948), Manchester (1950), Edinburgh (1953), Yale (1954), British Columbia (1954), Northwestern University Evanston (1954), Gen. Theol. Sem. New York (1957), Trinity College Dublin (1961), and Assumption University of Windsor, Ontario (1962). He was prelate of the Order of St John of Jerusalem (1946–67). He was awarded the Royal Victorian chain (1949) and became a freeman of the cities of London and Canterbury (1952) and of Croydon (1961).

The official portrait (1953) by Middleton Todd is in Lambeth Palace.

[W. E. Purcell, *Fisher of Lambeth*, 1969; Edward Carpenter, *Cantuar*, 1971; personal knowledge.]

Ian H. White-Thomson

published 1986

FLEMING Sir Alexander

(1881–1955)

Bacteriologist, was born 6 August 1881, the third of the four children of Hugh Fleming, farmer of Lochfield in Ayrshire, by his second marriage, to Grace Morton, the daughter of a neighbouring farmer. Hugh Fleming, whose ancestors probably came from the Low Countries, had four surviving children by his first marriage, was sixty at the time of his second marriage, and died when Alec was seven. Fleming was born at Lochfield, an upland sheep farm with some arable land, near Darvel. He had his early schooling in a small country school at Loudoun Moor, then at Darvel (four miles distant), and for eighteen months at Kilmarnock Academy. At fourteen he and his two brothers of the second marriage went to live with a doctor brother in London, where he continued his education for two years at the Polytechnic Institute in Regent Street. The next four years were spent as a clerk in a shipping office in the City, but on the advice of his brother and with the help of a small legacy Fleming, in 1901, became a student at St Mary's Hospital medical school, where, besides the senior entrance scholarship in natural science, he won virtually every class prize and scholarship during his student career. He took the conjoint qualification in 1906 and the MB, BS of London University in 1908 with honours in five subjects and a university gold medal. A year later he became FRCS, having taken the primary examination as a student. As Sir Zachary Cope has said, 'Surgery might have gained what bacteriology would have lost. Yet surgery gained infinitely more, as things fell out.' Fleming had a very good memory and learning was never a burden to him. But he was no bookworm; both as undergraduate and as postgraduate he was an active and proficient member of the swimming, shooting, and golf clubs and even took some part in the students' theatrical entertainments.

Immediately after qualification Fleming began his association with (Sir) Almroth Wright as an assistant bacteriologist in the inoculation department at St Mary's Hospital. He also held for some years the post of pathologist to the London Lock Hospital. He was appointed lecturer in bacteriology in St Mary's medical school in 1920 and eight years later he was given the title of professor of bacteriology in the university of London. He retired from the chair with the title emeritus in 1948, but continued until the end of 1954 as principal of the Wright–Fleming Institute of Microbiology in which he had succeeded Almroth Wright in 1946.

During his early postgraduate years at St Mary's medical school Fleming was to a considerable extent the apprentice of Almroth Wright, whose dominant character and fertile brain directed the general research of the inoculation department (later the Wright–Fleming Institute) for many years. But from the beginning of his career Fleming showed his ingenuity and originality in devising simple apparatus and techniques for tackling laboratory problems, for example, in his work on the opsonic index, recently introduced by Wright as a method for assessing the effect of vaccine therapy, and in a brilliant essay on 'Acute Bacterial Infections', published in *St. Mary's Hospital Gazette*, which won him the Cheadle gold medal. His capacity for original and accurate observation was also demonstrated in 1909 by a well-written article in the *Lancet* on the aetiology and treatment, with autogenous vaccines, of acne. About this time, Ehrlich had introduced salvarsan for the treatment of syphilis and Fleming made a typical contribution by devising a simple micro-method for the serological diagnosis of this disease.

Soon after the outbreak of war in 1914, Almroth Wright was invited by the Medical Research Committee to establish a research laboratory in Boulogne to study the treatment of war wounds. Fleming, who had joined the Royal Army Medical Corps as lieutenant (and later became captain), was a member of the team and although much of the work done during this period was published jointly with Wright and others, Fleming himself made some outstanding contributions to knowledge of the bacteriology and treatment of septic wounds. In a paper published in the *Lancet* a year after the outbreak of war, he noted the evil significance of *Streptococcus pyogenes*, which was also demonstrated in the blood of about a quarter of the more severe cases. He believed that the severity of wound infection was related to the presence of necrotic tissue in the wound and advocated early removal of this dead tissue at the same time as another Scotsman, Sir Henry Gray, had independently introduced surgical débridement to obtain healing by first intention. Later, with A. B. Porteous, Fleming showed that most streptococcal infections occurred *after* the patient was admitted to the base hospital, thus giving forewarning of the dangers of hospital cross-infection with this organism. He also made a significant contribution to knowledge of gas gangrene, and helped Almroth Wright in his advocacy of physiological principles rather than the use of antiseptics for the treatment of war wounds by devising numerous ingenious experiments.

In 1922 came the discovery of lysozyme, an anti-microbial substance produced by many tissues and secretions of the body, particularly in leucocytes, tears, saliva, mucus, and cartilage. Fleming probably regarded lysozyme, which he later called the body's natural antibiotic, as his most important discovery and, with V. D. Allison, he showed its wide distribution in nature, its enzymic quality and remarkable stability, and the interesting phenomenon of the development of bacterial resistance to its action. He also developed new techniques to demonstrate the diffusibility of lysozyme, techniques later to prove useful in his studies of penicillin.

In September 1928, Fleming made the world-famous observation which was to lead in time to the new antibiotic era. He was studying colony variation in the staphylococcus in relation to the chapter he was writing on that organism for the *System of Bacteriology.* This necessitated frequent examination of plate cultures of the organism over a period of days when 'It was noticed that around a large colony of a contaminating mould the staphylococcus colonies became transparent and were obviously undergoing lysis.'

As he himself often said, it was a chance observation which he followed up as a bacteriologist, and his previous experience with lysozyme which turned his alert mind aside from study of the staphylococcus instead of 'casting out the contaminated culture with appropriate language'. Fleming in his original paper, published in the *British Journal of Experimental Pathology* (June 1929), described most of the properties of penicillin which became universally known. Some of the conclusions of that historic paper are worth quoting to illustrate the appreciation of the potentialities of this new 'antiseptic' by a man who had been an active antagonist of antiseptics generally. 'The active agent is readily filterable and the name "penicillin" has been given to filtrates of broth cultures of the mould.' 'The action is very marked on the pyogenic cocci and the diphtheria group of bacilli.' 'Penicillin is non-toxic to animals in enormous doses and is non-irritant. It does not interfere with leucocytic function to a greater degree than does ordinary broth.' 'It is suggested that it may be an effective antiseptic for application to, or injection into, areas infected with penicillin-sensitive microbes.'

Fleming noted particularly, as advantages over the known antiseptics, its diffusibility, its activity in dilutions up to 1 in 1,000 against the pyogenic cocci, and its complete absence of toxicity on phagocytes. He mentioned that 'Experiments in connection with its value in the treatment of pyogenic infections are in progress' and a few years later he noted that penicillin 'has been used in a number of indolent septic wounds and has certainly appeared to be superior to dressings containing potent chemicals'.

Fleming undoubtedly had some appreciation of the potentiality of penicillin as a systemic chemotherapeutic substance before the Oxford team demonstrated it, for he suggested its *injection* into infected areas and predicted that it could be used in the treatment of venereal diseases. Some attempt was made to concentrate penicillin, but as Fleming said in his Nobel lecture, 'We are bacteriologists—not chemists—and our relatively simple procedures were unavailing.' Besides, as Sir Henry Dale has written, 'neither the time when the discovery was made nor, perhaps, the scientific atmosphere of the laboratory in which he worked, was propitious to such further enterprise as its development would have needed'.

Meanwhile Fleming turned his attention to the new sulphonamides and having shown that these drugs were bacteriostatic and not bactericidal and were inhibited by large numbers of living or dead bacteria, he believed, prophetically, that they would not be effective in the local treatment of septic wounds. Here again and later when penicillin became available for clinical use, he demonstrated his technical skill and ingenuity in devising micro-methods for measuring the concentration of these drugs in the patients' blood. Indeed, he was generally acclaimed as the most skilled technician among Almroth Wright's numerous colleagues and followers. He was his own technician to the end and it was always a joy to watch his deft and neat handling of glass slide and capillary pipette. But technical inventiveness is worth much more to the research worker than technical skill and Fleming was equally well endowed with both. He was keenly interested in staining methods and when India ink became unavailable after 1918 it was Fleming who introduced nigrosin as a negative method of staining and showed how it could be used for demonstrating spores and capsules. He was probably the first to grow bacteria and moulds on paper or cellophane placed on top of nutrient agar and he demonstrated the suitability of paper for bringing out the pigment of chromogenic bacteria. He left an interesting collection of 'coloured pictures' composed entirely of bacterial cultures which he was fond of showing to royalty and other visitors to the Institute.

The catalogue of Fleming's published work leaves little room for doubt that he had to an unusual degree the almost intuitive faculty for original observation coupled with a high degree of technical inventiveness and skill. He had in fact most of the qualities which make a great scientist: an innate curiosity and perceptiveness regarding natural phenomena, insight into the heart of a problem, technical ingenuity, persistence in seeing the job through, and that physical and mental toughness which is essential to the top-class investigator. He was a natural biologist, keenly interested in and very knowledgeable about birds, flowers, and trees. He appreciated the healthy atmosphere of his early upbringing in the country: tramping the upland moors and learning the shorter catechism, he once told a reporter, had been powerful influences in shaping his life.

Physically, Fleming was short and stockily built with powerful square shoulders and a deep chest, a fresh complexioned face with a fine broad forehead, intensely light-blue expressive eyes and for many years a good crop of snowy white hair. He had great powers of physical endurance and in the days when burning the midnight oil was a regular performance in the inoculation department, Fleming was always the first to appear, fresh and fit, the following morning. Later he seemed to stand up astonishingly well to the heavy journeyings and junketings he had to undergo, and he kept his freshness and jaunty step to the end. He was sensitive and sympathetic, enjoyed the simple things in life, and was not impressed with the grandiose. A collection of schoolchildren's signatures or a letter from a child or from some poor person who had benefited from penicillin gave him as much joy as the gold medals and honorary degrees. But, like most Scots, he had a 'guid conceit' of himself and readily commanded respect from his colleagues inside and outside the Institute. He was essentially a humble, simple man who to the end remained remarkably unspoiled and unchanged despite all the honours which were showered upon him.

Fleming had a natural combativeness and urge to win which was very apparent in the games he played. This determination to succeed was evident in his tackling of laboratory problems when he took delight in using his technical skill and inventiveness to overcome difficulties. On the other hand, Fleming never took kindly to administrative responsibility and shied away from problems, preferring to 'wait and see' rather than take immediate decisions. He had tremendous constancy and loyalty—to his friends and colleagues, to the inoculation department, to St Mary's and to its staff and students, and this quality of steadfastness inspired the confidence of his companions which was never misplaced. He had a quiet unruffled wisdom which made him a shrewd judge of men, but tolerant of weaknesses in his friends and colleagues. He was not heard to speak ill of anyone although he had decided likes and dislikes. He was not an easy man to know well, partly because of his natural reluctance to talk and express his feelings. He was not a conversationalist and awkward silences were sometimes broken by awkward remarks: as one visitor put it—talking with him was like playing tennis with a man who, whenever you knocked the ball over to his side, put it in his pocket. But this was shyness, not intentional rudeness, for he liked company and had many friends in various walks of life before he became famous. His association with the Chelsea Arts Club and some of its members gave him particular satisfaction and an outlet for his artistic sense, for he enjoyed beauty wherever he saw it.

Innumerable honours were conferred upon Fleming in the last ten years of his life. He was knighted in 1944, and was awarded the Nobel prize for medicine, jointly with Sir Howard (later Lord) Florey and (Sir) E. B. Chain, in 1945. He became a fellow of the Royal Society in 1943, of the Royal College of Physicians of London in 1944, of the Royal College of Physicians of Edinburgh in 1946, and an honorary fellow of the Royal Society of Edinburgh in 1947. Doctorates of medicine, science, and law were conferred on him by many British, European, and American universities. He was commander of the Legion of Honour in France, member of the Pontifical Academy of Sciences, fellow of important societies and academies in many countries, and the recipient of many medals and honorary lectureships. He was elected rector of the university of Edinburgh (1951–4), was a convocation member of the senate of the university of London from 1950, a member of the Medical Research Council (1945–9), and president of the Society for General Microbiology (1945–7). Besides becoming an honorary citizen of numerous cities in Europe, he was a freeman of the burgh of Darvel where he was born, of Chelsea where he lived, and of Paddington where his work was done.

There are several portraits of Fleming, of which perhaps the best known are those by T. C. Dugdale in the library of the Wright–Fleming Institute and by Anna Zinkeisen in the boardroom of St Mary's Hospital. The Imperial War Museum has one by Ethel Gabain. There is also a number of busts—those by E. R. Bevan and E. J. Clack are in the Wright–Fleming Institute, another by E. R. Bevan stands in the square of Darvel, Ayrshire, and one in bronze by F. Kovacs is in the Chelsea Town Hall. There is a memorial stone at Lochfield Farm, a plaque in the crypt of St Paul's Cathedral and there are several monuments abroad. The Ministry of Health building at the Elephant and Castle is called Alexander Fleming House, and streets and squares in several countries have been named after him.

He died suddenly from a heart attack at his home, in Chelsea, London, 11 March 1955. He was buried in St Paul's Cathedral. Fleming was twice married: first, in 1915, to Sarah (Sareen) Marion, daughter of a farmer, Bernard McElroy, county Mayo, Ireland, and herself a trained nurse, who died in 1949; secondly, in 1953, to Amalia Voureka Coutsouris, daughter of a Greek doctor, and herself a medically qualified bacteriologist. There was one son of the first marriage, who qualified in medicine and entered general practice.

[L. Colebrook in *Biographical Memoirs of Fellows of the Royal Society*, vol. ii, 1956; Robert Cruickshank in *Journal of Pathology and Bacteriology*, vol. lxxii, No. 2, October 1956; *British Medical Journal*, 19 and 26 March 1955; André Maurois, *The Life of Sir Alexander Fleming*, 1959; personal knowledge.]

R. CRUICKSHANK

published 1971

FLEMING Ian Lancaster

(1908–1964)

Writer, was born in London 28 May 1908, the second of the four sons of Valentine Fleming, who became Conservative member of Parliament for South Oxfordshire in 1910 and was killed in France in 1917, when he was posthumously appointed to the DSO. His mother was Evelyn Beatrice Ste. Croix, daughter of George Alfred Ste. Croix Rose, JP, of the Red House, Sonning, Berkshire. She was ambitious for her sons and her dominant personality was perhaps in some part responsible for Ian Fleming's early lack of confidence. Peter Fleming, the traveller and writer, was his elder, Richard Fleming, merchant banker, a younger, brother. Ian Fleming was educated at Eton where he was overshadowed by Peter's brilliance but proved an outstanding athlete, becoming victor ludorum two years in succession, a feat only once equalled. By the wish of his mother he entered the Royal Military College, Sandhurst, but he withdrew in the following year and continued his education privately in Austria, Germany, and Switzerland.

Having failed to enter the Foreign Office in 1931, he joined Reuters news agency and in 1933 reported the historic trial in Moscow of some British engineers on charges of espionage and sabotage, an experience he was not to forget. Between 1933 and 1939 he worked successively as a banker and a stockbroker in the City of London. Throughout the war he held a key position in the Naval Intelligence Division in Whitehall as personal assistant to the director of naval intelligence, rising to the rank of commander. His particular interest was the organization of 30 Assault Unit dedicated to the task of seizing material of value to intelligence. Soon after demobilization he became foreign manager of the Kemsley group of newspapers, and continued to hold the post after Roy Thomson (later Lord

Thomson of Fleet) acquired the concern, resigning finally at the end of 1959. For the last years of his life he worked only as a writer. In 1952 he had married Anne Geraldine Mary, eldest daughter of the Hon. Guy Lawrence Charteris, son of the eleventh Earl of Wemyss, and divorced wife of the second Viscount Rothermere. The Flemings' only child, a son, was born in that year.

The wedding had taken place in Jamaica, where Fleming had built a house in 1946, and where it was to become his habit to spend the winter months working on the successive adventures of his famous creation, the secret agent James Bond ('007'). Beginning with *Casino Royale* in 1953, one of these books appeared every year until 1966. The success of the series, though immediate, was not overwhelming until the publication in 1958 of *Dr. No*, the first of his books to be filmed. Thereafter his economic position and his worldwide fame were assured.

On the publication of *Casino Royale* it was apparent to many that a remarkable new writer had arrived on the scene, in the tradition of Buchan, Dornford Yates, and Sapper, although at that stage almost certainly more promising than any of these had been. Original in construction, the book contained many of the elements which were to become Fleming's hallmark: evident familiarity with secret-service activities (not least those of his country's enemies), portrayal of the kind of rich life to be found in exclusive clubs, smart restaurants, and fashionable resorts, obsessive interest in machines and gadgets and in gambling, an exotic setting, a formidable and physically repulsive villain, a strong sexual component, a glamorous and complaisant but affectionate heroine, and—of course—James Bond himself. Bond, at any rate on the surface, was a carefully constructed amalgam of what many men would like to be—and of what perhaps rather fewer women would like to meet: handsome, elegant, brave, tough, at ease in expensive surroundings, predatory and yet chivalrous in sexual dealings, with a touch of Byronic melancholy and remoteness thrown in.

Some would say that Fleming never surpassed, perhaps never quite equalled, his achievement in *Casino Royale*. Certainly there is a power and freshness about the book which in an age less rigidly hierarchical in its attitudes to literature, would have caused it to be hailed as one of the most remarkable first novels to be published in England in the previous thirty years. Yet, as the series continued, the author extended and deepened his range, attaining a new pitch of ingenuity and technological inventiveness while discovering in himself a gift for descriptions of landscape and of wild life, in particular birds and sea-creatures, pushing out in the direction of a more audacious fantasy, as in *Goldfinger* (1959), and also towards a greater realism, as in *The Spy Who Loved Me* (1962). In *You Only Live Twice* (1964) he produced a striking synthesis of these two impulses, though in narrative and other respects the book was unsatisfactory; and the last volume, *The Man with the Golden Gun*, published in 1965 after his death and written when his health had already begun to fail, was sadly the weakest of the series: it never received his final revision. It was during convalescence from a heart attack that he began to write the children's stories *Chitty-Chitty-Bang-Bang* which were later to be filmed.

It is arguable that *Dr. No* is at least as absorbing and memorable as any of the other books, with its unrelaxed tension, its terrifying house of evil, and the savage beauty of its main setting on a Caribbean island, a locale which Fleming made part of himself and which always excited his pen to produce some of his best writing. But one cannot forget *Moonraker* (1955) for the vivid, rounded depiction of its villain, Hugo Drax, and what is probably the most gripping game of cards in the whole of literature, nor *On Her Majesty's Secret Service* (1963) for its idyllic seaside opening and the vigour of its skiing scenes. Indeed, there is hardly a page in all the 3,000 and more of the saga that does not testify to Fleming's ability to realize a unique personal world with its own rules and its own unmistakable atmosphere. His style is plain and flexible, serving equally well for fast action, lucid technical exposition, and sensuous evocation of place and climate; if it falls here and there into cliché or the language of the novelette, it never descends to pretentiousness. The strength of his work lies in its command of pace and its profound latent romanticism.

Fleming travelled widely from an early age and his interest in foreign places is reflected in his journalism, of which two volumes are collected, as well as in his fiction. His pursuits included motoring, golf, bridge, and underwater swimming, but his reading and his cultural interests generally were wider and deeper than might be thought common in writers of his stamp. He acquired an unusual collection of first editions of books which marked 'milestones of human progress'. His friendships were many and enduring. He was humble about his work and, though totally professional in his approach to his task, did not take himself seriously as a literary figure, perhaps to the detriment of his standing in critical circles.

He died in Canterbury 12 August 1964 less than a month after the death of his mother. A portrait of him by Amherst Villiers was reproduced in the limited, signed edition of *On Her Majesty's Secret Service*.

[Fleming's own writings; John Pearson, *The Life of Ian Fleming*, 1966; *Burke's Landed Gentry*.]

KINGSLEY AMIS

published 1981

FLOREY Howard Walter

(1898–1968)

Baron Florey

Experimental pathologist and the main creator of penicillin therapy, was born in Adelaide 24 September 1898, the youngest child and only son of Joseph Florey, an Oxfordshire shoemaker who had emigrated in 1885. Joseph's first wife had died in 1886, leaving two daughters, and he married Bertha Mary Wadham, an Australian, in 1889, who bore him two daughters and a son. By 1906 he had built up a shoe manufacturing business with branches throughout Australia. Howard Florey went to Kyre College and St Peter's Collegiate School, Adelaide. He was clever, hard-working, and determined, winning six scholarships and many prizes. He was also good at games, representing his school (and later his university) at tennis, football, and in athletics. In 1916 he entered Adelaide University medical school, where he was usually first in his class (winning three scholarships). There his critical mind led him to thoughts of research. He qualified as MB, BS, in 1921. In 1918 his father died suddenly, his business was found to be insolvent, and the Florey family was translated from wealth to poverty. Florey's medical studies were secured by his scholarships, but his ambition for research rather than a well-paid post in Adelaide was maintained with some personal misgivings. In 1921 he was awarded a Rhodes scholarship and, having qualified in medicine, he worked his passage to England as a ship's surgeon, arriving 24 January 1922.

In Oxford, Florey enrolled in the Department of Physiology under Sir Charles Sherrington, and at Magdalen College. Sherrington recognized his drive and creative independence of mind, and became his most influential guide and friend. In 1923 Florey obtained a first class in the honour school of physiology, then stayed on, at Sherrington's invitation, to study the blood flow in the capillaries of the brain. He made some discoveries and devised a method for inserting transparent windows in living tissues which he later used in various parts of the body to answer questions by direct, simple observation. In October 1924 he moved to Cambridge as John Lucas Walker student in the Pathology Department under Professor H. R. Dean who, with Sherrington, felt that a more experimental approach to pathology could be achieved by an active young physiologist. Florey had spent the summer vacation with the third Oxford University Arctic Expedition as medical officer, and though it provided no major excitements, he never forgot this experience of human comradeship and of the colourful beauty of the Arctic. In Cambridge he continued his study of blood-flow changes in inflammation and thrombosis—problems which remained a major interest for the rest of his career. He submitted this work for an Oxford B.Sc. in 1925, and was congratulated by his examiners. In the same year he was awarded a Rockefeller fellowship to go to the United States to learn micro-surgical techniques. He spent three months with Dr A. N. Richards in Philadelphia and then went to Chicago to work out methods for the study of mucus secretion. Since his Arctic expedition Florey had suffered bouts of indigestion. Investigation had revealed a mucous gastritis and, experimenting on himself, he became interested in mucus, the mechanism of its secretion, and its importance in protecting the mucous membranes. It was a line that led by logical stages to his work on penicillin.

While in America, Florey accepted the offer of a Freedom research fellowship at the London Hospital. He took up this post in June 1926, but it proved not entirely congenial since the laboratories were more concerned with routine than research. But he found a collaborator in (Sir) Paul Fildes, with whom he experimented on a treatment for tetanus, and he often slipped away to work for a few days in Oxford or Cambridge. In 1926 he married Dr Mary Ethel Hayter, daughter of John Hayter Reed, an Adelaide bank manager, whom he had known as a medical student in Adelaide. London life suited neither of them, and when Florey was offered the Huddersfield lectureship in pathology at Cambridge he returned eagerly in October 1927 to the same room which he had occupied before going to America. He now had a new laboratory boy—the fourteen-year-old Jim Kent, who was to stay as his indispensable and devoted assistant for the next forty-one years, and who contributed so much to the success of his research projects. Florey had become a fellow of Gonville and Caius College and its director of medical studies, but he had (or made) ample time for research. He had embodied work on the flow of blood and lymph, in a thesis for a Cambridge Ph.D. which was conferred in 1927. During the next four years he began several fruitful lines of study and with various collaborators published twenty scientific papers. One of these lines in particular had momentous consequences. In 1922 (Sir) Alexander Fleming had accidentally discovered an agent in mucoid secretions which dissolved certain bacteria. He called it 'lysozyme' and supposed that it might normally prevent infection. It proved, however, to act only on relatively harmless bacteria, and little further work was done on it. Florey took up lysozyme in 1929, because he thought that its presence in mucus might explain an antibacterial action he had observed and also the natural immunity of some animals. He studied lysozyme in animals, publishing two papers in 1930. Though the results did not suggest that lysozyme was necessary to natural immunity, Florey retained a determination to discover its nature and mode of action.

In 1932 Florey was appointed Joseph Hunter professor of pathology at Sheffield University, a choice which surprised orthodox pathologists who still considered him a physiologist. However, there were experienced pathologists in the department who could maintain the routine work while Florey infused vitality into the teaching and research. One of his projects was on the control of the spasms in tetanus by curare combined with mechanical artificial respiration—the basis of the modern treatment. He made important advances in the field of gastro-intestinal function. Lysozyme remained a major interest, although one constantly frustrated by the lack of adequate biochemical collaboration.

In 1934 the chair of pathology in Oxford became vacant on the death of Georges Dreyer. Florey was appointed in 1935, being strongly supported by (Sir) Edward Mellanby, secretary of the Medical Research Council. The Sir William Dunn School of Pathology, designed by Dreyer himself on a grand scale, had become something of a mausoleum. Florey came into this partial vacuum with Dr Beatrice Pullinger (from Sheffield) and Jim Kent. Between them they brought the department to life at all levels—teaching, research, and technical assistance. They were hampered by lack of money and Florey had to spend much time in fund-raising. The Medical Research Council and the Rockefeller Foundation were his main benefactors, but the sums obtained now seem absurdly small. There was little to be had from the university, and Florey was disappointed that pre-clinical departments like his own did not receive any substantial help from the £2 million Nuffield benefaction which was mostly spent on clinical research and teaching at the Radcliffe Infirmary.

Florey brought his department to life largely by attracting young post-graduates who had their own grants. The quality of their research and his own work attracted others and within a few years the Oxford School of Pathology was among the best in the world. Florey expanded his own lines of research to include these new recruits, forming teams in which each contributed some special expertise, and over which he kept a general but not authoritarian control. One such project was the study of the lymphocyte; another was gastro-intestinal function; a third was the study of the micro-circulation by cine-photography. But the most productive of all —perhaps of all time—was the work which led to the practical use of penicillin.

Florey had interested a biochemist, E. A. H. Roberts, in lysozyme, who purified it by 1937. He had also engaged a young refugee biochemist, (Sir) Ernst B. Chain, and asked him to discover how lysozyme dissolves bacteria. Chain found that it is an enzyme which attacks a specific bacterial structure. Reviewing the literature on lysozyme, Chain read the paper by Fleming, published in 1929, describing the chance discovery of a penicillium mould that apparently dissolved bacteria. Since this 'penicillin' (as Fleming called the active agent) attacked a wider range of bacteria than lysozyme, Chain was interested. He found many earlier reports of the antibacterial action of other moulds and organisms, but he also found an actual culture of Fleming's mould in the School of Pathology, with which he began experiments in 1938. Florey had not been particularly interested in penicillin, even though Dr C. G. Paine in his own department in Sheffield had tried it locally, with some success, on eye infections: he had been more concerned with the antibacterial substances produced by the body than by moulds. But he agreed with Chain that a study of such extraneous activities might widen a research which now seemed to be reaching a dead-end in lysozyme, and they decided to work together on three known substances produced by micro-organisms, including penicillin. The project was mentioned to the Medical Research Council in January 1939, and again in September, when a request for a special grant yielded £25 and the possibility of £100 later. However, the Rockefeller Foundation granted $5,000 (£1,200) per annum for five years, a considerable sum in those days. Experiments showed that penicillin was the most promising of the substances chosen for study, and might have therapeutic as well as scientific importance. Thereafter the project became a team one. N. G. Heatley undertook the production of the mould filtrate; Chain, later joined by E. P. Abraham, worked on the chemistry, while Florey and Dr Margaret Jennings carried out the animal work and, with Professor A. D. Gardner, the bacteriology.

On Saturday 25 May 1940 there was enough partially purified penicillin to discover if it could protect animals from an otherwise lethal infection—a crucial test. Eight mice were injected with virulent streptococci, and an hour later four of these had injections of penicillin. All four untreated mice were dead in a few hours, all the treated mice were alive and well next day. Florey's remark, 'It looks promising', was a typically laconic assessment of one of the most important experiments in medical history. The results of a large series of such experiments, published in August 1940, completely confirmed the initial promise. Florey tried to persuade British drug firms to produce enough penicillin to treat human cases, but they were already hard-pressed by wartime needs and damage and when he failed he turned his own department into a factory. Descriptions of the physical, chemical, biological, and administrative difficulties fill many papers and books, and all that can be said here is that they were overcome by collaborative perseverance and ingenuity, and by Florey's energy, determination, and personal example. Beginning in January 1941, there was a limited trial under his direction by Dr C. M. Fletcher on patients at the Radcliffe Infirmary,

Oxford. The cases chosen were mostly those of otherwise hopeless infection. Though only six could be treated systematically, and even these with restricted doses, the results were practically conclusive. Penicillin had been shown to overcome infections which were beyond any other treatment.

In June 1941, with Mellanby's approval, Florey and Heatley went to the United States to try to enlist commercial help. Florey's old friend, Dr A. N. Richards, promised government support for firms prepared to develop large-scale methods of production, and three accepted. While Heatley remained to assist, Florey returned to Oxford to direct an even greater production effort in his department. This allowed a completely conclusive trial on 187 cases in 1942, largely carried out by Florey's wife. In the summer of 1943 Florey, with (Sir) Hugh Cairns, undertook on the battlefields of North Africa a trial of penicillin in the treatment of war wounds, and six months later he went to Russia with information on the new results. Meanwhile commercial production had, at last, begun in Britain, and this revealed that technical methods had been patented in America. Florey was criticized for having 'given away' a valuable commercial asset. But the information which Florey gave in America had been freely offered earlier in Britain, where it was then considered unethical for doctors to patent medical discoveries. Such discoveries continued to be made at the School of Pathology on later antibiotics, and the official attitude to patents had by that time changed. In 1949 a complete account of the Oxford work was published as a two-volume book, *Antibiotics*, by Florey and six of his collaborators. In all, he was also the author or co-author of thirty-two scientific papers and over thirty published lectures and reviews on the subject.

In scientific and medical circles the Oxford achievement had been recognized and applauded. Florey had been elected a fellow of the Royal Society in 1941, before the penicillin work had been established. Thereafter many other honours followed. He was knighted in 1944, and in 1945 he shared the Nobel prize for medicine with Chain and Fleming. The general public, however, tended to regard Fleming as the creator of penicillin therapy. He had, of course, discovered the antibacterial power of a rather rare sort of mould, shown that it was non-toxic to animals, and had used it, without much success, as a local antiseptic in a few cases. He had also suggested that it might be injected locally. But he had not during the next ten years developed his discovery or aroused interest in it, and, in any case, in the 1930s sulphonamides had captured the medical imagination. Fleming had taken no part at all in the Oxford work, although his cultures had prompted it. When the tremendous fact of penicillin therapy became popular news, Florey was unwilling to talk to reporters. Fleming had less reserve, and articles appeared in which he was portrayed as the hero of a long struggle to harness his discovery, producing large amounts of penicillin at St Mary's Hospital, London, for use there or at Oxford under his direction. Such distortions, continuing uncorrected for many years, created a general impression that only Fleming's name should be associated with penicillin.

After a period of work on the use of antibiotics in tuberculosis, Florey returned in the mid 1950s to his early research interests. He used electron microscopy and marker techniques in new studies of mucus secretion and of vascular changes which can cause thrombosis. As always, he encouraged young workers to participate, and because his interest in the leucocytes was leading into the wider fields of immunology and cytogenetics, his department was ready to move into another new era. Florey, always the best animal surgeon in the department, regularly did long experiments undistracted by his emergence as a public figure. In this latter role he surprised those who had known him as something of a firebrand, since he accepted high official responsibilities with patience and even pleasure. He was concerned with the foundation of the Australian National University, paid many visits to Canberra, and was personally involved with the design, building, and organization of the John Curtin School of Medical Research. Though he refused to become the School's director, he retained his association with the university and was its chancellor in 1965. In 1960 Florey was elected president of the Royal Society, and he brought to it a vitality which rejuvenated what was a rather staid organization and made of its officers and staff a team with a new sense of purpose. A major change was the move from the Society's elegant but cramped quarters in Burlington House to the far more spacious Carlton House Terrace. He also widened the Society's interests to include applied science and demography, and he opened its doors to lively discussion meetings and study groups which extended its already great influence.

In 1962 Florey became provost of the Queen's College, Oxford, and relinquished his chair of pathology. The move puzzled colleagues who thought that, after a life concerned with the clear objectives of science and scientists, he would find the clever meanderings of college politics tiresome. For a time, it seems, he did; but mutual adjustments led to a pleasant working relationship and he was able to contribute practical improvements, as he had done before in every appointment. The college gained its European studentships and the Florey Building, and something of a new outlook. In return, he received the pleasure of a gracious style of living. He had always appreciated the college system in Oxford and Cambridge, and had much enjoyed the fellowship of Lincoln College which he had held since 1935 (he was made honorary fellow in 1962). In 1965 he was created a life peer as Baron Florey and a member of the Order of Merit. He had become a commander of the Legion of Honour, and had received the USA medal of merit, the Royal and the Copley medals of the Royal Society, honorary degrees from ten British and eighteen foreign universities, and other world-wide honours, medals, and prizes.

In 1966 Ethel Florey died after some years of disabling ill health. They had one son and one daughter. In 1967 Florey married Dr Margaret Augusta Fremantle, daughter of the third Baron Cottesloe, and formerly wife of Denys Arthur Jennings. She had worked with him at the School of Pathology since 1936. For some years Florey had suffered from angina, unknown to his colleagues, and it was from a heart attack that he died suddenly in Oxford 21 February 1968.

As a scientist, Florey had an extraordinary flair for choosing expanding lines of research; the ability to reduce a problem to simple questions answerable by experiment; great industry and determination; and an honesty that allowed of no self-deception. Equally important, he could inspire others to work almost as hard and well as himself. He published over 150 scientific papers (excluding reviews and lectures) but the vast amount of experimental work entailed is only revealed by his notebooks. *General Pathology* (1954), the textbook edited by Florey and published in four editions, reflects the progressive teaching at his School. As a person, despite his outward geniality and humour, he was a man of profound reserve. He did not show his deeper feelings and he had few, if any, close friends. Ethel Florey's ill health and, in particular, her progressive deafness, had from the first marred the happy companionship which both had expected from their marriage. Yet she had made a supreme effort to overcome these physical handicaps in her work on penicillin. Outside his own laboratory, Florey's main enjoyment was in travel, which in later years became world-wide. From his first arrival in Oxford in 1922 he took every opportunity to go abroad, working in foreign laboratories, learning languages, and, above all, appreciating the history, art, architecture, and music of the countries he visited. His letters to Ethel before their marriage are full of these experiences, and they reveal him as sensitive, lonely, unsure of himself, and deeply concerned for human troubles—a picture of himself very different from the one he presented to the world. 'I don't think it ever crossed our minds about suffering humanity', he said publicly of his reasons for starting work on penicillin. But in 1923, in a letter to Ethel, he wrote of 'the appalling thing of seeing young people maimed and wiped out while one can do nothing'. He was referring to untreatable infections. He, perhaps more than anyone before him, helped to achieve their defeat.

There is a portrait at the Royal Society, London, by Henry Carr, at the

Sir William Dunn School of Pathology, Oxford, by Frederick Deane; at St Peter's Collegiate School, Adelaide, by William Dargie (1963); and by Allan Gwynne-Jones (1963) at Adelaide University. There is also a bronze head by John Dowie in Prince Henry Gardens, Adelaide.

[Gwyn Macfarlane, *Howard Florey. The Making of a Great Scientist*, 1979; Lennard Bickel, *Rise up to Life*, 1972; E. P. Abraham in *Biographical Memoirs of Fellows of the Royal Society*, vol. xvii, 1971; personal knowledge.]

R. G. MACFARLANE

published 1981

FORSTER Edward Morgan

(1879–1970)

Novelist and man of letters, was born in London 1 January 1879, the only son of Edward Morgan Llewellyn Forster, architect, and his wife, Alice Clara, daughter of Henry Whichelo. His great-grandfather was Henry Thornton of the Clapham Sect, and his great-aunt, Marianne Thornton, left him £8,000 which enabled him to go to Cambridge and be financially independent enough to exist as a writer. He repaid his debt by writing her biography in 1956. His maternal grandfather had been a drawing master and came of a family of artists. When Forster was an infant, his father died, and he was brought up by his mother and a gaggle of maiden aunts in an atmosphere suffused with doting care. His childhood home at 'Rooksnest' at Stevenage was evoked in his novel *Howards End*, but his mother moved in 1893 so that he might go as a day boy to Tonbridge School. He did not admire public schools or their products whom he described as having 'well-developed bodies, fairly developed minds and undeveloped hearts'. His unhappiness there melted and his potentialities appeared only when he went in 1897 as a classical exhibitioner to King's College, Cambridge, where, as he wrote later, 'They taught the perky boy that he was not everything, and the limp boy that he might be something'.

The man who taught him that he might be something was his supervisor, Nathaniel Wedd, who first encouraged him to write. Wedd gave him the confidence to be sceptical of worldly values. (So did Samuel Butler from whom he learnt that although money often distorted men's values, it was nevertheless important and could help them to discover what was really valuable in life.) His other mentor at King's, G. Lowes Dickinson, whose biography he wrote in 1934, suggested that the best undergraduate societies were those in which men sought truth rather than victory in discussion. He was an Apostle, and in that society first met the undergraduates, two to three years his junior, who were to form the Bloomsbury set with whom he was to remain always on affectionate terms though preserving a certain detachment. The essence of his undergraduate days is memorably recorded in the first chapter of his second (and his favourite) novel *The Longest Journey* (1907). He was placed in the second class of part i of the classical tripos (1900) and part ii of the historical tripos (1901).

On leaving King's, Forster travelled in Italy and Greece, countries which meant much to him and symbolized a style of life which he contrasted with the puritanism of northern Europe. He soon began writing short stories which were later gathered together in *The Celestial Omnibus* (1911) and *The Eternal Moment* (1928). But in 1905 he found his true medium and published his first novel *Where Angels Fear to Tread* in which one of the characters, Philip Herriton, was modelled on his friend at King's, the musicologist E. J. Dent, just as in his second the undergraduate Ansell was to some extent taken from another friend, Alfred Ainsworth. His third novel, set in Italy, *A Room with a View*, appeared in 1908 and *Howards End* followed in 1910. In 1912 he went with Lowes Dickinson for the first time to India. At this time when living with his mother at Weybridge he published little. He began a novel on India and another entitled *Arctic Summer* but got stuck in both after the first few chapters. Another, *Maurice* (1971), completed in 1914, came easily; but it was then unpublishable and he chose to allow it to appear only after his death. It is about homosexuality and Forster defiantly gave it a happy ending.

Forster asked his biographer not to dissemble about his private life. He in no way resembled Oscar Wilde or sought the milieu of international homosexuals: he longed only for a loving and stable relationship with someone not of his own class. This was denied him until the 1930s when he achieved such a relationship which endured with great happiness until his death. His homosexuality made the Greek poet, C. P. Cavafy, especially sympathetic to him when they became acquainted during the war, when Forster was serving with the International Red Cross in Alexandria, and he took pride in being the first to promote Cavafy's reputation in England in *Pharos and Pharillon* (1923).

In 1921 Forster returned to India where he became the private secretary of the Maharaja of Dewas State Senior, a curious experience which he described in *The Hill of Devi* (1953). This second visit had the effect of releasing what was to be judged his masterpiece, *A Passage to India* (1924).

It was awarded the Femina Vie-Heureuse and James Tait Black memorial prizes; and it led to his being invited to give the Clark lectures at Cambridge entitled *Aspects of the Novel* (1927), his most substantial piece of literary criticism. He continued to write criticism and biographies, and became a notable broadcaster. These essays and talks were collected in *Abinger Harvest* (1936) and *Two Cheers for Democracy* (1951). The latter reflects Forster's growing concern during the thirties and forties with political and social questions. He was twice president of the National Council for Civil Liberties, the liberty of the individual being the political cause nearest his heart. Despite his distaste for politics he thought it his duty to join other artists in the International PEN Club and protest against Nazism; he displayed more judgement than many of them in discerning what issues were at stake. After the war he helped to write the libretto of Benjamin Britten's opera *Billy Budd* and saw three of his novels dramatized for the stage. He became the sage of humanism.

When his mother died in 1945 Forster had to leave Abinger Hammer where for the past twenty years he had lived. He had been a fellow of King's in 1927–33 and in 1946 was elected an honorary fellow and invited to make his home there; he moved into the set of rooms which Wedd had occupied. Life at King's enabled him to make friends among each new generation of undergraduates. Friendship had always meant much to him. T. E. Lawrence and Siegfried Sassoon in the period between the two wars were particularly close, and he knew Thomas Hardy, D. H. Lawrence, and W. H. Auden well. On his eightieth birthday at a luncheon, friends from over the world came to honour him, among them George Seferis, the Greek poet and ambassador. Many writers of a younger generation admired him, among them William Plomer, Angus Wilson, and L. P. Hartley. Two of his dearest friends were Jack Sprott, professor at Nottingham University, and Joe Ackerley, the literary editor. He lived at King's until his death at Coventry 7 June 1970. He refused a knighthood, which after the war Attlee somewhat inappropriately offered him, but became a CH in 1953 and was admitted to the Order of Merit on his ninetieth birthday. He received eight honorary degrees.

These honours recognized that, second only to D. H. Lawrence, Forster was the most important British novelist of his generation. His works were translated into twenty-one languages, and his work began to be intensively studied, especially in America where Lionel Trilling's perceptive study in 1944 established his place in the canon. He was particularly venerated in India for his sympathy with the movement for independence and with both Hindu and Muslim culture. Whereas T. S. Eliot was the defender of the Christian and conservative heritage in English culture, Forster spoke for liberal humanism. No one wrote with greater simplicity or originality in defence of such well-worn concepts as liberty, democracy, and tolerance. He was unafraid of the contradictions in life which he believed liberals ought to face: that friendship may mean being hard on friends; that freedom and art depended on money and inequality; that racial prejudice was iniquitous but that it was folly to deny that chasms between cultures and races existed and that the bridges between them were flimsy; that his working-class friends needed houses but that the new housing estates meant the death of rural England and destroyed man's healing contact with nature. But if a choice had to be made he would make it. 'If I had to betray my country or my friend I hope I should have the guts to betray my country.' His works were full of aphorisms: 'panic and emptiness', 'the life of telegrams and anger', 'only connect'.

He distrusted size, pomp, the Establishment, empires, politics, the upper classes, planners, institutions. He put his trust in individuals, small groups and insignificant people, the life of the heart and mind, personal relations. His sense of humour and of the absurd was highly developed. In appearance diffident and his ragged hedgerow of a moustache unimpressive, he could be melancholy and low temperature—he once said 'I warmed both hands before the fire of life, And put it out'; his vitality went into the characters in his novels and his writing. He spent nothing on himself and hardly ever took a taxi. Money was spent on his friends, particularly on the young who came from the working class. He loved music, paradoxically for one who distrusted greatness, Beethoven and the romantics, but also much modern music so long as he could hear passion in it. Sharp though his judgements on people and events could be, and keen though his eye was for pretentiousness or anyone on the make, he had a natural courtesy, great powers of affection, and a gift of gnomic wisdom which appeared not only in his works but in his life.

Forster was drawn as a child by George Richmond. A portrait in oils by Edmund Nelson and a red chalk drawing by Sir William Rothenstein are at King's; a portrait in oils by Roger Fry (1911) is in a private collection in London.

[*The Times*, 8 June 1970; Patrick Wilkinson, *E. M. Forster at King's*, 1970; B. J. Kirkpatrick, *A Bibliography of E. M. Forster*, with a foreword by E. M. F., 1965; Lionel Trilling, *E. M. Forster, a study*, 1944; K. W. Gransden, *E. M. Forster*, 1962; Wilfred M. Stone, *The Cave and the Mountains, a study of E. M. F.*, 1966; *Aspects of E. M. Forster*, ed. Oliver Stallybrass, 1969; P. N. Furbank, *E. M. Forster, a Life*, vol. i, 1977, and vol. ii, *Polycrates Ring, 1914–1970*, 1978 (the authorized biography); Francis King, *E. M. Forster and his World*, 1978; personal knowledge.]

NOEL ANNAN

published 1981

FREUD Anna

(1895–1982)

Psychoanalyst, was born 3 December 1895 in Vienna, Austria, the third daughter and youngest of six children of Sigmund Freud, founder of psychoanalysis, and his wife, Martha Bernays. She was educated at the Cottage Lyceum in Vienna and qualified as a teacher. From her father, however, she received the educational experience that was to shape her entire life. As a shy young girl she used to sit quietly in the background in Freud's study when he discussed psychoanalysis with visitors. In her early twenties she was in analysis with her father, an extraordinary arrangement, demonstrating that Freud was not an orthodox Freudian. Neither, as it was to emerge, was she. While she remained Freud's most loyal representative, she went beyond his work in method and theory.

Her innovations were the result of continuous practical involvement with normal and disturbed children. In the 1920s she worked in a nursery for deprived Viennese children while conducting individual child and adult analyses, and taking courses at Wagner Jauregg's psychiatric clinic. At the same time she lectured to psychoanalysts, parents, and teachers, began to publish, and represented her cancer-ridden father publicly and acted as his secretary and nurse privately.

Her first paper appeared in 1922, her first book *The Ego and Mechanisms of Defence* in 1937 (in German in 1936). This book became a classic of psychoanalysis and was translated into many languages. In it she added to Freud's identification of nine ways in which the ego protects itself against inner conflict five more, of which 'identification with the aggressor' has become the best known. Her own life, however, was an outstanding example of an already established mechanism: sublimation. This period saw the beginning of her lifelong friendship with Dorothy T. Burlingham and of her lasting public controversy with Melanie Klein's approach to child analysis.

Hitler's invasion of Austria ended her Viennese career. For five hours she was interrogated by the Gestapo. Released with the help of powerful international friends, in 1938 she, her father, and his closest circle escaped to London, where they were warmly received by British psychoanalysts and officials. Four of Freud's sisters, all aged over eighty, perished, however, in concentration camps.

Anna Freud began the second half of her life under the shadow of her father's deteriorating health; he died in 1939. In 1940 she and Burlingham established the Hampstead Wartime Nurseries for children suffering from family disruption. At the end of the war (she was naturalized in 1946) she founded the Hampstead Child Therapy Course and Clinic, devoted to training, therapy, and research and offering educational and medical services. The Hampstead seminars in the late 1950s showed Anna Freud at the height of her powers. Sitting regally under a portrait of her father she dominated the proceedings not only intellectually but also by her unparalleled knowledge of every detail of the clinic's work. She knew every child, had read every clinical report, and was actively involved in research. With unflagging energy she continued individual analyses, supervised trainees, lectured in many countries, edited, and wrote profusely. In 1966 she published another important book, *Normality and Pathology in Childhood*, in which she summarized her innovations, demonstrated her openness to ideas and methods outside psychoanalysis, and recognized the importance of genetic equipment, medical conditions, and above all environmental influences.

Taking the child as her focus she branched out relatively late in life into relevant matters of law. The Yale Law School appointed her visiting lecturer. A number of papers on psychoanalysis and law concerning children followed, culminating in two widely read books co-authored with Yale faculty members.

Her appeal to diverse audiences owed much to the clarity of her written and spoken word, a clarity that could diverge into sharpness. Some people experienced her as authoritarian, particularly in guarding her father's legacy. She arranged for some of his papers to be withheld well into the twenty-first century. Those who knew her privately spoke of her charm, humour, modesty, and enjoyment of the good things in life, particularly her cottage in Ireland, where swimming and riding alternated with work. Her other hobby, knitting, she engaged in during analytic hours.

She received honorary degrees and fellowships from many universities and medical institutions in England, the USA, Germany, and Austria, of which a medical degree from the University of Vienna (1975) and a Ph.D. from the Goethe University in Frankfurt (1981) meant most to her. She was appointed CBE in 1967. She died 9 October 1982 in London. She was unmarried.

[Elizabeth Young-Bruehl, *Anna Freud: A Biography*, 1989; *The Writings of Anna Freud*, 8 vols., 1975; obituary by Clifford Yorke in *Journal of Child Psychology and Psychiatry*, vol. xxiv, 1983; obituaries by Joseph Goldstein, Leo Rangell, and Robert S. Wallerstein in *The Psychoanalytic Study of the Child*, vol. xxxix, 1984; personal knowledge.]

MARIE JAHODA

published 1990

GEORGE VI

(1895–1952)

King of Great Britain, Ireland, and the British Dominions beyond the seas, was born at York Cottage, Sandringham, 14 December 1895, the second of the five sons of the Duke and Duchess of York, afterwards King George V and Queen Mary. His birth on the anniversary of the deaths of the Prince Consort (1861) and Princess Alice (1878) was an occasion for apprehensive apology, but Queen Victoria was gratified to become the child's godmother and presented him with a bust of the Prince Consort as a christening present. He was baptized at Sandringham 17 February 1896, receiving the names Albert Frederick Arthur George, and was known thereafter to the family as Bertie.

A shy and sensitive child, Prince Albert tended to be overshadowed by his elder brother, Prince Edward, and his younger sister Princess Mary. A stammer, developed in his seventh or eighth year, inhibited him still further, and of all the children it was probably he who found it least easy to withstand his father's bluff chaffing or irascibility. The boy withdrew into himself, compensating with outbursts of high spirits or weeping.

Nevertheless life passed evenly enough in the 'glum little villa' of York Cottage and in the other residences to which the migrations of the court took them, interrupted by such events as the funeral of Queen Victoria or the coronation of King Edward VII. By 1902 Prince Albert and his elder brother had graduated to the schoolroom under the care of Henry Peter Hansell, an Oxford graduate, formerly tutor to Prince Arthur of Connaught. Although he gained the affection of his pupils, Hansell was not the man to inspire small boys with a desire for learning. He himself thought they should have been at school; but his earnest attempt to create the illusion that they were was not convincing. In the spring of 1907 Prince Edward departed for Osborne and Prince Albert, now 'head boy' with Prince Henry in second place, was left to struggle with the mathematics which seemed likely to prevent him from following suit. But here he showed that ability to face up to and overcome difficulties which was to be the marked characteristic of his career. When he passed into Osborne his oral French, despite his stammer, was almost perfect, and his mathematics 'very fair indeed'.

At Osborne and Dartmouth (1909–12), years which saw his father's accession to the throne, Prince Albert was never very far from the bottom of the class; but he was popular as a 'trier' and a good comrade, and there was a steady development of both character and ability. He was confirmed at Sandringham on 18 April 1912, a day he remembered as one on which he 'took a great step in life'.

After a training cruise in the *Cumberland*, during which he visited the West Indies and Canada, Prince Albert was posted in September 1913 as a midshipman to the *Collingwood* in the Home Fleet. To his great satisfaction he was able to see active service in her as a sub-lieutenant at the battle of Jutland, 31 May 1916. But the war years were in the main frustrating. Always a poor sailor, he was now suffering almost continuously from gastric trouble. An operation for appendicitis, performed in Aberdeen 9 September 1914, brought only temporary relief and there followed three years of misery before on 29 November 1917 an operation for duodenal ulcer proved more successful. The subsequent great improvement in the Prince's health was marked in 1920 by his winning the Royal Air Force tennis doubles with his comptroller, who had long been his mentor and friend, (Sir) Louis Greig. That he lost to Greig in the semi-finals of the singles did not surprise him.

Meantime the Prince had been forced to admit that life at sea was too much for him and in November 1917 he transferred to the Royal Naval Air Service and on 1 April 1918 was gazetted flight lieutenant in the new Royal Air Force. It was now that his interest in physical fitness was aroused through his work in the training of boys and cadets. He was in France when the war ended and was asked by his father to represent him when the King of the Belgians made his official entry into Brussels on 22 November: the first state occasion on which he acted for the King.

Returning to England in the following February, Prince Albert, disregarding his dislike of flying, became a fully qualified pilot, 31 July 1919, and received his commission as a squadron leader on the following day. But the time had come for him to leave Service life and take his share of the burden of public duties which falls to a royal family. As further preparation, in company with Prince Henry, he spent a year at Trinity College, Cambridge, which might have been more fruitful had they lived in college. He studied history, economics, and civics, and in particular the development of the Constitution; and tackled an increasing number of public engagements, each one an ordeal by reason of the stammer for which he had so far found no cure. He became president of the Industrial Welfare Society and thereafter until he came to the throne made it his special interest to visit industrial areas and seek to make contact with the people as informally as possible. His own personal contribution towards better relations between management and workers took the form of what became the famous Duke of York's camps for boys from public schools and industry which were held annually, with one exception, from 1921 until 1939. He remained keenly interested in them to the end and delighted in the informality of his visits to the camps when he always joined vigorously in singing the camp song 'Under the Spreading Chestnut Tree'.

In the birthday honours of June 1920 the King created his second son Baron Killarney, Earl of Inverness, and Duke of York. He had already conferred the Garter upon him in 1916 on the occasion of his twenty-first birthday and was to confer the Order of the Thistle on him on his wedding day. The Duke went on his father's behalf to Brussels in 1921 and twice in 1922 to the Balkans where his bearing during elaborate state occasions earned the highest praise.

On 26 April 1923 in Westminster Abbey the Duke married Lady Elizabeth Angela Marguerite Bowes-Lyon, youngest daughter of the fourteenth Earl of Strathmore and Kinghorne, and together they entered upon that path of domestic happiness and devotion to public duty which was to earn them the nation's gratitude. They made their home first at White Lodge in Richmond Park which had been Queen Mary's childhood home; then from 1927 at 145 Piccadilly, with, later, the Royal Lodge, Windsor Great Park, as their country residence. Two daughters were born to them: Princess Elizabeth Alexandra Mary (21 April 1926) and Princess Margaret Rose (21 August 1930).

Official visits to the Balkans (1923) and Northern Ireland (1924) and many public engagements at home were followed by a tour of East Africa and the Sudan in the winter of 1924–5 which gave the Duke and Duchess a welcome holiday and the opportunity for big-game hunting. On his return the Duke presided over the second year of the British Empire exhibition at Wembley. Public speaking was still an ordeal for him but in 1926 he first consulted the speech therapist, Lionel Logue, who over the years was able to help him to overcome his stammer so that speech came much more easily to him and the listener was aware of little more than an occasional hesitation. It was therefore with a lighter heart that he left with the Duchess in 1927 for a strenuous tour of New Zealand and Australia, the highlight of which was the opening on 9 May of the first meeting of Parliament at the new capital city of Canberra. The natural sincerity of the Duke and the radiance of the Duchess evoked an enthusiastic response throughout the tour. On their return to London they were met at Victoria Station by the King and Queen, the Duke having been forewarned by his father: 'We will not embrace at the station before so many people. When you kiss Mama take yr. hat off': attention to detail inherited by the Duke who was in many ways his father's son.

During the King's illness of 1928–9 the Duke, who had been introduced into the Privy Council in 1925, was one of the counsellors of State. In May 1929 he was lord high commissioner to the General Assembly of the Church of Scotland, and, as his father was not sufficiently recovered to visit

Scotland, he returned to Edinburgh in October to represent the King as lord high commissioner of the historic first Assembly of the two reunited Scottish Churches.

These were quiet years of home-making and of public duties faithfully performed, overshadowed perhaps by the King's failing health but with no realization of what was to come. With the death of King George V on 20 January 1936 and the abdication of his successor in the following December all this was changed. The Duke and his elder brother had always been on good terms, but after the latter's accession the Duke found himself increasingly excluded from the new King's confidence. It was with the utmost reluctance that he finally brought himself to accept the fact that the King was determined to marry Mrs Simpson even at the cost of the throne. Of this resolve the King informed him on 17 November. The days which followed were filled with 'the awful & ghastly suspense of waiting' until on 7 December the King told the Duke of his decision to abdicate. Two days later the Duke had a long talk with his brother but could do nothing to alter his decision and so informing his mother later in the day 'broke down & sobbed like a child'. On 12 December 1936 he was proclaimed King, choosing George VI as his style and title. His brother he created HRH the Duke of Windsor.

Thus there came to the throne a man who had 'never even seen a State Paper', at a time when the monarchy had suffered the successive blows of death and abdication. 'I am new to the job', the King wrote to Stanley Baldwin at the end of the year, 'but I hope that time will be allowed to me to make amends for what has happened.' To this task he brought his own innate good sense and courage in adversity, disciplined by his naval training and sustained by the strength which he drew from his marriage, the sterling qualities of his mother, and the goodwill of the nation. The King had the same simple religious faith as his father and the coronation which took place in Westminster Abbey on 12 May 1937 was a genuine act of dedication on the part of the new King and Queen. It was shared by millions of their people, for the service was broadcast by the BBC, an arrangement which had the full support of the King against considerable opposition.

The brilliance of a state visit to France in July 1938 brought a momentary gleam of light in a darkening international situation. The King had full confidence in his prime minister and like Neville Chamberlain believed that every effort must be made to avoid a war. Final disillusionment came in March 1939 when the Munich agreement was swept aside and the Germans finally destroyed Czechoslovakia. Shortly after the return visit to Great Britain by President and Mme Lebrun later in the month there was announced the Anglo-French guarantee of Polish independence against aggression. Two months later came the first occasion on which a reigning British monarch had entered the United States. The visit of the King and Queen to North America in May–June 1939 was a resounding success and gave them an increase of confidence. In Canada the King addressed the members of the Senate and the House of Commons and gave the royal assent to bills passed by the Canadian Parliament. At Hyde Park he was able to discuss with President Roosevelt the help which might be expected from the United States in the event of a European war. The warm regard which the two men felt for one another was thereafter maintained by correspondence. Nevertheless the King chafed in these years at his inability to influence the course of events. His successive suggestions of personal communications to Hitler, to King Victor Emmanuel, to the Emperor of Japan, were felt to be inadvisable by a Government which did not share his belief in communications between heads of State.

When, inevitably, war with Germany came, the King broadcast to the Empire on the evening of Sunday, 3 September 1939, a simple call to his people to fight for the freedom of the world. Of the issue he was never in doubt and it was no small part of his contribution in the years to come that he was able to transmit this unclouded confidence to more complex and fearful minds.

In October the King visited the Fleet at Invergordon and Scapa Flow and in December he spent some days with the British Expeditionary Force in France. At Christmas he resumed his father's tradition of broadcasting a personal message to the Empire, a custom maintained for the rest of his life despite his dislike of the microphone. When Chamberlain resigned the premiership in May 1940 the King was distressed to see him go and would have liked Lord Halifax to succeed him. But Chamberlain informed him that Halifax, being in the Lords, was 'not enthusiastic' and the King accordingly accepted the advice to send for (Sir) Winston Churchill. By September formal audiences had given way to a weekly informal luncheon and a somewhat guarded relationship had warmed into genuine friendship.

Throughout the war the King and Queen remained in London, sleeping at Windsor during the bombing. Buckingham Palace was hit nine times: in September 1940 it was bombed twice within three days. On the second occasion six bombs were dropped over the Palace by day and the King and Queen had a narrow escape—even the prime minister was not told how narrow. 'A magnificent piece of bombing', remarked a police constable to the Queen; but a tactical error. Prompt and indefatigable in their visits to bombed areas throughout the country the royal pair knew that it was realized that they too had suffered; it was now that they entered into the hearts of their people in a very personal way. It was the King's idea in 1940 to create the George Cross and Medal, primarily for civilian gallantry; and his idea two years later to award the Cross to Malta for heroism under siege. In that year of successive disasters to the Allies the tragedy of war touched the King more closely when his younger brother the Duke of Kent was killed on 25 August 1942 in a flying accident while on active service.

By 1943 the tide of the war had turned and in June the King visited his troops in North Africa where the Axis forces had surrendered. In two weeks he covered some 6,700 miles and although it involved some risk the tour included a visit to Malta, on which he was determined in recognition of the island's gallantry. After the surrender of Italy in September 1943 the King shared with J. C. Smuts some doubts about the wisdom of opening up a second front in France; they communicated their misgivings to Churchill who made it clear, however, that it was too late to change plans which were already well advanced. On 15 May 1944 the King attended the conference at St Paul's School at which the preparations for invasion were expounded. Before D-Day (6 June) he had visited all the forces bound for Normandy. Both he and Churchill wanted to witness the assault from one of the ships taking part. The King, on reflection, was able with his usual common sense to see the unwisdom of this course; it was not without difficulty that he prevailed upon Churchill to abandon the idea on his own count. Only ten days after D-Day the King had the satisfaction of visiting General Montgomery's headquarters in Normandy. For eleven days in July–August he was with his armies in Italy, and in October he again visited the 21st Army Group. When the European war ended on 8 May 1945, Londoners crowded towards Buckingham Palace in their rejoicing as they had done on 11 November 1918. In the evening the King broadcast a call to thanksgiving and to work towards a better world. There followed an exhausting fortnight of celebration which left the popularity of the monarchy in no doubt. There were state drives through London and services of thanksgiving at St Paul's Cathedral (13 May) and at St Giles' Cathedral, Edinburgh (16 May). On the 17th the King received addresses from both Houses of Parliament in the Great Hall of Westminster. Labour having withdrawn from the coalition, Churchill formed his 'caretaker' government and in July came the first general election of the King's reign. It proved a victory for Labour and, accepting Churchill's resignation, the King invited C. R. (later Earl) Attlee to form a government. When Attlee replied to the King's inquiry that he was thinking of Hugh (later Lord) Dalton as foreign secretary the King suggested that Ernest Bevin might be a better choice. This had indeed been Attlee's first thought but he had allowed himself to be influenced by Bevin's own desire for the Treasury. In the event it was Bevin who went to the Foreign Office.

The King opened Parliament on 15 August 1945, the day of the Japanese surrender, and ten days later he and the Queen left for Balmoral for a much needed rest. On his return to London in October he found that the advent of peace had done little to lighten his, or the nation's, burden. Great Britain, although still beset by austerity, was moving forward into the welfare State; the British Empire was evolving into the British Commonwealth of Nations; and Russian imperialism was on the march. Some of the new ministers lacked experience; while not out of sympathy with Labour there were occasions when the King felt that they were going ahead too fast and that he should exercise the right of the monarch to advise and even to warn. This he was able to do the more easily in that he now had a width of experience and a maturity of judgement which made it natural for people to turn to him for guidance.

In 1947 the King and Queen and the two princesses paid an extensive visit to Southern Africa where the King opened Parliament at Cape Town 21 February, and in Salisbury, Southern Rhodesia, 7 April, and where, also at Cape Town, the Princess Elizabeth celebrated her twenty-first birthday. It was always a matter of regret to the King that he was never able to visit India. The dissolution of the Indian Empire and the emergence of India as a sovereign independent republic within the British Commonwealth brought problems in the relation of the Sovereign to the Commonwealth in which he took great interest; but the necessary legislation had not been completed before he died.

On 20 November 1947 the Princess Elizabeth married Lieutenant Philip Mountbatten, RN, son of the late Prince Andrew of Greece, whose elevation to the peerage as Duke of Edinburgh was announced on that day. Five months later, 26 April 1948, the King and Queen celebrated their silver wedding and drove in state to St Paul's Cathedral for a service of thanksgiving. In the following October, for the first time since the war, the King opened Parliament in full state. He had, as usual, a heavy programme of engagements which included a visit to Australia and New Zealand in the spring of 1949. But symptoms of early arteriosclerosis had been apparent for some time and it now seemed that his right leg might have to be amputated. The first announcement of his condition was made on 23 November 1948 when the Australian tour was cancelled. A right lumbar sympathectomy operation was performed at Buckingham Palace 12 March 1949, from which the King made a good recovery although he was not restored to complete activity.

At the general election of February 1950 Labour was returned with but a narrow majority, and to anxiety at home over the uncertainty of government and a precarious economic situation was added anxiety over the outbreak of the Korean war. Both continued into the following year and even the Festival of Britain, opened by the King from the steps of St Paul's on 3 May 1951, could not dispel the gloom. Towards the end of the month the King succumbed to influenza. There followed convalescence at Sandringham and Balmoral; but he was found to have a malignant growth and on 23 September underwent an operation for the removal of his left lung. Attlee had already asked for a dissolution of Parliament and on 5 October the King was able to give his approval to the act of dissolution. With the return of the Conservatives with a small majority Churchill once more became his prime minister. From the list of government appointments the post of deputy prime minister, which had crept in during the war, was deleted on the King's instructions as being unconstitutional. As he did not fail to observe, it would have restricted his freedom of choice in the event of the death or resignation of the prime minister.

A day of national thanksgiving for the King's recovery was observed on 2 December and there followed a family Christmas at his beloved Sandringham. On the last day of January 1952 the King went to London Airport to see the Princess Elizabeth and the Duke of Edinburgh off on a visit to East Africa, Australia, and New Zealand. But their tour was perforce curtailed for after a happy day's shooting the King died in his sleep at Sandringham early on the morning of 6 February 1952. After lying in state in Westminster Hall he was buried on the 15th in St George's Chapel, Windsor, where a memorial chapel was built and dedicated in 1969.

Trained to service, although not to the throne, the King had served to the limits of his strength and of the confines of monarchy. Scrupulous in observing his constitutional position, he was nevertheless determined to exercise the role of monarch to the full in the service of his people. It was always an underlying frustration that he could not do more; and a mark of his modest diffidence that he failed to appreciate how much he did by being what he was. The whole of his reign was overshadowed by war and the fears and changes brought about by war. At such a time a nation needs not only the warrior leader which it found in Churchill but also the image of the way of life for which it fights, and this it found in the King. Lithe and handsome, good at sports, an excellent shot and a skilled horseman, he was the country squire, the racehorse owner, the freemason, and above all the family man. His approach to life was one of common sense and humour. He made no claims to brilliance of intellect yet had a questing mind for which the twentieth century held no fears; his keenness of observation and determination to get to the heart of the matter could open up new lines of thought in others. He had few hobbies but was well versed in all that concerned his *métier* as monarch. He was the King *malgré lui* whom the nation had watched grow into kingship with a steadfast courage which had earned him their respect, their gratitude, and their affection.

The King was painted by many of the leading artists of the day, the state portrait of him in his coronation robes being by Sir Gerald Kelly in 1938. There was, in addition, the statue in the Mall by William McMillan which was unveiled by the Queen on 21 October 1955.

[John W. Wheeler-Bennett, *King George VI*, 1958.]

HELEN M. PALMER

published 1971

GIBSON Guy Penrose

(1918–1944)

Airman, was born in Simla 12 August 1918, the younger son of Mr Alexander James Gibson, of the Indian Forest Service, and his wife, Nora Mary Strike. He was educated at St Edward's School, Oxford, where his housemaster, Mr A. F. Yorke, describes him as 'strong-minded without obstinacy, disarmingly frank and of great charm'. As a prefect, he exerted his authority without apparent effort, whilst at games, although he had no special aptitude, he forced himself into good teams by sheer determination, showing signs of that physical stamina which was later to stand him in such good stead.

Gibson left school somewhat early to join the Royal Air Force. He was granted a short-service commission in November 1936 and ten months later joined No. 83 (Bomber) Squadron as a trained pilot. He took part in the first attack—on the Kiel canal—of the war of 1939–45. In July 1940 he was awarded the DFC and shortly afterwards completed his first full operational tour. This would normally have earned him a rest at a training unit, but within two months his persistence had gained him access to Fighter Command where he carried out a further operational tour on night fighters, shooting down at least four enemy aircraft and gaining a bar to his DFC.

In April 1942, at the early age of twenty-three, he was promoted wing commander and returned to Bomber Command in command of No. 106 Squadron. At this time he had reached operational maturity and the quiet forcefulness of his character permeated the whole squadron, although it must be admitted that his relations with his aircrews had a special intimacy which he was never quite able to achieve with the groundcrews. He held command of the squadron for eleven months, an unusually long period and one covering the intensive fighting associated with the early attacks on the Ruhr, culminating in the first 1,000-bomber raid, and the difficult period in the winter of 1942–3. One who knew him well during this period said that he was the best captain he ever flew with and that it would have had to be a very smart night-fighter pilot to catch him out. It was during this period that he was appointed to the DSO and later awarded a bar, a recognition of the pre-eminence which the squadron had attained under his leadership, and his own exceptional contribution of 172 sorties.

By ordinary standards, Gibson should have been more than usually ready for a spell away from operations, but his rest proved short-lived, and after only a week at headquarters No. 5 (Bomber) Group, setting down his thoughts on bomber tactics, he was offered the command of No. 617 Squadron, which was then about to be formed for a special attack on the Möhne and Eder dams. He accepted with alacrity and thus entered a period which was to show the full measure of his leadership, in the intensive, and at times highly dangerous, preliminary training, and in the meticulous planning which alone made the subsequent operations possible. During the attack on the Möhne dam on the night of 16–17 May 1943 Gibson himself released the first weapon at low level in the face of heavy fire, and then flew so as to draw the fire of the defences from each crew as they went into attack. For this gallant act, and for his leadership throughout this highly successful action, he was awarded the Victoria Cross.

During the next twelve months Gibson undertook a variety of staff appointments, including a lecture tour in America, where his modesty, his straightforward approach to all problems, and the aura of operational success, made him a notable figure; but in June 1944 he was back once more in No. 5 (Bomber) Group where he took up the appointment of operations officer in No. 55 Base which included his old squadron, No. 617.

For some weeks Gibson strove hard for permission to fly on operations but met with a firm refusal. However, on the night of 19–20 September 1944, when the main Lancaster force of No. 5 Group was attacking a target involving only slight penetration into enemy-held territory, it was agreed that he should fly in a Mosquito and act as 'master bomber'. Gibson successfully directed the attack, wished the Lancaster force 'good-night' and turned for home in the normal manner. He did not reach base and it was subsequently learned that through some unknown cause his aircraft crashed in Holland. He was buried in the small cemetery at Steenbergen, Bergen-op-Zoom, Holland.

Thus ended a career which has few equals in the history of air warfare—a career of action, of which the mainspring was a wholly phenomenal faith. Given this faith, all things were possible, for if the devil ever temptingly suggested that a project was beyond him, he would unceremoniously order him where he belonged. In this attitude, there was nothing that was foolhardy, for every action which he took was planned in detail and he knew precisely what he would do in every emergency. Throughout, he had the loyal support of all who flew with him.

In 1940 Gibson married Evelyn Mary Moore; there were no children. A portrait by Cuthbert Orde hangs in the RAF officers' mess at Scampton, Lincolnshire. A drawing by Sir William Rothenstein is reproduced in his *Men of the R.A.F.* (1942).

[Guy Gibson, *Enemy Coast Ahead*, 1946; Air Ministry records; private information; personal knowledge.]

RALPH A. COCHRANE

published 1959

GRANT Cary

(1904–1986)

Film actor, was born 18 January 1904 at 15 Hughenden Road, Ashley, Bristol, as Archibald Alec Leach, the son of Elias Leach, tailor's presser, and his wife, Elsie Maria Kingdon, daughter of a shipwright. An earlier baby brother had died before his birth. Years later, after he had left England, a half-brother was born. He attended Fairfield Secondary School, Bristol. When he was ten, his mother disappeared and he thought she had died. However, she had been committed to a mental hospital, where she remained for many years. Discovering the exciting life backstage at the Bristol Hippodrome, he was fascinated by Bob Pender's Knockabout Comedians, a visiting troupe of slapstick, acrobatic, and stilt artists, and joined them when he was fourteen. For two years they toured Britain, and then had a long run in New York in 1920, after which they spent a year touring the United States. When the troupe returned to England Leach, now eighteen, stayed on in America and took various jobs in vaudeville, at Coney Island and as a sandwich-board man on stilts. After a speaking part in revue, Arthur Hammerstein, the producer, cast him in an operetta by his nephew Oscar in 1927. He spent several years working in Broadway musicals, in theatrical touring companies, and in repertory. In the 1920s he went to and fro between England and America.

In 1931 he easily obtained a Hollywood contract with Paramount, adopted the name Cary Grant, and began five years as a handsome romantic lead in many unremarkable films. *Blonde Venus* (1932) with Marlene Dietrich and two Mae West films may not have been great pictures, but the exposure was good for his career. *Sylvia Scarlett* in 1935, although another indifferent film, was a turning-point for him as he began to evolve a style of his own.

In 1937 he became freelance, which he remained, choosing his films carefully and developing a light comedy touch. Over the next thirty years he was to make many huge box-office successes, taking a percentage rather than a fee. He changed his name legally in 1941 and became an American citizen in June 1942. Among his many sophisticated and 'screwball' comedies, romantic comedies, and comedy thrillers, perhaps the best remembered are *Bringing Up Baby* (1938) and *The Philadelphia Story* (1940). He worked with some of the best directors and with stars such as Katharine Hepburn, Irene Dunne, Ingrid Bergman, and Grace Kelly. Above all, it was (Sir) Alfred Hitchcock who saw beyond the light comedian and jaunty man-about-town, giving him more subtle parts and being responsible for three of his best films, *Suspicion* (1941), *Notorious* (1946), and especially *North by Northwest* (1959). In 1966, at the age of sixty-two, he appeared in a part other than romantic lead for the first time. Not relishing the role of elderly character actor, and perhaps bored after seventy-two films, he made no more.

For many years one of the most glamorous and wealthy stars in Hollywood, playing opposite top actresses from Jean Harlow in the 1930s to Leslie Caron over a generation later, he was widely seen as an amiable performer who always played himself and, somewhat unjustly, was not taken seriously as an actor. He was nominated for the Best Actor award in 1941 and 1944 but did not win the Oscar. He finally got recognition from his peers in 1969 when, his film career over, the Academy belatedly gave him the survivor's consolation prize, an honorary award. The public loved him, however, and most of his films did well at the box office, some of them spectacularly so. He remained busy in old age, having a number of active directorships, including of the cosmetic firm Fabergé and Metro-Goldwyn-Mayer.

A tall, well-dressed man with thick dark hair and a marked cleft in his chin, he had a charming screen personality and self-deprecatory wit. He modified his west country working-class tones to an accent all his own, clipped and acceptable to American ears as upper-class British. So distinctive was his screen presence that it was easily mistaken for the man himself, but his private life suggests a deeply troubled individual. Rumoured to be bisexual, he had four unhappy marriages which collapsed quickly, with acrimony. His damaged childhood and vagabond youth had not equipped him for good personal relationships. Only a fifth marriage, when he was seventy-seven, to a much younger woman, seems to have brought him some tranquillity.

Cary Grant was married to actress Virginia Cherrill, formerly wife of

Irving Adler and daughter of James Edward Cherrill, of independent means, 1934–5; Woolworth heiress Barbara Hutton, daughter of Franklyn Laws Hutton and his wife Edna, one of Frank Winfield Woolworth's two daughters, 1941–5; actress Betsy Drake 1949–59; actress Dyan Cannon (whose true name was Samile Dyan Friesen, daughter of an insurance executive), by whom he had his only child, a daughter, 1965–8; and former public relations director Barbara Harris in 1981. The first four marriages ended in divorce. He died of a stroke in Davenport, Iowa, 29 November 1986.

[*The Times* and *Independent*, 1 December 1986; Nicholas Thomas (ed.), *International Dictionary of Films and Filmmakers*, vol. iii, 1992; Chuck Ashman and Pamela Trescott, *Cary Grant*, 1987; William Currie McIntosh and William Weaver, *The Private Cary Grant*, 1983; Charles Higham and Roy Moseley, *Cary Grant, the Lonely Heart*, 1989.]

RACHAEL LOW

published 1996

GREENE Sir Hugh Carleton

(1910–1987)

Journalist, broadcaster, and publisher, was born 15 November 1910 in Berkhamsted, the youngest of four sons and fifth of six children of Charles Henry Greene, headmaster of Berkhamsted School, and his wife Marion Raymond (his cousin), daughter of the Revd Carleton Greene, vicar of Great Barford. One of his brothers was the writer Graham Greene. He was educated at Berkhamsted School and at Merton College, Oxford, where he obtained a second class in both classical honour moderations (1931) and English (1933).

Having spent some time in Germany before he went to university, he joined the *Daily Telegraph*'s office in Berlin (1934) and became its chief correspondent in 1938. In May 1939, as a reprisal for the expulsion from London of a German correspondent, he was expelled from Germany. In his five years in Berlin he had become a forthright correspondent. He witnessed the rise of the Nazis and saw some of the evil at first hand, an experience which was a major influence in his life. As he put it: 'I learnt to hate intolerance and the degradation of character to which the deprivation of freedom leads.' The *Daily Telegraph* then stationed him in Warsaw. The Germans began to bomb Katowice on 1 September 1939 and within a week Greene had to leave Poland. He travelled to Romania, carrying only a bottle of beer and a gas mask. As the war spread, in the following months he reported from a number of European countries until in June 1940 he arrived at Falmouth, having left first Brussels and then Paris just ahead of the German armies.

After a brief period as a pilot officer in intelligence, while a member of the Royal Air Force Volunteer Reserve, he arrived at the British Broadcasting Corporation in October 1940 to become assistant news editor of the German Service. It was the beginning of a new career and a relationship with the BBC that was to last for thirty-one years. In 1942 he flew in a Mosquito bomber over German-occupied Norway to neutral Stockholm, to hear for himself how the BBC output sounded through the German jamming. As a result, he changed the style in which the German news was written and broadcast. He concentrated on news, being less interested in features programmes, and made many hard decisions to dismiss staff. The broadcasts put out by his department eased the job of the postwar occupation and reconstruction of Germany, because, as he later learned, they had made a genuine impact on Germany, providing the core of Britain's anti-Nazi propaganda.

After the war Greene was seconded in 1946 to the British Control Commission in Hamburg to reorganize German broadcasting. Although he returned to the BBC briefly (from December 1948, to the Eastern European Service), he was seconded again in 1950, this time to the Colonial Office, to supervise psychological warfare against the communists in Malaya, in the Emergency Information Service. When he returned to London in September 1951, he had no clear view of what he wanted to do. He made enquiries about various jobs in journalism and intelligence but nothing came of them. At the invitation of Sir Ian Jacob, director-general of the BBC, he went back to Bush House and took on a number of senior appointments, eventually becoming controller, Overseas Services (1955–6). By 1956 it was clear that Jacob was grooming Greene as his successor. But first he had to learn about the non-journalistic side of the BBC. For two years he was director of administration and then, in 1958, director of news and current affairs. He was the first holder of that post and he succeeded where his predecessor, Tahu Hole (head of the news division), had failed. He restored the eminence of news and current affairs. The 1959 general election was the first reported by the BBC in its news bulletins and the first in which there was questioning of party leaders and some discussion of the issues.

The arrival of Hugh Greene as director-general on 2 January 1960 was the most important thing to happen to the BBC since World War II. For the first time a BBC man had been promoted to the top job. He changed the BBC for the better by doing three things. He made it clear that he was the editor-in-chief, exercising general editorial control over the BBC's output of programmes; he gave priority to television over radio; and he made the BBC realize that competition could be stimulating. This was an exciting and exhilarating time for those who worked in the BBC. For those who watched and listened to it the changes were challenging and occasionally disturbing, with programmes such as *That Was The Week That Was* and *Till Death Do Us Part*, as well as the series of 'Wednesday Plays'. In Greene's view, the BBC did a great service to the country by widening the limits of discussion and challenging the old taboos. He was dismissive of those who did not share those views—too dismissive, some felt. He played a major part in the establishment of the Open University, allocating thirty-two hours of broadcasting time each week.

He ensured the future well-being of the BBC by convincing the committee of inquiry into the future of broadcasting (1960–2), chaired by W. H. (later Baron) Pilkington, that BBC television should have a second channel (BBC 2) and that colour television should call for an additional licence fee. Both these moves were delayed by the government. Financial pressures increased and so did criticisms of the BBC. Greene's relationship with the government became more testing and in 1967 Harold Wilson (later Baron Wilson of Rievaulx) switched Baron Hill of Luton from the chairmanship of the Independent Broadcasting Authority to the BBC. Greene was enraged and thought of resigning at once, but he was persuaded to stay. The strain of working under a chairman he did not respect became too much and on 31 March 1969 Greene resigned. Three months later he was translated to the BBC board of governors. It was a mistaken move and after less than two years he resigned in 1971 and left the BBC, not bitter, but disappointed and depressed.

In retirement he made some programmes for both Independent Television and the BBC, advised the Greek and Israeli governments on broadcasting, wrote several books on the rivals of Sherlock Holmes, and became chairman of Bodley Head (1969–81), the publishing house of his brother, Graham Greene. Greene was appointed OBE in 1950 and KCMG in 1964. He was given an honorary DCL by East Anglia (1969) and a D.Univ. by York and the Open University (both 1973). Germany honoured him with the Grand Cross of the Order of Merit (1977).

In appearance, Greene was immensely tall (six feet six inches), with a striking skull, a chubby, cheerful face, and heavy spectacles. He was a kind man, though he could be ruthless. He was incisive, but he could also ponder. He was quick-witted, but enjoyed listening to and telling long stories. He had few close friends, having an aloof personality, which partly explained the failure of his first two marriages. His first wife (1934) was Helga, daughter of Samuel Guinness, banker, of London. They had two sons and were divorced in 1948. In 1951 he married Elaine Shaplen, daughter of Louis Gilbert, accountant, of New York. They had two sons and were divorced in 1969. In 1970 he married Else Neumann (the German actress Tatjana Sais, with whom he had lived in 1948–50), daughter of Martin Hofler, of Frankfurt-am-Main, Germany. She died in 1981. In 1984 he married Sarah, daughter of David Grahame, concert manager, of Brisbane, Australia. Greene died of cancer in King Edward VII Hospital, London, 19 February 1987.

[Michael Tracey, *A Variety of Lives*, 1983; private information; personal knowledge.]

PAUL FOX

published 1996

GRIEVE Christopher Murray

(1892–1978)

Poet and prose writer, who used the pseudonym Hugh MacDiarmid, was born 11 August 1892, at Langholm in Dumfriesshire, Scotland, the elder son (there were no daughters) of James Grieve, postman, and his wife, Elizabeth, daughter of Andrew Graham, farmhand, of Waterbeck. He was educated at Langholm Academy, and his first published poem appeared in the *Eskdale and Liddesdale Advertiser* while he was in his teens. During a spell as a pupil-teacher in Edinburgh, he joined the Edinburgh branches of the Independent Labour Party and the Fabian Society. After working on various newspapers in Scotland and south Wales, he joined the army in July 1915, rising through the ranks to become a sergeant. In 1916 he was posted to the RAMC in Salonika from where he sent home poems to be read and judged by one of his previous schoolmasters; he contracted malaria and in 1918 he was invalided home. In June 1918 he married Margaret Cunningham Thompson Skinner (Peggy) (died 1962), a one-time colleague on the *Fife Herald*. They were to have a son and a daughter.

The end of the war found him in an Indian hospital in Marseilles, from which he was demobilized in July 1919. His first book, *Annals of the Five Senses* (1923), largely consisted of poems written in Salonika. After the war Grieve worked as a journalist, largely on the *Montrose Review*, and became widely known as the editor of three successive anthologies of current Scottish poetry called *Northern Numbers* (1920, 1921, and 1922).

From 1920 onwards a movement was started towards the revival of Scots as a literary medium. At first Grieve resisted this, believing it to be a 'backwater', but he finally started to experiment with it, assuming the pen-name of Hugh MacDiarmid. He employed a literary Scots based largely on the speech of his native countryside, but also using and reviving words from the Scots poets and prose writers of the past. In this medium he wrote the beautiful short lyrics of *Sangschaw* (1925) and *Penny Wheep* (1926), but his most notable use of it is in his long poem *A Drunk Man Looks at the Thistle* (1926). His method is best described in his own words: 'a long poem . . . split up into several sections, but the forms within the sections range from ballad measure to *vers libre*. The matter includes satire, amphigouri, lyrics, parodies of Mr. T. S. Eliot and other poets, and translations from the Russian, French and German. The whole poem is in braid Scots, . . . and it has been expressly designed to show that braid Scots can be effectively applied to all manner of subjects and measures' (1925). Hand in hand with this interest in Scots went his involvement with Scottish nationalist politics. When the National Party of Scotland was formed in 1927–8, Grieve was very active in encouraging it, and he became a founder member in 1928, but was expelled in 1933. He was a Labour member of the Montrose Town Council and a JP. He moved to Liverpool and London, becoming in 1928 editor of the short-lived radio journal *Vox*.

In 1932 his first marriage ended in divorce, and in 1934 he married a Cornishwoman, Valda Trevlyn Rowlands, who had borne him a son two years previously. After a brief spell in East Lothian, in 1933 they moved to Whalsay, a small remote island in the Shetlands, where they lived until Grieve was called up for war work, first in a factory, and later in the merchant navy. Grieve joined the Communist Party of Great Britain in 1934, but four years later was expelled for 'national deviation'. The long poems written during this period, which include two 'Hymns to Lenin' (1931 and 1935), are composed in a mixture of Scots and English, but during the later part of his life his poems are largely written in English. He continued his political involvement, standing as an Independent Scottish Nationalist candidate for Kelvingrove in 1945. In *Who's Who* he listed his recreation as 'Anglophobia'. In 1957 he rejoined the Communist Party and was the communist candidate for Kinross in 1964. In 1950 he visited Russia with members of the Scottish–USSR Friendship Society, and in the same year was awarded a Civil List pension; he went to China in 1956 as a member of the delegation of the British–Chinese Friendship Society. During this time he moved to the cottage in Biggar, Lanarkshire, where he lived until his death.

In 1957 an honorary LL D was conferred upon him by the University of Edinburgh, and in the following year he was presented with the Andrew Fletcher Saltoun medal for 'service to Scotland'. He was also honorary RSA. As part of the Robert Burns bicentenary celebrations in 1959 he visited Czechoslovakia, Romania, Bulgaria, and Hungary. In 1976 he was elected president of the Poetry Society of Great Britain. His most sustained work in prose is *Lucky Poet: A Self-study in Literature and Political Ideas, Being the Autobiography of Hugh MacDiarmid (Christopher Murray Grieve)* (1943); this also includes a 'Third Hymn to Lenin'. Of his overall contribution to Scots literature, he has characteristically written: 'My job, as I see it, has never been to lay a tit's egg, but to erupt like a volcano, emitting not only flame but a lot of rubbish.' He died in hospital in Edinburgh 9 September 1978.

[Gordon Wright, *MacDiarmid, an Illustrated Biography*, 1977; Kenneth Butley, *Hugh MacDiarmid* (*C. M. Grieve*), 1964; Hugh MacDiarmid, *Lucky Poet*, 1943, and *The Company I've Kept*, 1966 (autobiographies); Alan Bold (ed.), *The Letters of Hugh MacDiarmid*, 1984; *The Times*, 11 September 1978.]

John Wain

published 1986

HALLIWELL (Robert James) Leslie

(1929–1989)

Film buyer and encyclopaedist, was born 23 February 1929 in Bolton, Lancashire, the youngest child by thirteen years and only son in the family of three children of James Halliwell, cotton spinner, of Bolton, and his wife, Lily Haslam. He won a scholarship to Bolton School, and after national service in the Royal Army Education Corps he went to St Catharine's College, Cambridge, where he gained a second class (division I) in both parts of the English tripos (1951 and 1952).

Leslie Halliwell saw his first film at the age of four, and he spent his childhood going to the cinema, usually in the company of his mother. He claimed that at one time there were forty-seven cinemas within five miles of the centre of Bolton, and that he visited them all. At Cambridge, where he was editor of *Varsity*, he ran the university film society, and his first job after graduating was working as a journalist on *Picturegoer*.

At the end of 1952 Halliwell took on the job of running two cinemas in Cambridge. In 1956 he became a trainee publicity executive for the Rank Organization in London, moving in 1958 to Southern Television as a film buyer, and in 1959 he joined Granada Television as a film researcher, where he devised the *Cinema* series before moving to buy films for Granada from other companies.

In 1968 he became film buyer for the whole independent television network (ITV), and in 1982 Jeremy Isaacs, head of the new television channel, Channel 4, asked him to buy American films for Channel 4 as well. Isaacs described him as 'much more than a film buyer. Leslie Halliwell was a film buff, a walking encyclopaedia.' He visited Hollywood twice a year to search in the film libraries. At Channel 4 he was able to help schedule programmes, and he compiled very successful series such as *The British at War,* which he introduced himself. While he continued to buy for the other ITV companies, he earmarked interesting discoveries as 'obvious Channel 4 material', and his seasons of 'golden oldies', neglected films from the 1930s and 1940s, were very popular.

He was best known for his reference books. The first edition of *The Filmgoer's Companion*, the first comprehensive reference book of the cinema ever published, appeared in 1965, and revised editions appeared regularly thereafter. The first edition of *Halliwell's Film Guide*, with synopses and comments on 8,000 films, came out in 1977. Revised annually, it had grown to 16,000 entries by the time of the seventh edition in 1988. *Halliwell's Teleguide* (later with Philip Purser, *Halliwell's Television Companion*) was first published in 1979.

As well as compiling works of reference, Halliwell wrote about the cinema in such books as *The Clapperboard Book of the Cinema* (with G. Murray, 1975) and *Mountain of Dreams: the Golden Years of Paramount* (1965). In *Halliwell's Hundred* (1982) and its successor *Halliwell's Harvest* (1986) he considered some of his favourite films, claiming not that they were the greatest films ever made, or serious works of art, but that they all demonstrated an ability to entertain. In *The Dead That Walk* (1986) he wrote about horror films, with essays on films about Dracula, Frankenstein, and mummies, in which he argued that *Bride of Frankenstein* (1935) was the best horror film ever released. He also wrote a history of comedy, *Double Take and Fade Away* (1987). In the 1980s he published three books of short stories, wrote his autobiography, and also a novel, *Return to Shangri-La* (1987), a sequel to one of his favourite films, *Lost Horizon* (1937). After his retirement from ITV in 1986 he wrote a weekly television column in the *Daily Mail.*

Halliwell's work was directed at the general public, the middlebrow audience which went to the cinema for entertainment, and not at 'the egghead student of film culture who shuns commercial entertainments in favour of middle-European or Oriental masterpieces which never got further than the National Film Theatre' (introduction to the first edition of *The Filmgoer's Companion*). While he did not ignore foreign films, they did not appeal to him. Brought up in the 1930s and 1940s, he always regarded these years as the golden age of the cinema, the age when films were made in the studio in black and white. He liked very little that was produced after 1950, and lamented the demise of the old studio crafts and film techniques. He found modern films crude and violent, and the language offensive, and he felt that the wit and style of the early movies were lacking. He dedicated *Halliwell's Harvest* to the proposition that art should not be despised because it is popular.

His most distinctive physical feature was his very long chin, which he later covered with a beard. In 1959 he married Ruth Porter, who had one son and one daughter from her previous marriage. She was the daughter of Samuel Edward Turner, clerk and Baptist minister, of Nottingham. The Halliwells had one son. Halliwell died of cancer 21 January 1989 in the Princess Alice Hospice, Esher, Surrey. At a memorial meeting at the National Film Theatre excerpts from some of his favourite films were shown, including *Citizen Kane* (1941), which he regarded as the greatest film ever made.

[*The Times*, 23 January 1989; Leslie Halliwell, *Seats in All Parts: Half a Lifetime at the Movies*, 1985.]

ANNE PIMLOTT BAKER

published 1996

HAMBRO Sir Charles Jocelyn

(1897–1963)

Merchant banker, was born in London 3 October 1897, into a banking family of Danish origin, which settled in Dorset and the City in the first half of the nineteenth century. He was the elder son of (Sir) C. Eric Hambro (1872–1947), who was Conservative MP for the Wimbledon division of Surrey in 1900–7 and a partner in C. J. Hambro & Son, the family firm; his grandfather (Sir) Everard Alexander Hambro was a director of the Bank of England. His mother, Sybil Emily (died 1942), was the daughter of Martin Ridley Smith of Warren House, Hayes, Kent, and his wife, Cecilia, daughter of Henry Stuart (1808–80), of Montfort, Isle of Bute, a descendant of George III's prime minister, John Stuart, third Earl of Bute. In 1929 Hambro's parents were divorced and his father at once remarried. He had a younger brother and two sisters.

Hambro was at Eton from 1910 to 1915—in the cricket XI in 1914, and its captain in 1915, when he took seven wickets for six runs against Winchester. He went straight from school to Sandhurst, and by the end of the year was an ensign in the Coldstream Guards. He survived two years of the western front, receiving the military cross for conspicuous bravery in action. On demobilization in 1919 he went for a brief spell of training to the Guaranty Trust Company in New York, and then into the family firm, of which he soon became secretary. He played an important part in its merger with the British Bank of Northern Commerce, which led to the establishment of Hambros Bank in 1921. In 1928, when only thirty, he was elected a director of the Bank of England, and for a spell in 1932–3 he put all other work aside in order to establish, under the direction of Montagu C. (later Lord) Norman, the bank's exchange control division to deal with some of the consequences of the ending of the gold standard.

His commanding presence—he stood six feet three inches tall—and driving personality were backed by equal strength of character, loyalty, and charm. He made a notable impact in several spheres of work, particularly on the Great Western Railway, the most successful of the four great British railway companies. He became a director of it in 1928, and deputy chairman in 1934. From 1940 to 1945 he was nominally chairman, but war work took up much of his time.

On the outbreak of war with Germany in 1939, at the invitation of (Sir) Ronald Cross, the minister, Hambro joined the Ministry of Economic Warfare. In August 1940 Cross's successor Hugh (later Lord) Dalton brought Hambro into the new secret service he was forming under the Ministry's cover, the Special Operations Executive (SOE). SOE's purpose was to stimulate resistance in enemy-occupied territory, and Hambro's vigour, energy, and originality were valuable to it. He began in charge of Scandinavia, and visited Sweden in November 1940. There he arranged for some highly successful smuggling of ball-bearings, and for some sabotage in Swedish harbours, which provoked difficulties with the Swedes. He also, through the anti-Nazi journalist Ebbe Munck, initiated contacts with resistance-minded Danes, which bore useful fruit in the summer of 1944. Dalton thought highly of his Scandinavian work, and Hambro was created KBE in 1941.

From December 1940 to November 1941 he added to his responsibilities oversight of SOE's nascent French, Belgian, Dutch, and German sections, and from November 1941 for five months he was deputy head of the whole organization, in the rank of squadron leader, Royal Air Force. (Rank in SOE meant little.) He initiated an important development in January 1942, when he persuaded the Norwegians to help form an Anglo-Norwegian planning committee, from which several highly successful small operations derived, particularly the destruction on 27/8 February 1943 of the heavy-water plant at Vemork near Rjukan. When a further stock of heavy water was destroyed, in a separate operation, on its way to Germany, the Germans' search for an atomic bomb was utterly dislocated. By that time Hambro had become the executive chief of SOE (called CD) and been promoted to air commodore. Dalton's successor, the third Earl of Selborne, had appointed him in April 1942 to succeed (Sir) Frank Nelson when Nelson's health gave way—on the ground that a man who could run the Great Western Railway could run anything. An early and important task for Hambro was to arrange with Colonel William Donovan, his American opposite number, who visited London in June 1942, for co-operation between SOE and the American Office of Strategic Services. Occasional rivalries should not obscure a great deal of close and rewarding interchange.

Hambro's multifarious acquaintances in the business world were often useful to SOE. During his seventeen months of leadership, this small but lively service was transformed from a body still struggling to establish its worth into a recognized, and often highly efficient, military tool. Hambro cannot claim undue credit for this development, much of which arose from the general political and military course of the war, and some of it from the excellent work of his predecessor, Nelson, and from technicalities too abstruse even for him. A well-placed observer described him in retrospect as 'always the gentleman, among the professionals'; he was certainly not a professional in the secret-service world.

Hambro and Selborne could not agree over a protracted dispute about control over SOE by the commander-in-chief, Middle East; and early in September 1943 Hambro had to resign. Another weighty post was soon found for him. He spent the last eighteen months of the war in Washington as head of the British raw materials mission: this was cover for supervising the exchange of information between the United Kingdom and the USA which led to the first man-made nuclear explosions in July and August 1945.

He then returned to the City, and became prominent; not only in Hambros Bank, of which he was made chairman when his uncle Olaf died in 1961. He also diversified, through the Union Corporation, into mining, among other interests; supported several charitable trusts; worked himself harder than he worked his subordinates; and escaped whenever he could to Dixton Manor near Cheltenham to shoot. He married in 1919 Pamela (died 1932), daughter of John Dupuis Cobbold, DL, of Ipswich, and his wife, Lady Evelyn, daughter of Charles Adolphus Murray, seventh Earl of Dunmore; she bore him a son and three daughters. By his second wife, Dorothy (daughter of Alexander Mackay, of Oban), whom he married in 1936, he had another daughter; he had twenty-four grandchildren living when he died, in his Marylebone home, at the height of his powers and reputation, 28 August 1963.

[M. R. D. Foot, *SOE in France*, 1966, and *Resistance*, 1976; Bickham Sweet-Escott, *Baker Street Irregular*, 1965; *The Times*, 16 July 1915, 29 and 31 August, 2 and 3 September 1963; private information.]

M. R. D. Foot

published 1981

HANCOCK Anthony John (Tony)

(1924–1968)

Comedian, was born at Small Heath, Birmingham, 12 May 1924, the second of three sons of John Hancock, hotelier, and his wife, (Lucy) Lilian Thomas. He was educated at Durlston Court, Swanage, and Bradfield College, Reading. Much of his youth was spent in Bournemouth where his father, himself a part-time professional entertainer, ran a hotel. Here he met many people from the lighter side of the entertainment world. Attempts to find employment in ordinary life were less than successful. He was, briefly, in the Civil Service and his subsequent job, at a Birmingham tailor's, lasted just under three hours.

Enlisting in the RAF in 1942, Hancock toured with ENSA (Entertainments National Service Association) and the Ralph Reader 'Gang Shows'. Demobilized in 1946, in 1948 he appeared at the Windmill Theatre, a variety house whose girl-predominated turns had much pleased the mainly male wartime audiences and whose proud motto was 'We Never Closed'.

But it was to be with the BBC, both in radio and on television, rather than on the stage that Hancock's name was to be made. Graduating from such wireless attractions as 'Workers' Playtime', 'Variety Bandbox', and 'Educating Archie', where his catchphrase of 'flippin' kids!' became well known and widely copied, he was given on 2 November 1954 his own programme, 'Hancock's Half-Hour', which was an immediate success.

To add incongruity to his fictional and somewhat squalid East Cheam background, his name was elaborated into Anthony Aloysius St. John Hancock. The programme owed much to the presence in the cast with him of Bill Kerr, Kenneth Williams, and, particularly, Sid James. It owed perhaps most of all, for Hancock was incapable of producing his own material, to Alan Simpson and Ray Galton, his scriptwriters. The strength of the Half-Hour lay in the fact that it relied on comedy of character and situation rather than on set jokes and it had none of the musical interludes with which such programmes were normally interrupted. Hancock played an unsuccessful actor, full of pretentiousness and snobbery and deeply prejudiced. In one of the John Freeman 'Face to Face' interviews on BBC television, he said: 'The character I play isn't a character I put on and off like a coat. It's a part of me and a part of everybody I see.'

Throughout the 1950s television was becoming increasingly efficient and popular and vastly expanding (ITV appeared in 1955) and in due course in 1956 the Hancock programme was transferred to this medium and to the huge audience which it by then commanded. Here the success was even greater and for a few years there was no comedian of comparable popularity. His face fitted to perfection the character which had up to then been purely a wireless voice. There were the heavy jowls, the creases, the sunken and pouchy eyes, the turned-down corners of the mouth. There was a fresh catchphrase ('Stone me!'). Sid James, his partner in the constant disasters—financial, social, and professional—which beset them, had a face along similar lines. The programme frequently found them, bored to tears, after lunch on a Sunday afternoon and with rain falling. One of the episodes began with the following series of groans, treasured by the whole viewing public, from Hancock: 'Ahh. Oh dear. Mm. Oh dear, oh dear. Ahh, dear me. Ahhh. Stone me, what a life.'

Bored indeed with his by now familiar comedy routines, his attempts to branch out into other comic realms brought real disaster with them. Seldom has such a dazzling career disintegrated so swiftly. He abandoned Sid James and Galton and Simpson. He made three poor films. There was an unsuccessful ITV series. He began drinking heavily and could not remember his lines. His first marriage (to Cicely Romanis in 1950) broke up in 1965 and his second marriage to 'Freddie' Ross, his public relations agent, in the same year ended in divorce a week before his death.

Tony Hancock was the last of a cherished line of English comedians whose stock-in-trade it has been to have about them a seedy air of vanished sartorial grandeur and of better times, Burlington Berties every one of them. There was George Robey's bowler hat and frock-coat, with the red nose and heavy, arched eyebrows to go with them. There was Billy Bennett ('Almost a Gentleman') with his defiant bow-tie and dickey and boots. And with Hancock it was the Homburg hat, the shabby fur-collared overcoat, and the grand manner, all so splendidly out of place either in a fish and chip parlour or at home at 23 Railway Cuttings, East Cheam. And to accompany the run-down clothing there was the look of total gloom and despondency and a deep resentment against life.

J. B. Priestley, writing enthusiastically on the special characteristics of purely English humour, a brand so incomprehensible to other nations, says that Hancock, in the television sketches written for him by Alan Simpson and Ray Galton and which suited him so perfectly, 'seemed to combine an unconscious despair and hatred of show-business with more than a touch of genius for it, finally giving him deep at heart a deathwish'. Priestley was sadly right and in the end Hancock died by his own hand in Sydney, Australia, 25 June 1968.

[Roger Wilmot, *Tony Hancock—'Artiste'*, 1978; Eric Midwinter, *Make 'em Laugh*, 1979; *The Times*, 26 June 1968.]

ARTHUR MARSHALL

published 1981

HANDLEY Thomas Reginald

(1892–1949)

Radio comedian, was born in Liverpool 17 January 1892, the son of John Handley, a cowkeeper, and his wife, Sarah Ann Pearson. On leaving school he worked as a salesman but he had a good singing voice and was determined to go on the stage. He toured for a short time in *The Maid of the Mountains* and in 1917 joined the Royal Naval Air Service where he soon found himself a member of a concert party. After the war he went on tour and became well known on the halls in the sketch 'The Disorderly Room', a skit on army life which reached the London Coliseum and a royal command variety performance (1924). It was the British Broadcasting Company, however, which lifted him out of the rut of variety, and as early as 1925, when broadcasting was still a primitive medium, Tommy Handley was producing and acting in his own radio revues. Broadcasting, touring, and an occasional film kept him fully occupied until in 1939 he found the opportunity which made him the greatest British radio comedian of his generation.

When Handley died in 1949, for nearly ten years he had delighted a faithful audience of millions with his versatility and prowess in a weekly wireless extravaganza called ITMA. This household word, as it soon became, was an abbreviation, in the current fashion, of 'It's That Man Again!', a phrase first coined in veiled reference to Hitler, the bogey-man of that summer of 1939 when the show was first put on. ITMA was a radio cartoon of daily life in the war years and, week by week, relieved the tension of the times by the fun which it poked at the common hazards and endurances of the British public. In the Office of Twerps, war-time bureaucrats were ridiculed for their pomposity and mismanagement. As the strain of the war increased Handley, in a much-needed holiday mood, became mayor of the seaside resort, 'Foaming-at-the-Mouth', with its famous corporation cleanser, 'Mrs Mopp'. Another very popular figure was Funf the German spy. Handley later turned his attention to factory work, then to post-war planning, and after the war, taking a fresh leaf from the book of traditional satire, ITMA put on the map the Island of Tomtopia, where the austerities and vanished hopes of a brave new world were genially depicted. Such comic fictions as these—and there were scores of them—were sustained by Handley and his fellow clowns in a brand of vocal impersonation which brought the characters of these lampoons most vividly to life without benefit of vision. For this reason, ITMA was pure sound radio, so faithful to its subtle medium as to be incapable of translation into the terms of television. On 21 April 1942 ITMA made history by being chosen as the first royal command performance of a radio programme.

Tommy Handley was the leader of these weekly revels, but he was sustained in them by ten or a dozen other actors and actresses who learned from him the new alphabet of wireless comedy. They employed verbal mannerisms which were a kind of audio-shorthand; they exploited dialects, foreign accents, and sheer mumbo-jumbo in a wonderland of words where any absurdity was feasible. Tommy Handley was not only the keystone and inspiration of the actual performance of ITMA; he was one of the three men who invented it week after week. The script-writer was Ted Kavanagh, an old and shrewd hand at radio comedy; the producer was Francis Worsley; but it was Handley who fused the talents of this accomplished pair into a creative comic team. So much of his vital personality and quicksilver wit went into ITMA that the show perished on the day he died. For him there was no substitute, in either invention or performance.

Tommy Handley was as unique in radio as Charlie Chaplin was in the silent film. If, indeed, all the world spoke the same language, Tommy Handley would have been an international favourite. For he, too, in his own medium, had the power to identify and delineate those humours and absurdities which are common to mankind. There were differences, of course. Chaplin was best when he was in trouble; Handley when he was nimbly getting out of trouble. But their respective arts were different sides of the same medal: in their separate ways both of them personified the common man.

In 1929 Handley married a singer, Rosalind Jean (died 1958), daughter of Robert Allistone, a jeweller, and formerly wife of William Henshall; there were no children. He died suddenly in London 9 January 1949. A memorial service was held at St Paul's Cathedral. A bust by E. Whitney-Smith was in the possession of his widow.

[Ted Kavanagh, *Tommy Handley*, 1949; private information; personal knowledge.]

W. E. WILLIAMS

published 1959

HART Sir Basil Henry Liddell

(1895–1970)

Military historian and strategist, was born in Paris 31 October 1895, the younger son of the Revd Henry Bramley Hart, Wesleyan minister in Paris, and his wife, Clara, daughter of Henry Liddell. He was educated at St Paul's School. In 1913 he went up to Corpus Christi College, Cambridge, to read history, but on the outbreak of war in 1914 he obtained a temporary commission in the King's Own Yorkshire Light Infantry. Posted to France in September 1915, he was invalided home after a shell-burst at Ypres; he returned to the front in the spring of 1916, only to be rendered *hors de combat* by gas on the Somme. Deep thought about his intense experiences on the western front permeated his subsequent military ideas. As adjutant (temporary captain) of training units of the Volunteer Force in 1917–21, he evolved new methods of instruction and an original battle drill. These attracted the attention in 1919 of two generals, Sir Ivor Maxse and Winston (later Lord) Dugan, who were responsible for compiling a post-war *Infantry Training* manual, much of which, although junior in rank, Liddell Hart was to revise or compose. His concepts did not always survive the War Office sieve, but he promulgated them with characteristic assurance in articles and lectures. He transferred to the Army Education Corps in 1921 with a regular commission, but his health wrecked his professional career; he was placed on lieutenant's half-pay in 1924, and retired as captain in 1927 'on account of ill health caused by wounds'. Nevertheless, he was already launched as a military thinker.

Oppressed by the slaughter on the western front, which he ascribed to inflexible generalship and bull-at-a-gate offensives, he sought by intellectual analysis to prevent or ameliorate any recurrence, taking as his slogan 'if one wishes peace one should understand war'. His key concepts were the 'expanding torrent' and the 'indirect approach'. The former, drawing on techniques employed in the German offensive of March 1918, emphasized fluidity, continuous forward motion, and the vital need to reinforce spearheads by immediately available reserves. The latter stressed tactical and strategic outflanking, the paramount virtue of surprise, and the importance of striking not at an opponent's main body but at nerve centres such as headquarters and lines of communication. Between the wars he expounded these principles volubly, and his *Strategy—The Indirect Approach* appeared in different forms in six editions between 1929 and 1967. Some felt that as he elaborated his theories they became more a philosophy of life than a *vade mecum* for the commander, but it is unquestionable that their forceful and lucid reiteration had a seminal and liberating effect on educated soldiers at home and abroad.

With the inter-war pioneers of British armoured development—J. F. C. ('Boney') Fuller, (Sir) Percy Hobart, (Sir) Charles Broad, and (Sir) Giffard Martel—his affinity was two-way. They discussed with him their practical experiments and forward thinking; he stimulated in argument and provided a public forum for the unorthodox group, struggling as it was against conservatism and the 'cavalry spirit'. As military correspondent of the *Daily Telegraph* in 1925–35, and as correspondent and defence adviser of *The Times* in 1935–9, he assiduously charted the efforts of the pioneers of mechanization, while also turning a critical eye on broader aspects of the British military machine, and registering the progress of German rearmament. His intimate contacts with the Service hierarchy, both at unit levels and in Whitehall, gave him an unequalled insight into dead wood and growth points. He was cultivated by the alert, and rejected by closed minds.

Wide reading in military history gave his theories backbone. Over thirty books he wrote included studies of Scipio Africanus (1926), Sherman (1930), Foch (1931), and (1934) of T. E. Lawrence, with whom he had a warm *rapport*. A man of sturdy loyalty, he devoted much time to defending Lawrence against his denigrators, as he did in the case of David Lloyd George, whose war memoirs owed much to his assistance. His Lees Knowles lectures for 1932–3, on 'The Movement of Military Thought from the Eighteenth to the Twentieth Century', were published as *The Ghost of Napoleon* (1933). In 1930 *The Real War* (enlarged and reissued as *A History of the World War*, 1934) made a controversial indictment of the command of Earl Haig. Widely read by military students—indeed, often 'required reading' in military colleges—Liddell Hart's writings advanced his authority.

This seemed at a peak in 1937–8, when the war minister, Leslie (later Lord) Hore-Belisha, enlisted him as unofficial adviser. He gave a creative impulsion to Hore-Belisha's reforms, but when the connection waned in mid 1938 it had damaged him: the reforms (although mainly salutary) were resented and the minister himself was distrusted by the military establishment, where Liddell Hart was felt to have enjoyed an excessive influence—particularly over senior appointments. In November 1939 *The Times* accepted his resignation, tendered in August after mounting frustration over his inability to publish the truth as he saw it. He thus lost both power-bases, and the issue in July of *The Defence of Britain* had even raised doubts about the stability of his judgement. Its stress on the current need for defence rather than offence seemed inconsistent with his ardent advocacy of the 'expanding torrent'.

Throughout the war of 1939–45 he was excluded from positions of influence. This was not surprising, since he advocated a compromise peace and consistently opposed 'total war'. (Sir) Winston Churchill, who had sought his advice in the thirties, made no further overtures. Journalism and private consultation were his lot, and pain as he watched the Germans in 1940, and other belligerents later, apply the ideas he had preached. The latter were not his alone, but he had been an especially perceptive prophet: he had fertilized the British Army—particularly the Royal Tank Corps—and in Germany men like Field-Marshal Reichenau and General Guderian acknowledged his stimulus, although it was perhaps not so directly influential as their post-war confidences suggested.

After 1945 he recovered from his eclipse. *Persona grata* with captive German generals, he recorded his interrogations in *The Other Side of the Hill* (first issued 1948, and enlarged in 1951), for long a source-book on their attitudes, and his edition of *The Rommel Papers* (1953) became an enduring text. *The Tanks* (2 vols., 1959) lifted regimental history on to the highest plane, and years of preparation resulted in his posthumous *History of the Second World War* (1970). Here his strength as a military analyst was qualified by limitations, for in describing a total war he overlooked its totality in terms of sociological, economic, and political consequences.

During the post-Hiroshima years he denounced 'massive retaliation' and denied, in speech and writing, that the existence of nuclear weapons would proscribe warfare at lower levels, in which he was as prescient as in his warning that antidotes must be prepared for the coming plague of guerrilla insurgency. But in his Indian summer it was as a sage that he most happily contributed to military affairs. States House, Medmenham, became a place of multi-national pilgrimage; the gamut ran through chiefs of staff to graduate researchers. His study was lined with photographs of statesmen and soldiers with whom he had shared a dialogue—his 'rogues' gallery'—and a later collection, the 'young rogues', who represented the cream of a new generation of military historians, beneficiaries of his passionate tutorial dissection of their writing and the incessant dialectic of his conversation. His ideas, moreover, were still a weapon: in 1967 the Israelis affirmed that their war that year had been won by 'the true strategy of indirect approach', and Yigal Allon inscribed a photograph to 'the captain who teaches generals'.

Unusually tall, light of frame, with a busy inquisitive air, he struck one as like a secretary-bird. But his eyes were Robin Goodfellow's, puckish and smiling; his laughter effervesced, and an ill-concealed streak of vanity endeared more than it offended. Brocade waistcoats and an indefinably dandiacal pose reflected his eccentric but deeply informed studies of feminine fashion, about which the experts approached him on their own level. As a young officer he had reported for leading newspapers on lawn tennis and rugby, and his lifelong addiction to war games, chess, and croquet (in which he was described as a fiendish opponent) refreshed rather than reduced his competitive spirit.

In 1918 he married Jessie Douglas, daughter of J. J. Stone; they had one son. The marriage was dissolved, and in 1942 he married Kathleen, daughter of Alan Sullivan, of Toronto, and widow of Henry Philbrick Nelson, FRCS. In 1963 he was awarded the Chesney gold medal of the Royal United Service Institution, in 1964 Oxford made him an honorary D.Litt., and in 1965 he was elected an honorary fellow of Corpus Christi College, Cambridge. He was a founder-member of the Institute of Strategic Studies, president of the Military Commentators' Circle in 1953–70, and an honorary member of the United States Marine Corps. In 1965–6 he was visiting distinguished professor at the university of California, and also in 1965 he was presented with a Festschrift, *The Theory and Practice of War*, edited by Michael Howard. He was knighted in 1966. A unique archive, the hundreds of files containing his correspondence and voluminous papers, is lodged in King's College, London.

He died 29 January 1970 at his home at Medmenham. A drawing by Sava Botzaris (1938) and two portraits by Eric Kennington (1943) are in the possession of the family.

[Basil Liddell Hart, *Memoirs*, 2 vols., 1965; *The Times*, 30 January 1970; R. J. Minney, *The Private Papers of Hore-Belisha*, 1960; Kenneth Macksey, *Armoured Crusader: Major-General Sir Percy Hobart*, 1967; Sir Giffard Martel, *An Outspoken Soldier*, 1949; private information; personal knowledge.]

Ronald Lewin

published 1981

HARTY (Fredric) Russell

(1934–1988)

Broadcaster, was born 5 September 1934 in Blackburn, the only son and elder child of Fred Harty, greengrocer (who, his son claimed, introduced Blackburn to the avocado pear), and his wife, Myrtle Rishton. He was educated at Queen Elizabeth's Grammar School, Blackburn, and Exeter College, Oxford, where he read English and was taught by Nevill Coghill, who noted of an early essay on 'Sex in the Canterbury Tales', 'Energetic and zealous but very naïve'. He took a third-class degree (1957) and taught briefly at Blakey Moor Secondary Modern School in Blackburn before moving in 1958 to Giggleswick School in Yorkshire. Giggleswick was a school and a village with which he was to have close connections for the rest of his life. In 1964 there followed a spell at City College, New York, and at Bishop Lonsdale College of Education, Derby, but with many of his friends and contemporaries busy in the theatre and broadcasting he was increasingly dissatisfied with teaching.

In 1966 he made his first foray into television, an inglorious appearance as a contestant on Granada TV's *Criss Cross Quiz*; the only question he answered correctly was on Catherine of Braganza. It was such a public humiliation that his mother refused to speak to him. Still, it was a beginning and in 1967 he was taken on by BBC Radio as an arts programmes producer, his hankering to perform whetted by the occasional trip to the studio down the corridor whenever *Woman's Hour* wanted a letter read in a northern accent.

As an undergraduate Harty had invited Vivien Leigh round for drinks and this precocious appetite for celebrity stood him in good stead when, in 1969, he became producer and occasional presenter of London Weekend TV's arts programme, *Aquarius*. He might not have seemed the best person to film Salvador Dali, but the elderly surrealist and the boy off Blackburn market took to one another and the programme won an Emmy award; in another unlikely conjunction he set up an encounter on Capri between the eminent Lancashire exiles Sir William Walton and Gracie Fields. Harty was never abashed by the famous (his critics said that was the trouble), but it was his capacity for provocative half-truths and outrageous overstatement, which made him such a good schoolmaster, that now fitted him for a career as the host of a weekly talk show (*Eleven Plus* and later *Russell Harty*) and made him one of the most popular performers on television. Plump, cheerful, and unintimidating, he was particularly good at putting people at their ease, deflating the pompous and drawing out the shy.

In 1980 he returned to the BBC, but his output remained much as it had been for the last ten years, the same mixture of talk shows varied by occasional films like *The Black Madonna*, and his *Grand Tour*, shown in 1988. He wrote regularly for the *Observer* and the *Sunday Times*, publishing a book of his television interviews, *Russell Harty Plus* (1976) and also *Mr Harty's Grand Tour* (1988). He was a regular broadcaster on radio besides presenting the Radio 4 talk show, *Start the Week*.

'Private faces in public places are wiser and nicer than public faces in private places' (W. H. Auden) did not anticipate television, where the distinction is not always plain. For his friends Harty was naturally a private face but for the public he seemed a private face too and one that had strayed on to the screen seemingly untouched by expertise. That was why, though it infuriated his critics, so many viewers liked him and took him to their hearts as they never did more polished performers. He giggled, he fumbled and seldom went for the right word rather than the next but two, and though his delivery could be as tortured as his mother's on the telephone, it did not matter. It was all part of his ordinariness, his deficiencies, his style.

Harty never made much of a secret of his homosexuality. He did not look on it as an affliction, but he was never one for a crusade either. His funniest stories were always of the absurdities of sex and the ludicrous situations it had led him into, and if he was never short of partners, it was because they knew there would always be laughs, sharing a joke being something rarer than sharing a bed.

In the second half of the 1980s the spread of AIDS enabled the tabloid press, and in particular those newspapers owned by Rupert Murdoch, to dress up their muckraking as a moral crusade, and they systematically trawled public life for sexual indiscretion. Harty, who had not scrupled to question his more celebrated interviewees about their sex lives, knew that he was in a vulnerable situation. Early in 1987 a young man, who had had a previous fling with Harty, was wired up with a tape recorder by two *News of the World* reporters and sent to call on Harty at his London flat. To the reporters' chagrin nothing newsworthy occurred, but the paper fell back on printing the young man's account of the previous association, thus initiating a campaign of sporadic vilification in the tabloid press, which only ended with Harty's death just over a year later.

The cause of his death was liver failure, the result of hepatitis B, but in the hope that he was suffering from AIDS the press laid siege firstly to his home in Giggleswick and then to St James's Hospital in Leeds, where he was in intensive care. A telescope was trained permanently on the window of his ward and a reporter tried to smuggle himself into the ward disguised as a junior doctor, in order to look at his case notes. When Harty was actually on his deathbed one of the journalists responsible for the original 'scoop' could not be restrained from retelling the tale of her exploits on television.

He died in Leeds 8 June 1988 and is buried in Giggleswick, the gravestone evidence of the vulgarity from which he never entirely managed to break free.

[Private information; personal knowledge.]

ALAN BENNETT

published 1996

HEENAN John Carmel

(1905–1975)

Cardinal, eighth archbishop of Westminster, was born in Ilford, Essex, 26 January 1905, the youngest in the family of three sons and one daughter of James Carmel Heenan, a civil servant at the Patent Office, and his wife, Anne Pilkington. John Heenan's parents were Irish and he was brought up in an atmosphere of fervent Catholicism. He early showed a desire for the priesthood and was especially encouraged in this vocation by his mother and his parish priest at Ilford.

He was educated at St Ignatius' College, Stamford Hill, London, and began his studies for the priesthood at St Cuthbert's College, Ushaw, Durham. From there he was awarded a bursary at the Venerable English College, Rome, in 1924. While there he obtained doctorates in philosophy and theology. He was ordained priest in 1930 and, after completing his studies in Rome, was appointed assistant priest at the church of SS Mary and Ethelburga, Barking, in the diocese of Brentwood in 1931.

As a young priest, in 1936 Heenan visited the Soviet Union, disguised as a lecturer in psychology, in order to study conditions there. He had been encouraged in this venture by his old rector at the English College, Arthur Hinsley. On his return to England, Heenan was able to give a first-hand account of life in Russia to the cardinal and to the public.

He was appointed parish priest of St Stephen's, Manor Park, in 1937. During the next few years he became known as a public speaker at Catholic functions and also wrote a series of popular books explaining the Catholic faith. As a result of this work he was recommended to the BBC and during the early years of the war of 1939–45 he became a popular broadcaster. Heenan spent the whole of the war years with his parishioners at Manor Park.

In 1947 Heenan was asked by the Catholic bishops to become the superior of the re-established Catholic Missionary Society, a group of diocesan priests from England and Wales who were to give missions to Catholics and non-Catholics all over the country. After four years of this work, he was appointed bishop of Leeds in 1951. He showed himself extremely hard-working but admitted later that he was too impulsive and made many mistakes. During his time at Leeds, Heenan became an accomplished television speaker and the best-known Catholic bishop in the country.

In 1957 Heenan was translated to Liverpool as its eighth archbishop and metropolitan of the northern province. There his most notable achievement was the building of the Roman Catholic cathedral. Plans for the cathedral had been made about thirty years before, but by 1957 the cost had become prohibitive. Heenan decided that a more contemporary and necessarily cheaper design was needed and, by the time he left Liverpool, the new cathedral, designed by (Sir) Frederick Gibberd, was well on the way to completion.

On the death of Cardinal Godfrey in 1963 Heenan became the eighth archbishop of Westminster. Until 1966 most of his time was spent in attendance at the second Vatican Council. Even before the announcement of the Council, he had been appointed to the newly established Secretariat for Christian Unity. He was by no means the first Roman Catholic ecumenist in this country, but his appointment and his energy began for the first time to make an immediate impression on ordinary Catholics.

He was created cardinal in 1965. As leader of the English and Welsh bishops at the Council, Heenan was particularly active in the preparation of the Council's declaration on non-Christian religions and the decree on ecumenism. His work at the Council was particularly acceptable to the Jewish community in Britain, especially as he had already ensured, in the face of the Roman Curia's disapproval, the re-entry of Catholics into the Council of Christians and Jews in this country.

As archbishop of Westminster and president of the bishops' conference of England and Wales, Heenan had to put into practice the decrees of the Council. He managed to keep the Catholic church in England and Wales on an even keel in all the upheavals that followed the Council. This country was neither intellectually nor psychologically ready for all the changes, but the fact that Catholics remained a fairly cohesive body was largely the result of his handling of the situation.

Heenan had boundless energy and was almost a compulsive worker. He was regarded by most people as an expert politician and he certainly had the ability to say the right thing at the right time. He had great charm and seemed able to persuade whoever he was addressing that he was the most important person to the cardinal at the time. However, he also had great simplicity. His life was based on his simple belief in the goodness of God. While he accepted the changes that came from the second Vatican Council, he remained at heart a traditional Catholic. He realized that many of the changes brought about by the Council were good but he missed the certainty Catholics once had and hoped that they would soon settle down once more to a united church. He never reconciled himself to the number of priests leaving the priesthood—he could not understand how a priest could give up his vocation. He had had his greatest happiness in being a priest and looked on his time at Manor Park as the highlight of his life.

Heenan's last years were darkened by ill health. He had already decided to resign before his last illness. He died in Westminster Hospital 7 November and was buried beside the fourteenth station of the cross in Westminster Cathedral.

[Cardinal Heenan, *Not the Whole Truth*, 1973, and *A Crown of Thorns*, 1974 (autobiography); *A Tribute to Cardinal Heenan*, Catholic Information Services, 1976; personal knowledge.]

DAVID NORRIS

published 1986

HEPWORTH Dame (Jocelyn) Barbara

(1903–1975)

Sculptor, was born 10 January 1903 at Wakefield, Yorkshire, the eldest in the family of three daughters and one son of Herbert Raikes Hepworth CBE, civil engineer to the west riding of Yorkshire, and his wife, Gertrude Allison Johnson. She was educated at Wakefield Girls' High School. She entered the Leeds School of Art in September 1919, and a year later moved to the Royal College of Art in London to study sculpture. A fellow student in the sculpture departments at both Leeds and London was Henry Moore, who remained a friend and colleague for the whole of her working life.

Winning a scholarship for a year's study abroad, she left for Italy in 1924. She remained until 1926, marrying John Rattenbury Skeaping (died 1980), a fellow sculptor, in 1925 and living in Florence and Rome. Skeaping's father was Kenneth Mathieson, painter, of Woodford, Essex. They had one child, Paul, born in 1929, who was killed serving in the RAF in Malaya in

1953. In Italy she learned how to carve stone—not part of a regular sculptor's training at the time, and considered the work of a stonemason.

In 1928 she moved to 7 The Mall Studios, Parkhill Road, Hampstead, and had her first one-man exhibition at the Beaux Arts Gallery in London, showing stone carvings of figures and animals. Slowly, however, the forms in her work became more and more simplified, and by 1934 she was making totally abstract sculpture. This development was greatly furthered by her association with the painter Ben Nicholson, who became her second husband. Her marriage to John Skeaping was dissolved in 1933. Visits to Paris had put them in contact with an international avant-garde, in particular Brancusi, Picasso, Braque, and Mondrian. They were both members of the Paris-based group, Abstraction-Creation, from 1933, and in England of the Seven and Five Society, and of Unit One. By the mid-1930s Barbara Hepworth's studio in Parkhill Road had become the centre of the abstract art movement in Great Britain, as Nicholson, Henry Moore, the writer and art critic (Sir) Herbert Read, the Dutch painter Mondrian, and the Russian constructivist artist Naum Gabo were all living nearby.

In 1938 Barbara Hepworth was married to Ben Nicholson (died 1982), son of Sir William Newzam Nicholson, artist. In August 1939, with war in Europe imminent, they and their five-year-old triplet children (a son and two daughters) and the boy Paul left London for St Ives in Cornwall, at the invitation of the painter and critic, Adrian Stokes. This small Cornish fishing port and tourist centre, long a magnet for artists, was to become Hepworth's home for the rest of her life. During the war years she was able to make little sculpture (and much that had been done in London in the 1930s was abandoned and lost) but when she began working again in 1944 the influence of the Cornish landscape immediately made itself felt. Her sculpture was no longer austerely abstract, but now contained references to landscape forms, and to the patterns of nature. The movement of tides, pebble and rock formations, and the Cornish moorland landscape all enriched her work. The ancient standing stones of west Cornwall provided an analogy for her own sculpture which became increasingly a paradigm for the figure in a landscape, and an expression in abstract terms of man's relationship to his fellows, and to the world in which he lives. The inherent classicism of all Hepworth's work comes to the fore: her art always aspires to a timeless, universal concept of abstract beauty.

Though her marriage to Ben Nicholson was dissolved in 1951, he remained in St Ives until 1958, and the mutually beneficial influence of painter and sculptor on each other's work persisted. They regained their international reputation after the hiatus of the war of 1939–45. Barbara Hepworth had important retrospective exhibitions at the Venice Biennale in 1950, at the Whitechapel Art Gallery in 1954 and 1962, at the São Paulo Bienal, Brazil, in 1959 (where she was awarded the grand prix), and at the Tate Gallery in 1968. She exhibited her sculpture regularly in London and New York, and was shown throughout Europe and the United States, in Japan and Australia. The most important of her sculpture commissions was 'Single Form', outside the United Nations building in New York. It was unveiled in 1964 as a memorial to Dag Hammarskjöld, who was a personal friend. She made drawings, paintings, and lithographs, and designed the sets and costumes for the first performance in 1955 of (Sir) Michael Tippett's opera *The Midsummer Marriage.*

Barbara Hepworth won public recognition in the last years of her life, when she was widely regarded as the world's greatest woman sculptor. In her obituary the *Guardian* described her as 'probably the most significant woman artist in the history of art to this day'. No militant feminist herself, she asked simply to be treated as a sculptor, irrespective of sex.

She was appointed CBE in 1958 and DBE in 1965. Honorary degrees were awarded to her by the universities of Birmingham (1960), Leeds (1961), Exeter (1966), Oxford (1968), London (1970), and Manchester (1971), and by the Royal College of Art in London (1964), where she was also senior fellow (1970). She was made a bard of Cornwall in 1968, and in 1973 an honorary member of the American Academy of Arts and Letters. She served as a trustee of the Tate Gallery from 1965 until 1972.

Barbara Hepworth was small and intense in appearance, deeply reserved in character, and totally dedicated to her art. It was always a measure of surprise that such a frail woman could undertake such demanding physical work, but she had great toughness and integrity. She remained proud of her Yorkshire origins, though devoted to St Ives and the west Cornish landscape which provided her with enduring inspiration.

Barbara Hepworth died in a fire in her studio in St Ives 20 May 1975, after suffering serious illness for some time. As she herself had hoped, Trewyn studio, where she had lived from 1949, was presented to the nation by her executors in 1980, together with a representative collection of her work. It is now an outstation of the Tate Gallery, which also has a very considerable Hepworth collection. Her work is represented in more than a hundred public collections throughout the world, with particularly fine work in the Leeds and Wakefield City Art Galleries, in the Scottish

National Gallery of Modern Art, and in the Rijksmuseum Kröller-Müller at Otterloo in Holland.

[Herbert Read, *Barbara Hepworth*, 1952; J. P. Hodin, *Barbara Hepworth*, 1961; Alan Bowness, *The Complete Sculpture of Barbara Hepworth 1960–69*, 1971; Barbara Hepworth, *A Pictorial Autobiography*, 1970, 2nd edn. 1978; Margaret Gardiner, *Barbara Hepworth*, 1982; personal knowledge.]

Alan Bowness

published 1986

HILL William

(1903–1971)

Bookmaker, was born in Birmingham 16 July 1903, the second son and fourth of the eleven children (there were also a twin son and daughter who died at birth) of William Hill, journeyman coach-painter, and his wife Lavinia Knight, the daughter of a farmer, who also kept an inn on the border of Warwickshire and Leicestershire. Hill ran away from school at the age of twelve to work on an uncle's farm. After a short time working for his father he moved to a tool-making factory in Birmingham, where he took up bookmaking in a small way, by collecting bets on his motor bicycle. Shortly afterwards he became a more serious bookmaker, but plunged too heavily at first and lost all his capital. However, he started again in the cheaper rings, and after five years moved to London in 1929.

He started betting at greyhound stadiums, then extended to pony racing at Northolt Park, and in 1934 opened a one-room office in Jermyn Street. He soon moved to much larger premises in Park Lane, and later to even larger offices at Piccadilly Circus in 1947. By 1939 he had given up the dogs and the main business was credit betting, though he was still operating at Northolt Park.

In 1944 he produced the first fixed-odds football coupon, and set up a separate football company in 1944. In 1955 he gave up on-course bookmaking. In 1960 his great rivals, Ladbrokes, went into the football business, and Hill sued them for infringement of the copyright in his coupon. The case went to the House of Lords, where Hill won the £1 damages for which he had asked, with costs. In 1954 he bought, with Lionel Barber, 75 per cent of Holder's Investment Trust, to which he sold his interests between 1955 and 1961 for over £5 million. So successful was the business that Holder's shares rose from 2*s.* 10*d.* in 1956 to £18 10*s.* in 1960. This purchase of a 'shell' company was the first time that the manœuvre had been executed and the first time that a bookmaking company had been floated on the Stock Exchange.

Hill loathed the idea of betting shops, which were legalized in 1960, but rivals moved in and he followed in 1966. In the same year he reluctantly began to take bets on elections. He did not, as he said on 9 December 1958, when as owner of Be Careful he spoke at the Gimcrack dinner, object to bookmakers paying something towards the racing industry's expenses. However, as he wrote in the following May, it galled him to be expected to do so and still to be refused admission to the members' enclosures at smart meetings.

Hill's first stud was Whitsbury in Hampshire, which he bought in 1943. Nimbus was foaled there in 1946, and, having been sold for 5,000 guineas at the yearling sales, won the 1949 Two Thousand Guineas and Derby. In 1945 he bought Sezincote stud in Gloucestershire, where he stood his stallion Chanteur II, sire of Pinza, winner of the 1953 Derby.

William Hill was a great bookmaker, who had the courage to take enormous bets. He was an ebullient, sometimes irascible, charming man. In his latter years he took little day-to-day interest in racing, but was seen as an elder statesman of the turf. He had become accustomed to great wealth, but he had a social conscience and may even have considered himself a socialist.

In 1923 he married Ivy Burley, a ladies' hairdresser of Smallheath, Birmingham, who survived him. They had one daughter. Hill died in Newmarket 15 October 1971.

[*The Hill Story*, privately published, 1955; Richard Kaye, *The Ladbrokes Story*, 1969; *The Times*, 16 October 1971; Christopher R. Hill, *Horse Power: the Politics of the Turf*, 1988; William Hill Organization press release 4 February 1988; private information.]

CHRISTOPHER R. HILL

published 1993

HITCHCOCK Sir Alfred Joseph

(1899–1980)

Film director, was born 13 August 1899 in Leytonstone, London, the second son and youngest of the three children of William Hitchcock, a greengrocer and poulterer, and his wife, Emma Jane Whelan. He was educated at various Catholic boarding schools in London, and always spoke of his childhood as lonely and protected. But the memory of the period he most often quoted as having shaped his attitude towards authority, fear, and guilt, was being sent by his father at the age of five with a note addressed to the superintendent of the local police station, where he was locked in a cell for ten minutes and then released with the words, 'That is what we do to naughty boys'.

His father died when Hitchcock was fourteen and he left St Ignatius's College, a Jesuit institution in Stamford Hill, to study at the School for Engineering and Navigation, and then became a draughtsman and advertising designer with a cable company. After some free-lance work designing silent-movie titles, he obtained a full-time job at Islington Studios in 1920, and under its American owners, Famous Players–Lasky, and their British successors, Gainsborough Pictures, he gained a knowledge of all aspects of the business before the producer (Sir) Michael Balcon gave him the opportunity to direct his first picture, the extravagant melodrama *The Pleasure Garden*, in 1925.

The following year Hitchcock drew on his fascination with the classic English murders to make a movie about a man suspected of being Jack the Ripper, *The Lodger*, which was his first thriller and the first time he 'signed' a film by making a brief personal appearance. In 1929 he directed the first British talking film, *Blackmail*, another thriller. With its plot of a police officer in love with an accidental murderess, its innovative use of sound, and a finely staged climactic chase in the British Museum, *Blackmail* had all the characteristics of his mature work.

Although he directed adaptations of *The Manxman* (1928) by (Sir) T. H. Hall Caine, *Juno and the Paycock* (1930) by Sean O'Casey, and *The Skin Game* (1931) by John Galsworthy, Hitchcock soon came to specialize in thrillers, and after the success of *The Man Who Knew Too Much* (1934), only one film—a version of the Broadway comedy *Mr and Mrs Smith* (1941)—took him away from his chosen *métier*. Starting in the late 1920s, he cultivated the acquaintance of journalists and cinephiles, becoming one of the most articulate and frequently quoted exponents of his craft and winning the title 'master of suspense'. His pictures were meticulously planned before they went into production and he often said that the real interest lay in the preparation, the actual shooting being a necessary chore. The performers, however eminent their reputations, were there simply to realize his and his screenwriters' conception. This is what he meant when he said: 'Actors should be treated like cattle.'

Through such films as *The Thirty-Nine Steps* (1935), *Sabotage* (1936), and *The Lady Vanishes* (1938), the comedy-thriller many consider the finest achievement of his English period, Hitchcock became the most successful and highly regarded director in Britain. But he was increasingly attracted by the greater technical facilities, larger budgets, and more substantial international fame that working in America would bring him. Equally the apparent classlessness of American society afforded opportunities for social acceptance denied him in the hide-bound Britain of that time. So in 1939, after completing a film of (Dame) Daphne du Maurier's *Jamaica Inn*, he left for Hollywood where his first assignment for his new employer, David O. Selznick, was to adapt Daphne du Maurier's *Rebecca* (1940). It won an Academy award for the best film of the year.

Except for three brief sojourns in Britain—first making as a patriotic gesture two short films in French in 1944 for distribution by the Ministry of Information in newly liberated France, next directing *Under Capricorn* (1949) and *Stage Fright* (1950), then later his penultimate picture *Frenzy* (1971)—Hitchcock remained in Hollywood. A number of his early American films, however, had English settings, and most of his Hollywood productions featured British actors in key roles. He remained deeply attached to his native country and did not take out American citizenship papers until 1955.

During the 1940s and 1950s, Hitchcock developed a fascination for solving technical problems. His wartime melodrama *Lifeboat* (1943) is confined to the inside of a lifeboat after an American merchant ship has been torpedoed by a German U-boat. His version of Patrick Hamilton's play *Rope* (1948) is shot in a series of ten-minute takes so that the whole picture appears seamless and unedited. In 1954 he filmed another play, *Dial M for Murder*, using the three-dimensional camera, and in the same year he restricted the point of view of *Rear Window* to what a temporarily crippled photographer could see from the window of his New York apartment.

In the decade between his psychological thriller *Strangers on a Train* (1951) and his influential horror film *Psycho* (1960), Hitchcock produced within the perimeters of his chosen genre an extraordinarily varied range of work. It included *I Confess* (1952), the story of a Canadian priest prevented by the confidences of the confessional from clearing his name of a murder charge; *The Wrong Man* (1957), the reconstruction of a true story of a New York musician falsely accused of robbery; and *North by Northwest* (1959), an immaculate comedy-thriller that recaptured the light touch of his pre-war British films.

In this period his reputation advanced on two quite different fronts. In 1955 he began a ten-year association with television through his series of tales of mystery, crime, and the occult, *Alfred Hitchcock Presents* (1955–61) and *The Alfred Hitchcock Hour* (1961–5), some editions of which he directed, and all of which he introduced in his gentle, even London accent, and with his own brand of deadpan, often rather macabre, humour. This regular exposure on television, added to those eagerly awaited glimpses of him in the feature films, helped make his short portly figure (his weight varied between fourteen and twenty stones) and chubby face immediately recognizable and beloved by film-goers the world over. He became the only director in the history of the cinema to be instantly recognizable to the general public.

On another front, Hitchcock became the idol of the young French critics of the monthly journal *Cahiers du Cinéma* who were later to become the directors of the *nouvelle vague*. They regarded him as not merely a master film-maker with a unique ability to manipulate audiences, but also a profound psychologist, social observer, and Catholic moralist. A full-length study by Claude Chabrol and Eric Rohmer in the 'Classique du Cinéma' series (1957) was the foundation-stone for what by the end of Hitchcock's life was to be a substantial body of scholarship.

The English-speaking world at first resisted these larger claims that were being made for a man thought of largely as a skilled entertainer. But as film studies grew on the campuses of America, Hitchcock was accorded a similar status in his adopted and native countries. Honorary doctorates came his way, he received the Irving G. Thalberg memorial award (1972) from the American Film Academy, the Life Achievement award from the American Film Institute (1979), and finally in the 1980 New Year's honours list a KBE.

After *The Birds* (1963), the story of a mysterious avian attack on a small Californian community that initiated a cycle of ecological horror films, there was something of a decline in Hitchcock's work. His old-fashioned psychological melodrama *Marnie* (1964) was a throwback to the Freudian thrillers of the 1940s he had inspired with *Spellbound* (1945); his cold-war espionage pictures, *Torn Curtain* (1966) and *Topaz* (1969), and his film about a psychopathic murderer in London, *Frenzy* (1971), seemed dated, the products of a man not really living in the contemporary world. Then in 1976, working with a cast of mostly young American actors in the sprightly *Family Plot*, he showed himself once more the unchallenged master of the comedy-thriller, his set pieces as ingenious as ever, the Hitchcock touch as deft and definite. He was still discussing projects and planning a new film when he died in Los Angeles 29 April 1980.

In 1926 Hitchcock married Alma Reville (died 1982), the daughter of an employee of Twickenham Film Studio and herself a script girl and assistant editor. She collaborated on the screenplays of many of her husband's films. This man who took a gleeful delight in terrifying audiences with movies that were often violent, sadistic, and erotic in character (he often spoke of taking film-goers for an emotional roller-coaster ride), lived a happy, quiet domestic life of impeccable rectitude. When not busy filming, he devoted much of his spare time to indulging a gourmet's taste for good food and wine. The Hitchcocks had one child, a daughter Patricia, born in 1928, who trained as an actor at RADA in London and appeared in three of her father's films.

[John Russell Taylor, *Hitch*, 1978; *The Times*, 30 October 1980; private information.]

PHILIP FRENCH

published 1986

HOBBS Sir John Berry (Jack) (1882–1963)

Cricketer, was born at Cambridge 16 December 1882, the eldest of the twelve children of John Cooper Hobbs, a slater's labourer, and his wife, Flora Matilda Berry. As his father became a professional at Fenner's and later groundsman at Jesus College, cricket was immediately a central function of Jack Hobbs's life, and although he never had any formal coaching, he would get up at six to practise on Parker's Piece. He was educated at the local Church of England boys' school and the first cricket team for which he played was that of the church choir in which he sang. His promise in local cricket earned him a trial with Surrey in 1903 (after Essex had ignored his application), and he was paid 30*s.* a week, £1 in winter, while he qualified by residence.

Surrey were rebuilding after the triumphs of the 1890s and as in the previous season he had made 696 runs in 13 innings for Cambridgeshire, in 1905 Hobbs was given an immediate opportunity as soon as he was qualified. In his first match, against the Gentlemen of England, he made 18 and 88, and was awarded his county cap when he followed this with 28 and 155 against Essex in his first championship game, reaching the century in 2 hours. After three summers of consolidation under the guidance and example of Tom Hayward, his first great opening partner, he went to Australia in 1907–8. Left out of the first test, he made 83 at Melbourne and until his test career ended in 1930 he was never again omitted by England when he was available.

In 1909 he came within 81 runs of reaching a thousand in May, which he would probably have done had he not been rested against Oxford. In this prolific month he made 205 out of 371 in 165 minutes against Hampshire, 159 out of 352 against Warwickshire, and a century in each innings in the return match at Birmingham. Hobbs had established his authority in all English conditions, and he completed his apprenticeship when in 1909–10 he faced South Africa's battery of spin bowlers on their native matting.

The googly was a new weapon in the bowler's armoury and many of the leading batsmen of the era had been routed by it. Hobbs admitted that he could not yet spot it from the hand, but on this tour he subdued it by going down the pitch and attacking it off the front foot. Although the series was lost, his average in the tests was 67, the next highest being 33, and on the tour he made 1,194 runs. His mastery of spin, coupled with the bowling of S. F. Barnes, largely won the rubber in Australia in 1911–12, because after H. V. Hordern had taken 12 wickets in the first test, which was lost, Hobbs put him to the sword with centuries in the next three. At Melbourne he and W. Rhodes set up a record of 323 for the first wicket, made in $4\frac{3}{4}$ hours.

In South Africa in 1913–14 he made 1,489 runs, 700 more than anyone else, and in the following summer, when Surrey were champions for the only time in his career, he made 11 centuries, 3 of them over 200. At Bradford he hit 5 sixes and 11 fours in making 100 out of 151 in 75 minutes, and against Yorkshire at Lord's he and Hayward had the last of their forty century partnerships. This was his high noon, when he was unchallenged as the leading batsman in the world, the supreme technician on any sort of wicket. Although audacity was sometimes tempered by his increasing responsibility to the side, the characteristic style was a fluent aggression which dictated to the bowlers. The worse the conditions, the more he set himself to dominate through attack.

But the ripeness is all. By 1914 Hobbs had scored 25,587 runs, made 65 centuries, played in 28 tests. The war years should have been his prime, and at thirty-six he could not be certain of recovering his old ascendancy. But in the event all these figures were to be more than doubled, and he was to garner the richest harvest the game has known. When he retired in 1934 he had made 61,237 runs, at an average of 50·65, and 197 centuries, 98 of them after his fortieth birthday.

At first Hobbs showed much of the old aggression: 205 not out against the Australian Imperial Forces when the next score was 38; with J. N. Crawford 96 in 32 minutes, scored in bad light and drizzle, to defeat Kent in his postponed benefit match; with Sandham in 1920 190 in 90 minutes against Northamptonshire; a century in 65 minutes on a fiery pitch at Leicester. But in 1921 a muscle injury was followed by an ulcerated appendix which nearly cost his life. He played only 6 innings in that year of plenty and thereafter he tired more easily and his batting was less adventurous. Adapting his style to the physical possibilities, he now dominated the bowlers off the back foot. The runs rolled in, but their gathering was never mechanical. A Hobbs innings was scrawled with his personal signatures as, all technical problems now instinctively resolved, he deployed the fullness of his art.

At Bath in 1923 he made his hundredth century, and at Taunton two years later he both equalled and overtook the record of 126 centuries set up by W. G. Grace. In this season of 1925 he scored 10 of his 16 hundreds in the first 12 games, and he led the English averages with 3,024 runs at 70·32. Next year his 316 not out for Surrey was the highest innings ever played at Lord's and in the final test at the Oval, with Sutcliffe, a masterly century on a turning wicket helped to recover the Ashes from Australia. In 1928 he had an average of 82, and when he went to Australia in the winter a team-mate said that for him the tour was like a royal procession as he visited for the last time the grounds where he had given so much pleasure. At Melbourne his 49, made when the pitch was most lethal, enabled England to get 332 to win the match in conditions so bad that they were not expected to reach a hundred. Gradually, however, the years took their toll and he had to rest while minor strains and injuries took longer to clear up. His final century in first-class cricket was scored in Duckworth's benefit at Old Trafford in 1934, and the crowd sang 'Auld Lang Syne'.

All but 2 of Hobbs's 61 tests were played against Australia and South Africa: in 102 innings he made 5,410 runs at 56·94, with 15 centuries. In his career he shared in 166 opening century partnerships, an average of 1 every 8 innings, the highest being 428. Sixty-six were with Sandham, 40 with Hayward, 26 with Sutcliffe (15 in tests). Hobbs 6 times made 2 centuries in a match; he reached 1,000 runs in a season 26 times; he scored centuries both home and away against every county. In the Gentlemen v. Players fixture he had his own little cluster of records: an aggregate of 4,050, the highest individual score of 266 not out, and centuries at Lord's, the Oval, and Scarborough. In all grades of cricket he made 244 centuries, the last in 1941.

At medium pace with a late swerve he was also a useful bowler. He opened the bowling in three tests in South Africa in 1909–10, and in 1920 he even headed the English averages with 17 wickets at 11·82. In the field he was brilliant, lurking at cover with deceptive casualness to trap the unwary. In Australia in 1911–12 he ran out 15 opponents.

Surrey made Hobbs a life member in 1935, the MCC in 1949; his knighthood in 1953 was the first conferred on a professional cricketer; the Hobbs Gates at the Oval and a pavilion on Parker's Piece stand as tangible memorials of his career. But in a wider sense Hobbs was remembered as a potent symbol of the game, the small boy's idol, known to thousands who never saw him play. No other great player has inspired so much personal affection, nor permitted such a high degree of personal identification. His obvious integrity had something to do with this, his modest and disciplined way of life, his deep but unobtrusive religious beliefs, and his unassuming pleasure in his own achievement. But he was loved because he was so evidently an ordinary man, exceptional only in the endowment of a particular genius which he was humble enough to see in its proper perspective. He never expected to inherit the earth because of it, nor even to be hired as a radio pundit on matters outside his experience.

With the proceeds of his benefit in 1919 Hobbs opened a sports shop in Fleet Street in which he continued to take an active interest after he left the game. In 1906 he married Ada Ellen, daughter of Edward G. Gates, of Cambridge; they had three sons and a daughter. He died at Hove 21 December 1963, only a few months after his wife.

[J. B. Hobbs, *My Cricket Memories*, 1924, *My Life Story*, 1935; Louis Palgrave, *The Story of the Oval*, 1949; Ronald Mason, *Jack Hobbs*, 1960; *Wisden's Cricketers' Almanack*, 1936, 1963, 1964.]

M. M. Reese

published 1981

HUTTON Sir Leonard

(1916–1990)

Cricketer, was born 23 June 1916 in Fulneck, near Pudsey, Leeds, the youngest in the family of four sons and one daughter of Henry Hutton, builder, and his wife Lily Swithenbank, whose uncle, Seth Milner, had been a prominent cricketer in the 1880s. Fulneck, a Moravian religious community, had been founded in the 1730s by Count Zinzendorf, an exile from Bohemia. Generations of Huttons, some of whom became Moravian ministers, went to the community's school and chapel and were brought up in a terrace house dating from the eighteenth century. This moral, Nonconformist upbringing, which Len Hutton later described as 'strict but caring', gave him a reserved and thoughtful demeanour unusual among professional cricketers. He was educated at Littlemoor Council School, Pudsey.

His talent marked him out early for a career in the game, to which he took, he said, 'like a Sherpa to the mountains'. His three brothers all played Yorkshire league cricket for the Pudsey St Lawrence Club, where he joined them in the first XI at the age of fourteen. An important event in his life was the return to Pudsey of Herbert Sutcliffe, the opening batsman for Yorkshire and England, who had played in his youth with Hutton's father. Sutcliffe quickly saw the potential of the talented teenager who played on the concrete strip in Sutcliffe's garden and described him as 'a marvel—the discovery of a generation'. Hutton said he looked up to Sutcliffe at this time 'with the reverence that a pious Roman Catholic has for the Pope'.

It was Sutcliffe who introduced him to the Yorkshire County Cricket Club, where he was coached at the austere Headingley 'Winter Shed' in nearby Leeds by George Hirst, the former England all-rounder, who soon pronounced that he could 'teach him nowt'. In 1930, when he was fourteen, Hutton sat enthralled in the Headingley crowd as the great Australian, (Sir) Donald Bradman, scored 309 runs in a day on his way to the record total of 334 which, eight years later, Hutton was to break at the Oval in the most famous innings of his life.

Yorkshire was the most powerful cricket county in England in the 1930s, winning the championship five times in the seven years before World War II, and to break into that team at all was an achievement. Hutton did this in 1934, at the age of seventeen, albeit with a duck (a feat he repeated three years later on his début for England). But he confirmed his class with an early innings of 196. Yorkshire, with talent to spare, nursed the young Hutton through his early seasons to avoid putting too much strain on his fragile physique. He later claimed to have learned all he knew about cricket from listening to the dressing-room talk of great players like Sutcliffe, Hedley Verity, Maurice Leyland, and W. E. Bowes. It was an austere and rigorous apprenticeship designed to keep a young man, however talented, in his place. Even so, he was to say later of the Yorkshire dressing-room of his youth: 'Had I been ordered to walk on broken glass, I would have instantly obeyed.'

In 1937, just after his twenty-first birthday, he opened the batting for England against New Zealand and scored a century in his second test match. It was a year later, in the 'timeless' test at the Oval against Australia, that Hutton made history, scoring his record 364 in England's highest ever total of 903. It was a marathon feat of concentration over thirteen hours and seventeen minutes, the longest innings ever played, and the highest score by an England batsman. It made him an instant celebrity wherever cricket was played—a fame not entirely welcome to his reclusive personality.

In 1939, first in South Africa and then at home against the West Indies, he gave some of his finest batting performances and, in the view of many sound judges, was just reaching a peak when his career was interrupted by six years of war, when he served in the Royal Artillery and the Army Physical Training Corps. In Hutton's case the war was a double tragedy, for he dislocated a wrist badly in a gymnasium accident in March 1941 and was left, after skin and bone graft operations, with one arm more than two inches shorter than the other. He was discharged from the army and for some time it seemed unlikely that he could ever play cricket again.

He returned to the international arena in 1946, and over the next decade established himself as England's greatest opening batsman since Sir Jack Hobbs, scoring over 40,000 runs in his career, including 129 centuries, at an average of 55. But, as R. C. Robertson-Glasgow wrote, 'to admire Len Hutton merely for the quantity of his runs is like praising Milton for the length of *Paradise Lost* or Schubert for the number of his songs.' Despite the handicap to his left arm, which forced him to use a schoolboy's bat and restricted the range of his strokes, he was admired as a graceful, balanced, and classical batsman, perhaps the finest ever on a turning wicket. Only Bradman was unarguably his superior, and, for three or four years after Bradman's retirement in 1948, Hutton was undisputed as the greatest batsman in the world.

In 1951 he became England's first professional captain and never lost a series, recovering the Ashes against Australia in coronation year (1953) after a gap of fifteen years (and then retaining them in Australia). He was a cautious, uncommunicative captain, believing strongly in the use of fast bowlers, and was the first to slow down the over rate deliberately as a tactical ploy. In five series against the powerful Australian attack after the war he bore the brunt of the English batting, prompting the popular catchphrase 'Hutton out, side out'. The physical and nervous strain took its toll, forcing his early retirement in 1956. He was the first professional cricketer to be elected an honorary member of the MCC and the second (after Hobbs) to be knighted (1956).

Curiously, though, Hutton was never appointed captain of Yorkshire, an omission which may in part explain his exile in Surrey for the rest of his life. After his retirement he became a director of Fenners, the mining equipment manufacturers, who made good use of his worldwide cricketing contacts. Always a shrewd judge of the game, he also became an England selector and wrote on cricket for the *Observer* for thirty years. He published three books on cricket. Len Hutton mellowed in later life and amused his friends greatly with a cryptic sense of humour, delivered with a crinkled smile from wide-apart blue eyes. His strong moral outlook shaped and directed one of the best natural talents in the history of the game.

He married, in September 1939, Dorothy Mary, daughter of George Dennis, foreman joiner on Lord Downe's estate at Wykeham, Yorkshire. Her brother played cricket for Yorkshire. Their happy marriage was a powerful source of strength. Their two sons, Richard and John, were both cricketers; Richard played one season for England in 1971 and became editorial director of the *Cricketer*. In January 1990, in a bid to heal the county's divisions, Hutton was invited to be president of Yorkshire CCC, an honour he deeply appreciated, but, before he could have much effect, he died 6 September 1990 in Kingston upon Thames Hospital, of a ruptured aorta.

[Donald Trelford, *Len Hutton Remembered*, 1992; Len Hutton, *Cricket is My life*, 1950, and *Just My Story*, 1956; Len Hutton with Alex Bannister, *Fifty Years in Cricket*, 1984; Gerald Howat, *Len Hutton*, 1988; personal knowledge.]

DONALD TRELFORD

published 1996

HUXLEY Aldous Leonard

(1894–1963)

Man of letters, was born at Laleham, a house near Godalming, 26 July 1894, the third son of Leonard Huxley, an assistant master at Charterhouse and subsequently editor of the *Cornhill Magazine*, by his first wife, Julia Frances Arnold, a granddaughter of Thomas Arnold of Rugby and niece of Matthew Arnold. As a grandson of T. H. Huxley and great-grandson of Dr Arnold, Aldous Huxley inherited both a passionate interest in science and the pursuit of truth, and his high sense of moral purpose. Mrs Humphry Ward, the novelist, was his aunt; (Sir) Julian Huxley his eldest brother.

Huxley was educated first at Prior's Field, a successful avant-garde school founded by his mother, then at Hillside, a nearby preparatory school, from which he won a scholarship to Eton in 1908. Shortly after arriving there he suffered the first of three traumatic experiences: the premature death of his mother at the age of forty-five. Huxley was wholly devoted to her, and this sudden loss when he was only fourteen came as an appalling shock and deprivation. Then, scarcely more than two years later, he contracted an infection of the eyes (*keratitis punctata*) which sent him virtually blind and obliged him to leave Eton before the end of his eighth term. He faced this calamity with extraordinary determination and courage; taught himself to read braille, to type, and to play the piano; he continued his education doggedly with a series of tutors. In the spring of 1912 his sight had improved sufficiently for him to walk alone, to read large print with the aid of a magnifying glass, and to have hopes of going to Oxford. In October 1913 he went up to Balliol. There, despite his irreparably damaged sight, he read assiduously for a degree in English literature (in which he obtained a first, in 1916, as well as winning the Stanhope prize), developed a taste for Proust and the French symbolists, but also found time to play jazz and take part in amateur theatricals. By then Huxley was immensely tall (6 feet $4\frac{3}{4}$ inches), and so thin that he was accurately described as having to 'fold himself and his legs, like some gigantic grasshopper, into a chair'. But what people noticed most particularly was his unaffected charm, his extraordinarily mellifluous voice, his sense of humour, and, above all, his gentleness. In later life, many people who disagreed profoundly with some of his views and deplored his propensity for entertaining the most improbable hypotheses (a by-product of his immense intellectual curiosity) nevertheless found it impossible to quarrel with this most lovable of men. For in addition to gentleness, there was an innate modesty and a sweet reasonableness about him that disarmed contention. His first year at university was intoxicating and he took everything that Oxford had to offer. The spell was broken by the outbreak of war in August 1914, and almost simultaneously by the third of the personal tragedies which afflicted him before he came of age: the suicide of his gifted elder brother Trevenen.

It was while he was still an undergraduate that Huxley started writing poetry chiefly but also short stories, and first discovered that he had 'some kind of natural gift for it'—a gift that supported him and his family for the rest of his life. It was also while he was at Oxford that, towards the end of 1915, he was taken to Garsington, home of the pacifist member of Parliament Philip Morrell and his wife, Lady Ottoline, where he met most of the younger and more advanced writers and painters of the day. Huxley was both alarmed and fascinated by this immensely talented and varied *galère*, but after he left Oxford he spent part of the war years working on the land there (he was totally unfit for military service), and came to regard Garsington as one of the seminal factors in his education. More important, it was there that he met and became engaged to Maria Nys, the eldest daughter of a well-to-do Flemish family from Courtrai which had sought refuge in England; it was nearly three years, during which Huxley taught at Repton and Eton, before they could get married in July 1919. They set up house in Hampstead, and lived for some time in great financial stringency on Huxley's earnings as a journalist; their only child, Matthew, was born in April 1920.

The next ten years saw the emergence of Huxley as a novelist and short-story writer of marked originality, whose pungent wit, uninhibited dialogue, and frank discussion of subjects hitherto considered taboo in fiction, quickly won him a public, and a place as 'cultural hero' among the young. His first novel, *Crome Yellow* (1921), was shortly followed by *Antic Hay* (1923) and *Those Barren Leaves* (1925), all of which satirized contemporary society, through characters who challenged or flouted accepted conventions and were not always without resemblance to living people. The novels were interspersed by collections of brilliant short stories, including *Mortal Coils* (1922), *Little Mexican* (1924), and *Two or Three Graces*

(1926). In addition, volumes of essays and books of travel made a regular appearance, among them *On the Margin* (1923) and *Jesting Pilate* (1926): in all a dozen books in eight years—a remarkable achievement for a man almost bereft of sight. Moreover, they made him money, and amply justified the faith his publishers had shown by offering him a three-year contract, at £500 a year, as early as 1923—an arrangement which was renewed at intervals, in varying terms, up to his death. But it was 1928, the year in which his most ambitious novel to date, *Point Counter Point*, was published, which saw him become a best-seller both in Britain and America. The years 1925 to 1937 were among the happiest in Huxley's life. With the gradual easing of his financial position, he and his wife were able to spend more time abroad, especially in Italy, where they became close friends of D. H. Lawrence, whose *Letters* Huxley edited (1932); they also visited India and the Far East, as well as Germany, Spain, the West Indies, and Mexico; in 1928 they bought a house near Paris, and later a villa at Sanary, near Toulon, which they occupied on and off from 1930 to 1937. There Huxley painted a good deal as well as wrote, entertained, and visited friends. In the intervals, regular visits were paid to London for the publication of a book or the production of a play (Huxley remained mistakenly convinced that he could become a successful dramatist), or to Italy for refreshment of his delight in Italian painting and architecture.

Early in 1937 the Huxleys began a prolonged visit to America, and by 1938 they had finally decided to remain there. It has been suggested that this was a result of the threat of war already developing in Europe, that Huxley was turning his back on the ugly prospects ahead (he was an ardent supporter of the Peace Pledge Union, for which he lectured and wrote pamphlets). Huxley himself, however, believed that the clear sunlight of California would enable him to see and read better, and he heard encouraging reports of a new American method, invented by Dr W. H. Bates, of improving the vision of partially sighted people. In this, according to his own and his wife's reports, he was not disappointed. By the middle of 1939 he was able to read and write without spectacles, and in 1942 he published his conclusions in *The Art of Seeing*. By then his writing had taken an entirely fresh turn. The 'philosophy of meaninglessness', as Huxley himself described it in *Ends and Means* (1937), which had informed all his early work and proved so potent a liberating force for his readers, no longer satisfied him. Something positive, something transcendental, something which would set mankind on the road to a fuller realization of its potential, was what he sought. He found it, he believed, in a form of mysticism derived in part from oriental philosophy, but largely from his own intuitive aspirations. 'Men and women', he wrote, 'are capable of being devils and lunatics. They are no less capable of being fully human', and for the rest of his life he devoted himself to trying to persuade them to be so. The books which followed, *The Perennial Philosophy* (1945), *Science, Liberty and Peace* (1946), *Themes and Variations* (1950), and *Brave New World Revisited* (1958), and in a sense also *Grey Eminence* (1941), spelt out the temptations which life presents in the modern world with its materialist values and dangerous technological advances, and suggested ways of overcoming them. The ways were unorthodox, and of such originality that they inevitably exposed him to accusations of abandoning reason for mumbo-jumbo. Huxley was unmoved, and later his views found powerful support among some of the best minds of the day. Similarly, the novels of that period, *After Many a Summer* (1939) which won the James Tait Black memorial prize, *Time Must Have a Stop* (1944), *Ape and Essence* (1948), and *The Genius and the Goddess* (1955), were distinguished by a combination of irony and compassion with a profound regard for humanity which lifted them on to a different plane from his earlier novels. In that context, Huxley wrote two fictional Utopias: one, *Brave New World* (1932), was a nightmarish prognostication of a future in which humanity has been destroyed by science; and the other, *Island*, published exactly thirty years later, was a picture of the good life possible for humans if only they would behave rationally. It was ironic that the former, despite its pessimism, should prove easily his most popular (and many good judges continued to think his best) novel, while the latter was clearly unsatisfactory as fiction but comprised his most sustained, imaginative, and moving account of *la condition humaine*, which for Huxley was ever 'the beast in view'.

In 1953 Huxley's interest in the therapeutic value of hypnosis was extended to other methods of releasing the human body from the domination of its ego: notably the use of mescalin and other psychedelic drugs such as LSD. His own experiments with these, and the practical use which he believed could be made of them, he described in *The Doors of Perception* (1954) and *Heaven and Hell* (1956). He was subsequently much criticized for the part he was thought to have played in encouraging young people to take these drugs, although he had warned that they must be used with caution. The year before his first experiment, his wife, Maria—his 'dragoman', as he called her for her practical good sense and tact—was seriously ill; she died from cancer early in 1955. A year later Huxley married Laura Archera, an Italian concert violinist and psychotherapist from Turin, whom he had first met some years earlier. But it was not long before Huxley himself contracted cancer of the tongue, in 1960. The disease at first yielded to radium treatment (he refused surgery because it would have impaired his speech), and the next three years were spent indefatigably writing, lecturing, and attending conferences in America and all over Europe. This was interrupted, in May 1961, by the catastrophic fire which totally destroyed his home in Los Angeles, leaving him 'a man without possessions and without a past'. Huxley accepted the disaster philosophically, describing it as 'a sign that the grim reaper was having a good look at me'. A year later the cancer returned, this time incurably. By the autumn of 1963 his condition was hopeless, although he remained stoically detached and serene to the end. He died in Los Angeles 22 November 1963. In 1971 his ashes were returned to England and buried in his parents' grave at Compton cemetery, Surrey.

An oil portrait by his uncle, John Collier (1926), is privately owned; there is an ink and wash drawing by A. Wolmark (1928) in the National Portrait Gallery, and a drawing of Huxley and the Revd H. R. L. ('Dick') Sheppard by (Sir) David Low (1938) in the Tate Gallery. (Sir) William Rothenstein drew Huxley several times and one of these (1922) is reproduced in *Twenty-Four Portraits* (2nd series, 1923).

[*Listener*, 16 October 1947; *Aldous Huxley: a Memorial Volume*, ed. Sir Julian Huxley, 1956; *Letters of Aldous Huxley*, ed. Grover Smith, 1969; Laura Archera Huxley, *This Timeless Moment*, 1969; Sybille Bedford, *Aldous Huxley: a Biography*, 2 vols., 1973–4; personal knowledge.]

IAN PARSONS

published 1981

ISHERWOOD Christopher William Bradshaw (1904–1986)

Writer, was born 26 August 1904 at Wyberslegh Hall, Cheshire, the elder son (there were no daughters) of Francis Edward Bradshaw-Isherwood, professional soldier in the York and Lancaster Regiment, of Marple, and his wife Kathleen, the only child of Frederick Machell Smith, wine merchant, of Bury St Edmunds. He was educated at Repton, where he met his lifelong friend and the ultimate arbiter of his work, Edward Upward, with whom he wrote numerous surrealist-gothic stories about 'Mortmere', a 'fantastic village' they had invented. He followed Upward to Cambridge, where, at Corpus Christi College, he studied history. He left after deliberately failing his tripos, and began earning his living as secretary to the International String Quartet.

He was deeply affected by World War I, in which his father had been killed and the certainties of the Edwardian world destroyed. Much of his life may be seen as a search for some creed to replace the traditional, public-school, Christian values of his childhood, against which he began rebelling as a young man. In 1925 he was reintroduced to W. H. Auden, whom he had known at preparatory school, and through him met (Sir) Stephen Spender: the three men were to form a conspicuous literary, left-wing triumvirate of the 1930s. Isherwood's first novel, *All the Conspirators* (1928), is an oblique account of family discord, and is influenced by the work of Virginia Woolf and E. M. Forster. The conflict between mother and son was to be a frequent theme in his work (and, indeed, his life) and resurfaces in *The Memorial* (1932), a remarkably acute novel about the war between the generations, seen from both sides of the divide, and a key text of the period.

After a half-hearted attempt to train as a doctor at King's College, London (October 1928–March 1929), Isherwood followed Auden to Berlin, partly in order to pursue a homosexual life in the unfettered atmosphere of the Weimar Republic. He witnessed the rise of Nazism, and wrote two classic novels of the era, *Mr. Norris Changes Trains* (1935) and *Goodbye to Berlin* (1939). Both are sardonic tragi-comedies, and the latter contains the famous sentence 'I am a camera with its shutter open, quite passive, recording, not thinking', which (to Isherwood's increasing irritation) was often quoted as a summation of his fictional method. To this period also belong collaborations with Auden: the three plays written for London's experimental Group Theatre—*The Dog Beneath the Skin* (1935), *The Ascent of F6* (1936), and *On the Frontier* (1938)—and *Journey to a War* (1939), an account of their travels in China during the Sino-Japanese War. *Lions and Shadows* (1938) is an autobiography of the 1920s, in which many of Isherwood's preoccupations are outlined.

In January 1939 Isherwood and Auden emigrated to the United States, a controversial move seen in some quarters as little short of 'desertion'. Isherwood settled in Los Angeles, but, insecure, and wracked by feelings of guilt and literary impotence, he needed something to give form and order to his life. He found this in Vedantism and became a follower of Swami Prabhavananda, who had set up a temple in Hollywood. Isherwood had already worked in the British film industry (an experience he described in the novella *Prater Violet*, 1945), and now he found employment as a scriptwriter for Metro–Goldwyn–Mayer. His Hollywood career was largely undistinguished, and included scripts for *Diane* (1956), a lavish and miscast costume drama, and *The Loved One* (1965), a lamentably coarse adaptation of the novel by Evelyn Waugh.

In 1941 he went to work in a Quaker-run camp for refugees fleeing Europe. When America entered the war, he registered as a conscientious objector and enrolled at a Vedanta monastery, where he worked with Prabhavananda on a new translation of the *Bhagavad-Gita* (1944) and became co-editor of the movement's magazine, *Vedanta and the West*. He left the monastery in 1945, the year he became an American citizen, and set up house with Bill Caskey, an ebullient, argumentative, and hard-drinking Irish-American. *The Condor and the Cows* (1949) is an account of their travels in South America.

In 1953 Isherwood met Don Bachardy, a student almost thirty years his junior, who later became a renowned portraitist: they were to live together until Isherwood's death. His first attempt at an 'American' novel, *The World in the Evening* (1954), took a great deal of time and effort to write and pleased its author as little as it pleased the critics. He returned to form with *Down There on a Visit* (1962), an autobiographical novel of four interlinking sections.

Isherwood had begun teaching English literature at the University of California in 1960, and an Isherwood-like professor is the protagonist of *A Single Man* (1964), a witty, sly, and touching book about the outsider in society. It is perhaps Isherwood's masterpiece. During the 1960s he published further books on Vedanta and a novel on related themes, *A Meeting by the River* (1967).

His three last books were *Kathleen and Frank* (1971), a portrait of his parents in which his interest in heredity is fully explored; *Christopher and His Kind* (1976), which retells in more explicit fashion the story of his Berlin years; and *My Guru and his Disciple* (1980), an account of his relationship with Prabhavananda.

Isherwood's principal characteristic, both in his life and his work, was an apparent candour. He was also a professional charmer, and these two qualities offset his considerable vanity. He was of short stature, with a disproportionately large head, a prominent nose, and deep-set, penetrating eyes. Although he maintained a strikingly boyish appearance well into old age, he was a lifelong hypochondriac. He eventually died of cancer at the age of eighty-one 4 January 1986, at his home at 145 Adelaide Drive, Santa Monica, California.

[Peter Parker, *Christopher Isherwood*, 1996; Isherwood's autobiographical books (see above) and unpublished diaries and papers, in the possession of Don Bachardy; Brian H. Finney, *Christopher Isherwood: a Critical Biography*, 1979; private information.]

PETER PARKER

published 1996

ISSIGONIS Sir Alexander Arnold Constantine (1906–1988)

Motor engineer and designer, was born 18 November 1906 in Smyrna (later İzmir), Turkey, the only child of Constantine Issigonis, a marine engineer resident in Smyrna who was of Greek origin but had British citizenship, and his wife, Hulda Josephine Prokopp, whose family came from Bavaria and ran Smyrna's brewery. A comfortable childhood, during which 'Alec' was taught by private tutors, was abruptly ended by World War I, during which Greece and Turkey supported opposite sides and the Greeks in Smyrna were interned. Following the war, the city came under Greek control until 1922, when Turkey invaded and the Issigonis family was evacuated along with other British citizens. Constantine Issigonis died in Malta in 1922, and his wife and son travelled to London alone. Hulda Issigonis wanted her son to continue his broken education, but despite suggestions that his drawing talent pointed to art school, Alec enrolled at Battersea Polytechnic as an engineering student in 1923.

Though he failed his final exams because of his weakness in mathematics, Issigonis was determined to pursue an engineering career and joined Edward Gillett (London) in 1928, assisting in the design of a semi-automatic clutch. This earned him a job at Humber (Coventry) in 1934, as a technical draughtsman, and he began experimental designs for independent front suspension, which he continued after joining Morris Motors (Oxford) in 1936. During World War II Issigonis worked on various military projects, but simultaneously he began his first complete car design, which went into production in October 1948 as the Morris Minor. This small car was praised for its use of space, and its steering and road-holding capacities. It continued in production for twenty-four years, during which over 1.6 million were produced. Following this success, Issigonis was promoted to chief engineer in 1950. When Morris Motors merged with Austin Motors to form the British Motor Corporation (BMC) in 1952, he briefly moved to Alvis (Coventry), but in 1955 returned to BMC as deputy engineering co-ordinator, based in Birmingham.

Petrol-rationing, arising out of the 1956 Suez crisis, prompted motor manufacturers to think about small, fuel-efficient cars, and Issigonis was asked to head a team to design such a car for BMC. Just two years later, in 1959, the Mini was launched and was quickly recognized to be a revolutionary vehicle. A transverse-mounted engine with front-wheel drive gave maximum space utilization, with room for four adults, while the strikingly functional bodyshell, shaped like a box, and only ten feet long, resulted from Issigonis's insistence that a 'styled' car quickly dated. His instinct was vindicated by over three decades of continuous production, during which figures had reached 5 million by 1986. Though priced for the mass market, the Mini actually achieved its success as a 'cult' car, popular with the middle classes, particularly women, used by the rich and famous, and spectacularly successful in motor sport. It was probably the last great product of one man's vision the car industry is likely to see.

Issigonis's career was at its high point. In 1961 he became technical director of BMC, in 1963 he was given a seat on the board, and in 1964 he became engineering director. He continued to design successful cars, including the 1100/1300 range, launched in 1962 and the best-selling car of its day; but when BMC became part of the car giant British Leyland in 1968 innovation was sacrificed for 'market research', something Issigonis abhorred. In 1971 he officially retired, and though he was retained by the company as consultant, continuing to produce original designs for a steam-engined car and a gearless Mini, neither of these was ever manufactured.

Issigonis never married, but was a man of great personal charm, occasionally irascible, who formed enduring friendships. His working relationships seem to have been less relaxed, perhaps because of his need to be in complete control, his eye for detail, and his demanding work schedules. Colleagues were often irritated by his arrogant and impatient manner, but they also felt proud to be associated with one of his projects. His appearance was Mediterranean with his aquiline nose and large hands, yet his manner was very English and friends remembered his eloquent eyes and wry expression. He considered himself to be a creative artist rather than a number-cruncher, and his cars are very much the creation of an individual with a strong personality, not pieces of styled metal constructed by a committee.

His life was one of contrasts. His youth in Smyrna was relatively affluent but was followed by the privations caused by war. His middle years were spent in Oxford, where he built a career of personal achievement, while providing financial security for himself and his mother, who continued to live with him until her death. The years of his greatest success, which came when he was already over fifty, were spent in Birmingham, where he remained a man of simple tastes, which were reflected both in the practicality of his designs and the austerity which characterized his private life. His recreations were also modest, and included a model railway and love of Meccano sets.

His contribution to society brought him a number of distinctions. In 1964 he was elected a Royal Designer for Industry and appointed CBE. In 1967 he became a fellow of the Royal Society. In 1969 he was knighted for 'services to automotive engineering'. He died at his home in Birmingham 2 October 1988, after suffering for several years from a progressive illness.

[Andrew Nahum, *Alec Issigonis*, 1988; Laurence Pomeroy, *The Mini Story*, 1964; *The Times*, 4 October 1988; Sir Diarmuid Downs in *Biographical Memoirs of Fellows of the Royal Society*, vol. xxxix, 1994; private information.]

GILLIAN BARDSLEY

published 1996

JOHNSON Amy (otherwise Amy Mollison) (1903–1941)

Airwoman, was born at Kingston-upon-Hull 1 July 1903, the eldest daughter of John William Johnson, herring importer, by his wife, Amy, granddaughter of William Hodge, sometime mayor of Hull. The paternal grandfather was a Dane, named Anders Jorgensen, who sailed to Hull at the age of sixteen, settled down in England, changed his name to Johnson, and married a Devonshire woman named Mary Holmes.

Amy Johnson attended the Boulevard Secondary School at Hull and, intending to be a teacher, went to the university of Sheffield where she graduated BA in 1925; but she changed her mind and took a secretarial post in a firm of London solicitors. In the London Aeroplane Club at Stag Lane, Edgware, her interest in aviation was aroused, for she was fascinated by anything mechanical, and she spent nearly all her spare time there. She was the first woman in the country to be granted an Air Ministry's ground-engineer's licence, and she received the full navigation certificate. It was with no wider experience of flying than from London to Hull that on 5 May 1930 she started on her spectacular attempt to break the light aeroplane record in a solo flight to Australia in a tiny Moth with a Gipsy engine, purchased with the assistance of Lord Wakefield and named *Jason*, after the trademark of her father's firm. She arrived at Karachi in six days, breaking the record for that distance, but she failed to break the record to Port Darwin since she did not arrive there until 24 May. However, she flew on to Brisbane, but, either from weariness or inexperience, or both, she overshot the aerodrome and wrecked the machine. If her inexperience be borne in mind, the flight was an astonishing one; it aroused universal enthusiasm. She was appointed CBE, the *Daily Mail* made her a gift of £10,000, the children of Sydney raised a sum of money with which she bought a gold cup, now offered annually at Hull for the most courageous juvenile deed of the year, and when she returned to England she was met on arrival by the secretary of state for air, Lord Thomson.

Her very striking feat was the forerunner of other remarkable long-distance flights: in July 1931 across Siberia to Tokyo where she arrived in ten days, also a record, even as was the return journey; in 1932 she broke the record then held by her husband (Mr J. A. Mollison) for a solo flight to Cape Town; and her return journey was also a record; a non-stop flight in 1933 with her husband from England to New York via Newfoundland and Canada only failed for lack of petrol when within sixty miles of their destination. In 1934 they made a record flight to Karachi, and in May 1936 in a solo flight to the Cape and back she beat the records for both flights and for the double journey. This was the last of her long flights, but such a career fully bore out the opinion of aeronautical circles that she was a woman of unusual intrepidity and presence of mind. No diminution was apparent when in 1939 she joined the Air Transport Auxiliary. She was lost over the Thames estuary 5 January 1941 when ferrying a plane with material for the Air Ministry. Her death was presumed in the Probate Court in December 1943.

So remarkable a career fully justified the many honours which Amy Johnson received. Besides those already mentioned she received the president's gold medal of the Society of Engineers (1931), the Egyptian gold medal for valour (1930), the women's trophy of the International League of Aviators (1930), the Segrave trophy (1933), the gold medal of honour of the League of Youth (1933), and the gold medal of the Royal Aero Club (1936).

When Amy Johnson wrecked her machine at Brisbane in 1930, she was piloted to Sydney by James Allan, son of Hector Alexander Mollison, a consultant engineer, of Glasgow. She married him in 1932; there were no children of the marriage which was dissolved in 1938 when she resumed her maiden name. An oil portrait of her by J. A. A. Berrie is in the possession of her family; another, by Charles Gerrard, presented by Lord Wakefield, hangs in the Ferens Art Gallery at Hull, and a memorial bust by Siegfried Charoux is on loan from the Gallery for an indefinite period to the Kingston High School, Hull.

[*The Times*, 8 January 1941; private information.]

E. Underwood

published 1959

JOHNSON Dame Celia

(1908–1982)

Actress, was born 18 December 1908 at Richmond, Surrey, the younger daughter and second of three children of John Robert Johnson, physician, of Richmond, Surrey, and his wife, Ethel Griffiths. She was educated at Miss Richmond's private school and then at St Paul's Girls' School, Hammersmith. Having obtained a GCE first-year award to the Royal Academy of Dramatic Art, she won, during her training there, a special prize as well as a French prize.

In 1928 she played her first professional part as Sarah in *Major Barbara* at the Theatre Royal, Huddersfield. The following year she went south, to the Lyric Theatre, Hammersmith, to take over from Angela Baddeley as Currita in *A Hundred Years Old*. In *Cynara* (1930) she stole the notices from the two stars, Sir Gerald du Maurier and (Dame) Gladys Cooper. In 1931 she made her first trip to America to play Ophelia in *Hamlet*. Back in London the following year, she acted in *The Wind and the Rain*, a play set in a Scottish University. From that date she became a star, admired by all and unscarred by adverse criticism.

In 1935 she married (Robert) Peter Fleming (died 1971), traveller and author, the son of Major Valentine Fleming, a merchant banker. They had one son and two daughters. With a growing family in wartime, plus the prospect of her husband being overseas on active service, Celia Johnson faced difficulties. Typically, she solved them neatly. After playing Mrs de Winter in *Rebecca* in 1940 and then taking over from Vivien Leigh in *The Doctor's Dilemma* in 1942, she retired from the stage for five years, returning in 1947 to play the title role in *St Joan* with the Old Vic Company at the New Theatre. During the war she was an auxiliary policewoman. She starred in every kind of play, from Shakespeare to *Ten Minute Alibi* (1933), from Chekhov to *Flowering Cherry* (1957), by Robert Bolt. She also starred in four successful plays written by William Douglas-Home: *The Reluctant Debutante* (1955), *Lloyd George Knew My Father* (1972), *The Dame of Sark* (1974), and *The Kingfisher* (1977). She was, to put it in a single phrase, a playwright's dream.

As a film star, she was equally successful as the captain's wife in *In Which We Serve* (1942) and as the housewife in *Brief Encounter* (1945). Her other films included *A Kid for Two Farthings* (1955), *The Good Companions* (1956), and *The Prime of Miss Jean Brodie* (1969). She was rarely seen on television but gave excellent performances in *Mrs Palfrey at the Claremont* (1973), *The*

Dame of Sark (1976), and *Staying On* (by Paul Scott, 1980), in which she appeared with Trevor Howard, her co-star in *Brief Encounter.*

Though her dedication to her calling was immediately apparent to her public in the theatre, it rested on her shoulders lightly in her private life, which was devoted to her family, who lived in Nettlebed, Oxfordshire. She would often come out of a play before the end of its run in order to be with them. She seldom talked about the theatre and, when she did, approached the subject with a gay irreverence. She was a person of outstanding charm, with wide eyes, a retroussé nose, and a remarkable voice.

To her amused delight she was appointed CBE in 1958 and, to her great surprise, DBE in 1981. She died 25 April 1982, at Nettlebed, while playing bridge one weekend, during a pre-London run, in harness to the end.

[Personal knowledge.]

William Douglas-Home

published 1990

JOYCE William Brooke

(1906–1946)

Fascist and wartime broadcaster in English from Nazi Germany, was born in Brooklyn, New York, 24 April 1906, the eldest of three sons (there were no daughters) of Michael Francis Joyce, an Irish Catholic building contractor from county Mayo who emigrated to the United States, and his wife Gertrude Emily Brooke, the daughter of a doctor of Irish Protestant descent living in Shaw, Lancashire. The Joyces returned to Ireland in 1909, and William was brought up a Roman Catholic and educated at a Jesuit college where he excelled in Latin, French, and German. The Joyces were staunchly British, and, like many loyalists, felt betrayed by the Irish treaty of 1921. Two days after its signing, Joyce went to England and joined the army, but was discharged when it was discovered that he was only sixteen. An ardent patriot, he drifted into right-wing political movements, and in 1924, in an affray with communists in the East End of London, he received a deep razor-slash on the right side of his face, which left a permanent scar. He first came to prominence as a speaker when he joined the British Union of Fascists, founded by Sir Oswald Mosley, after some years at Birkbeck College where he obtained a first-class honours degree in English, and he helped to found a National Socialist party in London.

In 1933 he took out a British passport, falsely claiming his place of birth as Galway, Ireland. He renewed his passport in August 1939, and travelled to Berlin, where (not without difficulty) he persuaded Josef Goebbels's propaganda ministry to employ him as an editor and announcer for radio broadcasts in English. Joyce's drawling nasal delivery (the result of a broken nose in his schooldays) attracted widespread interest in Britain, where no restrictions were placed on listening to enemy broadcasts, and he was quickly dubbed 'Lord Haw-Haw', a kind of malign Bertie Wooster (see Sir P. G. Wodehouse), whose opinions were a subject only for entertainment. The authorities were disconcerted, however, when the broadcasts provoked an extraordinary wave of rumours, mostly concerned with town clocks, and suggesting that German spies were everywhere. In 1944 Adolf Hitler awarded him the cross of war merit, first class.

He was shot in the thigh while trying to avoid arrest at the Danish frontier in May 1945, and tried for treason in London in September. Although he was an American citizen, the prosecution argued that by taking a British passport he owed allegiance to the Crown. He was found guilty and sentenced to death, and, after his appeal to the House of Lords was rejected, he was hanged at Wandsworth prison 3 January 1946.

In 1927 he married Hazel Kathleen Barr. They were divorced in 1937 and in the same year he married Margaret Cairns White, daughter of a Lancashire textile-warehouse manager of Irish descent. There were two daughters of the first marriage and no children of the second.

[John A. Cole, *Lord Haw-Haw—and William Joyce: the Full Story*, 1964; John W. Hall (ed.), *The Trial of William Joyce*, 1946.]

A. T. Q. Stewart

published 1993

KEYNES John Maynard

(1883–1946)

Baron Keynes

Economist, was born in Cambridge 5 June 1883, the elder son of John Neville Keynes (1852–1949), for twenty-seven years lecturer in moral science and from 1910 to 1925 registrary in the university. Whereas Neville Keynes's most important work was his *Formal Logic* (1884), he was well known to economists of his generation for his *Scope and Method of Political Economy* (1891). He was a close friend of Alfred Marshall, as well as of Henry Sidgwick and Henry Fawcett. Economics then lay within the moral sciences tripos and Neville Keynes until 1919 was chairman of the special board which governed its teaching and examination. Through his father, Maynard Keynes thus grew up in close association with the Cambridge economists of the older generation, whilst through his mother he learned something of the social problems of the day. She was Florence Ada (died 1958), daughter of the Revd John Brown, long minister of Bunyan's chapel at Bedford, and author of a well-known study of Bunyan. A sister of Sir Walter Langdon-Brown, she had been an early student of Newnham College, and in addition to a wide interest in public and social work became justice of the peace, alderman, and mayor of Cambridge. Keynes's younger brother, Sir Geoffrey Langdon Keynes, achieved distinction as a surgeon and bibliophile; his sister, Margaret Neville, married Professor A. V. Hill, CH, secretary (1935–45) of the Royal Society.

Maynard Keynes went as a scholar to Eton where he was eventually elected to the Society. Educated in the classical tradition—he was in the Newcastle Select—he made his mark principally as a mathematician and the winner of the Tomline prize. An Eton scholarship in mathematics and classics took him to King's College, Cambridge. He was no more than twelfth wrangler in 1905. But at Cambridge, as at Eton and throughout his life, his interests were much wider than his formal studies. He won the Members' prize for an English essay on the political doctrines of Edmund Burke (1904), was president of the Liberal Club, and in 1905 president of the Union. His athletic activities at Cambridge were never strenuous. At Eton he had played the Wall game with enthusiasm and some skill and had rowed with energy rather than distinction; now, abandoning rowing after his first term, he engaged in a little occasional golf and riding and rather more strenuous bridge. The natural centre of attraction for this uncompromising pursuer of truth, companionable and argumentative by nature, rationalist and iconoclastic by conviction, was undoubtedly the group of brilliant undergraduate friends whose efforts to identify good states of mind, with the aid of (Professor) G. E. Moore's *Principia Ethica*, have been described by Keynes in 'My Early Beliefs' (*Two Memoirs*, 1949). They included Lytton Strachey and Mr Leonard Woolf—through whom he became a member of a small, select, and intimate society known as 'the Apostles'—James Strachey, Adrian and Thoby Stephen, and others who later, with Keynes, became identified as the Bloomsbury group. 'We were the forerunners of a new dispensation, we were not afraid of anything . . . water spiders gracefully skimming . . . the surface of the stream without any contact at all with the eddies and currents underneath.'

Within mathematics, Keynes's chief interest was in the borderland between that subject and philosophy; he continued for many years to work in this field, and his fellowship dissertation at King's was on the theory of probability. After taking the tripos, however, he turned to the study of economics and first came into working contact with Alfred Marshall and the teaching of Cambridge economics. Marshall, greatly impressed by Keynes's ability, expressed hopes that he might become a professional economist; although Keynes found economics 'increasingly satisfactory' he decided to sit for the Civil Service into which he passed second in 1906. Posted to the India Office at a time when it was still small and intimate, he found an interest in Indian currency and finance which later formed the theme of his first book (1913) in the field of economics. Meanwhile he was working on his fellowship dissertation, but to his great disappointment when he submitted this in 1908 he was not elected. At this moment Alfred Marshall offered him a lectureship in economics with a salary of £100 a year and Keynes decided to abandon the Civil Service and return to Cambridge. His revised dissertation was accepted in the following year, when he also won the Adam Smith prize for an essay on index numbers.

Until 1915 Keynes remained teaching in Cambridge; but wider claims upon him soon developed. In 1912 he became editor of the *Economic Journal* in succession to F. Y. Edgeworth. Through the journal, which he edited to within a year of his death, he exercised great influence over a younger generation of economists. In 1913 he became secretary of the Royal Economic Society, and in the same year he was a member of the Royal Commission on Indian finance and currency. The great impression which he made upon the chairman (Sir) Austen Chamberlain and others such as Sir Robert (later Lord) Chalmers, permanent secretary of the Treasury, was later to serve him well.

Through (Sir) Basil Blackett who had been secretary of the commission, Keynes advised successfully against the suspension of specie payments on the outbreak of war in 1914, and in January the following year he was invited to join the Treasury. By 1917 he had reached a position of considerable responsibility as head of the department dealing with external finance, and was appointed CB for his services. Despite these preoccupations and a widening circle of friendships which included the McKennas and the Asquiths, Bloomsbury was still the centre of his life in London. Prompted by his friend Mr Duncan Grant, he obtained permission to help the French balance of payments by the purchase of paintings for the National Gallery from the Degas collection. By purchases on his own account made at the same time he laid the foundations of his own collection.

Early in 1919 Keynes went to Paris as principal representative of the Treasury at the peace conference. He was present at the meetings of the Council of Four and acted as deputy for the chancellor of the Exchequer on the Supreme Economic Council. He was not himself a member of the Reparation Commission, to which Lloyd George had appointed W. M. Hughes (prime minister of Australia), Lord Cunliffe, and Lord Sumner, but no representative of either the Treasury or the Board of Trade, and thus Keynes could not directly influence the work of that body. He found himself in vigorous disagreement with much that was being advocated in respect both of frontiers and of reparations, and was convinced that the proposals were unjust and inexpedient and would jeopardize recovery from the war. He resigned in June and returned to England to write, with the encouragement of J. C. Smuts, *The Economic Consequences of the Peace* (1919), embodying his criticisms of the draft treaty. The book, outspoken and brilliantly written like all his work, provoked violent controversy in the United States and Europe as well as in England. It has more recently been suggested (for instance by Étienne Mantoux in *The Carthaginian Peace or the Economic Consequences of Mr. Keynes*, 1946), that his denigration of the peacemakers was the source of subsequent disaster in Europe. This view will not in fact bear investigation. In the United States, rejection of the treaty was certain before the book was published. But its influence on the economic negotiations of the next few years was beyond doubt.

Henceforth Keynes was in the centre of all controversy about the economic reconstruction of Europe. In a series of books and pamphlets, in articles and letters in the press, and at the Liberal summer schools, he brought his remarkable powers of lucid analysis and exposition to bear upon the urgent problems of the moment: reparations, exchange rates, the return to the gold standard, unemployment and effective demand. In 1923 he became chairman of the Liberal *Nation and Athenaeum* in which he wrote regularly until it merged with the *New Statesman* when he found himself increasingly out of sympathy with the policy of the joint venture. A 'real' rather than a 'true' Liberal, as he put it, his association with the Liberal Party was closer in these years than at any other time. He contributed much that was important to the 'Liberal Yellow Book', *Britain's Industrial Future* (1928); in the following year his conviction that unemployment could be cured if there was the will to cure it was apparent in Lloyd George's election claims, supported by Keynes in a pamphlet (with (Sir) Hubert Henderson), *Can Lloyd George do it?*

This conviction, and a more academic interest in work begun by (Sir) D. H. Robertson on the nature of saving and investment, and their relation to rising and falling prices, resulted in Keynes's most original contributions to economic thought, and those which have since been most closely identified with his name. Keynes's thought was developed, first in *A Treatise on Money* (2 vols., 1930) and later in the much more revolutionary *General Theory of Employment, Interest and Money* (1936) on which his fame as the outstanding economist of his generation must rest. This caused a furore almost equal to that of *The Economic Consequences of the Peace*. For Keynes was determined that his readers should face the full implications of his new ideas, and in particular the likelihood that the economic system had not an automatic tendency to full employment, as they had been taught by many generations of economists to believe. He expounded a new theory of the rate of interest and of the forms of short-period equilibrium. Almost equally important were his emphasis and development of a method of thought in which he had numerous predecessors: the study of flows of income and expenditure and the factors which determined their magnitude. For a time economists all over the world were divided into two violently opposed camps. In the following twenty years, while controversy on detail has persisted (particularly as concerns his theory of the rate of interest) and minor improvements have been formulated, his general approach to the effects of saving and investment has won wide acceptance.

The influences of Keynesian economics were not confined to a stimulus of academic discussion. As a member of the Macmillan committee on finance and industry (1929–31) which reported on Keynesian lines, and as chairman of a committee of the Economic Advisory Council, of which he was also a member, 'to review the present economic condition of Great Britain . . . and to indicate conditions of recovery', he found himself in controversy with 'the Treasury view' that measures to cure unemployment were likely to be ineffectual. The acceptance of some of his ideas for a planned economy by the Roosevelt 'New Deal' administration in the United States equally involved him in controversy, which made his name antipathetic to many who have unconsciously accepted the essentials of the policies he advocated. The fact that he wrote in the depression years of the 'thirties in terms of the stimulation of effective demand by low interest rates and public investment left a general impression that his ideas were essentially inflationary. Such a view will disappear when it is possible to publish some of the war-time official memoranda, in which he himself used the same concepts and techniques to handle the problems of inflation.

In the years between the two wars the stimulus of Keynes's rapid intelligence and financial skill were felt in many spheres. He had a remarkable ability not only to switch his complete attention from one subject to another, but also to bring each part of his varied activities to bear on the rest of his life. He was chairman from 1921 of the National Mutual Life Assurance Society and director of other companies. By investment and bold speculation he was amassing a very considerable fortune which owed its beginnings in no small part to the profits of his writings. This enabled him to pursue with increasing enthusiasm the discriminating collection of books, which he had begun whilst still at Eton; he acquired a valuable library, later bequeathed to his college, which included a comprehensive collection on the history of thought. He was always in close and intimate touch with the Bloomsbury group and a wider circle of writers and painters and proved himself a generous patron of the arts. He shared many interests with his friend Samuel Courtauld and with him founded the London Artists' Association. In 1925 he married Lydia Lopokova, famous in her own right as a dancer in the Imperial Ballet at St Petersburg and later in the remarkable company organized by Diaghilev. With her he several times visited Russia and through her he interested himself in the ballet. To Keynes's restless mind, interest meant constructive action and it was largely due to his efforts as well as hers that the Vic-Wells ballet became firmly established.

After his marriage Keynes acquired the lease of Tilton, Sussex, a property which had once belonged to his recusant forebears some of whom, such as George and John Keynes, had become Jesuits. There he spent his vacations, and began to take a knowledgeable interest in farming. In term-time he spent the middle of the week in London and went at the weekends to Cambridge where he had cut down his teaching commitments after 1919. In that year he had become second, and in 1924 first, bursar of King's College. To the problems of college finance, as to all else, Keynes brought a fresh and reforming mind. He challenged all the basic assumptions as to how a college should invest its funds and, with money at the free disposal of the college, adopted policies which to the bursars of the older tradition seemed dangerously unorthodox. In his hands these methods were successful in raising very greatly the income of King's College and endowing it with the resources for bold new ventures in building and expansion. It was characteristic that he should insist that the greater income was the means to greater expenditure and that he should be contemptuous of the colleges which hoarded reserves upon reserves. It was equally characteristic that his unorthodoxy had in a generation become orthodoxy which enabled those colleges which imitated his policies to weather the dangers of war and post-war inflation.

He was responsible too for the conception, building, and financing of the Arts Theatre in Cambridge (1935) which he designed to provide a home in Cambridge for the drama, cinema, opera, ballet, and music, under management which would maintain standards worthy of the town. He built the theatre almost wholly at his own expense, and then, after a brief period of trial, handed over his shares as a gift to trustees with funds to see the venture through its early years. This generous gift, designed in some sense as a memorial to the services of his parents to the town and university, provided Cambridge with a lively centre of experiment in those arts for which Keynes had a special affection.

In 1937 Keynes fell seriously ill with heart trouble and, forced to lighten his work, resigned most of his financial activities. When war broke out in 1939 he was still a sick man with severe limits on his activities. But when invited in 1940 by Sir Kingsley Wood, then chancellor of the Exchequer, to join the Treasury as one of his advisers, he accepted. At first he was primarily concerned with war finance, and was chiefly responsible for a new concept of budgetary policy, instituted in the budget of 1941, which aimed to estimate the flows of personal income and of goods for consumption, and to prevent inflation by framing taxation to equate expenditure with the goods available. In 1942, in recognition of these and other services, he was raised to the peerage as Baron Keynes, of Tilton, with the very appropriate heraldic motto *Me tutore tutus eris*.

Later, Keynes was more directly concerned with the problems of the transition from war to peace. In 1943, a British scheme for an international clearing union was published almost simultaneously with an American variation on the same theme. Both were intended to secure a satisfactory compromise between rigid exchange fixity and uncontrolled fluctuations. Both embodied ideas which Keynes had been advocating since the early 'twenties. An agreed scheme, which owed more to the original American concept than to the British, was referred to an international conference at Bretton Woods (1944) in which Keynes played a leading part. There emerged the International Monetary Fund and the International Bank for Reconstruction and Development which became the main instruments for the regulation of exchanges and foreign lending after the war. Although his swift sarcasm and pointed witticisms occasionally caused offence, they did much also to relieve tension and formality in the series of long and arduous meetings. His domination of the conference was acknowledged when he had moved the acceptance of the Final Act and the delegates rose to pay spontaneous tribute to him.

In May 1944 the coalition Government published a white paper on employment policy. This raised to the level of orthodoxy the ideas for which Keynes had been fighting almost single-handed in the early 'thirties. The final version owed little, if anything, to his pen, but served to show how much of his thinking had won acceptance, even among those who earlier had been his critics.

In the autumn of 1944 Keynes was engaged in negotiating the terms of 'lend-lease' aid from the United States in the event of the war with Japan continuing after hostilities with Germany had ceased. The complexities of Britain's post-war economic problems were for the first time revealed to the American authorities, but that they were not sufficiently appreciated became apparent when lend-lease was abruptly cancelled on the sudden termination of the Japanese war. In August 1945 Keynes was sent to the United States to join Lord Halifax and Mr R. H. (subsequently Lord) Brand in seeking financial arrangements to meet the emergency. Ever optimistic, Keynes set out with high hopes of convincing America that, in terms of sacrifice, Britain had borne more than her share and that an outright gift was justifiable. He developed the British case at length, but although his arguments were sympathetically received, the negotiations resulted only in a loan, coupled with the cancellation of the greater part of the lend-lease account. This offer, immensely generous as it was, fell far short of hopes entertained in London and negotiations were tortuous and protracted, the more so since the loan was conditional on the early establishment of the convertibility of the sterling earnings of other countries. Keynes came home to face widespread criticism. In the House of Lords, in one of the most effective speeches of his life, he was able to convince his hearers of the impossibility of much that was being demanded. The loan gave Britain a very essential breathing space. But the subsequent crisis of 1947, when convertibility was momentarily established, justified the fears of some of his critics.

Keynes returned exhausted. Ever since 1940, sustained only through his wife's unceasing care and vigilance, he had carried more than a fit man's load of work and responsibility despite constantly recurring heart trouble. Nevertheless in the spring of 1946 he went back to America for the sixth time in as many years to pilot the last stages of the Bretton Woods negotiations through the inaugural meetings of the Fund and the Bank, on both of which he had been made Britain's governor. Strong differences of opinion emerged; the moment was a delicate one, for the loan agreement was still before Congress. Keynes returned to England once more very near to collapse. Within a few days, on Easter Sunday, 21 April 1946, he had a sharp heart attack at his home at Tilton and died within a couple of hours, his death undoubtedly accelerated by the arduous labours of the past few years.

Ill health and great responsibilities had not narrowed his interests. In these last years he had become a fellow of Eton College, a trustee of the National Gallery, a director of the Bank of England, and high steward of the borough of Cambridge. He was chairman and leading spirit of the Committee for the Encouragement of Music and the Arts, and of the Arts Council into which it grew, and of the new trust which reopened the Royal Opera House at Covent Garden. He had been elected FBA in 1929, and among the honours conferred upon him none gave him greater pleasure than the degree of D.Sc. from Cambridge (1946). He died before his appointment to the OM could be announced. His wife survived him, but there were no children of the marriage and the title therefore became extinct.

The qualities in Keynes which most impressed themselves on his contemporaries were his immense vitality and activity, and his unfailing optimism and conviction that problems were soluble. Around Keynes, something was always happening. With him, to see a problem was to do something about it. And to do something involved almost always three stages: first, the intellectual solution; second, an administrative technique to achieve it; third, to persuade others of the need to accept his solution. He had a gift, particularly in the economic field, of seeing an emerging problem when it was still obscured to others. He had a still more remarkable gift for dissecting a problem and seeing in analytical terms the underlying issues which required intellectual solution before the problem could be handled administratively; his power to break down a problem and to stimulate thought on the basic issues is evident, both in the earlier discussions on reparations and the problem of transfer and in the later problems of unemployment and the determination of effective demand.

But Keynes was no hermit. He never thought in isolation. The intellectual solution was often reached, after he had posed the question, in discussion with his Cambridge and other friends. His stimulus to thought about the urgent problems of the world was seminal. What passed to the world as the product of Keynes's thinking was often that of himself and others in proportions which neither he nor they could possibly determine. It remains that without Keynes something of the essential vitality and urgency of earlier argument disappeared. It was remarkable, indeed, that his intellectual vitality seemed little if at all diminished by ill health. The body was tired, but the brain was indefatigable, even in the years after 1937.

The intellectual solution once discovered, there came the task of finding a practicable administrative technique of applying it. Keynes took pleasure always in the game of inventing technical solutions of his problems; for almost every major economic issue between the wars there was a Keynes plan. But these seldom represented the unique possible technical solution to the fundamental underlying problem, and Keynes often disconcerted his less discerning friends by switching from one possible technique of achieving his main objective to another. He acquired thereby a not wholly justified reputation for changing his mind—a quality which he himself regarded as more often worthy of praise than of blame.

And finally came the task of persuasion. While he had a great gift for persuading by word of mouth, which showed itself during the years of the two wars in meetings and conferences, and at a critical moment in the House of Lords, it was his pen which to Keynes was the main instrument. He enjoyed writing and took infinite trouble to get the effect he wanted from his words. While he wrote rapidly, as he did most other things in his life, he was the master of a concise, lucid English with an exquisite choice of words and an enchanting irony, which lent to all that he wrote an animation and a lively persuasiveness rivalled by few of his age. 'In one art, certainly', wrote Mr T. S. Eliot of him after his death, 'he had no reason to defer to any opinion: in expository prose he had the essential style of the clear mind which thinks structurally and respects the meanings of words.' In *Essays in Biography* (1933) Keynes's creative powers as an artist had freer rein than in his strictly economic writings; the delineation both of those whom, like Marshall and Edgeworth (or Dr Melchior in *Two Memoirs*, 1949), he loved and admired, and of those who were temporarily his antagonists, was superbly sharp and economical. The success of his advocacy, illustrated in *Essays in Persuasion* (1931), owed much to the beauty of the prose in which he argued his case.

It is almost a paradox to say of Keynes that his second great quality was his optimism. He had a reputation, and enjoyed it, of being a Cassandra. He was as quick as the most pessimistic to foresee trouble and to warn of the dangers ahead. But, unlike the pessimists, he was active to defeat trouble. He always assumed that a problem was soluble if the intelligence and the determination existed to solve it. He hated stupidity and defeatism because they were obstacles to the solution of the world's problems. And it was largely through this quality of optimism that Keynes created enthusiasm in his pupils and colleagues to fight for the solution of all the economic problems that confronted the world during the troubled years from 1914 to 1946. He could easily have retreated after Versailles, with his King's and Bloomsbury friends, into cynicism, or the discussion of states of mind, or have buried himself in mathematical philosophy. He remained determined to grapple with the problems of the world. And it is arguable that it was his optimism and determination, more than anything else, that has permanently changed the world's attitude to unemployment and has removed it from the list of inescapable disasters, to be fatalistically accepted, into the realm of the things which are under the control of human thought and action.

There is no major portrait of Keynes. A bust by Benno Elkan is in the library at King's College, Cambridge.

[R. F. Harrod, *The Life of John Maynard Keynes*, 1951; *Times Literary Supplement*, 23 February 1951; A. C. Pigou in *Proceedings* of the British Academy, vol. xxxii, 1946; *Economic Journal*, March 1947; *American Economic Review*, September 1946; *John*

Maynard Keynes, 1883–1946, a memoir printed for King's College, Cambridge, 1949; F. A. Keynes, *Gathering Up the Threads*, 1950; personal knowledge.]

E. A. G. Robinson

published 1959

KORDA Sir Alexander

(1893–1956)

Film producer, whose original name was Alexander Laszlo Kellner, was born 16 September 1893, at Pusztaturpaszto, Hungary. He was the eldest of the three sons of Henry Kellner, land agent to a large estate, and his wife, Ernestine Weisz. He was educated at Protestant gymnasiums in Nagykoros and Kecskemet and at a commercial school in Budapest. His father died when he was thirteen and to augment the family income he gave lessons in the evenings. Leaving school at seventeen, he became a proof-reader and newspaper reporter in Budapest and published a novel under the name of Alexander Korda. In 1911 he went to Paris where he became proficient in French but could find no work. Back in Budapest he had his first introduction to the infant film world by translating sub-titles from French into Hungarian. In 1912 he founded a film magazine, the first of its kind to appear in Budapest, and in 1913 with some friends he started to write and direct short film comedies.

Owing to his eyesight which was always weak Korda was not called up after the outbreak of war and was able to continue as a film director. In 1915, with the director of the Kolozsvar National Theatre in Transylvania, he formed a plan to make films with that company, using their actors, scenery, and costumes. The course of the war enforced a return to Budapest where he took over the company and built a studio, the Corvin. His first full-length film, *The Man of Gold* (1918), taken from M. Jokai's novel, was highly successful.

In 1919 there was unrest in Hungary and Korda, together with many other citizens, was arrested; by a fortunate chance he shortly obtained his release, and on returning home he took a bath, changed his clothes, and departed from Hungary for ever. In Vienna he joined the Sascha studios which at that time were making advanced films, and there he matured his film-craft. Among his films of this period were *The Prince and the Pauper* (1920) and *Samson and Delilah* (1922). In 1923 he moved to Berlin and in 1926 to Hollywood where amongst the films he made was *The Private Life of Helen of Troy* (1927) in which his wife, Maria Corda, played the title role.

Returning to Europe in 1930 Korda found work in Paris with the Paramount Film Company, for whom he made the classic film *Marius* (1931) from the play by Marcel Pagnol, in which Raimu played the leading part. In 1931 he went for Paramount to London to direct *Service for Ladies* which was an outstanding success and proved the turning-point in Korda's career, for he settled in London, formed his own company, London Film Productions, with Big Ben as trademark, and built the Denham studios and laboratories which when completed in 1937 were the most advanced in Europe. In the meantime Korda had become one of the most notable personalities of the film world with a series of pictures which obtained worldwide fame. They included *The Private Life of Henry VIII* (1933), *The Private Life of Don Juan* (with a script by Frederick Lonsdale, 1934), *The Ghost Goes West* (1935, directed by René Clair and starring Robert Donat), *The Scarlet Pimpernel* (1935, starring Leslie Howard), *Things to Come* and *The Man Who Could Work Miracles* (scripts by H. G. Wells, 1936), *Rembrandt* (1936), *Knight Without Armour* (1936), *Elephant Boy* (1936–7), *Fire Over England* (Vivien Leigh's first film, 1937), and *The Four Feathers* (1939).

No one in this country before or since Korda has equalled his range and brilliance of faculties for film-making. Building studios and making pictures need large sums of money and Korda seemed at this period to conjure them out of the air. His sense of romance and gift of story-telling produced excellent scripts; his knowledge, direction, and camera-work brought to his service the finest technicians, among whom were his two younger brothers, Zoltan and Vincent. His tact and talent, together with his generosity and personal magnetism, drew to him the best actors in the world.

With the worsening international situation financial backing was gradually withdrawn and in 1939 Korda had to give up the Denham studios. But he continued his film-making with *The Thief of Baghdad* (1939–40) and, immediately after the outbreak of war, the documentary *The Lion has Wings*. During the war years he moved between London and Hollywood where he directed *Lady Hamilton* (1941) and with his brother Zoltan produced *Jungle Book* (1941); in Britain he made *Perfect Strangers* (1944). After the war he revived London Films as an independent company, built studios at Shepperton, and once again under his management there came forth fine films, including *An Ideal Husband* (1947), *The Fallen Idol* (1948), *The Third Man* (1949), *The Wooden Horse* (1950), *Sound Barrier* (1952), and *Richard III* (1955). Working to the last, Korda died in London 23 January 1956.

In 1921 Korda married Maria Farkas, who acted under the name of Maria Corda, by whom he had one son, Peter. The marriage was dissolved in 1931. His second marriage (1939), to Merle Oberon, was dissolved in 1945. In 1953 he married a Canadian, Alexandra Irene Boycun (died 1966). Korda was naturalized in 1936 and knighted in 1942. He was made an officer of the Legion of Honour in 1950.

[Paul Tabori, *Alexander Korda*, 1959; private information; personal knowledge.]

RALPH RICHARDSON

published 1971

LANCASTER Sir Osbert

(1908–1986)

Cartoonist, designer, writer, and wit, was born in London 4 August 1908, the only child of Robert Lancaster and his wife, Clare Bracebridge Manger. His grandfather, Sir William Lancaster, became secretary of the Prudential Assurance Company and his father had a job in the City but enlisted in the army in 1914. He was killed in the battle of the Somme (1916). Lancaster was sent to St Ronan's preparatory school in Worthing, and then to Charterhouse, an appropriate school for a caricaturist, as John Leech, W. M. Thackeray, and (Sir) Max Beerbohm had all been there. (In the 1950s Lancaster received Beerbohm's warm compliments when he painted murals in the Randolph Hotel, Oxford, illustrating scenes from *Zuleika Dobson*.)

Lancaster did not shine at school (the headmaster's final report pronounced him 'irretrievably gauche') but was admitted to Lincoln College, Oxford, in 1926. Like his friend, (Sir) John Betjeman, Lancaster became a 'figure' at Oxford. He wore loud checks, sported a monocle, and grew a large moustache. He contributed cartoons to *Cherwell*, the university magazine. He and Betjeman were fascinated by the Victorians and their architecture, an interest which began half in a spirit of mockery, but ended in expert championship. Lancaster obtained a fourth-class degree in English (1930), after an extra year of study. Intended for the bar, he failed his bar examinations.

He then went to the Slade School of Art, where he met his first wife, Karen, the second daughter of Sir Austin Harris, vice-chairman of Lloyds Bank. The couple were married in 1933 and had one son and one daughter. Lancaster found work alongside Betjeman, as an assistant editor at the *Architectural Review*. In 1936 his *Progress at Pelvis Bay* began the long sequence of his books satirizing architecture and mores. He was appointed cartoonist to the *Daily Express* in 1939 and on 1 January the first of his pocket cartoons appeared in its William Hickey column. He was to draw roughly 10,000 cartoons, with only brief interruptions, over the next forty years. Lancaster's fusion of topicality and urbane wit was consistent. He depicted the world he knew—that of Canon Fontwater, Father O'Bubblegum, Mrs Frogmarch (the Tory lady), and, his most enduring creation, Maudie, countess of Littlehampton, and her dim, monocled husband Willy. Lancaster's satire was not splenetic, and, except in the cause of good architecture, he was never a crusader.

In World War II Lancaster joined the Press Censorship Bureau (1939) and then was sent to Greece, with which he fell in love, as a Foreign Office press attaché (1944–6). The British ambassador was being too high-handed with the press and Lancaster effectively smoothed things over. His first book to be published after the war was *Classical Landscape with Figures* (1947), a descriptive work based on his Greek experience. *The Saracen's Head* (1948) and *Draynflete Revealed* (1949) were in the manner of his pre-war satires, though the former was pitched as a children's book.

In 1951 Lancaster worked with John Piper on designs for the Festival of Britain. In the same year, on Piper's recommendation, he designed his first stage set, for *Pineapple Poll* at Sadler's Wells. This and the many stage designs that were to follow (several of them for Glyndebourne) released him from the austerity of line and allowed him to indulge in the Mediterranean colour he loved. In 1953 the Lancasters moved to Leicester House, a stucco Regency mansion at Henley-on-Thames. Karen died of cancer in 1964 and in 1967 Lancaster married Anne Eleanor Scott-James, the magazine editor and garden expert. She was the daughter of Rolfe Arnold Scott-James, journalist and author.

The 1960s, with their fashionable fads and fantasies, were perfect fodder for Lancaster's type of social satire. He would come into the *Express* office after having lunch at one of his four clubs and hold court for a while, telling jokes, before settling down with the day's newspapers. George Malcolm Thomson, right-hand man to Lord Beaverbrook, said of Lancaster: 'The annoying thing at the *Express* was, not only was he the only one who could draw; he could also *write* better than anyone in the building.' The prose, admittedly, was an acquired taste, and it had to be taken on its own terms. When Betjeman wrote to congratulate Lancaster on 'that deliciously convoluted prose you write', the implied censure was not lost on Lancaster. The prose had to be taken as part of the rich plum-cake fruitiness of the character Lancaster had created for himself. It was commonly said that he looked like one of his own cartoon characters and, as he aged, he resembled more and more an effigy of the English gentleman on a

French carnival float: bulging eyes, bulbous nose, buffalo-horn moustache, bald head, striped shirt, pinstripe suit from Thresher & Glenny, old-fashioned shoes with rounded toes.

'Osbert, it quickly becomes clear,' wrote the architect Sir Hugh Casson, 'was a performance, meticulously practised and hilariously inflated and at times disturbing.' What, he wondered, was behind that 'elaborately woven yashmak of subsidiary clauses, this defensive portcullis of anecdotes, cranked into place at one's approach?' Lancaster was a work of art as memorable as any he created. It was as if he had chosen to be a 'living museum' exhibit, representing not the period of his own life but that of his lost father.

He was appointed CBE in 1953 and knighted in 1975, in which year he also received an honorary D.Litt. at Oxford. He also had honorary degrees from Birmingham (1964), Newcastle upon Tyne (1970), and St Andrews (1974). He was a fellow of University College London (1967), an honorary fellow of RIBA and of Lincoln College, Oxford (1979), and was made RDI (1979). He died in Chelsea 27 July 1986 and was buried at West Wing, Norfolk.

[Osbert Lancaster, *All Done From Memory*, 1953, and *With an Eye to the Future*, 1967; *Strand Magazine*, February 1947; *Sunday Times*, 25 July 1954; *The Times*, 26 July 1986; Myfanwy Piper, 'Osbert Lancaster', *Spectator*, 1 August 1986; Edward Lucie-Smith (ed.), *The Essential Osbert Lancaster*, 1988; Richard Boston, *Osbert: a Portrait of Osbert Lancaster*, 1989; personal knowledge.]

BEVIS HILLIER

published 1996

LAUDER Sir Harry

(1870–1950)

Comedian, was born in Portobello, near Edinburgh, 4 August 1870, the eldest of the seven children of John Lauder, potter, of Musselburgh, by his wife, Isobella Urquhart Macleod, daughter of Henry MacLennan, of the Black Isle, Ross-shire. Lauder's assumption for stage purposes of Highland dress of a fanciful order was not therefore without ancestral justification. Before Lauder was twelve his father died, and the boy had to take what jobs he could, including work in a flax-mill in Arbroath as a half-timer (one day at work, the next at school), and in a pit-head in Hamilton. He subsequently became a miner, but his voice and his skilful, genial use of it were obviously his fortune. He was soon well known in his area through local concerts, and in a short time became a professional entertainer, at first travelling in concert-parties, and later appearing in the smaller music-halls. He was thirty before he reached London, but once there his conquest of the capital was immediate, rewarding, and unbroken. He began his London triumphs at a hall called Gatti's-in-the-Road, but soon he was the acknowledged 'bill-topper' of the central halls, including the Tivoli, Oxford, and London Pavilion. Such favourite ditties as 'Tobermory' and 'The Lass of Killiecrankie' were already in his repertory.

Lauder's vehicle was the song with an interlude of patter. With his growing popularity his turn became longer and would include four or five 'numbers'. He usually wrote the words and music himself, drawing with instructive shrewdness on traditional airs for the simple, ear-catching lilts which were so easily and widely remembered and so joyously re-sung—and not by Scotsmen only. As time went on, he developed a serious, almost a religious note. He liked to end his performance with 'Rocked in the Cradle of the Deep' or 'The End of the Road', and it was a sign of his genius that he could carry his music-hall audience easily from such frivolities as 'Stop your tickling, Jock' to the more serious ballad of his finale and even into listening patiently while he gave them what was almost a sermon.

At the height of his popularity Lauder was often 'working' four houses a night at an extremely high salary, and he was canny in his handling of the immense sums which he earned. He publicized his own thrift with good humour and some of the Harry Lauder stories were generally supposed to have been invented by himself.

Lauder gave a command performance before King Edward VII in 1908 and came increasingly to be the first citizen, as well as the first favourite, of the vaudeville stage. From 1907 he made nearly every year an immensely successful tour of the Empire and the United States. In the war of 1914–18, in which his only son was killed in action in 1916, he was an ardent recruiter, in speech and song, and a tireless contributor to troop concerts, at home and on the western front; he energetically renewed these efforts in 1939. He was knighted for his services in 1919, and in 1927 received the freedom of the city of Edinburgh. He published several volumes of memoirs.

In later years the serious youth of Scotland began to resent what was deemed to be Lauder's exploitation of a quaint, old Caledonia wherein a laughing wee man, in fantastic tartans and carrying a crinkly cromach, indulged in the sentimentalities and humours of the 'Kailyard School' which was in growing disrepute. Lauder's antics and equipment had indeed little to do with the real Scotland, but they were enormously pleasing to the expatriate Scots all over the world who richly enjoyed a nostalgic heart-glow at the thought of 'Roamin' in the Gloamin' ', and would happily fill a glass to the strain of 'A Wee Deoch-an-Doris'. The Scots are not notably a musical nation, but even those who were almost tone-deaf could appreciate, and even share without disgrace, a Harry Lauder chorus.

'Star-quality' on the stage is indefinable; roughly it means that its possessor has a magnetic, even a mesmeric, power which holds the audience immediately and maintains that grasp whatever the performer may be saying or doing. Lauder had that quality to the full. His patter, like his songs, had an elemental nature: he was never bawdy (at a time when the music-hall often was), never subtle, and never ingenious in the smart, 'wise-cracking' way which was to come. He wore his heart on his sleeve, and it seemed to be a heart of gigantic size. He sometimes executed part of his turn in the plain clothes of a trousered working-man; there was, for example, the unforgettable loon who lay in his bed crooning 'It's nice to get up in the morning' while his brother Jock the baker rose soon after midnight and was stumbling off to his ovens. In these features he struck a veracity absent from his gurgling, rollicking, absurdly kilted Highlanders. But the latter were the darlings of his public.

Lauder's strutting figure, short, broad, and tough, was that most common in the Lowland industrial districts, but his accent was more of Scotland in general than of any particular area. It was broad enough to give character, but not so broad as to puzzle any southern ear, a valuable factor in his music-hall victories.

Lauder married in 1890 Annie (died 1927), daughter of James Vallance, underground manager of a mine in Hamilton. When not working Lauder lived for a long while near Dunoon and later at Strathaven, nearer the scene of his pit-work and of his first successes as an amateur. He had a bad fall at the age of sixty-eight, but overcame a fractured thigh; he was taken very seriously ill in the autumn of 1949, but lived on beyond expectation until his death at Strathaven 26 February 1950. He had willed to 'keep right on to the end of the road', as he had so often counselled others in song. His friends in all ranks of life were countless; he had built up the reputation, in a half-humorous way, of never 'banging a saxpence' without much careful cogitation, but his kindnesses were quiet, many, and 'known to his own'. A portrait by James McBey is in the Glasgow City Art Gallery.

[*The Times*, 27 February 1950; Harry Lauder, *Harry Lauder at Home and on Tour*, 1907, *A Minstrel in France*, 1918, and *Roamin' in the Gloamin'*, 1928.]

IVOR BROWN

published 1959

LAUGHTON Charles

(1899–1962)

Actor and film star, was born 1 July 1899 at the Victoria Hotel, Scarborough, the eldest of three sons (there were no daughters) of Robert Laughton, a prosperous hotelier, and his wife Elizabeth Conlon. Laughton spent a childhood largely tormented by a glandular problem which made him constantly overweight and therefore unpopular at school and indeed at home, where his early determination to become an actor met severe parental opposition.

Brought up as a Catholic, he was educated at Stonyhurst, where even one of his few school friends described him as 'the ungainliest of boys with a huge head'. Laughton was sent, against his wishes, to study the hotel trade at Claridge's in London before being called up at the end of World War I; he was rapidly invalided out of the army after being gassed on the western front in 1918.

Returning to his parents in Scarborough, he continued to train in hotel management until in 1925 he at last defied the family and enrolled as a drama student at the Royal Academy of Dramatic Art in London, where two years later he won the gold medal and was immediately given his start in the professional theatre by one of his teachers, the Russian director Theodore Komisarjevsky. His earliest stage roles at Barnes and the Everyman in Hampstead in 1926 were in classic Russian plays but in 1928, at the Little Theatre in London, he first made his name in the type of role which was to become his hallmark: that of the neurotic, greedy, sinister villain in *A Man with Red Hair* by Hugh Walpole. From there Laughton progressed to two more familiar roles, Poirot and Pickwick, before scoring another big success as the Chicago gangster loosely modelled on Al Capone in *On the Spot* (1930) by Edgar Wallace. He then made his New York début in 1931 as the squalid murderer in *Payment Deferred*, before accepting a Hollywood offer which took him to California for *The Old Dark House* (1932) and his first Nero in *The Sign of the Cross* (1932).

It was back in England for (Sir) Alexander Korda [q.v.] in 1933 that Laughton made his screen name in *The Private Life of Henry VIII* at the start of a sequence of major cinema biographies (*The Barretts of Wimpole Street* (1934), *Mutiny on the Bounty* (1935), *Rembrandt* (1936), and the unfinished *I Claudius* (1936)), which were to see him at the very peak of his reflective, anguished talent for larger-than-life monsters of reality.

In 1933 he joined the Old Vic Company for an impressive range of stage work (*Henry VIII* again, *The Cherry Orchard*, *Macbeth*, *Measure for Measure*,

The Tempest) and in 1936 he was the first English actor ever to be invited to appear at the Comédie Française in Paris, where he played Molière's *Le Médecin Malgré Lui*. He then settled in California, where despite occasional returns to the theatre (notably in the first production of Bertolt Brecht's *The Life of Galileo* in 1947, which he also adapted) he focused mainly on such films as *Jamaica Inn* (1939), *The Hunchback of Notre Dame* (1939), *Witness for the Prosecution* (1957), *Spartacus* (1960), and *Advise and Consent* (1962), returning only rarely to Britain and only notably for David Lean's *Hobson's Choice* in 1954.

But then, as if aware that his time was running out and that his film career was waning, he returned to Britain in 1959 for one last remarkable Stratford season in which he played both *King Lear* and Bottom in *A Midsummer Night's Dream*: his last London appearance was in *The Party* (1958).

In 1929 he married the actress Elsa Lanchester, daughter of James Sullivan, an Irish worker in a black-lead factory, and Edith Lanchester, a Cambridge graduate and active speaker and member of the Social Democratic Federation. They had no children. Throughout his long marriage his homosexuality caused him great unhappiness, and if there was any one key to Laughton's greatness as an actor then it was surely his sense of being a misfit, uneasy in his own skin and forever on the outside of the social, sexual, and familial demands of his upbringing and conditioning. An American citizen from 1950, Laughton died in Hollywood 15 December 1962.

[*The Times*, 17 December 1962; Simon Callow, *Charles Laughton: a Difficult Actor*, 1988; Charles Higham, *Charles Laughton, an Intimate Biography*, 1976; Kurt D. Singer, *The Charles Laughton Story*, 1954; Elsa Lanchester, *Charles Laughton and I*, 1938; personal knowledge.]

SHERIDAN MORLEY

published 1993

LAUREL Stan

(1890–1965)

Comic, was born Arthur Stanley Jefferson at his grandfather's house in Ulverston, Lancashire, 16 June 1890, the second son in the family of four sons and one daughter of Arthur Jefferson, known as 'A.J.', of Bishop Auckland, theatre manager, and his wife Margaret ('Madge') Metcalfe, actress, of Ulverston. He attended schools in Bishop Auckland, Gainford, and Glasgow, after which his family connections helped him to gain entry to the music-hall, as a 'boy' comedian. It was while touring the United States with Fred Karno in 1912 that he tried his luck on American vaudeville, principally in a duo with his common-law wife, Mae Dahlberg, who suggested his stage name, Laurel, although he did not adopt it legally until 1934. In 1916 he saw the opportunities for music-hall pantomimists in the silent movies, and sought a mixed fortune in films and the stage. He lived in the USA from this period.

He became acquainted with Oliver 'Babe' Hardy in the early 1920s, but it was 1927, under the auspices of the Hal Roach studio, before they were first paired with any success. From that point they were to make over a hundred films together, some thirty of them silent ones, and with their best work probably deriving from the phase 1929–35, when they were engaged in creating coherent and sparse twenty-minute cameos.

The Laurel and Hardy set piece was the ordinary situation from which sprang a coiling spiral of disaster. Nervy, flustered, even tearful, Stan Laurel, 'the thin one', exacerbated these accumulating troubles, to the growing chagrin of 'the fat one', the ever-earnest Oliver Hardy. Laurel, in effect, made two contributions to the partnership: as Hardy was quick to concede, Laurel was the creator and rigorous controller of their comedy, as well as a member of what was widely recognized as the best comic double act of its time. An important reason for this was their eschewal of the conventional 'straight' man, two-dimensional and irritable. Each developed a detailed and complete persona of his own. The endearing bathos and crassness of Laurel found an admirable foil in the elephantine smugness of his rotund partner.

Laurel's marital toils were convoluted and confusingly reported. The nearest to an exact listing would be to record that he was married to Lois Neilsen in 1926; to Virginia Ruth Rogers in 1935 (after a possibly illegal ceremony in Mexico the previous year); to Illeana Shuvalova in 1938; to Ruth Rogers again in 1941; and to Ida Kitaeva Raphael, who survived him, in 1946. His only children were a daughter, Lois, who survived him, and a son, Stanley Robert, who lived but a few days: both were by his first wife. He died 23 February 1965 in Santa Monica, Hollywood, USA.

[Laurel and Hardy Museum, Ulverston; F. L. Guiles, *Stan*, 1980.]

ERIC MIDWINTER

published 1993

LEE Janet ('Jennie')

(1904–1988)

Baroness Lee of Asheridge

Politician, was born 3 November 1904 in Lochgelly, Fifeshire, the third of four children, two of whom died young, and only daughter of James Lee, miner and active member of the Independent Labour party, and his wife, Euphemia Greig. She was educated at Beath Secondary School from which she won her way to Edinburgh University and learned from the great English literature teacher, (Sir) Herbert Grierson, how to read and how to write. She described her Scottish childhood in *To-morrow Is a New Day* (1939), a socialist classic suffused with her vibrant compassion.

Taking the finals of her Edinburgh MA in June 1926 (she also gained an LL B, a teacher's certificate, and a diploma in education), she longed to return home, where the miners' struggle was reaching a fresh climax as their communities were ruthlessly destroyed by the coal-owners and the state. She began to earn her living as a schoolteacher, involved herself in politics, and, at a by-election in North Lanark in February 1929, she turned a Tory majority of 2,028 into a Labour majority of 6,578, and became the youngest woman ever elected to Westminster. Introduced into the House of Commons by Robert Smillie, the miners' leader she most admired, and James Maxton, she made many new friends, all on the left of the party: Ellen Wilkinson, Sir Charles Trevelyan, Aneurin Bevan, and, most especially, Frank Wise, with whom she fell in love (he died suddenly in 1933). All were outraged by the failure of their own government to tackle the scourge of mass unemployment.

After her defeat in the general Labour rout of 1931, she became involved in a classic battle with the Labour leaders about party discipline; she believed the rules binding MPs not to vote against party decisions to be an infringement of their duties and rights and said so forcibly. This involved her in arguments with many of her closest associates, notably Aneurin Bevan. She recorded in her book one famous argument with him: 'as for you, I tell you what the epitaph of you Scottish dissenters is going to be—pure, but impotent . . . Why don't you get you into a nunnery and be done with it? Lock yourself up in a separate cell away from the world and its wickedness. My Salvation Army lassie.'

Bevan's brilliant remonstrance may have been part of his wooing. On 24 October 1934 they were married at Holborn Registry Office. Bevan, the Labour MP for Ebbw Vale, was the son of David Bevan, a Welsh miner. Jennie Lee's ego, like his, could take a collective form. She wanted her beloved working class to acquire a touch of arrogance. She created a series of homes for Bevan, with the aid of her own mother and father, and, to the surprise of her parliamentary colleagues, put herself second. The first of those blazing, comradely firesides was established at Lane End Cottage at Brimpton Common in Berkshire in 1939; in 1944 they moved to Cliveden Place in Chelsea; and finally to Asheridge Farm in Chesham, Buckinghamshire. For their closest friends, these homes were political havens, heavens on earth. The Bevans had no children.

Outside Parliament Jennie Lee played a big part in the politics of the 1930s, always insisting on the international allegiance of her socialism. She undertook annual lecture tours in America and some journalism. She went to Vienna in 1934, soon after the fascist attack on the socialists there. She was stirred from the start by the fascist attack on the democratic government in Spain, yet shamed by the feebleness of the British government's response and, worse, by the initial Labour party response. When full-scale war did come, she, like Bevan, had no doubts that the contest must be fought on two fronts: to defeat the fascist enemy and to prepare for democratic socialist victory afterwards. She accepted a job with the Ministry of Aircraft Production touring the aircraft factories and in 1941 went on a propaganda tour to the United States: 'Don't come back,' said Bevan, 'until you've brought them into the war.' When Hitler attacked the Soviet Union, she wrote a speedy good seller, *Our Ally Russia* (1941).

In 1943, at a by-election in Bristol Central, she stood as an independent in support of the two-front war, but lost. As peace came, she in turn sought her peace with the Labour party. In 1945 she won the mining constituency of Cannock for Labour with a 19,634 majority. Soon after the formation of the Labour government in 1945, Aneurin Bevan became one of its foremost and controversial figures. He was the chief architect of the National Health Service and Jennie Lee could see more closely than anyone what difficulties he had to encounter. She too wanted to see these principles established over wider fields. In the process she made friends with many of his friends: Jawaharlal Nehru and Indira Gandhi in India, Yigal Allon in Israel, and Milovan Djilas in Yugoslavia. She could share his victories and his bitter defeats. She felt the attacks upon him more closely than anyone. When he died of cancer in 1960, she felt that he had been murdered.

However, even before the wounds were healed, she resumed her own political activity—notably in the Labour government formed by Harold Wilson (later Baron Wilson of Rievaulx) in 1964. The titles of her offices —parliamentary secretary at the Ministry of Public Buildings and Works (1964–5), parliamentary under-secretary of state, Department of Education and Science (1965–7), minister of state (1967–70)—give no proper indication of how she became one of the administration's most successful ministers. She was sworn of the Privy Council in 1966 and elected chairman of the Labour party the following year. She was, in effect, Britain's first 'minister for the arts', and thereafter no government could abandon the idea. She became an honorary fellow of the Royal Academy in 1981. Cambridge gave her an honorary LL D in 1974. Above all, she played the leading part in the establishment of the Open University. A commitment to experiment with a University of the Air had been included in Labour's manifesto and Wilson had always been an enthusiastic supporter. But, without Jennie Lee, the project would have been a pale imitation of a real university. She insisted that the highest academic standards must apply from the start. The new university received its first students in 1971, and by 1984 it was Britain's largest university, with 100,000 students.

Jennie lost her Cannock seat in the 1970 election and accepted a life peerage, as Baroness Lee of Asheridge. She lived happily at her Chester Row house in London for the next eighteen years, giving delight and good instruction to her family and friends. She never lost her zest for the causes of her youth, most of them celebrated in her last book of memoirs published in 1980, *My Life with Nye*. Dark, and strikingly beautiful in her youth, she had the physical, tough vivacity of many girls of mining families. She died 16 November 1988 at her London home, 67 Chester Row, Westminster.

[Jennie Lee, *To-morrow Is a New Day*, 1939, *This Great Journey*, 1963, and *My Life with Nye*, 1980; Michael Foot, *Aneurin Bevan*, 2 vols., 1962, 1973; personal knowledge.]

MICHAEL FOOT

published 1996

LEIGH Vivien

(1913–1967)

Actress, was born Vivian Mary Hartley in Darjeeling, India, 5 November 1913, the only surviving child of Ernest Richard Hartley and his wife, Gertrude Robinson Yackje. She spent the first six years of her childhood in India, where her father was a junior partner in a firm of exchange brokers in Calcutta. Her mother, who was of French-Irish descent, carefully superintended her small daughter's upbringing, and the books and music which early appeared in the nursery had a warm welcome. In 1920 the Hartleys returned to England and placed their daughter in the Convent of the

Sacred Heart in Roehampton, where Maureen O'Sullivan was a fellow boarder. Even as a child, Vivian Hartley was a leader in style, and her beautifully chosen clothes not a little coveted. Although bored by conventional school lessons, Vivian Hartley lost no opportunity in absorbing what interested her, and her letters home urged many extra lessons in ballet, piano, and violin. Visits to the theatre fed the child's dramatic instinct, and she took part each term in school productions, making her début as Mustardseed in *A Midsummer Night's Dream*.

When Vivian Hartley was thirteen, her parents extended her education by taking her on a European tour. This decision, which included study in schools and convents in France, Italy, and Bavaria, gave her fluency in three languages, and a liberal experience of great value. She made the utmost use of her five years abroad, visiting the great art galleries, attending opera, concerts, and the theatre, while her natural taste for beauty and quality was nourished by the international fashion designers. When she returned to England at eighteen, she was abundantly prepared to conquer the theatre world. Her clear green-blue eyes, chestnut hair, and delicate features were enhanced by a flawless complexion, and she walked with an assured grace.

Scarcely had she enrolled as a student at the Royal Academy of Dramatic Art, when she announced her engagement to a young barrister, Herbert Leigh Holman. The fashionable wedding which followed in December 1932 at St. James's, Spanish Place, and the establishment of a new pattern of living engrossed her until after the birth of her daughter in October 1933. Characteristically, this was recorded in her diary—'Had a baby—a girl'. Gradually, however, her ambition to become an actress again grew restless, and in August 1934 she interrupted a family yachting cruise to return home, just in case she should be called for a small part in a film. Her reward came in one line in the film *Things are Looking Up*, with (Dame) Cicely Courtneidge. More small parts now began to come her way, and she decided upon the stage name Vivien Leigh.

Less than a year after her entry into films, Vivien Leigh was given the stage opportunity she needed, when casting had been held up for a young actress to play a leading part in *The Mask of Virtue* by Carl Sternheim. Since the first requirement was exceptional beauty, Vivien Leigh conquered everyone concerned at the first interview. The play, produced at the Ambassadors Theatre in 1935, was not a success, but the young actress was acclaimed 'a star of unusual promise'. It was very much to her credit that the adulation she received did not turn her head, but like the good professional that she wished to be she took the exposure of her inexperience intelligently and began to learn her craft.

Within twenty-four hours of her successful press reviews, Vivien Leigh had signed a five-year contract with (Sir) Alexander Korda, but she had to wait another year before Korda was ready to cast her: in *Fire Over England* (1937). The occasion, when it came, was fateful, bringing her into professional relationship with Laurence (later Lord) Olivier. They were soon very much in love. She was already an admirer of his acting, and the four months working daily together on the film was deeply influential in her subsequent development. Aware of her limitations, and working constantly to overcome them, Vivien Leigh eagerly accepted the challenge to play Ophelia to Olivier's Hamlet, when the Old Vic production was invited to appear in Elsinore, Denmark, in June 1937. Under expert tuition, her voice—which had been light and small—gained in strength, and her willingness to learn so won her director's admiration that she was cast for Titania in the Old Vic production of *A Midsummer Night's Dream* at Christmas 1937.

With the offer to play Scarlett O'Hara in the film *Gone with the Wind* (1939), Vivien Leigh saw her first chance to break the image of a Dresden china shepherdess—a comparison she despised. Although she had no sympathy for Scarlett, the actress could recognize 'a marvellous part' when she saw one, and she seized and exploited every facet of her heroine, who gave her both an Oscar award and international status as a film star.

Following the dissolution of their previous marriages, Vivien Leigh and Laurence Olivier were married in California in August 1940. They made the film *Lady Hamilton* (1941), then returned to England—Olivier to service in the navy, and Vivien Leigh to establish a wartime home for them both. She was eager to return to the theatre, making her appearance in *The Doctor's Dilemma* by G. Bernard Shaw at the Haymarket in 1942. This was followed a year later by a three-month tour of North Africa, in which she appeared in a concert party with Beatrice Lillie for the armed services. In a letter home she confesses to 'one of the most exciting and often the most moving experiences I have ever had'.

Vivien Leigh had been an actress for almost ten years before her capacity to carry the action of a play was tested. In Thornton Wilder's *The Skin of Our Teeth* (Phoenix, 1945), as Sabina, she showed a new authority in her work, and evidence that she could now stand unsupported. In 1947 her husband was knighted. In a demanding ten-month tour of Australia and New Zealand with Olivier with the Old Vic Company, in 1948, she had abundant classical opportunities to prepare her for the tragic role of Antigone, in which she made a great impression when they returned to London in 1949. Critics, who had been cautious over her early successes, observed that 'this is a new Miss Leigh altogether', and complimented her on her extended vocal range and 'fanatical force of character'.

The actress was now seen in full maturity; and when she appeared as Blanche in *A Streetcar Named Desire* at the Aldwych in October of the same year she received a storming ovation for a performance of uncommon subtlety, and filled the theatre for eight months. Another Oscar award was given her for her film performance in the same role.

While she appreciated her film successes, it was more important to her to succeed as her husband's equal in the theatre. Her great joy was to act with Olivier, and in spite of her fears that she was not yet ready for the demanding variety of Cleopatra, she accepted the challenge to appear under their joint management in the two plays on alternate nights: *Caesar and Cleopatra* by Shaw and *Antony and Cleopatra* by Shakespeare, at the St. James's, 1951. Under her husband's direction, she gave a performance which satisfied both scholars and the general public.

The Oliviers' first season together at Stratford-upon-Avon in 1955 culminated in a powerfully effective production of *Titus Andronicus* by Peter Brook. In May 1957 this production was selected to represent the Memorial Theatre Company on a prestige tour of European capitals for the British Council. On such occasions, Vivien Leigh appeared in her natural element—a distinguished guest, a gracious hostess, and totally professional. Colleagues paid warm tribute to the unvarying quality of her performances, which remained constant throughout a gruelling social programme. Her tact and consideration for the press were tireless and individual. However, she repeatedly began to suffer from manic phases in which she lost physical control of herself and abused her husband verbally in public. Olivier finally decided that he could no longer tolerate the situation.

In 1957 Vivien Leigh and Laurence Olivier appeared together for the last time, at the Stoll Theatre in *Titus Andronicus*. It was during this run that Vivien Leigh interrupted a debate in the House of Lords to protest—without avail—against the projected demolition of the St. James's Theatre.

The last decade of her life, although marked by the same high level of performance, in plays by Jean Giraudoux and (Sir) Noël Coward, among others, had lost its radiance. Her marriage to Olivier was dissolved in 1960; they had no children. She continued to act, making a new reputation for herself in the musical *Tovarich* in New York, 1963, but her delicate constitution could not sustain a career single-handed; the fire of a shared grand passion for the theatre had gone out. Her career had been interrupted from time to time by nervous collapse when she drove herself too hard and by the tuberculosis which caused her death 8 July 1967, in London, during preparations for her appearance in Edward Albee's *A Delicate Balance*. That night the exterior lights of London's West End theatres were darkened for an hour.

Portraits of Vivien Leigh include an oil-painting (unfinished) by Augustus John, held in a private collection in America; an oil-painting, as Blanche DuBois in *A Streetcar Named Desire*, 1950, by A. K. Lawrence, given to the British Theatre Museum at Leighton House, London; and an oil-painting as Henriette in *The Mask of Virtue* by Diet Edzard, 1935, privately owned.

Vivien Leigh received the knight's cross of the Legion of Honour in 1957.

[Anne Edwards, *Vivien Leigh, A Biography*, 1977; *Who's Who in the Theatre*; Felix Barker, *The Oliviers*, 1953; Alan Dent, *Vivien Leigh—a Bouquet*, 1969; Gwen Robyns, *Light of a Star*, 1968; *Observer*, 16 February and 16 October 1949; private information.]

FREDA GAYE

published 1981

LENNON John Winston

(1940–1980)

Musician and composer of popular music, was born in Liverpool 9 October 1940, the only child of Alfred Lennon, a ship's steward, and his wife, Julia Stanley. The father was away when his son was born; the mother's sister, Mary, was present and named him John. Aunt 'Mimi' and her husband George Smith raised the boy at their house. Lennon attended Dovedale Primary and Quarry Bank High School. His academic work deteriorated as he cultivated a fondness for practical jokes, and he failed all his O levels by one grade. In 1957 he entered the Liverpool College of Art, but he obtained no degree.

That year a mutual friend brought (James) Paul McCartney to see Lennon's skiffle group the Quarrymen. One week later Lennon invited McCartney to join. He accepted, and in a few months brought his younger friend George Harrison into the group. In the four years that followed the act changed its name and its membership. In 1960 they became the Beatles and in August 1962 Ringo Starr became their drummer. None of the four could either read or write music.

It was while appearing in clubs in Hamburg from 1960 to 1962 and in the Cavern, Liverpool, in 1961–2 that the Beatles received invaluable experience. They played for hours, mastering a rock and roll repertoire while Lennon and McCartney wrote new songs. Lennon's controlled hysteria on the Isley Brothers' 'Twist and Shout' was an exciting example of rock and roll singing.

On 6 June 1962, the Beatles successfully auditioned for George Martin, the Parlophone label manager, and on 5 October they released their first single, 'Love Me Do', which was produced by Martin. It slowly climbed to number seventeen in the charts.

In 1963 the phenomenon known as Beatlemania swept Britain. 'She Loves You' was the first single to exceed sales of one and a half million in the United Kingdom. Hysterical crowds greeted the group's every appearance. In 1964 the fever spread to the United States, where six of their records reached the top of the charts in the first year. In one week in April, the Beatles held the top five positions in the national hit parade, an achievement never equalled. Throughout the 1960s the Beatles were the leading recording act in the world.

It is difficult to distinguish between the contributions of the individual Beatles at the beginning of their popularity. Lennon and McCartney were writing their songs together, and as a performing unit it was as John, Paul, George, *and* Ringo that they captivated the world as the 'Fab Four'. The Beatles were the first major pop group to write, sing, and play their own material; subsequent rock stars would be expected to do the same. The unprecedented demand for their long-playing discs put rock music on albums, which were previously predominantly the territory of film soundtrack or stage cast recordings.

The considerable foreign exchange the Beatles brought to Britain was a factor in their investiture as MBEs on 26 October 1965. On 26 November 1969 Lennon, who was passionately involved in left-wing and utopian politics, returned his MBE to the Queen as a protest against Britain's role in Biafra, Britain's support for American involvement in Vietnam, and the slipping sales of his Plastic Ono Band single 'Cold Turkey'. The other Beatles happily kept their decorations. The rebel of Dovedale Primary School never became an establishment figure, unlike Paul McCartney, who seemed to thrive on success and mass acceptance. After 1966 Lennon embraced transcendental meditation, drugs, and mystical religion.

The Beatles translated their success to other forms with a series of popular films and Lennon's two best-selling collections of stories and drawings, *John Lennon in his own Write* (1964) and *A Spaniard in the Works* (1965). It was around the time the latter work was published that Lennon and McCartney began to write songs individually. 'Help', 'In My Life', and 'Strawberry Fields Forever' were particularly outstanding Lennon pieces. In 1965 the Beatles released *Sergeant Pepper's Lonely Hearts Club Band*, which was considered the finest rock music album.

Lennon's association with the Japanese avant-garde artist Yoko Ono led him to lose interest in the Beatles, and by the time the group split in 1970 (the partnership was finally wound up in the High Court in 1971) Lennon had already made several 'solo' recordings. These almost inevitably included contributions from or were partly inspired by Yoko Ono. In 1971 Lennon composed 'Imagine', which became his best-known song. During the 1970s Lennon's relationship with Yoko Ono went through a rocky period, partly due to his use of drugs. He had difficulties with the United States Immigration Service which wanted to deny him permission to live there because of a British conviction for drug offences, but in 1972 the permission was granted.

Lennon's post-Beatle work was uneven but punctuated by heights of artistic achievement. His 1970 set *Plastic Ono Band* contains gripping examples of how emotional suffering can be conveyed musically. The single 'Cold Turkey' accurately recalls the agony associated with heroin withdrawal. 'Woman', from *Double Fantasy,* his 1980 collaboration with Yoko Ono, generates the warmth the artist himself was enjoying in his domestic life. For five years he had kept house and cared for his young son while Yoko Ono managed the business side of the marriage, buying property.

In 1962 Lennon married Cynthia, daughter of Charles Edwin Powell, commercial traveller. They had one son, (John Charles) Julian. This marriage ended in divorce in 1968 and on 20 March 1969 Lennon married Yoko, daughter of Eisuke Ono, of the Yokohama specie bank, Tokyo. They had one son, Sean Ono. Lennon was shot dead outside his New York City apartment 9 December 1980. The gunman made him a martyr in fans' eyes, proving that the words of 'All You Need Is Love' and 'Give Peace a Chance', which in moments of cynicism seemed trite, had meaning. At the time of his death Lennon's fortune was estimated at £100 million.

[Philip Norman, *Shout! The True Story of the Beatles*, 1981; *Sunday Times, John Lennon: The Life and the Legend*, 1980; personal knowledge.]

Paul Gambaccini

published 1986

LOW Sir David Alexander Cecil

(1891–1963)

Cartoonist and caricaturist, was born in Dunedin, New Zealand 7 April 1891, the third and youngest son of David Brown Low and his wife, Jane Caroline Flanagan. His father, a business man of wide interests, was of Scottish and his mother of Irish descent. Their families had emigrated to

New Zealand in the mid nineteenth century; neither had previously produced an artist.

Low's days at Christchurch Boys' High School ended when he was eleven, and thenceforth his youth was happily spent in the family house on the outskirts of Christchurch. There he read excursively in his father's library but devoted most of his time to drawing, rigging for himself a makeshift studio, and working from models, animate and inanimate, which he found available in the immediate surroundings. A determination to earn his living as an artist met with the usual parental opposition which was, however, tempered when one of his drawings was reproduced in the Christchurch *Spectator* before his twelfth birthday.

Although for a short period he attended a local school of art, he found it more profitable to learn by the hard process of trial and error, and to discover (in his words) that 'one could draw a thing if one understood it, but usually got lost if one did not'. A pile of old copies of *Punch* had introduced him to the work of Charles Keene and Phil May. 'Once having discovered Phil May', he later wrote, 'I never let him go.' Already encouraged by having many of his sketches accepted by local papers, he obtained his first regular appointment as political cartoonist on the *Spectator*, his second on the *Canterbury Times*. Success turned his thoughts and ambitions towards Australia and, eventually, England.

The Sydney *Bulletin* in Australia had a reputation for the fostering of talent, and no doubt this influenced Low in 1911 to accept an offer of six months as its Melbourne political cartoonist. There followed some years of general work for the *Bulletin* until in 1914 he became the paper's resident cartoonist at Melbourne. The *Bulletin*'s basic policy was to oppose established authority, particularly when power was wielded by politicians alleged to be taking themselves too seriously. By temperament and upbringing the young artist had radical leanings; and William M. Hughes, known in Australia as 'our Billy', who in 1915 became prime minister and was generally believed to be getting above himself, afforded just the target Low needed for the exercise of his pictorial wit. The artist did not spare Hughes, ridiculing both the man and his policy, and his cartoons were later collected in *The Billy Book* (Sydney, 1918) which had a wide sale. His portrait drawings of local worthies were more restrained; and when a selection was published in book form (Sydney, 1915) the artist confessed in a foreword that his caution derived from the fear of arousing resentment, a self-imposed curb on freedom of expression which his later career proved to be merely a temporary expedient.

Low's future as cartoonist was assured during these years in Australia. His technique matured from a highly finished, rather academic manner to the more confident economy of line which became so characteristic a feature of his later work.

His cartoons were now becoming known in England and the Cadbury Press offered him a place on the staff of one of its newspapers. In November 1919 he arrived in London, and for the next eight years he was political cartoonist to the *Star*, an evening paper with a strictly Liberal policy, vehemently opposed to the coalition Government of Lloyd George. Lloyd George, indeed, succeeded Hughes as the principal butt of Low's satire, and was often depicted astride the 'coalition ass', a grotesque and obstreperous double-headed animal, which the cartoonist had concocted to symbolize the alleged ineptitude of the coalition. Already, however, Low's cartoons relating to foreign affairs were of more serious import, and not infrequently prophetic, as, for example, the drawing (1922) of the intransigent Poincaré driving the democratic German Weimar Government at the point of the bayonet into the outstretched arms of totalitarianism.

In 1926 Lord Beaverbrook persuaded Low to join the *Evening Standard* as political cartoonist. Both proprietor and artist well knew that the policies in which Low believed would be frequently in conflict with those advanced in other parts of the paper. The agreement (by letter dated 6 December 1926) contained a clause that the artist was 'to have complete freedom in the selection and treatment of subject matter . . . and in the expression therein of the policies in which you believe; and that this fact will be given prominence in all our announcements . . . when you join the staff of the *Evening Standard*' (copy of letter in the Beaverbrook Library, London). Low's cartoons were often the subject of bitter criticism from readers, and occasionally of friendly remonstrance on Beaverbrook's part, but they were always printed except on the rare occasions when the paper's legal advisers raised the alarm.

In the years leading up to the war, although Low in his cartoons continued to record in the *Standard* the features and foibles of politicians at home, and to survey the national scene from his own highly critical and individual angle, affairs abroad, particularly those of countries under the heel of dictatorship, became his main theme. Hitler was depicted, often two or three times a week, as a militant pigmy strutting across the page; and Mussolini was also a constant subject of Low's derision, portrayed with dark half-shaven jowl and threatening mien, truculently defying the League and the irresolute democracies. In consequence, from 1933 the *Evening Standard* was banned from Germany, and later from Italy. The Nazis continued to be sensitive to criticism in the British press, and particularly resented Low's cartoons, as Lord Halifax was made well aware during his visit to Germany late in 1937. Goebbels, invited to meet Halifax at the British embassy, took the opportunity of contrasting the restrained behaviour of the German press at the time of the abdication in 1936 with 'the shameless fashion in which our Press was for ever attacking the Führer' (Lord Halifax, *Fulness of Days*, 1957). These reactions were later privately conveyed by Halifax to Low who so far relented as to introduce a composite character named 'Muzzler', fusing the features of Hitler and Mussolini without being identifiable as either; but after the invasion of Austria the cartoonist absolved himself from all such restraint.

In the immediate pre-war years Low's cartoons were reproduced by radio transmission throughout free Europe, the Americas, and the Commonwealth; and he thus became a figure of world-wide prestige, resented and feared in the totalitarian countries as Raemaekers and Will Dyson had been in the Germany of an earlier generation. In 1940 Low was reliably informed that he had been included in the Gestapo list for elimination.

In 1949 Low resigned from the *Evening Standard*. 'Black Friday' was how Beaverbrook described the day he received Low's letter of resignation. There was no quarrel: Beaverbrook's great admiration for Low's work and the close friendship between them remained constant until the end. Low needed a change, a need engendered by a characteristic fear of 'becoming a British institution', as he had already been described by a foreign newspaper; and the exigencies of post-war paper control no longer allowed him space for a full-sized cartoon, a technical point which decided the issue. In 1950 he joined the *Daily Herald*, then the mouthpiece of political and industrial Labour, and during the next three years either amused or bewildered readers by depicting the Trades Union Congress as an endearingly massive and clumsy draught-horse, the last and not the least famous of his pictorial symbols. From 1953, in semi-retirement, he contributed three cartoons a week to the *Manchester Guardian*.

Churchill described Low as 'the greatest of our modern cartoonists. The greatest because of the vividness of his political conceptions, and because he possesses what few cartoonists have—a grand technique of draughtsmanship' (*Thoughts and Adventures*, 1932). Certainly his technique of heavy black lines and masses, applied with brush and crayon, was peculiarly well adapted to modern methods of reproduction and, irrespective of content, aesthetically satisfying to the eye. Carried out under the stress of journalistic requirements—during the currency of the *Evening Standard* agreement he was contributing five cartoons a week—his drawing was bold in conception and execution, restoring to English caricature a vitality and irreverence which had been lacking since the early nineteenth century. Adopting a method begun by James Gillray, he portrayed living characters as butts, represented in varying shapes and images of fantasy, made familiar to the reader by constant use of accessories chosen as expressing the quiddity of the subject caricatured. Baldwin's pipe, for example, J. H. Thomas's dress-shirt (token of his alleged pleasure in dining out in full splendour), Goering's bemedalled girth, Neville Chamberlain's umbrella, all received regular attention. He also invented imaginary characters to symbolize policies and attitudes of mind, the most famous of whom was 'Colonel Blimp', a name added to the dictionaries to connote a muddle-headed type of complacent reactionary. The colonel was depicted by Low as an elderly gentleman, usually in a Turkish bath, bald and rotund, with a long white two-pronged moustache, delivering himself of self-contradictory aphorisms.

Although Low in his cartoons hit hard at folly and hypocrisy, and could state his theme with grim earnestness—the memorable drawings he contributed to the *Evening Standard* in the spring of 1940 perfectly reflected the mood of the nation—in the usual run his natural kindliness showed itself and 'cheerfulness was always breaking in'. His cartoons were sometimes bitter, occasionally perhaps brutal, but (except abroad) were seldom resented by those depicted, who were indeed often eager to obtain the original drawing. Low used to say he was incapable of disliking people whom he met, and he was frequently on friendly terms with those whose ideas he attacked in his cartoons. (Even the imaginary Colonel Blimp, for all his obtuse absurdity, became for many readers a not unlikeable figure of fun.) The pictorial commentary Low contributed to light-hearted articles on aspects of contemporary life in England was a popular feature of the papers for which he worked. The mocking self-portrait he introduced into these articles, as into many cartoons, of a squat gesticulating figure belied his real appearance which, with his heavy eyebrows, fine alert eyes, and dark pointed beard, was one of distinction.

Low throughout his career considered his work as a caricaturist to be at least as important as the political content of his cartoons. 'It lies within the bones of the caricaturist himself', he wrote, 'to decide whether he will be a mere drawer of funny pictures or a worthy satirist; . . . whether beneath the surface of his cartoons lies nonsense or the visible operation of human intellect in the presentation of truth' (from the foreword by Low to H. R. Westwood, *Modern Caricaturists*, 1932). Perhaps the finest examples of his work as a caricaturist, as distinct from that of a cartoonist, appeared in the *New Statesman*.

Many selections from Low's cartoons were published in book form. They include *Lloyd George & Co.* (1921); *Low's Political Parade* (1936); *Europe Since Versailles* (1940); *Low's War Cartoons* (1941); *Years of Wrath: A Cartoon History, 1932–45* (1949); and *Low Visibility: A Cartoon History, 1945–53* (1953). To the 'Britain in Pictures' series Low contributed *British Cartoonists, Caricaturists and Comic Artists* (1942). Mention too should be made of his ten double-page illustrations for H. G. Wells's *The Autocracy of Mr. Parham* (1930); and of his twelve double-page illustrations in water-colour for *The Modern 'Rake's Progress'* (1934) for which (Dame) Rebecca West wrote the words and in which he satirized the current scene in the Hogarthian manner. In 1956 his autobiography was published.

In 1920 Low married Madeline Grieve Kenning, of New Zealand; they had two daughters. He was knighted in 1962. He had been made an honorary LL D of the university of New Brunswick in 1958. He died in London 19 September 1963.

A self-portrait in oils is at the National Portrait Gallery which also possesses some 400 of his studies for caricature of a wide range of personalities. Letters and other papers in connection with Low's career are at the Beaverbrook Library, London, besides over 2,000 of his original drawings, mainly cartoons for the *Evening Standard*. In the library at New Zealand House, London, there are, besides seventy original cartoon drawings, a set of copies of books written or illustrated by the artist.

[*The Times*, 21 September 1963; *Low's Autobiography*, 1956; private information.]

D. PEPYS-WHITELEY

published 1981

McBEAN Angus Rowland

(1904–1990)

Photographer, was born 8 June 1904 in Newbridge, Monmouthshire, the elder child and only son of Clement Philip James McBean, surveyor, and his wife, Irene Sarah Thomas. He was educated at Monmouth Grammar School (1915–21) and, briefly, at Newport Technical College. His childhood was spent far away from the metropolitan sophistication which he later encountered in the 1930s and 1940s as Britain's most prominent and inventive theatre photographer. But photography had become significant to him long before he emerged as a professional. The teenage purchase of a simple Kodak camera gave him his first glimpse of the possibilities of the medium. Amateur dramatics, organized by an aunt, introduced McBean to the magical world of theatre—he designed posters and costumes, and began to experiment with the mask-making which intrigued him for the rest of his life.

McBean was a bank clerk from 1921 to 1924. After the death of his father in 1924, McBean's mother moved her family to London, and Angus joined the department store Liberty's (1926–33), as an antiques salesman. Like many of his generation, he was attracted by the Germanic cult of health and beauty and joined the Kibbu Kift movement, where he met Helena Wood, whom he married in 1923. They were separated in 1924 and there were no children.

By the end of the 1920s McBean was obsessed by theatre. He met the Motleys (Percy and Sophia Harris and Elizabeth Montgomery), three young stage designers who encouraged his interest in prop-making and helped him to secure his first design commission—work for the 1933 production of *Richard of Bordeaux*.

He continued to photograph, and in 1934 (after his first photographic exhibition, at the Pirates' Den teashop in London) he became assistant to the Bond Street portraitist Hugh Cecil. Though he disliked Cecil's soft-focus romanticism, he was an adept studio worker, and soon began to develop the aesthetic and technical skills which distinguished his later career. In 1935 McBean opened his own studio in London. He photographed Ivor Novello in *The Happy Hypocrite* in 1936. His stage photographs were boldly lit and dramatic, and soon he was photographing at the Old Vic, documenting now classic productions: Laurence (later Baron) Olivier in *Hamlet*, (Dame) Edith Evans in *The Country Wife*, and Diana Wynyard in *Pygmalion*. McBean's photographs were now appearing in all the London glossy magazines.

But it was the mounting in London of the 1936 exhibition of Surrealist art which inspired McBean to begin radical experiments with photographic portraiture. By 1937 he had begun to use the styles and devices of Surrealism to create fantastical portraits of theatrical stars —Vivien Leigh, enveloped in a plaster-of-Paris gown and posed among cotton-wool clouds, (Dame) Flora Robson erupting from a desolate landscape, the impresario H. G. ('Binkie') Beaumont as a giant puppet-master, and Patricia Hilliard emerging from a sea shell. He photographed himself too, in striped pyjamas with an umbrella, in a neo-classical aquarium, as King Neptune, and as a Roman bust, and sent the photographs out as Christmas cards to an ever-widening circle of friends and associates. With his flowing beard and his deep theatrical voice, he became a well known and much admired character in the London of the 1930s. Immediately after the end of World War II (during the course of which he spent some time in prison as a conscientious objector), he opened a bigger studio in Covent Garden, and during the 1940s and 1950s he was inundated with commissions from London's major theatre companies.

In the early 1960s McBean photographed the Beatles for the cover of their first long-playing record. But as the decade wore on, and fashions in both theatre and photography began to alter, McBean's style, so rooted in the aesthetics of the 1950s, became unpopular. McBean had made those he portrayed into elegant stars. On the new realist stage, however, actors simply wanted to look like ordinary people.

Angus McBean's appearance was flamboyant. His thick beard marked him out immediately as one who wished to be considered an artist rather than a craftsman, and his colourful and often handmade clothes indicated an enduring interest in design and costume. When McBean retired in 1970 and moved to Flemings Hall near the village of Eye in Suffolk, he became almost immediately obscure. He sold his glass plate negatives to Harvard University and in Suffolk moved back into the design work which had so fascinated him in his early years. Flemings Hall, where he lived with his companion (and long-time assistant) David Ball, became a fitting arena for McBean's fantastical imagination. When his photographs were shown in 1976, as a retrospective exhibition at Impressions Gallery, York (and two years later at the National Theatre), the significance of his work within the history of British photography was finally recognized. Acknowledged too was his place as an elder statesman of the burgeoning and culturally progressive international gay community. During the 1980s there were major exhibitions of his work, TV documentaries, and numerous photographic commissions. No longer a half-forgotten name from the unfashionable past, Angus McBean, much to his delight, was once more in demand. He died 8 June 1990 at Ipswich Heath Road Hospital, Ipswich. The Harvard Theatre Museum has a collection of his photographs and plates.

[Colin Naylor (ed.), *Contemporary Photographers*, 2nd edn., 1988; Adrian Woodhouse, *Angus McBean*, 1982; typescript of an unpublished autobiography *c.*1972, Angus McBean papers in a private collection; information from David Ball; personal knowledge.]

VAL WILLIAMS

published 1996

MACCOLL Ewan

(1915–1989)

Songwriter, singer, folk-song revivalist, and dramatist, was born James Miller 25 January 1915 in Salford, Lancashire, the youngest and only surviving child in the family of three sons and one daughter (one of each sex was stillborn and one son died at the age of four) of William Miller, iron-moulder, of Salford, and his wife Betsy Hendry, charwoman. He was educated at Grecian Street School, Salford. He left school at the age of fourteen after an elementary education and was immediately unemployed. He joined the Young Communists' League (he was not to leave the Communist party until the early 1960s) and then found work as a motor mechanic, factory worker, and street singer. He first began writing for factory newspapers, composing satirical songs and political poems, while also taking a keen interest in amateur dramatics, in 1931 forming a political street theatre group, the Red Megaphones, which performed sketches on the streets of Salford and Manchester. Both his parents were fine traditional singers, and he had begun to sing and write songs while a teenager. One of his first and finest protest songs, 'The Manchester Rambler', dealt with the 'mass trespass' campaigns of the 1930s, in which hikers fought pitched battles with gamekeepers when they invaded privately owned grouse moors.

It was two decades before he devoted his energies to music. He spent most of the 1930s involved in experimental theatre projects after joining forces with his future wife, Joan Littlewood, with whom he formed a 'workers' experimental theatre', the Theatre of Action, at Manchester in 1933. He wrote and co-produced a series of political satires and dance dramas, and was arrested and charged with disturbing the peace after the police stopped performances of his 'living newspaper', 'Last Edition'. In World War II he was called up, joined the army, and was arrested for desertion, although he claimed there had been a case of mistaken identity. He was discharged on medical grounds. He continued with his drama projects after the war, and he and Littlewood formed Theatre Workshop, for which he became art director and resident dramatist. He changed his name to Ewan MacColl in 1945. Between 1945 and 1952 he wrote eleven plays, including *Uranium 235* (1952), a drama with music, and *Landscape with Chimneys* (1951), which included one of his best-known songs, 'Dirty Old Town', written in a matter of hours on the opening night to cover a scene change.

He severed his links with Littlewood in 1952 and gradually withdrew from the Theatre Workshop. From 1952 onwards he worked to establish a folk-song revival in Britain. He saw folk music not as some quaint historical curiosity but as a political force, an expression of working-class culture, and he wanted to develop a style in which 'songs of struggle would be immediately acceptable to a lot of young people'. With help from American folklorist Alan Lomax and A. L. ('Bert') Lloyd, he mixed politics, British and American folk music, and jazz in a radio series, *Ballads and Blues* (1953). He founded the Ballads and Blues Club, later renamed the Singers'

Club, in London, and by the mid-1950s was considered one of the leading folk-singers in the country.

Initially, MacColl had encouraged the fashion for American folk and blues (he and Lomax had even started a skiffle group, which included another American singer and song-writer, Peggy Seeger, who was to become his third wife), but by the late 1950s he became concerned that British traditional music was being swamped by American styles. He therefore introduced his controversial 'policy rule'—singers had to perform songs from their own tradition, depending on whether they were British or American.

In 1957, when he claimed there were 1,500 folk clubs around Britain, he returned to experimental multi-media work, this time with a distinctively British flavour. The *Radio Ballads*, broadcast on the BBC Home Service (1958–64), dealt with the everyday lives of British workers, from railwaymen to boxers or fishermen, and used a montage of interviews and new songs written by MacColl. He wrote many of his best songs for this widely praised series, including 'Shoals of Herring' and 'Freeborn Man'.

A fiery, authoritative, opinionated figure, he never deviated from his staunch left-wing views. From 1965 to 1971 he trained young singers in folk-singing and theatre technique in his Critics Group, which performed an annual review of the year's news, the 'Festival of Fools'. He collected folk-songs, and co-wrote two books with Peggy Seeger (*Travellers' Songs from England and Scotland*, 1977, which was praised for its scholarship, and *Till Doomsday in the Afternoon, the Folklore of a Family of Scots Travellers*, 1986). With her he founded Blackthorne Records, which specialized in their own recordings. In the 1980s, by which time his jet-black hair and red beard had turned white, he wrote songs to support the miners' strike and the anti-apartheid movement. Considering his enormous and varied output, it was ironic that his only financial success came from his song 'The First Time Ever I Saw Your Face', a no. 1 hit in America for Roberta Flack in 1972. It won the Ivor Novello award in 1973. MacColl was awarded an honorary degree by Exeter University (1986).

In 1935 he married Joan Littlewood, who did not know the identity of her father, but was brought up by a stepfather, Jimmy Morritt, asphalter. They were divorced in 1948 and in 1949 he married Jean, daughter of William Newlove, a wartime director of regional supplies and part-time artist. They had a son, Hamish, and a daughter, Kirsty, a very successful singer-songwriter. They were divorced in 1974 and he married his third wife, the singer Peggy Seeger, with whom he had lived since the 1950s, in 1977. She was the daughter of Charles Seeger, musicologist, and sister of the singer Pete Seeger. MacColl died 22 October 1989 in the Brompton Hospital,

London, after complications following heart surgery, and his autobiography *Journeyman* was published the following year.

[Interview with Ewan MacColl; Ewan MacColl, *Journeyman* (autobiography), 1990; Joan Littlewood, *Joan's Book*, 1994; *Independent*, 30 October 1989; private information.]

Robin Denselow

published 1996

MACMILLAN (Maurice) Harold

(1894–1986)

First Earl of Stockton

Prime minister, was born 10 February 1894 at Cadogan Place, London, the youngest of three sons (there were no daughters) of Maurice Crawford Macmillan, publisher, and his wife, Helen ('Nellie') Artie, only surviving daughter of Joshua Tarleton Belles, surgeon, of Indianapolis, and his wife, Julia Reid. Nellie Belles's first husband, a young painter, died in November 1874, five months after their marriage. Ten years later she married Maurice Macmillan, a taciturn, austere workaholic, who left domestic matters exclusively to her. It has been often said, not least by Macmillan himself, that he was the grandson of a crofter. In fact he was the great-grandson; his grandfather Daniel left the croft at the age of eleven to become a bookseller's apprentice and to lay the foundations of the publishing firm which became one of the most prosperous and famous in Britain.

Nellie Macmillan was intensely and at times embarrassingly ambitious for her children. Neither Daniel ('Dan'), the brilliant donnish eldest son, nor Arthur, the gentle self-effacing second, were suitable instruments for her purpose. She concentrated on Harold, who later wrote: 'I can truthfully say that I owe everything all through my life to my mother's devotion and support.' But a price can be paid for matriarchal bossiness. Her constant vigilance and perpetual interference made her in the eyes of some members of the family 'a fiend'. Macmillan himself told a friend many years later when he was prime minister: 'I admired her but never really liked her . . . She dominated me and she still dominates me.' One asset she gave him was the ability to speak French. She had spent time in Paris before her marriage, and in London she employed French maids and insisted on her sons speaking French at meals 'downstairs'. Macmillan claimed that it was to be a help in dealing with General Charles de Gaulle.

The combination of a reclusive father and an obsessive mother, together with two much older and not very sympathetic brothers, resulted in a solitary life for a small boy. He found solace to some extent, like Sir Winston Churchill, in the affection of a devoted nanny, but he remained all his life a bit of a loner who found it hard, as did his brothers, to relate at all easily to his contemporaries, to his children, and to women. He was a shy and anxious child who hated to be conspicuous—curious characteristics in a future prime minister. To the end of his days he remained intensely nervous before making a speech. Of his famous 'unflappability' he said that people little knew how much his stomach flapped on those occasions. He suffered all his life from sporadic moods of deep depression. He was also a hypochondriac, although, since he lived to ninety-two, his health cannot have been too bad.

He was educated at Summerfields, Oxford, in those days a rather bleak factory programmed to produce scholars for the leading public schools. Although unhappy there, he gained a scholarship for Eton, where he was equally unhappy and from which in 1909 he was withdrawn early by his parents on grounds of health. Rumours of sexual impropriety have no foundation. Although he habitually wore an Old Etonian tie (that and the Guards' tie seemed in later life to be the only ones he possessed) he had little affection for the place. He never became a fellow and seldom revisited it.

To bridge the gap between leaving school early and the goal of Oxford set by his parents, a private tutor was needed. Their first choice was Dilwyn Knox, son of the Anglican bishop of Manchester, who proved cold and unsympathetic; their second choice was his brother 'Ronnie' Knox, an Eton and Balliol contemporary of Dan Macmillan and widely acclaimed at twenty-two as one of the intellectual stars of his time. He struck up a close friendship with his sixteen-year-old pupil. It was abruptly terminated in November 1910 by Nellie Macmillan, who may have suspected 'inordinate affection' and who certainly from her low-church angle disliked Knox's Anglo-Catholicism, which she saw, rightly in this case, as a stepping-stone to that arch-bugbear, 'Rome'. Their friendship was, however, renewed in 1912 at Oxford, where Macmillan was an exhibitioner at Balliol and Knox, also a Balliol man, had just become chaplain of Trinity College. Knox had loved Eton but was not keen on Balliol. Macmillan was exactly the opposite. He blossomed as never before at that supremely élitist college. He was secretary and then treasurer of the Oxford Union, and might well have become president but for World War I. He obtained a first class in classical honour moderations (1914). He made a host of friends, and many years later, when chancellor of the university, would dwell with nostalgia on the 'golden summer' of 1914—the last summer that so many of his Balliol companions were to see. Long after 1918, Oxford was to him a 'city of ghosts' and he could not bear to go back in the interwar years. Pictures show him at Oxford as a good-looking, dark-haired young man. He was tall and broad-shouldered. It was not till the war that he grew a bushy moustache which did not improve his appearance but which he kept for the rest of his life. Although he had the looks often associated with the Highlanders he had no trace of a Scottish accent but spoke the orthodox English of Eton and Oxford.

On the eve of war Macmillan, along with Knox and another Oxford friend, Guy Lawrence, seriously considered whether to 'Pope', in the jargon of their set. Lawrence did and Knox followed rather later, but Macmillan, to Knox's bitter disappointment, wrote in July 1915 to say that he intended to postpone a decision till after the war 'if I am alive'. In the end he resolved to remain an Anglican. He took his religion very seriously and continued to be a devout high churchman to the end of his life. In 1914 he was commissioned into the King's Royal Rifle Corps, but was soon transferred, thanks to wire-pulling by his mother, to the socially grander Grenadier Guards. He sailed to France in August 1915 and was wounded three times, a bullet permanently damaging his right hand on one occasion. The war left him with a limp handshake, a dragging gait, and sporadic pain. Mentally it gave him a deep sympathy with the largely working-class 'other ranks' and strong antipathy to the 'embusqués', who held office jobs far away from the front.

Yet, unlike so many 'demobbed' officers, he was financially secure, with a junior partnership in the publishing firm. Before taking it up he wanted to travel. His mother pulled wires again and in 1919 got him the job of aide-de-camp to Victor Christian William Cavendish, ninth Duke of Devonshire, governor-general of Canada. There he fell in love with one of the duke's daughters, Lady Dorothy Evelyn Cavendish, to the consternation of the formidable duchess ('Evie'), who had intended her for the heir of the Duke of Buccleuch. On 21 April 1920 they were married, amid suitable pomp and circumstance, at St Margaret's, Westminster. The bride's side was lined with royals and peers, the bridegroom's with Macmillan authors, including six OMs. It seems to have been a genuine case of love at first sight although, as Alistair Horne says in the official biography, it is not clear 'what exactly it was that drew Dorothy to the earnest crofter's great-grandson, the ambitious middle-class publisher's son, with his shy, somewhat stilted manners, his Groucho moustache, and the shuffling walk that was a legacy of his war wounds'.

Macmillan's life was not entirely easy. The publishing firm was dominated by his father and his two uncles. He lived during working days at his parents' home in Chester Square and on weekends at Birch Grove, the family house in Sussex, which his father intended to leave to him, although he was the youngest son. A set of rooms on the top floor was kept for him and for his wife and children, who lived there most of the while, apparently not disconcerted by the presence of the formidable American matriarch, though it was hardly an ideal arrangement. Nor was he at ease with the Cavendish clan and their closely related Cecil cousins. They called him 'the publisher' behind his back and regarded him as something of a snob. He certainly in those early days liked being a duke's son-in-law. But he was bored by the Cavendish passion for horse-racing, and they were bored by his prolixity. He cut a slightly uncomfortable figure at the vast Chatsworth house parties which, as Maurice Macmillan told Alistair Horne, must have been 'absolute hell' for his father. But he did genuinely enjoy shooting and made himself into a proficient, if slightly over-dressed, performer.

Macmillan, strongly encouraged by his mother, had for some time had parliamentary ambitions. Like more than one such aspirant he was not quite sure which side to join. He admired David Lloyd George (later first Earl Lloyd-George of Dwyfor) but he sensed that the Liberal party was on its way out. He stood as a Conservative for Stockton-on-Tees in the election of 1923 and lost, but he won a few months later in the election of 1924, which was a Conservative triumph. His diffident electioneering was compensated for by his wife's outgoing energy. But he made little impression on the House of Commons, and was regarded as an earnest bore, destined at best for some minor office.

In 1926 Birch Grove was rebuilt by Nellie and converted into a vast neo-Georgian mansion. The result was a house that could not be divided and the young couple had no refuge. This may have been a contributory cause of marital disaster. No one can say how far his mother's dominating presence affected Harold's relations with Dorothy, but in 1929—a year of calamity for Harold in every respect—she fell in love with Robert (later Baron) Boothby, a reckless, good-looking, 'bounderish' Conservative MP. The affair lasted in various ways till she died in 1966. She craved a divorce, but Macmillan, after some hesitation, decided against it and that, as the law then stood, settled the matter. They never separated. She continued to act as his hostess and canvass at his elections. But it was an empty shell of a marriage. They had three daughters and a son, Maurice, who died in 1984. Lady Dorothy claimed that their fourth child, Sarah, born in 1930, was Boothby's. But, although Boothby accepted responsibility, he did so with considerable doubt and it is by no means certain that she really was his daughter. Lady Dorothy's claim may have been a move to persuade Macmillan to divorce her. If so, it did not succeed. Sarah died in 1970.

The year 1929 brought another disaster. Macmillan lost his seat at Stockton and with it what slight chance he might have had of promotion when the Conservatives next regained office. After a brief flirtation with the 'New Party' run by Sir Oswald Mosley, he was returned for Stockton in the landslide election of 1931. Shortly before that he had a serious nervous breakdown, which lasted for several months. He embarked upon the uneasy currents of the 1931 Parliament in a state of doubt and anxiety, which he sought to alleviate by writing some dull quasi-Keynesian pamphlets and a book, *The Middle Way* (1938). Their *dirigiste*, corporatist, and collectivist tone seemed very un-Conservative even then.

He was again returned for Stockton in 1935. He supported Winston Churchill's criticisms of defence policy and appeasement and signalled his dislike of the government's foreign policy by resigning the party whip when sanctions against Mussolini were lifted in 1936, the only backbencher to do so. He was a rather solitary figure. His father and his two uncles died in 1936 and his mother in 1937. He now had far more responsibility as a publisher and found himself to be a good man of business. In politics and private life he ploughed a lonely furrow. In 1937 he applied successfully for the Conservative party whip, in the hope that the new prime minister, Neville Chamberlain, would impart drive instead of drift to national policy. Chamberlain did, but, from Macmillan's point of view, the drive was in the wrong direction. He was dismayed at the resignation of Anthony Eden (later the first Earl of Avon)—a heavy blow to the anti-appeasers. There were two groups, one centred on Churchill and called the 'Old Guard', the other on Eden and described by the whips as the 'Glamour Boys' Macmillan joined the latter. On terms of outward friendship with Churchill, he was never a member of his 'court'. The presence of Boothby there was one reason. Moreover, Macmillan had disapproved of Churchill's attitude to India, and with his strong high-church views, disapproved even more strongly of Churchill's attitude to the abdication crisis. Churchill never personally liked him.

The Munich agreement had an ambivalent effect of Macmillan. He cheered in the House of Commons when Chamberlain announced his third visit to Hitler, but later took the view that Britain should have fought rather than accept Hitler's terms. He campaigned unsuccessfully in the Oxford City by-election against Quintin Hogg (later Baron Hailsham of St Marylebone), and in favour of the anti-Munich candidate A. D. Lindsay (later first Baron Lindsay of Birker), the master of Balliol. For this rebellion he narrowly missed 'deselection' and expulsion from the Carlton Club.

When war came, Chamberlain had to give office to Churchill and Eden, but their followers were excluded. Macmillan was briefly involved in a fact-finding mission to Helsinki in January 1940, the idea being a possible Anglo-French expedition to help the Finns in their war with the USSR. Fortunately—though not thanks to Macmillan—this insane project came to nothing; the Finns had to sue for peace before any troops could be sent. The fall of Chamberlain in May 1940 at last brought Macmillan some recognition. He became parliamentary under-secretary to the Ministry of Supply (1940–2). His Civil Service private secretary was John Wyndham (later first Baron Egremont), who was to be closely associated with him as aide and personal friend till he died in 1972. In June 1941 the first Baron Beaverbrook became minister of supply, with quasi-dictatorial powers. As spokesman in the Commons Macmillan moved up a rung in the ladder. He coped with his strange and formidable chief both warily and successfully, laying on flattery, but keeping his distance, for he knew that Beaverbrook could morally seduce men as easily as he physically seduced women. To the end of Beaverbrook's life they remained on excellent terms. In February 1942 a reconstruction of the ministry suggested by Macmillan himself meant that Beaverbrook would cease to be represented by a parliamentary under-secretary in the Commons. Macmillan was shunted into the Colonial Office to represent the first Baron Moyne and then Viscount Cranborne (later fifth Marquess of Salisbury). It was, he said, 'like leaving a madhouse in order to enter a museum' But he had the consolation of being made a privy councillor (1942), in those days a rare honour for a junior minister.

In the autumn of 1942 came the turning-point of his career. Churchill appointed him—his second choice—minister resident with cabinet rank at Allied Forces Headquarters in Algiers (1942–5). It was a make or break situation. It made Macmillan. He displayed remarkable diplomatic skill in dealing with such disparate characters as generals Eisenhower, Giraud, and de Gaulle, and with Robert Murphy, his American opposite number. He was helped by his American ancestry and his fluency in French. At the Casablanca conference shortly after his arrival he acquitted himself with notable success and was warmly congratulated by Eden. This warmth was not destined to last. Despite being badly burned and nearly killed in a plane accident soon afterwards, Macmillan was able to continue in his important office, much appreciated by Churchill, till the end of the war. He was head of the Allied Control Commission in Italy and thus in effect, as John Wyndham described him, 'viceroy of the Mediterranean'—a situation far from palatable to Eden.

His next major problem was Greece, where German withdrawal in October 1944 had left a situation of civil war between the Greek communists and the forces of the centre and the right. Macmillan spent some uncomfortable weeks during the bitter winter of 1944–5 in Athens, where the British army of occupation was very thin on the ground and the embassy was a beleaguered garrison under constant sniper fire. In the end Churchill and Eden made a personal foray; despite the hostility of the

Americans and the *bien pensant* left–liberal media in England, the communists were ousted.

Then came the highly controversial question of the 'repatriation' of Soviet citizens who had been captured by the Germans. To be a prisoner at all was unforgivable by Stalin, and some of them had fought on the German side. Repatriation had been agreed at the Yalta conference (1945), but it did not apply to White Russians, who were also involved but had never been Soviet citizens. When the war ended large numbers of both categories were in British hands in northern Yugoslavia and Austria. Macmillan discussed the matter on 13 May with General Sir Charles Keightley, who commanded V Corps at Klagenfurt. It is clear that repatriation (which also involved handing Chetniks and Ustasi over to Tito's partisan forces in Yugoslavia) was effected in deplorable circumstances of force and fraud, but there is no evidence of a conspiracy on the part of Macmillan, who had no executive authority nor any part in decisions taken at Yalta or the orders for their implementation made in Whitehall. The charge of being a war criminal, made many years later, haunted Macmillan in his old age, but it was baseless.

On 26 May 1945 Macmillan returned to Britain. By now he had made his mark. Churchill appointed him air minister in the caretaker government, pending the verdict of the general election to be announced on 26 July. The result was a disaster for the Conservatives and for Macmillan personally. The party was defeated by a huge majority and he lost Stockton. He might have been out of the house for two or three years and become a forgotten man but for a lucky chance. The sitting member for Bromley, a safe Conservative seat, died just before the election figures were announced. Macmillan was promptly adopted as candidate and was back in November with a majority of over 5,000.

For the next six years he devoted himself to the postwar problems of publishing and the opposition front bench. He had no difficulty in holding his seat in 1950 and 1951. On the personal side he had come to a bleak but balanced *modus vivendi* with his wife. She continued to support him socially and politically but her obsession with Boothby never waned. Politically Macmillan was active in trying to adapt the Conservative party to the challenge of its defeat. His theme was the occupation of the 'middle ground'—a Conservative heresy thirty years later but reasonable at the time, though it gave him a reputation among the right of being a 'neo-socialist', as Brendan (later Viscount) Bracken described him. He hoped for an alliance with the Liberals and even toyed with proportional representation.

In foreign policy he was a 'European' up to a point. He regarded Clement (later first Earl) Attlee's refusal in June 1950 to join the discussions of the six European nations about the Schuman plan as a disastrous error. But, like Churchill and other prominent Conservatives, he blew hot and cold. Although he served for three years on the Council of Europe at Strasburg, he wrote in 1949 'the Empire must always have first preference for us'.

When Churchill returned to office with a precarious majority in October 1951 he offered Macmillan the ministry of housing and local government. Macmillan nearly refused and only accepted with reluctance. The Conservative party conference, in a rush of blood to its collective head, had insisted on a mandate to build 300,000 houses a year compared with the 200,000 or so achieved by Labour. The target was widely regarded as unattainable—or only attainable at the unacceptable expense of industrial investment and infrastructure. Injecting into the ministry something of the hustle and bustle he had experienced under Beaverbrook, Macmillan reached the figure in 1953. He was helped inside the ministry by Dame Evelyn (later Baroness) Sharp, the first woman to become a permanent under-secretary, outside it by Sir Percy Mills, a Birmingham businessman. Equally valuable was his junior minister Ernest (later Baron) Marples, who had also made his fortune from humble origins, as an engineer and road-builder. He introduced American principles into the torpid British building industry, with notable success. Macmillan told Alistair Horne: 'Marples made me PM: I was never heard of before housing.' The critics were probably right about the damage done to the balance of the economy, but politically the achievement was a notable feather in the caps of both the party and the minister.

In October 1954 there was a cabinet reshuffle and Macmillan became minister of defence for five unhappy months. At housing Churchill backed him and left him to get on with it. At defence he did neither and Macmillan became irritated at the ceaseless flow of memoranda on the most detailed topics from the aged prime minister. Perhaps this experience prompted him to take the lead in persuading Churchill to retire in favour of Eden. It was high time, but he was never forgiven by Clementine, Lady Churchill, who had always mistrusted him. Eden succeeded on 5 April 1955, and the ensuing general election in May resulted in a Conservative majority of fifty-nine. Macmillan became secretary of state for foreign affairs, the post which he most wanted and believed would be the culmination of his political career. He was very much Eden's second choice. The prime minister would have preferred the fifth Marquess of Salisbury (the former Viscount —'Bobbety'—Cranborne), but feared a row about a peer in this position—unnecessarily, in view of the later appointments of lords Home and Carrington.

Like Churchill over defence, Eden could not keep his hands off foreign policy. At the end of the year he used the ill health of R. A. Butler (later Baron Butler of Saffron Walden) to move him to the leadership of the Commons and replace him as chancellor of the Exchequer by Macmillan, who was replaced by Selwyn Lloyd (later Baron Selwyn-Lloyd). Macmillan resented the change. He had never liked Eden, nor Eden him. He only introduced one budget. His more radical proposals were vetoed by the prime minister. The budget is mainly remembered for the introduction of premium bonds. The second half of 1956 was dominated by the Suez crisis. Macmillan does not come well out of it. He was a leading 'hawk', and he totally misjudged the American reaction. On 25 September he had a conversation with Eisenhower at the White House, from which he inferred that the American president would support British military action against Gamal Abdel Nasser, the Egyptian leader. Sir Roger Makins (later first Baron Sherfield), the British ambassador, was present and took notes. He was astonished to learn later that Macmillan had sent a dispatch to this effect to Eden, for the discussion in no way warranted such a version of the president's attitude. But the report inevitably reinforced Eden's already erroneous view of the American reaction.

Macmillan's second major error was one of omission. The Suez operation constituted an obvious risk to sterling. He took no precautions and failed to do what the French did, draw out a tranche of funds from the International Monetary Fund well in advance of the invasion. The ensuing run on the pound was exactly what a chancellor of the Exchequer might have anticipated and avoided. Instead he panicked and with all his power pressed the case for withdrawal. 'First in, first out,' was the justified jibe from Harold Wilson (later Baron Wilson of Rievaulx). Macmillan was unhappy about his role for ever afterwards. It was, he said, 'a very bad episode in my life'.

Credulous adherents of the conspiracy theory of history have seen in Macmillan's conduct a plot to oust and replace Eden. There is no evidence at all for this implausible theory. Eden resigned on 9 January 1957 on genuine grounds of health. He made no recommendation to the queen about his successor, merely advising her private secretary to consult Lord Salisbury as a senior peer who could not be a runner himself. He and the lord chancellor interviewed each member of the cabinet separately and took slightly perfunctory soundings in the parliamentary party and the National Union. The result was a strong preference for Macmillan rather than Butler, whose attitude over Suez had been ambivalent, indecisive, and obscure. Macmillan was appointed by the queen at 2 p.m. next day.

The outlook for the Conservative party could hardly have been bleaker. Suez had been a fiasco and it looked as if Labour would have a walk-over at the next general election. Macmillan transformed the situation. He soon dominated the House of Commons and his apparent confidence radiated out to the electorate. He also dominated his party, taking in his stride the resignation of Lord Salisbury over the release of Archbishop Makarios in March 1957, and the resignations of Peter (later Baron) Thorneycroft, Enoch Powell, and Nigel Birch (later Baron Rhyl)—the whole Treasury 'team'—nine months later in protest against his refusal to accept expenditure cuts of £50 million in the next budget. On the eve of his departure on a Commonwealth tour he dismissed the resignations as 'little local difficulties'. Meanwhile he had mended fences with Eisenhower and, in the 1958 crisis involving Iraq, Jordan, and Lebanon, the USA and Britain acted in harmony. Despite some awkward negotiations with the trade unions, he approached the election of 1959 at the head of a party in far better shape than in 1957. His ebullient behaviour caused the cartoonist 'Vicky' to depict him ironically as 'Supermac'. The joke backfired and made him in Horne's words 'something of a folk hero'. He was accused by many moralists of excessive 'materialism'. A famous phrase which he used—'most of our people have never had it so good'—was wrenched out of its context, which was a warning against rising prices and contained a forgotten qualification: 'Is it too good to be true?' On the foreign and colonial front there were difficulties—Cyprus, the Hola incident in Kenya, and other episodes. But Macmillan kept calm, plumped for autumn 1959 rather than spring for the election, and won easily, almost doubling the majority he had inherited from Eden.

His premiership lasted for another four years. But after the major triumph of the general election and the minor one of defeating Sir Oliver (later Baron) Franks in 1960 for the chancellorship of Oxford University, the tale is anything but a success story. It is clear now—and many people thought so then—that he spent too much time on foreign and post-colonial affairs, and too little on matters at home. These years were the period when France and Germany caught up and surpassed Britain in terms of economic success. The major British problems—trade-union power and chronic inflation—were never recognized by Macmillan, who was not helped by two singularly mediocre chancellors of the Exchequer, nor by the expansionist advice of his economic guru, Sir Roy Harrod. When unemployment rose from 500,000 to 800,000 Macmillan, obsessed by his memories of Stockton-on-Tees in the 1930s, was horrified. Attempts at an 'incomes policy' flopped as they always have. No serious effort was made to amend trade-union legislation. In July 1962 Macmillan got rid of his second chancellor of the Exchequer, Selwyn Lloyd, but made the major error of combining his dismissal with a reconstruction of the government, which involved sacking a third of the cabinet. It looked like panic and probably was. His prestige never recovered. He was not helped by the general anti-establishment sentiment that dominated the early 1960s. It was not exactly pro-Labour, but it was certainly anti-Conservative.

In external affairs Macmillan achieved a certain *réclame* in 'liberal' circles by his speech at Cape Town in 1960, on Monday 3 February, warning of the 'wind of change' which was blowing through Africa. To the Tory right it was anathema—'Black Monday'—and led to the formation of the Monday Club. Macmillan was of course correct about the strength of African nationalism, which was affecting the Central African Federation of the two Rhodesias and Nyasaland (later Zimbabwe, Zambia, and Malawi). The Federation had to be dissolved but the labyrinthine and disingenuous process won few friends even among the Africans and bitterly alienated its prime minister, Sir Roy Welensky, and his white supporters. They felt they had been double-crossed.

Macmillan was determined to keep in with America. He played the card of his American ancestry for all it was worth. The Cavendishes were related by marriage to the Kennedys, and the president genuinely admired the wit and wisdom of the older man. During the Cuban crisis of 1962 he kept in touch with Macmillan more closely than with any other European leader, but there is no evidence to suggest that the prime minister gave any advice which affected the course of events. He did, however, extract from Kennedy some concessions about the British independent nuclear deterrent, and the president paid full tribute to Macmillan for his part in negotiating the Atmospheric Test Ban treaty with the USSR on 5 August 1963. Macmillan came to regard this as one of the principal achievements of his premiership.

But long before that he had been in major trouble. Britain had applied in July 1961 to accede to the Treaty of Rome. From the start it was clear that President de Gaulle was hostile, but it was not clear that he could carry France with him till the referendum on the presidency in October 1962, followed by a sweeping electoral victory for his party a month later. Despite his earlier policy—he had tried to wreck the European Economic Community by setting up the European Free Trade Association in May 1960—Macmillan now put much political capital into accession to the EEC. But Britain was doomed. On 29 January 1963 de Gaulle delivered his formal veto. 'All our policies at home and abroad are ruined,' Macmillan wrote in his diary.

If that was not enough, a series of scandals, connected with espionage, security, and sex, erupted, culminating with the famous John Profumo affair when the secretary of state for war denied in Parliament in March 1963 a charge that he had slept with a woman who shared his favours with those of the Russian military attaché A few weeks later Profumo had to retract and resign from public life. Macmillan was unfairly criticized as gullible and out of touch. Nigel Birch made a long-remembered attack, quoting Robert Browning's *The Lost Leader*, 'Never glad, confident morning again'. The government tottered but survived.

An election was due at the latest by autumn 1964. Macmillan, now nearly seventy and feeling none too well, had to decide whether to fight it himself or pass the lead to someone else. But whom? He resolved to go ahead. On the eve of the Conservative conference at Blackpool he was taken ill with an inflamed prostate gland, which necessitated an immediate operation. A prostate operation was a relatively minor matter but Macmillan, hypochondriac as ever, convinced himself that the malady was malignant and decided to resign at once. In fact it was not, and there was no need to retire at this singularly awkward political moment. He was to regret his decision for ever after.

When the operation was over, it was indicated that the queen would welcome his advice about the succession. He did not have to give it. Perhaps it would have been better if he had politely declined, like Bonar Law in 1923 and Eden in 1957. But he was determined, despite later disclaimers, to block the obvious heir presumptive, R. A. Butler, whom he regarded as a ditherer. After complicated indirect consultations with the cabinet and other elements of the party—which have been the subject of controversy ever since—he plumped for the fourteenth Earl of Home (later Baron Home of the Hirsel) in preference to his first choice, Quintin Hogg, who was then second Viscount Hailsham. Both of them had taken advantage of a recent Act to disclaim their peerages. It was the last occasion when this informal and secretive system of consultation was employed.

Macmillan left the House of Commons at the election of October 1964. He declined for the time being the traditional earldom offered to ex-prime ministers. He recommended a barony for John Wyndham but took nothing for himself. He did not wish to damage the prospects of his only son Maurice, now at last a minister. He may also have dreamed of being recalled to office himself in a crisis as head of an all-party coalition. In 1966 his wife died. He missed her despite their latterly loveless marriage, but the Chatsworth connection remained and the reigning duke and duchess of Devonshire made ample hospitable amends for any snubs by an earlier Cavendish generation. Another consolation for his rather lonely life in the chilly emptiness of Birch Grove was Garsington Manor near Oxford, where he often stayed with Sir John Wheeler-Bennett. Then there was clubland, which he regularly frequented.

In the long twilight—or perhaps Indian summer—of his career his chancellorship of Oxford University (from 1960) meant much to him. It also meant much to Oxford. He attended the various occasions—dinners, centenaries, laying of foundation stones, and the like—more assiduously than any previous chancellor. Dons and undergraduates alike were fascinated by his speeches and his conversation—an inimitable combination of wit, emotion, and nostalgia, which made it almost incredible that he had once been regarded as a parliamentary bore. He travelled a good deal, especially in America, where he raised money for Oxford. He even paid a visit to China, where he was fêted. He spent much time on his memoirs in six volumes (1966–73), published profitably by his firm, in which he took a renewed interest. They are in places somewhat heavy going but essential for historians. Much more 'fun', to use a favourite word of his, are his *The Past Masters* (1974), a series of political sketches and reminiscences from 1906 to 1939, and his diary of his time as minister resident in the Middle East, *War Diaries: Politics and War in the Mediterranean 1943–1945* (1984). He frequently appeared on television, almost always with great success. In the last ten years of his life he gave many long interviews at Birch Grove to Alistair Horne, his chosen official biographer. His relations with Margaret (later Baroness) Thatcher, who always treated him with respect, were ambivalent. She sought and followed his advice about the Falklands war in 1982. But he had led his party from left of centre whereas she did so from the right. Towards the end his coded criticism of her economic policy was abundantly clear.

He changed his mind about the peerage and, on his ninetieth birthday in 1984, his acceptance of an earldom was announced. Maurice was very ill (he died on 10 March) and the main reason for refusal had gone. Macmillan took the title of Earl of Stockton, after his old constituency. By now he was almost blind—a great blow to such a voracious reader though relieved by his discovery of 'talking books'—and he made his thirty-two-minute maiden speech in November without a single note. It was a wonderful performance, which those who heard it will never forget.

Macmillan's political hero was Benjamin Disraeli (first Earl of Beaconsfield), who had something of the same mixture of wit, irony, cynicism, romance, and sheer play-acting. To the end of his days Macmillan loved to put on a show. His last performance was a speech to the Tory Reform Group in November 1986. By now well distanced from Margaret Thatcher he compared privatization to 'selling the family silver'—a specious simile since the silver was, after all, being sold to the family. It is arguable whether Disraeli was a great prime minister, but he was certainly a great character. The same can be said of Harold Macmillan.

Macmillan was sworn of the Privy Council in 1942 and admitted to the Order of Merit in 1976. He became an honorary fellow of Balliol (1957), honorary DCL of Oxford (1958), and honorary LL D of Cambridge (1961).

He died 29 December 1986 at Birch Grove, Hayward's Heath, East Sussex. He was succeeded in the earldom by his grandson, Alexander Daniel Alan Macmillan (born 1943).

[Macmillan's own writings mentioned in the text; Alistair Horne, *Macmillan, the Official Biography*, 2 vols., 1988, 1989; George Hutchinson, *The Last Edwardian at No 10*, 1980; Nigel Fisher, *Harold Macmillan, a Biography*, 1982; private information; personal knowledge.]

BLAKE

published 1996

MACTAGGART Sir William

(1903–1981)

Painter, was born 15 May 1903 at Loanhead, Midlothian, the elder son and third of four children of Hugh Holmes MacTaggart, mechanical engineer, and his wife, Bertha, daughter of Robert Little, businessman, of Edinburgh. His father was the eldest son of the Scottish landscape painter William McTaggart. Although he always revered his grandfather's memory MacTaggart established his artistic personality from the beginning and even his earliest pictures owe nothing to his illustrious namesake. As a child MacTaggart suffered from ill health and was educated privately. From an early age he determined to become a painter. In this he received every encouragement from his father whose collection of pictures not only contained an excellent representation of the elder McTaggart but also pictures by Boudin and Le Sidaner. Between 1918 and 1921 he attended the Edinburgh College of Art as a part-time student. It was at this time he met the painters (Sir) W. G. Gillies, Anne Redpath, and John Maxwell who were to remain lifelong friends. The person who had the greatest influence on MacTaggart at this period, however, was the artist William Crozier (1893–1930). He had studied in Paris with André Lhote, had travelled extensively, and brought an intellectual approach to painting which was important to MacTaggart.

Between 1922 and 1929 MacTaggart went regularly to the South of France for the sake of his health, sometimes in the company of Crozier: to Cannes, Le Cannet, Cassis, Bormes, and Grimaud. He took advantage of these visits to paint, and a six-week period at Cannes in 1923 was particularly important. The pictures from this period are bright and strong in colour and show an affinity with those of the Scottish colourists, particularly S. J. Peploe. It was appropriate therefore that in 1927 MacTaggart joined the Society of Eight, of which Peploe and F. J. Cadell were also members. MacTaggart held an exhibition of his work at St Andrews church hall, Cannes, in 1924. His first one-man show in Edinburgh took place at Aitken Dott & Son in 1929.

The inclusion of twelve pictures by Edvard Munch in the annual exhibition of the Society of Scottish Artists in 1931–2 was the occasion for MacTaggart meeting the person who was largely responsible for bringing them to Edinburgh: Fanny Margarethe Basilier, daughter of General Ivar Aavatsmark, of Oslo. She was perhaps the most important influence in his life. She gave him confidence in his work and broadened his outlook. Together they visited Matisse in the summer of 1936 and after their marriage in July 1937 they paid regular visits to Norway. MacTaggart was president of the SSA between 1933 and 1936, during which period paintings by Klee and Braque were shown at their annual exhibitions in Edinburgh. In 1933 he began his teaching career at the College of Art, Edinburgh, an association that lasted until 1956. In 1937 he was elected as associate of the Royal Scottish Academy. (He became a full member in 1948 and was president between 1959 and 1969.)

Between 1939 and 1945 MacTaggart again turned his attention to the landscape of East Lothian which remained an important source of inspiration for the remainder of his life. Visits to Scandinavia resumed after the war and between 1947 and 1952/3 the MacTaggarts stayed regularly at Orry-la-Ville, just north of Paris. The Rouault exhibition at the Musée d'Art Moderne in 1952 had a profound effect on MacTaggart's technical approach to painting. The palette becomes more sombre and the paint surface more richly worked. In the landscapes and still lifes of this period, especially those of flowers seen through an open window against a night sky, colours take on an inner glow. The most important example of the 'window' theme which he often repeated throughout the 1960s is the 'Starry Night, the New Town', 1955 (Coll. Laila Aavartsmark, Oslo). MacTaggart gave up painting directly from nature in the mid-1950s and increasingly worked from sketches boldly executed on the spot in black chalk.

The MacTaggarts were a focal point of social life in Edinburgh and entertained constantly at 4 Drummond Place, which was their home from 1938. In the later 1960s and 1970s the routine of work, parties, and official functions was broken by the annual visit to the spa town of Skodsborg in Denmark. MacTaggart was a man of great personal charm with a gift for friendship. Position and honours were important to him, if only to prove that he had been able to conquer adversity and ill health. He had an honorary LL D from Edinburgh University (1961), was knighted in 1962, and became a chevalier of the Legion of Honour (1968). He was elected ARA in 1968 and RA in 1973.

MacTaggart's range as an artist was limited and he was no innovator. But he spoke with a distinctive voice and the East Lothian landscapes of the 1960s in which harvest fields and ploughed land glow under an incandescent sun belong to the visual imagery of the Scottish scene and make a small but distinctive contribution to a larger Nordic tradition in painting. He was very popular in his lifetime and his pictures always sold well. MacTaggart stopped painting about 1976. He died in Edinburgh 9 January 1981, and his wife died nine days later. They had no children. An unfinished portrait by W. G. Gillies (*circa* 1935) is in the Scottish National Portrait Gallery (2496). A bronze bust by Benno Schotz, RSA, belongs to the Royal Scottish Academy who commissioned it in 1970. Both are good likenesses.

[The MacTaggart Papers, National Library of Scotland, MS Acc. 8636, 8416, 8755; catalogue (by Douglas Hall) of the retrospective exhibition at the Scottish National Gallery of Modern Art, Edinburgh, 1968; H. Harvey Wood, *W. MacTaggart* (Modern Scottish Painters 3), Edinburgh, 1974; catalogue of the Studio Sale, Christie's & Edmiston's at 4 Drummond Place, Edinburgh, 2 July 1981, pp. 45–74; personal knowledge.]

HUGH MACANDREW

published 1990

MARKHAM Beryl

(1902–1986)

Aviator, horse trainer, and author, was born 26 October 1902 at Westfield House, Ashwell, Rutland, the younger child and only daughter of Charles Baldwin Clutterbuck, farmer and formerly a lieutenant in the King's Own Scottish Borderers, from which he was cashiered for absence without leave, and his wife Clara Agnes, daughter of Josiah William Alexander, of the Indian Civil Service. The Clutterbucks went to British East Africa in 1904 and in the following year bought Ndimu farm at Njoro, overlooking the Rift Valley, where they built a timber and flour mill. In July 1906 Clara left for England with her son and soon divorced her husband. Left with her father, Beryl did not see her mother again until she was twenty-one. She lived a wild childhood with the farm's African children, particularly Kibii (whose name after initiation was arap Ruta), a Kipsigis boy.

In 1911 Beryl was sent to Nairobi European School, from which she was expelled in her third term. She returned to the farm and a possibly promiscuous early adolescence, not being sent to school again until 1916, when an army officer paid for her to attend Miss Seccombe's School in Nairobi, providing he could marry her. She was again expelled. On 15 October 1919, at the age of sixteen, she married the officer—Captain Alexander Laidlaw ('Jock') Purves, son of Dr William Laidlaw Purves, founder of the Royal St George's Golf Club in Scotland. Purves bought land adjoining Ndimu farm, but the marriage lasted only six months. Beryl began to train horses, as her father had done, and in 1921 left her husband to live on Soysambu, the farm on the floor of the Rift Valley owned by the third Baron Delamere. She stayed there as a trainer until 1924, when she left for London, where she discovered she was pregnant. She claimed the child's father was Denys Finch Hatton, the lover of Karen Blixen, who later wrote *Out of Africa* (1937), but she had been so free with her sexual favours that any of a number of people could have been responsible. She had a late abortion and returned to Kenya, where she met Mansfield Markham, the son of Sir Arthur Basil Markham, first baronet, Liberal MP and owner of collieries in the north of England. He was wealthy and they married in 1927.

In 1928 Edward, Prince of Wales, and his brother Henry, Duke of Gloucester, visited Kenya. Beryl became mistress to Henry. She agreed to go to London to be with him, and he established her in a suite at the Grosvenor Hotel. On 25 February 1929 she had a son, about whom there was much speculation. However, he cannot have been fathered by Prince Henry, because Beryl must already have been pregnant when she met him. The boy was given to Markham's mother to bring up. When Markham threatened to cite Henry as co-respondent in a divorce, Queen Mary, in an effort to avoid scandal, made Henry settle on Beryl a capital sum of £15,000, which provided her with an annuity of £500 until her death.

Beryl stayed in England until 1929, and learned to fly. Back in Kenya, she obtained her commercial pilot's licence in 1933. Following a dare, she decided to fly the Atlantic from east to west. On 4 September 1936 she took off from Abingdon, near Oxford, in a Vega Gull, without a radio. After 21 hours 35 minutes she landed in a bog at Baleine cove, near Louisburg, Nova Scotia, 100 yards from the ocean, having run out of fuel. She was the first woman to fly the Atlantic from east to west, and the first person to make a solo non-stop crossing in that direction.

Fêted in America, she returned there in 1939, and met Raoul Cottereau Schumacher, son of Henri Schumacher, farmer, of Minneapolis. A well-read and articulate man, Schumacher worked as a ghost writer. In 1942 Beryl married him, having divorced Markham in the same year. In June

1942 *West with the Night*, by Beryl Markham, was published in America. A remarkable account of her African childhood, it reached thirteen best-seller lists. The book was lyrically written, with many classical and Shakespearian allusions, and in a style similar in places to that of Antoine de Saint-Exupéry, who had befriended Beryl in Hollywood and who may well have been a help with the manuscript. Beryl later claimed that he encouraged her to write the book. Some short stories she wrote were later gathered together by her biographer, Mary Lovell, and published as *The Splendid Outcast* (1987). Schumacher divorced Beryl in 1960 and died in 1962.

In 1950 Beryl returned to Kenya without Schumacher. Her remaining days were spent training horses in Kenya, South Africa, and Rhodesia. She won the Kenya top trainer's award five times and the Kenya Derby six times. In 1971 her son, whom she had seldom seen, died after a car accident in France, leaving two daughters, and Markham died three months later.

In 1979 the Jockey Club of Kenya allocated Beryl a bungalow at its racecourse. *West with the Night* was republished in 1982 and hailed as a lost masterpiece. By 1987 140,000 copies had been sold and royalties began to pour in. At the last count the book had sold over a million copies.

Beryl Markham was five feet eight inches tall, of willowy build, with blue eyes, fair hair, slightly wide-spaced teeth, and slim, boyish hips. Her beautiful long oval face had a determined chin. She was exceptionally promiscuous, but retained the loyalty of her male friends. Women found her often ruthless and selfish, although they admitted her stamina, physical prowess, courage, and ability to withstand pain. She died in Nairobi Hospital, from pneumonia which followed a broken hip, 3 August 1986.

[Beryl Markham, *West with the Night*, 1942; Mary S. Lovell, *Straight on till Morning*, 1987; Errol Trzebinski, *The Lives of Beryl Markham*, 1993; private information; personal knowledge.]

C. S. NICHOLLS

published 1996

MARKS Simon

(1888–1964)

First Baron Marks of Broughton

Retailer and business innovator, was born in Leeds 9 July 1888, the only son of Michael Marks and his wife, Hannah Cohen. His father, who only a few years earlier had come to England as a poor Jewish immigrant from Poland, set up in 1884 a stall in the open Kirkgate market with a slogan 'Don't ask the price—it's a penny'. In 1894 he went into partnership with Thomas Spencer; in 1903 the firm became a private limited company; and when Michael Marks died in 1907 Marks and Spencer Ltd. was a chain of sixty penny bazaars.

Simon Marks was educated at Manchester Grammar School and spent two years on the Continent studying languages and business methods. He joined his father shortly before his death and became chief merchandiser. He was appointed director in 1911, and in 1916 assumed control as chairman, the position he occupied for forty-eight years during which he transformed the company into one of the most progressive retail organizations in the world and a national institution.

He was greatly influenced by his father and was fond of saying that he learned his social philosophy 'from Michael Marks and not Karl Marx': to put people always first. He maintained that there were three factors of success for a retail business: the customers, the suppliers, and the staff, all of whom must derive benefits and contentment from their association.

At school Marks met Israel (later Lord) Sieff who married in 1910 his eldest sister, Rebecca. Marks married Sieff's sister, Miriam (died 1971), in 1915 and asked him to join the board of Marks and Spencer. The two men, who were to be friends, partners, and associates for over sixty years, shared the same outlook on life and business; 'that David and Jonathan relationship had permeated throughout our lives', wrote Marks.

During the war of 1914–18 he joined the Royal Artillery as a signaller, but following the issuing by the British Government of the Balfour Declaration he was seconded to Chaim Weizmann to establish and direct the Zionist headquarters in London. He had met Weizmann in 1913 who was then teaching biochemistry at the university of Manchester and this friendship converted Marks to a fervent belief in technology and gave him his first experience of statesmanship.

By 1916 Marks was in full command of his father's business, following a Chancery court's ruling against the executors of the Spencer estate who wanted to have its control. In 1926 Marks and Spencer was incorporated as a public company and in that year Sieff left his family textile firm to become its full-time vice-chairman and joint managing director.

Marks called the twenties the formative years when, following an intensive study and a fruitful visit to America in 1924, he laid down the principles which not only revolutionized his own business but were to have an effect on the whole of British retailing and beyond it. 'We believe', said Marks at the first annual general meeting in 1927, 'that we are filling a long-felt want in providing sound quality goods at inexpensive prices, which the public cannot get elsewhere . . . It is our aim and object to get as much produced in this country as possible.'

The war put an end to the penny price point. During his American visit Marks had been impressed by the goods offered there within the dollar limit. On his return, the new pricing policy, with a five-shilling ceiling, enabled Marks and Spencer to use economies of co-ordinated large-scale production and distribution to create a range of clothing for the family. To ensure better and more consistent quality, the company established its own technological organization to research and test materials and garments, to set specification standards, and to enforce quality control. This was a revolutionary step for a retailer to take.

'St Michael', the brand name of Marks and Spencer, was registered in 1928 and gradually all the goods sold in the stores were to be produced under this name to the company's own specifications. Since the company would not own factories, a massive educational programme was required for suppliers and soon Marks was able to say that 99 per cent of the goods were British made.

The capital available from the public issue of shares made it possible to implement the policy of progressive enlargement, rebuilding, and modernization of the stores, and of the continuous improvement of standards, both for the customers and the staff. Very little was spent on advertising. Marks always laid great stress on the importance of direct communications through good human relations and personal contact; he introduced efficient stock control to speed up the flow of goods directly from factories to stores. 'The stores were for him a kind of fairyland', wrote the company's historian; 'it gave him deep pleasure to see the transformation.' He took particular pride in the affectionate nickname of 'Marks and Sparks' by which his organization had become known to the public.

Over the years he built up a wonderful relationship with the customers, the suppliers, and the staff. He was the most human of employers and the social amenities for his staff were outstanding. From the beginning, the company initiated an enlightened welfare policy, starting with the provision of a good hot midday meal and extending to medical, dental, catering, and social services, generous pensions, and comfortable quarters. All this created a family-like atmosphere. Marks, though a perfectionist himself, was very protective towards people who worked for him.

During the war of 1939–45, while the company helped with its welfare services, for instance feeding evacuees, Marks served as deputy chairman of the London and South Eastern Regional Production Board and as adviser to the Petroleum Warfare Department. A co-founder of the Air

Defence Cadet Corps before the war, he served as one of the first directors of British Overseas Airways.

Marks, with his genius for merchandising, will be remembered especially as the initiator of high-quality clothing at reasonable prices. His retailing revolution was based on the principle that the main function of distribution was to tell the manufacturer what the public needed, and assist with expert advice on technology, production engineering, and so on. His dynamic and imaginative reform reached its climax after the Second World War, when he helped to bring about a social revolution by attracting customers in every class and making it possible for every woman to be well dressed. The expansion into foodstuffs followed a similar path, with emphasis on quality and freshness as he himself had an almost fanatical interest in hygiene and cleanliness.

His sensitivity almost amounted to intuition and with it went the faculty of criticism and self-criticism. He was always ready to examine and re-examine both merchandise and systems, to reconsider any approach that had taken root, even though he had brought these ideas into being, or had approved them. He often said to those he led and guided: 'I am the greatest rebel of you all.' Very impatient with rising costs, he started in 1956 the 'good housekeeping campaign' to simplify his business and eliminate unproductive paperwork. This led to higher efficiency, lower prices, and a greater sense of involvement among the staff.

This 'operation simplification' was widely reported and caught the popular imagination, bringing civil servants, administrators, and business men to study it. Marks had a strong sense of social responsibility and was ready to give generous help to those who wanted to learn from his success. Also, personally, he was warmly and lavishly generous. His interests included the Royal College of Surgeons, University College, London, Manchester Grammar School, the British Heart Foundation, and always Israel. 'Rich men must learn to give,' he once said, 'for some it is the hardest lesson of all and some of them never learn it.'

Marks was knighted in 1944 and raised to the peerage in 1961; the speeches he made in the House of Lords showed pride in British achievement and a desire to enhance it. Parallel with his love for England was a passionate commitment to Zionism which could always claim his high-pressure energy and resourcefulness and the services of his family. He was president of the Joint Palestine Appeal and honorary vice-president of the Zionist Federation.

Honours conferred on him included the honorary D.Sc. (Economics) of London, LL D of Manchester and Leeds, Ph.D. of the Hebrew University of Jerusalem; the honorary fellowship of the Royal College of Surgeons, of the Weizmann Institute of Science, and of University College, London. In 1962 he was the first recipient outside the United States of the Tobé award for the most distinguished retailers.

Marks conveyed an impression of youthful enthusiasm and spontaneous warmth, with his sensitive and mobile features, a small agile body, and quick expressive gestures. His soft and appraising eyes, under heavy eyebrows and a full head of hair, would light up with intense curiosity or emotion. His spirit was vibrant but his manner and humour were understated. He had a mercurial personality: soft in sympathy but passionately relentless in determination, with an earthy sense of fun, particularly at the expense of pomposity.

He had great personal charm and was a good companion, with an extraordinary zest for life and a capacity to surprise. He liked to be surrounded by his family in his Grosvenor Square flat or the Berkshire farm; he had one son and one daughter. Once an ardent tennis player, he enjoyed the theatre and concerts, collecting French Impressionists or antique furniture, and reading. Most of all, he liked people: he was very modest and simple in his approach, able to talk with all kinds of people and quick to understand their problems and points of view. He died in London 8 December 1964 at the head office of Marks and Spencer, where his portrait by Frank O. Salisbury hangs in the boardroom. He was succeeded in his title by his son, Michael (born 1920).

[Goronwy Rees, *St. Michael, A History of Marks and Spencer*, 1969, and *The Multi-Millionaires*, 1961; S. J. Goldsmith, *Twenty 20th Century Jews*, New York, 1962; Woodrow Wyatt, *Distinguished for Talent*, 1958; Marshall E. Dimock, *Administrative Vitality*, 1959; *The Times*, 9 December 1964; *Observer*, 30 June 1968; Israel Sieff, *Memoirs*, 1970; private information; personal knowledge.]

SIEFF

published 1981

MEDAWAR Sir Peter Brian

(1915–1987)

Biologist and Nobel prize-winner, was born 28 February 1915 in Rio de Janeiro, the elder child and only son of Nicholas Agnatius Medawar, a Brazilian businessman of Lebanese extraction, and his British wife, Edith Muriel Dowling. He was educated at Marlborough College and Magdalen College, Oxford, where he took a first-class degree in zoology in 1935 and a D.Sc. in 1947. At Oxford he was successively a Christopher Welch scholar and senior demy of Magdalen (1935), a senior research fellow of St John's (1944), and a fellow by special election of Magdalen (1938–44 and 1946–7). From 1947 to 1951 he was Mason professor of zoology in the University of Birmingham, from 1951 to 1962 Jodrell professor of zoology and comparative anatomy in University College London, and from 1962 to 1971 director of the National Institute of Medical Research, Mill Hill. From 1971 to 1986 he was head of the transplantation section of the Medical Research Council's clinical research centre, Harrow.

He created a new branch of science, the immunology of transplantation. During the Battle of Britain in 1940 a plane crashed near Oxford, and Medawar, engaged there in research on tissue growth and repair, was asked whether he could help the badly burned pilot. Although he had nothing to offer at the time, this awoke in him an interest in transplantation of skin, which was to form the core of his scientific achievement. With the Glasgow surgeon Thomas Gibson he discovered the 'homograft reaction', the process whereby an immunological response causes the rejection of tissue that has been transplanted between unrelated individuals. It took another two decades and the work of many people to find ways of overcoming this reaction, by means of immunosuppressive drugs, but it was Medawar's first decisive step that made possible organ transplantation as it was later known.

Along the way he and his small research group, especially Leslie Brent and Rupert Billingham, made other important discoveries, most notably of immunological tolerance in 1954. The immune system discriminates efficiently between skin grafts of foreign and self origin, and under certain experimental conditions, which Medawar and his colleagues first defined, it can be misled into treating as self what is in fact foreign. Just as a new branch of surgery sprang from Medawar's seminal work on the homograft region, so also a new branch of developmental biology sprang from his work on tolerance. For this discovery he was awarded the Nobel prize for medicine in 1960, jointly with (Sir F.) Macfarlane Burnet.

It must not be thought that a scientist as clear-minded and creative as Medawar was never wrong. Indeed, it is precisely those qualities which make his few mistakes easy to identify. A conspicuous example was his idea, during the early 1950s, that pigment spreads in the skin by cell-to-cell passage of infective particles.

To a wider public he was known for his eloquent projection of ideas in and about biology. He was passionately convinced of the power of the scientific method not only to create what he called a magnificent 'articulated structure of hypotheses', but also to solve human problems. His deepest contribution was to expound the deductive view of scientific activity. For Medawar the place of honour is occupied by the 'act of creation', in which a new idea is formulated; experimentation has the humbler (but entirely necessary) role of verifying ideas. He happily accepted the consequence that an idea can never formally be proved true. Even the faintest whiff of induction was dismissed with contumely. He took pleasure in searching out the roots of this position in the English thinkers of the last three centuries. In all of this he was much influenced by his friends the philosophers T. D. ('Harry') Weldon, Sir Alfred Ayer, and Sir Karl Popper. He conveyed these convictions with eloquence, elegance, and an unfailing sense of humour in ten books published between 1957 and 1986— including *The Uniqueness of the Individual* (1957), *The Future of Man* (1960), *Advice to a Young Scientist* (1979), and *The Limits of Science* (1984)—and in some 200 articles and reviews. His 1959 Reith lectures on the future of man powerfully rejected the gloom-and-doom view of the impact of science on ordinary life. 'Is the Scientific Paper a Fraud?' (BBC Third Programme, 1963, reprinted in P. B. Medawar, *The Threat and the Glory*, 1990) was much enjoyed in scientific circles.

His autobiography, *Memoir of a Thinking Radish* (1986), relates that the Oxford senior common-rooms taught him to regard no subject as intellectually beyond his reach. Throughout his life he was quick to respond to the ideas of those around him: colleagues, students, friends, and family. How delighted were the undergraduates who attended his tutorials to find themselves acknowledged in his profound 1947 review of cellular inheritance and transformation. He never ran a large laboratory, and even as director of the National Institute of Medical Research he and two or three junior colleagues occupied just two rooms (where he continued to do his own research and his own washing up, on the Tuesdays and Thursdays that he kept free of administrative duties). He laughed at gigantic research programmes, and the possibility that government might perceive the practical benefits of research better than the individual scientist who carried it out. In his own experimental work, and above all in his writing, he set a standard which inspired the postwar flowering of immunology.

He needed and received the total love and support of his wife, from their first meeting as undergraduates at Oxford to his last paralysing illness. She was Jean, daughter of Charles Henry Shinglewood Taylor, surgeon; they had two sons and two daughters. Jean entered fully into his professional life, filling first their house in Edgbaston, and then successively Lawn House and Holly Hill, their large houses in Hampstead, with his students and colleagues, many of whom became her own friends. They had a wide circle of friends in the media, in music, and especially in opera, which he enjoyed intensely. A sudden visit to Covent Garden or Glyndebourne was one of the joys of his University College days. His wife collaborated in his later writings, and maintained a strong interest in birth control and in the environment.

Medawar was tall, physically strong (an excellent cricketer), with a voice which could hold a lecture theatre in suspense or reassure a doubting student. Always accessible and open to argument, he had no doubts about his own capacity: sitting at his typewriter in University College, cigarette in his mouth, he told James Gowans that 'It takes an effort to write undying prose'. His books are lucid and beautifully written.

He was elected a fellow of the Royal Society (1949), appointed CBE (1958) and CH (1972), knighted (1965), and admitted to the Order of Merit (1981). He became an honorary FBA in 1981. He was an honorary fellow of many colleges and was awarded numerous honorary degrees.

During his last fifteen years at the clinical research centre at Harrow he was partially paralysed from a stroke suffered in 1969, while reading the lesson in Exeter Cathedral at the British Association for the Advancement of Science (of which he was president in 1968–9), but his ideas continued to flow, and he both inspired and received support from devoted colleagues. He suffered several more strokes and eventually died from one, 2 October 1987, in the Royal Free Hospital, London.

[P. B. Medawar, *Memoir of a Thinking Radish*, 1986; N. A. Mitchison in *Biographical Memoirs of Fellows of the Royal Society*, vol. xxxv, 1990; personal knowledge.]

AVRION MITCHISON

published 1996

MERCER Joseph

(1914–1990)

Footballer and football manager, was born 9 August 1914 at 32 Queen Street, Ellesmere Port, Wirral, Cheshire, the eldest in the family of three boys and one girl of Joseph Powell Mercer, professional footballer, of Ellesmere Port, and his wife, Ethel Breeze. He was educated at Cambridge Road School and John Street Senior Mixed School, Ellesmere Port, playing football for the Cheshire schools' team. His father, a former Nottingham Forest player, was wounded in World War I, and became a bricklayer. He died when Mercer was twelve. After leaving school, Mercer worked for Shell in a variety of unskilled jobs, and played football first for the village of

Elton Green and the Shell Mex team, and later for Ellesmere Port. Spotted at Elton Green by an Everton scout, he played for Everton as an amateur for two years before signing on as a professional in 1931. He became a regular first-team player during the 1935–6 season as a wing-half, and got his first England cap in 1938. He appeared five times for England during the 1938–9 season, in which Everton won the League championship. In September 1939 Mercer joined the army after (Sir) Stanley Rous, secretary of the Football Association, had circularized footballers urging them to join the Army Physical Training Corps, so that they would keep fit. He became a sergeant-instructor, and ended the war as a sergeant-major. He played in twenty-seven wartime internationals, captaining England on several occasions, and also played for Aldershot.

After the war he was unhappy at Everton, and suffered from knee trouble. He was contemplating retirement in order to devote himself to running a grocery business in Wallasey when Arsenal offered £7,000 for him in November 1946. He agreed to go on condition that he could live and train in Liverpool, and he continued to do so throughout his eight years with Arsenal. He became a half-back, and went on to captain Arsenal to two League championships, in 1948 and 1953, and to success in the FA Cup Final against Liverpool in 1950, a few days after being voted Footballer of the Year. In April 1954 he broke his leg, playing against Liverpool, and retired.

For the next twenty years Mercer pursued a successful career as a football manager. He became manager of Sheffield United, who were relegated to the second division at the end of his first season there, in 1955—an inauspicious start. In December 1958 he replaced Eric Houghton as manager of Aston Villa, who were also relegated at the end of the season. But, under his management, Aston Villa came top of the second division in the 1959–60 season, and won the League cup in 1961. Mercer had a nervous breakdown in 1964, after a disappointing season when the club came nineteenth in the League championship, and he resigned.

He was out of football for fourteen months before becoming manager of Manchester City in 1965. He brought in Malcolm Allison as assistant manager and coach, and for five seasons this was a highly successful partnership. Manchester City came top of the second division in Mercer's first season there, won the League championship in 1968 and the FA cup in 1969, and in 1970 won both the League cup and the European Cupwinners' cup, beating the Polish team, Gornik Zabrze, 2–1 in the final. It was the first English club to win a domestic and a European trophy in the same season. Mercer's relationship with Allison soured after Allison, ambitious for promotion, became involved in boardroom intrigues, and Mercer left in 1972 to become manager of Coventry City. In May 1974, after the resignation of Sir Alf Ramsey, the England manager, Mercer agreed to be caretaker manager for the rest of the season. He was in charge for seven matches, with a record of three wins, three draws, and one loss. He was appointed OBE in 1976.

Mercer was regarded as the greatest wing-half of his generation, and had the war not interrupted his career he would have won many more England caps. As a manager, his greatest successes were with Manchester City, previously overshadowed by their neighbours and rivals, Manchester United. He was a popular manager, much loved for his amiable manner and his big smile. He was famous for his bandy legs and was often mistaken for the jockey Joe Mercer.

In 1942 he married Norah Fanny, daughter of Albert Edward Dyson, provision merchant. They had one son. Mercer died 9 August 1990 in Manchester.

[*Independent*, 11 August 1990; Joe Mercer, *The Great Ones*, 1964; Eric Thornton, *Manchester City*, 1969; Andrew Ward, *The Manchester City Story*, 1984.]

ANNE PIMLOTT BAKER

published 1996

MILNE Alan Alexander

(1882–1956)

Author, was born 18 January 1882 at Henley House in Kilburn. He was the youngest of a family of three sons, a fact which seems to have suggested to him as he grew up the romantic approach to life of a fairy-tale. His father, John Vine Milne, a Scotsman of Aberdonian descent, had married, at Buxton, Sarah Maria, daughter of Peter Heginbotham, a manufacturer. Both parents at the time conducted private schools. While the mother is remembered chiefly as an embodiment of all the domestic virtues, his father was an educational enthusiast, hero and mentor to his sons. H. G. Wells was for a time a science master at Henley House and remained always a family friend.

A. A. Milne obtained a Westminster scholarship at the age of eleven, an unprecedented achievement, and proceeded to Trinity College, Cambridge, where he disappointed his tutor by accepting the editorship of the *Granta* and preferring journalism to the mathematical tripos, in which he gained a third class (1903). It was not only his ambition to write, but to write exactly as he pleased, and returning to London he became in 1906, after various less successful ventures, assistant editor of *Punch* under (Sir) Owen Seaman. In this capacity he showed a remarkable gift for light and witty dialogue and a sense of dramatic form, which soon attracted the attention and admiration of a large circle of readers.

The war interrupted his literary career. He served as a signalling officer in the Royal Warwickshire Regiment in England and overseas, but he was able in 1917 to stage his first fantasy, *Wurzel-Flummery*, which was followed in 1920 by the far more considerable comedy, *Mr. Pim Passes By*.

Leaving the staff of *Punch* in 1919, Milne thereafter devoted the greater part of his time to stage comedy. Clearly the success of Sir J. M. Barrie was a guiding influence: the paradoxical situation, the mingling of much laughter with a little pathos, and, if need be, the fairy wand. But Milne had a fancy and a style which were all his own, and if his dream world was not so wistful as Barrie's, it was whimsical enough and his characters could sustain ingenious and airy conversations which never failed to amuse.

His first successes were followed by a long series of plays in which the attempt to create genuine characters became more marked. The most notable of these were *The Truth About Blayds* (1921), the story of a poetical imposter, which provided an excellent part, as the unmarried daughter, for (Dame) Irene Vanbrugh; *The Dover Road* (1922), a light-hearted homily on divorce, in which Henry Ainley appeared; and *The Great Broxopp* (1923), in which the role of a romantic advertising agent was assumed by Edmund Gwenn. Later came *To Have the Honour* (1924); *The Fourth Wall* (1928), a cleverly contrived murder mystery; *Michael and Mary* (1930); and *Other People's Lives* (1932). *Toad of Toad Hall*, his dramatization of *The Wind in the Willows* by Kenneth Grahame, was first staged in 1929.

Milne also wrote *The Red House Mystery*, a detective story (1922); two novels: *Two People* (1931) and *Chloe Marr* (1946); and many essays in various moods, some of them an expression of his serious views on world politics and peace. But he had found a new and wider public as early as 1924 when he published *When We Were Very Young*, a series of verses for children dedicated to his son, Christopher Robin, who was born in 1920. *Now We Are Six* followed in 1927. In the same genre, but in prose, he produced *Winnie-the-Pooh* (1926) and *The House at Pooh Corner* (1928), which bring to life the unforgettable character of a child's nursery toys, a thought suggested to him by his wife. On both sides of the Atlantic and in other languages, including Japanese and Bulgarian, these enchanting stories with their attractive illustrations by E. H. Shepard acquired a popularity which seemed almost likely to rival an earlier Wonderland.

Milne married in 1913 Dorothy (Daphne), daughter of Martin de Sélincourt, a City merchant. He died at his home at Hartfield, Sussex, 31 January 1956. The National Portrait Gallery has a drawing by Powys Evans.

[*The Times*, 1 February 1956; A. A. Milne, *It's Too Late Now*, 1939; private information; personal knowledge.]

E. V. Knox

published 1971

MITFORD Nancy Freeman-

(1904–1973)

Novelist and biographer, was born at 1 Graham Street (now Terrace), Chelsea, 28 November 1904, the eldest child in the family of six daughters and one son of David Bertram Ogilvy Freeman-Mitford, the second Baron Redesdale, and his wife, Sydney, daughter of Thomas Gibson Bowles, MP. In different ways her grandfathers were remarkable men: the first Baron Redesdale being a diplomat, oriental traveller (author of *Tales of Old Japan*, 1871), horticulturist, and intimate friend of King Edward VII, whereas Gibson Bowles, the creator of *Vanity Fair*, was a brilliant *enfant terrible* backbencher. Through her Redesdale grandmother, Lady Clementine Ogilvy, Nancy had the blood of the Stanleys in her veins. She was to edit two volumes of their correspondence, *The Ladies of Alderley* (1938), of whom one was her great-grandmother, and *The Stanleys of Alderley* (1939). She was also directly descended from William Mitford the historian. With these antecedents it is hardly surprising that, in spite of a conventional upbringing, the six sisters and one brother Thomas David (killed in action in Burma, 1945), all endowed with striking good looks and gifts, have emerged in different degrees of fame and notoriety as a legendary family.

After her father succeeded to the Redesdale title and estates in 1916 Nancy Mitford's childhood was spent in the Cotswolds—at Batsford Park (sold in 1919), Asthall Manor (sold 1927), and Swinbrook Manor, a rather cumbersome house designed by her father. Her education was sketchy. Her father would not hear of her being sent to an ordinary boarding-school, deeming education of his daughters quite unnecessary, if not reprehensible. All her life Nancy Mitford deplored her lack of academic education, which she held against her parents. Yet she became an early and avid reader of biographies, memoirs, and letters which she found in the library her father had inherited but never himself looked at. For he was, in spite of natural intelligence and humour, a professed low-brow, whom

Nancy Mitford caricatured mercilessly but affectionately as the blustering 'Uncle Matthew' of her novels. Indeed he was the source of most of her family jokes.

After a short spell at a finishing school at Hatherop Castle, Gloucestershire, and then as an art student at the Slade School under Henry Tonks (where she did not excel) she was sent, heavily chaperoned, to Paris. The French way of life immediately captivated her. After a first taste she was obliged to return to England in order to 'come out'. For three seasons she flung herself into London balls and country house parties where she was extremely popular. She soon met a group of Bohemian contemporaries —Evelyn Waugh, Robert Byron, Brian Howard, Mark Ogilvie-Grant, John Sutro, Christopher Sykes, and (Sir) Harold Acton, to name a few. They were fascinated by her intelligence, vivacity, wit, and beauty. On the fringe of these clever, sophisticated, provocative, and bright young people was James Alexander (Hamish) St Clair-Erskine, a beguiling younger son of Lord Rosslyn, but improvident, impecunious, and five years her junior. For five unsatisfactory years they were engaged.

Not until she was twenty-four was Nancy Mitford able to break away from her family. In 1928 she took a room in the London flat of Evelyn Waugh and his first wife (Evelyn Gardner), then a close friend. But when the Waughs' marriage collapsed Nancy's sympathies were transferred to the 'he-Evelyn'. She soon took to writing, precariously supporting herself by articles for *Vogue* and *Harper's Magazine*. In 1931 her first novel, *Highland Fling*, was published. *Christmas Pudding* (1932), in which Hamish Erskine and (Sir) John Betjeman were thinly disguised, and *Wigs on the Green* (1935) followed.

In 1933 she married Peter Murray Rennell Rodd (died 1968), a younger son of the first Baron Rennell; he was handsome and intelligent, with a certain panache. But he was impecunious, with no regular job. Moreover he was from the start unfaithful and neglectful. The marriage was not happy although his wife would never brook any criticism of him by her friends. When she could no longer tolerate his escapades she left him and at his request agreed to a divorce in 1958. There were no children. In 1939 she followed him to Perpignan where he was working in a camp for Spanish refugee victims of Franco's regime. The experience made her violently anti-fascist and turned her into a socialist.

On the outbreak of war in 1939 she became an ARP driver. Then once again she worked for evacuees, this time from Nazi-invaded countries. In 1940 her fourth novel, *Pigeon Pie*, a skit about the phoney war, was published. In March 1942 she became employed as an assistant in Heywood Hill's Curzon Street Bookshop. She helped make this shop into a favourite wartime rendezvous of intellectuals who were drawn by her astonishing knowledge of the books she sold, her cheerfulness and vaunted enjoyment of the war. On her retirement in 1946 she was made a partner of the firm.

Almost overnight her state of poverty and insecurity was turned to affluence by the publication of her fifth novel, *The Pursuit of Love* (1945). It was a wild success and sold over a million copies. The theme was a consequence and the reflection of the most important crisis of her life, namely her meeting and falling deeply in love with Gaston Palewski, a member of the Free French forces, a gallant and cultivated follower of General de Gaulle, who was to become one of his closest advisers and future ministers. The 'Colonel', as he was known to her friends, aroused in Nancy a latent capacity for hero-worship and a total dedication to France and all things French. Henceforth the 'Colonel' was transmuted into the idealized characters of her future books, whether the Duc de Sauveterre in *The Pursuit of Love*, or Louis XV in *Madame de Pompadour* (1954). When the war was over Nancy went straight to Paris. In 1947 she rented the ground floor of an old 'hotel' in the rue Monsieur where she lived with her faithful maid, Marie, until obliged to move to a house in the rue d'Artois, Versailles, in 1967.

Until she was forty Nancy Mitford was not a public figure. Her excitement and pleasure in her sudden popularity and comparative riches were endearing. With *Love in a Cold Climate* (1949) and *The Blessing* (1951), the most accomplished of her novels having for theme fashionable French society, she had changed from amateur to professional status. Her writing was now compact, terse, and simple. Her plots were subtle, satirical, and humorous. In Parisian circles she was in great demand because of her renown, elegance (beautiful clothes from Dior), sparkling wit, and mischievous fun. Yet for all her extolling of France and the French and her disparagement (occasionally tiresome) of England and the English, her most intimate friends were her own countrymen.

In the 1950s she turned to biography, of which *Madame de Pompadour* was her first and most lively. She was an industrious researcher who soaked herself in the court life of Louis XV's reign. In spite of an air of self-confidence she went in much anxiety and fear of reviewers. However, their reception of the book was generally rapturous. It was followed by *Voltaire in Love* (1957), the profusely illustrated *The Sun King* (1966), a life of Louis XIV on whom and whose satellites she also became a specialist, and *Frederick the Great* (1970), whose battles she revelled in. During her biographical phase she wrote one more novel, *Don't Tell Alfred* (1960), a story centred on the British embassy, which she frequented during the ambassadorships of her friends the Duff Coopers and Gladwyn Jebbs.

Her one attempt at drama was a translation of André Roussin's farce,

The Little Hut. In 1950 it appeared in the provinces and London where it was highly acclaimed. Her contribution, more serious than comical, to *Noblesse Oblige* (1956) on correct upper-class usage of words brought her prominently into the limelight as arbiter of social conduct. Of all her books *The Water Beetle* (1962), a collection of fourteen short essays, perhaps shows her to greatest advantage as a writer. In these succinct, perceptive, evocative, and extremely funny stories and anecdotes she shared her private jokes and prejudices with her readers. They are the nearest approach to the as yet unpublished correspondence with her family and friends. She took her writing extremely seriously and mastered an unmistakably individual style, which at first was marred by too frequent lapses into the exclusive jargon of her class and generation. For she was essentially a child of the twenties. Yet with all her sophistication she remained fastidious, abstemious, and seemingly spinsterish. She was a marvellous guest, staying for weeks on end with friends, whom she entertained during the intervals of her reading and writing.

She was much photographed by (Sir) Cecil Beaton. She was painted as a young woman by William Acton and in middle age by Mogens Tvede (1947), seated at her writing-table in the rue Monsieur. She was slim and vivacious. She had dark brown hair and delicately moulded features. Her dancing blue-green eyes and downward-sloping brows were vibrantly expressive of her moods which alternated from insatiable curiosity to mockery and merriment.

In January 1969 she was stricken with agonizing pains which persisted, with intermittent periods of relief, until her death 30 June 1973 at no. 4 rue d'Artois, Versailles. She bore these cruel sufferings with almost superhuman courage and cheerfulness. In 1972 she was awarded the Légion d'Honneur, which gave her inordinate pleasure, and appointed CBE, of which she remarked, 'I've never heard of the CBE but of course I'm delighted to have it . . . I hear it ranks above a knight's widow, oh, good.'

[Harold Acton, *Nancy Mitford, a Memoir*, 1975; Selina Hastings, *Nancy Mitford*, 1985; private information; personal knowledge.]

James Lees-Milne

published 1986

MONTGOMERY Bernard Law

(1887–1976)

First Viscount Montgomery of Alamein

Field marshal, was born in St. Mark's vicarage, Kennington Oval, 17 November 1887, the third of the six sons and fourth of the nine children of the Revd Henry Hutchinson Montgomery, son of Sir Robert Montgomery, lieutenant-governor of the Punjab, and his wife, Maud, third daughter of Canon (later Dean) Frederic William Farrar, author of *Eric, or Little by Little* (1858). Their family was to grow up in Tasmania where Henry Montgomery became bishop in 1889.

A self-willed larrikin of fourteen, at odds with a mother as determined as he was, Bernard went with a brother as a day-boy to St Paul's School, when the Montgomerys finally returned from Hobart in 1902, to live frugally in Chiswick; but high-spirited family holidays—there were eight children by now (a daughter died young and a son later died as a schoolboy)—were spent at New Park, the property at Moville, Donegal, which the bishop had inherited from his father.

Good at games and eager to lead, Bernard was 'very happy' at St Paul's and at nineteen (and 5 ft. 7 ins.) 'the Monkey' eventually managed to pass, not very impressively (seventy-second out of 177), into Sandhurst. Lucky to be allowed to continue there after a cruel jape, he failed to pass out high enough (he was thirty-sixth) to make the coveted Indian Army; instead, he was commissioned, 19 September 1908, into the Royal Warwickshire Regiment with which he had no previous connection. Entirely dependent upon his pay and never having tasted alcohol, he was posted in December to the 1st battalion, then on the North-West Frontier at Peshawar. He rode hard at everything, his chosen profession and the study of Urdu and Pushtu. He always wanted to win, whether an argument or a steeplechase. Wilful and opinionated, he was continually straining at the leash.

Returning to England by 1913 in time to play hockey for the army and to pass out top of the musketry course at Hythe, Lieutenant B. L. Montgomery was acting adjutant when the 1st Warwickshire Regiment was mobilized at Shorncliffe in August 1914, and he crossed to Boulogne 23 August with the 10th brigade in the 4th division. Scarcely twenty-four hours after disembarkation they were under fire at Le Cateau. A notably fearless young officer, Montgomery was reported missing, gravely wounded and left for dead at Meteren, but survived in hospital at Woolwich to learn that he had been appointed, 13 October 1914, as a temporary captain of twenty-seven, to the DSO—the Military Cross was not instituted until December—for his bearing at the first battle of Ypres.

There followed early in the New Year a formative posting to Lancashire as brigade-major, 112th (later 104th) brigade, which enabled him not only to survive (which his return to a battalion would have rendered most improbable) but to begin to take on responsibilities and to uncover that flair for training which characterized his whole career. He pierced impatiently into the heart of matters to discover the most straightforward tactical solution to be used by the new armies which Lord Kitchener was raising to succeed the original British Expeditionary Force. Montgomery's written orders tingled with clarity; he was becoming highly professional.

His dedication soon inspired trust; he was brigade-major, 104th brigade on the Somme, January 1916; GSO 2, 33rd division (at Arras again), 1917; then, from July 1917, GSO 2 of IX Corps at Passchendaele; thereafter, from 16 July 1918, until the war ended, GSO 1, 47th (London) division. Then, at Cologne, with the connivance of Sir William Robertson, he contrived to get himself selected for the Staff College at Camberley for January 1920. A brevet-major (3 June 1918), he had been mentioned in dispatches six times, wounded thrice, and awarded the French croix de guerre.

He came to ponder his experiences deeply only after he had left Camberley. In 1921 he was posted to Cork as brigade-major, 17th (the largest) Infantry brigade, in a war to him 'far worse' than the one he had survived. During the next few years in England, under sympathetic leadership, he became determined that costly mistakes should not be perpetrated again: there should be no more 'useless' carnage under remote generals and their cosy staffs; future battles were to be fought with decent economy and orchestrated artillery—metal saving flesh. Hence it was important to have accurate information, good communication and wireless, and the use of aircraft; there was also a need for sound understanding between effectively trained officers and an informed soldiery. All these considerations underlined the importance of training to which Montgomery now devoted his single-minded bachelor career. He was brigade-major, 8th Infantry brigade at Devonport, then GSO 2, 49th West Riding Territorial division at York where he lived in the same friendly mess as (Sir) F. W. de Guingand, his future chief of staff. In March 1925 he went back to his regiment at Shorncliffe, but the turning point, Montgomery himself believed, was his posting in January 1926 to the Staff College, this time as an instructor, alongside Alan Brooke (later Viscount Alanbrooke), (Sir) Bernard Paget, and (Sir) Richard O'Connor. Their pupils included Harold Alexander (later Earl Alexander of Tunis), (Sir) Miles Dempsey, (Sir) Oliver Leese, (Sir) Richard McCreery, (Sir) Archibald Nye, Brian Robertson (later Lord Robertson of Oakridge), (Sir) Gerald Templer, and A. F. ('John') Harding (later Lord

Harding of Petherton). Montgomery was an inspired teacher, unforgettably clear-headed.

To everybody's surprise he married, 27 July 1927, Elizabeth, widow of Captain Oswald Armitage Carver, a sapper officer killed at Gallipoli, the sister of P. B. S. Hobart, and the daughter of Robert Thompson Hobart, Indian Civil Service, of Tunbridge Wells. She had two sons at preparatory school. They had met on successive skiing holidays in Switzerland. The marriage, which opened new horizons to the monastic, dogmatic soldier, was intensely happy.

Contentment did not attenuate a marked independence of spirit and not infrequent clashes with authority. Set to revise, as secretary of a War Office committee, the manual of *Infantry Training* in 1929, Montgomery, by his own account, published his personal version ignoring amendments; 'exploitation' was a significant omission. Three years followed while he fulfilled a natural ambition, the command of his own first regiment, in Jerusalem, Alexandria, and Poona. His seniors noted 'a certain high-handedness' as a possible handicap to future advancement.

In 1934 he succeeded Paget as chief instructor at Quetta, where he remained until 1937, experiencing the earthquake in May 1935. Then, at the instigation of A. P. (later Earl) Wavell, he was posted May 1937 to Portsmouth to command 9th brigade. Tragedy struck. After ten enjoyable years of their marriage, 'Betty' Montgomery died of septicaemia (19 October 1937) after an insect bite on the beach at Burnham-on-Sea. Montgomery, left a widower with a young son, was utterly desolate. He hid himself in the army and was never the same man again: he had lost his firm base.

Lonely wilfulness could land him in trouble. War Department land at Southsea was let without reference to authority for an August fairground, the rent being spent on garrison amenities. The solitary brigadier found himself for a while 'dicky on the perch', but Wavell (at Southern Command) was never a man to waste eccentric talent, and a successful career was resumed in October 1938 with Montgomery's promotion to Palestine to command the 8th Infantry division from Haifa. O'Connor's 7th division was stationed to his south. Their grip was soon felt: terrorism was dealt with rigorously and the civilian administration regained confidence. By now evidently a most promising major-general, Montgomery was told that, should war break out in Europe, he might expect to command the 3rd division in the proposed expeditionary force. At this moment he was suddenly struck by a feverish illness affecting the lung which had been penetrated in 1914. Taken on board at Port Said on a stretcher, he forced himself to walk confidently ashore at Tilbury and proceeded to badger the military secretary until on 28 August 1939 he received the command he had been promised.

With Brooke, his Corps commander in II Corps, and with Alexander, he was one of the few to emerge from the inglorious campaign in Belgium with an enhanced reputation. However, before the fighting began Brooke had to protect him—not for the last time—from the consequences of acting off his own bat. In this instance, he had issued a tactless ordinance about brothels, which had started an outcry.

Highly trained and diligently rehearsed, Montgomery's 'Third Division worked like clockwork', the Corps commander noted, from the Dyle and Louvain back to Dunkirk where he and Alexander were responsible for the rearguard. Montgomery was appointed CB (1940).

The 3rd division was the first to be re-equipped in England but in July 1940 Montgomery left it to succeed Sir Claude Auchinleck (promoted to Southern Command) as commander, V Corps. Cheerfully disobedient, he held that the way to repel the expected invasion was not on the beaches but by counter-attack after the enemy had landed; yet the army still lacked mobility and he himself had had to beg the prime minister at Brighton that summer for buses for his own division. Brooke, the only soldier Montgomery genuinely respected, and who was to become his surrogate conscience, besought him (3 August 1940) not to let him down 'by doing anything silly'.

In April, having lost all his worldly goods in an enemy bombing raid on Portsmouth in January, Montgomery moved from V Corps to XII Corps, and thence to command South-Eastern Army (17 November 1941). It was from this spell in England that, by his own reckoning, his 'real influence on the training of the army began' and with it the growth of the legend (which reached the Middle East) of the abstemious, dedicated widower, the ruthless oddity who made physical fitness a fetish and declared war on 'dead wood', wives, and complacency. Once the threat of invasion abated (and Montgomery spotted this sooner than most) the army in England had to be made ready for aggressive warfare in all weathers overseas, and this he set about achieving in a series of formidable exercises.

In mid-1942 planning for a Canadian raid on Dieppe was put in train and Montgomery was involved (although in later years he was inclined to be reticent on this score). He felt that since secrecy had been forfeited, another venue should be sought. The raid took place on 19 August 1942; Montgomery had left the United Kingdom nine days earlier.

He had been told to be ready to succeed Alexander (who had been sent to Cairo to succeed Auchinleck as C-in-C Middle East) in command of First Army, which was to invade French North Africa (Operation Torch) under General Eisenhower's overall command. Then, when W. H. E. Gott was killed, Montgomery was dispatched to take his place at El Alamein, in command of Eighth Army. Placing his son David in the care of his friends the Reynolds, he reached Cairo on 12 August. He knew in his bones that he was stepping into history.

Disregarding instructions, he took over in the Western Desert two days early and at once set about imposing his strong will. He was unprepossessing in appearance, skinny, sharp-faced 'like a Parson Jack Russell terrier', and his English knees were still white, but he knew exactly what he wanted: an abrupt change of 'atmosphere', the end of 'bellyaching' (the discussion of orders rather than their execution) and of looking over one's shoulder. There was to be no withdrawal. Eighth Army would fight and die at the Alamein position where the enemy had been halted by Auchinleck's resolution in July. De Guingand was promoted from brigadier general staff to chief of staff, to free the army commander from detail. New corps commanders and a new brigadier Royal Artillery were summoned from England, the 44th division was ordered up imperiously from the delta, and the army headquarters was set down by the sea alongside the desert air force. The armour was rehearsed in its defensive role, dug in or hull down.

Montgomery quickly imposed his personal authority as he quickened the pulse of his new command. In a crisis of confidence among men far from home he provided reassurance and certainty. His army (or enough of it) soon became convinced, as they saw him darting about in unexpected headgear, that, despite his sartorial eccentricity, he knew what he was up to, talked sense (in an odd but readily quotable vocabulary), would deliver the goods, and, above all, not waste their lives. It was a new and exciting technique of command. The model defensive battle (from 31 August) at Alam Halfa, in which the air force played a substantial role, furnished Montgomery with the mastery and Eighth Army with the morale demanded in the major offensive battle to follow. Although he himself came to exaggerate the uniqueness and novelty of his own contribution and to maintain that everything went according to preconceived plan, the unfamiliar sight of Rommel's forces on their way back (3 September) through the minefields they had penetrated with such difficulty heartened Eighth Army enormously and hardened belief in 'Monty' and his self-assurance.

There was political pressure on him to resume battle, partly because the Martuba airfields in the North African bulge had to be regained by mid-November to allow for air cover for the last convoy leaving Alexandria to replenish Malta's almost exhausted aviation fuel, and partly because the departure of 'Torch' in early November would have been hazarded had news reached England of any apathy. With Alexander's imperturbable backing, Montgomery took his own time to mount his offensive. He had to learn to master the new American Sherman tanks and anti-tank guns, to improve the training (especially in dealing with minefields), and to institute deception measures for what was inevitably frontal attack on the strong enemy defences at El Alamein between the sea and the virtually impassable Qattara depression. These requirements, together with the state of the moon and of the Eighth Army's readiness, set the date for 23 October. By then, of course, the enemy defences were deeper and stronger.

His design (Operation Lightfoot) was to feint in the south whilst cutting corridors through the northern Axis positions in a moonlit operation with massed artillery support, to hold off the German armour during the 'crumbling' operations which would ensue, and in this 'dogfight', lasting perhaps twelve days, to hold the initiative so as to deprive the enemy armour of firm bases from which to manoeuvre or within which to refurbish.

By 23 October the desert air force had conclusively won the air battle and thereafter successfully devoted its full attention to the close support of the land forces, which had already been so effective at Alam Halfa. By 25 October Eighth Army had gained a bridgehead in the northern Axis positions, which was slowly developed into a salient increasingly menacing the coastal road. With controlled flexibility Montgomery alternated the direction of his thrusts—until, fearful of his ultimate line of advance, the main German forces were congregated, not without severe losses, in the northern sector about Sidi Abd al Rahman. Maintaining his apparent thrust line, Montgomery, who, by shrewd regrouping since 26 October had been accumulating reserves as steadily as the returning Rommel had been forced to commit his, early on 2 November cut through south of the main German concentrations into the preponderantly Italian positions (Operation Supercharge). A quickly improvised Axis anti-tank screen prevented immediate breakthrough but on 4 November this was forced back and the overextended Axis defences crumpled. Those with vehicles could attempt retreat; for the rest, mainly Italian, surrender was the only option. Eighth Army's casualties were 13,500.

It was a considerable victory. With air supremacy and, on the ground, unparalleled numerical superiority in armour and artillery, Montgomery could call on resources denied to his predecessors. But he used them (and a remarkable flow of intelligence) in a unique revelation of determination and skill to enforce the attrition. It was 'a killing match'.

He could be criticized—there were willing critics of, for example, the way he used his armour and the cumbersome arrangements of corps commands with which he began. This was strange indeed in a general who made tidiness a shibboleth. Yet Montgomery retained throughout those twelve days in that chaotic man-made dust storm a clinical control of the mine-filled battlefield, a serenity and balance in his own deployments, and, above all, an intense unswerving determination which dominated the situation and compelled both his own troops and their adversary to submit to his unremitting will. By insisting when it was all over that it had all gone according to plan, he did not do justice (a curious sacrifice) to his own generalship, his trained skill, and his power to improvise in an emergency.

A compulsive student of the military art, he could pierce with fierce concentration into the essence of a battlefield. This talent for simplification could be pressed to excess, as the nuances or rougher edges became subsumed in an overriding certainty. Personal vanity nourished in him a deliberate (and infectious) self-assurance. Within a self-compelled taut serenity lay genuine physical bravery: he made himself ignore danger. There was always too a didactic note: lessons must be drawn from all that was happening. To this educational concern was added a capacity to inspire, an unexpectedly Messianic quality. He had the gift of seeing into the hearts of men, of sensing what was worrying them; they must be convinced (despite a spinsterly voice) that what he and they were going to do together was the best recipe, and it must be readily, memorably explicable. Therefore every battle must be seen to go according to plan, in order to persuade and inspire men to undertake it and sustain their morale for future campaigns.

A caustic critic of others, he was far too intelligent not to know that matters do not go according to plan, but he was often too vain to admit this publicly, too much wrapped up in what he was doing to unravel the problems fully afterwards. In convincing others (or some of them), he came to convince himself too.

He became a full general and was appointed KCB (11 November 1942). The tight control of the battlefield was momentarily relaxed. Montgomery would argue that the sluggish pursuit was ensuring that the Rommel bogey laid at Alamein should never return—to disturb the assiduously nourished morale which had made the victory possible. Eighth Army did not think itself as slow as the outside world found it: it throve on carefully planned success, the build-up which avoided the unnecessary casualty, the assured maintenance before the next hammer-blow by orchestrated artillery, air, infantry, and armour. The brilliant improvisation which cut off the retreating Italians at Beda Fomm in February 1941 was not in Montgomery's repertoire: he wanted Rommel finally expelled from El Agheila, his original springboard. In the event he was unable to cut Rommel off at Benghazi, El Agheila, or Buerat. He personally superintended from his

'Tac HQ' the drive on Tripoli (Eighth Army's perennial target) which he reached on 23 January 1943 because storms in Benghazi had made his maintenance more tenuous than he liked. On the way he prepared a training pamphlet on *High Command in War* which could scarcely have enhanced his popularity outside Eighth Army; neither did the 'teach-in' in Tripoli and the parades there for Churchill's benefit.

Knowing that Rommel, having savaged the Americans at Kasserine in mid-February, would turn on Eighth Army before it was fully ready to tackle the Mareth Line, Montgomery hastened up his tanks by transporter and gave himself time to arrange his anti-tank guns for another model defensive battle at Medenine (6 March). At Mareth an uncharacteristic attack on the coastal flank was repulsed (20 March), but Montgomery cut his losses, swiftly reinforced his attacking forces on his left, and forced the Axis switch-line (27 March) west of the hills before El Hamma. The Akarit position remained to be stormed (6–7 April). A day or so later Eighth Army's armoured cars made contact with tanks of US II Corps on the Gabes–Gafsa road, and Eighth Army's private war was over.

When he arrived in Sfax (10 April 1943) Montgomery tactlessly insisted that as payment of a bet made in Tripoli with General Walter Bedell Smith, Eisenhower's chief of staff, he should receive a Flying Fortress aircraft with its American crew, for his personal use: an early sign that he was to be a difficult ally to work with. Despite his quite remarkable understanding of his own soldiers and his staff, he made no attempt to comprehend American sensibilities.

He was now anxious for the speedy termination of the North African campaign to release his troops and staff to prepare for the invasion of Sicily. He overestimated the ease of the problem and was rebuffed at Enfidaville: even Eighth Army could not move mountains; but he swiftly recognized that, by switching some of his troops and commanders to First Army, Tunis might rapidly be captured.

Meanwhile he had emphatically rejected the plans proposed for the capture of Sicily, and insisted that his army and the Americans (under General George S. Patton) should invade the south-east corner, side by side, a proposal eventually adopted although not without argument and friction. He became increasingly offhand with Alexander, his old pupil, whose headquarters was to co-ordinate the invasion, and, although in the event the campaign took only thirty-eight days, his selfishness in insisting upon Eighth Army's priorities led to further wrangling. But, as at Enfidaville, he could make himself realize better ways of accomplishing military purposes, and to Patton's surprise he deliberately yielded the capture of Messina to him.

Before Sicily was invaded (10 July 1943) he had taken some leave in London where he found himself a popular hero, an enjoyable discovery which made him less and less amenable to subordination or advice. He had come to regard himself as the greatest fighting commander alive. He was ready to lay down the military law and he had no hesitation in criticizing anyone. His hold on his soldiers remained secure and he took great trouble about them, but senior officers of other services and nations became increasingly critical of his unbridled self-importance.

He was thus disconcerted to learn at Taormina in August that in the invasion of Italy his was to be a minor role, since Eisenhower planned to employ forces at Salerno under General Mark Clark quite separately from Eighth Army, which was allocated the secondary task of getting across the straits of Messina and then switching from Reggio to the heel of Italy, to secure the Foggia airfields and the ports of Taranto and Brindisi. The task was over-elaborately performed (3 September 1943) and did little to take pressure off the Allied forces at Salerno.

When it became evident that the Germans (with more than twenty divisions) proposed to hold a line as far south in Italy as they were able, Montgomery was faced with a slow slog up the Adriatic coast until checked at the end of 1943, after an expensive battle, at the Sangro. From the start he was highly critical of the campaign: no master plan; no operational grip; and administratively, 'a dog's breakfast'.

He was therefore overjoyed at Christmas in Vasto to be posted to England to command 21st Army Group in the cross-Channel invasion of France.

As with the Sicilian campaign, his decisive contribution to the Normandy invasion was his insistence upon the invasion plan he himself had proposed. On his way back to the United Kingdom Churchill at Marrakesh showed him the draft plans, which Montgomery sulkily criticized. He was authorized by Eisenhower, the new supreme commander for Operation Overlord, to undertake the initial role of C-in-C of the ground forces, and he insisted upon a widening of the frontage, an increase in the invading forces, two armies to go in side by side, and the consequent postponement of the proposed D-Day until early June to allow additional landing craft to become available. From the first, the British on the left were to go for Caen and the airfield country beyond, the Americans for the Cotentin peninsula to gain the port of Cherbourg. To decisiveness he added inspiration. Having secured the major decisions he required from the navy and air forces and General Omar Bradley, the American army commander, he set about enthusing not only those who would actually take part in the invasion, the troops on the ground, but also the populace who would sustain them. Detailed planning, once the major decisions had been agreed (in a surprisingly short time considering their importance), was left to the staff to get on with: they were more grateful for what they inherited than Montgomery would show himself to be. Instead, he occupied himself in an astonishing revivalist campaign in which he toured the country addressing not only troops but railwaymen, dockers, factory workers, and the City. Since the darker days of 1940 there can scarcely have been a more enthusiastically united nation as the weeks before D-Day lessened: people came to believe that the invasion would happen, and were convinced of victory at last. The whistle-stop tour was interrupted for Montgomery to give a quite remarkable exposition of his assault plans on 15 May at St Paul's School, Hammersmith (his temporary headquarters before moving close to Portsmouth to be ready for D-Day) to a spellbound senior audience which included the King, the prime minister, J. C. Smuts, Sir Alan Brooke, and Eisenhower, the supreme commander.

With complete air supremacy, the landings of 6 June, though fiercely opposed, were very successful and a firm bridgehead was established fairly rapidly. The danger was stalemate, and Montgomery, whilst the deception plan was still holding enemy reinforcements in the Pas de Calais, managed to sustain the initiative in Normandy by forcing Rommel to commit more and more of his Panzer divisions to plugging holes against expensive British thrusts in the Caen sector until such time as the Americans, having secured Cherbourg, could turn south, then wheel to drive the enemy against the Seine. He was criticized for the slowness of his progress by an impatient supreme commander awaiting more rapid results, by the air marshals anxious to secure their promised airfields, and by the prime minister and the press, especially the American press. From the serenity of his 'Tac HQ' at Creuilly, or later at Bray, with his young liaison officers keeping him well informed of the battlefield (as Ultra did of his enemy), Montgomery's confidence never wavered and he carried with him that of his troops. He was supported by the sturdy loyalty of Dempsey at British Second Army and Bradley at American First Army who both well understood his overall purpose and saw him daily. It was an anxious period, more anxious the further removed one was from Normandy, and there were cries for Montgomery's head. The American break out which he had patiently awaited eventually started on 25 July, the British and Canadian forces having successfully tied down enough of the German Panzers on the further flank; Montgomery's balanced arrangements paid off when, through Hitler's intervention, the enemy launched a desperate counter-offensive on 7 August at Mortain directed towards the coast at Avranches, to cut the Americans in two. But Bradley kept his nerve: the American right was ordered to wheel north whilst the Canadians thrust south to create 'the Falaise pocket'. Fighting was intense and casualties very heavy indeed, and though the enemy left many dead, many escaped to cross the Seine to fight again. However, Montgomery's determination and sustained initiative, together with the punishment meted out by the air forces, resulted in Allied victory and German losses of 400,000—half of them prisoners.

It had always been the intention as Montgomery himself well knew, that around 1 September, once Eisenhower's headquarters were established in France and there were two Army Groups each of two armies under his overall command, the supreme commander would assume direct control of the ground forces himself. Montgomery however was so sure that he had the military answer, just proven by substantial success, that in his heart of hearts he never genuinely accepted the simple political fact: had the Americans considered him the best available commander of ground forces (they did not), it was still impossible, once the restricting emergencies of Normandy had been successfully surmounted, for a British general, however distinguished, to continue in overall command when, through manpower shortages, the British contribution—at first roughly equal—was shrinking and the American effort becoming daily more preponderant.

Normandy was followed by an unseemly period of patronizing, querulous, and insubordinate disagreement about how the campaign should develop and whose ideas should prevail, until eventually a long-suffering Eisenhower was girding himself to demand Montgomery's dismissal when de Guingand intervened and prevailed upon the supreme commander to hold his hand and Montgomery his tongue.

Meanwhile Montgomery had become a field marshal (30 August 1944) and 21st Army Group had reached Brussels and Antwerp. He wanted the Allied advance to be concentrated in a powerful thrust of some forty divisions (which he hoped to command) north-east to cut off the Ruhr. Eisenhower however preferred to advance to the Rhine on a broader front and refused to give Montgomery priority in fuel supply by rationing American advances further south.

As the Allied front broadened, so distance widened the difference of opinion. Whereas it appeared to Montgomery's staff that the first priority was to get the Schelde river open to nourish further advances (especially after the uncovenanted capture of Antwerp on 4 September), Montgomery himself persuaded Eisenhower that this might be delayed (or conducted *pari passu*) whilst an operation was mounted to advance into Germany by vaulting the great Dutch rivers with airborne troops. Eisenhower released his strategic reserve to Montgomery. The subsequent operation (Arnhem, 17 September) was neither well planned nor well conducted. Communications were erratic, the intelligence was untuned, and Montgomery paid the penalty for acting impulsively and out of character in the first and only defeat of his military career. He hoped (it may be supposed) that had he succeeded, the whole Allied *Schwerpunkt* would be dragged north-east, but in his desire to have his own way, the war over, and the sites of the missiles assailing London cut off from their supply, he underestimated both the extent of German recovery and the marked reluctance of American generals to return under his governance. Defeat at Arnhem cost him his bargaining arm and thereafter the northern flank ceased to figure importantly in SHAEF's priorities.

Montgomery bounced back into the forefront when, on 16 December 1944, a surprise German offensive in the Ardennes drove a wedge between the strung-out American divisions. He was called upon to command those north of the new German salient. He rose to the opportunity, and sorted out the front with his former clarity and verve, but the manner of his coming (as if 'to cleanse the temple') and the cocksureness of his subsequent press conference (7 January) left much bitterness, and once the campaign was successfully resumed he was kept increasingly out on a limb. American speed in crossing the Rhine at Remagen (First Army) and Oppenheim (Third Army) was in sharp contrast to the deliberation with which Montgomery prepared to cross at Wesel. Having forfeited his infallibility at Arnhem, he reverted to his proven ways, overinsurance which might lose pace but made for certainty.

The argument about having a ground forces commander (as distinct from Eisenhower's direct command from SHAEF in Versailles) was inextricably entangled with the personality—and nationality—of Montgomery himself. Montgomery even volunteered, how genuinely it is difficult to guess, to serve under Bradley. But this was difficult to envisage, and Churchill's clumsy intervention was too late in the day to bring back Alexander from Italy in the role Montgomery himself objected to. The dispute spilled over into contention over control of US Ninth Army and whether it should be comprised within Bradley's left or Montgomery's right wing. Montgomery's trouble was that he could not achieve his aims without considerable American support; his own forces were by now inadequate for a 'master plan' finishing in Berlin. He was not therefore brought back into the middle of matters but left with the limited role of closing off the entrances to Scandinavia before the Russians reached them. His troops reached Wismar on 2 May 1945 and two days later the German forces in north-west Germany, Holland, and Denmark were surrendered to him on Lüneberg heath.

All his life Montgomery's methods and personality provoked controversy and animosities. By cutting himself off from SHAEF which he visited but once and maintaining, instead, a running correspondence with the War Office, from his sanctuary in 'Tac HQ', he was encouraged by the chief of the imperial general staff and P. J. Grigg, the secretary of state, in an anti-American bias which hindered his getting on with the job. His was not the only way to win the war, and he paid all too little recognition to American resourcefulness, Bradley's dour professionalism, or Patton's outstanding talent for exploitation.

Montgomery—perhaps uniquely—knew how to handle large amounts of military equipment without becoming overwhelmed by them and to inspire large bodies of men (and not just his own fellow countrymen) for military purposes. It was easy to deride his strut, his preoccupation with personal publicity, his two-badged beret, his evangelical messages to his troops; but, whatever one's distaste for 'Montification', he was not 'just a PR general'. He was a very professional soldier, and citizen soldiers at the sharp end felt 'safe' in his hands, a belief their families came to share. It was not just a prolonged stunt: his care for his men was deep-seated. He might rile military clubland by the frankness of his 'ungentlemanly' self-aggrandizement; yet there is not much room for 'nice' men in war. In the dread trade, to which his life was dedicated, of killing considerable numbers of enemy in the most economical way possible, he exhibited a clinical concentration on the essential with morals taking a major share in the calculations. His talents and his behaviour were evidently best fitted to circumscribed command in which he got his own way—he was at his best in the Western Desert commanding Eighth Army in whom he instilled his own especial arrogance, the army of the film *Desert Victory.* As an army group commander, which eventually entailed working loyally alongside allies, he was less well placed. One is tempted to conclude that he had got beyond his ceiling—it was his own view that each officer has his ceiling—yet any account of his command in Normandy would go a long way to challenge that evaluation.

Most awkward to serve alongside, impossible to serve over, he was an excellent man to serve under, especially on his staff. The staff he had mostly inherited from Auchinleck he retained until the war ended. He was indulgent to the young aides-de-camp and liaison officers whom he picked, trusted, and trained.

His sense of fairness and especially of truth were not as other men's. In his convictions he was ruthless, even baleful, yet his insensitively arrogant self-confidence was combined with an indiscreet, mischievous, schoolboyish sense of humour which buoyed up the spirits of those far from home. Above all, he trusted those who worked with him to get on with the job, treating them as experienced professionals. His competence as a general, his economy in the use of his troops, the clarity of his commands, and, quintessentially, his decisiveness made a profound impression. One felt that he would get the war over, so that 'we could all pack up and go home again'. Until that happened, he won ready allegiance.

Montgomery became C-in-C of the British forces of occupation and the British member of the Allied Control Council in Berlin. Having secured what he believed mattered most—the establishment of order, the restoration of communications, the demobilization of the German armed forces, the reopening of the mines, and the sowing of the harvest—he left the fuller implementation to able subordinates: Sir Ronald (later Lord) Weeks and then Brian Robertson in Berlin, and Gerald Templer in the British zone.

In 1945 he was advanced to GCB. Honours were now showered upon him by nations, cities, and universities. He was granted a peerage in the New Year honours of 1946. He took the title Viscount Montgomery of Alamein, of Hindhead, in the county of Surrey. In December 1946 he was installed as a Knight of the Garter. All these were accolades which he enjoyed to the full.

Accounts of his campaigns (ghost-written in the main by 'David' Belchem and issued ostensibly as training manuals for the Rhine Army) were soon published generally: *El Alamein to the River Sangro* (1948) and *Normandy to the Baltic* (1947). Bedell Smith remarked that he now knew that Montgomery's battles had always gone according to plan 'from end to beginning'.

In June 1946 Montgomery, discarding de Guingand like yesterday's shirt, succeeded Alanbrooke ('Brookie'), the only man he recognized as a better soldier, as chief of the imperial general staff. It was a virtually unavoidable succession but the appointment brought out some of his less admirable qualities. He was too set in his ways. He clashed again with Lord Tedder, who was now chief of the air staff: a lack of rapport dating from Alamein. He got on well with C. R. (later Earl) Attlee and Ernest Bevin, and in the War Office itself was soon on nickname terms with Emanuel ('Manny') (later Lord) Shinwell, but he became increasingly at odds with the less convincing A. V. Alexander (later Earl Alexander of Hillsborough) at the Ministry of Defence. After two uncomfortable years for everybody, Montgomery was eased out of Whitehall to become chairman of the Western Union commanders-in-chief, a stop-gap appointment until he became, in March 1951, deputy supreme commander to Eisenhower, commanding the Allied forces of NATO in Europe. He continued to serve as a sort of inspector-general under three other successive supreme commanders until he retired in September 1958. He took the task seriously and, given his limitations, was thought to have performed it well. He had adjusted to the anti-climax with surprising willingness.

The first drafts of his *Memoirs* were in his own clear pencilled handwriting: they were published with too few changes in 1958 and were so much in character that no opinions were altered by them. Publication ended an uneasy friendship with Eisenhower, by then president of the United States. Hackles were also raised in Italy. The book sold well everywhere.

Montgomery lived in active retirement, amidst mementoes and portraits, in a reconstructed mill at Isington on the river Wey near Alton in Hampshire. Tidiness and punctuality were the order of the day. He was a thoughtful and generous host, himself as abstemious as ever. He remained very fit and was to travel widely (though rarely without raising controversy). He wrote in the press about his visits to the USSR (1959), China, and South Africa and published an account of them in *Three Continents* (1962). He was an occasional broadcaster and lecturer and sometimes spoke in the House of Lords, with all his old vigour and habitual reiteration; but he was not well enough to act as pallbearer at Churchill's funeral in 1965. Four years later, however, he performed that office for Field Marshal Alexander and later in the year carried the Sword of State at the opening of Parliament (although in the following year he had to yield it to another). He also had to abandon going to the annual Alamein reunions in London. He used to spend Christmas with the Griggs at the mill and he also enjoyed his seaside arguments with Basil Liddell Hart. His own *History of Warfare* (1968) was mostly by other hands and he recommended his surviving friends to read only those sections he specified as written by himself, but the preface made it clear that his interests were well maintained and was revealing about the commentaries which had impressed him. He continued to be a good correspondent and remained the eager listener he had always been, and he brooded, as he always had, on what he had heard or read. He had come to believe his own legend and to wrap himself in memories which excluded the inconvenient. He died full of years on 25 March 1976 and was succeeded as viscount by his son David Bernard (born 1928). The funeral service was in St. George's chapel, Windsor, and he was buried in a country churchyard at Binstead, Hampshire, a mile from his home.

A statue by Oscar Nemon outside the Ministry of Defence in Whitehall was unveiled by the Queen Mother on 6 June 1980, the anniversary of D-Day.

Montgomery's formidable military skills were best exhibited in the defensive battle, yet it fell to him to mastermind and infuse the two great frontal assaults which heralded the Axis defeats in North Africa and in western Europe, two victories most needed in this country, which forced him, warts and all, into the company of the great captains: the best British field commander, it has been held, since Wellington himself.

[*The Times*, 25 and 26 March 1976; Nigel Hamilton, *Monty, the Making of a General, 1887–1942*, 1981, *Monty, the Master of the Battlefield, 1942–1944*, 1983, and *Monty, the Field Marshal, 1944–1976*, 1986; Ronald Lewin, *Montgomery as Military Commander*, 1971; C. J. C. Malony, *The Mediterranean and the Middle East* (vol. v of the official war history), 1973, pp. 510–13; Michael Howard, *The Causes of Wars*, 1983, pp. 208–23; Corelli Barnett, *The Desert Generals*, 2nd edn., 1983; Max Hastings, *Overlord*, 1984; Stephen Russell F. Weigley, *Eisenhower's Lieutenants*, 1981; Brian Montgomery, *A Field Marshal in the Family*, 1973; Goronwy Rees, *A Bundle of Sensations*, 1960, pp. 113–51; T. E. B. Howarth (ed.), *Monty at Close Quarters*, 1985; private information; personal knowledge.]

E. T. Williams

published 1986

MOORE Henry Spencer

(1898–1986)

Sculptor, was born 30 July 1898 at Castleford, Yorkshire, the youngest of four sons and seventh of eight children of Raymond Spencer Moore, coal-miner, of Castleford, and his wife Mary, daughter of Neville Baker, coal-miner, of Burntwood, Staffordshire. He was educated at Castleford Secondary (later High) School, where his natural talents were immediately recognized by the young art mistress, Alice Gostick.

Moore's father held responsible positions in the colliery, and the family lived on a newly built estate, with the children attending modern, well equipped schools. Raymond Moore was a self-improving man, with a taste for music and literature, and, as was the case with the family of D. H. Lawrence, living not so far away in the Nottinghamshire coalfield, he saw schoolteaching as the way in which his clever children could better themselves and lead a more satisfying and less arduous life than his own. It was expected, therefore, that Henry would become a schoolteacher, like his older brother and his sisters. In 1915, on leaving school, he returned as a student teacher to his old elementary school at Castleford, in order to gain some practical experience before going to teacher training college. Meanwhile, his private ambition was to become a professional sculptor.

With a world war in progress, and compulsory conscription introduced in January 1916, Moore knew that his training was going to be interrupted. Rather than await his call up, he decided in 1917 to volunteer for a regiment of his own choice. Travelling to London for the first time, he tried for the Artists' Rifles—an indication of his secret wishes—but was rejected, and went into the Civil Service Rifles instead. After a brief training, Private Moore was sent in August 1917 to the front line in France; in December 1917 he was gassed in the assault on Cambrai and returned to England as a stretcher case, very fortunate to survive. After convalescence he returned to duty as a physical training and bayonet instructor, with the rank of lance-corporal. He went back to France just before the armistice was signed in November 1918, but as a teacher he was entitled to early demobilization, and he was back at his old school in Castleford in February 1919.

In later life, Moore rarely spoke about his wartime experiences, and then often in a somewhat light-hearted manner. He admitted to being a callow young man, pleased to have broken away from the parental home, and at the time unaware of the tragic implications of the war—in sharp contrast to slightly older contemporaries such as the Yorkshire-born (Sir) Herbert Read, later to become Moore's close friend and champion.

It was expected that Moore would become a teacher specializing in art, and in September 1919, with an ex-serviceman's grant, he began his formal training at the Leeds School of Art, commuting by train from his home in Castleford. It was immediately clear that he was an outstanding student, and he completed the two-year drawing course in his first year. In his second year at Leeds Moore asked for sculpture lessons, and his progress was remarkable enough for him to win a scholarship to the Royal College of Art in London, which was, with the Slade School, the leading art school in Britain.

Moore studied in the sculpture school of the Royal College of Art from September 1921 until the summer of 1924, when he was awarded his diploma. He learned little from his teachers, but won the interest and support of the college's principal, (Sir) William Rothenstein, and enjoyed the company of his fellow students, particularly those who had come with him from Leeds, the painters Raymond Coxon and Edna Ginesi, and the sculptor five years his junior, (Dame) Barbara Hepworth. Together they visited exhibitions, made their first trips to look at art in Paris, and worked very hard with great confidence and dedication. Moore lived mainly in Hammersmith in west London, and for a time attended drawing classes in the local studio of the sculptor and painter, (G. C.) Leon Underwood. Drawing always mattered for Moore, who saw it as the essential adjunct to sculpture.

The decisive experience for the young Moore was his hours spent studying the sculpture in the Victoria and Albert and, more importantly, the British Museum. The tradition of western sculpture had reached a culmination in the work of Auguste Rodin, and Moore knew instinctively that his generation would need to form a new language for this powerful but difficult three-dimensional art if it was to speak with a clear and distinctive twentieth-century voice. Following the examples of (Sir) Jacob Epstein, Henri Gaudier-Brzeska, and Constantin Brancusi, Moore felt that the way forward must be to look at those other sculptures outside the classical/medieval/Renaissance/Rodin tradition: namely archaic Greek, Egyptian, Assyrian, and more significantly sculptures that until the twentieth century had not been recognized as art at all but as antiquities or curiosities, from pre-European Mexico, Africa, and Oceania.

It was this broad sculptural heritage, to which might be added such great archaeological remains as Stonehenge, that the young Moore studied. He visited Italy on a six-month travelling scholarship in 1925, and though he admired the paintings of Giotto and Masaccio he seems not to have wanted to look at sculpture: perhaps this is the reason why he surprisingly never competed for the prix de Rome. His appreciation of Donatello and Michelangelo came later in life. At the time Moore preferred to return to London, where he had a part-time teaching position in the sculpture school of the Royal College of Art. This gave him both financial security and enough time to make his own sculptures, and prepare for that crucial test that faces any artist—a first one-man exhibition.

This came for Moore in January 1928 at the Warren Gallery, where the artist showed forty-two sculptures and fifty-one drawings. Though giving rise to some controversy, it was an undoubted success. 'A very "advanced" show and one that will shock the orthodox, it contains much sculpture of overwhelming power,' said the *Daily Herald*. Moore was particularly pleased that among the purchasers of his work were artists of the calibre of Augustus John and Jacob Epstein. There followed immediately, later in 1928, Moore's first public commission. On Epstein's recommendation he was asked to carve a relief for the façade of the new London underground headquarters near St James's Park, symbolizing the west wind, part of a decorative scheme to which (A.) Eric Gill and Epstein himself also contributed. But providing sculpture for buildings was not the route forward that Moore wished to pursue, and in general he always avoided such commissions. At this stage in his career he also avoided making modelled sculpture for casting in bronze, believing that the future lay in the direct carving of wood and stone.

In July 1929 Moore married a student at the Royal College of Art, Irina Anatolia Radetzky. The daughter of Anatol Radetsky, who was lost in the Russian revolution, from an upper-class mercantile family, she had been born in Kiev in 1907 and had come to England in 1921–2 to stay with step-grandparents in Little Marlow, Buckinghamshire. A woman of striking and exotic beauty, she was Moore's support and best critic for the whole of his long career. They had one daughter. Irina died in 1989.

On their marriage, the Moores moved into a ground-floor studio with accommodation above at 11A Parkhill Road in Hampstead. The apartment was found by Barbara Hepworth, who lived nearby in The Mall Studios with, from 1931, the painter Ben Nicholson. The poets Herbert Read and Geoffrey Grigson, the writer Adrian Stokes, and the painters Paul Nash and Ivon Hitchens were all close neighbours. This Hampstead circle became the most receptive to modern ideas in the visual arts in Britain, and its interests reflected the rival continental avant-garde movements of abstraction and Surrealism. At this time Moore's sculpture entered its most experimental phase, and, though still relatively small in size, his carvings in stone and wood, and the pages of drawings for sculpture, showed an astounding originality of invention, on which rests his international fame.

With the outbreak of war in September 1939 everything changed. During the 1930s Moore had led a regular and productive life, teaching part-time at the Chelsea School of Art, working in his Hampstead studio, and during the holidays making larger works in the garden of his cottage in Kent. The war stopped his teaching, and the bombing and the threat of invasion made it impossible to work in London or Kent. When his Hampstead studio was damaged by bombs in October 1940, he took the house at Perry Green, Much Hadham, Hertfordshire, in which he was to live and work until his death. With the gradual addition of land and studios this was the centre of all his later activity, rarely left for long.

Moore had more or less stopped making sculpture, and from 1940 to 1942 worked as an official war artist in the scheme supervised by Sir Kenneth (later Baron) Clark, director of the National Gallery, and an admirer of Moore's art. He had begun to draw the women and children sheltering from the bombing on the platforms of London underground stations at night, and the coloured finished drawings he made from his sketches quickly won international attention. An artist hitherto associated exclusively with the avant-garde seemed uncannily able to capture the resignation and resistance felt by the ordinary people of London.

When Moore returned to sculpture in 1943–4 it was with two public commissions—a madonna and child for St Matthew's church, Northampton, and a family group, originally intended for the Village College at Impington, Cambridgeshire. In both cases Moore knew he had to make a sculpture that would speak directly to a wide community, and this led to fundamental changes in both his art and materials and techniques used to make it. Moore always held broad socialist principles, supporting the

Labour party; he believed that the artist had a social responsibility, and he was pleased to find that his work could be appreciated in a public situation, and that his own obsession with the female human form could be shared by others.

This social commitment also led Moore to give his time generously to serve on public bodies. He was a trustee of the Tate Gallery (1941–8 and 1949–56), and of the National Gallery (1955-63 and 1964–74); a member of the Arts Council (1963–7), and of its art panel for many years from 1942 onwards. He was appointed a member of the National Theatre board in 1957 and the Royal Fine Art Commission (1947–71). He was elected a fellow of the British Academy in 1966. He accepted many prizes and twenty-one honorary degrees, and membership of a number of foreign academies.

In 1946 the first fully retrospective exhibition of Moore's work was held at the Museum of Modern Art in New York. Two years later he won the international sculpture prize at the Venice Biennale, and in 1956 he was commissioned to make a sculpture for the new Unesco headquarters in Paris. By the time he was sixty Moore was generally regarded as Britain's greatest artist and the world's greatest living sculptor. More than 200 museums worldwide own examples of his work, with particularly strong holdings in the Art Gallery of Ontario, Toronto, and the Tate Gallery, London. In over fifty cities his sculpture stands in prominent public places, notably outside the National Gallery of Art in Washington, the Lincoln Center in New York, the Houses of Parliament in London, and in Dallas, Chicago, Amsterdam, Zurich, Berlin, Singapore, and Hong Kong. By the time of his death he had had more exhibitions than any other artist, with the exception only of Pablo Picasso; particularly celebrated were those in Florence in 1972, Paris in 1977, and New York in 1983. The official bibliography devoted to his work published in 1992 lists over 10,000 publications.

Despite this public acclaim and celebrity, Moore's work in his last phase took on a more personal and private quality. Throughout the 1950s he had made a series of large seated and reclining female figures, but in the 1960s the sculptures became distinctly more abstract. The reclining figure was broken up into two, three, or even four parts, and sometimes made on a grand, monumental scale, much larger than life size. In such sculptures—the 'Sheep Piece' of 1971–2, the 'Three Piece Vertebrae' of 1968 and 1978–9, and the 'Large Four Piece Reclining Figure' of 1972–3, for example—Moore is at his most majestic, making work of a boldness no other sculptor has attempted. The figure references almost disappear, and in the big 'Arch' of 1963/9, 'Hill Arches' (1972), or the 'Mirror Knife

Edge' in Washington (1977), the work takes on a powerful architectural quality that enhances the feeling of some mysterious timeless memorial.

Moore's working methods remained much the same from 1944 onwards: ideas were developed by the artist as plaster maquettes, no more than hand size, which he could alter and shape like small carvings. Then, with the help of assistants, the forms could be enlarged to a human dimension or, if appropriate, to a monumental scale. The plaster sculpture was usually cast in bronze, the most durable material a sculptor can use, and works were sold in editions of three to ten copies. Nearly 1,000 works are listed in the complete catalogue of Moore's sculptures, and, as most were issued in editions, the probable complete tally must be over 6,000.

Such a production, spread over more than sixty years, made Moore a very wealthy man. In the mid-1970s he was paying over £1 million a year in tax, and it was partly this that led him in 1977, with the assistance of his only child Mary, who had been born in 1946, to set up the Henry Moore Foundation. This charitable foundation was established to advance public appreciation of the fine arts and in particular of the works of Henry Moore, and by the time of Moore's death it was already playing an active role arranging Moore exhibitions worldwide, and funding fellowships, publications, galleries, and exhibitions devoted to sculpture.

Moore's fame as a sculptor was matched by the renown that his drawings, water-colours, and graphic works brought him. As he grew older, so he spent more time drawing, not so much studies for sculpture, but drawings made for their own sake, of rocks, roots, and landscapes, as well as the human form. It was the natural world, and the human presence in it, that lay at the heart of all Moore's work, in whatever medium. He did not seek to express beauty, rather an image of power and vitality. Though without formal beliefs, Moore had a religious sense of life, and it is perhaps this quality that has given his best work a universal relevance which speaks to people of whatever race and religion in a way that no artist before Moore had been able to achieve. He was regarded as, and is likely to remain, a towering figure in twentieth-century art.

In personal appearance and manner Moore belied such an impression. It was often said that he looked more like a successful farmer than an artist. He had an attractive modesty that hid great self-confidence and ambition. He kept a light Yorkshire accent all his life, and expressed himself in simple straightforward terms, avoiding any philosophizing. Interpretations of his work he left to others; he was the maker, driven by some creative force that he could not and perhaps did not wish to understand. At times he seemed almost surprised at his own reputation, expressing a boyish delight at visits from prime ministers and presidents, accepting a CH in 1955 and the OM in 1963 but declining any title. Moore died at Perry Green, Much Hadham, 31 August 1986, and was buried there.

[Herbert Read, *Henry Moore*, 1965; Donald Hall, *Henry Moore*, 1966; John Russell, *Henry Moore*, 1973; William Packer, *Henry Moore*, 1985; Roger Berthoud, *The Life of Henry Moore*, 1987; Susan Compton, *Henry Moore*, 1988; David Mitchison and Julian Stallabrass, *Henry Moore*, 1992; personal knowledge.]

ALAN BOWNESS

published 1996

MORISON Stanley Arthur

(1889–1967)

Typographer, was born at Wanstead, Essex, 6 May 1889, the only son and second of three children of Arthur Andrew Morison and his wife, Alice Louisa, daughter of Charles Cole, clerk, of Hackney. His father, an unsuccessful and intemperate commercial traveller, deserted the family when Morison was fourteen, a sufficient reason for Morison's leaving Owen's School, Islington, in 1903 and finding paid work. After a phase of sharing his mother's agnosticism, he was received into the Roman Catholic Church in December 1908. Unhappy as a clerk with the London City Mission (1905–12), he spent his spare time in museums and public libraries. *The Times* printing supplement of 10 September 1912 concentrated his mind on the study of letters, printed and written, and early the following year he was fortunate in securing a post as assistant in the office of the *Imprint*, a new monthly periodical devoted to design in printing. When the *Imprint* seemed likely to fail in the following year, the editor recommended Morison to Wilfrid Meynell, husband of Alice Meynell and managing director of Burns & Oates, Roman Catholic publishers, who took him on his staff. Morison afterwards felt deeply grateful to the Meynell family for help and encouragement.

In 1916 he made known his conscientious objection to war service. His appeal against conscription on religious and moral grounds was dismissed, and on 7 May 1916 he was taken to prison. Eventually he accepted alternative employment and by the time the war ended he was engaged in farm work. Meanwhile, on 18 March 1916 he had married Mabel Williamson (died 1961), a schoolteacher. Not until many years later did Morison learn that she was not seven but seventeen years older than himself. Morison never spoke of his marriage: late in 1926 he made a settlement on his wife and they separated. He had formed a close relationship, undoubtedly amorous but as certainly chaste, with the American typographer, Mrs Beatrice Lamberton Warde, who was by his bedside when he died.

After the war Wilfrid and his son, (Sir) Francis Meynell, found him temporary employment until, in June 1921, he went as typographer to the Cloister Press near Manchester. The press was liquidated in July 1922, and Morison was never again full-time employed. He acted as freelance consultant to several publishers; but his position as Britain's greatest authority on letter-design was won by the success of a programme for the production of a series of typefaces proposed to the Monotype Corporation in 1922 leading to a part-time appointment as typographical adviser lasting until 1954. A dozen typefaces made to his specifications, some rendering old designs, others drawn by living artists, became those most commonly used for book-printing in Great Britain and to a large extent abroad.

Morison's writings, some two hundred books, articles, collections of specimens, reviews, and prefaces, strongly affected the taste and enlarged the knowledge of experts and amateurs concerned with book-production. A succession of learned essays in the annual the *Fleuron* (1923–30), founded in conjunction with Oliver Simon, discovered much that was of value in the history of type and its relation to the work of scribes and writing masters. The final one, 'First Principles of Typography', was reprinted as a book (1936) in thirteen editions and seven languages during Morison's lifetime. On weekly visits to Cambridge, where he was part-time typographical adviser to the University Press, he was the perfect collaborator for the printer, Walter Lewis, from 1923 until 1945 and his successor, Brooke Crutchley, until 1959.

Morison's great services to *The Times* over thirty years made him known to a wider public and as more than a technician. His appointment as typographical adviser was the result of his caustic comments on the paper's drab and old-fashioned look made in 1929 to a representative. His views, reported to the manager, were taken seriously at the highest levels and led eventually to his being asked to submit proposals. That he did throughout 1930 and 1931, advocating typographical changes including the abandonment of the ornamented gothic for the title. As a consequence a new typeface was cut and when the paper first appeared in *The Times* New Roman on 3 October 1932 almost all correspondents found it a relief to their eyes. Morison's position at *The Times* developed into something much more than adviser on printing. He edited and largely wrote the four-volume *The History of The Times* (1935–52) and was for two years, 1945–7, editor of *The Times Literary Supplement*. He was consulted about organization and appointments of personnel, and even for a time about editorial policy; but this last anomaly ended in 1952. He retired from *The Times* in 1960. His researches in newspaper history brought him in touch with Lord Beaverbrook, who entertained him in the years 1948–63 to winter holidays in the Bahamas and on the Riviera.

Morison's involvement with the *Encyclopaedia Britannica* began in 1949, when he met the publisher, William Benton, and in 1961 he was added to the editorial board. He made periodic visits to Chicago (the city that came nearest to rivalling London in his affections) and enjoyed Mediterranean cruises in Senator Benton's yacht.

During the war of 1939–45 he seldom spent a night out of London. The preface to *Black-letter Text* (1942) describes his experiences in a catastrophic air raid when his rooms, most of his books, and his work in progress were destroyed.

Morison far excelled other typographers of his day in point of erudition; and his choice of type-designs, prompted by a fastidious mind and a sensitive eye, was enduring. His capacity for gaining the confidence of managements and commanding the skill of technicians made him a leader in his profession of consultant. Consequently, his influence on book-printing was powerful, and he exerted it in favour of an austere and traditional style, with an improved repertory of type. His reform of *The Times* unfortunately failed to survive a need for stringent economy. As a scholar he was quick to grasp essentials but inaccurate in details, and in the lectures of 1957, delivered when he was James P. R. Lyell reader in bibliography at Oxford in 1956–7, he undertook a task for which he had insufficient knowledge.

Cambridge University, where he had been Sandars reader in 1931, honoured him with the degree of Litt.D. in 1950, and so did Birmingham and Marquette (Wisconsin, USA). He was elected FBA in 1954 and appointed Royal Designer for Industry in 1960; but he declined three offers of knighthood. His lesser honours would make a long catalogue.

He was vigorous and did not spare himself. In middle life he worked very hard and travelled a great deal in search of information. His talk was pugnacious in a humorous way. Victorian in morals, on other subjects he would differ without bitterness, though he had no doubts. In politics he was radical: spoke contemptuously of the Roman Curia, resented monarchy, and thought capitalism was wrong but invincible. Communist friends dissuaded him in 1921 from applying for membership of their party. Apart from the breviary, which he always carried, he read only for information, increasingly about liturgy and ecclesiology: in music he cared only for plainchant. His fine collection of books (presented by Sir Allen Lane) is kept in a 'Morison Room' at Cambridge University Library.

He was of spare build; wore spectacles (steel-rimmed) from his youth up, the lenses thickening as he aged. Dressed invariably in a black suit with a white shirt and black tie, outdoors with a rather small black hat, he struck strangers as looking like a Jesuit.

Given handsome parting presents from *The Times* and the Monotype Corporation and a generous subsidy from Senator Benton, he lived his declining years in great comfort in a double suite of rooms in Whitehall Court, Westminster, and indulged a discriminating taste in food and wines. He was still visiting Chicago in 1966; but by May 1967 he had taken to a wheelchair because of spinal weakness and he could hardly see. He died at home, 11 October 1967. He had taken a close interest in the form of the requiem Mass offered in Westminster Cathedral on 18 October.

There is a charcoal drawing (1924) by (Sir) William Rothenstein at Cambridge University Press. A sketch for this drawing, dated 1923, is in the possession of the Monotype Corporation.

[Nicolas Barker, *Stanley Morison*, 1972; S. H. Steinberg in *Proceedings* of the British Academy, vol. liii, 1967; personal knowledge.]

H. G. Carter

published 1981

MORRIS William Richard

(1877–1963)

Viscount Nuffield

Industrialist and philanthropist, was born in Worcester 10 October 1877, the son of Frederick Morris, who was then working for a draper in Worcester, and his wife, Emily Ann, daughter of Richard Pether, of Wood Farm, Headington. He was the eldest of a family of seven of whom only a sister survived beyond an early age. His father was an Oxford man and to Oxford he returned to farm when Morris was three. The boy grew up in Cowley and went to the village school. After a short period with a local bicycle firm he started on his own at the age of sixteen with a capital of £4. By 1901 he could advertise himself as 'Sole maker of the celebrated Morris cycles'. In 1902 he showed a model of a motor cycle of his own design, and about this time he started on motor-car repairs. In 1903 he went into partnership but this soon got into financial difficulties, and he salvaged only his personal kit of tools. He resumed business under his own name and by 1910 he was described as motor-car engineer and agent and garage proprietor. He was by then well advanced on his project for a car of his own; the Morris-Oxford was announced at the 1912 Motor Show when he received an order for 400 cars. The first was produced in April 1913: the original bull-nosed 8.9 hp two-seater which did 35–50 miles to the gallon, had speeds ranging up to 50 miles per hour in top gear, and was priced at £165.

Morris was a hard-working, conscientious, enthusiastic, and attractive young man, with plenty of self-confidence. He had no formal training as an engineer, but was good with his hands and had a shrewd eye for the potentialities of the newly developing internal combustion engine. In a rapidly expanding industry he had a large number of competitors, but in some ways being in Oxford was an advantage. The richer undergraduates, and even senior members of the university, were interested in the motor car and Morris was quick to learn from the variety of cars which passed through his hands. Not having the wide-ranging engineering facilities of some industrial towns he had to concentrate largely on assembling components made by others. This gave him greater flexibility and involved much less capital. He was also free to concentrate on design and improvement. He was a shrewd bargainer with, but also a reliable customer for, his suppliers. He had the courage, flair, farsightedness, and singlemindedness of the successful business man, who knew how to choose men and attract their loyalty.

Since his premises in Longwall, next to New College, were unsuitable for large-scale production Morris acquired property at Temple Cowley, including the buildings of what had formerly been Hurst's Grammar School, where his father had gone to school. Early in 1914 he visited the United States to secure components for his second model—the 11.9 hp Morris-Cowley. During the war of 1914–18 the Cowley factory made a small number of cars but was engaged mainly on munitions. For his services Morris was appointed OBE in 1917.

He was quickly ready to produce cars to meet the post-war boom: the firm of Morris Motors Ltd. was incorporated in July 1919 and by September 1920 was selling around 280 cars a month. Then came the slump. By February 1921 the company had a large bank overdraft, owed even more to suppliers, and production was obstructed by the accumulation of supplies and unsold cars. Morris then took the dramatic decision which proved the turning-point in his career: to cut the price of the 4-seater Morris-Cowley by £100 to £425 and other models by smaller sums. Within three weeks all the completed cars had been sold and the factory was running short of supplies—400 cars were sold in March 1921. Other manufacturers reduced their prices but at the Motor Show in the autumn Morris made further reductions. By 1923 Morris Motors were producing some 20,000 cars a year and by 1926 some 50,000, or about a third of the national output. Morris had established himself as one of the major producers of the popular car.

In that year Morris joined with other companies to finance the Pressed Steel Company, located at Cowley, to supply car bodies to the industry. And in the same year the new public company of Morris Motors (1926) Ltd. was established to take over Morris Motors Ltd. and three other firms already owned by Morris, supplying bodies, engines, and radiators. The City advised that an issue only of preference shares would not attract the investor and that either Morris should market some ordinary shares or allow the preference shares some part of the profits. He declined the advice; the issue of £3 million cumulative preference shares was oversubscribed and he retained the ownership of the whole of the ordinary shares with a nominal value of £2 million. He combined this policy with ploughing back the surplus trading profit. Thus in 1924–5 Morris Motors Ltd. had paid £2,030 on its preference shares, nothing on its ordinary shares, and retained net profits of £822,000 in the business which was thereby provided with cheap capital for its expansion.

The company weathered the depression of the early thirties by shifting the emphasis to smaller models: the Morris Minor of 1931 sold at £100 and claimed to do 100 miles per hour and per gallon. In the meantime in 1930 Morris had registered the MG Car Company which produced the famous MG sports car; and acquired the Wolseley Company in 1927, as well as the SU Carburettor Company which in 1927 became Morris Industries Ltd., the holding company for all Morris's interests. In 1935 Morris Motors acquired the Wolseley and MG companies from him and in 1939 Morris Commercial Cars, Morris Industries Export, and the SU Company. By now the ordinary share capital of Morris Motors consisted of £2,650,000 in 5*s.* shares, all owned by Lord Nuffield as he had now become. In 1936 one-quarter of these was issued to the public at 37*s.* 6*d.* and at the end of the first day their price closed some 4*s.* higher. This put Nuffield's financial interest in the company at some £16 million, and with Morris Garages and another company he wholly owned, and the proceeds of the sales, he had a fortune of over £20 million.

Although Morris had started to give money away as early as 1926, when he endowed the King Alfonso XIII chair of Spanish studies at Oxford, his major benefactions started from around the period of the public issue; indeed, in order to fulfil his desire to become a public benefactor on a large scale he had to have large sums more readily available. During his lifetime Nuffield gave away some £30 million, with the main general aim of reducing human suffering. His £2 million endowment in 1936 for the medical school at Oxford made the university one of the main centres for medical research and teaching. He claimed he had always wanted to be a surgeon and in 1948 he gave a quarter of a million to the Royal College of Surgeons for the establishment and maintenance of a residential college. He was a generous benefactor of the Oxford hospitals and also of Guy's, St Thomas's, Great Ormond Street, and hospitals in Birmingham, Coventry, Worcester, and elsewhere. His especial sympathy for the crippled was shown in his provision for what became the Nuffield Orthopaedic Centre at Oxford, in the Nuffield Fund for Cripples (1935–7), and the Fund (1935–45) for orthopaedic services in Australia, New Zealand, and South Africa. In 1939 he gave over a million pounds to form the Nuffield Provincial Hospitals Trust; and in the same year over a million and a half for a Forces Trust.

The very imaginative Trust for the Special Areas, created in 1936 by a grant of £2 million, with the important contribution it made to bringing new industries to depressed areas, was part of the general pattern. The primary purpose of Nuffield College, founded in 1937 with the grant of a site in Oxford and some £900,000 in cash, was the study of social, economic, and political problems. And the first three objects of the Nuffield Foundation, founded in 1943 by the gift of 4.8 million ordinary shares (then worth about £10 million), were the advancement of health and the prevention and relief of sickness; the advancement of social well-being; and the care and comfort of the aged poor. Most of the good Nuffield did lived after him, for the bulk of his money went on endowments and buildings. The Nuffield Foundation continued to distribute its large annual income among a wide-ranging variety of research projects and pioneering activities.

Although Nuffield declined to participate in the shadow factory scheme devised before the war because he disagreed with the basis upon which it was organized, he set up organizations for the manufacture of tanks in 1937 and of aircraft in 1938. During the war of 1939–45 Cowley became the headquarters of the Civilian Repair Organization. After the war Morris Motors went on to produce its two-millionth car in October 1951. In the following year the company merged with the Austin Motor Company in the formation of the British Motor Corporation, of which Nuffield became first chairman. Six months later he retired and became honorary president. He continued regularly to attend his office in the headmaster's study in the former Hurst's Grammar School, but he was no longer the dominant figure. Since the late thirties he had spent an increasing amount of his time on his numerous benefactions and on his annual long sea trips, on which he excelled at deck games. Unlike many rich men he did not develop new pursuits or figure in the gilded world. His pleasures were simple—the Huntercombe Golf Club and the company of convivial friends and kindred spirits. He was an uncomplicated man with a strong belief in the old-fashioned virtues of hard work and honesty. He was an individualist who disliked committees and took very little part in organized public affairs. When he did, his views were of the same homespun variety combined with a firm belief in the freedom and opportunities afforded by private enterprise. He knew his own mind, and could make large and imaginative decisions of which there is plenty of evidence in his careers as industrialist and benefactor. He was essentially a kindly man, concerned at the sufferings of others. He read very little and notwithstanding all the money he gave for academic activities and research was not greatly interested in the results—only medical problems and progress excited his direct interest.

In 1929 Morris was created a baronet, in 1934 a baron as Lord Nuffield, and in 1938 a viscount. He was appointed GBE in 1941 and CH in 1958. He was an honorary DCL of Oxford (1931) and in 1937 received an MA which made him a voting member of the university and 'one of us'. He was a doctor of six other universities, three of them Australian. He was elected FRS in 1939 and honorary FRCS in 1948. He was an honorary fellow of St Peter's, Pembroke, Worcester, and Nuffield colleges in Oxford and an honorary freeman of seven towns, including the cities of Oxford, Worcester, Cardiff, and Coventry.

In 1904 Morris married an Oxford girl, Elizabeth Maud (died 1959), daughter of William Jones Anstey; they had no children. His heirs were the numerous benefactions which he liked to bear his name. He died at Nuffield Place 22 August 1963 and was cremated at a simple private service and his ashes buried in the parish church at Nuffield. He showed his confidence in the college carrying his name by making it his residuary legatee and assigned to it his coat of arms. Nuffield Place, his home for thirty years, became the responsibility of the college.

Nuffield College has a bronze bust by Madame Lejeune and a portrait of Morris by Sir Arthur Cope which was presented to him by the staff and workpeople of Morris Motors in 1929. It shows him as a youngish man standing on Shotover, with Oxford spires in the background.

[P. W. S. Andrews and Elizabeth Brunner, *The Life of Lord Nuffield*, 1955; Robert Jackson, *The Nuffield Story*, 1964; personal knowledge.]

D. N. Chester

published 1981

MORRISON Herbert Stanley

(1888–1965)

Baron Morrison of Lambeth

Labour politician, was born in Brixton, London, 3 January 1888, the youngest in a family of four girls and three boys of Henry Morrison, police constable with a weakness for the bottle, and his wife, Priscilla Caroline Lyon, daughter of a carpet fitter in the East End of London. His mother had been in domestic service and, with six surviving children, the early years were hard but not marked by lack of the basic necessities. An eye infection shortly after birth deprived Morrison of the sight of his right eye, although this was a handicap which he generally overcame. He was educated at one of the Board schools set up under the 1870 Education Act, and, from the age of eleven, at St Andrew's Church of England School, Lingham St., which he left at the age of fourteen to become an errand boy. After a spell as a shop assistant and as a switchboard operator (which gave him more time for reading), minor journalistic efforts helped to provide a living, and from 1912 to 1915 Morrison worked as circulation manager for the first official Labour paper, the *Daily Citizen*. From April 1915 he became part-time secretary of the London Labour Party and thereafter politics, either as an organizer or as a member of Parliament, was his sole occupation: and politics to Herbert Morrison meant the Labour movement. In his early years he took part in the local forums, heard such famous figures as George Bernard Shaw and Keir Hardie, and in 1906 he joined the Brixton branch of the Independent Labour Party. Following a common trend among left-wingers in London, he found this a rather pro-Liberal, north of England or Nonconformist type of organization, and himself preferred the more direct socialism of the Social Democratic Federation to which he transferred in 1907. To the London Left, free trade, anti-landlordism, and Home Rule for Ireland were all meaningless; Morrison was preoccupied—it was his lifelong preoccupation—with transport, health, education, and housing as provided by the local authorities for the citizens of the larger towns, and, above all, for London. Later he left the SDF and rejoined the ILP because he saw that it was more likely to win elections and achieve actual changes. As part of this interest he attended the Lambeth Metropolitan Borough Council—he was often the sole visitor—and unsuccessfully contested the Vauxhall ward for the ILP in 1912. In 1910 he had become secretary of the South-West London Federation of ILP branches and his work led steadily to the decision of the London Trades Council to call a conference and form the London Labour Party. After he became secretary to this new organization, in 1915, Morrison talked less and less about political theory, though he was opposed to the war of 1914–18 and to conscription. His concern was entirely with winning elections and carrying out pragmatic reforms, the common feature of which was to remedy social grievances in a manner which showed no prejudice against either governmental action or state ownership. If he resisted Popularism, he also rigorously opposed any Communist move 'to pour sand' into the Labour Party machine.

In many respects Morrison's greatest achievements in politics were in London between 1920 and 1940. He began by bringing his organization intact through the war of 1914–18, going on to win fifteen out of 124 seats in the 1919 London County Council elections. He realized that more was gained by steady work and preparation, by mastery of the immediate subject and its possibilities, than by all the street-corner oratory which so delighted the older generation of socialists. This work required the finding and training of candidates not only for the LCC but for the elections in twenty-eight boroughs. Once elected, these men had to be taught how to make speeches, conduct committees, and actually run the machinery of local government. In late 1919 the London Labour Party won a majority or became the largest party in sixteen boroughs. In 1919 Morrison became mayor of Hackney and in 1922 a member of the London County Council. He was soon the dominating figure.

Elected to Parliament for Hackney South in 1923 and 1929, Morrison was a strong supporter of Ramsay MacDonald and in the second Labour Government became minister of transport (1929). He proved to be a first-class minister, and was responsible for the 1930 Road Traffic Act and for the London Passenger Transport Bill of 1931. In the latter case, Morrison had been leading the Labour group on the LCC in opposition to a proposal to form a privately owned monopoly of London Transport. He became minister of transport just in time to prevent the Bill from passing and introduced his own measure, the creation of the London Passenger Transport Board. As a progenitor of the Board, Morrison was a firm believer in the autonomous public corporation as the best instrument for controlling a nationalized industry. He argued the case in his book *Socialization and Transport* (1933), which was in part a defence of his views against criticism from within the Labour Party. Other possibilities, such as workers' or joint control of an industry or management by a government department, had a strong traditional appeal to some socialists. By winning acceptance for his own view, Morrison in effect determined the form which was later given to the post-war nationalization Acts. He also insisted on fair compensation for stockholders and on the obligation to demonstrate the advantages of nationalization industry by industry. Because, as he thought, the case had not been made out for nationalization of the steel industry, he was opposed to that commitment in Labour's programme.

It was in the 1930s that Morrison achieved his greatest hold on the Labour Party. In part this was due simply to his personality and ability. A short, stocky figure with a quiff of hair combed back from his forehead, he was a first-rate debater and public speaker. He could put his party's view in the most reasonable, lucid, and engaging manner while never suggesting weakness and he was always ready to counter every attack. Also his achievements in London were a tonic to the Labour Party just when it most needed one. The annual conference found him in his element.

After Labour's exhilarating rise to power in the early 1920s, there had been the disappointing experiences of the two minority Governments, the defection of Ramsay MacDonald, and the débâcle of the 1931 general election. Morrison had begun in 1931 by wishing to remain in office with MacDonald, but after much hesitation he eventually stayed with the rest of the party when the 'national' Government was formed. In the face of these setbacks, the capture of the LCC in 1934 and the steady achievements thereafter were a most welcome sign that Labour could win and govern, achievements which in London were due to Herbert Morrison. Under him the LCC reformed public assistance, kept Poor Law officers out of the hospitals, built a new Waterloo Bridge despite government opposition, introduced the green belt, and pushed ahead with slum clearance and school building. Morrison was, in fact, a rather unusual type of Labour leader. He had not come up through the trade-union movement, nor was he one of the middle-class intellectuals who formed the other major group in the senior ranks. A working-class boy who was largely self-educated, he had risen by virtue of his organizational, tactical, and argumentative skills and he had no signs of a social inferiority complex. Indeed his bearing was a mixture of cockney brashness and the self-confidence which arose from knowledge, competence, and a solidly based political position. His clothes and his furniture were always bought at the Co-op. A further facet of Herbert Morrison's character which emerged strongly after his re-election in 1935 was his love of the House of Commons. As might have been expected, despite a shaky start, he took pleasure in mastering its rules of procedure. He was never overawed by the Palace of Westminster, but he valued its historical traditions and became an expert at using the House of Commons as part of the machinery of government.

His absence from the Commons from his defeat in 1931 until the general election of 1935, when he was re-elected for Hackney South with a majority of 5,000 was, however, to have a crucial effect on his subsequent career. Clement Attlee, hitherto junior to Morrison, who had been a Cabinet minister already, found himself deputy leader of the small group of Labour MPs in 1931 and when the leadership fell vacant in 1935 on George Lansbury's retirement, Attlee's claims were preferred to those of Morrison or Arthur Greenwood. When a 'national' Government was formed in 1940, Morrison became minister of supply and then, from October, home secretary and minister of home security. In large part this appointment arose from his close knowledge of London and Londoners because the chief task was to reassure the citizens that all possible measures were being taken to preserve them from air attack.

Herbert Morrison visited all the areas and units involved in Civil Defence, and, after some reluctance to remove fire-fighting from its local government base, he created the National Fire Service to secure better co-operation and more rapid action, and provided a proper Civil Defence uniform. This did much for morale, as did the Morrison indoor table shelter; and he went on to institute a Fire Guard with regular fire-watching duties. In all these activities Morrison typified the irrepressible London civilian who made a joke out of nights at the office or the factory, who rallied round after the raids, and would not let any German actions depress him.

In many ways, the climax of Morrison's career was the Labour landslide of 1945. He had prepared the ground for it in several respects. In the actual chain of events leading to the election, Morrison had played a considerable part. In 1940 he had insisted that the Labour Party divide the House at the end of the debate on the Norwegian fiasco and had thus given the impetus which led to the resignation of Neville Chamberlain. As one of the small group of Labour leaders who successfully occupied high office through the war, he had shown that such men could rule most effectively. And, when Churchill asked the Labour Party to continue with the Coalition until Japan was defeated, Morrison was instrumental in insisting that this was unsatisfactory and that the country wanted a general election.

It has often been said that Morrison constructed and managed the machine which channelled the enthusiasms of 1945 into decisive action at the ballot box. Of this there is less evidence. The Conservative Party had almost totally abandoned its organization while Transport House had kept in operation. But there was no expert electioneering on either side. As with the LCC campaigns, all that was done was to provide candidates, explain the legal position, and produce a manifesto and some centrally directed propaganda. But because Morrison had done this before in London and played a large part in the similar process at a national level in 1945, he, not unfairly, received a large measure of the credit for the victory.

Although he had many subsequent achievements and his highest offices and honours were bestowed after 1945, some aspects of his career raised doubts and Morrison himself had disappointments, which made this period perhaps less happy than the previous years had been. As the results of the election of 1945, when Morrison was elected for Lewisham East, became known, he suggested that Attlee should not accept the royal commission to form a Government until the parliamentary party had met to elect a leader. Ernest Bevin and Attlee himself resisted this argument; Sir Stafford Cripps and Harold Laski agreed with Morrison; Attlee ended the matter by going to the palace. Morrison in his *Autobiography* (1960) denied that, in supporting delay, he was seeking the post of prime minister for himself. Yet Laski, Ellen Wilkinson, and the others who were active on this occasion were quite clear that their candidate was Morrison and that he had given them his complete support. In fact, Morrison pressed his case in meetings of various Labour groups for several days after Attlee had been designated prime minister.

Again, in 1947, when Cripps was alarmed about the lack of leadership on economic affairs, Morrison became involved in the situation. But, in spite of these frictions, not uncommon in all Governments, few would deny Morrison the credit for many of the successes of the post-war Labour Government. When he was minister of supply in 1940, Morrison had had some difficulty with economic problems, a field which he never mastered as thoroughly as he had general administration and the social services. This difficulty cropped up again between 1945 and 1947, when he was responsible, as lord president of the Council, for economic planning and co-ordination. In 1947 this task was given to Cripps at a new Ministry of Economic Affairs and Morrison was left to lead the House of Commons and to plan and carry through the legislative programme of the Government. In this task he excelled. His experience over the London Passenger Transport Act made him the authority on all the earlier nationalization measures, particularly of transport and electricity. Experienced members of the press lobby said it was a joy to watch him introduce these Bills, picking his way through the complexities and skirting the dangers like a cat walking across a mound of cans and broken bottles.

When it came to the question of steel, he was never adamant about public ownership and had wanted this item omitted from the 1945 election programme. Then, when the Cabinet took up the measure, Morrison was responsible for negotiations with (Sir) Ellis Hunter and (Sir) Andrew Duncan, the steel-masters' leaders. They produced a plan for increasing the powers of the Iron and Steel Board and allowing it to take over any firm which was not amenable to control. Aneurin Bevan, Bevin, and Cripps resisted this scheme throughout the summer of 1947 (when part of the time Morrison was seriously ill). In August the Parliamentary Labour Party discovered the situation, insisted on full nationalization, and the Bill was put in hand in October of that year. Although Morrison was much criticized for his 'hybrid measure', it was the most that could be achieved if the co-operation of the steel-masters was to be retained; and it would have given the Government a substantial measure of control.

In September 1947 Cripps openly admitted that he felt Bevin should take over from Attlee as prime minister, Hugh (later Lord) Dalton should become foreign secretary, and Attlee could remain as chancellor of the Exchequer. Cripps was almost equally critical of Morrison but still tried to win him over. Morrison said that he felt he should be prime minister and he went no further with the conspirators when it was clear that their objective was to elevate his chief enemy, Bevin. He left Cripps to put the proposal to Attlee who stopped the whole business by appointing Cripps to the Exchequer. Morrison's account of this in his *Autobiography* is not entirely frank. Eventually he agreed to be lord president of the Council, in which office he would have to co-ordinate Labour's policies.

When Bevin fell ill in 1950, Morrison dithered over whether he wanted to become foreign secretary. The following year Attlee noted that: 'He seemed to want it badly and turned down every other suggestion I made to him, so in the end I appointed him. Rather bad luck for him, as it turned out.' This was because Morrison lacked all feeling for foreign affairs and was unhappy and uncomfortable in it so that his reputation suffered as a result. It is generally agreed that much of Morrison's touch, his sure-footedness in all matters of domestic policy and administration, deserted him when he moved to the Foreign Office in 1951. It has been suggested that for the first time his eyesight troubled him, when so much had to be read. More seriously, his judgement faltered. Even friendly critics pointed out that he knew Londoners perfectly, other English fairly well, the Scots and Welsh were strangers to him, and foreigners incomprehensible. This may not have been fair, but his tenure of the Foreign Office was neither successful nor fortunate. A Morrison Plan for Palestine was quickly disregarded but the chief problem confronting him was the decision of Mr Mossadeq's Government to take over the British-owned oil-wells at Abadan. Morrison was in favour of recovering them and admonishing the Persian Government by direct military action. It was left to Attlee to veto any such idea, pointing out that world and particularly Asian opinion would react violently, that the Persians could not be denied the right to nationalize such assets, and that strong-arm action in defence of commercial interests could no longer be tolerated. Unable to act as he had wanted, Morrison's performance lacked clarity or decisiveness and his short spell at the Foreign Office did considerable harm to his political standing.

In opposition after 1951, Morrison played a prominent part but many felt that he was getting older and was not as effective as he had been in the 1940s. In 1955 Attlee retired and Morrison entered the leadership contest. In his *Autobiography* he says that his weakness was his 'inability to intrigue'. Yet there is small evidence of intrigue on the side of the victor, Hugh Gaitskell. There is little doubt that Attlee held on to the leadership until 1955 in order to prevent Morrison's succeeding. He resigned only when Morrison was sixty-seven and then after declaring that the Labour Party needed a leader who was born in the twentieth rather than in the nineteenth century. As deputy prime minister from 1945 to 1951 and as deputy leader of the party since then, as a man who had contested the leadership with Attlee as far back as 1935, Morrison had undeniable claims to the topmost position. There was also a definite campaign to prevent his succeeding, all of which may justify his meeting such efforts with all the resources open to a politician.

'In politics', it is said, 'there is no friendship at the top', and this appears to have been the case among some of the Labour leaders. Attlee was always on reasonable terms with Morrison but he complained that 'Herbert cannot distinguish between big things and little things' and this was probably one motive behind his desire to prevent Morrison from obtaining the leadership. It was while Attlee was ill in hospital in early 1951 and Morrison was presiding over the Cabinet that divisions arose and Aneurin Bevan and (Sir) Harold Wilson resigned. Attlee blamed Morrison for this and complained that the issue was not kept open for long enough—'he lost me two of my ministers'.

Herbert Morrison had not got on well with Bevan, but the most publicized disharmony was between Morrison and Ernest Bevin. For some reason, very possibly over trade-union representation on public bodies, the massive leader of the Transport and General Workers Union had decided as early as 1924 that Morrison was anti-union and to this he added a distaste for disloyalty of which he accused Morrison in 1945 when the attempt was made to replace Attlee. While Cripps's move to oust Attlee in 1947 apparently never riled Bevin, he continued to suspect Morrison. A major reason why Attlee had placed Bevin at the Foreign Office in 1945 was the feeling that his relations with Morrison were not easy enough to permit the close co-operation which would have been required had both men occupied posts on the home front.

After the Labour Party lost power in 1951, Morrison remained as a leading and very effective opposition spokesman. He had been elected a visiting fellow of Nuffield College, Oxford, in 1947 and was much aided there by (Sir) Norman Chester, especially when he turned to writing and in 1954 published *Government and Parliament, a Survey from the Inside*. The book was at once acclaimed as a notable account of British government and Morrison himself hoped it would become another Erskine May, the authoritative description which would be renewed every few years and continue long after he had died. While the book had considerable merits, especially in the lucid accounts of parliamentary procedure, the legislative programme, and the nationalized industries, it never attained the stature Morrison hoped for. One reason was that he lacked the academic turn of mind and, while the exposition was excellent, there was little analysis. Deeper criticisms are that the book is a first-rate description of how the system worked in theory, but that Morrison put in too few of the by-ways and circumventions of practice. A brilliant intuitive politician, he did not explain how he played by ear, but set out the actual score as it was on the official hymn sheet.

After his defeat for the party leadership, he rejected all attempts to persuade him to remain as deputy leader, although until the end of that Parliament he was still a frequent contributor to debates, as jaunty and pugnacious as ever. In the dissolution honours of 1959 he was made a life peer and the following year extended his activities by accepting the presidency of the British Board of Film Censors.

Morrison's *Autobiography* appeared in 1960. It provided little new information or insights into the period, but did give some interesting sidelights on the author and his relations with his colleagues. In it Morrison says of Attlee that 'he was one of the best mayors that Stepney ever had'. It would be true to say that Morrison himself was almost certainly the best leader whom the London Labour Party and the LCC have ever had, but it would not be enough. He was a great parliamentarian, effective in debate, a master of legislative and administrative detail, the father of an important account of British government and a man whose sincere desire to create better conditions for all was recognized by everyone engaged in British politics.

He died in Queen Mary Hospital at Sidcup 6 March 1965, and his ashes were scattered in London, on the river.

Morrison married in 1919 Margaret (died 1953), the daughter of Howard Kent, of Letchworth, a clerk at Euston station; they had one daughter. It was not a particularly happy marriage. He married, secondly, in 1955, Edith, daughter of John Meadowcroft, of Rochdale. She wrote an enjoyable account of his second marriage (1977).

There are two portraits in chalk of Morrison, both in the National Portrait Gallery, one by Juliet Pannett (1961), the other by Sir David Low.

[Lord Morrison of Lambeth, *An Autobiography*, 1960; Bernard Donoughue and G. W. Jones, *Herbert Morrison, Portrait of a Politician*, 1973.]

JOHN P. MACKINTOSH

published 1981

NAMIER Sir Lewis Bernstein

(1888–1960)

Historian, was born 27 June 1888 at Wola Okrzejska, to the east of Warsaw, the only son of Joseph Bernstein (originally Niemirowski), advocate and landowner, by his wife, Ann, daughter of Maurice Theodor Sommerstein. Both parents were Polonized Jews who no longer adhered to the Jewish religion. Ludwik Bernstein was educated privately, and after brief periods at Lwow and Lausanne universities came to England where he spent a year at the London School of Economics and entered Balliol College, Oxford, in 1908. He took a first in modern history in 1911 and was awarded a share in the Beit prize in 1913. Throughout his life Oxford, and especially Balliol, had a high place in his affections. He took British nationality in 1913 and changed his name by deed poll.

In 1913 Namier went to the United States to take up a post with one of his father's business associates. There he began research on eighteenth-century parliamentary history, and he returned to England in 1914 with the intention of writing a book on the British Parliament during the American revolution. On the outbreak of war he joined the army and served as a private in the Royal Fusiliers, but his knowledge of east European affairs led to his transfer to the Foreign Office where he worked from 1915 to 1920, first in the propaganda, then in the political intelligence, department. He was much concerned with the settlement of Polish affairs at the Paris peace conference.

Namier spent 1920 and 1921 as a tutor at Balliol. He had hoped to resume his historical work but found teaching occupied too much of his time, and in 1921 he again entered business in order to amass a competence. He became the European representative of a firm of Manchester cotton manufacturers, with his headquarters in Czechoslovakia, and a correspondent of the *Manchester Guardian*. From 1924 to 1929 he was occupied fully with historical research. He had no private income, and when his capital ran out he lived on his earnings from journalism, loans from friends, and two grants from the Rhodes Trustees. The results of his labours, *The Structure of Politics at the Accession of George III* (1929) and *England in the Age of the American Revolution* (1930), were immediately recognized as epoch-making for the study of the eighteenth century and established him in the front rank of British historians. Yet they represented only the first instalment of what was intended to be a multi-volumed study of Parliament during the period of the American revolution—a project which Namier did not resume until over twenty years later.

While rejecting the Jewish religion Namier had early become a Jewish nationalist, and his sympathy with Zionism increased during the post-war period. In 1929 he became political secretary to the Jewish Agency for Palestine, but his position was ambiguous and in 1931 he left to take up the chair of modern history in the university of Manchester. This he retained until his retirement in 1953. From 1931 to the outbreak of war his historical work took the form largely of essays and lectures, notably the Ford's lectures in 1933–4 on 'King, Cabinet and Parliament in the Early Years of George III'. What time he could spare from university teaching was spent in helping Jewish refugees from Germany. In 1939 he was adviser to Chaim Weizmann at the Palestine conference, and from 1940 to 1945 he was again engaged on full-time political work with the Jewish Agency. The events of the war reawakened his old interest in European history, and in 1946 he published *1848: The Revolution of the Intellectuals*, an expanded version of the Raleigh lecture delivered to the British Academy in 1944, the year of his election as a fellow. This masterly study of the revolutions in eastern Europe was followed by one on the German revolution of 1848, delivered as a series of lectures at Magdalen College, Oxford.

Namier had been a determined opponent of the policy of appeasement, and during the war of 1939–45 he settled down to study the diplomatic origins of the conflict. Although the principal documents were not then available, he was able to talk with men who had taken part in the events he narrated and much of *Diplomatic Prelude* (1948) was based on their recollections and notes. This was followed by two further volumes of essays on pre-war diplomatic history (*Europe in Decay*, 1950, and *In the Nazi Era*, 1952), and in 1951 Namier returned to what he described as his chosen field of British parliamentary history. He had been a member of the Treasury committee set up in 1929 to consider plans for writing a history of Parliament, and when the scheme was revived in 1951 he was appointed to the editorial board and given responsibility for the period 1754–90. The last nine years of his life were devoted almost entirely to this task, despite the handicaps of increasing deafness and a paralysed right hand which made writing almost impossible. He lived to see the biographies and constituency histories almost completed, but the introductory survey, in which he had planned to sum up the results of a lifetime's research, was hardly begun, when he died suddenly in London 19 August 1960. The work was completed by his chief assistant John Brooke and published in three volumes in 1964.

Namier was both a stimulating and a controversial figure. His foreign birth and his experience in business and politics gave him an attitude towards history which was not shared by most of his academic contemporaries, and with scholars he was ill at ease. An historical sense, he once remarked, is 'an intuitive understanding of how things do not happen'. He had vast learning and creative imagination of a high order, but was unable to discipline either, so that his published work represents but a fragment of what he had intended to do. Two problems in history particularly interested him: the composition and working of legislative assemblies (particularly the British Parliament) and the growth of nationalism in modern Europe. But *England in the Age of the American Revolution* stops short before the American revolution has even begun, while instead of the history of Europe during the nineteenth century which he had planned to write he left only detached essays on isolated subjects. Many of Namier's profoundest observations on history and historical problems are scattered in essays which he wrote as *pièces d'occasion* or in the guise of book reviews and afterwards republished in book form (in particular, *Avenues of History*, 1952, *Personalities and Powers*, 1955, *Vanished Supremacies*, 1958, and *Crossroads of Power*, 1962). In part Namier's failure to achieve his aims was due to his meticulous concern for accuracy and an exact prose style, but in part also it was due to his inability to correlate ends to means. Although he believed that 'what matters in history is the great outline and the significant detail', he could never resist the temptation to wander down some fascinating by-path of his story, regardless of his main theme, and his books are spoilt for the general reader by the proliferation and over-elaboration of his footnotes.

Despite these defects in his work, Namier exerted a greater influence over historians than perhaps any other scholar of his generation. Although strongly criticized, especially in his later years, his view of eighteenth-century political history has been generally accepted, and it is impossible to write on this period in terms of the pre-Namier era. It is in the field of his method and technique that his critics have gained most ground. He believed that in order to understand an institution or a society it must be broken up into its component parts, and these studied in isolation and then in relation to the whole. When he began work on *The Structure of Politics* he tried to find out all he could about every member who sat in the Parliament of 1761 and then to study 'how they consorted together' (in the words of a quotation from Aeschylus which he took as the motto for the book). Critics have pointed out, not always unfairly, that he was more interested in the parts than the whole, and that his method of structural analysis ignored the importance of ideas in history. What in fact Namier did was to bring to the study of history the post-Freudian conception of the mind: the belief that the reasons men give for their actions are rationalizations designed to cloak their deeper purposes. This led him to distrust political ideas as the explanations of historical movements and to stress the determinism underlying history.

It would be more correct to say that Namier paid insufficient attention to culture, of which ideas are but a part. Although a tireless searcher after historical material, he was little acquainted with the art, music, literature, or science of the period he studied. As a result he placed a low value on human achievements. His mind was powerful but his interests were narrow, and while for those of similar tastes he could be a fascinating companion he lacked the ability to make himself generally agreeable. A Conservative in politics in the tradition of Burke and a Calvinist in religion, he had also great sympathy for human distress and weakness. The dominating passion in his historical work was the search for truth: he would take immense pains to check the most insignificant details; and he dealt harshly and not always wisely with the errors of others. Yet he could also accept criticism or correction of his own work, and would praise a research student who had discovered a mistake in one of his books. He could win loyalty, and his assistants on the *History of Parliament* were devoted to him.

Namier was a tall, heavily built man, with a serious if not grim expression, lightened by vivacious eyes. Although a master of written English, he habitually spoke with a foreign accent; and he had a wide command of languages. In later years he mellowed considerably, under the influence of his second marriage and the general recognition of his work. He was knighted in 1952; was an honorary D.Litt. of Durham (1952), Oxford (1955), and Rome (1956); honorary Litt.D. of Cambridge (1957); and honorary DCL of Oxford (1960). Perhaps he derived most pleasure, however, from his election to an honorary fellowship of Balliol in 1948 and from the invitation to deliver the Romanes lecture at Oxford in 1952.

In 1917 Namier married Clara Sophie Edeleff, a widow, and daughter of the late Alexander Poniatowski, doctor of medicine. She died in 1945. He married secondly, in 1947, Iulia, daughter of the late Mikhail Kazarin, barrister at the Russian Law Court, and widow of Nicholas de Beausobre. There were no children.

[Lucy S. Sutherland in *Proceedings* of the British Academy, vol. xlviii, 1962; Sir Isaiah Berlin, 'Lewis Namier: A Personal Impression', in *A Century of Conflict, Essays for A. J. P. Taylor*, ed. Martin Gilbert, 1966; Arnold J. Toynbee, *Acquaintances*, 1967; private information; personal knowledge.]

JOHN BROOKE

published 1971

NIVEN (James) David (Graham)

(1910–1983)

Actor and author, was born 1 March 1910 in Belgrave Mansions, London, though in his best-selling autobiographies he later followed the example of his own Hollywood studio publicists by listing the more romantic and picturesque birthplace of Kirriemuir in Scotland. He was the youngest of four children, two sons and two daughters, born to William Edward Graham Niven, a landowner, and his wife Henrietta Julia, daughter of Captain William Degacher, of the South Wales Borderers. At the outbreak of World War I, Niven's father enlisted in the Berkshire Yeomanry and was killed in action at Gallipoli on 21 August 1915, leaving a widow to bring up their children in somewhat reduced circumstances until she remarried, in 1917, (Sir) Thomas Platt (from 1922 Comyn-Platt), a businessman who contested, for the Conservative Party, Southport (1923) and Portsmouth Central (1929).

Niven neither knew his father well nor cared for his stepfather at all, his childhood being largely spent at a succession of preparatory boarding schools (from one of which, Heatherdown in Ascot, he was summarily expelled for stealing) and then at Stowe where he at last found in the pioneering headmaster J. F. Roxburgh the father figure he so lacked at home. It was at Roxburgh's urging that Niven was taken into the Royal Military College at Sandhurst in 1928, and his final school report on Niven was unusually prescient: 'Not clever, but useful to have around. He will be popular wherever he goes unless he gets into bad company which ought to be avoided because he does get on with everybody.'

It was while at Sandhurst that, in a college production of *The Speckled Band*, Niven made his first notable stage appearance, though there was as yet little indication of any desire to enter the acting profession. Instead he was dispatched from Sandhurst in 1929 into the Highland Light Infantry as a junior officer and stationed on Malta, which conspicuously lacked the social and night life to which he had now become accustomed as a young man about London. After several military pranks born of tedium had misfired, and his army future looked extremely bleak, he sent a telegram to his commanding officer in the summer of 1933 reading simply 'Request Permission Resign Commission', a request which was met with evident relief and almost indecent haste.

With no immediate job prospects in England, his mother recently deceased, and only a vague idea that he might perhaps quite like to be an actor, Niven set sail for Canada: he was just twenty-three and it seemed as good a place as any to start out on a new life. Within a matter of weeks he had travelled south to New York and found work as a whisky salesman before joining a dubious pony-racing syndicate in Atlantic City. From there he travelled on to Los Angeles and began to seek employment as an extra in minor westerns. His Hollywood fortunes distinctly improved when he formed a romantic attachment to Merle Oberon however, and by 1939 as a contract artist at the Goldwyn Studios he had made starring appearances in *The Charge of the Light Brigade* (1936), *The Prisoner of Zenda* (1937), *The Dawn Patrol* (1938), *Raffles* (1939), and *Wuthering Heights* (1939), among a dozen other and lesser films. His Hollywood image was that of the 'grin and tonic' man, a veneer actor who traded in a kind of jovial good fortune, that of the happy-go-lucky adventurer who once shared a beach house with Errol Flynn known locally as Cirrhosis-by-the-Sea on account of its constant stock of alcohol.

In truth, Niven was a considerably more serious, astute, and talented man, one whose behaviour at the declaration of World War II showed characteristic courage: abandoning a lucrative studio contract and a career which was at last successful, he was the first of the few English actors to return from California to enlist. He rejoined the army as a subaltern in the Rifle Brigade, was released to make three of his best films (*The First of the Few*, 1942, *The Way Ahead*, 1944, and *A Matter of Life and Death*, 1945), and returned to Hollywood in 1946 accompanied by his beloved first wife Primula Susan, whom he had married in 1940, and their two young sons, David and James. Primula was the daughter of Flight-Lieutenant William Hereward Charles Rollo, solicitor, grandson of the tenth Baron Rollo. Within a few weeks of the Nivens' arrival in California however, 'Primmie' was killed in a fall down a flight of cellar stairs, and although Niven was to marry again in 1948 (the Swedish model Hjördis Paulina Tersmeden, who survives him and with whom he adopted two daughters, Kristina and Fiona) a certain sadness was now discernible behind the clenched grin of the gentleman player.

Niven's post-war career as an actor was remarkably undistinguished, coinciding as it did with the collapse of the Hollywood Raj of expatriate British officers and gentlemen on screen. By 1951, however, with the publication of a first novel (*Round the Rugged Rocks*) Niven had discovered a second career as a writer, and in the 1970s he was to publish two anecdotal volumes of memoirs (*The Moon's a Balloon*, 1971, and *Bring on the Empty Horses*, 1975) which were the most successful ever written by an actor and ran into many millions of paperback reprints. Shortly before his death he also published a second novel (*Go Slowly, Come Back Quickly*, 1981) and had become a regular guest on British and American television chat shows where, as himself, he gave some of his best performances.

In 1958 Niven deservedly won an Oscar for *Separate Tables*, in which he played an army officer who invented a private life when his own proved unsatisfactory, a habit often endorsed by Niven himself in his autobiographies. His later films of note included *The Guns of Navarone* (1961), *Paper Tiger* (1974), and *Murder by Death* (1976), but during an author tour for his last novel in 1981 he was stricken by motor-neurone disease which condemned him to a lingering and painful death, one he approached with all the courage and good humour that were the hallmarks of his life. Niven died 27 July 1983 at his home in the Swiss village of Château d'Oex where he spent many of his later years skiing. He was buried there. There was a memorial service at St Martin-in-the-Fields in London attended by more than five thousand people.

[David Niven, *The Moon's a Balloon*, 1971, and *Bring on the Empty Horses*, 1975 (autobiographies); Sheridan Morley, *The Other Side of the Moon*, 1985 (biography); private information; personal knowledge.]

SHERIDAN MORLEY

published 1990

OLDFIELD Sir Maurice

(1915–1981)

Head of SIS (Secret Intelligence Service), traditionally known as 'C', was born 16 November 1915 in the village of Over Haddon, near Bakewell, Derbyshire, the eldest of eleven children of Joseph Oldfield, tenant farmer, and his wife, Ada Annie Dicken. He was educated at Lady Manners School in Bakewell, where he learned to play the organ and began his lifelong devotion to the Anglican Church. In 1934 he won a scholarship to Manchester University and specialized in medieval history. After the award of the Thomas Brown memorial prize, in 1938 he graduated with first class honours in history and was elected to a fellowship. The war upset his plans for an academic career.

After joining the Intelligence Corps, his service was spent mostly at the Cairo headquarters of SIME (Security Intelligence Middle East) where his talent was spotted by Brigadier Douglas Roberts. Oldfield finished the war as a lieutenant-colonel with an MBE (1946). When Roberts joined SIS at the end of 1946 as head of counter-intelligence, Oldfield became his deputy from 1947 to 1949. There followed two postings to Singapore from 1950 to 1952 and from 1956 to 1958, first as deputy and later as head of SIS's regional headquarters covering South East Asia and the Far East. It was here that he established himself as a flyer. In 1956 he was appointed CBE. Throughout his life he never lost interest in the family farm and kept up his organ playing and regular attendance in church, both at home and abroad. Although there was never any hint of indiscretion in his private life, a number of his colleagues put the standard interpretation on why he had reached middle age without getting married.

Following a short spell in London from 1958 to 1959, he was selected for the key post of SIS representative in Washington, where he remained for the next four years, with the main task of cultivating good relations with the CIA. In 1964 he was appointed CMG. His close ties with James Angleton, the head of the CIA's counter-intelligence branch, were reinforced by their shared interest in medieval history. But Angleton also persuaded Oldfield to swallow the outpourings of the KGB defector, Anatoli Golitsyn, who was claiming, *inter permulta alia*, that the Sino-Soviet conflict and President Tito of Yugoslavia's breach with Moscow were clear cases of Soviet disinformation. Soon after leaving Washington, Oldfield withdrew his belief in most of Golitsyn's fairy stories. If, however, he confessed his errors when on his knees, there was, understandably, no overt explanation of how someone of his calibre had been led up the garden path.

On his return to London he became director of counter-intelligence and in 1965 'C's' deputy. He therefore had reason to feel aggrieved when he was passed over in 1968 in favour of Sir John Rennie from the Foreign and Commonwealth Office, whom he later succeeded as 'C' in 1973. This made Oldfield the first member of the post-war intake to reach the top post. Under his leadership, SIS benefited from the good relations he cultivated with both Conservative and Labour ministers at home and from its improved standing with friendly foreign intelligence services with which he kept in personal touch. Oldfield was appointed KCMG in 1975 and GCMG on his retirement in 1978: the only 'C' so far to have received this award. He was also the first to cultivate chosen journalists at meetings in the Athenaeum. This led to the smile on his pudgy face behind horn-rimmed glasses appearing in the press.

All Souls made him a visiting fellow in 1978, where he began a study of Captain Sir Mansfield Cumming, the first 'C', but soon lost interest in it through lack of material. He therefore welcomed Margaret Thatcher's proposal in October 1979 to appoint him co-ordinator of security intelligence in Northern Ireland. In Belfast he did his best to improve relations between the chief constable and the new GOC, but the strains of office soon told on him. It was not only incipient cancer, but also alleged evidence on his unprofessional contacts that caused his return to London in June 1980. Subsequent interrogation resulted in the withdrawal of his positive vetting certificate, after he confessed he had lied to cover up his homosexuality. There is, however, no evidence that his private life had prejudiced the security of his work at any stage in his career. He died in London 11 March 1981. He never married.

[Richard Deacon, *'C': A Biography of Sir Maurice Oldfield*, 1984; private information; personal knowledge.]

NIGEL CLIVE

published 1990

OLIVIER Laurence Kerr

(1907–1989)

Baron Olivier

Actor and director, was born in Dorking 22 May 1907, the second son and youngest of three children of the Revd Gerald Kerr Olivier, assistant priest at St Martin's church there, and his wife, Agnes Louise Crookenden. Educated at St Edward's School, Oxford, he showed precocious acting ability, which was recognized even by his clerically blinkered father, and made his stage début at the age of fifteen as Kate in a boys' performance of *The Taming of the Shrew* at the Shakespeare festival theatre, Stratford-upon-Avon. After leaving school, he won a scholarship to the Central School of Speech Training and Dramatic Art, founded by Elsie Fogerty, and went on to join the touring company run by Lena Ashwell and then (in 1927) the Birmingham repertory theatre, directed by (Sir) Barry Jackson.

His first years on the stage were marked by fierce ambition and energy, but no clear sense of direction. An outstandingly good-looking young actor, he was in some danger of falling into the matinée idol trap—as when, having created the role of Stanhope in the try-out of *Journey's End*, by R. C. Sherriff, he abandoned that fine play for the option of a short-lived lead in *Beau Geste* (1929). At the invitation of (Sir) Noël Coward (to whom he remained lastingly in thrall) he took the tailor's dummy role of Victor Prynne in *Private Lives* (1930–1). He also began uncertainly in Hollywood as a Ronald Colman look-alike; he was fired from the cast of *Queen Christina* in 1933 at the request of Greta Garbo.

After the failure of *Beau Geste* he went on to play five leading parts in under two years without ever achieving a decent run; an ominous experience for a young star in a hurry, though it forecast one of the greatest strengths of his maturity: the refusal ever to please the public by repeating himself. Late in his career, when he played James Tyrone in Eugene O'Neill's *Long Day's Journey into Night* (1971), there was a sense of personal horror in his portrait of a once hopeful young talent destroyed by years of profitable type-casting.

In Olivier's own view, the turning point in his career came with the 1934 production of *Queen of Scots*, by Gordon Daviot (the pseudonym of Elizabeth Mackintosh): a long forgotten play which, again, met with small success, but which marked the beginning of a group of lifelong professional friendships with, among others, George Devine, Glen Byam-Shaw, Gwen Ffrangçon-Davies, and, supremely, the show's director, (Sir) John Gielgud. Olivier the fiery egoist had discovered his need for a family, and with it his future course as a company-based classical actor. The first fruits of this discovery were bitter when—playing Romeo to Gielgud's Mercutio (1935)—he ran into opposition from the London critics, who did not like his verse speaking. The fact that he then turned a flop into a triumph by switching roles with Gielgud, did not really heal the wound.

Olivier described his duel with Gielgud as one between 'earth and air'. The two stars were, and remained, opposites. But it was not long before the public learned to value both; to relish Olivier's animal magnetism, physical daring, and power to spring surprises, as much as his conversion of speech into another form of action. He struggled to extract every ounce of dramatic meaning from the text, often driven into harsh sardonic resonance and shock inflections, and detonating isolated words. Following Gielgud (whose theatrical families kept breaking up), Olivier's other main partnership was with his friend from the Birmingham rep, (Sir) Ralph Richardson, with whom he played in two Old Vic seasons in the late 1930s—consolidating his Shakespearian position in a sequence of contrasted leading roles (Toby Belch, Henry V, Macbeth, Hamlet, Iago, and Coriolanus) before their reunion (with John P. Burrell) as directors of the postwar Old Vic company.

In the flush of his pre-war Shakespearian success, Olivier was wary of another summons from Hollywood. However, in 1939 he deigned to accept the role of Heathcliff in *Wuthering Heights*, and suffered a baptism of fire from his director, William Wyler, who criticized him unmercifully for his theatrically exaggerated style and patronizing attitude towards the art of film. Made ill by this treatment, Olivier endured it and emerged from the experience as a major star. 'Wyler,' he later acknowledged, 'taught me how to act in movies; taught me respect for them; taught me how to be real.' It was another victory for naturalism; and an apprenticeship in film-making which swiftly led to mastery in the first and best of his own films: *Henry V* (1943–4), probably the first successful Shakespeare film ever made, at once for its cunning blend of picturesque artifice and point-blank realism, and for Olivier's outstanding performance, which long outlived its patriotic morale-boosting intentions.

Olivier had entered the war in 1941 with the intention of putting acting away for the duration, and qualified as a pilot in the Fleet Air Arm. An incompetent aeronaut, he destroyed five aircraft in seven weeks. He was seconded into propaganda entertainment by the Ministry of Information and saw no active service. On completing *Henry V*, he led the Old Vic company in 1944 from their bombed-out Waterloo Road house into temporary West End premises at the New theatre. The company flowered as never before. These were the years of Olivier's Richard III, Hotspur, and Lear; and the inspired double bill of *Oedipus*, and *The Critic* by R. B. Sheridan, in which Olivier, as Puff, was whisked off, still talking, up to the flies. Coupled with Richardson's Falstaff (to Olivier's Shallow) and Peer Gynt (to which Olivier, in a supreme stroke of luxury casting, played the tiny part of the Button Moulder) these seasons formed a glorious chapter in the Old Vic's history. But neither that, nor the knighthood Olivier received in 1947, inhibited the theatre's governors (headed by Viscount Esher) from picking a moment in 1948 when Olivier was leading the troupe on a tour of Australia, to inform him that the directors' joint contract would not be renewed.

Indignantly repulsing Esher's subsequent offer to re-engage him as sole director, Olivier set up his own management at the St James's theatre for a mixed classical and modern repertory, in which he directed and co-starred with his wife, Vivien Leigh. These seasons included premières of plays by (Sir) Terence Rattigan and Christopher Fry, new work from Thornton Wilder and Tennessee Williams, and two Cleopatras from Vivien Leigh, with Olivier paying successive court to her as Shakespeare's Antony and G. B. Shaw's Caesar.

By this time, Olivier had reached the summit of his worldly ambitions. All his desires had been satisfied: as an actor, for whom audiences would queue all night, he was the undisputed monarch of the London stage; he had succeeded as a director and as a manager; unlike Gielgud and Richardson, he also had an international film career, known to a vast public who had never set foot in a theatre. He had made a fairy-tale marriage; his residence was a twelfth-century abbey including a home farm. But under the glittering public image he felt he had come to a stop; his work had again lost its sense of direction, and his private life was becoming a hostage to Vivien Leigh's increasing manic depression.

To repair the 'aching void' he made some random career changes: embarking on an unconvincing singing début in the film of *The Beggar's Opera* (1952), which at least forged an alliance with Peter Brook, with whom he again broke new Shakespearian ground in the 1955 Stratford production of *Titus Andronicus*; and directing and playing the title role in the film of Rattigan's *The Prince and the Showgirl* (1957), in which he was outshone by Marilyn Monroe. By that time he had already discovered the route to renewal in the English Stage Company's new play-writing revival at the Royal Court theatre, under his old friend George Devine. Unlike the other leading actors of his generation, Olivier took the plunge into the new wave and, to the dismay of some admirers, appeared as Archie Rice, the seedy bottom-line comedian in John Osborne's *The Entertainer* (1957), which became one of his favourite parts. He discarded his West End wardrobe with zest, swaggering on in a loud check suit, exchanging all the obligations of eminence for the free speech of the dregs of the profession. 'Don't clap too loud, lady,' he leered out to the house; 'it's a very old building.' This was the time of the Suez crisis.

At the Royal Court (where he also played in Eugène Ionesco's *Rhinoceros*, 1960) he met the actress Joan Plowright, whom he married after divorcing Vivien Leigh. His attachment to the Court became crucial in 1963 when, after running the first seasons of the Chichester festival theatre, he achieved his ultimate professional goal as first director of the newly formed National Theatre, where he confirmed his alliance with the young generation by engaging Devine's protégés, John Dexter and William Gaskill, as his associate directors, and appointing the *Observer*'s campaigning critic Kenneth Tynan (formerly an arch foe) as his literary manager. Just as he transformed his stage physique from role to role, Olivier instinctively altered his public identity according to the mood of the times; and as head of the National Theatre he put off West End glamour and re-emerged in the likeness of a go-ahead bank manager, thoroughly at home in the new world of state subsidy and permanent companies. He was uniquely qualified for the job, as a natural leader who commanded the loyalty of the whole profession, and as an artist who had nothing more to prove.

There remained one unscaled Shakespearian peak, *Othello*, which he played (directed by Dexter) in 1964 in a final burst of incandescent sensuality. Otherwise, though he was a regular NT player in roles ranging from punishing leads like Edgar in August Strindberg's *The Dance of Death* (1967) to walk-on parts like the Jewish divorce lawyer in *Home and Beauty* (1969) by W. Somerset Maugham, his main energy went into creating an ensemble that could tackle any play in the world. The opening seasons were a surprise: plays by Harold Brighouse, Noël Coward, Henrik Ibsen, Georges Feydeau—works with nothing in common beyond the fact that almost every one of them brought the theatre another success and redefined the reputation of the playwright.

One criticism of the National Theatre—voiced, among others, by Olivier's former Old Vic colleague, Sir W. Tyrone Guthrie—was that the ensemble was failing to present Britain's leading actors. With the exception of Sir Michael Redgrave, no actor approaching Olivier's own rank became a member of the team; and Olivier unceremoniously sacked Redgrave and took over his role in Ibsen's *The Master Builder* (1965), mistaking the onset of Redgrave's Parkinson's disease for drunkenness. Possibly the criticism he received for importing Peter O'Toole over the heads of the regular troupe for the opening production of *Hamlet* (1963–4) made him shut his door against visiting stars. What he did achieve was a theatre that became a second home to its actors and which developed its own stars—including Colin Blakely, Derek Jacobi, Edward Petherbridge, Geraldine McEwan, and Joan Plowright.

Olivier's years at the National Theatre were wracked with troubles of which the general public knew little or nothing. His artistic associates' support for controversial work such as Frank Wedekind's *Spring Awakening* and Rolf Hochhuth's *Soldiers* brought him into collision with the governors and completely estranged him from their chairman, the first Viscount Chandos. For the first time in his career, Olivier also became plagued with stage fright and memory loss. He suffered five major illnesses—including thrombosis, cancer, and muscular dystrophy—and came through them by sheer force of will. But after appearing in Trevor Griffiths's *The Party* (1974)—delivering a twenty-minute speech as an old Glaswegian Trotskyite—his stage career was at an end. In the previous year, with mixed feelings, he handed over the directorship of the National Theatre to (Sir) Peter Hall, who led the company from the Old Vic theatre into its new South Bank premises.

In his remaining years Olivier had a busy film and television life, though (with a few exceptions, such as the roles of Dr Christian Szell in *Marathon Man*, 1976, and Loren Hardemann in *The Betsy*, 1978) his film work consisted of cameo parts which he took to support his new young family. He was more scrupulous when it came to television, and the last flowering of his talent can be seen in his performances of Lord Marchmain in the Granada adaptation of Evelyn Waugh's *Brideshead Revisited* (1981), the blind protagonist of John Mortimer's *A Voyage Round My Father* (1982), and a valedictory *King Lear* (1983). In his last decade he also published two books: *Confessions of an Actor* (1982) and *On Acting* (1986), both absorbingly informative but no guide to the man himself. As an author, as on stage, he disappeared into a role. He left behind a Dickensian gallery of characters, each one composed with the copious observation and imaginative investment of a novelist. Olivier did more to advance the art of acting than anyone since Sir Henry Irving, and just as Irving had become the English theatre's first knight, so Olivier, in 1970, became its first life peer. In 1981 he was admitted to the Order of Merit. He had honorary degrees from Tufts, Massachusetts (1946), Oxford (1957), Edinburgh (1964), London (1968), Manchester (1968), and Sussex (1978). He had numerous foreign awards and in 1979 was given an honorary Oscar.

In 1930 he married an actress, Jill Esmond (died 1990), daughter of Henry Vernon Esmond, whose original surname was Jack, actor and playwright; they had one son. The marriage was dissolved in 1940 and in the same year he married the actress Vivien Leigh (died 1967), daughter of Ernest Richard Hartley, exchange broker in Calcutta, and former wife of Herbert Leigh Holman, barrister. There were no children and the marriage was dissolved in 1961. In the same year he married the actress Joan Ann Plowright, daughter of William Ernest Plowright, editor of the local newspaper in Brigg, Lincolnshire, and former wife of Roger Gage. They had one son and two daughters. Olivier died 11 July 1989 at his home in Steyning, West Sussex.

[Laurence Olivier, *Confessions of an Actor*, 1982, and *On Acting*, 1986; Felix Barker, *Laurence Olivier*, 1984; Melvyn Bragg, *Laurence Olivier*, 1984; Donald Spoto, *Laurence Olivier*, 1991.]

IRVING WARDLE

published 1996

O'NEILL Terence Marne

(1914–1990)

Baron O'Neill of the Maine

Prime minister of Northern Ireland, was born 10 September 1914 at 29 Ennismore Gardens, Hyde Park, London, the third son and youngest of five children of Captain Arthur Edward Bruce O'Neill (2nd Life Guards), of Shane's Castle, Randalstown, county Antrim, MP for mid-Antrim and eldest son of the second Baron O'Neill, and his wife, Lady Annabel Hungerford Crewe-Milnes, eldest daughter of the Marquess of Crewe, statesman. Terence O'Neill's father became the first MP to die at the front (5 November 1914) and his mother married again in 1922. The young O'Neill was educated at West Downs School in Winchester, and at Eton. He spent much time in Abyssinia, where his stepfather was consul, and during the 1930s had several jobs, ending up at the Stock Exchange. After being commissioned at Sandhurst in May 1940, O'Neill joined the 2nd battalion of the Irish Guards, serving in Normandy and Holland. Both his brothers were killed in World War II.

In October 1946 O'Neill was returned unopposed as the Unionist member for Bannside in the Stormont parliament. He became parliamentary secretary to the minister of health in February 1948 and to the minister of home affairs in 1955. In 1956 he was sworn of the Privy Council (Northern Ireland) and became minister of home affairs and then of finance, forming a politically important relationship with a reform-minded private secretary, (Sir) Kenneth Bloomfield. Another important member of O'Neill's circle, *Belfast Telegraph* editor Jack Sayers, was 'never able to satisfy my mind about the Prime Minister's liberalism—it is far more intellectual than emotional and even then much of it emanates from Ken Bloomfield'. Nevertheless, the fact remains that when in 1963 O'Neill became prime minister of Northern Ireland—unlike his three Unionist predecessors—there was no trace of anti-Catholic bitterness on his record. Yet he was to disappoint some, at least, of his liberal friends.

The subsequent intensity of the sectarian conflict has obscured the fact that in his early years in office he was primarily concerned to win back Protestant support which the Unionist party had lost to the Northern Ireland Labour party in the period since 1958. 'Stealing Labour's thunder'—to use O'Neill's own term—rather than allaying Catholic resentments, was his main preoccupation.

O'Neill had a generous, even impulsive, streak and was capable of the occasional conciliatory grand gesture, such as his famous visit to a Catholic school. In the main, however, he espoused a rhetoric of planning and modernization by which nationalist grievances would be dissolved by shared participation in the benefits of economic growth. He saw little role for structural reform. His speeches in this early period resonate with a pious little-Ulsterism in which devolution emerges not just as an inevitable and reasonable historical compromise but as a responsive communal form of government superior to that of the class-based party system in the rest of the United Kingdom. That UK system was, however, economically sustaining the Stormont regime: a fact of which O'Neill was more aware than the Unionist electorate.

O'Neill's early lack of responsiveness to Catholic grievances was sharply criticized by liberal unionist groupings, such as the leadership of the Northern Ireland Labour party and the *Belfast Telegraph*, but in the short term O'Neillism was quite effective politically. The O'Neillite manifesto for the 1965 election crystallized the ideology of modernization—'Forward Ulster to Target 1970'. The result showed an average swing to the Unionist party of 7 per cent and was a major defeat for Labour.

Despite this electoral success, even then O'Neill was widely perceived to be a poor party manager. Normally secretive and aloof, at times he was capable of indiscreet and hurtful sarcasm at the expense of prickly senior colleagues. And, ironically, his 1965 triumph played a key role in marginalizing a party (Labour) which gave radicals from the Catholic community an outlet.

The emergence in 1968 of the civil rights movement, which included many such radicals, presented O'Neill with an excruciating dilemma: placating the reformers was likely to mean the consolidation of the internal unionist opposition. O'Neill chose the path of moderate, even modest, reform—'the five-point programme' of November 1968. For a brief moment, he seemed to have a real chance of gaining significant Catholic support whilst retaining that of a majority of Protestants. But the tactics of the radical wing of the civil rights movement, responding more to leftist politics than nationalist impulses, were to frustrate him.

The civil rights march led by the People's Democracy group in January 1969 was of decisive importance. This march was attacked at Burntollet bridge by Orange partisans and the subsequent deterioration in communal relations made O'Neill's position exceptionally difficult. Caught between the pressures generated by loyalist and nationalist militants, and having almost lost his seat in a snap election he called in February, he resigned in April 1969, though he retained substantial Protestant support even at the end. He accepted a life barony in 1970. In 1967 he had received an honorary LL D from Queen's University, Belfast.

O'Neill's legacy is ambiguous. Even the reputation of his path-breaking talks in 1965 with the taoiseach, Sean Lemass, suffered, amongst unionists at any rate, from later claims by Lemass's widow (bitterly repudiated by O'Neill) that they had been about 'Irish unity'. His famous statement on resignation continues to haunt his reputation: 'It is frightfully hard to explain to Protestants that if you give Roman Catholics a good job and a good house, they will live like Protestants . . . they will refuse to have eighteen children on National Assistance . . . in spite of the authoritative nature of their church.' He was a patrician figure out of touch with large sections of the population. O'Neill's political failure is made all the more tragic by the fact that he was essentially a man of decent tolerant instincts.

In 1944 O'Neill married (Katharine) Jean, daughter of William Ingham Whitaker, of Pylewell Park, Lymington. They had a daughter and a son. O'Neill died 12 June 1990 at his home in Lymington, Hampshire.

[*Ballymena Observer*, 13 November 1914; Terence O'Neill, *The Autobiography of Terence O'Neill*, 1972; Andrew Gailey (ed.), *John Sayers, a Liberal Editor*, 1993; Paul Bew and Henry Patterson, *The British State and the Ulster Crisis*, 1985.]

PAUL BEW

published 1996

PARTRIDGE Eric Honeywood

(1894–1979)

Lexicographer and etymologist, was born 6 February 1894 in the Waimata Valley, a farming district near Gisborne in New Zealand, the son of John Thomas Partridge, grazier, and his wife, Ethel Annabella Norris. About 1907 his family emigrated to Australia and he attended Toowoomba Grammar School before entering the University of Queensland in 1914. His studies were interrupted by the war and he served with the Australian Imperial Forces at Gallipoli and on the western front. He completed his BA at the University of Queensland in 1921.

A travelling scholarship took him to Oxford, where, as a non-collegiate student, he wrote a thesis on Romantic poetry of the eighteenth century before the Lyrical Ballads as the requirement for his University of Queensland MA. In 1923 he completed a B.Litt. thesis for the University of Oxford on English and French literature of the Romantic period. Both were published as books in Paris in 1924.

He was a lecturer in English literature at the universities of Manchester, 1925–6, and London, 1926–7. In 1927 he left the academic world in order to become a writer and a publisher. He founded the Scholartis Press with a capital of £100, and it published a number of works, including some of his own, before it went out of business in the economic depression of the early 1930s. Using the pseudonym 'Corrie Denison' he wrote three novels, but they went unregarded.

Other works that he wrote or edited at about this time pointed the way to his later obsessional interest in popular vocabulary: *Songs and Slang of the British Soldier (1914–1918)* with John Brophy (1930); *American Tramp and*

Underworld Slang, with G. Irwin (1931); and *Francis Grose's Classical Dictionary of the Vulgar Tongue* (1931), reprinted from the third edition of 1796.

His most celebrated work, *A Dictionary of Slang and Unconventional English*, was published in 1937. He revised it at regular intervals rather in the informal way in which a child extends a hastily constructed sand-castle.

In the war of 1939–45 he served first in the Army Education Corps (1940–1) and later in a propaganda department of the RAF (1942–5) with H. E. Bates and other writers. These duties appear not to have greatly impeded his own writing and he produced an astonishing number of books in the 1940s. The best known of these were *A Dictionary of Clichés* (1940), *Usage and Abusage* (1942), *A Dictionary of RAF Slang* (1945), *Shakespeare's Bawdy* (1947), and *A Dictionary of Forces' Slang, 1939–45* (with W. Granville and F. Roberts, 1948).

By the end of the 1940s Partridge had established his reputation partly by using a technique well known to eighteenth-century lexicographers—the taking over, more or less verbatim, of material published at an earlier date, and wrapping it in a cloak of evidence he had gathered himself. In 1949 some of the contents of his *Dictionary of the Underworld British and American* was found to be closely related to work published by an American scholar, David W. Maurer. The matter was settled out of court in Maurer's favour.

Much of his primary lexicographical evidence came from a kind of proletariat army of devoted correspondents. Thousands of scholars and laymen throughout the world accepted his invitation to submit details of local usage. For Partridge—the great word peasant—these other peasants were the equivalent of staff, as he continued to work, otherwise without assistance, at the same desk, K1, in the British Museum. He rewarded the more productive of them with autographed copies of his books and with his autobiographical Christmas cards.

The pattern remained the same for the rest of his life. He compiled new editions of his dictionaries and wrote many books about English usage. Two works of more enduring value stand out from the rest: *Origins: a Short Etymological Dictionary of Modern English* (1958); and *A Dictionary of Catch Phrases: British and American from the Sixteenth Century to the Present Day* (1977).

Amateur enthusiasts of words who knew him through his books spoke of him with unqualified admiration and sympathy. Edmund Wilson called him 'the word king', and Benny Green 'the Middleweight Champion of the Word'. Others caught from him 'a sense of passionate and infectious curiosity about words'. This may have been his greatest contribution, for his professional contemporaries judged his work as partially flawed by its derivative nature and by a quirky mode of presentation.

In appearance a cheerful, rather shambling, and self-effacing figure, he was obsessively interested in tennis and cricket. He played tennis himself and for many years forecast the Wimbledon results in *Time and Tide*. He was a member of the Surrey and Middlesex cricket clubs and often went to The Oval and Lord's on working days. His other main obsession, apart from his work, was an incurable belief in his own impecuniosity, though in the end his estate was, by any normal standard, substantial.

In 1964 the University of Queensland awarded him the honorary degree of Doctor of Letters.

In 1925 he married Agnes Dora (died 1978), daughter of Arthur James Vye-Parminter, an architect. They had one daughter. Partridge died 1 June 1979 at Moretonhampstead, Devon.

[David Crystal (ed.), *Eric Partridge in his Own Words*, 1980; private information; personal knowledge.]

ROBERT BURCHFIELD

published 1986

PEAKE Mervyn Laurence

(1911–1968)

Artist and author, was born at Kuling, China, 9 July 1911, the younger son of Ernest Cromwell Peake, MD, Congregational missionary doctor, of Tientsin, by his wife, Amanda Elizabeth Powell. Peake was educated at Tientsin Grammar School, Eltham College, Kent, and the Royal Academy Schools where he won the Hacker prize (1931). After finishing at the Academy Schools he spent two years in an 'artists' colony' of friends on the island of Sark; on the strength of his work he was offered a position at the Westminster School of Art in 1935, where he taught life drawing until 1939. There, too, he met Maeve, youngest of the six children of Owen Eugene Gilmore, MD, FRCS; they married in 1937, and had two sons and a daughter. During the war Peake served in England in the Royal Artillery, being later transferred to the Royal Engineers, but was invalided out in 1943 after a nervous breakdown. For the next two years he was attached to the Ministry of Information, and it was not until just after the end of the war that he was appointed war artist with the rank of captain. In 1946 he returned to Sark with his family, where they spent three serenely happy years; but a retainer from his publisher and a few commissions could not continue to meet the needs of a growing family, and in 1949 they came back to England where Peake secured a part-time teaching post at the Central School of Art, Holborn; this, together with commissioned paintings and illustrations for books, and to a lesser extent his writing, formed the often uneven ground on which he supported his family. From 1957, after the failure of his first and only West End play, *The Wit to Woo*, which was to have solved all their financial problems, he became increasingly incapacitated by what was eventually diagnosed as a form of Parkinson's disease, and by 1960 he was obliged to give up teaching.

After his death in 1968 Peake became best known for his three 'Titus' novels, *Titus Groan* (1946), *Gormenghast* (1950), and *Titus Alone* (1959), which describe the growth of Titus, the seventy-seventh Earl of Groan, in his ancestral home Gormenghast castle, his rebellion against Gormenghast and his restrictive duties, and his attempt to find a new identity for himself in another land. Although showing the influence of Dickens, Lewis Carroll, and Kafka, these books defy ready classification. The term 'fantasy' is perhaps the least inadequate, although Peake's work has nothing of the lightweight or evasive commonly implied by the word: but it is fantasy in being the creation of a fully realized 'other' world, ontologically separate from our own. The strength of *Titus Groan* is the thoroughness with which it is imagined, and the dialectical play throughout of the static, unchanging nature of the castle against the dynamic of the enemies within it. In Gormenghast Peake found the perfect literary expression for his interests as an artist: the slow, heavily descriptive method of the style and the delight in the individualities of people and objects are paralleled in the unmoving character of the castle, the obsessive preoccupation with minutiae which epitomizes the ritual laws which govern it, and the eccentric personalities it produces. Gormenghast castle is the natural home of Peake's imagination, a home to which he was irresistibly drawn, even while as a man and an artist he wished to escape it and explore new worlds. The undertow of Gormenghast drains the life from the portrayal of Titus's rebellion, and the imaginative unity and power of *Titus Groan* is increasingly lost in the succeeding volumes. Yet, considered as a whole, the 'Titus' books remain a massive achievement.

During his lifetime, Peake was known more as an artist, particularly as an illustrator of books. The finest examples are his work for the editions of Lewis Carroll's *The Hunting of the Snark* (1941) and the *Alice* books (1946 and 1954); Coleridge's *The Rime of the Ancient Mariner* (1943); the Grimm brothers' *Household Tales* (1946); and R. L. Stevenson's *Dr. Jekyll and Mr. Hyde* (1948) and *Treasure Island* (1949). Peake also illustrated much of his own work; and his children's books, *Captain Slaughterboard Drops Anchor* (1939) and *Letters from a Lost Uncle from Polar Regions* (1948) are composed round his brilliant drawings. In collections of his individual sketches, *The Craft of the Lead Pencil* (1946) and *The Drawings of Mervyn Peake* (1949), Peake also outlined his views on art as at once intensively subjective and objective. The primary concern of Peake's drawings is with the human figure, rather than with landscape: of Gormenghast he has left us scarcely a pictorial trace. One of the most frequent and powerful of his effects is the portrayal of the frail verticality of his figures struggling against a dense and crushing atmosphere, or else bent or deformed by it: this is also his vision of the lives of the personages of Gormenghast, and of those who rebel against the castle. Later publications, such as his *Writings and Drawings* (1974) and his *Drawings* (1974), showed a return of interest in Peake the artist.

Peake was also recognized in his own day as a poet. Poetry was for him the most moving form of human expression. Much of his poetry for adults appeared in his *Shapes and Sounds* (1941), *The Glassblowers* (1950), *The Rhyme of the Flying Bomb* (1962), and *A Reverie of Bone* (1967). For *The Glassblowers* (and *Gormenghast*) he was awarded the W. H. Heinemann Foundation prize of £100 and an honorary fellowship of the Royal Society of Literature (1951). He is at his best when an experience and its significance for him are fused, as for instance in 'The Glassblowers' or the frightening 'Heads Float About Me', rather than when he reflects on or self-consciously tries to proportion his feelings to his experience. A recurrent motif in his poetry is the idea of a face or body as a building or city, and vice versa: this transference is also seen in the interrelations of Gormenghast and its inhabitants. Peake also wrote children's and nonsense poetry (the latter often in the vein of Lewis Carroll). His poetic impulse is as divided between the serious and the comic as is his *Gormenghast*: Peake would have written more good poetry, as he did the prose of *Titus Groan*, had he fused both sides of his nature in the making of it.

Tall, thin, dark, and haggard, Peake was a romantic figure, whose passionate and intense nature exhausted him: he lived always on 'this desperate edge of now', and wrote to pour himself forth, to empty himself of all his 'golden gall'. In some ways shy and reserved, he was innocently open and generous to all who asked his help. He was enormously sensitive to human suffering, and a visit to Belsen in 1945 (commissioned by the *Leader* to sketch what he saw) left him emotionally scarred. In character he was gentle, gracious, unworldly, and unpractical. He lived in many ways outside convention, wearing strange clothes and behaving in a gently whimsical fashion which puzzled the ordinary. He did not care for 'arrangements' in life: he would gather materials for drawings simply by walking the streets of central London and stopping interesting subjects for on-the-spot sketches; and he would write in the midst of his family circle.

It was in part Peake's very proximity to and delight in life which produced his fantasy, and his sense of the individual his art of exaggeration: 'Anything,' he once said, 'seen without prejudice, is enormous.'

Peake died at Burcot, Berkshire, 17 November 1968. Several portraits done by his widow, Maeve Gilmore, remained in her possession. A Mervyn Peake Society was formed in 1975.

[Maeve Gilmore, *A World Away: A Memoir of Mervyn Peake*, 1970, and *Peake's Progress*, 1979; John Watney, *Mervyn Peake*, 1976; private information; personal knowledge.]

C. N. Manlove

published 1981

PEVSNER Sir Nikolaus Bernhard Leon (1902–1983)

Architectural historian, was born in Leipzig 30 January 1902, the younger son (there were no daughters) of Hugo Pewsner, a successful fur trader, settled in Leipzig, and his wife, Annie Perlmann, both of Jewish extraction. The elder brother died in 1919, the father in 1940, his widow committing suicide two years later to avoid internment in a concentration camp. Pevsner was educated at St Thomas's School, Leipzig, and attended the universities of Leipzig, Munich, Berlin, and Frankfurt. His doctoral dissertation focused on the baroque merchant houses of Leipzig and led to the writing of his first book, *Leipziger Barock* (1928). Meanwhile in 1924, he joined the staff of the Dresden gallery as a 'Voluntär' or unsalaried assistant, remaining there till 1927 and contributing the volume on Mannerist and baroque Italian painting to the *Handbuch der Kunstwissenschaft* series (1928). Also in the Dresden years he was attracted to the social history of art, on which nothing yet had been written. An eventual outcome was his *Academies of Art, Past and Present*, published in England in 1940.

In 1928 Pevsner was attached to the University of Göttingen as a *Privatdozent*. In 1930 he visited England for the first time and thereafter lectured on English architecture in the art history department and occasionally in the philosophy faculty. His experience of the arts in England induced a profound curiosity about the contrast between the English arts and their equivalents on the Continent. 'The contrast was complete and it was, against all expectations, agreeable too!'

In 1933, notwithstanding that he had become a Lutheran when he was nineteen, Pevsner was forced to stop teaching under the Nazi race laws.

He decided to leave Germany and move to England, making the acquaintance of Philip Sargant Florence of Birmingham University. Florence suggested that he should undertake an investigation into English industrial design. From 1934 Pevsner worked mainly in Birmingham, his findings eventually crystallizing in *An Enquiry into Industrial Art in England* (1937). In the course of his work he met (Sir) S. Gordon Russell and became his firm's adviser on modern furniture design.

Pevsner had early recognized the validity of the Modern movement in architecture. He was conscious, however, of the need for clarification of the movement's sources and in 1936 appeared his *Pioneers of the Modern Movement from William Morris to Walter Gropius*. The book was widely influential and was translated into many languages.

With the outbreak of hostilities in 1939, Pevsner's status became technically that of 'enemy alien' and in 1940 he was interned for a short period in the Isle of Man under the war-time regulation 18B. His friends in academic circles quickly secured his release and he briefly took employment as a labourer clearing rubble from bombed London streets. From this he was rescued by an offer of employment by the Architectural Press and from 1942 to 1945 the editorship of the *Architectural Review* was almost entirely in his hands. He was naturalized in 1946.

Also in 1942 he was appointed to a part-time lectureship at Birkbeck College, University of London. He lectured there till his retirement in 1969, having in the meantime been appointed (1959) professor of the history of art. His approach to architectural history is reflected in the Pelican Book written in 1941, and first published in 1942, *An Outline of European Architecture*. Consisting only of 160 pages and selling at a very modest price, it placed the history of architecture in a new perspective. 'The history of architecture', Pevsner wrote in the introduction, 'is the history of man shaping space.' By the adroit selection and analysis of only a few buildings in each period, he penetrated deeply into the social and philosophic roots of architectural form.

For Penguin Books Ltd. Pevsner edited, from 1941, the series of 'King Penguins', miniature picture books with short texts by distinguished scholars; of these his own study of *The Leaves of Southwell* (the carved foliage in the chapterhouse), 1945, was one of the most original.

Following the success of the Pelican *Outline*, the publisher, Sir Allen Lane asked Pevsner what he would like to tackle next. Pevsner made two suggestions. One was for a comprehensive series of histories covering the whole world of art and architecture, of which he would be the editor. The other was for a series of county-by-county guides to the architecture of Britain. This he would undertake to write entirely himself. Lane reacted promptly in favour of both proposals. In the event, the guides, *The Buildings of England*, were launched first, in 1951, and completed, in forty-six volumes, in 1974. The 'Pelican History of Art', launched in 1953, is still in progress.

If *The Buildings of England* was Pevsner's most conspicuous and widely acclaimed achievement, he was constantly engaged in writing and lecturing on a wide range of subjects. He was Slade professor of fine art at Cambridge in 1949–55 and at Oxford in 1968–9. In 1955 he delivered the annual Reith lectures on the BBC, taking as his subject 'The Englishness of English Art'. This had always been for him an absorbing theme. The talks were made into a book, published in 1955.

In 1964 he produced *Sources of Modern Art* (reissued as *Sources of Modern Architecture and Design* in 1968). *Some Architectural Writers of the Nineteenth Century* followed in 1972. His last published work was *A History of Building Types* (1976), a valuable collection of notes made over the whole period of his career.

Pevsner's continuous production of books, articles, and lectures left him little leisure for social activities which indeed, he constantly declined. His only recreations were walking and swimming. He participated, however, in the work of commissions and committees which he considered important, serving on the Royal Fine Art Commission, the Historic Buildings Council, the Advisory Board on Redundant Churches, and the National Council for Diplomas in Art and Design. He was a founding member of the Victorian Society and chairman from its inception in 1958 till 1976, after which he was president for life.

He received many honours and awards. He was appointed CBE in 1953, elected FBA in 1965, and knighted 'for services to art and architecture' in 1969. In 1967 he received the RIBA Royal gold medal for architecture. Honorary doctorates were awarded to him by the universities of Oxford, Cambridge, East Anglia, Keele, the Open University, the Heriot-Watt University of Edinburgh, Pennsylvania, and Zagreb. In 1969 he was decorated with the grand cross of the Order of Merit of the Federal Republic of Germany.

In appearance Pevsner was tall, slim, and fresh complexioned but with the somewhat 'owlish' mask of the scholar. In conversation he was lively and responsive, with a keen sense of humour; his letters were always concise and sometimes witty. He lived simply, worked incessantly, and was wholly dedicated to scholarship and the arts, especially to the architecture of his adopted country, to the study of which he may be said to have contributed more than any man of his time.

Pevsner married in 1923 Karola ('Lola') Kurlbaum, who has been described as 'the most important influence on his life'. She was the daughter of Alfred Adolf Kurlbaum, by his first wife, who was of Jewish descent, though Kurlbaum himself was not. He was a lawyer who practised at the Supreme Court in Leipzig. By her Pevsner had two sons and a daughter, all of whom survived him. She died in 1963. Pevsner's last years, during which he was incapacitated by Parkinson's disease, were spent at 2 Wildwood Terrace, Hampstead, which he had occupied since 1941. He died there 18 August 1983.

[*The Times*, 19 August 1983; Peter Murray in *Proceedings* of the British Academy, vol. lxx, 1984; information from Stephen Games; personal knowledge.]

JOHN SUMMERSON

published 1990

PHILBY Harold Adrian Russell ('Kim') (1912–1988)

Soviet agent, was born 1 January 1912 at Ambala in the Punjab, the only son and eldest of four children of Harry St John Bridger Philby, Indian civil servant, explorer, and orientalist, and his wife Dora, daughter of Adrian Hope Johnston, of the Indian public works department. With unconscious prescience they nicknamed him Kim. He was educated at Westminster and Trinity College, Cambridge, where he joined the university Socialist Society and became a convinced communist. He obtained a third class in part i of the history tripos (1931) and a second class (division I) in part ii of the economics tripos (1933). Philby was of medium height with a seductive smile. In 1933 he went on a trip to Vienna, where he met Alice ('Litzi') Friedman, an Austrian communist, whose father was Israel Kohlman, a minor government official of Hungarian Jewish origin. They witnessed the street fighting, which ended with the defeat of the socialists in February 1934, when they had a hurried marriage and left for England. By this time she had persuaded him to become a Soviet agent. While he was in Vienna, the NKVD (the Soviet secret service) had talent-spotted Philby as a potential recruit.

In June 1934, at a secret meeting in Regent's Park, Philby was approached by Arnold Deutsch, a Czech undercover Soviet intelligence officer operating in London. Philby welcomed the suggestion that he should penetrate 'the bourgeois institutions'. Another of his controllers was Teodor Maly, a Hungarian who had renounced the priesthood and become an idealistic convert to Bolshevism. Beginning his career as a journalist, Philby was instructed to sever all links with his communist past and swing over to the far right. Hence his involvement with the pro-Nazi Anglo-German Fellowship. First as a freelance and later for *The Times*, he went to Spain in February 1937 to cover the Spanish civil war from the point of view of General Franco (whose planned assassination was part of his original brief), who awarded him the red cross of military merit. He left Spain in August 1939 with his overt right-wing credentials established, while his covert faith in Joseph Stalin remained untarnished by the Terror of the mid-1930s, although he had an ambivalent attitude to the Nazi–Soviet pact in August 1939. His luck never deserted him, especially permitting him to survive the ups and downs of an alternating relationship with the Moscow centre.

After the outbreak of World War II Philby went to France as a war correspondent. Returning to England after Dunkirk, he was recruited, thanks to Guy Burgess, his friend from Cambridge and a fellow NKVD agent, into the SIS (the Secret Intelligence Service or MI6) in July 1940 and soon joined Section Five (counter-intelligence) in 1941. A base in London eased his domestic problems with Aileen Furse (the daughter of Captain George Furse of the Royal Horse Artillery) with whom he had been living and producing children since 1940, but whom he did not marry until December 1946, a week after his divorce from Litzi. By then he was a rising star, having become in 1944 head of Section Nine, whose remit was 'to collect and interpret information concerning communist espionage and subversion'. When Section Nine was merged with Section Five in 1945, he alerted Moscow to the intended defection in Istanbul of Konstantin Volkov, who could have unmasked Philby. He was appointed OBE in 1946.

In 1946 the SIS posted him to Turkey and in 1949 he became their representative in Washington, where he kept Moscow informed of Anglo-American intelligence collaboration. He also saw how the net was closing in on Donald Maclean. In 1950 Guy Burgess was posted to Washington and lodged with Philby. When Maclean and Burgess fled to Moscow, Philby was summoned back to London and interrogated by MI5, who were persuaded of his guilt, but lacked the evidence of a confession to convict him. The SIS, however, in return for Philby's voluntary resignation, gave him a golden handshake. After his name had been cleared by Harold Macmillan (later the first Earl of Stockton) in 1955, the SIS fixed his cover as a correspondent for the *Observer* and the *Economist*, based on Beirut, where he arrived in August 1956.

Aileen died in 1957. There were three sons and two daughters of the marriage; Philby had no other children. In 1959 he married Eleanor, from Seattle, who was formerly married to Sam Pope Brewer, Middle East correspondent of the *New York Times*. In Beirut, Philby was successfully reincarnated as a journalist until Anatoli Golitsyn's defection to the CIA in 1962 filled in the gaps in the case against him. The SIS and MI5 then confronted Philby with a prosecutor's brief in January 1963, plus an offer of immunity if he returned to London and made a full confession. Philby admitted he had been a Soviet agent but said no more. He quietly arranged his escape and arrived in Russia at the end of January 1963. Five months later he was granted Soviet citizenship.

Eleanor soon joined him, but she so disliked life in Moscow that she left for good in 1965; she died in America in 1968. Meanwhile, Philby had been awarded in 1965 the Order of Lenin and the Order of the Red Banner. He began an affair with Melinda, the wife of Donald Maclean, who had also defected to Moscow, but this did not last. Heavy drinking and smoking dominated his life until 1970, when George Blake, another defector, introduced him to Rufina Ivanova, half Polish and half Russian, whom he married in 1971. She was the daughter of an expert on the chemical treatment of furs. In 1980 his award of the Order of Friendship of Peoples preceded his East German, Hungarian, Bulgarian, and Cuban decorations. He died in Moscow 11 May 1988, receiving his final recognition in an elaborate funeral organized by the KGB. A private buyer purchased the lion's share of Philby's papers, which were auctioned at Sotheby's in July 1994.

[Christopher Andrew, *Secret Service*, 1985; Christopher Andrew and David Dilks (ed.), *The Missing Dimension*, 1984; Nicholas Bethell, *The Great Betrayal*, 1984; John Costello, *Mask of Treachery*, 1988; John Costello and Oleg Tsarev, *Deadly Illusions*, 1993; Phillip Knightley, *Philby, the Life and Views of the KGB Masterspy*, 1988; Patrick Seale and Maureen McConville, *Philby, the Long Road to Moscow*, 1973; Hugh Trevor-Roper, *The Philby Affair*, 1968; Kim Philby, *My Silent War*, 1968; Eleanor Philby, *The Spy I Loved*, 1968; Genrikh Borovik, *The Philby Files*, 1994; Yuri Modin, *My Five Cambridge Friends*, 1994; personal knowledge.]

NIGEL CLIVE

published 1996

RAMBERT Dame Marie

(1888–1982)

Ballet director and teacher, was born Cyvia Myriam Ramberg 20 February 1888 in Warsaw, Poland, the youngest of the three children, all daughters, of Yakov Ramberg, a bookseller of Jewish descent whose father's surname was Rambam, and his wife, Yevguenia Alapina. For a time she called herself Myriam Ramberg, but when she came to London she assumed the name by which she was thereafter to be known, Marie Rambert. She was educated at the Gymnasium in Warsaw, and in 1905 was sent to Paris with the intention of studying medicine. Instead she began to associate with the artistic world, attracting the attention of Raymond Duncan, brother of Isadora, with whose free style of dancing she first identified. Between 1909 and 1912 she worked in Geneva under Emile Jaques-Dalcroze, whose influence was central to her artistic development.

Towards the end of 1912 she was engaged by Serge Diaghilev to give classes in Dalcroze eurhythmics to the dancers of his Ballets Russes and more especially to assist Nijinsky in the difficult task of choreographing *Le Sacre du Printemps*. Shortly after that ballet's riotous première she accompanied the company on its visit to South America. From her association with the Diaghilev Ballet she received a lasting legacy: a profound interest in classical dance. Her engagement was not renewed when the company returned to Europe, and she went back to Paris, moving to London on the outbreak of war in 1914. There she met the playwright Ashley Dukes (died 1959), whom she married on 7 March 1918, and by whom she had two daughters. Dukes was the son of the Revd Edwin Joshua Dukes, Independent minister. Rambert became a British subject by this marriage. After the war she became an assiduous pupil of the celebrated ballet teacher, Enrico Cecchetti, and was soon teaching ballet on her own account, gathering around her, as time went by, students of exceptional promise, among them (Sir) Frederick Ashton, Harold Turner, and Pearl Argyle.

Such talented young dancers needed stage experience to fulfil themselves, and in the later 1920s Rambert began to supply this, first with the ballet, *A Tragedy of Fashion* (1926), which she persuaded Ashton to choreograph: it was his first ballet, and can now be seen as a historic landmark, from which a national ballet tradition was to spring. In the years that followed her students continued to make occasional appearances under the name of the 'Marie Rambert Dancers'. When Diaghilev died in 1929, there was a sudden dearth of ballet in London. In 1931, to fill the void, Rambert formed the Ballet Club with the object of forming a permanent ballet company with a theatre of its own. She even had a theatre—the minuscule Mercury Theatre near Notting Hill Gate, purchased by her and her husband out of their savings. It was to be the home of their ballet until 1939, and for many years housed their remarkable collection of historic ballet lithographs (now in the Theatre Museum).

Rambert possessed a unique gift for discovering and nurturing young choreographers, and Ashton, Antony Tudor, and Andrée Howard were all greatly in her debt for the cultural enrichment that she brought them. Under her inspired direction, Ballet Rambert (renamed thus in 1934) became part of the fabric of the growing English ballet tradition, although it was to fall to (Dame) Ninette de Valois' Vic-Wells Ballet to be chosen as the national company. Owing to the tiny dimensions of the Mercury Theatre, Ballet Rambert operated as 'chamber ballet', but the absence of spectacle was compensated for by exquisite taste and attention to detail. During World War II the company became larger and outgrew the Mercury. But it never lost its strong interpretative quality, and in 1946 Rambert herself staged a production of *Giselle* that was remarkable for its dramatic content.

Towards the end of her active life Rambert guided the steps of another budding choreographer, Norman Morrice, who succeeded her as director in 1966 and launched Ballet Rambert on a new course with greater emphasis on modern dance. Rambert's support of this bold move was an indication of her extraordinarily active and receptive mind. She enjoyed a long retirement and lived on to 12 June 1982, when she died at her London home in Campden Hill Gardens.

Considered as one of the architects of British ballet, she was appointed CBE in 1953 and DBE in 1962. In 1957 she became a chevalier of the Legion of Honour; she received the Royal Academy of Dancing's Queen Elizabeth II Coronation award in 1956. The University of Sussex awarded her an honorary D.Litt. in 1964.

She had inexhaustible energy (she could turn cartwheels until she was seventy), an infectious sense of fun, and a very retentive memory (displayed in reciting poetry by the page). Above all she gave inspiration to others, without which British ballet would today be much poorer.

[Mary Clarke, *Dancers of Mercury*, 1962; Marie Rambert, *Quicksilver*, 1972 (autobiography); Richard Buckle, *Nijinsky*, 1971, and *Diaghilev*, 1979; Clement Crisp and others (ed.), *Ballet Rambert: 50 Years and On*, 1981; Mary Clarke, obituary in *Dancing Times*, July 1982.]

IVOR GUEST

published 1990

RAMSEY (Arthur) Michael

(1904–1988)

Baron Ramsey of Canterbury

Archbishop of Canterbury, was born in Cambridge 14 November 1904, the younger son in the family of two sons and two daughters of Arthur Stanley Ramsey, a Cambridge mathematics don and Congregationalist elder, and his wife (Mary) Agnes, daughter of Plumpton Stravenson Wilson, vicar of Horbling, Lincolnshire. His elder brother Frank Ramsey (died 1930) became the well-known Cambridge philosopher. Educated at Repton and then as a classical scholar at his father's college, Magdalene, he became a leading debater and president of the Cambridge Union (1926). He was committed to the Liberal party and was adopted as the Liberal candidate for Cambridgeshire. But during his third year at university he became convinced, to the surprise of his friends, that he should take holy orders. He gained a second class in part i of the classical tripos (1925) and a first class in part i of the theology tripos (1927). He then went to Cuddesdon College, near Oxford, to be trained for the priesthood. This training was almost wrecked, first by the death of his mother in a car accident in 1927, and then by the need for psychiatric treatment.

He was ordained to the curacy of St Nicholas, Liverpool, in September 1928 but stayed in the parish only eighteen months. He then became subwarden of the theological college at Lincoln. Here he published in 1936 his best-known book, *The Gospel and the Catholic Church*. It was at once a persuasive to Protestants to take seriously the Catholic tradition of ministry and devotion, and a persuasive to Catholics to take seriously the Protestant conviction of the central biblical truths. The book was original in form and range of ideas and made him well known to the thinking and reading members of the church. After another curacy at Boston (Lincolnshire, 1936–8) and a year as vicar of St Benet's in Cambridge (1939–40), he was chosen in 1940 to be professor of divinity at Durham University. The post carried with it a canonry at the cathedral.

At Durham (1940–50) he was soon valued as the leader of sane Catholic thought and devotion in the Church of England, and after the war as an Anglican leader prominent in the ecumenical movement and the World Council of Churches. After a brief spell as regius professor of divinity at Cambridge, with a fellowship at Magdalene College (1950–2), during which he was also canon and prebendary of Lincoln Cathedral (1951–2), he was chosen successively as bishop of Durham (1952–6), archbishop of York (1956–61), and archbishop of Canterbury (1961–74). As bishop of Durham he had the historic duty of standing at the queen's right hand during her coronation; his vast bald dome and mobile eyebrows attracted comment when the event was televised and introduced his colourful personality to the nation. His shining face, which looked old from the age of thirty-five, was attractive, though not at all handsome, with its abundant, beaming smiles.

His term at Canterbury coincided with the introduction of reforming legislation, in which he took a prominent part. He was weighty in the abolition of capital punishment, in changes in the laws on abortion, divorce, and homosexuality, and, especially, on the subject of race relations. As prime minister, Harold Wilson (later Baron Wilson of Rievaulx) made him the chairman of the national committee for Commonwealth immigrants, and as such he was in public dispute with Enoch Powell over immigration. His term also coincided with a prising apart of church and state. He was determined that Parliament should no longer have the final say in the doctrine and worship of the Church of England. To that end he helped with the creation of the general synod to secure a representative government for the church, with legislation to allow modern experiments in worship, with the abolition of the historic subscription by clergy to the Thirty-nine Articles of 1571, and with the transfer of the power over forms of prayer and doctrine to the authorities of the church instead of the state. This involved the repeal of the Act of Uniformity and was the biggest change in English church government since the restoration of Charles II.

What made Ramsey world-famous was his visit in March 1966 to Pope Paul VI, who received him with all honour and gave him his own bishop's ring. He had undertaken the mission with a certain reluctance, but once it was decided threw himself into its spirit of affection and charity. In public opinion the visit became an important symbol of the happier relations between churches in the modern age and the new attitudes of the Roman Catholic Church after the second Vatican Council. Afterwards, as Ramsey travelled the world on his visits to the Anglican provinces, he was much in demand as a speaker on the unity of the churches. He had long had an understanding of the eastern Orthodox tradition of spirituality and valued much that was best in the western Catholic inheritance. He stated his views in numerous books, of which the last was *Be Still and Know* (1982). His essays and addresses he gathered into three volumes.

His part in the movement for Christian re-union made him, despite his Anglo-Catholic convictions, an eloquent advocate of the proposed plan for union between Anglicans and Methodists. He just failed (1969 and 1971) to persuade a sufficient majority of his church to accept the plan. This was a blow to his confidence in the wisdom and charity of the representatives, to whom he was engaged in transferring authority from Parliament.

One strength of the Church of England had lain historically in its links, unconfessed, with the more tolerant sides of the Conservative party. Ramsey, however, swung away and became a Liberal advocate in the House of Lords, causing much criticism. He was accused of sanctioning modern services which lost the beauties of a beloved Prayer Book; of being kind to homosexuals; of being friendly to an open policy of immigration; of not denouncing the bishop of Hong Kong when he ordained two women as priests; and, above all, of sanctioning in 1965 military action by Britain to stop Ian Smith from making a racialist state in Rhodesia. This last matter incurred the strong displeasure of the far right, and Ramsey did not bear their abuse without suffering.

The attribute which commanded a vast discipleship and affection was Ramsey's obvious devotion. Despite an enchanting sense of humour, he was not good on television and was accused of sounding like a bumbling old parson. But his faith, and experience of God, and prayerfulness, came over unmistakably to nearly everyone who met him. He was an incompetent administrator if he was bored by the subject—such subjects included finance, the structure of a parish system, and constitution-mongering. Yet, where the subject interested him, where it concerned religion or religious thought, or something he otherwise cared about, he was a very good administrator. At conducting a retreat he was inspiring and lovable, at hearing confessions he was wise, and when he celebrated a quiet little sacrament it lifted the souls of the people heavenward. He distrusted his pastoral colleagues when they needed distrust, but occasionally he trusted too much someone who had won his confidence. His conversation was fascinating when he was interested; his silences were profound when he was not or when he wanted to think about God. Some who sat next to him at dinner, especially women, despaired of making him say anything. His hobby was brass-rubbing.

Ramsey was an honorary master of the bench (Inner Temple, 1962), president of the World Council of Churches (1961–8), a trustee of the British Museum (1963–9), and an honorary FBA (1983). As well as a number from overseas universities, he held ten honorary degrees from universities in Britain, including Cambridge (1957) and Oxford (1960). He was an honorary fellow of several Oxford and Cambridge colleges, was sworn of the Privy Council (1956), and became a life peer in 1974.

In 1942 he married Joan Alice Chetwode Hamilton and the marriage, though childless, was happy. She was the daughter of Lieutenant-Colonel Francis Alexander Chetwode Hamilton. She shared her husband's vocation and helped him through the worst of the silences, especially when he was a host.

In 1974 he retired first to Cuddesdon, where he hoped to teach at his old college, and then in 1977 to Durham, where he loved to renew his association with the cathedral. He still paid many visits abroad to lecture. Nashotah House, Wisconsin, a college for training priests, became almost a second home, for he felt there a spirit in devotion and theology that he valued highly. In 1986 Ramsey and his wife began to age and moved to a ground-floor flat in the archbishop's house at Bishopthorpe outside York, and then to St John's Home in Oxford, where Ramsey died, 23 April 1988.

[Owen Chadwick, *Michael Ramsey*, 1990; J. B. Simpson, *The Hundredth Archbishop of Canterbury*, 1962; Michael De-la-Noy, *A Day in the Life of God*, 1971, and *Michael Ramsey, a Portrait*, 1990; D. L. Edwards, *Leaders of the Church of England*, 2nd edn., 1978; Adrian Hastings, *A History of English Christianity 1920–1985*, 1986; personal knowledge.]

OWEN CHADWICK

published 1996

RANSOME Arthur Michell

(1884–1967)

Journalist and author, was born in Leeds, 18 January 1884, the eldest in the family of two sons and two daughters of Cyril Ransome, professor of history, who died when Arthur was thirteen, and his wife, Edith, daughter of Edward Baker Boulton, who had been a sheep farmer in Australia. He was educated at the Old College, Windermere, and Rugby, but he was a reluctant pupil. Doggedly determined from early adolescence that he was going to be a writer, he spent two unprofitable terms at Yorkshire College, Leeds (later to become Leeds University), reading science before he threw in his hand and left for London where he found a job for eight shillings a week at Grant Richards, the publishers. He was then seventeen.

His bohemian life in London, with a brief period in Paris, lasted for some twelve years. He scratched a living by writing stories and articles, some of which appeared in book form; he reviewed and ghosted. His literary friends included Edward Thomas, Lascelles Abercrombie, Gordon Bottomley, Robert Lynd and his wife Sylvia, and Cecil Chesterton, brother of G. K. Chesterton. There were also actors and artists with whom he would celebrate the sale of an article or a picture by a flagon of Australian burgundy and a meal of macaroni cheese. Many of these met at the studio 'evenings' of Pamela Colman Smith—'Pixie'; he later said that it was from her telling of Negro folk-stories that he learnt so much of the art of narration. He was very poor but nevertheless avidly buying books, and he later attributed his chronic stomach troubles to the meagre and erratic meals of that period.

If there was time for a brief holiday and he could scrape together the fare, he found himself hurrying 'through the big grey archway at Euston that was the gate to the enchanted North' on his way to the Lake District where, before his father had died, his family had spent summer months so happy that the rest of his life seemed an anticlimax. Here he passed much of his time with the family of W. G. Collingwood, adopted as an honorary nephew by the parents, and camping and boating with the children, one of whom was Robin Collingwood. Later, the four children of Dora, the oldest daughter (later Altounyan), were to identify themselves as the Walker children in his books. He hoped to marry Barbara, the second daughter, but this never came about, and it was to escape the unhappy marriage that he did make, to Ivy Constance, daughter of George Graves Walker, in 1909, that he went to Russia in 1913.

The winter of 1912–13 had been one of continual nightmare. A book commissioned by Martin Secker on Oscar Wilde had landed Ransome in a suit for libel issued by Lord Alfred Douglas, and though judgment was given against Douglas in April 1913 it was a scarring experience. Meanwhile, seeing Russian folklore as the material for a new book of folk-stories retold in a simple vernacular style, he decided to visit Russia itself. Arriving there in 1913, he taught himself Russian, collected folklore, and busied himself with writing a guide to St Petersburg commissioned by an English firm. After the outbreak of war (which prevented the guide from being published), he supported himself as a newspaper correspondent for the *Daily News*. In 1916 was published *Old Peter's Russian Tales*, the result of Ransome's investigations into Russian folklore. It had considerable success and was reprinted several times. Paying regular brief visits to England, he stayed in Russia until 1919, becoming friendly with Lenin and other Bolshevik leaders, especially Karl Radek, and making himself unpopular with the British Foreign Office by his opposition to foreign intervention in Russian affairs. For a time in 1918 a British mission in Moscow was headed by (Sir) Robert Bruce Lockhart, of whom Ransome said '. . . [he] was soon on better terms with Trotsky than I was'. In *Six Weeks in Russia in 1919* (1919) he gave a picture of Moscow in those days of starvation and high hopes, and in *The Crisis in Russia* (1921) he defended the Russian revolution and pleaded for a more balanced view of its aims.

By that time he was living in Estonia with Evgenia, daughter of Peter Shelepin (she had been Trotsky's secretary), whom he was to marry in 1924 when his first marriage had been dissolved. His long association with C. P. Scott and the *Manchester Guardian* started in 1919, and such time as he could spare from his newspaper reports he spent in the fishing and sailing that all his life were an absorbing passion. In the *Racundra*, a thirty-ton ketch, built to his specifications at Riga, he cruised round the Baltic in 1922. The log of this holiday was published in *'Racundra's' First Cruise* (1923).

At the end of 1924 Scott sent him as correspondent to Egypt and then in

1925–6 to China, but he was growing increasingly weary of political journalism and longing to settle to his own writing. In March 1929 he began to write *Swallows and Amazons*, an account of four children and their holiday camping and sailing in the Lakes, an evocation of the supreme happiness of his own boyhood holidays. Published in 1930, it was slow to sell. Jonathan Cape, the publisher, had received it politely but was more interested in his fishing essays, *Rod and Line* (1929). Nevertheless he persisted, following it up with a further account of the Walker children and their allies the Blacketts sailing Lake Windermere and exploring the fells—*Swallowdale* (1931). But only with his third story, *Peter Duck* (1932), did he soar into the popularity that made his nine other books for children best-sellers. (It was in *Peter Duck* that he first attempted his own illustrations, a practice he was to continue.) *Winter Holiday* (1933) recalled a winter he had spent on the Lakes when he was at preparatory school. There were books such as *Coot Club* (1934) about bird-watching and sailing on the Norfolk Broads, near which he lived for a time from 1935 on the river Orwell, in Suffolk. For *Pigeon Post* (1936) he received the Library Association's first Carnegie medal for the best children's book of the year. He became an honorary D.Litt. of Leeds University in 1952 and was appointed CBE in 1953. He published his last book, *Mainly about Fishing*, in 1959.

Bald, vastly moustached as he became in later life, habitually dressed in a fisherman's sagging tweeds and a thimble of a tweed hat, he still contrived to retain much of the appearance of the round, rosy, bright-eyed schoolboy that can be seen in the early photographs. With it went a boyish charm of manner with its mingling of enthusiasm and fierce indignation; a deftness of fingers—especially where tying flies was concerned—and a stimulating ability to say something new and unexpected about almost any subject.

He died 3 June 1967 at Cheadle Royal Hospital, Manchester. His second wife died in 1975. He had one daughter by his first marriage. There is a portrait by John Gilroy, 1958, in the Garrick Club.

[*The Times*, 6 June 1967; Hugh Shelley, *Arthur Ransome*, 1960; *The Autobiography of Arthur Ransome*, ed. Sir Rupert Hart-Davis, 1967.]

GILLIAN AVERY

published 1981

RATTIGAN Sir Terence Mervyn

(1911–1977)

Playwright, was born in Cornwall Gardens, Kensington, 10 June 1911, the second of two children, both sons, born to (William) Frank (Arthur) Rattigan and his wife, Vera Houston. His father, Frank, was the son of Sir William Rattigan, at one time chief justice of the Punjab and, later, MP for North-East Lanark. Frank's career was less distinguished than his father's had been. He resigned from the Diplomatic Service in 1922 after a disagreement with the foreign secretary, the Marquess Curzon of Kedleston, over the best approach to the Chanak crisis. (Frank, who was assistant high commissioner at Constantinople, favoured intervention on behalf of Greece.) Thereafter the finances of the family were never soundly based.

Vera was seventeen when she married. She outlived her husband who, by all accounts, had a lifelong attachment to 'fluffy blondes' (his second son's expression) which may have steered that impressionable boy, not only into the arms of his mother but also, in true Freudian style, down less conventional emotional paths in later life. One of his mother's Houston relatives had, in 1863, given a public lecture, later published (Arthur Houston, 'The English Drama. Its Past History and Probable Future' in *The Afternoon Lectures on English Literature*, 1863), in which may be read the following prophetic passage: 'The highest type of dramatic composition is that which supplies us with studies of character, skilfully worked out, in a plot not deficient in probability, and by means of incidents not wanting in interest.' No truer definition of the future products of his relative, as yet unborn, is ever likely to be penned.

In 1920 Rattigan went to Sandroyd, a preparatory school near Cobham in Surrey. For one summer holiday his mother took a cottage, in which the bookshelves held nothing but plays, from a drama critic, Hugh Griffiths. Rattigan read them all and, as he said in later years, that holiday determined his career. In 1925 he won a scholarship to Harrow, thus relieving his now hard-up father from the onus of financing him. He wrote a one-act play in French, which the French master marked two out of ten, conceding that the 'theatre sense was first class'. He also wrote an article, in the *Harrovian*, on modern drama, in which he discussed 'the ceaseless conflict between Entertainment and Instruction'. Broadly speaking, the position he adopted in that article foreshadowed the stance he took, forty years on, in his battle with the New Guard drama critics, during which, in his own words, 'I had no chance with anything. They didn't give me reasons for it. They just said, "It must be bad".'

At Harrow he played cricket for the school and took the Bourchier history prize. In 1930, having won a minor scholarship to Trinity College, he went up to Oxford. By now he was a fair-haired, charming youth, with one foot on the playing-fields, the other firmly planted in the Oxford University Dramatic Society. His father, whose ambition was that he should be a diplomat, sent him to France in his first long vacation. Rattigan came home with the idea for his first successful play already in his mind.

In 1932 he and a friend, Philip Heimann, collaborated in the writing of *First Episode*, produced in 1933 at the Q Theatre and transferred to the Comedy in 1934. This play, though adolescent in conception and, indeed, in plot—the scene was set in Oxford—earned mild praise from the reviewers (not excluding James Agate, of the *Sunday Times*). At once, the fledgling dramatist left Oxford with his father's grudging blessing and a small allowance from the same source.

In November 1936 the play he had conceived in France, *French Without Tears*, came on at the Criterion. From curtain-fall until the day of his death, forty-one years later, in the same month, Rattigan was famous and his name a household word. Unhappily, the path Rattigan trod, as an outstanding British dramatist, was not invariably strewn with roses. None the less, for more than twenty years in London and New York, his touch was golden. Audiences felt not only confidence but also fulfilment in his company.

French Without Tears, his greatest comedy success (in spite of Agate's strong aversion to it) was succeeded by another triumph. With *Flare Path* (1942), based on his RAF experience, he proved himself to be a good all-rounder, capable of writing with uncanny skill on any theme that took his fancy. He reverted to light comedy, in 1943, with *While the Sun Shines*; then—his war service concluded—he again took up more serious themes—*The Winslow Boy* (1946), *The Browning Version* (1948), *The Deep Blue Sea* (1952), and *Separate Tables* (1954). His screen-plays, too, were equally successful. Many of them were produced by Anatole de Grunwald and directed by Anthony Asquith, with both of whom he worked in total harmony.

In later life the quality of Rattigan's plays fell somewhat short of what it had been at its zenith. It was never less than adequate, however, and did not merit the hostile criticism it received. His obituary in *The Times* (1 December 1977) states: 'Rattigan's opponents, at an hour of theatrical rebellion, took every chance to belittle a probing storyteller.' Kenneth Tynan called him 'the Formosa of the British Theatre', asserting that he had betrayed the revolution (the New Wave) by staying with the Old Guard. None the less, although the argument around which this sad controversy raged was sterile from the start, it needled Rattigan beyond endurance and—unwisely—to the point of fighting back, thus provoking the New Wave with his constant references to his middle-class 'Aunt Edna'—a fictitious figure he invented—whose tastes, so he said, deserved as much attention as the avant-garde.

Rattigan was a homosexual and never married. He received a knighthood in 1971, having been appointed CBE in 1958. He came to England from Bermuda, for his last play *Cause Célèbre* (1977), aware that he was dying. '*Cause Célèbre*', wrote Bernard Levin, in the *Sunday Times*, 'betrays no sign of failing powers.' Its author died, back in Bermuda, 30 November 1977. *The Times* described him as an 'enduring influence in the English theatre'. Sir Harold Hobson, in the *Sunday Times*, wrote that 'he had the greatest natural talent for the stage of any man in this century'.

In a memoir for the *Sunday Telegraph* William Douglas-Home said: 'Consider *Separate Tables*. Here, most notably, in all the goings-on concerning an unhappy army officer, the many gifts bestowed on Rattigan by providence are on parade, his humour, his integrity—above all, his compassion. There is not one character who does not speak true. There is not one sentiment expressed which is not grounded in humanity, not one line that, in any way, diminishes the dignity of man. And, as for the compassion, that most Christian of all Christian virtues, it is there in such full measure that no member of the audience, unless his heart be made of stone, will go into the street at curtain-fall, without a lift in spirit and a fuller understanding of mankind as his companion. That is Rattigan's achievement and his triumph. That, so long as theatres exist and players strut their hour upon the stage and speak the dialogue he wrote for them, is his eternal monument.'

[Michael Darlow and Gillian Hodson, *Terence Rattigan. The Man and his Work*, 1979; personal knowledge.]

William Douglas-Home

published 1986

READ Sir Herbert Edward

(1893–1968)

Writer on art, critic, and poet, was born 4 December 1893, the eldest of the three sons of Herbert Read, of Muscoates Grange, Kirbymoorside, in the North Riding of Yorkshire, and his wife, Eliza Strickland. Of farming stock, he was always proud of his peasant origins, and gave a memorable account of them in *The Innocent Eye*, a fragment of autobiography (1933). They were also the inspiration of *Moon's Farm*, a poem written for the radio in 1951. When he left his birthplace to go to the Crossley and Porter Endowed School for orphans in Halifax, he wrote that 'no wild animal from the pampas imprisoned in a cage could have felt so hopelessly thwarted'. After employment as a clerk in the Leeds Savings Bank at the age of sixteen, he entered Leeds University, and felt the literary influence of Blake and Tennyson. At the same time he came under the spell of Nietzsche. On the outbreak of war in 1914 he was commissioned into the Green Howards, and rose to the rank of captain, winning both the MC and the DSO—the type of 'resolute soldier' who organized his men for battle as he would afterwards try to organize the world for peace. His distinguished military record, which included a mention in dispatches, lent an added authority to his pacifism.

He had also, like Guillaume Apollinaire, fought 'on the frontiers of culture'. There was a certain discrepancy between a man so traditional in his way of life, so concerned to create a 'cell of good living' for himself and his family, and the tireless apostle of the avant-garde in literature and art. He was an early pioneer of the modern movement, where his friendship with T. S. Eliot and T. E. Hulme, Ben Nicholson, (Dame) Barbara Hepworth, and Henry Moore, counted for much. Read's imagination was essentially visual. This set him apart from a poet like W. B. Yeats for whom poetry was always, in some degree, incantation, and ranked him with the Imagists who held that only free verse could guarantee to the picture its sharp outline, and to the emotion its unblurred significance. Read's output of verse was not large, but at its best—that is to say, at its most direct and concrete, and at its least explanatory—it had a moving honesty, precision, and power.

Herbert Read was aware of the two forces which shaped his life and gave it a creative tension. As he wrote in *Moon's Farm*: 'the instinctive voice that flows like water from a spring or blood from a wound and the intellectual voice that blares like a fanfare from some centre in the brain.' It was this second voice which, as time went on, was more generally heard. His public appointments registered an increasing interest in the visual arts. After a short period at the Treasury (1919–22), he became an assistant keeper at the Victoria and Albert Museum (1922–31), and Watson Gordon professor of fine art in the university of Edinburgh (1931–3). From 1933 to 1939 he edited the *Burlington Magazine*. In these years he published *Art Now* (1933), *Art and Industry* (1934), and *Art and Society* (1937), all of which were many times reprinted. Only the outbreak of war prevented the establishment of a Museum of Modern Art in London of which he would have been the first director—for his championship of the Surrealist Exhibition (1936) had marked him out as the principal theorist of non-figurative painting and sculpture, where the intention—as Paul Klee had put it—was 'not to reflect the visible, but to make visible'. In 1947 he founded, with Roland Penrose, the Institute of Contemporary Arts—not as yet another place for study or exhibition, but as 'an adult play-centre . . . a source of vitality and daring experiment'.

Through all these activities, and the numerous publications which accompanied them, Read became an international authority and indeed something of a sage. It was not a role to which he ever pretended, for he was a man of conspicuous modesty, and quite capable himself of resting in uncertainty about the essential matters of life and death. His somewhat uncritical welcoming of the new experiment often reflected his dissatisfaction with the old one. But he believed, profoundly, in the dialectic of tradition and innovation, of anarchy and order, which alone could preserve society from sclerosis. This was the meaning of his single novel, *The Green Child* (1935). His anarchism was philosophical, not political, although he was generally found subscribing to any protest on behalf of personal freedom, and he sat down with the others in Trafalgar Square while Bertrand (Earl) Russell was warning the world against the imminent threat of self-destruction. This nonconformity did not prevent the offer and acceptance of a knighthood in 1953. His anarchist friends were dismayed, but it was observed that the Queen had never dubbed a knight to whom the epithet of 'gentle' was more perfectly applicable.

Read's poetry was the classical expression of a romantic temperament, and his literary criticism emphasized his sympathy with romanticism. His Clark lectures on Wordsworth (1930) showed how a passionate love affair and a passionate political *parti-pris* had simultaneously inspired so much of Wordsworth's greatest poetry, and how its incandescence grew faint when the first had cooled and the second had been betrayed. *In Defence of Shelley* (1936) rescued the poet from the denigrations of T. S. Eliot, with whom Read remained on terms of the closest friendship, although Eliot had quoted Read's opposition of 'character' and 'personality' as an example of 'modern heresy'. Read's philosophy might not unfairly be described as 'aesthetic materialism', but the purpose of his preaching in one book after another was to link the good life with the good artefact. *Education Through Art* (1943) indicated how this might be done.

In 1950 Read returned to his Yorkshire roots at Stonegrave, only a few miles from his birthplace. A beautiful stone house was filled with pictures illustrating the achievement of the school whose prophet he had become. For some years he was a director of Routledge & Kegan Paul, and this, among other things, brought him to London for a few days every alternate week. And these years saw the publication of his Concise Histories of *Modern Painting* (1959) and of *Modern Sculpture* (1964). Much of his time, however, was spent abroad, as a speaker at international congresses. He was not at all a voluble person, but it was remarked that 'when Read does at last open his mouth, you know there's nothing more to be said'. In the last years of his life the poet and the peasant, the philosopher and the paterfamilias, seemed to have realized their separate vocations in a serene and unified way of living. He was twice married: first, in 1919, to Evelyn May Roff, by whom he had one son; and, after the dissolution of the marriage in 1936, to Margaret Ludwig, by whom he had three sons and a daughter. He died at Stonegrave 12 June 1968.

The National Portrait Gallery has a portrait by P. Heron given by Dame Barbara Hepworth and Henry Moore.

[Private information; personal knowledge.]

Robert Speaight

published 1981

REED Sir Carol

(1906–1976)

Film director, was born 30 December 1906 in Wandsworth, London, the fourth son (there were subsequently another son and a daughter) of (Sir) Herbert Beerbohm Tree, actor-manager, and his friend, (Beatrice) May Pinney, who took the name of Reed by deed poll in 1904. She named Herbert Reed, of independent means, as the father on the birth certificate, but in 1911 she altered the birth certificate by statutory declaration, leaving the father's name a blank. Tree shared his time between his wife and three daughters and his family by May Pinney. Carol Reed was educated at King's School, Canterbury. After a brief spell of farming in America he returned to London to become an actor. In 1924 he walked on in *St. Joan* by G. B. Shaw, starring (Dame) Sybil Thorndike, at the New Theatre but his first credited appearance was later that year in *Heraclius* at the Empire Theatre, Leicester Square. There followed three years of touring before he returned to the West End as understudy and assistant stage manager at the Lyceum in 1927. The play was *The Terror* whose author, R. H. Edgar Wallace, became an important influence in Reed's life. Reed produced and performed in Wallace's plays and gained his first film experience with Wallace's company at Beaconsfield Studios. After Wallace's death in 1932 he joined Basil Dean at Ealing Studios as a dialogue director and it was there, in 1935, that he directed his first film, *Midshipman Easy*, a vigorous and amusing version of the book by Captain Frederick Marryat.

During the next seven years Reed's many films included an adapted play, *Laburnum Grove* (1936); a backstage comedy, *A Girl Must Live* (1939); a mining drama, *The Stars Look Down* (1939); two entertaining thrillers, *Night Train to Munich* (1940) and *The Girl in the News* (1940); and a pair of costume pieces, *Kipps* (1941) and *The Young Mr Pitt* (1942). All showed a flair for story-telling in cinematic terms and a sympathetic interest in the lives of ordinary people. Now Reed was beginning to tackle weightier and more expensive projects, often as his own producer, but his real maturity as a film-maker came with work he did for the army, which he joined in 1941. He made a training film showing raw recruits being turned into efficient fighting men, *The New Lot* (1943), and the military authorities asked for an expanded version to be shown to the public. The result was *The Way Ahead* (1944), one of Britain's best war films. Reed went on to collaborate with the Americans on an actuality film about the European campaign, *The True Glory* (1945), which won the American Academy award (Oscar) for the best documentary.

Reed was now Britain's leading director. His next film, *Odd Man Out* (1947), an account of the dying hours of an Irish gunman, was hailed as a masterpiece. He followed with two collaborations with Graham Greene, *The Fallen Idol* (1948) and *The Third Man* (1949), both studies in disillusion, which confirmed his status as an international figure. These three films and the next, *Outcast of the Islands* (1952), a version of the book by Joseph Conrad, share a dark view of the world; their visual style, using sharp black and white photography and unusual camera angles, is deliberately disturbing. They reflect what one critic has described as 'a humane pessimism'. They form a body of work unsurpassed in the British cinema, a peak of achievement that Reed never quite scaled again. In 1952 he was knighted for his services to the cinema.

There was a further successful collaboration with Graham Greene, this time in a lighter vein, with *Our Man in Havana* (1960) but Reed's return to international acclaim came with his first musical, *Oliver* (1968), adapted from Lionel Bart's version of *Oliver Twist*. It was visually splendid, making full use of colour and the wide screen, and had a truly Dickensian gusto. It won an Oscar for the best film of the year and another for Reed as the best director, as well as four more for technical qualities.

Carol Reed was a meticulous craftsman and a brilliant technician who had a special sympathy with actors. He worked closely with script-writers and editors but he saw himself as an interpreter rather than an initiator of ideas. His most characteristic films were made in Britain and he never seemed entirely at ease in Hollywood. Indeed, he was temperamentally averse to much of the Hollywood ethic. A quiet, gentle man, he shunned publicity, gave few interviews, and protected his private life. He was very tall but his commanding presence belied a likeable modesty.

In 1943 Reed married the actress Diana Wynyard (died 1964), daughter of Edward Thomas Cox, master printer. The marriage was dissolved in 1947 and there were no children. In 1948 he married Penelope (died 1982), also an actress, daughter of William Dudley Ward, MP for Southampton, and former wife of Harry Anthony Compton Pelissier, son of H. G. Pelissier and Fay Compton. They had one son. Reed died in London, 25 April 1976.

[Madeleine Bingham, *The Great Lover. The life and Art of Herbert Beerbohm Tree*, 1978; Oliver Reed, *Reed All About Me* (autobiography), 1979; Brenda Davies (ed.), *Carol Reed*, British Film Institute, 1978.]

BRENDA DAVIES

published 1986

REED Henry

(1914–1986)

Poet and playwright, was born in Birmingham 22 February 1914, the elder child and only son of Henry Reed, master bricklayer and foreman in charge of forcing at Nocks Brickworks, and his wife, Mary Ann Ball. He was educated at King Edward VI Grammar School, Birmingham, where he specialized in classics. Since Greek was not taught, he taught himself, and went on to win the Temperley Latin prize and a scholarship to Birmingham University, gaining a first-class degree (1934) and an MA for a thesis on the novels of Thomas Hardy (1936).

Like many other writers of the 1930s, he tried teaching and, again like most of them, hated it and left to make his way as a freelance writer and critic. In 1941 he was conscripted into the Royal Army Ordnance Corps, in which he served—'or rather *studied*', as he preferred to put it—until 1942 when, following a serious bout of pneumonia and a prolonged convalescence, he was transferred to the Government Code and Cipher School at Bletchley. At first employed as a cryptographer in the Italian section, he was subsequently moved to the Japanese section, where he learned the language and worked as a translator. In the evenings, he wrote much of his first radio play, *Moby Dick* (1947), and many of the poems later to be published in *A Map of Verona* (1946).

The most famous of these—indeed, the most famous English poem to emerge from World War II—derived from Reed's experience of basic training in the RAOC. A brilliant mimic, he would entertain his friends with a comic imitation of a sergeant instructing his recruits. After a few performances, he noticed that the words of the weapon-training instructor, couched in the style of the military manual, fell into certain rhythmic patterns which fascinated him and eventually provided the structure of 'Naming of Parts'. In this and two subsequent 'Lessons of the War', the military voice is wittily counterpointed by the inner voice—more civilized and still civilian—of a listening recruit with his mind on other matters. At approximately the same point in each of the first four stanzas, the recruit's attention wanders from the instructor's lesson in the unnatural art of handling a lethal weapon, back to the natural world: branches, blossom, Edenic life as opposed to death. The dialectical opposition of two voices, two views of a landscape associated with sexual desire, is a strategy refined in two remarkable poems of Reed's middle years: 'The Changeling', a brilliantly condensed (and disguised) autobiography, and 'The Auction Sale', a Forsterian or Hardyesque short story. Both deal with the loss of Eden, for which Reed, an unmarried, unhappy homosexual, would continue to search in vain. He came to associate the Great Good Place with Italy, the setting of some of his later poems, such of his radio plays as 'Return to Naples' and *The Streets of Pompeii* (1971), and two fine verse plays about another poet whose work he was translating and with whom he identified strongly, Giacomo Leopardi.

In the mid-1950s Reed made a major liberating decision: he abandoned a projected biography of Hardy, which for years had burdened him with guilt like the Ancient Mariner's albatross. That failed quest, perhaps related to the failure of his earlier quest for lasting love, played out a dominant theme of his radio plays: from failure as a biographer, he turned to triumphant success in a radio play about a nervous young biographer, Herbert Reeve, engaged on just such a quest as he had himself abandoned. Reed's hero (whose name owes something to that of Herbert Read, the poet and critic, with whom he was tired of being confused) assembles a mass of conflicting testimony about his author, the novelist Richard Shewin. His witnesses include a waspish brother, his wife, two spinsters of uncertain virtue, and (the finest comic role he was to create for radio) the twelve-tone female composer Hilda Tablet. The success of 'A Very Great Man Indeed' (1953) prompted six sequels, the best of them 'The Private Life of Hilda Tablet' (1954), in which Reeve is browbeaten into switching the subject of his biography from the dumb dead to the exuberantly vocal living female composer.

The modest income that Reed's work for radio brought him he supplemented with the still more modest rewards of book reviewing and translation. The reviewing was to result in a British Council booklet, *The Novel since 1939* (1946), and his published translations include Ugo Betti's *Three Plays* (1956) and *Crime on Goat Island* (1960), Honoré de Balzac's *Le Père Goriot* (1962) and *Eugénie Grandet* (1964), and Natalia Ginzburg's *The Advertisement* (1969). Several of his translations found their way into the theatre, and in the autumn of 1955 there were London premières of no fewer than three.

Reed's greatest imaginative investment, however, was in his poems, but as a perfectionist he could not bring himself to release what he must have recognized would be his last book until it was as good as he could make it, and it never was. Only with the posthumous publication of his *Collected Poems* (1991) would he take his rightful place 'among the English poets'. In his last years he became increasingly incapacitated and reclusive, but devoted friends never ceased to visit him in the London flat he continued to occupy in Upper Montagu Street, thanks to the generosity of a long-suffering landlady, until, removed to St Charles Hospital, Kensington, he died there 8 December 1986.

[Henry Reed, *Lessons of the War*, 1970, *The Streets of Pompeii and Other Plays for Radio*, 1971, *Hilda Tablet and Others, Four Pieces for Radio*, 1971, *Collected Poems*, ed. Jon Stallworthy, 1991.]

JON STALLWORTHY

published 1996

REITH John Charles Walsham

(1889–1971)

First Baron Reith

Creator of the BBC, wartime minister and peacetime administrator, was born 20 July 1889 at Stonehaven, Kincardineshire, the fifth son and the last of the seven children of the Revd George Reith, a Glasgow minister of the Free Church, and his wife, Adah Mary, daughter of Edward Weston, a London stockbroker. He was educated at Glasgow Academy, at Gresham's School in Norfolk, and at the Royal Technical College, Glasgow. He was apprenticed in 1908 to the Hyde Park works of the North British Locomotive Company, Glasgow. In February 1914 he obtained employment with S. Pearson & Son Ltd. at the Royal Albert Dock extension in London.

He had been keen on military activities from his youth, joining various Cadet and Officers' Training Corps. He went to France in November 1914 with the 5th Scottish Rifles, and despite quarrels with his colonel and adjutant he had, as he noted in his diary, 'a thoroughly happy war'. Early evidence of one of his major characteristics is a 1915 entry. After seeing Sir John French (later Earl of Ypres), the commander-in-chief, and 'crowds of brass-hatted Olympians', he thought he 'could do their jobs—some of them anyhow—as well as they'. When turning these war diaries into his book *Wearing Spurs* twenty-two years later (but not published till 1966) he added 'I am sure of it now'. During the battle of Loos in October 1915 a sniper's bullet gashed his face and ended his fighting.

Back in Britain he first had a post in the Ministry of Munitions, then a rewarding eighteen months (1916–17) in America, controlling contracts for munitions. He got on well with Americans all his life. America's entry into the war in April 1917 brought him home again, to work on an Admiralty construction project. He ended his World War I service in the Ministry of Munitions.

The war gave him the greatest boon of his life. In 1918 he fell in love with the driver of his colonel's car. She was Muriel Katharine, younger daughter of John Lynch Odhams, head of the publishing firm of that name. They were married in 1921. Through the fifty years of Reith's public life, which were increasingly unhappy in spite of all the successes and honours that they brought him, his wife was, in the last resort, a powerful stabilizer, a calm companion in the midst of every storm.

In 1920 Reith joined William Beardmore & Co. as general manager at Coatbridge. Seeing no path there for his growing ambition, he resigned and moved to London. Ever since youth he had envisaged a political career. In 1914, 'awfully keen to go into Parliament', he had approached the Liberals. In March 1920 he sounded J. R. Clynes of the Labour Party. In October 1922 he worked for Sir William Bull, Conservative MP for Hammersmith, in the preparations for the general election following Lloyd George's fall. An advertisement offering the post of general manager of the British Broadcasting Company, then being formed, caught his eye. He applied and was appointed in December 1922. Not only was he on the threshold of his greatest achievement; he had been saved from inevitable disaster. Reith's strengths and weaknesses prohibited his ever becoming a successful politician. He could be neither subtle nor supple. He spurned compromise.

Reith's accomplishment in creating the BBC must be measured by the void that confronted him. He had no precedents, no rules, no standards, no established purpose to guide him. There was doubt whether the new device would last. Even the prophetic H. G. Wells saw little future for it. Disregarding all doubts Reith was determined from the beginning to give broadcasting status and purpose. The high proportion of his staff recruits from Oxford and Cambridge became a matter of criticism in later years. He battled ceaselessly to get radio's importance accepted. He persuaded Robert Bridges to include some lines on broadcasting in *The Testament of Beauty.* C. F. Garbett, later archbishop of York, told how Reith had formed a religious broadcasting advisory committee in the earliest days. When its members failed to attend meetings he would upbraid them individually for their lack of vision. He restricted broadcasting on Sundays. He insisted his staff should be chaste.

When, after four years, the manufacturers-owned British Broadcasting Company was replaced under royal charter by the British Broadcasting Corporation, he was its architect as a public service. His claim to have originated the idea has been disputed. Whatever the exact sequence of events, it was what he wanted and built. He had outlined the ideals and policy of the company in *Broadcast Over Britain* (1924). As first director-general of the Corporation he made no change in his policies. Education, religion, and culture were to have their places alongside information and entertainment. The most eminent speakers and musicians were invited to broadcast. Anyone going to the microphone at Savoy Hill or Broadcasting House was given a sense of occasion. Development of regional broadcasting must not weaken the BBC as a national unifying force. Reith's engineering background determined him to have the finest and most efficient system in the world.

While the BBC's charter had settled its status for a quarter of a century, it had given Reith new problems. The governors who replaced the former directors could not be so easily handled. The Earl of Clarendon, the corporation's first chairman, became one of Reith's *bêtes noires*. Viscountess Snowden, a member of the Board of Governors, was an even greater one. When ex-Speaker J. H. Whitley replaced Clarendon in 1930 there came not only peace but mutual affection.

More important was the opposition to Reith growing outside the BBC. The general strike of 1926 had willy-nilly taken the company into politics. The corporation was a fair target for critics in Parliament. Reith was accused of being dictatorial, of poor staff relations (in fact the staff's loyalty to 'Sir John'—he was knighted in 1927—was great), and of bias. He was not deterred. He had the satisfaction of seeing what he had created copied in other parts of the Commonwealth. In 1936 he inaugurated British television.

By 1938 all was going too well for his peace of mind. The BBC was stretching him (a favourite term) no longer. He became bored. He let it be known he would welcome a call to some new national challenge. The government responded. The prime minister, Neville Chamberlain, told him he should leave the BBC to become chairman of Imperial Airways. He went.

The 1938 move soured the rest of his life. 'Stupendous folly', he was to call it in his autobiography *Into the Wind* (1949). Immediately he quarrelled with the BBC governors because they would not give him a major role in choosing his successor. Many and outstanding as were his subsequent achievements, they could not kill his sense of loss. If he had held on for just another year, the problems of broadcasting in wartime, the vast extension and ramifying of the BBC's activities, the establishing of television throughout the kingdom on the standards he had set for radio, all would have given him in war and in peace the new challenge he had been seeking. But patience was never one of Reith's virtues. For the rest of his life the BBC remained a lost Shangri-La.

The imminence of war has been given as the reason for Reith's achieving little in his new post. He did become in 1939 the first chairman of the new British Overseas Airways Corporation, but his heart was not in the job. In January 1940 Chamberlain made him minister of information and on 1 February he became National MP for Southampton. In May (Sir) Winston Churchill, having become prime minister, made him minister of transport, and within five months of that minister of works and a peer (he became first Baron Reith). Early in 1942 Planning was added to his Ministry. The combined posts seemed to promise Reith the scope he craved. In fact he was never at ease with politicians. In a government reshuffle ten days after the last announcement Churchill dismissed him. After the war, on 1 January 1946, Reith wrote a remarkable rebuke to Churchill for never having tested his full powers. Churchill's reasoned soft answer did not mollify him. Reith's hatred of Churchill stayed virulent for his remaining twenty-five years.

Out of office and unemployed Reith turned to the Royal Navy. As a lieutenant-commander RNVR he rationalized coastal forces, and in 1943–4, as a captain and director of Combined Operations, Material Department, Admiralty, planned the movements of all supplies, materials, and transport for the D-Day landings. Tributes from those qualified to assess what he had done declared the work to have been wellnigh perfect. Reith valued the CB (military) he was awarded for this in 1945 above almost all of his many other honours.

Meanwhile, Reith had begun to diversify into other work. In 1943 he joined the board of Cable and Wireless. After leaving the navy he made in 1945 a world flight of 45,000 miles to study future Commonwealth communications. He was chairman of the Commonwealth Telecommunications Board in 1946–50. In 1945–6 he was chairman of the New Towns Committee, and from 1947 to 1950 was chairman of the board of the Hemel Hempstead development corporation. In 1949–50 he chaired the National Film Finance Corporation. His last major achievement was to rescue, revivify, and make viable the ailing Colonial Development Corporation (1950–9). But here his scant respect for his political masters led to bitterness. Commercial appointments were to the boards of Tube Investments, Phoenix Assurance, and British Oxygen, of which he became vice-chairman, characteristically chafing because he was not the chairman. His administrative drive was felt wherever he went. His only fault was sometimes to take his logic beyond what was practical.

His closing years were sad. Not until almost the very end of a long life would he give up hope of being called upon for one last great national effort. When such posts became vacant he would ask friends to mention his name to the prime minister. He would sit by his telephone for hours, waiting for the call that never came. A solitary solace was his appointment to be lord high commissioner of the General Assembly of the Church of Scotland in 1967 and 1968, leading to his being appointed Knight of the Thistle in 1969. He was a member of the Queen's Body Guard for Scotland and of the Royal Company of Archers.

Reith was outsize physically as well as in character. Six feet six inches in height, the scar of his war wound added to his gauntness. He was a man of fierce hates, unrelenting and unforgiving. At the same time he won deep affections. His personal kindness could be overpowering. To ask of him a small service was to switch on a dynamo of energy. He had no wit, but a sense of fun. Some of his quirks, such as misnaming people of whom he did not approve, could become tiresome. But to be with him was to be taken on to a higher and more exciting level.

He accepted no limits to his capabilities. He believed his gifts fitted him for posts for which he had the wrong qualifications. Both as viceroy of India and British ambassador in Washington—two posts he openly confessed to have coveted—he would have been miscast. Even his lord rectorship of Glasgow University (1965–8) was not altogether happy. He was a man of fixed principles. An instinctive leader, he showed when in the navy that he could work happily under authority he could respect. While he justly regarded all he did after he left the BBC as anticlimax, a number of his successes would singly have made the reputation of less extraordinary men.

Reith's honours in addition to those already mentioned included the GBE (1934), GCVO (1939), PC (1940). He had LL Ds from Aberdeen and Manchester (1933), DCL Oxford (1935), and LL D Glasgow (1951). Worcester College, Oxford, made him an honorary fellow in 1962. Reith died in Edinburgh 16 June 1971. His only son Christopher (born 1928) disclaimed the peerage in 1972. The heir to the barony became the Hon. James Harry John Reith (born 1972). Lady Reith, who unveiled a memorial to her husband in Westminster Abbey in 1972, died in 1977. Their only daughter, Marista, married the Revd Dr Murray Leishman.

The BBC has portraits of Reith by (Sir) Oswald Birley (*circa* 1934), by Sir Gerald Kelly (1967), a drawing by (Sir) Max Beerbohm (1938), and a bust (1929) by Lady Scott (later Lady Kennet). There is a chalk drawing by Sir William Rothenstein in the National Portrait Gallery. The portrayal of the inmost man will remain Charles Stuart's fine volume of *The Reith Diaries* (1975).

[*The Times*, 17 June 1971; works above mentioned; personal knowledge.]

WILLIAM HALEY

published 1986

RICHARDS Sir Gordon

(1904–1986)

Jockey and racehorse trainer, was born 5 May 1904 in Ivy Row at Donnington Wood, a district of Oakengates, Shropshire, the fourth child and third son of the eight surviving children (four died) of Nathan Richards, coalminer, and his wife Elizabeth, a former dressmaker, daughter of William Dean, miner and lay preacher. He was given a strict Methodist upbringing, and educated at the Infant School at Donnington Wood. In 1917 he became a junior clerk in the warehouse of the Lilleshall engineering works, Oakengates. Finding the work monotonous, he answered a newspaper advertisement for an apprentice to Martin Hartigan, who had the Foxhill stable near Swindon, Wiltshire, and on New Year's day 1920 left home for the first time to go to Foxhill.

Short, stocky, and very strong for his weight, he had the ideal physique for a jockey. He had dark brown eyes and a thick shock of black hair, which gave him the nickname of 'Moppy'. He weighed out at six stone nine pounds for his first mount in public on Clock-Work at Lingfield on 16 October 1920, and rode his first winner on Gay Lord at Leicester on 13

March 1921, but it was not until he had ridden forty-nine winners, and lost his apprentice allowance, in 1923, that his career got under way.

After coming out of his apprenticeship in 1924, he was first jockey to Captain Thomas Hogg's stable at Russley Park, Wiltshire, in 1925, and became champion jockey by winning 118 races. By the outset of 1926 his career was put in jeopardy by the diagnosis of a tubercular lung after he had ridden just five more winners, and he spent the rest of the year in a sanatorium. In the 1927 season he regained the championship with 164 winners. The first claim on his services in 1928 was held by the shipping magnate the first Baron Glanely, to whom Captain Hogg had become private trainer at Newmarket. Richards obtained his first classic successes in 1930 by winning the Oaks on Rose of England and the St Leger on Singapore for Lord Glanely, but he narrowly lost the championship. After landing the Manchester November handicap on Lord Glanely's Glorious Devon, on the final day he had ridden one more winner than Freddie Fox, but Fox won the fourth and fifth races to be champion with 129 successes.

Richards was champion again with 141 winners in 1931, during which the Beckhampton trainer Fred Darling offered a substantial sum for first claim on him. With typical loyalty, he first asked Lord Glanely to match the offer, but on Glanely pleading poverty, he became first jockey to the Beckhampton stable. Always immensely popular with the public, Richards was a national hero in 1933, as he bid to break the seasonal record of 246 winners established by Frederick Archer in 1885. After eleven consecutive successes at Chepstow in October, he rode his 247th winner on Golden King at Liverpool on 8 November, and finished the season with 259 winners. In 1934 he rode Easton to be second in the Derby, a race he was yet to win, and in 1936 may have been unlucky not to win it on the Aga Khan's Taj Akbar, who was badly hampered before being runner-up to the Aga Khan's second string Mahmoud. By 1938 his bad luck in the Derby was proverbial. That year Darling ran both Pasch, on whom Richards had won the Two Thousand Guineas, and the recent French importation Bois Roussel. Richards elected to ride Pasch, and was third to Bois Roussel.

As his tubercular record made him ineligible to serve in the armed forces, Richards continued to ride during World War II, but, after breaking a leg at Salisbury in May 1941, he missed the remainder of that season and lost the championship for the third time. In 1942 he wore the colours of King George VI when winning substitute races for the One Thousand Guineas, Oaks, and St Leger on Sun Chariot. He also won a substitute Two Thousand Guineas for the king on Big Game, and was champion again. In 1943 he surpassed Archer's career total of 2,748 winners on

Scotch Mist at Windsor, and was champion for the sixteenth time. After winning the Two Thousand Guineas by an extraordinarily easy eight lengths on that great miler Tudor Minstrel in 1947, Richards seemed certain to win the Derby at last. Heavily backed by the public, Tudor Minstrel started hot favourite, but failed to stay the course and finished only fourth. Champion for the twentieth time in 1947, Richard broke his own record of 1933 by riding 269 winners. After the retirement of Fred Darling at the end of that season, the Beckhampton stable continued to hold first claim on him when it was taken over by (Sir) Noel Murless. The best horse he rode for Murless was the brilliant grey sprinter Abernant, on whom he won the Nunthorpe Stakes at York in 1949 and 1950.

The knighthood that Richards received in the coronation honours in 1953 was as much in recognition of his exemplary integrity as of his professional achievement. A few days after the queen had conferred it upon him, he won the Derby at his twenty-eighth and final attempt by riding Sir Victor Sassoon's Pinza to beat the queen's colt Aureole. A little over a year later, Richards had to retire from riding after breaking his pelvis and four ribs when he was thrown by Abergeldie in the paddock at Sandown Park on 10 July 1954.

With his body slewed round to the left, so that his weight was unevenly distributed as he rode his powerful finish, Richards had a most unorthodox style. All the same, horses ran as straight as a die for him. From 21,843 mounts, he rode 4,870 winners and was champion jockey twenty-six times.

Subsequently he trained at Beckhampton, Ogbourne Maisey, and finally Whitsbury, Hampshire. Although his success was not comparable to that which he had enjoyed as a jockey, he won a number of valuable races, notably the Middle Park Stakes with Pipe of Peace, who was to be third in the Derby in 1956, and the Champion stakes with Reform in 1967. Richards also managed the horses of Lady Beaverbrook and (Sir) Michael Sobell. He closed his stable in 1970. He was elected an honorary member of the Jockey Club the same year.

On 1 March 1928 Richards married Margery Gladys (died 1982), daughter of Thomas David Winckle, railway carriage fitter. They had two sons and a daughter. A third son, the daughter's twin, lived only a few hours. Richards died of a heart attack at his home at Kintbury, Berkshire, 10 November 1986.

[Sir Gordon Richards, *My Story*, 1955; Michael Seth-Smith, *Knight of the Turf*, 1980; *Sporting Life*, 11 November 1986; personal knowledge.]

Richard Onslow

published 1996

RUSSELL Bertrand Arthur William

(1872–1970)

Third Earl Russell

Philosopher and social reformer, was born at Trelleck in Monmouthshire 18 May 1872, the younger son of Viscount Amberley (the eldest son of the first Earl Russell, previously Lord John Russell) and his wife, Kate, daughter of the second Baron Stanley of Alderley. Russell's mother died of diphtheria in 1874 and his father died in 1876, before Russell was four. The Amberleys were a highly progressive couple, holding unconventional beliefs in morals, politics, and religion. They chose John Stuart Mill to be a kind of secular godfather to Russell. The atheist guardians they appointed to look after their orphaned children were set aside by the courts and replaced by their paternal grandmother, the second wife, and, after 1878, widow of the first Earl Russell, and daughter of the second Earl of Minto.

Russell remained in the firm and unremitting care of his grandmother until he went up to Cambridge in the autumn of 1890 at the age of eighteen. The other adults in the household were some unmarried aunts and there were visits from uncles of varying degrees of eccentricity. Russell's education until he left home was in the hands of governesses and tutors. Russell and his elder brother lived in this curious state of sequestration in Pembroke Lodge, a grace-and-favour house in Richmond Park, allocated to Russell's grandfather as a former prime minister. Russell's grandmother, the chief influence on his early development, was a woman of strong, high-minded opinions, morally puritanical, and the adherent of a radical form of liberalism in politics.

Later Russell recalled various impingements of the outside world on Pembroke Lodge in his autobiographical writings, notably being alone with Gladstone at dessert as the great man wondered why he had been served such good port in a claret glass. Russell seems to have had reasonably unobstructed access to his grandfather's large and comprehensive library and valuably exploited the tedium of his childhood years to lay up massive stores of attentive reading for future use. Significant developments of later years announced themselves in a modest way. In 1883 his elder brother, trying to teach him geometry, disappointed him by insisting that the axioms had to be accepted without question. That, Russell subsequently claimed, set him off on his passionate quest for ultimate mathematical truth. A year later his grandmother gave him a Bible for his twelfth birthday, inscribed with the text: 'thou shalt not follow a multitude to do evil'. For all their differences he was to remain as faithful to that text as she did.

In his teens Russell began to have religious doubts, ascribing some influence in this to John Stuart Mill's *Autobiography.* Also important was an atheistic tutor he had when he was sixteen. Soon after that he went to an army crammer's in north London to bring his mathematics up to the state of technical polish required for entrance to Cambridge. Contact with future army officers was deeply shocking to the protected and priggish adolescent Russell. In December 1889 he sat for the scholarship examinations at Trinity College, Cambridge, and with the support of A. N. Whitehead, who recognized his still unpolished brilliance, was elected to a minor scholarship.

The Cambridge to which Russell went up in October 1890 was a marvellous place for any intelligent young man fortunate enough to find his way there. To Russell, arriving from the narrow rectitude and bleak avoidance of pleasure practised at Pembroke Lodge, it seemed like paradise. His remarkable qualities of mind were soon detected by his contemporaries and he was made one of the Apostles. He became friendly with many gifted and interesting people: the philosopher J. E. M'Taggart, G. Lowes Dickinson, the Trevelyan brothers—Charles, G. M., and Robert—and, perhaps most important of all, G. E. Moore, at first a classicist, but eventually a philosopher, the strongest early influence on Russell's strictly philosophical thinking.

Russell was placed as seventh wrangler in part i of the mathematical tripos of 1893 and decided to stay up for a further year to read 'moral sciences' (in other words, philosophy). In September of that year he read *The Principles of Logic* of the Oxford idealist F. H. Bradley and formed an admiration of him from which nothing short of the persistent, hardheaded commonsensicality of Moore could rescue him and then only by a process of conversion lasting several years. Closest to Bradley among Russell's philosophical teachers was James Ward; he learnt less from Henry Sidgwick and G. F. Stout. After a year he secured a first class with distinction in the moral sciences tripos. For a few months he served at the British Embassy in Paris. On 13 December 1894 he married Alys Whitall (died 1951), daughter of Robert and sister of Logan Pearsall Smith, at the Quaker meeting-house in St Martin's Lane. Robert Pearsall Smith came from a family of rich Philadelphia Quakers and had settled near Hindhead on an evangelical mission. Russell's family opposed the match, in part because of Alys's age (she was five years older than he), in part because of a strain of madness in his own background which seemed to count against his becoming a father. As it turned out he and Alys had no children together.

In 1895 Russell and Alys paid a visit to Bernard Berenson and his wife (who was a sister of Alys's) in Italy. In the same year Russell was elected to a fellowship at Trinity on the strength of a dissertation which was published in 1897 as *An Essay on the Foundations of Geometry*, his first philosophical book. It was closer in subject than in doctrine to his main contributions to philosophy, being concerned to adjust a fundamentally Kantian conception of geometry as the *a priori* science of space to the emergence of non-Euclidean geometries. But even in the pursuit of this somewhat untypical goal Russell was already showing the superbly crystalline style that served him and his readers so well from the 1890s to the splendid memorandum on his association with Ralph Schoenman that he wrote shortly before his death.

After his election at Trinity he and Alys travelled to Berlin. There he studied the theory and practice of Marxism, accumulating the material which formed the basis of lectures at the London School of Economics in 1896 and, later that year, of his first book: *German Social Democracy*. An initial chapter neatly expounds the main theses of Marx and Engels, and crisply affirms their invalidity; the main bulk of the text is more straightforwardly historical. During the year 1896 Russell paid the first of his numerous, frequently eventful, and often profitable visits to the United States. He and Alys visited Johns Hopkins and Bryn Mawr, at both of which he lectured, and they stayed with William James at Harvard. The conclusion to the first, more or less dependent, phase of his life ended with the death of his grandmother in 1898. Later he was to blame himself for his lack of feeling about this at the time.

It was in the following year that Russell established himself as a seriously professional philosopher, with his first work of genius his *A Critical Exposition of the Philosophy of Leibniz*. M'Taggart, intending to spend the Lent term in New Zealand, persuaded Russell to give his lectures for him. The result was more than anyone had bargained for. Instead of journeyman lectures by a substitute there was a brilliantly imaginative reinterpretation of a major philosopher effected by one of the few qualified to do it. In the course of the task Russell rebelled against the idealism which he and M'Taggart had previously shared.

The main work of the closing years of the nineteenth century for Russell was his great *The Principles of Mathematics*. This was not published until 1903 but the first draft was completed by 31 December 1900. Two important influences were first brought to bear on Russell in the last year of the old century. The first was that of Guiseppe Peano, whom Russell met and talked with illuminatingly at the International Congress of Philosophy in Paris. The other was Gottlob Frege, whose *Grundgesetze der Arithmetik* Russell acquired, to discover that they had been working along similar lines.

The central idea of their two philosophies of mathematics was the reducibility of mathematics to logic, first by the definition of the basic mathematical concept of number in terms of the logical concept of class and, secondly, by the derivation of the principles about number from which Peano had shown all pure mathematics to be deducible from more fundamental principles of a logical kind.

Frege had carried out this logicist programme with greater thoroughness and rigour than Russell was ever to do, even in the full formal development of *Principia Mathematica*. Furthermore, Frege based his work on a much more sophisticated theory of meaning than Russell was ever to develop. But he used an obscure diagrammatic notation and he failed to notice the paradoxical consequences which Russell saw resulted from an unrestricted use of the concept of class. Russell first perceived the paradox about the class of classes that are not members of themselves (viz. that if it is a member of itself it is not and if it is not then it is) in June 1902. It preoccupied him to a point of exasperation that could be called agonizing for the next four years until the discovery, or perhaps invention, of the theory of types.

The strain of these years of unrelenting thought of the most powerful originality at the outer limits of abstraction revealed itself in various ways. In February 1902 Russell realized he no longer loved his wife, bluntly told her so, and yet continued to live with her in considerable tension for the next nine years. He seems to have fallen in love with Evelyn Whitehead, the wife of his teacher and collaborator, a love it was impossible for him to declare in public in any way. For many of these years he and Alys lived in grim proximity in a small house in Bagley Wood near Oxford. In 1903 he published his well-known, stylistically rather over-ripe, declaration of cosmic defiance 'The Free Man's Worship' in the *Independent Review*. In 1905 his article 'On Denoting' appeared in *Mind*, perhaps the most influential philosophical article of the twentieth century, for all the uncharacteristic muddle of its expression. In 1907 the public Russell stood for Parliament in Wimbledon as women's suffrage candidate. In 1908 he was elected a fellow of the Royal Society.

By 1909 another large change was about to occur in Russell's life. His work on *Principia Mathematica*, for which he wrote most of the crucial first volume and most of the explanatory philosophical material in the introduction, was nearing completion. In the autumn Logan Pearsall Smith, Alys's brother, brought Lady Ottoline Morrell to visit the Russells in Bagley Wood, setting in motion the first of Russell's major love affairs. Appointed a lecturer at Trinity College, Cambridge, for five years in 1910 he spent a good deal of time there, away from Alys. He canvassed for Ottoline's husband Philip in the election of that year. The first volume of

Principia Mathematica came out, as also did a volume of collected *Philosophical Essays* of the preceding years. The two later volumes of *Principia* came out in 1912 and 1913.

In 1911, still under forty, Russell was elected president of the Aristotelian Society. He and Alys finally separated and in the spring Ottoline Morrell became his mistress. In October he first met Ludwig Wittgenstein, who was to be the stimulus of a bout of original thinking in general philosophy almost as profound as the mathematical philosophizing of his previous decade. Before long he was Wittgenstein's academic supervisor, but was learning as much as he was teaching. One lesson he absorbed with a reluctance he never wholly overcame was that logic and mathematics are essentially tautological in nature, that they do not describe the relations between independently existing abstract entities, but merely register the consequences of our linguistic and notational conventions.

During the years just before World War I, the period of his closest contact with Wittgenstein, Russell was laying out the main lines of that combination of the major assumptions of traditional empiricism with the techniques of the revolutionized formal logic he had himself so much developed that was to remain his basic philosophical position until his last words on the subject in the late 1940s, as well as coming to be the position of the main group of analytic philosophers of the twentieth century. (Sir) Alfred J. Ayer, in many ways the most Russellian of Russell's interpreters, has rightly observed that Russell's conception of philosophy is somewhat old-fashioned: 'He makes the now unfashionable assumption that all our beliefs are in need of philosophical justification.' From 1911 onwards in a series of powerful and lucid essays (later brought together, for the most part, in *Mysticism and Logic* in 1918), in the remarkable and remarkably durable *The Problems of Philosophy* (1912) that Russell wrote for the Home University Library and in his Lowell lectures of 1914—*Our Knowledge of the External World*—his ideas about perception, causation, knowledge, truth, and the nature of philosophy itself were elaborated.

Other interests were not extinguished by this outpouring of philosophical creativity. He wrote more sympathetically than at any other time about religion in the *Hibbert Journal*, perhaps revealing the influence of Ottoline Morrell, and tried his hand at fiction in a long story, 'The Perplexities of John Forstice'. In 1913 the Morrells bought Garsington Manor, and thus provided the scenery for a good deal of English intellectual life in the ensuing years. Russell met Joseph Conrad and greatly admired him, giving Conrad's name to both of his sons. A long manuscript he wrote at this time on the theory of knowledge (in his papers but still not published) was devastatingly criticized by Wittgenstein with a damaging effect on Russell's philosophical self-confidence.

In March 1914 he left for the United States to give the Lowell lectures at Harvard. There he met T. S. Eliot who was to report Russell's appearance in cultivated circles in Boston in his poem 'Mr Apollinax'. He also met John Dewey on this visit for the first time, the philosopher who was to be in a way his closest counterpart in the United States, combining as he did large and influential philosophical productivity with a conspicuous public position as social and educational reformer. He also met Helen Dudley who was to follow him fruitlessly to England in the war, one of the more pathetic victims of his amorous energies.

By 1915 Russell was becoming increasingly and turbulently involved in resistance to the war. Around the time that Trinity College was renewing his lectureship he joined the rather militantly pacifist No-Conscription Fellowship. A leaflet whose authorship he acknowledged brought him a fine of £100 in 1916 and, more seriously, removal from his lectureship at Trinity. A brief friendship with D. H. Lawrence flared up around this time and soon died away in mutual recrimination: on Lawrence's side in the portrait of 'Sir Joshua Malleson' in *Women in Love* (1921), on Russell's with an uncharacteristically bitter recollection in *Portraits from Memory* (1956). He was seeing a good deal of T. S. Eliot and his attractive, unbalanced wife Vivienne, supplying money to the husband and a not precisely discoverable degree of amorous affection to the wife. In June of 1916 he met Dora Black, who was to be his second wife, for the first time, and in July Colette O'Niel (Lady Constance Malleson), perhaps his greatest love.

His most coherent and well-organized political book *Principles of Social Reconstruction* was a product of the war years, delivered as lectures at Caxton Hall and then published in 1916. Invited to the United States he was refused a passport by the Foreign Office. In 1917 he gave an initial welcome to the Russian Revolution and, increasingly at odds with the leadership of the No-Conscription Fellowship, resigned from it. Early in 1918 he returned to philosophy with a series of eight lectures, 'The Philosophy of Logical Atomism' (*Monist*, 1918 and 1919), in which the influence of Wittgenstein is much more evident than in anything he had written before, epistemological considerations being altogether outweighed by purely logical ones.

An article he wrote in May 1918, suggesting that American troops would be useful in this country in the strike-breaking role to which they were accustomed in their own, led to his being sentenced to six months in prison (for sedition rather than silliness). Secured the comforts of the 'first division' by the exercise of elevated interest on his behalf, he settled down to write his sparklingly lucid *Introduction to Mathematical Philosophy* (1919), which perhaps owes its smoothness of development and coherence of organization to the monotonous circumstances in which it was composed.

Comparing it with some of his later books, often spasmodic and casual, one might wish he had been imprisoned more often.

The end of the war allowed for a measure of tidying-up in his life. He was in poor financial circumstances with no job and with a deserted wife to support. An admirably succinct and informative pot-boiler, *Roads to Freedom*, gave only temporary relief. A fund raised by G. Gilbert Murray enabled him to deliver at the London School of Economics the lectures that were to be published in 1921 as *The Analysis of Mind*, in which a strong leaning towards behaviourism is evident, but not total acceptance of it. Helen Dudley conveniently returned to the United States. He managed to disentangle himself from his involvements with Ottoline Morrell, for some time an increasingly unwilling object of his desires, and Mrs Eliot. Something like normality seemed to have been regained when in November 1919 Trinity College agreed to reinstate him, the vengeful emotions of wartime having cooled down sufficiently and the surviving younger fellows having come back from the war to outvote their more bellicose seniors.

With the help of J. M. (later Lord) Keynes, Wittgenstein's manuscript of the *Tractatus Logico-Philosophicus* had been got out of its author's prison camp. A return to academic life might have seemed, therefore, both practicable and intellectually exciting. What ruled out the possibility was Russell's desire for a family. Believing that Colette O'Niel was unwilling to have children he took up with Dora Black who was not. Early in 1920 he and Dora travelled to Russia where he formed the unalterable conviction of the coarseness and cruelty of the Bolsheviks expressed in *The Practice and Theory of Bolshevism* (1920), a work he was rightly content to see republished without change in 1949, nearly thirty years later.

Their next trip together was to China, which Russell admired as much as he had disliked Russia. That too inspired a book: *The Problem of China* (1922). A bad attack of pneumonia led to reports that Russell was dead. Dewey, also travelling in China, came to his aid. Returning to England in July 1921 Russell resigned the lectureship at Trinity in which he had been reinstated. For in September he got his divorce from Alys and at once married Dora Winifred Black who presented him with a son in November. She was the daughter of Sir Frederick Black, formerly director-general of munitions supply.

In the early twenties Russell established the style of life he was to follow until the war of 1939, which, after a troublesome start for him, left him financially secure and in a condition of unprecedented respectability. He was able to undertake a certain amount of original and seriously reflective philosophical writing. The main instance of that between *The Analysis of Mind* in 1921 and *An Inquiry into Meaning and Truth* in 1940 is *The Analysis of Matter* of 1927, originally given as Tarner lectures in Cambridge in 1925. He put a good deal of work into a new edition of *Principia Mathematica* in 1925, getting a grumpy reaction from Whitehead for his efforts. But most of his writing was popularization or journalism, always lively and amusing, often shallow and somewhat mechanical. *The Prospects of Industrial Civilisation* (1923), which he wrote with Dora, was serious enough, as was *On Education* (1926). Other writings were of lighter weight, the excellent *ABCs* of *Atoms* (1923) and *Relativity* (1925) as good as any popular accounts of the new developments in physics, *Marriage and Morals* (1929) arguing for what most would now see as reasonable permissiveness, *The Conquest of Happiness* (1930), a book that Wittgenstein found quite unbearable, *The Scientific Outlook* (1931), *Education and The Social Order* (1932), *Religion and Science* (1935), and *Power* (1938). Of the same quality are the highly readable essay collections—*Sceptical Essays* (1928) and *In Praise of Idleness* (1935). It was with these, and other, yet more fugitive, writings, that Russell earned his living, met the obligations arising from his and his elder brother's earlier marriages, and sustained such enterprises as his standing as the Labour candidate for Chelsea in the general elections of 1922 and 1923 and the money-engorging progressive school, Beacon Hill, which he and Dora founded in 1927.

Lecturing in the United States was a reliable resource in these financially anxious years. Russell clearly enjoyed the work and threw himself into it with energy and appetite. He was an excellent debater, able to disagree wholly with an opponent without being in any way personally offensive to him. He carried out lecture tours in 1924, 1927, 1929, and 1931. After leaving Dora and the school in 1932 his need for money was a little less pressing, fortunately, perhaps, in view of the state of the American economy.

Beacon Hill School was started in 1927 at Telegraph House, in the country near Petersfield, which Russell had rented from his elder brother. It was not of the utmost progressiveness; although Russell would not have children forced to do academic work, he required them to show a measure of consideration for others. But his reputation ensured that there would be many problem children in the school and a number of rather singular teachers. Carried on by Dora after she and Russell parted, it managed to survive until war began in 1939. They had agreed to tolerate moderate deviations from strict marital fidelity in one another but that proved hard in practice. In 1930 Dora, who had also had a daughter of Russell's, had a daughter by a young American and two years later a son by the same father. It is not surprising that Russell should have fallen in love with Marjorie Helen Spence, who changed her name to Patricia ('Peter'), and who was originally in the household as a holiday governess for the Russells' own children. Russell and Dora were divorced finally in 1935 and he married Peter Spence the following year. She was the daughter of Harry Evelyn Spence.

Towards the end of the 1930s Russell, now in his sixties, was beginning to favour the idea of a return to the calm and regularity of academic life. He had inherited the title from his brother Frank on the death of the latter in 1931. In 1937 he had been obliged to sell Telegraph House, to which he was devoted, and in the same year he and Peter had a son. He made some tentative gestures towards Cambridge but G. E. Moore was not helpful. He and Moore had examined Wittgenstein for the Ph.D. in 1929, his last academic act for a long time. Unsuccessful at home he turned next to the United States, to the Institute for Advanced Study at Princeton, but nothing came of it. A series of lectures, 'Words and Facts', delivered in Oxford in 1938 (published two years afterwards as *An Inquiry into Meaning and Truth*) showed that he could still take part in the most advanced and up-to-date type of philosophical discussion. He wrote in the book's preface that it was the result of 'an attempt to combine a general outlook akin to Hume's with the methods that have grown out of modern logic'.

In these difficult circumstances George Santayana, unexpectedly enriched by writing a best-selling novel *The Last Puritan* (in which a character based on Russell's brother took a notable part), generously agreed to subsidize Russell with a sum of £1,000 a year. As it turned out he was not called on for very long, since the university of Chicago offered a visiting professorship for the next year starting in the autumn of 1938. Russell and his family left England soon after the death of Ottoline Morrell broke another link with the past. In the autumn of 1939, with the outbreak of war in Europe, Russell moved to another visiting professorship, at the university of California in Los Angeles. Conflict with an unsympathetic right-wing president induced him to leave California before his time was up for what proved to be a bird in a very prickly bush, a chair at the City College of New York.

As a municipal institution City College was exposed to citizen litigiousness and a lady was induced to sue the New York Board of Higher Education for offering employment to an alien atheist and exponent of free love. A ludicrous judge upheld her plea, Mayor La Guardia was happy to placate conventional opinion which carried a lot of votes, and the outraged protests of a great number of liberal-minded and intelligent Americans went for nothing. Harvard counteracted the insult by inviting him to give the William James lectures there later in 1940 but the practical problem of economic survival remained.

Dr Albert Barnes, inventor of argyrol, came to the rescue, appointing Russell lecturer at his 'Foundation' in Philadelphia at a fairly generous stipend. Russell's duty was to lend a certain broad intellectual respectability to Barnes and his remarkable collection of pictures by lecturing on the history of philosophy. At first things went well enough but eventually Barnes, enraged, it seems, by Peter Russell's knitting during the lectures, found a pretext for ending Russell's contract, which he understood to rule out outside lectures by Russell. At the end of 1942 Russell was given three days' notice to leave. But better times were at hand.

Later in 1943 Russell won an action against Barnes for wrongful dismissal, receiving $20,000 in place of withheld salary. He was invited to lecture at Bryn Mawr. He pushed ahead with the work he had undertaken for Barnes and which was soon delivered to the publisher as *A History of Western Philosophy*, an immediate success from the moment of its publication in 1945 on both sides of the Atlantic and a complete guarantee of financial security to Russell for the rest of his life. By no means a scholarly work it combines lively passages on philosophical themes of the past where they happen to have caught Russell's interest, entertaining biographical material rather in the manner of G. H. Lewes, and amusingly processed historical matter of only the most marginal relevance to his main exposition derived from readily accessible sources. To close a splendid year Trinity College once again invited him to rejoin it.

With the war coming to its end he was able to take up this suggestion in the October of 1944. The seal of approval from the philosophical profession of which he had been such a fitful and wayward member was given by the appearance of a volume on his philosophy by a largely distinguished cast of contributors in the 'Library of Living Philosophers'. Once in England again he was quickly recruited by the BBC, and his voice became available for widespread imitation on the popular Brains Trust programme for which his brand of mental agility and definiteness of opinion was ideal. Now seventy-two he was still avid for romantic episodes, falling in love with the writer Gamel Brenan in 1944 and enjoying an affair with the young wife of a lecturer at Cambridge the year after.

The dropping of atomic bombs on Japan instantly commanded his attention and preoccupied his energies, along with connected political interests, for the rest of his life. At an early stage of his thought on the subject he conceived the idea of coercing Russia, if necessary by the threat of war, to agree to international control of atomic energy, expressing it publicly in 1947. His subsequent denials of this and very limited and reluctant admissions in the face of plain evidence of the fact pose a problem which his biographer Ronald Clark reasonably solves with the conjecture that it was not that Russell had forgotten but that he saw himself as lying in the best of all possible causes, that of getting the human race, as he put it, 'to acquiesce in its own survival'. But his anti-nuclear preoccupation was not to reach its full intensity until 1954.

In the late 1940s and early 1950s Russell was in the happiest circumstances, universally revered, loaded with honours, provided with unlimited opportunities for speaking his mind. He made lecture tours in a great variety of places, among them Switzerland, Scandinavia (during which his flying-boat capsized in Trondheim fjord), Australasia, and, of course, the United States. In his homeland he gave the first Reith lectures on the radio in 1949, published as *Authority and the Individual*. He was admitted to the Order of Merit in 1949, and awarded the Nobel prize for literature in 1950. His private life continued its undulating course. His marriage to Peter Spence collapsed in 1949 and she left with their young son. In the same year he met Alys again. More significant for the future was a new meeting with Edith (died 1978), daughter of Edward Bronson Finch, of New York. He had first met her at Bryn Mawr in the war years, and she was to become his wife in 1952 after his third divorce and to bring him, at last, complete marital contentment. In 1955 they went to live at Plas Penrhyn, Merionethshire, Wales.

A personal cloud over this generally agreeable scene was cast by what he, not unreasonably, took to be the low opinion shared by most philosophers of the new generation of his last major philosophical book: *Human Knowledge* (1948). The book itself was not one of his best. Apart from its last section on inductive reasoning (where he fell back on a method of postulation which he had once criticized as 'having all the advantages of theft over honest toil'), there was little in it that had not appeared in his earlier books. It so happened that the academically ascendant philosophy of that moment was radically opposed both to Russell's idea that the ultimate task of philosophy is justification and to his methodological reliance on formal logic. He and his old pupil Wittgenstein were now totally estranged, particularly after a risible scene at the Cambridge Moral Sciences Club, where Wittgenstein swept out in a hysterical tantrum.

From then on Russell's literary work was largely confined to his own past, as in *Portraits from Memory* (1956), *My Philosophical Development* (1959), and the three volumes of his fascinating but rather fragmentary *Autobiography* (1967, 1968, 1969), and to the political present as in his *Common Sense and Nuclear Warfare* (1959), *Has Man a Future?* (1961), and *Unarmed Victory* (1963).

His most active period as a campaigner against nuclear weapons can be dated from a broadcast of 1954, 'Man's Peril', inspired by the Bikini H-bomb tests. In 1955 he organized a manifesto, signed by Einstein and other scientists. He took part in the first Pugwash conference in 1957 and in 1958 became the first president of the Campaign for Nuclear Disarmament. Two years afterwards, in 1960, he split the CND to form the more militant Committee of 100, dedicated to civil disobedience in pursuit of its aims. It was in that year that Ralph Schoenman first came into Russell's life, which he was to stage-manage, to Russell's increasing discredit, during his tenth decade.

That is not to say that Russell did not take part with full consent in the mass sit-down in Whitehall in February 1961 and in a demonstration the following August, as a result of which he and his wife were sentenced to two months in prison, but detained only for a week because of age and ill health. It was Russell too who said that J. F. Kennedy and Harold Macmillan were more wicked than Hitler. In 1962 in the Cuba crisis Russell wrote powerful letters appealing to various heads of state and retained enough sense of proportion to doubt whether they had any effect whatever. But as he moved into his nineties he became more and more the instrument of Schoenman's one-sided campaign to blame the United States for all the world's misfortunes. Letters written in villainously sub-literate American English appeared over Russell's signature in *The Times*. He became the figurehead of the long-drawn-out buffoonery of a 'war crimes trial' whose bench consisted exclusively of apologists for Russian imperialism, most notably the egregious Sartre. Finally, in 1969, Russell took the step that had driven many of his allies and friends to abandon him politically; he disowned Schoenman and wrote a funny, lucid, rather insufficiently apologetic account of the relations between them. Shortly afterwards, on 2 February 1970, within three months of his ninety-eighth birthday, he died at his home, Plas Penrhyn.

If Russell's political reputation was low at the time of his death, his philosophical reputation had taken an upward turn from the trough of the late 1940s and the 1950s. The heroes of 'linguistic philosophy', Wittgenstein and J. L. Austin, died in 1951 and in 1960, and although Wittgenstein at least remained an object of close and interested study, and even of more or less convincing impersonation in some circles, up to and beyond the date of Russell's death, the influence of Austin effectively died with him. The philosophers of greatest standing in the Anglo-Saxon analytic tradition in the 1960s and 1970s—W. V. O. Quine, Davidson, Putnam, Kripke—have all been more Russellian than anything else.

Although Frege was a more profound philosopher of mathematics than Russell he was not as influential. No one had had a more fundamental and persistent effect on the course of academic, technical philosophy in the English-speaking world than Russell did. Less original than Wittgenstein, and even in some respects than his original mentor, G. E. Moore, he served as a listening-post for his age in which a vast range of movements of thought were perceptively picked up, helpfully simplified, and then sent forth to the world in a lucid and readily digestible form. At times his style, for the most part a magnificent expository instrument, is a little remorseless and mechanical in its determined brightness but he managed to be entertaining about topics that had never been seen before as joking matters.

Russell was an attractive and sociable man, generous with time, money, and attention, no respecter of persons, but the same to all men, even if somewhat ruthless in, and after, his pursuit of women. He was short in stature, but quite sturdy from middle life. In his early manhood he wore a somewhat fleecy moustache. This was removed in deference to the wishes of Ottoline Morrell in 1911 and was not seen again. In his long life he had various quite severe illnesses, among them, not surprisingly, a collapse through nervous exhaustion. But only a very reliable constitution could have kept him going for nearly a hundred years with little diminution of mental vigour and, to the end, with a fair degree of physical capacity. A great pipe smoker, he had a sharp, slightly raucous voice and a highly recognizable whinnying laugh. His articulation was amusingly precise and pedantic.

There is a pencil drawing of him by Sir William Rothenstein (reproduced in *British Philosophers* by Kenneth Matthews, 1943) and a bust (1953), which he commissioned himself, by (Sir) Jacob Epstein. Another bust (also 1953) was fashioned by Eric L. Edwards. Two portraits in oils, by David Griffiths and Lewin Bassingthwaighte, were painted in the last two years of Russell's life. In the National Portrait Gallery is a portrait by Roger Fry (*c.* 1923). There are many excellent photographs of him in comparatively old age: the best, perhaps, being that by Philippe Halsman in 1958 (reproduced in Ronald Clark's biography).

[Ronald W. Clark, *The Life of Bertrand Russell*, 1975; Alan Wood, *Bertrand Russell—The Passionate Sceptic*, 1957; Bertrand Russell, *Portraits from Memory*, 1956, *Autobiography*, 3 vols., 1967, 1968, 1969; Rupert Crawshay-Williams, *Russell Remembered*, 1970.]

ANTHONY QUINTON

published 1981

RUSSELL Dora Winifred

(1894–1986)

Feminist writer and campaigner, was born 3 April 1894 at 1 Mount Villas, Luna Road, Thornton Heath, Croydon, the second of three daughters and second of four children of (Sir) Frederick William Black, clerk in the Admiralty and later senior civil servant, and his wife, Sarah Isabella Davisson. She was educated at Sutton High School and Girton College, Cambridge, where she was awarded a first class in the medieval and modern languages tripos in 1915. She began research on eighteenth-century French philosophers at University College London, but in 1917 went to the United States as personal assistant to her father, who was head of a special government mission to persuade the American government to re-route some of its oil tankers to Britain. She was appointed MBE for this (1918). Shortly after her return she was elected to a fellowship by Girton, and returned to Cambridge in 1918.

In 1916 she had met Bertrand Russell, already famous as a mathematician and philosopher, and notorious as a pacifist. Bertrand Arthur William Russell was the grandson of Lord John Russell, first Earl Russell, prime minister in 1846–52 and 1865–6, and the son of John Russell, Viscount Amberley, MP for Nottingham. He became third Earl Russell in 1931. They began an affair in 1919. She visited Russia in 1920, and on her return took to wearing peasant-style clothes. She remained an enthusiastic supporter of the Soviet Union all her life. In 1921 she wrote 'The Soul of Russia and the Body of America', which was finally incorporated in *The Religion of the Machine Age* (1983). She resigned her Girton fellowship in 1920 in order to accompany Russell to Russia and China.

Russell was married, although separated, and had no children. Although Dora disapproved of marriage she agreed to marry him when she became pregnant, as he was anxious to produce a legitimate heir. On their return from China he divorced his wife and married Dora in the same month, September 1921, two months before their son John, later fourth Earl Russell, was born.

They bought a house in Chelsea, and Dora soon became aware of the difficulties involved in being married to a much older, famous man. Although Russell supported women's suffrage, he believed that women were less intelligent than men, and that their main function was to be wives and mothers. His friends adopted a patronizing attitude towards Dora, assuming that any ideas she might express came from him. She was determined to have an identity separate from that of her husband, and to escape from the shadow of his reputation. She joined the Labour party, and stood unsuccessfully as Labour candidate for Chelsea in the autumn of 1924. She helped to form the Workers' Birth Control Group in 1924, and threw herself into the campaign for birth-control advice to be given to all women. In 1925 she published *Hypatia, or, Women and Knowledge*, followed by *The Right to Be Happy* in 1927.

In 1927 Dora and Bertrand Russell started Beacon Hill School at Telegraph House, on the South Downs, in order to educate their own children in the company of others, because no existing school seemed satisfactory. The plan was to do away with excessive discipline, religious instruction, and the tyranny of adults. It was a joint venture, although Dora was responsible for the day-to-day organization, while Bertrand financed it through writing popular books and lecture tours in the United States. The school was ridiculed in the press, and Bertrand Russell later claimed it was a failure, but it embodied many progressive ideas. Dora published *In Defence of Children* in 1932.

Betrand Russell left Dora, and the school, in 1932, after she had had two children by Griffin Barry, an American journalist. Although they had always insisted on their freedom to have affairs with other people, Russell could not accept her extending this to the freedom to have another man's child. They were divorced in 1935. She managed to carry on the school alone, moving several times after leaving Telegraph House in 1934. She had a brief affair with a communist, Paul Gillard, before he was murdered, and in 1940 married his friend, Gordon Grace ('Pat'), a working-class Irish communist who was helping her to run the school. He was the son of Patrick Grace, clothier, and he died in 1949.

She closed the school in 1943, and went to London to work at the Ministry of Information, moving to the Soviet relations division in 1944 to work on *British Ally*, a weekly paper published by the British government in Moscow. When the paper was closed down in 1950 she lost her job. Unable to find another, she devoted herself to feminist causes and the women's peace movement. She was a member of the Six Point Group (a discussion and political pressure organization) and the Married Women's Association. She attended peace conferences, and went to New York in 1954 to the United Nations Commission of Women, on behalf of the Women's International Democratic Federation. In 1958 she organized the Women's Caravan of Peace, a group of women who travelled across Europe to Moscow and back, protesting against nuclear weapons and calling for total disarmament, with the banner 'women of all lands want peace'.

In 1962 she returned to Cornwall, to Carn Voel, Porthcurno, the house she and Russell had bought in 1922. She devoted most of her time to writing, and to the care of her son John, who had had a mental breakdown in 1954. She continued to campaign for peace, leading a London CND rally in a wheelchair at the age of eighty-nine, and just before her death she took part in an anti-nuclear demonstration at the RAF base at St Mawgan, Cornwall. Dora Russell died 31 May 1986 at home in Porthcurno. She had four children, one son and one daughter from her first marriage, and one son and one daughter with Griffin Barry. The younger son was crippled in a mining accident in 1952 and was an invalid until his death in 1983.

She loved campaigning, enjoying public speaking—she had always wanted to be an actress—and writing letters to the press. A chain-smoker, she was small, red-haired, and untidy, and claimed to have been one of the first women in England to wear shorts, in the 1920s. Throughout her life she campaigned for sexual freedom for women. She believed passionately that hope for the future lay in women. Many of her ideas anticipated those of the feminist movement of the 1970s and 1980s.

[Dora Russell, *The Tamarisk Tree*, 3 vols., 1975, 1980, and 1985 (with portrait); Dora Russell, *The Dora Russell Reader: 57 Years of Writing and Journalism, 1925–1982*, 1983; Dale Spender, *There's Always Been a Women's Movement This Century*, 1983; Bertrand Russell, *The Autobiography of Bertrand Russell*, vol. ii, 1968; Caroline Moorehead, *Bertrand Russell*, 1992.]

ANNE PIMLOTT BAKER

published 1996

RYLE Sir Martin

(1918–1984)

Radio astronomer and Nobel prize-winner, was born at Brighton, Sussex, 27 September 1918, the second son and second child in the family of three sons and two daughters of John Alfred Ryle, professor of medicine, and his wife, Miriam Power, daughter of William Charles Scully, civil servant, of Cape Town, who came from a land-owning family in county Tipperary. His uncle was the philosopher Gilbert Ryle. When Ryle was five years old the family home was established at 13 Wimpole Street, London, where he was first educated by a governess. Later he attended Gladstone's preparatory school in Eaton Square and entered Bradfield College at the age of thirteen. He gained an exhibition in the scholarship examination in 1932 and in 1936 entered Christ Church, Oxford, to read physics. He obtained a third class in natural science honour moderations (1937) and a first in physics (1939).

Ryle then joined J. A. Ratcliffe's ionospheric research group at the Cavendish Laboratory, Cambridge. On the outbreak of World War II Ratcliffe joined the Air Ministry Research Establishment (later TRE) and Ryle followed him in May 1940. For two years he worked mainly on the design of aerials and the development of test equipment. In the summer of 1942 he became the leader of a group in the newly formed radio counter-measures division. Ryle played a prominent part in various radar jamming and radio-deception operations amongst which the electronic 'spoof invasion' on

D-Day, which led the Germans to believe that the invasion was taking place across the Straits of Dover, was particularly important. In this complex field of counter-measures the technical response often had to be immediate. Ryle's extraordinary inventiveness and immediate scientific insight were of great importance in this work and often led him to be intolerant of those not similarly blessed.

At the end of the war Ryle obtained an ICI fellowship and returned to research work at the Cavendish Laboratory. He did not find the ionospheric research sufficiently stimulating and Ratcliffe transferred his interest to an entirely new and challenging research problem. The German jamming of the British radars which enabled the battleships *Scharnhorst* and *Gneisenau* to pass through the English Channel from Brest to Kiel on 12 February 1942 was referred to J. S. Hey of the Army Operational Research Group for investigation. Two weeks later Hey found that an apparently similar case of jamming of the anti-aircraft radars was caused by an intense outburst of radio waves from the sun, associated with a solar flare and large sunspot group. Ratcliffe suggested to Ryle that he should investigate whether in such cases the radio emission came from the region of the sunspots or from the whole solar disc. The solar disc subtends an angle of 0.5 degrees and spots and flares occupy only a very small area of the disc so that the broad beam aerials then available to Ryle were useless for settling this question. He solved this problem by using two simple aerials, which he could move apart, connected by cable to the same receiver. Later, Ryle stated that he did not at first realize that he had invented the radio analogue of the optical interferometer used by A. A. Michelson thirty years earlier to measure the diameter of stars.

This elegant method of obtaining the resolving power equivalent to a very large aerial had far-reaching consequences in astronomy. Ryle's interest soon turned to the study of the cosmic radio waves. He discovered that there were sources of strong radio emission of small angular extent in the universe, and with his colleagues he made a catalogue of the positions and intensities of two thousand of these objects, few of which could be identified optically. He concluded that the number-intensity distribution of these objects provided the evidence that the universe had evolved from a dense and concentrated condition some ten billion years ago. When these results were published in 1955 a historic dispute arose with those astronomers who supported the steady state, continuous creation theory.

In 1954 the idea appears in Ryle's notebooks that he could extend the two aerial interferometers to synthesize a complete large aperture aerial. By moving the two aerials to successive positions and using a digital computer to combine the records he successfully demonstrated the *aperture synthesis* method in 1960–1. He then developed a number of such systems culminating in 1971 with the synthesis of a radio telescope of 5 km. aperture by using eight 13-metre aperture radio telescopes, four fixed and four moving on a railway track. The succession of maps of radio sources with a definition of about an arc second produced by this system revealed the complexity of their structure and raised major problems about the nature of the power sources in the distant galaxies.

An important consequence of the investigations of the radio sources by Ryle's group was the discovery of pulsars (neutron stars) in 1967 by Antony Hewish and Jocelyn Bell. In the joint award of the Nobel prize to Ryle and Hewish in 1974 the development of aperture synthesis was specifically itemized as Ryle's major contribution.

Ryle's early post-war research in Cambridge was carried out at the Grange Road rifle range. In 1956 the research was moved to the site of a former Air Ministry bomb store at Lord's Bridge. On 25 July 1957, in recognition of support from Mullards, the site was named the Mullard Radio-Astronomy Observatory. Ryle was the director from 1957 until his retirement in 1982.

In 1972 Ryle was appointed astronomer royal, the first appointment of an astronomer royal who had not been director of the Royal Greenwich Observatory in the 300 years of its existence. Ryle's appointment coincided with the development of a serious illness and he was unable to exercise the authority which had hitherto been associated with that office, which he relinquished in 1982. In his later years Ryle began experiments on the generation of electricity by wind power. He was deeply concerned about the misuse of science and protested publicly against nuclear armaments.

Ryle's outstanding brilliance as a scientist was widely recognized. He was made lecturer in physics at Cambridge in 1948, became a fellow of Trinity College in 1949, and was appointed to the Cambridge chair of radio astronomy in 1959 (until 1982). He was knighted in 1966, elected FRS (1952), and awarded the Hughes (1954) and Royal (1973) medals of the Royal Society. He was awarded the gold medal of the Royal Astronomical Society in 1964, the Henry Draper medal of the US National Academy of Sciences and the Holweck prize of the Société Française de Physique in 1965, the Popov medal of the USSR Academy of Sciences, the Faraday medal of the IEE, and the Michelson medal of the Franklin Institute of the USA in 1971. He was elected a foreign member of the Royal Danish Academy of Sciences and Letters (1968), of the American Academy of Arts and Sciences (1970), and of the USSR Academy (1971). He was made an honorary D.Sc. of the University of Strathclyde (1968), Oxford (1969), and Torun (1973).

Ryle's chief recreation was sailing and his skill as a craftsman enabled him to construct his own sailing ships. On 19 June 1947 Ryle married Ella Rowena, eighth of the ten children of Reginald Palmer, tradesman, of Mildenhall in Suffolk. There were one son and two daughters of the marriage. Ryle died 14 October 1984 at Cambridge.

[Francis Graham-Smith in *Biographical Memoirs of Fellows of the Royal Society*, vol. xxxii, 1986; Bernard Lovell in *Quarterly Journal of the Royal Astronomical Society*, vol. xxvi, pp. 358–68, 1985; M. Ryle, *Les Prix Nobel en 1974*, pp. 80–99, Stockholm, 1975; personal knowledge.]

BERNARD LOVELL

published 1990

SARGENT Sir (Henry) Malcolm (Watts) (1895–1967)

Conductor, composer, pianist, and organist, was born in Ashford, Kent, 29 April 1895, the only son of Henry Edward Sargent of Stamford, Lincolnshire, and his wife, Agnes Marion Hall, daughter of a Hertfordshire landscape gardener. Henry Sargent, employed in a coal-merchant's business, was a keen amateur musician, an organist, and choirmaster, who carefully fostered his son's talent from the beginning: but the most important early influence was that of Frances Tinkler, an inspiring local teacher who greatly helped Sargent and, some years later, (Sir) Michael Tippett. At Stamford School Sargent was soon noted for irrepressible high spirits and quick intelligence. But his interests were never academic, and other possibilities were elbowed aside in the determined drive towards a career in music.

On leaving school in 1912 Sargent was articled to Haydn Keeton, organist of Peterborough Cathedral, and was one of the last to be trained in that traditional system, so soon to disappear. The discipline involved daily contact between master and pupil in a severe but balanced curriculum: and Keeton was an exacting tutor, old-fashioned perhaps, but highly professional. He taught the counterpoint of Fux, organ-playing in the style of Samuel Sebastian Wesley, and piano-playing in that of Mendelssohn and Sir W. Sterndale Bennett. Score-reading and continuo-realization were learnt not as academic subjects but in the daily practice of cathedral music, performed from the scores of William Boyce and Samuel Arnold. It was hard work, and Sargent loved it all. 'We had no money', he said in later years, 'and our future was quite uncertain: but it was music, music, music all the way.'

By the end of his articles Sargent was already recognized as a fine player, a composer of marked talent, and a well-equipped professional whose charm, vitality, and technical accomplishment were outstanding. But his ambitions, though ample, were not yet defined. Sometimes he thought of being a solo-pianist and, like a Rachmaninov, playing his own compositions all over the world. He could probably have done this. After a performance of *The Dream of Gerontius* in 1912, however, he told a group of friends about his intention to be 'a second Elgar'. For that destiny he was less well suited.

In 1914 Sargent was appointed organist of Melton Mowbray, and found himself among people able to appreciate his talent and to give him substantial help. It was made possible for him to have piano-lessons from Benno Moiseiwitch; a good orchestra was created for him to conduct in Leicester; opportunities were offered generously. In his Leicester concerts he appeared as pianist, composer, and conductor, and won the approval of Sir Henry J. Wood, who invited him to conduct, in the 1921 Promenade Concert season, his tone-poem 'Impressions of a windy day'. The performance was a triumph: but it was as conductor rather than composer that the young man was acclaimed, and on that evening the pattern of his career was settled. For a time he continued to work from his base in the Midlands, but in 1923, invited to join the staff at the Royal College of Music, he moved to London, where in the following year he married Eileen Laura Harding Horne, by whom he had two children, a son, Peter, and a daughter, Pamela. The marriage was terminated by divorce in 1946.

The ten years after 1923 were decisive in Sargent's career, and were a time of unremitting hard work and social activity. He was a restless man, for whom dancing till dawn after a concert seemed to be a necessary relaxation. With no private income and increasing responsibilities, as well as a natural inclination to spend freely, he was obliged to undertake whatever work was offered; and his schedule involved much travel, with varied programmes on limited rehearsal time. Only a musician of great talent and resilience could have done what he did. But he might have been wise to be more selective, even if the experience made him a general-purpose conductor of extreme efficiency, sometimes criticized for not being fastidious but also admired for being totally reliable.

Sargent's responsibilities at this time included the Robert Mayer concerts (1924), the Diaghilev Ballet (1927), the Royal Choral Society (1928) including the spectacular productions of *Hiawatha*, the Courtauld-Sargent concerts (1929–40), and the D'Oyly Carte Opera Company (1930). He conducted many performances of the British National Opera Company and numberless concerts in cities outside London. Among the works entrusted to him for first performance were *Hugh the Drover* by Ralph Vaughan Williams, (Sir) William Walton's *Belshazzar's Feast*, and Walton's opera *Troilus and Cressida*.

Success so brilliant and an enjoyment of its glamour so uninhibited were bound to provoke hostility and to 'excite the common artifice by which envy degrades excellence'. There began to be troubles with orchestras which Sargent tried to discipline. Methods that delighted his devoted choralists were less acceptable to experienced orchestral players: harsh things were said on both sides. Some critics described his performances as brash and superficial, and purists objected to adjustments that Sargent made in the scoring of well-known works, even though these were always effective, and generally less drastic than those made by other conductors. Sargent seemed to disregard these attacks: in fact he was deeply hurt, and they added to the strain under which he worked, a strain that was beginning by 1930 to affect the quality of his performances and his health.

In 1932 he suffered a complete breakdown, and there was doubt whether he would recover from the tubercular infection that involved serious abdominal operations. For two years he was out of action, but when he did reappear his performances had all the old zest and a new depth.

In 1944 a fresh blow fell when his much-loved daughter Pamela was smitten with polio and died. For months Sargent was almost a broken man, but music saved him, and he seemed in time to draw inspiration from the experience. There were, however, works that he never conducted again except as a kind of memorial to Pamela, and not a few of his many generous but strictly private benefactions to other sufferers were really an offering to her.

In 1950 Sargent was chosen to follow Sir Adrian Boult as conductor of the BBC Symphony Orchestra and entered the final, most influential, stage of his career. With that orchestra, the BBC Chorus, the Royal Choral Society, the Huddersfield Choir, the Promenade Concerts, and many appearances as guest conductor with other ensembles, he enjoyed unrivalled opportunities for music-making on a great scale. Old prejudices had largely evaporated, and his interpretations were now seen to be equal to those of any conductor in the world; as an accompanist, he was regarded by many exacting soloists as pre-eminent.

His influence in these years was extended by appearances on the Brains Trust, where he effectively represented the common sense and decency of the ordinary citizen, and proved himself more than a match for the plausible intellectuals who often appeared with him. In this as in other activities he used his gifts of personality and showmanship to spread the love of music and to insist upon its place in a good life.

Sargent was now accepted as a valuable ambassador for music, and especially British music, in many parts of the world; and it was on one of his numerous foreign tours that he was taken ill. There was a temporary recovery, and he returned to conducting, but again collapsed in Chicago in July 1967. On his return he was seen to be dying. During the months that remained he continued to present himself with courage and something of the old panache, and made an unforgettable farewell visit to his devoted audience on the last night of the Proms. He died a day or two later at his home in London 3 October 1967.

Sargent's death provoked a remarkable demonstration of public sorrow and admiration. During a career in which social success had played no small part he had won the affection and loyalty of countless ordinary music-lovers who recognized his sincerity and came to share his buoyant love of life and music. He once said in jest that his career had been based on the two Ms, Messiah and Mikado, and there was an element of truth in the comment, which was a characteristic example of his unguarded spontaneity. But he could have added that it also rested on a long record of fine performances, an unfailing devotion to music, and natural endowments of exceptional brilliance.

Sargent's character was a strange blend of simplicity and sophistication, of apparent self-confidence and a deep sense of insecurity. He was an extremely generous man, but could sometimes appear vain and arrogant, displaying a frank enjoyment of fame and success which more cautious persons would have concealed, not from modesty but from fear of ridicule.

The circumstances of his early life had permanently influenced him. If he had enjoyed the privilege of attachment to a great professional orchestra and its conductors he might have become a different musician but not necessarily a better one. As it was, in the tough campaign to make his own way, he won the equipment necessary for the work he had to do, a work that greatly forwarded the interests of British music. After Sir Henry Wood's death in 1944 there was nobody except Sargent who could carry on his particular task; and when Sargent himself passed from the scene his place was not filled.

Sargent was appointed honorary D.Mus. (Oxford) in 1942 and honorary LL D (Liverpool) in 1947, the year in which he was knighted. Among his many other honours were honorary RAM, honorary FRCO, FRCM, honorary FTCL, and FRSA.

There is a bronze bust by William Timyn in the Royal Albert Hall and a portrait in oils by Sir Gerald Kelly. Another portrait in oils by John Gilroy (1967) is in the Garrick Club.

[Charles Reid, *Malcolm Sargent*, 1968; private information; personal knowledge.]

THOMAS ARMSTRONG

published 1981

SCHOLES Percy Alfred

(1877–1958)

Musical writer and encyclopedist, was born at Headingley, Leeds, 24 July 1877, the third child of Thomas Scholes, commercial agent, and his wife, Katharine Elizabeth Pugh. Ill health limited his attendance at school (he was a lifelong sufferer from severe bronchitis), but he gave much time to miscellaneous reading and the assiduous study of the elements of music. After a couple of years earning 10*s*. a week as assistant librarian of the Yorkshire College (later the university of Leeds), he taught music at Kent College, Canterbury (1901), and Kingswood College, Grahamstown, South Africa (1904). On his return to England at the age of twenty-eight his career began to take a more definite direction. He became an extension lecturer to the university of Manchester on what was coming to be known as 'musical appreciation', and continued in this way very successfully for the next six years. Meanwhile he took his A.R.C.M. diploma and (after a false start at Durham) entered St Edmund Hall, Oxford, gaining his B.Mus. in 1908.

In 1907, following a series of lectures for the Co-operative Holidays Association, he formed the Home Music Study Union, whose organ, *The Music Student* (in later years *The Music Teacher*), he edited from its foundation in 1908 until 1921. He married in 1908 and in 1912 made the decisive step of moving to London, his only guaranteed income being £40 a year as assistant to J. S. Shedlock, music critic of the *Queen*. With the support of such men as H. C. Colles and (Sir) Percy Buck, he was soon making his mark as a journalist and as an extension lecturer for the universities of Oxford, Cambridge, and London. From 1913 to 1920 he was music critic of the *Evening Standard*.

When war broke out in 1914 he was on a lecture tour of colleges in the United States and Canada. On his return he headed, until 1919, the 'music for the troops' section of the Y.M.C.A. in France, further developing his twin gifts of detailed organization and the ability to hold the attention of the unpractised listener. From this work came his very successful *Listener's Guide to Music* (1919).

Early in 1920 he became music critic of the *Observer*, following the abrupt departure of Ernest Newman who had accepted a substantial offer from the rival *Sunday Times*. For the next five years Scholes filled the position with notable success. His style, always fluent and readable, gained distinction. He continued to regard his role as primarily that of an educator, and was undoubtedly among the first to see the educational potentialities of broadcasting, the gramophone, and the player-piano. He gave a weekly radio talk commenting on the previous week's broadcasts: from 1926 to 1928 he was musical editor of the *Radio Times*. He was usually at work on several books at once. His home was a busy office with as many as six or more typists and co-workers, including his devoted wife.

A contract to provide pianola roll annotations for the Aeolian Company provided him with the means to detach himself from journalism. In 1928 he moved to Switzerland, and thenceforward lived in the neighbourhood of Montreux. The following year he organized an 'Anglo-American Music Educators' Conference' at Lausanne, which was repeated in 1931. He made four further lecture tours of the United States. He was now able to give time to more solid scholarship and his thesis on 'The Puritans and Music' gained him in 1934 his D.ès L. from Lausanne University.

For some time Scholes had planned a more comprehensive work, tentatively called 'Everyone's Musical Encyclopedia', for the great new body of listeners brought into being by radio and the gramophone. The book finally appeared as the *Oxford Companion to Music* in the autumn of 1938. Scholes's varied experience as teacher, lecturer, journalist, critic, and scholar was at last drawn together in one accomplishment—'the most extraordinary range of musical knowledge, ingeniously "self-indexed", ever written and assembled between two covers by one man' (*Grove*).

In 1940 he made his way to England just before the fall of France; his wartime homes were first at Aberystwyth, then at Oxford, where he was elected to the board of the faculty of music. He completed a monumental biography of Dr Charles Burney (2 vols., 1948, James Tait Black memorial prize), a model of humane scholarship, and continued his lexicographical labours with his *Concise Oxford Dictionary of Music* (1952) and *Oxford Junior Companion to Music* (1954). After the war he returned to Switzerland, and built a house at Clarens. In 1950 the devaluation of the pound drove him back to Oxford, where he spent the next six years losing inch by inch his battle against the complications in his lifelong bronchitis brought on by advancing age and an inimical climate. Every winter he returned to Switzerland; and there, at Vevey, he died, 31 July 1958. He was survived by his wife, Dora Wingate, daughter of Richard Lean, civil engineer. There were no children.

Scholes was of middle height, and although not robust, an active walker. He worked long hours with great concentration, with methodical interruptions for exercise. His conscience was strongly protestant, totally divorced from any conventional religious expression. He was warmly humanitarian; a long-standing and articulate vegetarian and opponent of blood sports. There were those for whom his clarity of thought, total absence of humbug and affectation, and ironic humour made him seem something of a philistine. He was charitable in good causes, warm and generous in personal dealings, at the same time disinclined to give ground in business matters. Traces of his native Yorkshire speech remained with him to the end. In a letter to his publisher he once wrote, 'the epitaph I should desire for myself, were it not already applied to another and a greater man, would be "The common people heard him gladly" '.

Scholes valued his well-earned academic distinctions which in addition to those already mentioned included: from Oxford the honorary degree of D.Mus. (1943), MA (by decree, 1944), and D.Litt. (1950), and from Leeds an honorary Litt.D. (1953). He was an honorary fellow and trustee of St Edmund Hall, Oxford; an officer of the Star of Romania (1930), FSA (1938), and OBE (1957). His remarkable library, one of the largest of its kind in private hands, was acquired by the National Library of Canada, Ottawa.

[Private information; personal knowledge.]

John Owen Ward

published 1971

SCOTT Sir Giles Gilbert

(1880–1960)

Architect, was born in Church Row, Hampstead, 9 November 1880, the son of George Gilbert Scott, a noted exponent of the Gothic revival in Britain, and his wife, Ellen King-Sampson. He was a grandson of Sir George Gilbert Scott, chiefly remembered for that courageous work, the Albert Memorial. He was educated at Beaumont College; then became, in 1898, a pupil of the architect Temple Moore in whose office, probably, he saw the possibility of designing in Gothic, without reproducing all its detail. There too, by working at night, he went in for and won the competition for the new Liverpool Anglican cathedral. This remarkable feat embarrassed the selection committee when it discovered the winner to be a young man of twenty-two, of no experience, and furthermore a Roman Catholic. Scott himself was surprised. Nevertheless he was appointed architect for the cathedral, with G. F. Bodley, once a pupil of Sir Gilbert Scott, as collaborator. That imposition was removed when the plans were finally drawn up and the first contract placed in 1903.

This great undertaking covered an area almost twice that of St Paul's. Scott made all the drawings and only one major revision: he abandoned the twin towers of his winning design in favour of a much larger central tower. Looking at the whole exterior sixty years later one is struck by the dependence on mass rather than intricacy, and on well-proportioned stone surfaces, deftly pierced by windows betraying no more than a Gothic ancestry. The cathedral shows both a knowledge of structure and a belief in its anatomy as the chief factors in architectural design.

Naturally such an early triumph launched Giles Scott on an evenly successful career. The other churches he was asked to design in the ensuing years all had a quality traceable to the parent building at Liverpool: the same reliance on mass for effect; a look of strength always; together with an imaginative and wise handling of detail. He never repeated himself; but, when he was able to incorporate it, he preferred a strong square tower at the west end. An exception to this is St Alban's at Golders Green, where a very squat central tower draws together happily the sloping tiled roofs grouped round it. Another is the chapel for Charterhouse School. This is no more than a long, narrow, and lofty edifice, almost in the class of industrial architecture; but admirably proportioned and lit by tall narrow windows with deep reveals. More interesting is the large chapel for Ampleforth Abbey in Yorkshire, which took over twenty years to build. One is impressed again here by the massive piling up of the exterior; and, internally, by the roughly plastered surfaces between the piers and arches. Scott was inspired by the narrowness of the site allowed to the chapel to form a crypt under the south half of the slope of the ground, which provides space for side chapels and is reached most attractively by a wide stone staircase taking up much of the south transept. Moreover, the high altar, standing roughly in the centre, is a double one facing east and west. A strong richly designed stone baldachino rises darkly to a great height above it.

Other churches which must be mentioned are St Michael's, Ashford, Middlesex; St Francis, Terriers, Buckinghamshire; St Andrew's, Luton; and St Maughold's, Ramsey, Isle of Man. The last two have west end towers. The church Scott built in Oldfield Lane, Bath, differs from those four in that it achieves unusual charm from its great simplicity inside. The aisles are divided from the nave by very short fat round columns, joined by thick semi-circular arches, which spring from sculptured capitals reminiscent of ninth-century work in the Vosges. Then there is Oban cathedral, built for the Roman Catholic diocese of Argyll and the Isles; a late work, and not very well known; but finished in time for Scott to see it. All his churches with west end towers are crowned by this instance: the massive square feature, built in roughly hewn granite—grey with a touch of pink—stands very dominantly almost on the edge of the sea, facing the Atlantic blasts. It is anchored there by twin porches at its base, rising unusually high but effectively integral with the tower itself. Although a small cathedral, it looks large inside, due partly to the absence of subdivisions in its length and partly to the extreme simplicity—almost innocence—of the treatment. The nave piers are very tall and very plain; and a rugged look is given by the roof, seemingly constructed of old ships' timbers. The high altar, again, richly outshines all the other furnishings. Oban cathedral is a notable example of a design most suitable to its site and, in every way, to its purpose. It was Scott's power to grasp clearly the practical object of a building and design it on that basis. Appearance followed from the expression of this more than from a preconceived idea of beauty.

The University Library which Scott built for Cambridge is little more than a towering bookstack. Fortunately it is not overwhelmingly too near the ancient colleges. But the large addition to the Bodleian at Oxford had of necessity to be in the centre of the city to provide storage for millions of books within easy reach of the ancient reading-rooms. An immense stack on a corner site in Broad Street would have been impossible. Hence the new structure, deeply sunk into the earth and screened by two elevations no higher than its neighbours. In an attempt to be polite to these—which vary from late Gothic to Victorian Tudor—Scott produced a not very impressive neo-Jacobean design. If this is compared to the addition he made to Clare College, Cambridge, the Bodleian extension loses interest. For the former is the straight provision of two blocks of rooms in a simple Georgian idiom, linked by a memorial arch of great beauty. The unexpected value of this lies in its showing that Scott could design in the spirit of the late eighteenth century with a facility equalling his handling of Gothic.

Scott was appointed architect for the new Waterloo Bridge in 1932; and it was opened to traffic in 1945. This is an engineering work married to architecture most properly and in sharp contrast to the fanciful liaison of Tower Bridge. The clean sweep of the five unadorned arches reflects admirably the invisible steel anatomy. One feels and enjoys the tension expressed in the form. The great spans bounding across the Thames testify to the purpose of the structure—the rapid conveyance of traffic. And again, the right collaboration between engineer and architect can be appreciated in the great Battersea power-station. Its high walls of plain good brickwork seem as if they encased big machinery; while the huge chimneys—as pleasant to look at as many campaniles—hint, in the strength and delicacy of their design, at the puffing of smoke in tall clouds.

Some restoration of buildings damaged or destroyed by enemy bombing in the war of 1939–45 fell to his lot. The mid-Victorian Gothic-revival Carmelite church in Kensington, popular but of little charm, with a number of altars in the sugary fourteenth-century style much favoured at that time, was practically obliterated. Scott made no attempt to reproduce it; as the church was hemmed in closely by narrow streets at each side, he made the new building follow the plan of the old but lit it with top lights inserted in the curve of the roof. His restoration of the Guildhall consisted chiefly of saving what remained and strengthening the roof with steel, inserted above the old timbers. In what amounted to a rebuilding of the House of Commons, Scott was instructed by the select committee to re-state the Chamber in its original form, but to eliminate much of the ecclesiastical Gothic detail and ornament. The foundation stone was laid in 1948 and the new Chamber first used in October 1950.

Scott was elected an associate of the Royal Academy in 1918 and a full academician in 1922. He was knighted in 1924 and appointed to the Order of Merit in 1944. He was an honorary DCL of Oxford (1933) and LL D of Liverpool (1925) and of Cambridge (1955). He received the Royal gold medal of the Royal Institute of British Architects (of which he became a fellow in 1912) in 1925; in 1933–5 he was president of the Institute which celebrated its centenary in 1934. When in 1949 Princess Elizabeth presented him with the Albert medal of the Royal Society of Arts she hailed him as 'the builder of a lasting heritage for Britain'.

This excellent architect was a man of medium height and, at first sight, not unduly impressive, in view of his high distinction. He was very modest and approachable, with a charming sense of humour. Golf was his great recreation. He married in 1914 Louisa Wallbank Hughes who died in 1949, leaving two sons. Scott himself died in London 8 February 1960. The National Portrait Gallery possesses drawings of him by Robin Guthrie and Powys Evans and a painting by R. G. Eves.

[Private information.]

A. S. G. Butler

published 1971

SCOTT Sir Peter Markham

(1909–1989)

Conservationist, painter, naturalist, sportsman, writer, and broadcaster, was born at 174 Buckingham Palace Road, London, 14 September 1909, the only child of Captain Robert Falcon Scott, Antarctic explorer, and his wife Kathleen Bruce, sculptor, daughter of Canon Lloyd Stewart Bruce. His father died in 1912 and in 1922 his mother married Edward Hilton Young, who became first Baron Kennet. There was one son of this marriage. In his last message home before he died Scott had urged his wife to make his son interested in natural history, which was better than sport. In the event, Peter Scott came to excel at both. He was an energetic child, with a passion for natural history, who spent much time drawing and painting. He also shone at sports, ice-skating, and sailing in small boats. From his preparatory school, West Downs, he went to Oundle. He then studied at Trinity College, Cambridge (1927–30), where he hoped to take the natural sciences tripos, but failed his part i (1930). He stayed on for an extra term and obtained an ordinary degree in December 1930 (zoology, botany, and history of art). During his Cambridge days he took up wildfowling, and in 1929 *Country Life* magazine printed two articles on the sport written and illustrated by him.

From Cambridge he went to the Munich Academy for a term, and then spent two years at the Royal Academy Schools in London. In 1933 he held his first one-man exhibition, which was a huge success, at Ackermann's Galleries in London. He was able to make his living as a painter of wildfowl, producing his first book (entitled *Morning Flight* and published by *Country Life*) in 1935. This was followed by *Wild Chorus* in 1938. Lavishly illustrated with his paintings, both books became very popular and ran to twelve editions.

Scott excelled at sailing and won a bronze medal in the 1936 Olympic Games, for single-handed yachting. He also won the prestigious Prince of Wales cup for international fourteen-foot dinghies in 1937, 1938, and 1946. In the late 1950s he developed a passion for gliding, and won the British gliding championships in 1963.

At the outbreak of war in 1939 he volunteered for the Royal Naval Volunteer Reserve. After training he spent two years in destroyers, mainly in HMS *Broke* in the Western approaches, becoming a first lieutenant, and then he served in the coastal forces in steam gunboats. He became senior officer of the flotilla, was awarded a DSC (1943) and bar, and was thrice mentioned in dispatches. He also invented a night camouflage scheme for naval ships. His final appointment was the command of a new frigate, as a lieutenant-commander. With the war coming to a close, Scott was adopted as the Conservative candidate for Wembley North, but he failed to be elected by 435 votes, having had only two weeks to prepare for the election.

While visiting the river Severn at Slimbridge in Gloucestershire in 1945, in search of a rare goose amongst the wintering white-fronted geese, he decided to establish a research organization, which he had planned for many years, to study the swans, geese, and ducks of the world. The Severn Wildfowl Trust was set up at Slimbridge in 1946 and soon boasted the largest collection of wildfowl in the world. Later known as the Wildfowl and Wetlands Trust, it expanded into nine centres around Britain. Scott remained its honorary director until he died. Scientific research took Scott to Iceland in 1951 to study pink-footed geese on their breeding grounds, and to the Perry river region of northern Canada, where in 1949 he mapped this unknown area while in search of the breeding grounds of the ross goose. Scott did more than any British contemporary to save wildlife species from extinction.

When the BBC founded a television centre in Bristol Scott helped to establish the Natural History Unit there, planning a programme on natural history called *Look*, which he hosted for seventeen years. Many of the early programmes contained his own film which he shot on his travels. He took part in *Nature Parliament*, a radio programme which ran for twenty-one years, and was the narrator in many other programmes.

In the early 1950s Scott became involved with the International Union for the Conservation of Nature and Natural Resources (IUCN). He helped build up the Species Survival Commission of the union and became chairman (1962–81). With two friends, in 1961 he founded the World Wildlife Fund (later the World Wide Fund for Nature) to raise the money needed to finance nature conservation around the world. As its chairman from 1961, he designed its panda logo and invented the red data books listing endangered species. He travelled abroad extensively on behalf of the Fund, establishing national appeals, advising on conservation issues and areas for reserves, lecturing, and fund-raising. He was also involved in numerous other conservation and naturalist societies. He became as much of an expert on coral fish as he was on birds and his records have proved scientifically useful.

His autobiography, *The Eye of the Wind*, was published in 1961 and was reprinted many times. He was a prolific author and illustrator, his final books being the three volumes of *Travel Diaries of a Naturalist*, published in 1983, 1985, and 1987 respectively.

He was elected rector of Aberdeen University (1960–3) and appointed chancellor of Birmingham University (1974–83). Appointed MBE (1942) and CBE (1953), he was knighted in 1973. In 1987 he became both CH and a fellow of the Royal Society. He had honorary degrees from the universities of Exeter, Aberdeen, Birmingham, Bristol, Liverpool, Bath, Guelph, and Ulster. He was also awarded numerous medals, prizes, and foreign honours.

Strongly built and of average height, Scott was warm and friendly, tackling everything with enthusiasm. He liked to paint every day. In 1942 he married the novelist Elizabeth Jane Howard, daughter of David Liddon Howard, timber merchant. They had a daughter. This marriage was dissolved in 1951 and in the same year he married (Felicity) Philippa, daughter of Commander Frederick William Talbot-Ponsonby, of the Royal Navy, and his wife Hannah (née Findlay). They had a daughter and a son. Peter Scott died from a heart attack in hospital in Bristol 29 August 1989.

[Peter Scott, *The Eye of the Wind* (autobiography), 1961; Jonathan Benington, *Sir Peter Scott at 80: a Retrospective* (catalogue including a biography), 1989; Elspeth Huxley, *Peter Scott*, 1993; personal knowledge.]

PAUL WALKDEN

published 1996

SELLERS ('Peter') Richard Henry

(1925–1980)

Comedian, was born in Portsmouth 8 September 1925, the only child of William Sellers, a pianist of modest ability, and his wife, Agnes ('Peg') Marks, who was one of the Ray Sisters entertainers, and the great-granddaughter of Daniel Mendoza, the pugilist. Although his mother was Jewish, he was primarily educated at St Aloysius College in Hornsey Lane, Highgate, a Roman Catholic school run by the Brothers of Our Lady of Mercy. He left school at fourteen and entered the theatre world, doing most backstage jobs. He then developed a desire to play drums in a dance band. At this he became very proficient and, but for his ability at mimicry, might well have stayed a jazz drummer.

Called up into the RAF during the war despite his mother's desperate efforts to have him disqualified on medical grounds, he finally ended up in its Entertainment Section in India, Ceylon, and Burma with Ralph Reader's Gang Show. Within a short time of leaving the Services in 1947, such was his confidence and his ability as an impressionist, that he duped a BBC producer, Roy Speer, by using the voice of Kenneth Horne. The producer was duly impressed, and gave him a small part in a comedy show.

In a short space of time he had appeared in the following series: 'Petticoat Lane', 'Ray's a Laugh', 'Variety Bandbox', 'Workers' Playtime', 'Third Division' (the first comedy show to come on the erudite Third Programme), finally reaching the highest acclaim in the revolutionary *The Goon Show,* which began in 1951 and ran for nine years. During this period he also appeared in Variety, including the Royal Command Performance. There were a few second-rate films: *Penny Points to Paradise* (1951), *Orders are Orders* (1954), *John and Julie* (1955), and *The Smallest Show on Earth* (1957). Then came a strangely original short film written and directed by Spike Milligan, entitled *The Running Jumping Standing Still Film* (1957–8), which won numerous awards because of its innovatory ideas. Sellers's big commercial break came with *The Ladykillers* (1955), but he received world acclaim for his outstanding performance in *I'm All Right Jack* (1959).

There followed a series of quality films, some successful and some not, including *The Millionairess* (1960), where he played opposite Sophia Loren, and *Waltz of the Toreadors* (1962), and one produced and directed by himself, *Mr. Topaze* (1961). He soared to new heights in his multi-character *Dr. Strangelove.* He did some black comedy films, one being *What's New Pussycat?* (1965), with Peter O'Toole and Woody Allen. But the watershed in his career was his portrayal of Inspector Clouseau, in *The Pink Panther* (1963). There followed a period of indifference, and it would appear at one time that his career might have come to a conclusion. However, there followed *The Return of the Pink Panther* (1974) and *The Pink Panther Strikes Again* (1976), which renovated his career and made him a millionaire.

To summarize him, one would say that he had one of the most glittering comic talents of our age, but what few people knew was that he never reached or was allowed to perform the levels of comedy that he delighted in most: the nonsense school. To his dying day he said his happiest days were performing in the Goon Shows. He made a desperate attempt to recreate *The Goon Show* atmosphere by making the film *The Fiendish Plot of Dr. Fu Manchu* (1980), which he co-wrote. But the fact that he never was a writer, or ever would be, and the collaboration with Americans, who had no like sense of humour, made the film a failure. However, most extraordinarily, he gave his finest performance in his last but one film, *Being There* (1979). This showed his incredible ability to recreate a character, in which Peter Sellers himself seemed to be totally excluded. His last wry contribution to comedy was having Glen Miller's 'In the Mood' played at his cremation.

Sellers was appointed CBE in 1966. He won many awards: Best Actor for 1959 (British Film Academy award); the Golden Gate award, 1959; the San Sebastian film award for the best British actor, 1962; Best Actor award,

Tehran Film Festival, 1973; and the *Evening News* best actor of the year award, 1975.

Sellers suffered from a heart condition for his last fifteen years which made life difficult for him and had a debilitating effect on his personality. None of his marriages lasted long. His first one, in 1951, to Anne Howe produced two children, Michael and Sarah, but was terminated in 1964. In the same year, after a whirlwind romance, he married the starlet, Britt Ekland. There was one daughter of this marriage, Victoria, but the marriage was dissolved in 1969. In 1970 he married Miranda, daughter of Richard St John Quarry and Lady Mancroft; the marriage was dissolved in 1974; there were no children. His last marriage, in 1977, to Lynne Frederick, also underwent emotional undulations, and all the signs point to a marriage that had failed; they had no children.

Sellers died in the Middlesex Hospital, London, 24 July 1980. Among the many who attended a later service of thanksgiving in London were Spike Milligan, Harry Secombe, and Michael Bentine, his former colleagues on *The Goon Show.*

[Peter Evans, *The Mask Behind the Mask, a Life of Peter Sellers*, 1968 and 1969; Alexander Walker, *Peter Sellers*, 1981; Michael Sellers with Sarah and Victoria Sellers, *P.S. I Love You*, 1981; personal knowledge.]

SPIKE MILLIGAN

published 1986

SLIM William Joseph

(1891–1970)

First Viscount Slim

Field-marshal, younger son of John Slim, an iron merchant of Bristol, and his wife, Charlotte, daughter of Charles Tucker, of Burnham, Somerset, was born in Bristol 6 August 1891. The family moved to Birmingham at the turn of the century and he began his education at St Philip's Catholic School and went on to King Edward's School where he showed a flair for literature and the clear thinking which remained a distinctive trait. He was not notable at games but was a keen member of the Officers' Training Corps and his great ambition was to be an army officer. But his parents could not afford to send him to Sandhurst or guarantee the allowance then almost essential for young officers. He took a post with the engineering firm of Stewarts & Lloyds and at the same time succeeded in getting himself accepted by the Birmingham University OTC.

In August 1914 Slim was commissioned in Kitchener's army and posted to the Royal Warwickshire Regiment. With the 9th battalion he first saw active service at Cape Helles and in August 1915 was so seriously wounded at Sari Bair that it seemed unlikely he would ever again be fit for active service. He was posted to the 12th (holding) battalion, but in October 1916, although still officially unfit for active service, went with a draft to his old battalion in Mesopotamia where he was again wounded, gained the MC, and was evacuated to India. He had been granted a regular commission, with seniority from 1 June 1915 in the West India Regiment, but in 1919 he transferred to the Indian Army. From November 1917 until January 1920 he was on the staff at army headquarters, India, becoming a GSO 2 and temporary major in November 1918. In March 1920 he was posted to the 1/6th Gurkha Rifles; as he had not been applied for by the regiment his reception was not cordial, but his ability was soon recognized and he was appointed adjutant. Efficient and strict, he yet became well liked and respected.

In January 1926 Slim entered the Staff College, Quetta, and although he had not the interest in games and horsemanship which counted there for so much, he soon gained the respect and friendship of his contemporaries and was without doubt the outstanding student of his time. On passing out in 1928 he was appointed to army headquarters, India, as a GSO 2 and received a brevet majority in 1930. In 1934 he became Indian Army instructor at the Staff College, Camberley, where colleagues and students testified to the brilliance which earned him the brevet of lieutenant-colonel in 1935. After attending the 1937 course at the Imperial Defence College he went back to India to command the 2/7th Gurkhas and a little over a year later was sent to command the Senior Officers School at Belgaum, with the rank of brigadier, a few months before the outbreak of war in 1939.

Slim was now given command of the 10th Indian Infantry brigade of 5th Indian division which went to Eritrea in the autumn of 1940. The Italians had occupied Gallabat on the Sudan-Abyssinia border and Slim was sent with a brigade group to retake it and to ensure that the Italians did not advance into the Sudan. Though Gallabat was captured after a hard fight, it was untenable unless the near-by Italian border post, Metemma, could also be taken before the Italians could move up their large reserves. Rather than risk being caught off balance Slim pulled out of Gallabat to positions from which he could prevent the Italians reoccupying it. Subsequent information indicated that the enemy had panicked and would have abandoned Metemma. Of his failure to attack Metemma Slim wrote later 'I could find plenty of excuses for failure, but only one *reason*—myself. When two courses of action were open to me I had not chosen, as a good commander should, the bolder. I had taken counsel of my fears.' Acceptance of blame if things went wrong and praise for his subordinates in victory were characteristic of Slim throughout his career.

Soon after Gallabat he was wounded in a surprise low-flying attack on a vehicle in which he was travelling. On recovering, in May 1941 he was given command, with the rank of major-general, of the 10th Indian division in Iraq and Syria, where he carried out a brief and successful campaign against the Vichy French forces. There followed an advance into Persia where a brisk minor action and much tactful firmness helped to ensure that Persia gave no further trouble during the war.

Much to his disappointment Slim was next recalled to India but his fears of becoming chairborne were dispelled when, on 19 March 1942, Sir A. P. (later Earl) Wavell sent him to Burma to organize a corps headquarters, which carried the rank of lieutenant-general, to take control of the two British-Indian divisions of the army retreating from Rangoon. He brought 'Burcorps' out battered and exhausted but in good heart, and on its disbandment was given command of XV Corps.

Slim's next task was to pull the chestnuts out of the fire in the closing stages of the disastrous Arakan campaign of 1942–3. His handling of this critical situation brought him into conflict with the commander-in-chief Eastern Army, who wished to relieve him of his command; but he had his way, and events vindicated his methods.

By this time Slim had evolved the strategy which was to put an end to the hitherto unbroken success of Japanese infiltration: to cover the approaches to vital areas (at this time Chittagong and Imphal) with well-stocked strongholds which were to stand fast if by-passed, to be supplied by air if necessary, and to cut the supply lines of the infiltrators. The strongholds would thus become backstops against which army or corps reserves would destroy the infiltrators before moving straight into the counter-offensive.

On being given command of the newly formed 14th Army in October 1943 Slim began to build up the administrative organization, including a highly developed air supply system, to underpin his new strategy. At the same time he saw to it that all units in the 14th Army knew what was expected of them. Wherever he went—and he went everywhere—he inspired confidence. In early 1944 the Japanese launched the grand offensive which they hoped would so shatter the Allied forces on the India–Burma border that there would be revolt in India which could be exploited by the so-called Indian National Army. In Arakan the offensive was broken in three weeks and the counter-stroke drove the Japanese from their North Arakan stronghold. At Imphal/Kohima the Japanese 15th Army suffered a disastrous defeat and over 50,000 casualties, of whom more than half were dead, and withdrew in disorder to the Chindwin. These victories earned Slim the CB and KCB and international fame.

During these critical battles Slim was harassed by two unusual command problems. General Stilwell commanding the American–Chinese forces refused to serve under the 11th Army Group, but eventually agreed to take orders from Slim until his own force reached Kamaing within striking distance of his objective of Myitkyina. Fortunately the friendship between Slim and Sir George Giffard, who commanded the 11th Army Group, ensured that this awkward situation caused no trouble. The second problem was presented by Major-General Orde Wingate. Though Slim admired Wingate's gift for leadership his confidence in Long Range Penetration was limited, he felt unsure about Wingate himself, and he strongly disapproved of fragmenting tested formations like 70th division to furnish the Chindit columns which seemed to him a private army working for private purposes. Wingate's attempt to exploit his connection with Churchill was a particular embarrassment. But operation Thursday was an Anglo-American commitment, and on 5 March it was Slim who, at the take-off airfield, authorized the fly-in of the Chindit striking force despite last-minute evidence from air-photographs of Japanese attempts to block the landing-strips.

In the reconquest of Burma, Slim's task was to capture Mandalay and consolidate on the line of the Irrawaddy from there south-westwards to its junction with the Chindwin about 100 miles distant. When on 12 November 1944 11th Army Group was replaced by Allied Land Forces South East Asia (ALFSEA) under Sir Oliver Leese, the 14th Army advance on Mandalay had already begun. Slim had hoped to trap and destroy the reconstituted Japanese 15th Army west of Mandalay on the plain bounded by the Chindwin and Irrawaddy, but by mid December he realized that it had seen its danger and withdrawn across the Irrawaddy. On 17 December he sent ALFSEA a revised plan and the next day gave his corps commanders verbal orders to put it into operation at once. Slim had taken the bit between his teeth and this, added to the fact that earlier he had refused to fly a division into north Burma to contact the American-Chinese forces advancing under General Sultan, was perhaps the beginning of a rift between him and the commander-in-chief ALFSEA which had serious repercussions later, although events had vindicated Slim's handling of the operations.

The new plan put in motion a great two-pronged battle designed to cut the Japanese communications to their main base at Rangoon, envelop and destroy the 15th and 33rd Japanese Armies in north Burma, and isolate the 28th Japanese Army in Arakan for destruction later. The Japanese life-line was to be cut at Meiktila, some 80 miles south of Mandalay, while the two

Japanese armies in north Burma were to be held there by what was to be made to seem the advance of the whole 14th Army on Mandalay; a deception which made full use of the romantic appeal of 'the road to Mandalay'. While XXXIII Corps, headed by a division known by the Japanese to have been in IV Corps, drove eastwards on Mandalay, IV Corps, in wireless silence, moved unostentatiously south and established a bridgehead near the confluence of the Chindwin and Irrawaddy. Thence a motorized and armoured column burst through to Meiktila, there to be supplied and reinforced by air.

Great in conception, brilliant in execution, the manœuvre mystified and misled the Japanese who took the thrust south to be the deception and so concentrated on trying to stop the thrust on Mandalay. Thus they were unable to prevent Meiktila being overrun. Their desperate efforts to retake Meiktila collapsed by the end of March and meanwhile the garrison of Mandalay left to fight to the last were destroyed. The failure to retake Meiktila sealed the fate of the Japanese Burma Area Army whose commander-in-chief described it as 'the master stroke'.

On 1 April 1945 Slim began the drive on Rangoon. One corps, with most of the armour, pursued the remnants of the 15th and 33rd Japanese armies down the Mandalay–Rangoon road while another drove down the Irrawaddy valley against the 28th Japanese Army, the remnants of which got penned in the Pegu Yomas and as planned were destroyed later. On 5 May 1945 the 14th Army linked up with the amphibious force which had landed unopposed in Rangoon two days earlier. So ended the brilliant series of victories which went far to substantiate Lord Mountbatten's view that 'Slim was the finest general the Second World War produced'. Throughout the campaign Slim was invariably at hand at vital moments to help if needed.

The day after Rangoon was taken over by 14th Army Slim was told by the commander-in-chief of ALFSEA that he proposed to make a change in the command of 14th Army for the invasion of Malaya, and offered him Burma Command. Slim refused it and said that as it seemed that the high command had lost confidence in him he would apply to the commander-in-chief in India to be allowed to retire. There was dismay in 14th Army and at GHQ India, and it was not long before the direct intervention of the CIGS, Lord Alanbrooke, resulted in Slim's supercession being cancelled.

He was promoted full general 1 July 1945 and was shortly afterwards himself appointed commander-in-chief ALFSEA, taking up the appointment on 10 August 1945. At the beginning of 1946 he was recalled to England to resuscitate the Imperial Defence College and on completion of his two years as commandant he retired from the army and was appointed deputy chairman of the Railway Executive. This appointment was short-lived for on 1 November 1948 he was recalled to the army to be chief of the imperial general staff and two months later was promoted field-marshal. He visited every British command overseas as well as India, Pakistan, Canada, the United States, Australia, and New Zealand. Before his term had expired he was nominated the next governor-general of Australia. He took office in 1953 and soon established himself in the affections of the Australian people as 'a human being who understands how human beings think'. Lord Casey considered that Australia was very fortunate in having him as governor-general. Slim made it his business to seek out Australia and the Australians and meet them as a man who had something to contribute, and when he relinquished office after an extended term the prime minister of Australia gave it as his opinion that there never had been two people who achieved a greater hold on the affections and regard of the Australian people than had Sir William and Lady Slim.

On leaving Australia in 1960 Slim accepted four active directorships and membership of the board of advice of the National Bank of Australasia. Eleven universities, including Oxford and Cambridge, conferred honorary degrees on him and in 1962 he was master of the Clothworkers' Company. He was a freeman of the City of London and between 1944 and 1960 was colonel of three regiments. In 1963 he was appointed deputy constable and lieutenant-governor of Windsor Castle and became constable and governor the following year, a post which he held until shortly before his death. Before 1939 he published many short stories under the pen-name of Anthony Mills. His book, *Defeat into Victory* (1956), was considered one of the finest published on the war of 1939–45 and sold over a hundred thousand copies. His other two books, *Courage and other Broadcasts* (1957) and *Unofficial History* (1959), a collection of reminiscences many of which had appeared in *Blackwood's*, were also very successful.

His robust appearance and determined jutting chin gave an impression of ruthlessness, but nothing could be further from the truth. Kindly and approachable with a quiet sense of humour so evident in his book, *Unofficial History*, he possessed tremendous fortitude and determination and, in all walks of life, he inspired the confidence given to a great leader. Once a course of action had been decided he carried it through whatever the difficulties: he lived up to his tenet that 'the difficult is what you do today, the impossible takes a little longer'. His humility about his own achievements is exemplified by a remark he made to a friend on learning that he was to be chief of the imperial general staff 'I only hope I can hold it down'.

Slim was appointed CBE (1942), to the DSO (1943), CB and KCB (1944), GBE (1946), GCB (1950), GCMG (1952), GCVO (1954), KG (1959), and was created a viscount in 1960. He married in 1926 Aileen, daughter of the Revd John Anderson Robertson, minister at Corstorphine, Edinburgh. He had one daughter and one son, John Douglas (born 1927), who also entered the army and who succeeded him when he died in London 14 December 1970. After a public funeral with full military honours at St George's Chapel, Windsor, Slim was cremated privately.

The National Army Museum has a portrait by Leonard Boden. There is also a portrait by T. C. Dugdale.

[Lord Slim's own writings and his record of service; biographical record in the Australian National Library; S. Woodburn Kirby (Official History), *The War Against Japan*, vols. ii–v, 1958–69; Sir Geoffrey Evans, *Slim as Military Commander*, 1969; Ronald Lewin, *Slim: the Standardbearer*, 1976; private information; personal knowledge.]

M. R. Roberts

published 1981

SOPWITH Sir Thomas Octave Murdoch

(1888–1989)

Engineer and pioneer airman, was born 18 January 1888 at 92 Cromwell Road, Kensington, west London, the eighth child and only son of Thomas Sopwith (1838–1898), managing director of the Spanish Lead Mines Company of Linares in southern Spain, and his wife Lydia Gertrude, daughter of William Messiter, of Wincanton, Somerset. Sopwith was educated at the Cottesmore School, Hove, Sussex, and, from 1902, the Seafield Park Engineering College at Lee-on-Solent, where he pursued his already deep interest in early motor cars, motor cycles, and all things mechanical. His childhood was deeply affected by an incident on a boating expedition during the family's annual summer holiday on the Isle of Lismore, off Oban in Scotland, when a gun, lying across the ten-year-old Sopwith's knee, went off and killed his father. This haunted Sopwith for the rest of his life. A substantial inheritance of £52,000 was divided, chiefly, between Sopwith and his mother, because five of the seven daughters had already married well.

Thus provided, on leaving Seafield Park in 1905, without academic attainments, but with a good, practical grasp of basic engineering, Sopwith plunged into the enjoyable pursuits of ballooning, motor-racing at Brooklands, and sailing in Channel waters. He bought a single-seat Avis monoplane and taught himself to fly (he gained the aviator's certificate no. 31). Before the end of 1910 he set up a British distance and duration record of 107 miles and 3 hours 10 minutes and, in December, with a flight of 169 miles in $3\frac{3}{4}$ hours, won the £4,000 Baron de Forest prize for the longest flight of the year from Britain into Europe. He won further prize money in America, which enabled him, in February 1912, to found the Sopwith School of Flying and, in June, the Sopwith Aviation Company Ltd.

By the outbreak of war in August 1914 the Sopwith Aviation Company had become one of the leading early British aircraft manufacturers, supplying aircraft to both the Admiralty and the War Office. Moreover, a Sopwith Tabloid on floats—a precursor of all subsequent single-seat fighters—had won for Britain the second Schneider Trophy air race at Monaco. Between August 1914 and November 1918 more than 18,000 Sopwith aircraft, of thirty-two different types, were designed and built for the Allied air forces. They included 5,747 Sopwith Camel single-seat fighters. The Camel was one of the most successful military aircraft of World War I, with 1,294 confirmed victories in air combat.

Sopwith's contribution to the war was recognized by his appointment as CBE in 1918, but from the end of the war until September 1920 the Sopwith Company built only fifteen aircraft, while vainly endeavouring to maintain the employment of as many as possible of its workers by building motor-car bodies, motor cycles, and even aluminium saucepans. In September 1920 Sopwith put the company into liquidation while he was still able to pay creditors in full. Two months later he launched the H. G. Hawker Engineering Company Ltd., with himself as chairman, Fred Sigrist as chief engineer, and Harry Hawker as designer/test pilot. In June 1928 the Hawker Company's fortunes were truly founded, following the first flight at Brooklands of the outstanding Hawker Hart, a two-seat day bomber, designed by (Sir) Sydney Camm, who had joined the Hawker Company in 1923. During the next ten years 3,036 Harts, and its seven variants, were built to form a substantial portion of the Royal Air Force.

Until 1963, under Sopwith's leadership and with Camm's design team, 26,800 aircraft of fifty-two different types flowed from the production lines of Hawkers and its associated companies. Chief among them was the Hawker Hurricane, a single-seat fighter, first flown on 6 November 1935, and put into production by Sopwith three months before an Air Ministry order had been received. Thanks to that hazardous but calculated risk, an additional 300 Hurricanes were able to be in service when the Battle of Britain began in 1940—a factor which contributed to Britain winning the world's first decisive air battle.

Meanwhile, in July 1935, with acumen and skill Sopwith had begun to weld a major portion of the British aircraft industry into the Hawker Siddeley Group—a combination of the Armstrong-Whitworth, Avro, Gloster, and Hawker aircraft companies, with the Armstrong Siddeley aero-engine and motor-car company and Air Service Training. During World War II the group delivered more than 40,000 aeroplanes of fifteen different types. They ranged from the Avro Lancaster bomber to the Gloster Meteor jet fighter. In 1959 the de Havilland Aircraft Company was added to the group and, in 1963, Blackburn and General Aircraft Ltd. Sopwith remained steadfastly in charge as chairman of the board, skilfully delegating his responsibilities until in 1963, at the age of seventy-five, he retired as chairman, but remained on the board until, on his ninetieth birthday, he was elected founder and life president. He was knighted in 1953.

Throughout his long life Sopwith maintained his cherished pursuits of fishing, shooting, and boating. In 1913 he set up a world speed record for powerboats of 48 knots, and between 1928 and 1930, with seventy-five first prizes, he became the leading British 12-metre yachtsman. In 1930 he was elected a member of the Royal Yacht Squadron. With his J-class sloop, *Endeavour*, he came close to winning the America's Cup for Britain in 1934. In 1937 he tried again, with *Endeavour II*, but lost to a better boat. In later years he confided, 'My one great regret is that I didn't bring home that Cup.' Between 1937 and 1939 Sopwith revelled in the ownership of the 1,600-ton, ocean-going diesel yacht, *Philante*, built to his own requirements.

Sopwith was six feet tall, somewhat chubby-faced, with full cheeks, and a high, broad, and clear forehead, topped by a mass of thick dark hair, always parted to the right. He had somewhat heavy eyebrows, hazel eyes, a broad, straight nose, a wide mouth, and a rather thin upper lip. In 1914 he married the forty-three-year-old Beatrix Mary Leslie, divorced wife of Charles Edward Malcolm and daughter of Walter James Ruthven, Baron Ruthven. To his great distress, she died of cancer in 1930. In 1932 he married Phyllis Brodie Leslie, daughter of Frederick Philip Augustus Gordon, inspector of gaols in the Indian Civil Service. She died in 1978. They had one son. In his ninetieth year Sopwith became completely blind, but he lost none of his memory, nor his interest in aviation, sport, and meeting old friends. In 1988 a great assembly of Sopwith's legion of friends attended a hundredth birthday party held for him at Brooklands, at which they contacted him in Hampshire by land line (a discreet telephone line). He died at his home, Compton Manor, at Kings Somborne in Hampshire, 27 January 1989.

[Bruce Robertson, *Sopwith the Man and His Aircraft*, 1970; Horace F. King, *Sopwith Aircraft 1912–1920*, 1981; Alan Bramson, *Pure Luck, the Authorized Biography of Sir Thomas Sopwith*, 1990; private information; personal knowledge.]

PETER MASEFIELD

published 1996

SPENCER Sir Stanley

(1891–1959)

Artist, was born at Cookham-on-Thames, Berkshire, 30 June 1891, the seventh son in a family of eleven children of William Spencer, an organist and music teacher, and his wife, Anna Caroline Slack. His brother Gilbert was born in the following year. Spencer had no formal education, attending only a class which met in a corrugated iron building in the Spencer garden and was presided over by his sister Annie, who, he said, despaired of him.

In 1907 Lady Boston, who had been giving Spencer private drawing lessons, sent him to the Technical School at Maidenhead. A year later she sent her protégé to the Slade School with introductions to Professors Tonks and Brown. He was accepted but continued to live at home catching an evening train back—a routine which nourished his gifts: his already vivid imagination was rooted in Cookham and its surroundings and inhabitants. The subject-matter of his art was already clear and distinct in his mind; the Slade developed his powers to express the vision. In 1912 he gained the Melville Nettleship prize (a scholarship) and the composition prize for a painting 'The Nativity'

Spencer painted a series of memorable canvases while still a Slade student: 'Two Girls and a Beehive' (1910), 'John Donne arriving in Heaven' (1911), 'Joachim among the Shepherds' (1912), 'Apple Gatherers' (1912–13), the last of which was acquired by the Tate Gallery. In 1912, his last year at the Slade, he began one of his finest paintings, 'Zacharias and Elizabeth' (1912–13).

Spencer had attained both technical and imaginative maturity while still a student. In the introduction he contributed in 1955 to the catalogue of the Tate Gallery retrospective exhibition of his work, Spencer himself commented on what he considered the best period of his painterly life. He described the 'state of sureness' he was in before the war of 1914–18, a state which after the war continued to about 1922–3 'when I did the Betrayal. At this time I did the series of drawings for the Burghclere Memorial and also the drawing for the 1927 Resurrection. So that all the painting I was to do from 1922 to 1932 was settled in nearly every detail: ten years of solid bliss were ahead of me. But I knew in 1922–3 that I was changing or losing grip or something. I was, I feared, forsaking the vision and I was filled with consternation. All the ability I had was dependent on that vision.'

The vision he lived with was a vision of heaven in Cookham's streets and of the incidents of Christ's life, with which the family Bible-readings had enkindled his imagination, as enacted there; it was a vision in which Cookham scenes and biblical stories were simultaneously in focus and interpenetrated. This private and ecstatic way of seeing so engrossed him that even in so large (and so vivid) a family circle he lived much within himself, and when not painting his 'vision' was walking alone along the river or around the village seeing the everyday things in which he delighted all the more sharply for their irradiation in a light of heaven.

These were the seminal years of Spencer's career. This trance-like life was interrupted by the war. He joined the Royal Army Medical Corps in 1915 and was sent to Macedonia in the summer of 1916. In 1917 he volunteered for the infantry (the 17th Royal Berkshires), also in the Macedonian theatre, and served there until demobilization.

While still in Macedonia he had been commissioned to do a war painting, and this he carried out on his return home—'Travoys arriving with Wounded' (Imperial War Museum). He also finished 'Swan Upping' (Tate Gallery), which he had left two-thirds completed four years earlier.

To the years 1919–23 belong either in execution or in conception most of his finest and also most mature works: paintings such as 'The Robing of Christ' and 'The Disrobing of Christ', of 1922 (Tate Gallery); the drawings for the great 'Resurrection, Cookham' which he painted in 1923–7—the completed picture was exhibited in Spencer's first one-man exhibition in 1927 and bought by Sir Joseph (later Lord) Duveen and presented to the Tate Gallery; and the drawings for one of his 'chapels in the air', which subsequently became the Burghclere murals. For in 1926–7 Mr and Mrs J. L. Behrend built a war memorial chapel at Burghclere in Berkshire, in commemoration of their relative Harry Willowby Sandham, in order to make it possible for Spencer to realize this cycle of drawings. The painting of these murals occupied him without interruption from 1927 to 1932 and they are his most impressive achievement.

In 1925 Spencer had married Hilda Anne Carline. Two daughters were born: in 1925 and 1930. The marriage was a failure (his wife showed progressive symptoms of mental ill health) and by the time Spencer returned to Cookham in 1932 it had broken. But he continued to see Hilda frequently until her death in 1950 and his love for her remained the one enduring bond of his life. In the early thirties he grew acquainted with Patricia Preece, whom he married in 1937 after divorce from Hilda.

This new emotional relationship in his life was largely responsible for a radical change in his painting. He now had two women to provide for, in addition to two daughters (one of whom was cared for by relatives). Until this period in his life he had been virtually maintained by friends and patrons (from 1919 to 1923, for example, he had lived in the houses of friends), but now, back in Cookham, he had to stand on his own feet and to earn all the money he could: 'I was making big demands on life at the time', he subsequently wrote, 'and had to paint far more than I would have wished.' He turned out what he called his 'pot-boilers', landscapes and flower-pieces, at the rate of one a week or every ten days. These pictures, rendered in pre-Raphaelite exactitude, are often beautiful, sometimes mechanical, but they afforded no joy of creation to their maker.

Moreover, since (according to Spencer) the relationship with Patricia had no physical fulfilment, his sexuality sought expression in erotic paintings and in erotic writings in the form of a diary-letter to Hilda. The paintings had little appeal and were largely unsaleable.

The thirties were years of artistic frustration for Spencer, although he painted some figure-pieces which brought him further acclaim and were bought by many art galleries both in the provinces and in London. Among his best paintings of these years are 'Sarah Tubb and the Heavenly Visitors' (1933); 'Separating Fighting Swans' (1933) and 'Hilda, Unity and Dolls' (1937), both at the City Art Gallery, Leeds; 'St. Francis and the Birds' (1935); and 'The Cedar Tree, Cookham' (1934–5). Among the erotic paintings were a number of nudes of Patricia Preece, some of which were bought by W. A. Evill. 'Promenade of Women' (1937) and a series entitled 'The Beatitudes of Love' (1937–8) were among Spencer's own favourites of the period.

In 1935 he resigned from the Royal Academy, to which he had been elected as an associate member three years before, on its rejection of two of his pictures for the summer exhibition. He rejoined as a full RA in 1950. In 1938 twenty-two of his paintings were exhibited at the Venice Biennale, at which he had also been represented six years earlier.

Although he was prolific of landscapes and flower-pieces and also of portraits, and although they sold well, Spencer was sued by Hilda on a number of occasions during the thirties for arrears of maintenance. Even the tiny sum of fifty shillings a week for herself and their daughter Unity was not forthcoming. Spencer himself lived on about forty shillings a week or less. The shock of appearing in court together with years of over-work on his pot-boilers brought on, in 1938, a breakdown of several months' duration, during which he was quite unable to paint at all. At this time his dealer and friend, Dudley Tooth, however, agreed to take over the management of his finances, paying a weekly allowance to each of the dependants as well as a small sum to Spencer himself. He also paid off the many debts contracted in the thirties and the arrears of income-tax.

The tribulations of these years, when Spencer was also without a home and (as he said) felt himself a vagrant, were the inspiration for a series of small paintings of 'Christ in the Wilderness'; four of the series belong to

1939, two to 1940, one to 1942, while the eighth and last was painted in 1953. The first of them was made in lodgings in London, for in the autumn of 1938 Spencer left Cookham on account of personal unhappiness. He had never lived with his second wife.

In 1940 Spencer was commissioned by the war artists advisory committee to paint pictures of shipyards. He began work at Port Glasgow, making visits to the shipyards for studies for larger paintings until the end of the war. While in Port Glasgow the sight of a cemetery—cemeteries were always powerful imaginative stimulants for him—inspired him to another series of resurrection canvases; he painted eight in all. It had been his earnest wish that the complete cycle might hang together, but the pictures were bought separately: 'Resurrection: Tidying' (1945) by the City Art Gallery, Birmingham; 'Resurrection: Reunion' (1945) by the Aberdeen Art Gallery; 'Resurrection with Raising of Jairus's Daughter' (1947) by the Southampton Art Gallery; 'Resurrection: the Hill of Sion' (1946) by the Harris Museum and Art Gallery, Preston; 'Resurrection: Port Glasgow' (1947–50) by the Tate Gallery.

In 1945 Spencer returned to his native Cookham and remained there until his death, devoting his time principally to an enormous cycle of about sixty drawings of 'Christ preaching at Cookham Regatta' and later to the painting of it. He worked on these canvases until too weak to continue. Another huge painting of his last years, an altar-piece in praise of Hilda, was also not completed by the time of his death.

A retrospective exhibition of Spencer's work (68 paintings and 27 drawings) was held at Temple Newsam House, Leeds, in 1947, and another (83 paintings) at the Tate Gallery in 1955. He was appointed CBE in 1950 and knighted in 1959. In 1958 the vicar of Cookham organized an exhibition of Spencer's paintings in Cookham church and vicarage; it drew large crowds and, set in his own beloved Cookham, gave particular gratification to Spencer himself. The following winter he fell ill and he died in hospital at Cliveden 14 December 1959 and is buried in Cookham churchyard.

Stanley Spencer was the outstanding—the most potent and fertile—imaginative painter of the English-speaking people in the first half of the twentieth century. As he himself often said and wrote, the quality of his imaginative work deteriorated after the twenties; after the completion of the Burghclere murals both the intensity and the focused and integrated unity of inspiration which animated his early works and fused into one his dual vision of the commonplace and of the divine consistently evaded him. How this came about has been suggested above, but it may be added that Spencer was in no sense strongly rooted in a religious faith nor had he any clear or reasoned convictions, so that in the pressures of life his early poetic empathy with the New Testament faltered and waned and the dual vision was no longer possible. Cookham became no longer the suburbs of heaven but suburbs; the later Resurrections are just vast conversation-pieces crammed with anecdote. His figure painting, including much which was in intention religious, came to be an expression of grotesquerie and whimsy. The ordinary things and objects and events of life he loved with passion, and in his painting he wanted to show them as being, in what they are, heavenly and somehow divine—this is why his Resurrections are insistently filled with incidents of trivial daily life—but it was an aim which in the second half of his life he could no longer successfully achieve.

Spencer's early paintings were not only strong in their draughtsmanship and composition; they were distinguished by painterly qualities as well. Later on, however, he came to take delight only in the drawing and in the composition of his pictures. With the painting of them he was, he admitted, bored. His paintings, therefore, came to be coloured drawings, conceived as drawings, rather than paintings conceived in terms of paint. It was another element in the fragmentation of his imagination in consequence of which, in place of a dominant and unifying intensity, there is an evenly distributed intensity over his themes, so that everything is illumined but nothing is picked out and the whole is but the sum of its parts.

It was Spencer's proud claim to be an ordinary Cookham villager. 'My mother was just a little village biddy.' In appearance, even to the end of his life, he was like a village urchin. So tiny was he that his clothes were always too large, but as he quite often wore his suit over his pyjamas, which, even so, peered out at ankle and wrist, this was an advantage.

His hair, unparted, hung in an unkempt fringe over his eyes. His glasses he usually bought at Woolworths. They did not fit and slid to the end of his nose, so that, to keep them in balance, Spencer had a habit of tilting his head slightly backwards.

In repose his features were without distinction; his eyes looked tired and sleepy. When he was aroused, however, by enthusiasm (over his own work or imaginings) or by anger, the eyes widened and glittered. His speech, which was ordinarily a village diction uttered in a squeaky nasal voice, would then become resonant with language cast in biblical words and phrases. On such occasions—and they were very numerous—he was a fierce, prophet-like presence, and a compelling speaker.

Spencer drew and painted innumerable self-portraits. The first, painted in 1913, hangs in the Tate Gallery. The central, nude, figure in 'The Resurrection, Cookham', also in the Tate, is the painter himself. The last self-portrait, and the finest, was painted in 1959 and became the property of Mrs. Dennis Smith.

[*Stanley Spencer, a Retrospective Exhibition*, Tate Gallery, 1955; *Stanley Spencer: Resurrection Pictures (1945–1950)*, 1951; Gilbert Spencer, *Stanley Spencer*, 1961; John Rothenstein, *Modern English Painters*, vol. ii, 1956; Elizabeth Rothenstein, *Stanley Spencer*, 1962; private information; personal knowledge.]

ELIZABETH ROTHENSTEIN

published 1971

STIRLING Sir (Archibald) David

(1915–1990)

Founder of the Special Air Service Regiment, was born 15 November 1915 at Keir, Stirlingshire, the third son and fourth child in the family of four sons and two daughters of Brigadier-General Archibald Stirling of Keir, of the Scots Guards and later MP for West Perthshire, and his wife Margaret Mary, daughter of Simon Fraser, fifteenth Baron Lovat. His childhood, mostly spent at Keir, was a happy one. He was educated at Ampleforth and, for a brief period, at Trinity College, Cambridge. Soon after leaving Cambridge, without a degree, he decided that he wanted to climb Mount Everest and, with this in mind, spent some time climbing in Switzerland and later in the American and Canadian Rockies. On the outbreak of war in September 1939 he returned from North America to join the Scots Guards Supplementary Reserve, of which he had become a member the previous year.

Early in 1941 the newly raised Guards Commando, for which he volunteered as soon as he had been commissioned and which he found more congenial than ordinary regimental soldiering, sailed for the Middle East as part of Layforce, consisting of three commando units commanded by a friend of his, Brigadier (Sir) Robert Laycock. Later in 1941 Layforce was disbanded, leaving Stirling at a loose end, but at least in a theatre of war. This offered him the opportunity he needed. The war in the desert had by this time settled down into a slogging match between the opposing armies and Stirling turned a fertile mind to the overall strategic situation. What he quickly grasped was the possibility of turning the enemy's flank by sending well-equipped raiding parties through the allegedly impassable Sand Sea to strike at worthwhile targets far behind the enemy's front line.

Gaining access to the commander-in-chief Middle East, General Sir Claude Auchinleck, by what can best be described as shock tactics, Stirling, still to all appearances an unremarkable subaltern of twenty-five, with little or no military experience, managed to win his confidence, convince him of the soundness of his ideas, and gain from him authority to recruit at the end of July 1941 six officers and sixty other ranks, a small-scale raiding force to be known, misleadingly, as L detachment Special Air Service brigade. He was promoted to captain.

Stirling's first operation, in November 1941 by parachute, was a total failure. But he did not let this deter him, and General Auchinleck, greatly to his credit, continued to back him. Fortunately L detachment's next, land-borne, raids, which followed immediately and were carried out with the invaluable help of the Long Range Desert Group, were spectacularly successful. In two weeks ninety enemy aircraft were destroyed on the ground. They were the first of a succession of no less brilliant operations planned and led by Stirling himself, who was quickly promoted to major (January 1942) and then to lieutenant-colonel (July 1942). In their planning he showed remarkable imagination and resourcefulness. In their execution his personal courage and utter determination were unsurpassed. He possessed above all the ultimate quality of a leader, the gift of carrying those he led with him on enterprises that by any rational standards seemed certain to fail and convincing them that under his leadership they were bound to succeed. Stirling was appointed to the DSO in 1942, and also became an officer of the Legion of Honour and of the Order of Orange Nassau.

By the time Stirling was taken prisoner in Tunisia in January 1943 the potential value of the SAS and of his contribution to military thinking had been generally recognized. As he had intended it should, the regiment went on to play an important part in the Mediterranean and later in the European theatres where, without their founder's outstanding leadership, but using his methods, they achieved a series of remarkable successes.

Stirling escaped from prison in Germany four times and was eventually shut up in Colditz. On his return to Great Britain in May 1945, his first thought was to take full advantage of the obvious opportunities for SAS operations offered by the war against Japan. But before he could put his plans into execution, the war in the Far East was over and by the end of 1945 the SAS had been disbanded. In due course the SAS was, however, reconstituted in the shape of one regular and two territorial regiments. With these Stirling, who as founder had been active in securing their reconstitution, remained in continual contact.

After the war Stirling's imagination was captured by Africa and its problems, to which he was thereafter to devote much time and energy. He settled in Southern Rhodesia and in 1947 became president of the newly founded Capricorn Africa Society, set up, largely on his initiative, to help find a solution to Africa's innumerable racial, economic, social, and political problems, which he felt could not safely be ignored. His efforts were overtaken by political events and he returned to Britain in 1961. In 1974 he organized GB75, to run essential services, such as power stations, in the event of a general strike. He then turned to fighting left-wing extremism in trade unions, by backing the Movement for True Industrial Democracy (Truemid).

Six feet six inches tall, with a deceptively vague and casual manner, Stirling had a very strong personality. He was appointed OBE in 1946 and knighted in 1990 by when, half a century on, the full extent of his achievement had finally been recognized. He died in the London Clinic 4 November 1990. He never married.

[Alan Hoe, *David Stirling*, 1992; John Strawson, *A History of the SAS Regiment*, 1984; personal knowledge.]

FITZROY MACLEAN

published 1996

STOPES Marie Charlotte Carmichael

(1880–1958)

Scientist and sex reformer, was born in Edinburgh 15 October 1880, the elder daughter of Henry Stopes, a man of private means whose passionate hobby was archaeology, by his wife, Charlotte Carmichael, a pioneer of women's university education who had studied at Edinburgh University, and who became well known for her research on Shakespearian questions. Marie Stopes sometimes called herself a child of the British Association, for her parents first met at one of its meetings, and as a girl she attended them regularly. When she was six weeks old her parents moved to London. Her mother tried to initiate her at the age of five into Latin and Greek, but she showed no aptitude, becoming far more interested in her father's large collection of flint implements. She had little formal education until at the age of twelve she went to St George's, Edinburgh, then two years later to the North London Collegiate School. At University College, London, in 1902 she obtained at the same time first class honours in botany and third class honours in geology and physical geography. After a year of research under F. W. Oliver, she went with a scholarship to Munich where she obtained her Ph.D. for work on the cycad ovules which proved fundamental to the understanding of the evolution of integumentary structures.

In the same year she was appointed assistant lecturer and demonstrator in botany at Manchester where she was the first woman to join the science faculty. She obtained her D.Sc., London, in the following year. In 1907–8 she spent some eighteen months in Japan with a grant for research from the Royal Society. After a further period as lecturer in palaeobotany in Manchester she settled in London after her marriage in 1911, and from 1913 to 1920 she was lecturer on the same subject at University College, London, of which she became a fellow in 1910.

In the same year she published an elementary textbook *Ancient Plants*. Her main interest at this time was the Cretaceous floras on which she was invited to work by the British Museum: her *Catalogue of the Cretaceous Flora* in the British Museum was published in two volumes (1913–15). Meantime the advent of war had turned her attention increasingly to coal itself. She published a number of memoirs of fundamental importance, mainly with R. V. Wheeler, with whom she collaborated in a standard work, *The Constitution of Coal* (1918). A short paper which the Royal Society published in 1919, *The Four Visible Ingredients in Banded Bituminous Coal: Studies in the Composition of Coal*, changed the attitude of palaeontologists and chemists to its structure, and her later classification of coal ingredients (*Fuel*, 1935) was almost universally adopted.

It was, however, for her work for sex education and birth control that Marie Stopes became widely known. Her concern was undoubtedly aroused by her first marriage, to a Canadian botanist, Reginald Ruggles Gates, whom she met in America and married in Montreal in 1911. The marriage was annulled in 1916 on her suit of non-consummation. In 1918 she married Humphrey Verdon-Roe (died 1949), who had joined his brother, (Sir) Alliott Verdon-Roe, in the manufacture of aircraft. He was already interested in birth control and the marriage was initially a perfect union of common interests: together they founded the Mothers' Clinic for Birth Control in London in 1921, the first of its kind in England. Dr Stopes, who retained her maiden name in both her marriages, relinquished her lectureship and henceforth her dominating interest was family planning and sex education for married people.

Her first book on the subject, *Married Love* (1918), had been drafted in 1914 to crystallize her own ideas. It became an immediate success and was eventually translated into thirteen languages, including Hindi. Its frank discussion of sexual relations for the ordinary public was, by the standards of the time, sensational, and it caused a furore. The book dealt scarcely at all with birth control but she received so many requests for instruction on the subject that she published later in 1918 a short book, *Wise Parenthood*, with a preface by Arnold Bennett. This too was an immediate success and quickly outstrode its predecessor: within nine years it had sold half a million copies in the original English edition alone. (Like other of her works it was banned in several states of America.) For some twenty years Dr Stopes's books were leading popular works on their subject. She published some ten others of which *Radiant Motherhood* (1920) and *Enduring Passion* (1928) were, to judge by their sales, the most influential. By the time of her death their romantic presentation had become outmoded, but she was still regarded as the great pioneer fighter for the movement. And a fighter she was, for, especially in the early days, she was attacked sometimes to the point of persecution, notably during her prolonged libel action against Halliday Sutherland which she won on appeal but lost when the case went to the House of Lords.

Marie Stopes's great achievement was the transformation of the subject of birth control into one which was openly discussed. Her advocacy of birth control was based on her wish to see woman's lot become a happier one—a pursuit of a general happiness which she did not herself attain. Her elder son was stillborn, while both her younger son and her husband eventually became alienated from her. But this fearlessly dedicated woman, with a touch of the mystic, for all her arrogant argumentativeness and vanity which made co-operation so difficult, had very many loyal friends and supporters among leading churchmen, doctors, and writers as well as social workers. For a quarter of a century the personalities of the day corresponded with or visited her at Norbury Park, her fine eighteenth-century mansion near Dorking. Friendship with Dr Stopes was a prickly, demanding, but always stimulating business. Her demonic advocacy of planned parenthood never waned; but towards the end of her life her interest in her own poetry and in literature generally occupied more of her time; in the forties she took an almost naïve pride in reading a paper on her friend, Lord Alfred Douglas, to the Royal Society of Literature of which she was a fellow and to which she bequeathed Norbury Park and the residue of her estate. Almost all her publications after 1939 were volumes of verse, of which her long poem, *The Bathe* (1946), a sensuous and rather high-flown work, was typical.

Convinced until almost the end that she would live to be 120, Marie Stopes died at Norbury Park 2 October 1958. She left her portraits by Sir Gerald Kelly and Augustus John to the National Portrait Gallery and that by Gregorio Prieto to the National Gallery of Edinburgh.

[Aylmer Maude, *The Authorized Life of Marie C. Stopes*, 1924; Keith Briant, *Marie Stopes*, 1962; *The Times*, 3 and 8 October 1958; *Nature*, 1 November 1958; private information; personal knowledge.]

JAMES MACGIBBON

published 1971

TAWNEY Richard Henry

(1880–1962)

Historian, was born in Calcutta 30 November 1880, son of Charles Henry Tawney, principal of Presidency College, and his wife, Constance Catherine Fox. The boy was sent to Rugby, and proceeded as a classical scholar to Balliol College, Oxford, in 1899, a year before William Temple. After a first in classical honour moderations and being *proxime* for a Craven scholarship (1901), Tawney only got a second in *literae humaniores* (1903); his father enquired how he proposed to 'wipe out the disgrace', but Edward Caird, the master, told (Sir) Frank Fletcher, 'I grant you his mind was chaotic; but the examiners ought to have seen that it was the chaos of a great mind'. Tawney himself learned more from Rugby and Balliol than he would subsequently acknowledge; typically, he never proceeded to his Oxford MA, although he became a fellow (1918–21), and in 1938 an honorary fellow, of his college.

Tawney himself would trace the major preoccupations of his life to the six years between going down, when he lived for a while at Toynbee Hall, and his marriage in 1909 to Annette Jeanie ('Jeannette'), sister of William (later Lord) Beveridge, one of his closest college friends. After Oxford, Tawney 'found the world surprising'; already by 1909, however, he had established himself as a historian and a devoted and inspiring teacher, and had formulated the outlines of a distinctive version of socialism which was later to guide the Labour Party for many years. He had also become a forceful critic of the public schools and Oxford and Cambridge as privileged institutions, and he showed little interest in his comfortable origins or his father's links with India. He was embarking in his own style on a course of his own which eventually inspired Beatrice Webb to dub him a 'saint of socialism' (1935) and Hugh Gaitskell to describe him as '*the* democratic socialist *par excellence*' (1962).

By 1909 Tawney's historical interests had focused on the late sixteenth to early seventeenth century and its relationships with both the medieval world and the nineteenth and twentieth centuries. His first book, *The Agrarian Problem in the Sixteenth Century* (1912), immediately established him as an authority on economic and social history. It was dedicated to Albert Mansbridge and William Temple, successive pillars of the Workers' Educational Association, which had been formed in 1903; Tawney joined the executive committee in 1905. In 1906–8 he taught political economy at Glasgow University alongside Thomas Jones, under Professor William Smart who was busy with the royal commission on Poor Law reform; in

1908 Tawney accepted the pioneer post of teacher for the WEA tutorial classes under Oxford University, which he held until 1914. This proved to be his first source of inspiration, and *The Agrarian Problem* acknowledged a debt to the students of Tawney's tutorial classes, whom he regarded as fellow workers—a class of one tutor and twelve students was, to him, a class of thirteen students. He learned much about English society in those classes, and from them sprang his belief that the only effective way of making necessary changes in society was through education.

His first WEA classes—which quickly became legendary—were held at Rochdale in Lancashire and Longton in the Potteries, and soon after their marriage the Tawneys settled in Manchester at 24 Shakespeare Street, where they lived until just before the outbreak of war in 1914. In Manchester George Unwin, occupant of Britain's first chair of economic history, was one of his early mentors; in 1927 Tawney wrote a memoir of Unwin prefacing his collected papers. Two other Manchester friends, also economic historians, were T. S. Ashton, who became one of his closest colleagues during the last years of his life, and A. P. Wadsworth. Tawney developed in both himself and his pupils a strong sense of affinity with peasants, and found no difficulty in proving the social relevance of a study of the agrarian history of a remote century, even in the industrial environment of northern England: capitalism had preceded industrialism just as enclosed farms had preceded power-driven factories, and it was in the sixteenth century, he believed, that the erosion of old values and their conflict with the new had become clear. Yet Tawney never showed much enthusiasm for the industrial revolution or the nineteenth century, and was more interested in restraints on economic drive than on commercial or industrial enterprise; he was always suspicious of treating economics as an objective science. He selected themes in economic and social history, therefore, which were concerned with shifts of values in attitudes and relationships, rather than with measurement of economic indicators, like the growth of national income. In 1914 he co-edited with A. E. Bland and P. A. Brown *English Economic History: Select Documents*.

The young WEA prided itself that while it demanded the highest academic standards it was also a thoroughly democratic body at the class level. Tawney, who never thought of himself as an 'educationist', plunged into both the teaching and organizing sides of adult education; he became a champion of extended provision and helped to write, for example, the conference report *Oxford and Working-Class Education* (1908). He remained a member of the WEA executive committee for forty-two years, was vice-president from 1920, and president in 1928–44. He always considered himself not so much a leader as an active member of a 'movement'; the distinction between 'movement' and 'organization' seemed to him crucial, as did that between 'membership' (whose virtues he stressed) and 'service' which seemed to him to have Rugby-cum-Balliol overtones. It was through WEA experience that Tawney hammered out his ideas about 'equality'; his thought developed from the tradition of Ruskin and Morris, but he extended it through his emphasis on activity rather than on reading.

Tawney's socialism was less intellectual than that of most of his non-working-class contemporaries; at its core was a simple faith in Christian principles, and in this respect also he represented a tradition of Christian socialism which he never fully elucidated. When he talked of the erosion of values, or conflicts between spiritual and materialistic values, he had biblical values in mind: 'Give me neither riches nor poverty, but enough for my sustenance' was both a personal rule and a precept for society. Tawney did not shout either his Christianity or his socialism from the house-tops. He joined the Fabian Society in 1906, and was a member of its executive (1921–33); in 1909 he joined the Independent Labour Party. He had little sympathy with the Marxist-influenced Social Democratic Federation which provided some of the members of his first tutorial classes: he found it sloganizing and sectarian, concerned not with education but with indoctrination. In later years he disagreed with the Webbs about the merits of Communism, and also with Harold Laski. The moral basis of socialism seemed to him beyond argument; in a future socialist society the dominant values would be those which had been appreciated long before Marx or MacDonald.

At the outbreak of the war in 1914, Tawney was director of the Ratan Tata Foundation at the London School of Economics for the study of poverty, and had just produced a monograph (1914) on *Minimum Rates in the Chain-Making Industry*; he was to serve on the Chain-Making Trade Board, 1919–22, but meanwhile the war itself did much to widen and clarify Tawney's beliefs. He enlisted in 1915 as a private in the 22nd Manchesters, and rose to the rank of sergeant, having characteristically refused a commission. During this period he learned to appreciate the French people, especially the peasants, and asserted that in the trenches he discovered more about his fellow countrymen than he had in his tutorial classes. His stress on 'fellowship' acquired a deeper dimension when associated with the fellowship of 'comrades in misery' and sacrifice for the future. Tawney was wounded in courageous action at Fricourt in July 1916 and invalided home to an army hospital in Oxford—a coincidence typical of a life which he once described as 'that terrible thing, an unplanned economy'. He described the other-ranks hospital as a 'workhouse', and, after a surprise visit from Bishop Gore, was shocked when the matron asked him 'Why didn't you *tell* us you were a *gentleman*?'—the one word which Tawney never wished to have applied to himself. 'He never suffered stuffed shirts gladly.' The refusal to be fussed over, to be thought a 'gentleman', went even deeper than his refusal to accept high honours in the form of a peerage, which he was to be offered first by MacDonald and again by Attlee.

On his recovery, Tawney served briefly in the Ministry of Reconstruction, and continued to write articles for periodicals; he returned to his old preoccupations in 'A National College for All Souls' which appeared in the *Times Educational Supplement* in February 1917. He was also one of the draughtsmen of an Anglican report on 'Christianity and Industrial Problems' in December 1918. Many phrases from this period of his career have become folk memory. For example: 'It is right that there should be a solemn detestation of the sins of Germany, provided that we are not thereby caused to forget our own.' The remarkably rich prose style was unmistakable: long, sometimes rambling, sentences with upward cadences which were prominent in his lectures; wild, often clashing, imagery referring to the natural world (tadpoles and tigers) as much as to the world of human history; maxims which sounded biblical even when they were not: had English soldiers 'slaved for Rachel' only to come back to have to 'live with Leah'? Avoiding sentimentality, irony was one of his more powerful weapons.

Tawney mistrusted the hasty abolition of economic controls after the war of 1914–18, and wrote an admonitory article on the subject in 1943; he also deplored the unemployment which followed the immediate post-war boom. He stood unsuccessfully as Independent Labour candidate in the general elections of 1918, 1922, and 1924, but between 1918 and 1928 he became a major political influence. He was a powerful member of the Coal Industry Commission under Sir John (later Viscount) Sankey which reported in 1919, and became, as a result, something of a national figure. Working closely with the trade-unionists, Tawney proved a devastating questioner of the coal-owners, and during this commission he developed his views on the disastrous consequences of 'functionless property'. In 1921 the publication of *The Acquisitive Society* persuaded many of Tawney's readers that his was the only correct and constructive way of looking at national problems. He appealed to basic 'principles'—fundamentals which, he claimed, his fellow countrymen usually took for granted. The critique was more powerful than the somewhat vague remedies suggested, and the lack of attention to both economic and international issues reflected a failure to go far beyond moralizing. There were similar weaknesses in the Labour Party manifesto of 1928, *Labour and the Nation*, which was largely Tawney's work; it too was imprecise, particularly with regard to policies dealing with unemployment and the deteriorating business situation, despite its brave statement that socialism was 'neither a sentimental aspiration for an impossible Utopia, nor a blind revolt against poverty and oppression'.

Tawney's writings on education were more incisive than those on industry; indeed, two Labour Party reports, *Secondary Education for All* (1922) and *Education: the Socialist Policy* (1924), went further than many party members wished, in urging the abolition of all fees in secondary schools and a system of maintenance allowances; similarly, it was he who urged the introduction of a system of comprehensive schools twenty years later. Tawney's belief that politics would be sterile without adult as well as school education was made clear both in party publications and in a large number of newspaper articles. He served as a member (1912–31) of the consultative committee of the Board of Education, and was on its panel of reformers who produced the 'Hadow Report' of 1926, recommending *inter alia* the raising of the school-leaving age to fifteen. For Tawney, education was at the heart of social policy and it was the duty of a democratic state to provide it. He believed that 'to serve educational needs without regard to the vulgar irrelevancies of class and income is part of the teacher's honour'.

In 1919 he served for a time as the WEA's first resident tutor in north Staffordshire, but in 1917 he had become lecturer in economic history at the London School of Economics—an institution to which he returned in 1920 and with which he was to remain associated until 1949, becoming reader in 1923 and professor in 1931. With Eileen Power, his colleague there, he produced *Tudor Economic Documents* (1924). He preferred LSE to Oxford or Cambridge for its 'simplicity, . . . its freedom from formality and inhibitions'; yet Tawney eventually became an honorary fellow of Peterhouse, Cambridge, as well as of Balliol, and an honorary doctor of Oxford, Glasgow, Manchester, Birmingham, Sheffield, London, Chicago, Melbourne, and Paris. He was also proud of his membership of the American Philosophical Society, and of his fellowship of the British Academy in 1935; in 1941 he delivered the Academy's Raleigh lecture. He made the first of five tours to the United States in 1920, and one of his last and happiest academic visits was with his wife to Australia in 1955. Nevertheless, he remained an essentially insular figure, although there was one country about which he showed considerable insight and sympathy. During the thirties he paid two visits to China and in 1932 published *Land and Labour in China*, a brilliant survey of agrarian problems, which in the light of later Chinese Communist history contained a prophetic element; interesting affinities have been noted between Tawney's social thought and that of Mao Tse-Tung. They might have surprised Tawney, although he would doubtless have attributed them to peasant influence.

The Economic History Society which Tawney helped to found in 1926 brought him into contact with a new generation of scholars, and he co-edited the *Economic History Review* from 1927 to 1934, with Ephraim Lipson. 'What historians need', he told them, 'is not more documents but stronger boots!' He insisted that the society, like the WEA, should meet in simple surroundings for its conferences, not in expensive hotels; his simplicity could, indeed, sometimes be carried to embarrassing extremes. His house at Mecklenburgh Square was probably the untidiest in London; he smoked heavily, his pipe filled with a cheap mixture bought in bulk, ashes of which were scattered upon carpets rumoured to cover manuscripts of more unpublished masterpieces. His Cotswold cottage at Elcombe was described as 'a charming slum'. But if unaffected humility characterized Tawney's private and public life, his writings during the twenties and thirties certainly did not lack confidence. His reputation as a scholar was consolidated by his best-known historical work, *Religion and the Rise of Capitalism* (1926), based on his Scott Holland lectures of 1922, and dedicated to Bishop Gore. It provoked continuing international controversy about the relationships between religious beliefs and conduct and economic behaviour. A further contribution to what came to be called 'Tawney's century' appeared in 1941: the article on 'The Rise of the Gentry' in the *Economic History Review*, supplemented, after various sharp exchanges, by a postscript in the same journal in 1954. It was a measure of the power of Tawney's historical scholarship that it stimulated counter-attack; while he did not really enjoy academic debate and preferred to withdraw, muttering, into his shell, his private comments remained devastating.

Equality, his Halley Stewart lectures delivered in 1929 and published in 1931, served as a driving-force behind many of the policies of the Labour Government after 1945: although Tawney himself was suspicious of 'trends' and never liked the term 'welfare state', he was one of its principal architects. But, alarmed by the rise of 'the Nazi tyranny' and unsure what ought to be done about it, he was less productive during the later thirties. He mistrusted great concentrations of power as much as the irrationalism of crowds; Hitler was a 'frantic dervish' dealing in 'hoary sophisms', menacing the freedom of the world. When the war began, Tawney was as optimistic as he had been in 1914 that from it a better society could be constructed. Just as he had resumed wearing his old sergeant's tunic during the general strike of 1926, he now joined the Home Guard, wrote an article for the *New York Times* 'Why Britain Fights', and for a year held the post—at times frustrating—of labour attaché at the British Embassy in Washington. He was more at ease as an air-raid warden on patrol in the Gloucestershire hills with the dog which would also accompany him into church.

After the war Tawney continued to follow most of his earlier patterns of activity, and he remained as magnificent a lecturer as ever, tousled, inspiring, and defiant of humbug. He gave the Webb Memorial Trust lecture in 1945, and an inspiring National Book League lecture in 1950. He was a member of the University Grants Committee from 1943 to 1948, stayed on as vice-president of the WEA from 1944 to 1948, and was a main speaker at its jubilee celebrations in 1953; he was also for a time president of the Council for Educational Advance. He had friends and admirers in all sections of the Labour movement, and his eightieth birthday was celebrated by a Festschrift and a dinner at the House of Commons, where people from the world of education, politicians, trade-unionists, and historians, gathered to honour him—notwithstanding his fidgetiness about being treated as a historical figure before he was dead.

His last book, *Business and Politics under James I: Lionel Cranfield as Merchant and Minister* (1958), was as much concerned with shifting values as his first had been. It dealt with 'that seductive border region where politics grease the wheels of business and polite society smiles hopefully on both'. It was a mature and meticulous work, vintage Tawney in style, and dealt with real people, forgotten perhaps, but not abstractions; if the historian 'visits the cellars', he had said, 'it is not for love of the dust but to estimate the stability of the edifice'. Yet the closing years of his life were not, on the whole, very happy. He was disturbed about the state of society and uncertain about the future; the sudden transition from national austerity to affluence made him ponder yet again on what seemed to him false values. He had little sympathy with current fashions in political argument, and felt that even the WEA had lost some of its force. After his wife died in 1958 he was never quite the same, although his marriage had not been without its problems, for his wife had often exasperated him and was wildly extravagant. They had no children. Other deaths, too, affected him, and his dwindling circle of friends were increasingly worried to see his simplicity becoming shabbiness and his humility degenerating into complete lack of care for himself. 'Never be afraid of throwing away what you have,' he had written in his diary in 1912. 'If you *can* throw it away, it is not really yours.'

Tawney died in London 16 January 1962. He was buried at his wife's side at Highgate, and there was a vast congregation at his memorial service at St Martin-in-the-Fields on 8 February. Psalm XV was appropriate, Hugh Gaitskell gave the address, and the large number of WEA members present must have approved of one additional reading—an unpublished fragment of Tawney's Chicago lecture (1939): 'Democracy a society where ordinary men exercise initiative. Dreadful respect for superiors. Mental enlargement . . . Real foe to be overcome . . . fact that large section of the public *like* plutocratic government, and are easily gullible. How shake them!'

A portrait for Tawney's seventieth birthday by Claude Rogers hangs in the London School of Economics, where there is also a sketch by 'Vicky' of the *New Statesman* (1960); a drawing by John Mansbridge (1953) is in the National Portrait Gallery.

[*The Times* and *Guardian*, 17 January 1962; R. H. Tawney, *The Attack and Other Papers*, 1953, *The Radical Tradition*, ed. Rita Hinden, 1964, and *Commonplace Book*, ed. J. M. Winter and D. M. Joslin, 1972; J. R. Williams, R. M. Titmuss, and F. J. Fisher, *R. H. Tawney, A Portrait by Several Hands*, 1960; T. S. Ashton in *Proceedings of the British Academy*, vol. xlviii, 1962 (which includes an admirable photograph of an unexpectedly tidy Tawney); R. Terrill, *R. H. Tawney and His Times*, 1973; J. M. Winter, 'Tawney the Historian' in *History and Society: Essays by R. H. Tawney*, 1978; Christopher Hill in the *Balliol Record*, 1974; private information; personal knowledge.]

ASA BRIGGS

published 1981

TAYLOR Alan John Percivale

(1906–1990)

Historian, journalist, and broadcaster, was born 25 March 1906 in Birkdale, Lancashire, the only son (and sole surviving child) of Percy Lees Taylor, Preston cotton merchant, and his wife, Constance Sumner Thompson, schoolmistress. His well-to-do Edwardian Liberal parents subsequently became ardent Labour supporters, which shaped Taylor's lifelong commitment to left-wing causes, notably the first Campaign for Nuclear Disarmament. Precocious, learned, and spoilt, he was educated at Bootham School in York and Oriel College, Oxford, where, as something of a gilded youth who flirted with the Communist party, he took a first class in modern history as a medievalist in 1927.

Abandoning his intention of becoming a labour lawyer, Taylor went to Vienna in 1928 as a Rockefeller fellow to work on modern diplomatic history. Appointed a lecturer at Manchester University in 1930, he came under the influence, which he later denied, of his professor, (Sir) Lewis Namier, and wrote the first of his more than thirty books, *The Italian Problem in European Diplomacy, 1847–1849* (1934) and *Germany's First Bid for Colonies, 1884–1885* (1938), both mischievous products of hard work, rarely repeated thereafter, in the archives. He schooled himself to lecture (and speak publicly) without notes, a craft he later brought to perfection; contributed regularly as reviewer and leader-writer on the *Manchester Guardian* under A. P. Wadsworth; travelled widely; and cultivated his vegetable garden at Disley in the High Peak.

With Namier's crucial support, Taylor returned to Oxford in 1938 as a fellow of Magdalen College, to which he remained devoted until his retirement in 1976. Soon established as an outstanding tutor of responsive undergraduates and a charismatic, early-morning lecturer, he began to make a wider name for himself as an incisive speaker on current affairs, in person and on the radio. Throughout World War II his house at Holywell Ford was a centre for writers young and old, wayward musicians, and the grander Slav refugees clustered in north Oxford as well as his pupils coming on leave. In 1941 he published the most elegant of his books, the elegaic first version of *The Habsburg Monarchy*, and this was followed in 1945 by his initial best seller, *The Course of German History*, a graphic, opinionated *pièce d'occasion* and the clue to much of his later work in its anti-German assumptions.

Notorious as an early critic of the cold war, Taylor emerged as a national figure with the advent of television. On *In The News* and *Free Speech* he caught the viewers' fancy as a quick-witted debater, a Cobbett-like scourge of 'the establishment', and, quite simply, something of a card, much appreciated by the 'man on the Clapham omnibus', in the phrase of his exemplar, Lord Macaulay. First of the television dons, he retained this primacy into old age as he delivered unscripted lectures direct to the camera on historical themes to a vast audience. Meanwhile he was taken up by Lord Beaverbrook, a lover of maverick left-wingers, as the charms of Oxford faded. A highly paid, sometimes outrageous columnist on the *Sunday Express*, and the first (and last) director of the Beaverbrook library, Taylor paid uneasy tribute to an improbable but close friend in *Beaverbrook* (1972), the last of his substantial works and dedicated to the only man who ever persuaded him to cross the Atlantic.

Long before, Taylor had consolidated his academic reputation. In 1954 *The Struggle for Mastery in Europe, 1848–1918* was at once recognized as a model analysis, with its careful attention to the records. This massive work, with the brief but perceptive *Bismarck* (1955) and the self-indulgent Ford lectures, *The Trouble Makers* (1957), fully justified his election to the British Academy in 1956. (Perversely, he resigned on libertarian grounds in 1980 when Anthony Blunt relinquished his fellowship.) Contrary to many expectations, however, Taylor was not appointed regius professor at Oxford in 1957. This failure, in which Namier played some part, remains a subject of uncertain legend, but it did not prevent an embittered man denigrating the university he loved. Thereafter he was consoled by honorary doctorates at Bristol, Manchester, New Brunswick, Warwick, and York, as well as honorary fellowships of both Magdalen (1976) and Oriel (1980).

Superficially, Taylor was an old-fashioned historian, holding that 'politics express the activities of man in society', with the addendum that economic and social circumstances must be taken into modest account. A master of narrative but essentially an analyst, he founded no school, despite his influence upon younger historians, and his methods could be a dangerous model. In his heyday Taylor came to rely upon assiduous reading in five languages and sheer intuition—'green fingers', in Namier's envious phrase. There was no elaborate filing system, but a prodigious memory could usually supply some evidence for the thousand words tapped out each well-organized morning. Despite his commitment to popular journalism, he was also a superb and creative essayist, and published several volumes based upon serious reviews in the learned journals and the *Observer.*

Ultimately, Taylor's scholarly standing depends upon three major achievements. *The Struggle for Mastery* remains unrivalled as a totally authoritative study of international relations in a complicated period. *English History, 1914–1945* (1965) is an enthralling, highly idiosyncratic account of his own times, regarded by some as his best book. *The Origins of the Second World War* (1961) was a dazzling exercise in revisionism, which earned him a mixture of international obloquy and acclaim. Whatever its flaws, this treatment of Hitler as a product of German tradition summed up Taylor's paradoxical, provocative, and inventive approach to historical explanation. A pragmatic loner, suspicious of philosophies of history and a brilliant stylist, he was admired even by his many critics for the range of his erudition, his clarity of presentation, and the fertility of his hypotheses.

Though he enjoyed portraying himself as a simple, true-born Englishman, Taylor was a cosmopolitan intellectual, with an expert knowledge of European architecture, music, and wine. An admirable but frugal host, his table talk was inimitable; a shrewd if nervous man of business, he was soothed by domestic chores; and in old age he became an indefatigable walker in town and country. Short, stocky, and bespectacled, he was vain about his appearance, but always happiest in a crumpled tweed or, more often, corduroy suit, invariably accompanied by a flamboyant bow-tie.

An emotional man, despite the brash exterior, Taylor was three times married and devoted to his six children. In 1931 he married a musician, Margaret, the daughter of Harold Adams, an English merchant trading in India; they had two sons and two daughters. Margaret was later an over-indulgent patron of Dylan Thomas. This marriage was dissolved in 1951 and in the same year he married Eve, daughter of Joseph Beardsel Crosland, under-secretary at the War Office. There were two sons of this marriage, which was dissolved in 1974. In 1976 he married the Hungarian historian, Eva Haraszti, daughter of Mitse Herczke, a textile merchant in Budapest. Taylor's last years were clouded by Parkinson's disease and he died at a nursing home in Barnet, 7 September 1990.

[Taylor's works *passim*, but especially *A Personal History*, 1983, and *Letters to Eva*, 1991; Adam Sisman, *A. J. P. Taylor*, 1994; C. J. Wrigley, *A. J. P. Taylor, a Complete Annotated Bibliography*, 1980; Chris Wrigley in *Proceedings of the British Academy*, vol. lxxxii, 1992; personal knowledge.]

A. F. THOMPSON

published 1996

THOMPSON Flora Jane

(1876–1947)

Writer, was born in Juniper Hill, a hamlet in north-east Oxfordshire, 5 December 1876, the eldest child in the family of four daughters and two sons of Albert Timms, a stonemason, originally from Buckingham, and his wife Emma, a nursemaid, daughter of John Dibber from Stoke Lyne, an 'eggler', who took his pony and cart around local farms, collecting eggs and selling them in the market town. Her favourite brother Edwin, born in 1879, was to die in 1916 during the battle of the Somme. After elementary education at the village school in Cottisford she became, at the age of fourteen, an unofficial post-office counter clerk in the Oxfordshire village of Fringford. Until her marriage in 1903 she worked in post offices in Buckinghamshire, Essex, and Hampshire.

In 1911 she won a magazine essay competition and went on to write short stories, newspaper articles, and during the 1920s two long series of articles for the *Catholic Fireside* magazine. In alternate months she wrote nature articles and literary pieces. She was a dedicated if self-taught naturalist. An anthology of her nature articles called *The Peverel Papers* was published in 1986. The literary articles were the result of her home study of literature—she had grown up during the establishment of the free library system in Britain, which she used extensively to supplement her elementary education. Her first published book was *Bog Myrtle and Peat* (1921), a volume of poems which she was persuaded to submit for publication by her friend and literary mentor Dr Ronald Campbell Macfie. In 1938 she sent essays on her country childhood to the Oxford University Press. These were published as *Lark Rise* (1939), the story of the Oxfordshire hamlet where she was born. *Over to Candleford* (1941) was followed by *Candleford Green* (1943). These popular books were issued as the trilogy, *Lark Rise to Candleford* (1945), with a perceptive introduction by H. J. Massingham.

Flora Thompson was a reserved woman of little confidence who was astonished when reviewers praised her work and Sir Arthur Bryant rated her books as high as *Cranford*. The books, which have become classics of country writing, evoke the vigorous life of a hamlet, a village, and a country town in the England of the 1880s. They are social history but also the lightly disguised story of Flora Thompson's youth. Her last book, *Still Glides the Stream*, was published posthumously in 1948.

In 1903 she married John William Thompson, a post-office clerk and telegraphist from the Isle of Wight, son of Henry Thompson, formerly a chief petty officer in the Royal Navy. They had two sons and one daughter. In 1941 her much-loved younger son Peter was lost at sea when the ship on which he served was torpedoed in mid-Atlantic; she never recovered from this loss. She died 21 May 1947 in Brixham, Devon.

[Margaret Lane, *Flora Thompson*, 1976; Gillian Lindsay, *Flora Thompson: the Story of the Lark Rise Writer*, 1990.]

GILLIAN LINDSAY

published 1993

TITMUSS Richard Morris

(1907–1973)

Social historian, was born 16 October 1907 at Stopsley, near Luton in Bedfordshire, the second child of an unsuccessful small farmer, Morris Titmuss, whose wife, Maud Louise Farr, of rather less modest farming origins, bore him four children. The family lived an isolated and impecunious life in Bedfordshire and, from the early 1920s, in Hendon where, as a haulage contractor, Morris was no more successful than as a farmer. He died in 1926, leaving Richard to support the family, and particularly to accommodate his mother's emotional and financial needs until her death in 1972.

Titmuss's education was not untypical of the son of a petty proprietor in his day. He began at St Gregory's, a small preparatory school at Luton, and was 'finished' at Clark's Commercial College to which he went at the age of fourteen for a six-months course in bookkeeping. He was then employed as an office-boy in Standard Telephones until aged eighteen when he was engaged as a clerk by the County Fire Insurance Office, and there he served for sixteen years.

He never sat an examination or secured a formal credential. Nor did he regret his uncertified career, preferring instead to applaud the public library as among the most precious of British social services, and to hold the Ph.D. in sceptical suspicion. Yet in 1950 he was elected to the chair of social administration at the London School of Economics. In the years between, and indeed as a child often absent from school with poor health, he had been an indefatigable and imaginative autodidact. Afterwards, when fellowship of the British Academy (1972) and honorary degrees from the University of Wales (1959), Edinburgh (1962), Toronto (1964), Chicago (1970), and Brunel (1971) were conferred on him, he remained a devotee of the spirit rather than the conventions of academic institutions. He was also appointed CBE in 1966.

The first step out of obscurity was made in 1934 in a Welsh Youth Hostel where Titmuss met Kathleen Caston ('Kay') Miller who became his wife in 1937, and his encouraging companion for the rest of his life. His first unpublished writing in 1936 was under his wife's middle name. Her father, Thomas Miller, was a sales representative for a cutlery firm. They set up house at St George's Drive near Victoria Station, Titmuss still working for the County Fire Insurance Office, his wife supporting his efforts to write in the evenings and stimulating his social and political interests.

Titmuss's first book, *Poverty and Population* (1938), reflected both his wife's influence in its social concern, and his insurance work in its mastery of vital statistics and statistical technique. It was noticed enthusiastically by Lord Horder the physician, Eleanor Rathbone, Harold Macmillan (later the Earl of Stockton), and the liberal intellectuals of the day, including the Laytons, the Rowntrees, and the Cadburys. It established his place in the distinctive English tradition of political arithmetic which runs from Sir Thomas More to R. H. Tawney, and bears a literature down the centuries of responsible social criticism based on private numerical enquiry into public issues. Titmuss became the main inheritor and exponent of this tradition of humanistic social accounting.

The second step towards distinction eventually yielded a book which made him nationally and internationally well known, the official history *Problems of Social Policy* (1950). Titmuss had been invited by (Sir) W. Keith

Hancock to join the group of historians commissioned to write the official civil histories of World War II and to cover the work of the Ministry of Health. So Titmuss entered Whitehall, became industriously familiar with the social services, and was recognized by Hancock as possessed of 'really creative insight into human problems' and 'the most unusual gift for asking the right questions'.

The answers led Titmuss from his pre-war allegiance to the Liberal Party, through active interest in the short-lived Commonwealth Party, to the Fabian wing of the Labour Party. Not that his passions for social justice and equality ever made him a strident politician, for he was always essentially a private citizen and scholar, a teacher and adviser, rather than a political leader, though he was strenuously dutiful in public service, whether as a member of the fire-watching squad at St Paul's during the war, or as deputy chairman of the Supplementary Benefits Commission from 1968. His socialism was as English as his patriotism, ethical and non-Marxist, insisting that capitalism was not only economically but socially wasteful, in failing to harness individual altruism to the common good. The most startling and impassioned statement of his conviction was in his book, *The Gift Relationship: From Human Blood to Social Policy* (1970), in which, on the basis of characteristically meticulous statistical enquiry, he expounded the theory of a Gresham's law of selfishness such that commercialized blood markets undermine social integration.

This book, and many others, were the product of over twenty years as the incumbent of the LSE chair. From that position he established the academic respectability of social administration, and taught it to a generation of university teachers, administrators, and social workers from New York and Toronto to Mauritius and Tanganyika, until he died in the Central Middlesex Hospital 6 April 1973.

He was indeed a remarkable figure. Indefatigable in his obligation to his colleagues and students, unsparing in his loyalty to his college and his country, a bench-mark of integrity and virtue for the vast majority of those who knew him, whether at work in Houghton Street or at his modest house in Acton with his wife and their daughter, who was born in 1944. In another age he might have been an ascetic divine, painted by El Greco, with his long, thin body and large, round compelling eyes. In fact, he was no saint, but a secular agnostic—in Sir Edmund Leach's phrase, 'the high priest of the welfare state'.

[*The Times*, 9, 12, 15, and 16 April 1973; Margaret Gowing in *Proceedings* of the British Academy, vol. lix, 1975; personal knowledge.]

A. H. HALSEY

published 1986

TIZARD Sir Henry Thomas

(1885–1959)

Scientist and administrator, was born at Gillingham, Kent, 23 August 1885, the only son among the five children of Thomas Henry Tizard, navigator of the *Challenger* and later assistant hydrographer of the navy, and his wife, Mary Elizabeth Churchward. He came of stock distinguished in engineering and the fighting Services; a remote ancestor was Sir Paul Rycaut, FRS. Unable to enter the navy because of defective eyesight, Tizard went first as an exhibitioner, later as a scholar, to Westminster where he studied science and mathematics and learnt to write good English. Elected to a science demyship at Magdalen College, Oxford, in 1903, he went up in 1904 and gained a first class in mathematical moderations (1905) and in chemistry (1908). His tutor was Nevil Sidgwick, with whom he formed a lifelong friendship. After starting research with Sidgwick in Oxford, he spent a semester with Nernst in Berlin, when he met F. A. Lindemann (later Viscount Cherwell). Ten years later Tizard's support was a major factor in Lindemann's election to lead the Clarendon Laboratory in Oxford. As neither of the projects chosen for him by Nernst showed any promise, Tizard returned to Oxford for the summer of 1909 and then spent a year at the Royal Institution, investigating the colour changes of indicators. The papers he published revealed a clarity and elegance of approach which established Tizard's reputation as an investigator. His report in 1911 to the British Association on 'The Sensitiveness of Indicators' was published *in extenso* in the report of the Portsmouth meeting.

In 1911 Tizard returned to Oxford as a tutorial fellow at Oriel, and he also held a demonstratorship in the electrical laboratory, which led to several papers on the motion of ions in gases of which he was a part author. August 1914 found him on board a ship with Sir Ernest (later Lord) Rutherford bound for the meeting of the British Association in Australia. He came home at once and joined the Royal Garrison Artillery, where his unorthodox methods of training recruits were supported by higher authority. In June 1915 R. B. Bourdillon, who had just started experimental work on bomb-sights with G. M. B. Dobson at the Central Flying School at Upavon, secured Tizard's transfer to the Royal Flying Corps as an experimental equipment officer. Tizard, whose eyesight had improved, soon learned to fly, an indispensable qualification for understanding the airman's problems. From bomb-sights Tizard turned his attention to the testing of new aircraft and in 1917 Bertram Hopkinson, who was responsible for research and development in aeronautics, put him in charge of the testing of aircraft at the experimental station at Martlesham. There Tizard developed a scientific system for investigating the performance of aircraft which he described in a paper published by the Aeronautical Society in 1917. Martlesham was the prototype of future experimental stations such as Boscombe Down. Tizard flew as one of his own test pilots, showing skill and imaginative foresight as well as courage. When Hopkinson went to the headquarters of the Ministry of Munitions at the end of 1917 Tizard went with him as his deputy with the rank of lieutenant-colonel and after Hopkinson's death in 1918 Tizard carried on in his place.

In the spring of 1919 Tizard returned to Oxford and early in 1920 he was made reader in chemical thermodynamics. Meanwhile he had been working in a new and important field. During the war when supplies of aviation fuel were short owing to loss of tankers, Tizard had suggested the addition of gasworks benzole which gave excellent results, apart from the freezing of the benzene at low temperatures. Toluene from Borneo petroleum proved to be equally good and did not freeze. This brought Tizard into contact with (Sir) Harry Ricardo who was investigating the performance of petrol engines. He invited Tizard and (Sir) David Pye to join him. Tizard agreed, on condition that the results of the work were published, to which (Sir) Robert Waley Cohen, of Shell who were financing the work, agreed.

By the summer of 1919 Tizard and Pye had prepared an analysis of the physical and chemical properties of the range of fuels which were to be examined and Ricardo had built a new variable compression engine. Tizard's help was particularly valuable in devising ingenious tests and in his astuteness in analysing the results. As they expected, the incidence of detonation was found to be the most important single factor limiting the performance of the petrol engine. Tizard suggested the term 'toluene number' to express the detonation characteristics of each fuel. Toluene was the least prone to detonate of all the fuels they examined, and the 'toluene number' was the proportion of toluene that was added to heptane, the most prone to detonation, in order to match the performance of each fuel they examined. Several years later the Americans substituted the use of iso-octane for toluene and the expression 'octane number' became universal. The results of this classic investigation were published in a series of papers which were Tizard's major contribution to scientific literature. They marked a new era in the understanding of the internal combustion engine.

In 1920 Tizard accepted an invitation from Sir Frank Heath to go to the Department of Scientific and Industrial Research as assistant secretary. He had realized that he was unlikely to do outstanding work in pure research and had seen the great opportunities offered in the application of science to practical problems, for which he felt himself to be better suited. He was first in charge of a new division created to implement a government decision charging the D.S.I.R. with the co-ordination of the scientific work of the defence and civil departments. Several co-ordinating research boards were set up which led to numerous cross-contacts at scientific working level between the departments, and this continued when the rather cumbrous machinery of the boards was abandoned. Meanwhile they gave Tizard a most valuable bird's-eye view of what was happening. In 1924 he saw the need to co-ordinate scientific research in the Air Force and suggested the appointment of a director with similar responsibilities to (Sir) Frank Smith, the director of scientific research in the Admiralty. Pressed to accept the post himself, Tizard declined and H. E. Wimperis, the deputy director, was promoted to it in 1925.

In 1922 Tizard had become principal assistant secretary and in 1927 he succeeded Heath as permanent secretary. During these years he exercised an increasing influence on the policy of D.S.I.R. and was largely responsible for establishing the Chemical Research Laboratory at Teddington, renamed later the National Chemical Laboratory. He left the D.S.I.R. in 1929 when he became rector of the Imperial College, an office he held until 1942. Tizard's decision to go to Imperial College was influenced by his conviction of Britain's need for more scientists and engineers. He soon raised funds to complete the new Beit building and his great service to the College was his imaginative grasp of the site planning needed for its future expansion. He fought tooth and nail and with his customary opportunism to secure the use of the whole site north of Imperial Institute Road for education and to move all museums south of it. His foresight undoubtedly made the later development of the College possible. In many other ways the College benefited by his imaginative approach to its problems such as the introduction of an undergraduate course in chemical engineering, and a scheme for entrance scholarships for boys who had not specialized in science at school. He had the great gift of being able to talk on seemingly equal terms to people of all kinds and all ages and find out what they were thinking so that he kept his finger effectively on the pulse of the organization and inspired people with his own enthusiasm for getting things done.

Meantime Tizard was increasingly occupied with the problems of defence. He had been a member of the Aeronautical Research Committee since 1919 and in 1933 he became chairman. He was also chairman of the engine sub-committee. It was a period of revolutionary advances in aircraft and engines and Tizard, with his background of experience in the first war and his knack of selecting the significant factors, was an admirable choice. While he did not contribute much in the way of original ideas he was a most stimulating chairman and he gave great encouragement to those like (Sir) Frank Whittle, with his jet engine, who were endeavouring to break fresh ground. One important suggestion arising out of his work with Ricardo was that new engines should be tested at pressures higher than those reached with normal fuel so that they could use higher octane fuels when they became available. In 1938 at the end of his five-year term of office he was invited by the Air Council, who wished to retain his 'invaluable assistance', to serve for a second five years and he continued as chairman until 1943.

Baldwin's statement in November 1932 that 'the bomber will always get through', underlined by the air exercises in 1934, had the merit of concentrating attention on this issue. Lindemann in August 1934 wrote a letter to *The Times* calling for action. His papers show that on 15 November he met Tizard and told him of his plan for a sub-committee of the Committee of Imperial Defence, since it was too important to be dealt with by a departmental committee. He noted that Tizard promised his help if possible.

Meanwhile Wimperis at the Air Ministry a few days earlier had recommended the appointment of a small committee, with Tizard as chairman, Dr A. V. Hill, P. M. S. (later Lord) Blackett, and himself as members, and Dr A. P. Rowe as secretary, to consider how far recent advances in scientific and technical knowledge could be used to strengthen defence against hostile aircraft. His recommendation was accepted, and all three men agreed to serve.

In December Lindemann, unaware of these proceedings, wrote to the air minister pressing for a C.I.D. committee. When he was told of the existence of the Tizard committee he regarded it as a plot by the Air Ministry and Tizard to circumvent his own proposal. This was the start of the unfortunate quarrel between them which was to loom so large over the next five years. Both were convinced of the importance of science in future warfare and each anxious to play his part. With this common objective they might have worked together, but the trouble lay largely in their different avenues of approach. Tizard relied on his influence with the air staff and civil servants, whom he understood and whose confidence he had won. Lindemann relied on the politicians which, in Tizard's mind, implied intrigue and was anathema to him.

The Tizard committee met first on 28 January 1935 when Wimperis told them of (Sir) Robert Watson-Watt's view that it might be possible to detect the presence of aircraft by a radio beam. At the next meeting on 21 February they had a memorandum by Watson-Watt and, after a successful experiment to detect an aircraft in flight at Daventry on 26 February, Sir

Hugh (later Lord) Dowding, air member for research and development, agreed to an expenditure of £10,000 to carry out experiments at Orfordness. By June, planes were detected at fifteen miles. The Tizard committee was only advisory, without executive functions, but Tizard kept the air staff in close touch with its proceedings so that they were actively concerned with its deliberations from the start.

Meanwhile Lindemann and (Sir) Winston Churchill combined to press for a C.I.D. committee to deal with the political and financial problems of air defence and in April such a committee held its first meeting under the chairmanship of Sir Philip Cunliffe-Lister (later the Earl of Swinton), soon to become air minister. The Tizard committee became its sub-committee, responsible for research. In June Churchill joined the C.I.D. committee, of which Tizard was a member, and Lindemann became a member of Tizard's committee.

From his first meeting Lindemann was at odds with his colleagues over both projects and priorities. The crisis came in June 1936 when Lindemann went behind the backs of his colleagues by arranging a meeting between Churchill and Watson-Watt, who said that he was dissatisfied with the rate of progress under the normal ministry machinery. This led to a stormy meeting of the Swinton committee when Churchill attacked Tizard. Shortly afterwards Lindemann announced his intention of standing for Parliament where he could raise the question of the country's air defences. Four days later A. V. Hill sent his resignation to Swinton; this was followed by Blackett's and Tizard's. In October Swinton reconstituted the committee, substituting (Sir) Edward Appleton for Lindemann, and in 1939 (Sir) T. R. Merton was added as a member.

In spite of these controversies, the development of radar had continued and when Tizard reported progress to the Swinton committee the large sums needed for the work were always forthcoming. In September 1935 Watson-Watt moved to Bawdsey and in December 1935 sanction was given to build the first five radar stations. In the summer of 1936 Tizard told the air staff that the time had come for the Royal Air Force to learn how to use RDF, as it was called, in combat and to find out the ground organization which would be needed. On 4 August 1936 Tizard met the officers of the bombers and fighters who had been detailed to Biggin Hill for such trials and explained to them that they were to investigate the best way of intercepting a formation of enemy bombers, if they were given fifteen minutes' warning of its approach and its position and altitude at minute intervals. Hitherto the normal procedure was to put fighters up on patrol at suitable points in anticipation of attacks. The Biggin Hill trials were a classic instance of operational research. Methods were gradually evolved for tracking the bombers which gave their position by wireless, thus enabling the fighters to take off and secure an interception. Tizard took an active part in the trials and on one occasion simplified procedure by pointing out an easier means of determining the correct course of the fighter: this was generally adopted and known as the 'Tizzy angle'.

The trials having proved the practicability of this new method of interception, Fighter Command then took over the introduction of the new technique into the defence organization. This was a complex task and it had its difficulties, but Tizard kept in close touch with developments, ever ready with help and advice. He was largely responsible for the introduction of the 'filter room' by means of which the corrected courses of enemy aircraft were clearly presented to the controller in the operations room. When war broke out both the radar chain and the means of using the information it obtained were ready, thus providing a new system of air defence by day.

The Biggin Hill trials were only one of the practical steps which Tizard took to ensure the effective use of radar. In 1938 he persuaded (Sir) Mark Oliphant, then at Birmingham, to drop some of his nuclear research and concentrate on the development of an improved source of short-wave radiation. This led to the invention by (Sir) John Randall and Dr H. A. H. Boot of the cavity magnetron, a major advance in radar technique. Foreseeing the numbers of scientists that would be required to service the radar stations, Tizard early in 1938 told (Sir) John Cockcroft, then working in the Cavendish Laboratory, what was on foot and took him to one of the new radar stations. After a visit by Watson-Watt to Cambridge, scientists were enlisted and shown the stations. Large-scale trials were planned for 1 September 1939, so that when war broke out all the stations were manned for action.

The ground radar stations were not effective by night and much effort was directed to various means of night defence. Tizard realized that the solution lay in the development of airborne radar, and, thanks to his encouragement, the research team led by E. G. Bowen had produced in 1939 an airborne radar set, AI, which needed considerable development before it was suitable for operational use. Tizard gave it his full support in its early stages when doubt was cast on its operational value. Success depended on intimate co-operation between the radar observer and the pilot and gradually the difficult art of interception was learnt. The aircrews' confidence in AI owed much to Tizard's advice on his visits to the squadron. He was also responsible for the night interception committee, and the fighter interception unit for carrying out scientific trials of AI in combat, which paid a dividend in its later stages. Tizard's advocacy won the day and airborne radar played a decisive part in the air war by land and sea.

Intelligence was another field in which Tizard's initiative was to prove decisive. In 1939 we knew little or nothing of what Germany was doing in military research and in April Tizard persuaded Pye, Wimperis's successor, to ask for someone to be appointed in the Air Ministry to deal with scientific intelligence. (Professor) R. V. Jones, known to Tizard by his work on infra-red radiation, then in the Admiralty research laboratory, was selected for the appointment. He was not released by the Admiralty until 1 September, but from then on his flair for interpreting intelligence reports, backed by his shrewd scientific judgement, played a vital part in our defences.

During the first ten months of the war Tizard had advised the chief of the air staff on scientific matters in addition to continuing the chairmanship of the Defence and Offence committees which in October 1939 amalgamated as the Committee for the Scientific Survey of Air Warfare. Its most important decision was to form the Maud committee under (Sir) George Thomson in March 1940 to investigate the feasibility of an atomic bomb after Oliphant had given Tizard the remarkable memorandum by (Professor) O. R. Frisch and (Sir) R. E. Peierls.

When Churchill went to the Admiralty in 1939 with Lindemann as his scientific adviser, and in 1940 became prime minister, Tizard's position gradually became more difficult and when Sir Archibald Sinclair (later Viscount Thurso) became air minister he also sought Lindemann's advice. This uncertainty as to his responsibility led to Tizard's resignation in June 1940 from all his Air Ministry commitments, with the exception of the Aeronautical Research Committee.

From the outbreak of war Tizard was seized with the importance of winning the sympathy and technical support of the United States of America. At his suggestion, A. V. Hill went to Washington in 1940 as 'supernumerary air attaché' to Lord Lothian. Hill's exploration of the position made it clear that the President would welcome a proposal from Britain to share all scientific knowledge of weapons and equipment. Lothian strongly supported the plan to send a British scientific mission and the mission, led by Tizard, went to America in August 1940. Very wisely he went first to Canada, taking details of Britain's war inventions and a list of problems in which Canada might help. This gave Canada her first start in war research and won for Tizard the regard and affection of all the Canadians he met. Subsequently he was frequently their guest and they attached great value to his advice on their military and scientific problems. When he left for Washington Tizard took with him Professor C. J. Mackenzie as Canada's representative on his mission. It was a stroke of genius on Tizard's part to take with him a mixed team of scientists and serving officers from the Army, Navy, and Air Force with battle experience. This gave him the entrée to the armed Services in Washington, not easy for civilians at that time, and within a few days Tizard, Cockcroft, and other civilians were lecturing to the military Services and establishing a confidence and co-operation which were maintained throughout the war. Tizard also took with him in his famous black box the prints of Britain's war devices such as radar and a specimen of Randall and Boot's 9·5 c.m. resonant cavity magnetron which gave the American work on radar a new stimulus. Tizard's brilliant leadership of the mission was one of his greatest services to Britain.

After his return from America in the autumn of 1940 Tizard became a semi-official adviser to successive ministers of aircraft production, sitting on the Aircraft Supply Committee and representing the Ministry on the Air Council from June 1941. He was particularly active in securing the flow of up-to-date information to Washington. In April 1941 after the jet engine had left the ground on a taxiing run, he sent a verbal message to Dr Vannevar Bush, unintelligible to the bearer, but sufficient to keep Bush informed of progress. The development of (Sir) Barnes Wallis's dam-busting bomb owed much to Tizard's support. His influence was felt in the greater use of scientific evaluation of our military operations, such as (Sir) Solly Zuckerman's mission to North Africa, and in the expansion of operational research. When in March 1942 Cherwell recommended bombing built-up areas of Germany in order to break the spirit of the German populace, Tizard queried his estimate of the number of bombers available and the amount of damage to be expected, concluding that the policy would not be decisive and by concentrating bombers on the offensive might risk losing the war through inadequate defence. But by this time Cherwell's influence with the prime minister was much greater than Tizard's.

In 1942 Tizard felt that his whole-time service in the Ministry was no longer needed and he accepted the presidency of Magdalen College, Oxford, at a time when the college was preparing for the adjustments which would be needed in a post-war world. Tizard quickly acquired an admirable grasp of the rather complicated college statutes and he gave much thought to the financial fortunes of the college, incidentally reorganizing the bursary. He soon made up his mind about what he wanted the college to do and he gave a clear lead to those who worked closely with him in small committees. He was less successful in handling a large college meeting when he had to pilot controversial issues through a very varied and independent-minded body of fellows. Perhaps he had too authoritarian a back-ground to fit easily into the democratic ways of a college.

During the years at Magdalen, Tizard's advice was much in demand by the Service chiefs, both here and in the dominions. In 1943 he was preparing to lead a mission to Russia on the same lines as his mission to

America, but eventually this was abandoned. He was then invited by the Australian Government to spend three months visiting defence establishments and advising them on scientific developments, particularly in relation to the Pacific war. Tizard's experiences of government machinery and his personal knowledge of people in key positions enabled him to help the Australians to clarify a number of war problems and to secure the co-ordination of their war research with developments at home.

In 1944 Tizard was chairman of a committee set up by the chiefs of staff to assess the probable effects of new weapons on defence policy. Soon after its report in 1945 the Labour Government turned to Tizard for advice on the place of science in post-war development. In September at a meeting of the chiefs of staff Tizard pressed for the formation of a scientific organization under a defence ministry to keep scientific development under continuous review. He developed this idea in October in a paper on 'The Central Direction of the Scientific Effort' advocating the appointment of a scientific adviser who would act as chairman of a deputy chiefs of staff committee and would also serve on a new body to consider science in relation to civilian needs. These recommendations were approved but a year elapsed before action was finally taken. Meanwhile in the spring of 1946 Tizard had acted as chairman of a Commonwealth conference on defence science at which he advocated the dispersal of scientific effort and the encouragement in the dominions of great centres of scientific education and research. In 1945 he had already made suggestions which led directly to the Woomera rocket range. In August 1946 Tizard was invited to undertake the chairmanship of the two committees he had suggested, involving his resignation of the presidency of Magdalen. He was divided in his mind and asked the advice of his colleagues, who suggested combining one chairmanship with the presidency. A large majority wished him to remain at Magdalen, but since it was not a unanimous decision he resigned.

So in January 1947 Tizard found himself again in Whitehall. Both positions, as chairman of the Defence Research Policy Committee and the Advisory Council on Scientific Policy, were fraught with difficulties. Tizard's instinct was always for action, but with the end of the war the motive of urgency had disappeared, people were tired, including Tizard, and needed time for recovery. Moreover, they were looking again to their own immediate interests and resented any encroachment of their authority. The authority of the Defence Ministry was as yet uncertain and the Services were inclined to stand on their own. The fact that the Defence Committee was debarred from discussing nuclear weapons did not help.

It was an uphill fight and some of Tizard's most effective work was done in the dominions, during visits to Canada and Australia. However, Tizard, in his position of authority as chairman of the Defence Research Policy Committee, succeeded in establishing the position that science had an extremely important part to play in framing the policies of the defence departments and the later organization evolved directly from his efforts.

On the civil side Tizard had a more difficult task, lacking the prestige and record of achievement with other scientific administrators that he had earned so fully with the Services. There was less belief amongst the interested parties that co-ordination of their activities towards the formation of a national scientific policy was necessary, let alone achievable. The bodies concerned, the Research Councils, under their own autonomy, had already achieved much success.

Nevertheless Tizard succeeded in laying some foundations. A small fact-finding staff was created and a forum for discussion provided, but the body was far less executive than was even its military counterpart, and Tizard undoubtedly felt frustration. But he had three important successes. He was able strongly to influence the need for a long-term plan for the training of scientists, particularly technologists. His influence in ensuring that scientific views were fed in at the policy-forming stage was pervasive and effective, and he succeeded in securing the appointment of a chief scientist, who had the necessary powers and appropriate access, in Ministries which lacked such senior scientific officers and needed them most.

The long strain had told on Tizard's health and in 1949 he had wished to retire. Finally in 1952 he left Whitehall for the last time. 'These last six years of his active life were in a real sense the fulfilment of his quarter-of-a-century-old belief in the importance to the life and prosperity of Great Britain of a close relationship between the administrative and scientific worlds . . .' (P. M. S. Blackett, Tizard memorial lecture to the Institute for Strategic Studies, 11 February 1960).

The rest of Tizard's life was directed partly to his educational interests as pro-chancellor of Southampton University and chairman of the Goldsmiths' education committee and partly to his services on the board of the National Research Development Corporation and of several chemical concerns. He took an active interest in their affairs, frequently visiting their plants and research laboratories where his presence gave encouragement to younger chemists and engineers. He foresaw the need for a large expansion of university education and his advice was eagerly sought on his visits to Southampton. He died of a cerebral haemorrhage at his home at Fareham 9 October 1959. His ashes were buried in the floor of the ante-chapel of Oriel College, Oxford.

Tizard had a quick, alert, well-stored mind, great moral and physical courage, and a high sense of integrity which was a handicap in political infighting. Without marked scientific originality, he was quick to see the practical issues raised by new discoveries and indeed to foresee the fields in which research was most needed. He could draw out the best from young scientists or engineers or Service officers. Wit and humour were his in abundance. On his own wide range of topics he was an excellent critic, reserving his more barbed shafts for his equals, superiors, or the scientifically arrogant. He was at his best when faced with a problem calling for a decisive answer as he saw so clearly the practical issues involved and could explain them in simple words. This made him the ideal interpreter between the Services and the scientists, having the confidence of both; it was in this respect that Britain had the advantage over Germany.

Tizard received many honours: an Air Force Cross in 1918, a CB in 1927, KCB in 1937, and GCB in 1949, and the American medal for merit in 1947. He was elected FRS in 1926, was foreign secretary of the Royal Society in 1940–5, and vice-president (1940–1 and 1944–5). He was an honorary doctor of ten British and Commonwealth universities, an honorary fellow of Oriel and Magdalen at Oxford, and of the Imperial College and University College in London. He was awarded the gold medals of the Royal Society of Arts and the Franklin Institute, and the Messel medal of the Society of Chemical Industry. Many learned societies acclaimed him as an honorary member. In 1948 he was president of the British Association; and from 1937 until 1959 he served as a trustee of the British Museum.

In 1915 Tizard married Kathleen Eleanor (died 1968), daughter of Arthur Prangley Wilson, mining engineer; they had three sons.

There is a portrait of Tizard by Bernard Hailstone in the Imperial War Museum; one by Cuthbert Orde at the Imperial College; and a pastel by William Dring at Magdalen College, Oxford.

[Sir William Farren (and R. V. Jones) in *Biographical Memoirs of Fellows of the Royal Society*, vol. vii, 1961; R. W. Clark, *Tizard*, 1965; R. V. Jones in *The Times*, 6, 7, and 8 April 1961 and *Oxford Magazine*, 9 May 1963; C. P. Snow, *Science and Government*, 1961; C. Webster and N. Frankland, (Official History) *The Strategic Air Offensive Against Germany, 1939–45*, vol. i, 1961; Sir Harold Hartley in *Proceedings* of the Chemical Society, May 1964; *Nature*, 5 March 1960 (P. M. S. Blackett, Tizard memorial lecture); *Journal* of the Royal Aeronautical Society, August 1967 (A. R. Collar, Tizard memorial lecture); private information; personal knowledge.]

HAROLD HARTLEY

published 1971

TOYNBEE Arnold Joseph

(1889–1975)

Author, scholar and historian, was born in London, 14 April 1889, the only son and eldest of the three children of Harry Valpy Toynbee, worker for the Charity Organization Society, and his wife, Sarah Edith Marshall. He gained a scholarship to Winchester College and another from there to Balliol College, Oxford, in 1907. He acquired a remarkable knowledge of Latin and Greek, obtaining first classes in both classical honour moderations (1909) and *literae humaniores* (1911). He then became a tutor in ancient Greek and Roman history at Balliol; his scholarship was renewed and he was encouraged to travel. In 1911 and 1912 he explored Greece and Italy alone and on foot. For a year he became a student at the British School of Archaeology at Athens. He contracted dysentery which rendered him unfit for the army (the death on active service of many contemporaries haunted him all his life) and he spent most of the war years in government work, notably in the Political Intelligence Department of the Foreign Office. He was a member of the British delegation to the Paris peace conference of 1919, after which he was appointed to the Koraes chair of Byzantine and Modern Greek language, literature, and history at London University. He resigned in 1924.

Toynbee had married in 1913 Rosalind, daughter of G. Gilbert Murray, scholar, poet, and author. There were three sons, of whom the eldest died in 1939. (Theodore) Philip (died 1981) was a distinguished novelist and journalist, and Lawrence is a gifted artist. The marriage was dissolved in 1946 and in the same year Toynbee married Veronica Marjorie (died 1980), daughter of the Revd Sidney Boulter. This marriage, a very happy one, continued a working partnership which had begun in 1925, when Toynbee went to Chatham House (the Royal Institute of International Affairs), as director of studies. Miss Boulter, already on the Chatham House staff, soon became his collaborator, sharing with him until 1946 the writing of the annual *Survey of International Affairs*. Simultaneously he was research professor of international history in the University of London. During World War II Toynbee was director of the Foreign Office Research Department (called the Foreign Research and Press Service before 1943). He retired from Chatham House and his chair in 1955.

When still a very young man he had made a programme of what he wished to accomplish in his writing, and he carried it through, with the aid of a large number of small notebooks, filled with ideas and references to be used, sometimes years later, in fulfilment of the plan. It was in about 1914 that it struck him that, with the outbreak of World War I, our world had entered on an experience that the Greek world had been through in the Peloponnesian war. That flash of perception gave him the idea of making comparisons between civilizations. As a result, *A Study of History* in twelve volumes was published by the Oxford University Press between 1934 and 1961, and it is largely on this great work that Toynbee's fame rests. His theory of 'challenge and response' in relation to civilizations brought him many critics, two of the most vociferous being Pieter Geyl and Hugh Trevor-Roper (later Lord Dacre of Glanton). Toynbee was untroubled by their views, since he had every confidence in his own. A venture which made the *Study* accessible to a vast new public was the abridgement prepared, on his own initiative, by David C. Somervell, and to the publication of which Toynbee gave his reluctant approval. Volumes i–vi appeared in 1946; volumes vii–x in 1957; the complete edition, in one volume, in 1960. Much later (1972) the illustrated version, in which Toynbee had the collaboration of Jane Caplan, reached another new public.

He was a writer of prodigious output and many of his books became bestsellers, though they often attracted controversy. Mention should be made here of *Hannibal's Legacy* (1965) and *Constantine Porphyrogenitus and his World* (1973) for their profound scholarship. His two 'personal' books, *Acquaintances* (1967) and *Experiences* (1969), reveal a great deal about their author, and the few short travel books show another facet of this many-faceted man. He was a regular contributor to the *Manchester Guardian* and the *Observer* and wrote a weekly column in the *Economist* between 1930 and 1939. His lectures, notably the Reith lectures of 1952 and the Gifford series of 1953 and 1954, were published in book form. His last major published works, both of which appeared posthumously, were *Mankind and Mother Earth* (1976) in which his aim was 'to give a comprehensive bird's-eye view of mankind's history in narrational form' and *The Greeks and their Heritages* (1981).

His main publishers, the Oxford University Press, found him a co-operative and appreciative author. He was genuinely interested in the minutiae involved in book production. In 1972 the Press, in conjunction with the National Book League, mounted an exhibition of his work at the League's premises. Called 'A Study of Toynbee', and consisting mainly of photographs, manuscripts, and copies of his books (including translations into twenty-five languages), it attracted a large number of visitors.

Toynbee's preoccupation with religion is well documented. He became an agnostic early in life, but was convinced that Man was not the highest form of creation; he believed in an 'ultimate spiritual reality', but he could not conceive of a god who was both all-loving and all-powerful. He was, in fact, a deeply religious agnostic, and his writings on, or touching on, religious subjects indicate that perhaps his agnosticism was nearer belief than the belief of some practitioners of conventional religion.

Toynbee was a quiet, charming, courteous, and kindly man. A generous host, he had a personal life-style that was simple to the point of austerity. His regular (and early) hours enabled him to produce the maximum amount of work every day. He wasted nothing, least of all, time. He admitted that his need to work was obsessional and was able to produce reasons for the obsession.

He had a deep feeling for the countryside, and a historical vision of landscape. He loved travel, and visited many countries of the world, sometimes on his own, but often with his wife, Veronica. (It was in a ship between Panama and Auckland, in 1956, that he learned of the offer of his appointment as a Companion of Honour, which he accepted.) A holiday 'for pleasure', though, he would have seen as a waste of time. Not for him the superficial sightseeing trip or the 'beach' holiday. All that he saw and did was transmuted into books or articles or lectures.

Toynbee received many honours apart from his CH. He was elected FBA in 1937, made an honorary fellow of Balliol in 1957, and presented with honorary degrees from many universities including Oxford, Cambridge, and Princeton. It delighted him when, in 1968, he was made a *membre associé de l'Institut de France*, taking the place of Sir Winston Churchill. But what was perhaps the crowning honour came in 1974, when he was received *ad portas* at his old school, Winchester College. His reply, in Latin, written in his minute, beautiful handwriting, was in his pocket, but his memory did not falter: he had no need to refer to it.

In the same year he suffered a severe stroke. From then on he had little power to communicate, and none to work. He longed for death and died in Purey Cust nursing home in York fourteen months later, 22 October 1975. His ashes lie in the burial ground at Terrington, near his Yorkshire home.

[S. Fiona Morton, *A Bibliography of Arnold J. Toynbee*, 1981; family papers; personal knowledge.]

LOUISE ORR

published 1986

URQUHART Robert Elliott

(1901–1988)

Major-general, was born in Shepperton on Thames 28 November 1901, the eldest in the family of three sons and one daughter of Alexander Urquhart, MD, physician, and his wife, Isabel Gillespie. After attending St Paul's School and the Royal Military College, Sandhurst, he was commissioned as a second lieutenant in the Highland Light Infantry in 1920. Two years at the Staff College, Camberley (1936–7), were followed by staff appointments in India—staff captain (1938), deputy adjutant and quartermaster-general at army headquarters (1939–40), and deputy assistant adjutant-general and AA & QMG (3rd division, 1940–1), until he was given command of the 2nd battalion of the Duke of Cornwall's Light Infantry in 1941. In 1942 he became general staff officer grade 1 of the 51st Highland division and went through the campaign in North Africa which destroyed the Afrika Korps. He was given command of 231st brigade in Malta in 1943, and its distinguished performance in Sicily and Italy brought him appointment to the DSO.

He was then brigadier general staff of XII Corps and was chosen in 1944 for command of the 1st Airborne division. He led it in Operation Market Garden, which was designed to cross three main river obstacles in Holland in September 1944 and to join up with XXX Corps arriving from the south, to swing through into the German industrial heartland. Since Urquhart was over six feet tall, of robust build, and possibly at forty-two rather too old for parachuting, he moved into battle by glider. He faced immediate difficulties. British troops arrived in a piecemeal fashion over three days and had to move five miles to their allotted positions around Arnhem. Their route was blocked by German armour reorganizing after Normandy, and, to compound the difficulties, the Germans captured the plans of the entire operation on the body of an American soldier shot down in a glider. Communications were rarely satisfactory and the weather was atrocious, making air support and replenishment difficult. The worst stroke of ill luck was Urquhart's enforced absence (he was obliged to take refuge in the attic of a house surrounded by German troops) from his headquarters for thirty-six hours soon after his arrival, when decisive command was imperative and was lacking. Urquhart made mistakes: the high ground at Wester Bouwing, for example, dominating the divisional bridgehead, and the heavy ferry at Heveadorp were never secured, but he fought a great battle. The high morale of the troops under his command reflected his own, but the battle of Arnhem was a defeat for the British and the advance of XXX Corps was delayed. The remnants of Urquhart's division, withdrawn on 25 September 1944 across the Lower Rhine, numbered some 2,600 men of the 10,000 he had brought in.

Urquhart, appointed CB after Arnhem (1944), was next used to command an *ad hoc* airborne force, styled 1st Airborne division, which was sent to Norway to rescue King Haakon, but his division was never reconstituted and was disbanded in November 1945. He became a colonel in 1945 and major-general in 1946. He was awarded the Netherlands Bronze Lion (1944) and Norwegian Order of St Olaf (1945).

Urquhart's career thereafter puzzled and disappointed many who knew his qualities. For fourteen months while the Territorial Army was being reorganized he was its director-general (1945–6). He was general officer commanding 16th Airborne division, Territorial Army (1947– 8), and commander, Lowland District (1948–50). In 1950 he was given command of 17th Gurkha division in Malaya and in the same year became general officer commanding Malaya. He moved to Austria in 1952 for three years as GOC-in-C British troops, in an agreeable if uninspiring assignment, which was his last in the service. From 1954 he was colonel of his regiment, the Highland Light Infantry, but when the Army Council decreed its amalgamation with the Royal Scots Fusiliers in 1957 he became embroiled in a disagreement, which concerned style, title, and above all dress. Would the new regiment be in kilt or trews? The two colonels negotiated an agreement, with the lord lyon's support, that the kilt should be worn with the tartan dress Erskine. The War Office insisted on trews and both colonels had to go (1958).

After Urquhart's retirement from the army in December 1955 he lived for some years at Drymen in Stirlingshire and thereafter at Bigram, Port of Menteith, nearby. In 1957 he joined the Davy & United Engineering Co., where his sound judgement and administrative experience found useful scope, first as personnel manager and then as director, in an industrial environment whose technical aspects were not perhaps among his deepest interests. He moved into complete retirement in 1970.

In 1939 Urquhart, always known as 'Roy', married Pamela, daughter of Brigadier William Edmund Hunt Condon, of the Indian Army. They had one son and three daughters. Urquhart died 13 December 1988 at his home in Port of Menteith.

[R. E. Urquhart, *Arnhem*, 1958; Sir John Hackett, *I Was a Stranger*, 1977; private information; personal knowledge.]

JOHN HACKETT

published 1996

VAUGHAN WILLIAMS Ralph

(1872–1958)

Composer, was born 12 October 1872 at Down Ampney, Gloucestershire, into a family of mixed Welsh and English descent whose members went chiefly into the law or the Church. Sir Edward Vaughan Williams was his grandfather, Sir Roland Vaughan Williams his uncle. He was the younger son of the vicar, the Revd Arthur Vaughan Williams, and his wife, Margaret, daughter of the third Josiah Wedgwood, grandson of the potter, who had married his cousin, Caroline Darwin, niece of Charles Darwin. His parents' two families had come to live at Leith Hill in Surrey in the middle of the nineteenth century and Ralph Vaughan Williams was to continue his association with the Leith Hill musical festival until the middle of the twentieth. He was brought up at Leith Hill Place because his father died when he was only two. There was music in both families but the child was no precocious genius. He wrote a little piece four bars long for piano when he was six, and by the time he was eleven he was playing the violin quite well, but, when he was an undergraduate at Cambridge his Darwin cousins thought he was wasting his time trying to be a composer, and he was thirty by the time he had found his real idiom. However, he relates in a musical autobiography contributed to *Ralph Vaughan Williams* (1950) by Hubert Foss that while he was still at Charterhouse he organized a concert at which one of his own works was played. Before he went up to Trinity College, Cambridge, in 1892 he spent two years at the Royal College of Music studying composition with (Sir) Hubert Parry and (Sir) Charles Stanford and he was able to take his Mus. Bac. in 1894 while still reading history in which he obtained a second in 1895. He then put in another year at the Royal College but he still had not found himself and went off to Berlin to work with Max Bruch. Years later he was still dissatisfied with his technique and in 1907–8 worked for some months at refining it with Ravel in Paris. But he had taken his Cambridge doctorate in 1901. Thereafter he was known to the world, since he declined a knighthood, as Dr Vaughan Williams and later to younger generations as 'Uncle Ralph'.

Vaughan Williams was by creed and practice a nationalist, like those Slavonic, Latin, and Scandinavian musicians who in the nineteenth century turned against the long hegemony of German and Italian music to native sources of inspiration in order to secure emancipation for themselves and the ultimate enrichment of European music. Chief of these sources for Vaughan Williams was English folksong, but other influences were hymnody, including plainsong, to which he was led by his editorship of *The*

English Hymnal (1906), Purcell, of whose works he edited a volume of the Welcome Odes for the Purcell Society (1904–6), and the Elizabethan madrigals to which he was devoted all his life both publicly and domestically. In him English music secured independence of the continental dominance which had been exerted by the powerful figures of Handel and Mendelssohn for a century and a half. He was assisted in this movement by his friend Gustav Holst, but he did not in the end establish a school, for the emancipation when it came was complete, and nationalism had spent most of its force in the early twentieth century.

Vaughan Williams had the integrity and independence of his middle-class origins, the lively conscience and streak of puritanism of his formal education, and an impressive physical presence. He belonged to that small class of Englishmen who are by temperament and upbringing radical traditionalists or conservative liberals; he could even be described as an agnostic Christian, in that while cherishing the main traditions of English life, its folksong, its hymnody, its ecclesiastical occasions, its liberal politics, its roots, he was forward-looking, outspoken, and quick to protest at official obscurantism, timidity, or intolerance, as when he publicly deprecated the banning of Communist musicians from access to the radio during the war of 1939–45. In the war of 1914–18 he enlisted as a private in the Royal Army Medical Corps and went to France and then to Salonica, but in 1917 he was transferred to the Royal Garrison Artillery and given a commission. He was sent again to France in March 1918 at the time of the great retreat. During his time in the army he had organized such music as was possible in recreation huts and after the armistice was made director of music, First Army, B.E.F., France, until he was demobilized.

His earliest music, apart from student and prentice work, consisted of songs, of which 'Linden Lea' (1902), the first published work, became and remained a classic. Another early song, 'Silent Noon' (1903), which was, however, one of a sequence of six settings of sonnets by Dante Gabriel Rossetti, also achieved a wide and lasting currency. In retrospect Rossetti seems less suited to his robust imagination than R. L. Stevenson (*Songs of Travel*, 1904) or Walt Whitman (*Towards the Unknown Region*, 1907) who provided texts for more characteristic music. By the time the latter had been given at the Leeds Festival of 1907 and had proclaimed that a new voice was to be heard in English music, a crisis in style had been resolved by Vaughan Williams's discovery of English folksong. He had been attracted in youth by Christmas carols and such few folksongs as came his way—'Dives and Lazarus' was a favourite which years later was to give him the 'Five Variants of "Dives and Lazarus" ' for harp and string orchestra (1939)—but in December 1903 he collected 'Bushes and Briars' in Essex, the first of several hundreds of authentic folksongs taken down from the lips of traditional country singers in the course of the next few years. The modal character of these tunes unlocked for him the idiom which had been struggling to erupt and the first-fruits of the emancipation were three orchestral 'Norfolk Rhapsodies' (1906–7) and the *Fantasia on Christmas Carols* (1912). The rhapsody and the fantasia were the forms found by all nationalist composers to be more suited to thematic material derived from national tunes than conventional sonata form, which is recalcitrant to extended melody. He continued to compose songs on and off throughout his life but in diminishing numbers after about 1930, although his last completed work was a set of 'Four Last Songs' (1958).

Vaughan Williams would not have been the traditionalist he was had he failed to contribute to the long tradition of English choral music. After the success of his Whitman cantata at Leeds in 1907 it was natural for him to provide something more substantial for the premier choral festival: the *Sea Symphony*, with words again by Whitman, for the festival of 1910. More than Beethoven's Ninth is this a true choral symphony since all its four movements are vocal and at the same time are cast in one or other of the symphonic forms. As Vaughan Williams's mind gradually turned towards the symphony, which was eventually to form the central corpus of his output, this large-scale cantata took its place as the first in the canon of his nine symphonies. There is only one oratorio actually so called among his choral works with biblical words, *Sancta Civitas* (1926), of which the words are derived from the Apocalypse and prefaced by a quotation from Plato. *Hodie* nearly thirty years on (1954), however, is, in fact if not in official nomenclature, a Christmas oratorio. Of the other choral works some are occasional pieces, *Benedicite* (1929), *Dona nobis pacem* (1936), *Flourish for a Coronation* (1937), *A Song of Thanksgiving* (1944), and only *Five Tudor Portraits* (1935) is of the dimensions of a secular oratorio, although *An Oxford Elegy* and *Fantasia on the 'Old 104th'* (both 1949) employ a chorus, the one with an obbligato for a speaker, the other with an obbligato for pianoforte.

His first purely instrumental symphony was the *London*, completed before the war but revised before publication in 1920. Two other of his nine symphonies bear titles, No. 3, the *Pastoral* (1922), and No. 7, *Sinfonia Antartica* (1952), which was an overflow from the music he had composed for a film, *Scott of the Antarctic*. Nos. 4 (1935) and 6 (1948) are so angry and disturbing that they have also suggested a submerged programme, which the composer himself firmly deprecated. No. 5 (1943) had an avowed connection with *The Pilgrim's Progress*, on a setting of which the composer was contemporaneously working. Nos. 8 (1956) and 9 (1958) show a preoccupation with formal experiment and tone colour. No. 9 was performed only four months before his death and while it showed no lack of vigour it did sound a note of something like resignation not previously heard in his music. The range of experience covered is wide, although the subjective emotions explored by the German symphonists are not prominent.

Vaughan Williams also composed a good deal of dramatic music, which includes incidental music to pageants, masques, Shakespeare, Greek plays (of which the overture and suite for *The Wasps* of Aristophanes, 1909, is the chief and has an independent existence), film scores, ballets, and operas. These last are heterogeneous, ranging from the quasi-ballad opera to the text of Harold Child, *Hugh the Drover* (1924), to the full-length comedy *Sir John in Love* (1929); from the farcical extravaganza *The Poisoned Kiss* (1936) to the word-for-word setting of the tragic *Riders to the Sea* (1937) and the 'morality' *The Pilgrim's Progress* (1951). In none of these is the dramatic touch as certain as in the symphonies and choral works and they are not wholly proof against theatrical mischance, yet the work which is not only utterly characteristic but reveals supreme mastery is a stage work, the ballet *Job* (1931).

Many of his most characteristic works are not classifiable in the normal categories. Such are the *Serenade to Music* (1938) dedicated to Sir Henry Wood, *Flos Campi* (1925) which is a suite scored for solo viola, small orchestra, and small chorus, and his most important chamber work is a song sequence 'On Wenlock Edge' (1909) with accompaniment for string quartet and piano. There is an element of cussedness in his attitude to the concerto: he wrote four so called, besides two 'Romances' and a suite, for instrumental solo with orchestra. Those for violin are not virtuoso works; that for piano the composer rearranged for two keyboards to make it more effective; on the other hand it was a particular performer's virtuosity which evoked the concerto-type works for viola, oboe, harmonica, and tuba.

There is no side of music which Vaughan Williams did not touch and enrich, although some of his compositions were primarily of occasional and local significance, and for piano and organ he wrote little. His settings and arrangements of folksongs, however, are a valuable parergon. He conducted the Bach Choir from 1921 to 1928 and taught composition at the Royal College of Music for twenty years. His literary output consisted mostly of pamphlets and lectures, which were reprinted in book form, the chief being *National Music* (1934) in which his aesthetic creed was formulated. He did his share of committee work, notably in connection with the English Folk Dance and Song Society, of which he became president in 1946. The honours which came to him, an honorary doctorate of music from Oxford (1919), an honorary fellowship of Trinity College, Cambridge (1935), and the Order of Merit (1935), were no doubt for his eminence as a composer, but they were also a recognition of the manifold services he rendered to English music. It was not until he was an old man that it was realized that there was no formal portrait of him. The Royal College of Music therefore commissioned one from Sir Gerald Kelly which hangs in the college. The Manchester City Art Gallery has a bronze by Epstein and the National Portrait Gallery drawings by Juliet Pannett and Joyce Finzi and a bronze by David McFall.

In 1897 Vaughan Williams married Adeline (died 1951), daughter of Herbert William Fisher and sister of H. A. L. and Sir W. W. Fisher. In 1953 he married Ursula, daughter of Major-General Sir Robert Lock and widow of Lieutenant-Colonel J. M. J. Forrester Wood. He died in London 26 August 1958 and was buried in Westminster Abbey.

[Ursula Vaughan Williams, *R.V.W.: A Biography of Ralph Vaughan Williams*, 1964; Michael Kennedy, *The Works of Ralph Vaughan Williams*, 1964; personal knowledge.]

FRANK HOWES

published 1971

WAKEFIELD (William) Wavell

(1898–1983)

First Baron Wakefield of Kendal

Sportsman and politician, was born 10 March 1898 at Beckenham, Kent, into an old and respected Westmorland Quaker family, the eldest of four sons (there were no daughters) of Roger William Wakefield, a medical practitioner in Beckenham, and his wife, Ethel Mary, daughter of John Frederick Knott, of Buxton, in Derbyshire. He was educated at the Craig Preparatory School, Windermere, and at Sedbergh, which he left in 1916 to serve in the Royal Naval Air Service and later in the Royal Air Force. He went to Pembroke College, Cambridge, in 1921, on the first RAF course arranged at the university, and took a BA in engineering (1923).

He was a tremendous enthusiast in everything he did, and he was already an England rugby international when he went to Cambridge. He won two blues and was captain of the university in his second year. Typically, he discarded the traditional selection procedures in that year, and combed the colleges for talent. He took players from obscurity, moved them into different positions, and moulded them into such an effective team that they beat Oxford, the hot favourites, by what was then a record score. He went on to win 31 caps for England, which remained a record for forty-two years.

He retired from the RAF as a flight lieutenant in 1923, having reached the rank of captain in his wartime service and having been mentioned in dispatches. On leaving the RAF he joined Boots, the chemists, and qualified as a pharmaceutical chemist during his four years with the firm. In those years he established himself as one of the great players of Rugby Union football and as one of the best-known Englishmen of his time. He played cricket for the MCC and was also an exceptionally gifted athlete. He won the RAF 440 yards championship, and in sprint training at Cambridge he was fast enough to extend Harold Abrahams, who went on to win the gold medal for the 100 metres in the 1924 Olympic Games. That speed, then unusual in such a big man, enabled Wakefield to transform forward play in rugby football, and such was his enquiring mind and innovative nature that he was in the forefront of introducing specialization to the various forward positions. With his white scrum cap laced firmly on his fair hair and round his strong, open face, he played for England for eight years and captained his country to the most successful period in its rugby history since the breakaway of the northern clubs which formed the Rugby League in 1892. Wakefield was elected to the Rugby Union while he was still a player, and he went on to become president in 1950–1 and to represent England on the International Rugby Football Board.

He maintained an active interest in skiing and water-skiing throughout his life. He won the Kandahar gold and became president of the Ski Club of Great Britain. In the summer months he was fond of water-skiing and subaqua diving in his beloved Lake District where he lived and where he had some of his family banking and business interests. After he left the RAF he continued flying as a pilot in the Reserve and in 1939 was recalled to active service for flying duties. He was then transferred to the Air Ministry as parliamentary private secretary and in 1942 was made director of the Air Training Corps.

He stood unsuccessfully for Parliament in a by-election at Swindon in 1934, but a year later, at the general election, he won the seat for the Conservatives. In 1945 he left Swindon and won St Marylebone. He held that seat until 1963, when he was created a baron. He had been knighted for public services in 1944. He served on the committees of the YMCA and the National Playing Fields Association, and was president of various manufacturing and transport associations. He also held a wide range of company directorships, including those of Rediffusion Ltd., Skyways Engineering, and the Portman Building Society.

In 1919 he married Rowena Doris (died 1981), daughter of Llewellyn Lewis, medical practitioner. They had three daughters. Wakefield died in Kendal 12 August 1983. The barony became extinct.

[Family information; personal knowledge.]

JOHN REASON

published 1990

WALEY Arthur David

(1889–1966)

Orientalist, was born at Tunbridge Wells 19 August 1889, the second of the three sons of David Frederick Schloss, economist and Fabian socialist, and his wife, Rachel Sophia, daughter of Jacob Waley, legal writer and professor of political economy, whose surname the family adopted in 1914. He was the brother of Sir Sigismund David Waley.

Arthur Waley was brought up in Wimbledon and sent to school at Rugby (1903–6), where he shone as a classical scholar and won an open scholarship at King's College, Cambridge, while still under seventeen. He spent a year in France before going up to the university in 1907; he obtained a first class in part i of the classical tripos in 1910 but was obliged to abandon Cambridge when he developed diminished sight in one eye due to conical cornea. Rest and Continental travel saved the second eye from being affected and made him fluent in Spanish and German. Although he had got to know (Sir) Sydney Cockerell at Cambridge it was through Oswald Sickert, a brother of the painter, that he was led to consider a career in the British Museum. Sickert was one of a group of friends, mostly either on the museum staff or researchers in the library, who used to meet regularly for lunch in the years before 1914 at the Vienna Café in New Oxford Street, at which Laurence Binyon was one of the 'regulars'. In 1912 Sir Sidney Colvin retired from his keepership of prints and drawings and Waley was a candidate for the vacancy in February 1913, supported by both Sickert and Cockerell. In June he started working in the newly formed sub-department of oriental prints and drawings under its first head, Binyon. Waley's task was to make a rational index of the Chinese and Japanese painters represented in the museum collection; he immediately started to teach himself Chinese and Japanese. He had no formal instruction, for the School of Oriental Studies was not founded till 1916; but by that date Waley was privately printing his first fifty-two translations of Chinese poems, and in 1917–18 he added others in the first numbers of the

Bulletin of the School and in the *New Statesman* and the *Little Review.* By 1918 he had completed enough translations of poems, mainly by writers of the classic T'ang period, to have a volume entitled *A Hundred and Seventy Chinese Poems* accepted for publication by Constable largely on account of a perceptive review in the *Times Literary Supplement* of the 1917 *Bulletin* poems. In 1919 (Sir) Stanley Unwin became his publisher and remained his constant friend and admirer.

During his sixteen years at the museum Waley's only official publications were the index of Chinese artists (1922), at that time the first in the West; and a catalogue of the paintings recovered from Tun-huang by Sir Aurel Stein and subsequently divided between the Government of India and the British Museum (1931). His *An Introduction to the Study of Chinese Painting* (1923) was a by-product of his unpublished notes on the national collection and its relation to the great tradition of Chinese painting. He also set in order and described the Japanese books with woodcut illustrations and the large collection of Japanese paintings. He retired from the museum on the last day of 1929 because he had been told that he ought to spend his winters abroad. Waley had started to ski as early as 1911 and he liked to get away into the mountains whenever he could, generally to Austria or Norway and not to the regular runs but as a lone figure on the high snow slopes.

In 1925 began the publication of Waley's largest and probably best-known translation—of the *Genji Monogatari* by Murasaki Shikibu, the late tenth-century classical novelist of Japan, the sixth volume of which did not appear until 1933. This was not the first of Waley's Japanese translations, for it had been preceded by two volumes of classic poetry, selections from the *Uta* (1919) and Nō plays (1921); in these he was more concerned with the resonances of the Japanese language, whereas in the *Genji* he aimed rather at an interpretation of the sensibility and wit of the closed society of the Heian court, described in the idiomatic English of his day. Inevitably this already shows signs of dating as the idiom itself becomes remote, but it may be long before it is again possible to enter so sympathetically into the spirit of that refined and élitist world.

The translations of Chinese poetry which he continued to produce for the rest of his life show Waley more as a creative poet, though his lives of Po Chü-i and Li Po show how closely he was aware of their milieux. In his verse translations Waley not only wanted to evoke the mood and intention of the original text but also to convey in the English mode the stresses of Chinese verse form. He denied the influence of G. Manley Hopkins in his use of 'sprung rhythm' but said that he was influenced by him in the phrasing of the Nō plays. In fact the level of his speech rhythm is naturally different from that of Hopkins, with none of its urgent acceleration but rather with the clear phrasing of the flute which he enjoyed playing.

Waley moved with the smooth grace of the skier, his gesture was courtly in salutation, but more characteristic was the attentive, withdrawn pose of his finely profiled head with its sensitive but severe mouth. His voice was high-pitched but low-toned and unchanging, so as to seem conversational in a lecture, academic in conversation. In later life he had a slight stoop which accentuated his ascetic appearance. He enjoyed meeting the sympathetic and their conversation but never spoke himself unless he had something to say; he expected the same restraint in others. His forty years' attachment to Beryl de Zoete, the anthropologist and interpreter of Eastern dance forms, brought out the depth of feeling and tenderness of which he was capable.

As a scholar Waley aimed always to express Chinese and Japanese thought at their most profound levels, with the highest standard of accuracy of meaning, in a way that would not be possible again because of the growth of professional specialization. He was always a lone figure in his work though he was not remote from the mood of his times. Although he never travelled to the Far East and did not seek to confront the contemporary societies of China or Japan, he was scathingly critical of the attitude of the West to their great cultures in the world in which he grew up: hence his scorn for the older generation of sinologists and his hatred of imperialism, as shown in his *The Opium War through Chinese Eyes* (1958).

For over forty years Waley lived in Bloomsbury, mostly in Gordon Square. Although he had many connections with the Bloomsbury group of artists and writers, he was never a member of a clique and his friendships with the Stracheys, the Keyneses, and with Roger Fry dated from his Cambridge days. He was elected an honorary fellow of King's in 1945 but was not often seen there. Other honours also came to him late, election to the British Academy in 1945, the Queen's medal for poetry in 1953, CBE in 1952, and CH in 1956. Aberdeen and Oxford universities awarded him honorary doctorates. After the death of Beryl in 1962 he went to live in Highgate where he was looked after by Alison Grant Robinson, an old friend from New Zealand, who was formerly married to Hugh Ferguson Robinson, and to whom he was married a month before his death at home from cancer of the spine 27 June 1966.

A volume of appreciation and an anthology of his writings was edited by Ivan Morris, under the title *Madly Singing in the Mountains* (1970), a phrase taken from a poem by Po Chü-i which Waley had translated in 1917 and chosen because of its 'joyfulness', as expressed in the lines:

Each time that I look at a fine landscape:
Each time that I meet a loved friend,
I raise my voice and recite a stanza of poetry
And am glad as though a God had crossed my path.

Two notes that Waley wrote on his own work when over seventy, while not factually reliable, contain his own assessment of his translations; that he had made them to the measure of his own tastes and sensibilities, in a 'recherche esthétique'. Forty years earlier he had written: 'If I have failed to make these translations in some sense works of art—if they are mere philology, not literature, then I have indeed fallen short of what I hoped and intended.' It can be asserted that his intention was fully realized.

A bibliography of Waley's work was published by F. A. Johns in 1968. A portrait drawing by Michael Ayrton is in King's College, Cambridge, and a pencil drawing by Rex Whistler is in the National Portrait Gallery.

[Introduction to the second edition of *170 Chinese Poems*, 1962; Ivan Morris (ed.), *Madly Singing in the Mountains*, 1970; *The Times*, 28 June 1966; L. P. Wilkinson in *King's College Annual Report*, 1966; private information; personal knowledge.]

BASIL GRAY

published 1981

WALLIS Sir Barnes Neville

(1887–1979)

Engineer, was born at Ripley, Derbyshire, 26 September 1887, the second child and second son in the family of three sons and one daughter of Charles George Wallis, general practitioner, and his wife, Edith Eyre, daughter of the Revd John Ashby. He was educated at Haberdashers' Aske's School at Hatcham and at Christ's Hospital in London.

Early in Wallis's childhood, his father, who had moved to London, became handicapped by poliomyelitis and although he struggled to maintain his practice, his family felt the need for rigid economy and his wife Edith had to shoulder the family responsibilities. It was due to her encouragement that Wallis, at the age of twelve, entered Christ's Hospital by way of a competitive examination. In spite of frequent illness and some attacks of migraine, he did well, particularly in English, science, and mathematics. He was afterwards always grateful to the school, especially to his science master, and to his mother for the sacrifices she made to keep him there.

Seeking to earn his living as early as possible, he chose to become an engineer and left school at the age of seventeen to become an apprentice in the Thames Engineering Works at Blackheath. Later he moved his indentures to J. S. White's shipyard at Cowes. There he did well, and after attending local evening classes, passed the London matriculation examination. Throughout, he kept in touch with his mother, under whose leadership he had become, and remained throughout his life, a devout Anglo-Catholic.

Two events now occurred that were to have much influence on his life: first, his mother died in 1911, leaving him with a permanent sense of loss and a determination to do his best for his family; and second, a new recruit to Cowes, H. B. Pratt, came to work alongside him.

Pratt had worked for Vickers at Barrow when the first British rigid airship, the R 1, was built there, and in 1913 he was recalled by Vickers to start on the design of a new airship, the R 9. He persuaded Wallis to join him, and it was not long before both, caught by the romance of these great ships of the air, were working long hours every day of the week. Under Pratt, who had already appreciated Wallis's design flair, Wallis became chief designer, and J. E. Temple, another Vickers engineer, was placed alongside him as chief calculator. The R 9 was completed in 1916. It closely followed Zeppelin practice and became popular in the navy for the training of officers and men for subsequent airships. The same team later produced the R 23 and the R 26, which entered naval service too late to contribute much to the 1914–18 war effort. Meanwhile Wallis served in the Artists' Rifles and RNVR in 1915.

After the war Pratt and Temple moved out of airship work and Wallis started upon the design of his favourite airship, the R 80. It was intended for Atlantic convoy work and was to be faster and more manoeuvrable than previous airships. Wallis, impressed by the results of aerodynamic tests on some airship models at the National Physical Laboratory, boldly stepped away from the cigar shape of the wartime Zeppelins and adopted a streamline form for the R 80. It first flew in 1920 and, after some minor troubles and modifications, was soon acclaimed as the best rigid airship of its day. However, government airship work ceased in 1921 after the R 38 disaster, and Vickers closed their airship department.

Wallis, in despair, and suffering increasingly from migraine, sought without success an airship appointment in the USA. He turned to studying for an external degree in engineering of London University, which he gained in 1922, and then went to Switzerland to teach in a school there. He proved a good teacher and discovered the ability to lecture with clarity and charm for which he was well known for the rest of his life.

Meanwhile, largely due to the advocacy of (Sir) C. Dennistoun Burney of Vickers, ideas for large airships for commercial purposes were astir in England and the government was considering an airship service to India. The Zeppelin Company had started upon the design and construction of the Graf Zeppelin, the most successful of all commercial airships. Wallis, full of enthusiasm, returned to Vickers and at Howden was put in charge, under Burney, of the design of the R 100, one of the two great airships finally authorized by the government in 1924. The other, the R 101, was to be built at the Royal Airship Works at Cardington. Both ships were to be much larger, even, than the Graf Zeppelin and were to be capable of carrying a hundred passengers to India with a single stop in Egypt, using diesel engines to reduce fire risks in the tropics.

For the R 100 Wallis again adopted a streamline form, this time adjusted to enable the ship to be handled in and out of the large shed provided for it at Cardington. Its structure, as in the R 80, followed in layout the best Zeppelin practice and was built mainly of duralumin. However, the great increase in size introduced new problems. The structure of a rigid airship consists primarily of longitudinal girders arranged around a number of transverse frames. The gasbags fit between these frames and the whole structure is covered by fabric supported by the longitudinals. Wallis had difficulties—as did the designers of the R 101—with all of these components and solved them in his own way.

To try to save weight, Wallis spaced his longitudinals more widely than ever before, and so had to use a stronger fabric covering and fit internal wiring to pull it taut to prevent flapping. This gave the R 100 a rather 'hungry horse' appearance and did not leave it entirely free from outer cover troubles. Moreover, for the booms of the widely spaced longitudinals Wallis found he needed four-inch diameter tubes, a size beyond available manufacturing equipment. He met this in characteristic fashion by inventing a new process for manufacturing large duralumin tubes from strip, a fine example of his skill as a mechanical engineer. The wire bracing of the ship's structure followed Zeppelin practice, but the wiring to contain the gasbags and transmit their lift to the frames was novel. For this he developed a system of intersecting helical wires to which he gave the name 'geodetics', an arrangement later to influence his aeroplane structures.

Meanwhile, development of suitable diesel engines for the R 100 and R 101 was proving difficult, and in view of their excessive weight Wallis pleaded to forgo diesel power (and hence the ability to travel safely to India) and revert to well-tried petrol engines. It was this that led to the successful demonstration flight of the R 100 across the Atlantic instead of to the east.

All this was not done without hard work and nervous stress. Burney, who had retained Temple as a personal assistant, sometimes sought to influence Wallis on technical matters; and while Wallis usually managed to reject such interventions, he did so only with great nervous strain. Migraine troubles and a strike by fitters brought matters to a head and in 1928, beset by insomnia, Wallis had a nervous breakdown and went away to Menton with his wife. When he returned, he had made up his mind to move to aeroplane design. He stayed at Howden to see the R 100 off on its first flight to Cardington, and then went to Weybridge to start a new life as chief designer (structures) alongside R. K. Pierson, chief designer at Vickers Aviation there. Pierson welcomed Wallis as a leader in duralumin construction and as a colleague with a common interest in long-range aircraft.

It was not long before Wallis began to experiment with a geodetic structure for a biplane fuselage. His intersecting spiral structure surrounded four main longerons both to brace them and to support the fabric covering. Following the success of this arrangement, Wallis applied the method to a monoplane wing by wrapping his geodetics around a single spar to form the basis of the wing profile. For long range, Pierson had planned for wings of unusually high span to chord ratio, which called for high wing stiffness in torsion to prevent flutter and related troubles. This stiffness Wallis achieved and the Wellesley bomber was born. At first the geodetics were made by hand, but the ingenuity of Wallis and the production team at Vickers soon mechanized the process. In 1938 a Wellesley flew to Australia to establish a record range of 7,158 miles non-stop, a triumph for both Pierson and Wallis. Nearly 180 of these bombers were built, a large number for pre-war aeroplanes.

With the approach of the war of 1939–45, larger bombers were called for, and Pierson and Wallis started upon the design of a twin-engine bomber with a shape and structure based on the Wellesley. The resulting bomber—the Wellington—came into production before the war started, and remained in service throughout. In all, nearly 12,000 Wellingtons were built. The Wellington proved popular with the RAF, particularly when it was found to fly well when its fabric covering or some of its geodetics had been damaged by gunfire. But its speed was high for a fabric-covered aeroplane and Wallis had often to deal with flapping and tearing troubles. Towards the end of the war a more fundamental trouble emerged. Most bombers had very short flying lives, but some Wellingtons survived an unusual 1,500 flying hours and began to develop fatigue cracks in the wing spar booms at their joints. It was a knowledge of this metal fatigue problem—the first of its kind in aeroplane structures—that led N. S. Norway, who had worked under Wallis on the R 100, to write, as Nevil Shute, his famous novel *No Highway* (1948).

The Wellington had its rivals among English bombers and was finally outclassed by the Lancaster, a metal-covered four-engine bomber designed by Roy Chadwick of Avro, Manchester. Wallis strangely failed to recognize the merits of metal covering which, unlike fabric, contributed substantially to the strength and stiffness of aeroplane structures; so he made further efforts to produce a new larger geodetic aeroplane. This never went into production and he came to accept, with the generous co-operation of Chadwick, variants of the Lancaster for the delivery of the great bombs to which he began to devote his energies.

By 1941 he had become convinced of the need to attack German industry at its roots—its sources of power—and persuaded Sir Henry T. Tizard, then scientific adviser to the Ministry of Aircraft Production, to support him in the development of a mode of attacking the great Möhne dam in the Ruhr. He first thought of using a large bomb which, if it could be delivered nearby, would set up shock waves in the ground at the base of the dam sufficient to crack it. However, experiments conducted with the help of (Sir) W. H. Glanville of the Road Research Laboratory quickly showed that, to be effective, impracticably large bombs would be needed unless they could be made to explode very close to the dam face. It was this impasse that led Wallis to think of a spherical bomb to be sent on a ricochet path over the water with a spin to ensure that when it struck the dam face it would roll down it and explode at a depth predetermined by a pressure fuse. As a result of many experiments in government research establishments and in Wales, he was able to convince Bomber Command of the feasibility of his scheme. The attack on the Möhne and Eder dams, using spinning bombs in cylindrical form, took place in May 1943, with complete success. Soon afterwards Wallis produced much bigger deep penetration bombs for dropping from high altitude on vital targets such as the launching sites for German flying bombs, and submarine pens. With the improved aiming methods by then available in the RAF, Wallis's great bombs were often dramatically successful; in the words of Sir Henry Tizard, he had made the 'finest individual technical achievement of the war'.

The war over, (Sir) George R. Edwards, who had been at Weybridge since 1935, had become interested with Pierson in metal-covered aeroplanes. Vickers Aviation was reorganized and while Edwards went on to design the successful Viscount civil aeroplane, Wallis was moved to head a special research department. Encouraged by Tizard, Wallis now sought to develop a new type of aeroplane, one with variable geometry wings and no tailplane, as the basis for a high-speed, high-altitude bomber. The scheme was beset with difficulties, many of which Wallis overcame, but changes in government and air staff views rendered his work abortive.

His mind turned to other fields. Waterloo bridge had just been replaced and a scheme for another road bridge over the Thames, near Charing Cross, was mooted. Wallis enjoyed advancing the idea of spanning the Thames there with a glorious single duralumin arch, incorporating an ingenious automatic control over its deflections. But collapse of the backing for the proposed bridge led to the scheme being abandoned.

Reverting to his early interest in marine engineering, he made, without success, a somewhat similar invasion into submarine design, advancing the idea of a large submarine as a cargo ship, less vulnerable to enemy action than surface ships.

Wallis's last major engineering activity was more successful. The astronomer royal, at the instance of Tizard, invited him to attend a committee considering the design of the new Isaac Newton telescope, for which a specially rigid frame was required. His suggestions proved too unconventional for the British astronomers, but caught the interest of those concerned in Australia with the design of a large radio telescope comparable with that at Jodrell Bank. The construction of the disc and the control of its movement interested Wallis, and he made valuable contributions in both respects to its final design by Freeman, Fox, & Partners. Wallis, thus active, did not finally retire from Vickers until 1971, when he was eighty-four.

At the end of the war of 1939–45 Wallis became an almoner at Christ's Hospital. Thus started a new association with his old school, for which he worked with devotion for the rest of his life. It led also to his establishment of a foundation for the education at the school of children of RAF personnel, an expression of his deepest loyalties. Later, when Wallis had become school treasurer, he led an appeal for funds that resulted in the collection of nearly £1,000,000.

Wallis had a deep spiritual approach to life that was manifested not only by formal religious observances but also by his generous help to others, typified by his foundation. He was intensely patriotic as well as very loyal to his school and to Vickers. Professionally, however, he was a severe master, demanding hard work and high standards from all under him. He was always willing to seek advice from specialists, but when his mind was made up he was intolerant of the ideas or criticisms of others. He could, nevertheless, be very persuasive and charming, characteristics that led many to support his work.

His achievements were honoured in 1943 by appointment as CBE, in 1945 by election as FRS, by honorary doctorates from six British universities (Bristol, Cambridge, Heriot-Watt, London, Loughborough, and Oxford), and by a knighthood in 1968. He was an honorary fellow of the Royal Aeronautical Society (1967) and became an RDI in 1943. He was awarded the James Alfred Ewing medal in 1945, the Albert gold medal in 1968, and the Royal medal in 1975. He was an honorary fellow of Churchill College, Cambridge, from 1965 and a freeman of the city of London.

In 1925 Wallis married Mary ('Molly') Frances (died 1986), his step-cousin, daughter of Arthur George Bloxam, managing director of the firm of Abel & Imray, patent agents, of Hampstead. They had two sons and two daughters, and also adopted Molly's sister's two sons (aged ten and eight), who were orphaned in 1940. Wallis died in Leatherhead Hospital 30 October 1979.

[J. E. Morpurgo, *Barnes Wallis, a Biography*, 1972; Sir Alfred Pugsley and N. E. Rowe in *Biographical Memoirs of Fellows of the Royal Society*, vol. xxvii, 1981; personal knowledge.]

A. G. PUGSLEY

published 1986

WALTON Sir William Turner

(1902–1983)

Composer, was born in Oldham, Lancashire, 29 March 1902, the second son in the family of three sons and one daughter of Charles Alexander Walton, the son of an Inland Revenue official, and his wife, Louisa Maria Turner, the daughter of an upholsterer. Both his parents were singing teachers, who instructed pupils at their home. Charles Walton, one of the first enrolments at the Royal Manchester College of Music, had sung oratorio and operatic roles there. As the organist and choirmaster of St John's, Werneth, he had an excellent choir, which included both William and his brother Noel.

In 1912, at the age of nine, Walton took a voice test for a probationer chorister at Christ Church Cathedral Choir School, Oxford, and, on being accepted, became a boarder at the school, remaining there for six years. Then, after being squeezed into Oxford University (Christ Church) at the age of sixteen, without much secondary education, he studied under (Sir) Hugh Allen, the professor of music, and on 11 June 1918 passed the first part of the Bachelor of Music examination, but failed responsions at three attempts. He passed the second part of the examination on 8 and 9 June 1920.

While an Oxford undergraduate, Walton completed the writing of a string quartet and a piano quartet. After being revised in the early 1920s, the first of these was performed at the festival of the International Society of Contemporary Music at Salzburg on 4 August 1923; the latter gained a publication award from the Carnegie Trust Fund in 1924. Among his boyhood compositions were three notable works: *Tell Me Where is Fancy Bred* (1916), a Choral Prelude on *Wheatley* for organ, and *A Litany*, a setting of a poem by Phineas Fletcher. Despite early influences acquired from the study of other composers, Walton's own characteristics soon showed in his music.

During this period he made enduring friendships with the poets Siegfried Sassoon and I. Roy Campbell, and the novelist Ronald Firbank. He also met (Sir) Sacheverell Sitwell, who, designating him a musical genius, brought his brother (Sir) Osbert Sitwell to Oxford in February 1919 to meet him and to hear him play his Piano Quartet. Osbert Sitwell was greatly impressed by the music, and as a result the young composer, after leaving Oxford, went to live with the Sitwells at Swan Walk, Chelsea, and at Osbert's house, 2 Carlyle Square, London, in effect becoming another member of the family.

His 'adoption' by the Sitwells, already achieving some literary fame, opened up exciting vistas of opportunity. Combining with Dr Thomas Strong, the dean of Christ Church, and with Lord Berners and Sassoon, in guaranteeing him an income of £250 a year, they enabled him to spend his life composing. By introducing him to famous writers, musicians, and painters, they helped to broaden his cultural and social outlook. In the spring of 1920 and on subsequent occasions, he visited Italy with his benefactors; an experience which undoubtedly influenced his music. If he was short of money, his generous friend Sassoon provided it. He even found some for the impoverished Baroness Imma Doernberg, with whom Walton had a romantic association. Born the Princess Imma of Erbach-Schönberg on 11 March 1901, she was the daughter of Alexander, Prince of Erbach-Schönberg. Fortune smiled on the composer in 1932 when Elizabeth Courtauld, wife of Samuel Courtauld the industrialist, died, bequeathing him a life annuity of £500.

Walton had gone to live with the Sitwells in 1919 and he remained with them until 1934, when, having started a romance with Alice, Viscountess Wimborne, he moved into her house. The younger daughter of the second Baron Ebury and a cousin of the Duke of Westminster, she married Ivor Guest, first Viscount Wimborne, heir to the Guest Steel fortune, in 1902. Walton's affair with Imma Doernberg seems, at some time in 1933, to have gone adrift. While staying with the Sitwells, he had composed several works, including *Façade, Portsmouth Point*, the *Sinfonia Concertante*, the Viola Concerto, the First Symphony, and *Belshazzar's Feast*.

Drawn to the world of film music by Dallas Bower, he was commissioned by the British and Dominion Film Corporation in 1934 to write a score for *Escape Me Never*, in which the young (Dame) Margot Fonteyn appeared. The fees for this and other commissions helped him to purchase his own house in Eaton Place, London. In 1935 he collaborated with (Sir) C. B. Cochran by writing a short ballet, *The First Shoot*, which formed part of *Follow the Sun* (1935), a spectacular review. After King George V died,

Walton was commissioned by the BBC to provide a Symphonic March for the coronation of King George VI in Westminster Abbey on 12 May 1937, and he wrote *Crown Imperial*, which was played for the entry of Queen Mary just before the ceremony began.

He was in America in the spring of 1939, completing the Violin Concerto commissioned by Jascha Heifetz, who gave him some useful technical advice. In the same year Paul Czinner's film *A Stolen Life*, for which Walton had composed music, had its première at the Plaza Theatre, London.

On 28 December 1940, during World War II, he finished work on his comedy-overture *Scapino*, and, about the same time, was attached to the films division of the Ministry of Information as a composer. Walton wrote several film scores for the MOI and these included *The Next of Kin* (1942), *The Foreman Went to France* (1941), *The First of the Few* (1942), and *Went the Day Well?* (1942). Released by the MOI in 1945, he completed his Second String Quartet; then, towards the end of the year, he accepted an invitation from six Scandinavian orchestras to tour Scandinavia, conducting his own music. Imma Doernberg died on 14 March 1947 and Lady Wimborne on 17 April 1948, the latter leaving him £10,000, Lowndes Cottage in Westminster, and various effects. Shortly after settling in a new home on the island of Ischia, off the coast of Italy, in 1949, Walton started work on his opera *Troilus and Cressida*, completing it in 1954. Following the death of King George VI in 1952, he composed a coronation march, *Orb and Sceptre*, and a *Te Deum*: these were performed at the Coronation of Queen Elizabeth II in Westminster Abbey on 2 June 1953.

In the years that followed, Walton wrote many fine works. They included such orchestral pieces as the film music for Laurence (later Lord) Olivier's *Richard III* (1956), the *Johannesburg Festival Overture*, the Cello Concerto, the *Partita* for Orchestra, and the Second Symphony. He composed a one-act opera, or extravaganza, *The Bear*, and among the choral and vocal pieces were *Anon in Love* (1960), *A Song for the Lord Mayor's Table* (1962), a Missa Brevis, and a Magnificat and Nunc Dimittis (1975).

Walton toured the United States in 1955 and appeared there for the first time as a conductor, leading a performance of his *Crown Imperial* at the United Nations. In 1963 he made a return visit, conducting an all-Walton concert at the Lewisohn Stadium, New York.

In January 1957, while travelling along a road near Rome, he was involved in a car crash, sustaining a cracked pelvis and other injuries. He made his first visit to Canada in February 1962 and shared a Canadian Broadcasting Corporation programme with the American composer Aaron Copland and Louis Applebaum from Canada; then in June the same year he was in Los Angeles for the American première of his *Gloria*. He went to Israel in 1963 and conducted three concerts of his own music there, one taking place in July, when the first performance of *Belshazzar's Feast* in Hebrew was given by the Tel Aviv Choir and the Israeli Philharmonic Orchestra in Tel Aviv, Haifa, and Jerusalem. In the first half of 1964 he toured New Zealand and Australia, again acting as an ambassador for, and conductor of, his own compositions. Commissioned by United Artists Ltd. to write music for a new film, *Battle of Britain*, he showed bitter anger when, after he completed the score in February 1969, it was rejected because there was not enough music to fill a long-playing record.

Walton visited Russia for the first time in 1971, accompanying André Previn and the London Symphony Orchestra, whose performance of his First Symphony before a Moscow audience was described by the *Financial Times* as 'a phenomenal success'. His seventieth birthday was celebrated in Britain by special concerts and tributes from press, radio, and television. Edward Heath, then prime minister, gave a concert for him at 10 Downing Street on 29 May 1972, with the Queen Mother heading the distinguished guests.

Walton's manifestations of ill health surfaced alarmingly in November 1976, when, after attending all the performances of *Troilus and Cressida* at the Royal Opera House, he returned to Ischia, showing definite signs of a stroke, and became a very sick man, unable to work. He made only a partial recovery, but, with characteristic gallantry, visited Britain in March 1977 and 1982, for the London concerts given to celebrate his seventy-fifth and eightieth birthdays. Back on Ischia, a semi-invalid in a wheelchair, with a restricted range of movement and energy, Walton continued to compose in a small way, but the end was near.

To look back over his life is to realize the lofty scale of his achievements. Like Sir Edward Elgar, he was largely self-taught as a composer, but, like Elgar, he became a supreme professional. For many people, *Façade*, skittish, catchy, and beautiful by turns, marked him as the brilliant English counterpart of the Parisian playboys of the 1920s, and although this work, which uses strange, capricious poems by (Dame) Edith Sitwell, was booed and hissed at its première, it was soon recognized as a concept of rarest originality. The public waited for Walton to repeat the phenomenon. He never did. Between the first performance of *Façade* in 1923 and that of the *Sinfonia Concertante* in 1928 he averaged only one small piece a year, the most impressive of which was *Portsmouth Point* (1926).

The poet in Walton came into his own with the Viola Concerto (1929), when he could with complete conviction write what the critics and music lovers of the day seemed to want. This composition, closely modelled on Elgar's Cello Concerto, has maintained its pre-eminence, like the Violin Concerto (1939), a miracle of delicate, haunting lyricism and elegiac feeling. Between Walton's two concertos came *Belshazzar's Feast* (1931), whose high-flying drama and savage ferocity, offset by passages of songful serenity, broke the bonds of conventional oratorio.

Most of the great masters of the previous generation had avoided the symphony, arguing that it had no relevance to the musical situation of the day, but there was in the early 1930s a definite movement backwards towards this large-scale form. Walton felt sure that he could speak eloquently through the symphony, but his confidence had been shaken by the rather cool response to *Belshazzar's Feast* shown at the 1933 ISCM Festival. Despite doubts and difficulties, his First Symphony proved to be a masterpiece. He was, for a time, unable to find a satisfactory solution to the problem of writing the final movement, and on 3 December 1934 he allowed the symphony to have a première in its unfinished state. Almost a year elapsed before he completed the last movement, and not until 6 November 1935, in London, did the public hear the full score. The tragic nature of the work, with a scherzo marked 'Presto con malizia', reveals the influence of Sibelius.

Walton wrote music for fourteen films, of which *Dreaming Lips* (1937) is not usually included in his list of credits. The score for *Henry V* (1944) is magnificent. He drew a fine line between true 'background' music and those elements of musical pastiche that were needed to evoke the atmosphere of a particular historical period. The most thrilling facet is the Agincourt battle sequence, where the sound effects of horses' hooves, rattling harness, and clinking armour, make the charge of the French knights fearsomely real. Outstanding among the film scores which he wrote for the Ministry of Information during World War II is *The First of the Few* (1942), from which the 'Spitfire Prelude and Fugue' was later published as a separate concert piece.

The comedy-overture *Scapino* (1941), a brittle portrayal of a rascally character of the *commedia dell'arte*, contains the best of all the exhilarating tunes he ever wrote. Both this work and *Portsmouth Point* are superior to the *Johannesburg Festival Overture* (1956). One of his most glorious achievements at this time was the massive and picturesque score which he created for the BBC's radio drama *Christopher Columbus*, used in a transatlantic broadcast on 12 October 1942, the 450th anniversary of the great explorer's first voyage to America.

Walton's String Quartet in A minor (1947) has an air of easy composure, despite the rhythmic vitality of the scherzo and the finale, while the slow movement has a gentle inwardness that emphasizes the Ravelian aspect of much of his art. Like the First Symphony, it was not ready for the publicized première. It seems that, at different stages of his life, unease and doubt over the direction he was taking interrupted his flow of inventiveness.

Uncertainty and discontent haunted him also while he was composing *Troilus and Cressida* (1954), and sometimes irascibility surfaced between him and his librettist, Christopher Hassall. He knew that there was a feeling of disillusionment about English opera, *Gloriana* by Benjamin (later Lord) Britten and *The Midsummer Marriage* by (Sir) Michael Tippett having been poorly received. *Troilus and Cressida*, a love story in the grand manner, with a Chaucerian text, struck some critics as being old-fashioned, but Walton's passionate score, full of gorgeous harmonies and luminous orchestration, inspired much praise after the initial reaction.

His second coronation march *Orb and Sceptre* (1953), enriched by music of coruscating brilliance, proved to be more complex than the previous one, *Crown Imperial* (1937), a work of simple, diatonic grandeur. The other new coronation piece he composed, the *Te Deum* (1953), covered a big expanse of sound and, in its noble utterance, outshone most of the remaining choral works that were sung on this great occasion. Walton's Cello Concerto (1957) also captivated the listener, revealing a warm, Italianate glow and a really fresh invention.

In complete contrast to its mighty predecessor, his Second Symphony (1960) showed him in a more subdued, reflective vein: gone were the truculence, the spiky rhythms, and the restless unease of former years. Because of this, some people complained that he had taken a wrong turning, that he had failed to 'advance' in his style. But after the Cleveland (Ohio) Orchestra, under George Szell, made their splendid recording of the symphony, it was recognized as a feat of orchestral virtuosity which few, if any, British composers could match. The music not only represented a natural development from the preceding period, but introduced entirely fresh ideas that were treated in a quite different way.

Walton's second opera, *The Bear* (1967), has a witty libretto with rhyming lyrics by Paul Dehn based on a short play of the same title by Chekhov, and is a comedy of manners, not of plot. His pungent, high-spirited score never holds up the pace of the merry making, and there is fun for the listener in identifying in the music certain droll parodies of contemporary composers.

He used a spare melodic style of scoring in *Improvisations on an Impromptu of Benjamin Britten* (1970), just one of a stream of finely crafted works too numerous to catalogue fully here. They include the dreamy, skittish miniature *Siesta* (1926), piano pieces *Duets for Children* (1940), a Spenserian ballet *The Quest* (1943), the exquisite setting of the poem by John Masefield *Where Does the Uttered Music Go?* (1946), the *Partita* for Orchestra (1958), the *Gloria* (1961), and the elegant, poetic *Variations on a*

Theme of Hindemith (1963). Walton was always a slow, painstaking perfectionist, who revised a number of his scores after publication.

At a time when a reaction against nineteenth century romantic music had set in, he had to work extremely hard to find a personal idiom and he did, in fact, create a tone and a rhythm that were unmistakably his own. His pre-1939 compositions were very popular in the concert halls of Europe and America: so that, in winning a reputation abroad, he also acted as an ambassador for his own country. Walton introduced no pioneering techniques into his music, but he demonstrated, most eloquently, that to scale lofty heights a man of genius looks, not necessarily for new forms, but simply for the best means to express his own ideas.

As he grew older, during the post-1945 phase of his career, the inventive quality in his music declined, but he became more prolific, with a greater variety of expression. One example is the *Capriccio Burlesco* (1968), with its sly musical gesticulations and saucy ideas. Walton could not possibly have written this in his so-called *enfant terrible* days.

In the matter of gramophone recordings, Walton conducting Walton became a revelatory, as well as definitive, experience. Sir Eugene Goossens, renowned for his brilliance in handling contemporary scores, taught the young composer a technique for mastering the swift nervous changes of rhythm in his own music. Most of Walton's recordings, especially those made for Columbia in the 1950s, are bright, unpretentious, and vibrant with life.

Despite occasional flashes of anger and hostility, there were many appealing facets to his character. He had an endearing habit of self-denigration and once described *Belshazzar's Feast* as 'a beastly noise'. There was no pomposity in his make-up. He loved to tease his friends. A very private person, he often retreated into a haven of brooding silence when questioned about his music or his views. Walton had a curious way of smoking his pipe, balancing it precariously on his lower lip in the centre of his mouth.

He was knighted in 1951, given the freedom of the borough of Oldham in 1961, and admitted to the Order of Merit in 1967. He held honorary doctorates from the universities of Durham (D.Mus. 1937), Oxford (Mus.D. 1942), Dublin (D.Mus. 1948), Manchester (D.Mus. 1952), Cambridge (D.Mus. 1955), London (D.Mus. 1955), and Sussex (D.Litt. 1968). He had a number of honorary fellowships, including those at the Royal College of Music (1937), the Royal Academy of Music (1938), and the Royal Manchester College of Music (1972). Appointed an honorary member of the Royal Swedish Academy of Music (1945) and an Accademico Onorario di Santa Cecilia (Rome) (1962), he was awarded the Benjamin Franklin medal (1972), the gold medal of the Royal Philharmonic Society (1947), and the medal of the Worshipful Company of Musicians (1947).

In 1948 he married Susana Valeria Rose Gil Passo, daughter of Enrique Gil, a prosperous Buenos Aires lawyer. After their marriage the couple settled on the island of Ischia, where 'La Mortella', a beautiful villa with an exotic garden, was built specially for them. Walton died there 8 March 1983. He had no children.

[Neil Tierney, *William Walton: His Life and Music*, 1984; Susana Walton, *William Walton*, 1988; Michael Kennedy, *Portrait of Walton*, 1989; information from Lady Walton and Dr Stewart R. Craggs; private letters and documents.]

NEIL TIERNEY

published 1990

WAUGH Evelyn Arthur St John

(1903–1966)

Novelist, was born in Hampstead 28 October 1903, the younger son of Arthur Waugh, publisher and author, and his wife, Catherine Charlotte, daughter of Henry Charles Biddulph Colton Raban, of the Bengal Civil Service. The family originally came from the Scottish Lowlands, and Waugh's mother's family also came from Scotland, for she was directly descended from Henry, Lord Cockburn. Arthur Waugh, in the previous year to Evelyn's birth, had become managing director of Chapman and Hall, once famous as the publishers of Charles Dickens, although by the end of the century the firm had very much contracted, and Arthur Waugh did not have a particularly easy or lucrative life. Himself educated at Sherborne he had sent his elder son there. But the storm created by Alec (Alexander Raban) Waugh's novel based on his school days, *The Loom of Youth* (1917), made it necessary to find another school for Evelyn who was five years younger.

He was sent to the high Anglican public school, Lancing, after some happy years as a day boy at a preparatory school in Hampstead. At first he was unhappy, at a time when the privations of the war years were at their most severe, and when it was the general condition of new boys to be given a bad time at public schools. But he developed his artistic interests, in painting, drawing, and calligraphy, and became editor of the school magazine. He crowned his Lancing career by winning a history scholarship to Hertford College, Oxford, in December 1921. He chose Hertford in preference to his father's old college, New College, out of consideration for his father's strained purse, because the scholarship at Hertford was of greater value. He went up immediately in January 1922, and took happily to Oxford life. At first he was overshadowed by his brother's name, but he soon made many friends in many colleges, and lived a high-spirited life in which social and somewhat rowdy drinking played a larger part than academic study. He developed a lasting antipathy for his history tutor, C. R. M. F. Cruttwell, dean, and later head, of the college, who wrote him a severe letter when he obtained a bad third in 1924. Waugh subsequently used the name Cruttwell for derogatory characters in his fiction. Conversely, the origins of many of his characters were to be found in real people.

The next three years, the unhappiest of his life, saw Waugh in a succession of posts as an assistant master, first at a school in Denbighshire, caricatured in *Decline and Fall* (1928), then at Aston Clinton in Buckinghamshire, and finally for half a term at a day school in Notting Hill Gate. In his autobiography, *A Little Learning* (1964), he ends what was intended to be only the first volume with an account of a rather half-hearted attempt to drown himself towards the end of his time at the school in Wales. Leaving a Greek inscription on his clothes, he swam out to sea, only to find himself in a shoal of jellyfish which caused him to turn back and decide to live. As a schoolmaster he was easy-going and not unpopular with the boys, but had the candour to recognize that he was very unsatisfactory from the headmaster's point of view. He managed to pursue an active social life; he had made particularly close friends with the Plunket-Greene family and fell deeply in love with the daughter, Olivia, a devout Catholic. She did not reciprocate, but his close friendship with the family had a great influence on him.

While still a schoolmaster Waugh wrote an essay on the *Pre-Raphaelite Brotherhood* which was printed privately in 1926. It came to the notice of the publishing house of Duckworth who suggested that Waugh should write for them a book on Rossetti. By April 1927 Waugh and the teaching profession had had enough of one another. In the autumn of the year he decided to study carpentry seriously with a view to becoming a maker of fine furniture, and he always said that this work gave him greater pleasure than writing ever did. In December Waugh became engaged to Evelyn Florence Margaret Winifred Gardner, daughter of the late Lord Burghclere, whose widow (daughter of the fourth Earl of Carnarvon) was strongly against her daughter engaging herself to a young man with neither income nor occupation. His book on Rossetti was published in 1928 and received some good reviews, but did not solve any problems. It was made very clear to Waugh that if he wanted to marry he must earn some money, and this was the genesis of *Decline and Fall*. When Duckworths jibbed and wanted more alterations than the author would agree to, its publication was undertaken by Chapman and Hall in the absence of his father who might have hesitated to publish his son's work. The book was an immense success, enthusiastically praised, notably by Arnold Bennett who enjoyed a unique position as a critic of fiction, and Waugh's financial troubles were ended.

In the meantime Waugh had married Evelyn Gardner in June 1928 without the knowledge of her mother. The success of his first novel was soon soured by domestic trouble. While Waugh was writing his next novel, *Vile Bodies* (1930), which proved that he was not a man of one book, but a writer with a rich and developing talent, his young wife was unfaithful to him, and in 1930 he obtained a divorce. When in that year Waugh was received into the Roman Catholic Church by Father Martin D'Arcy at Farm Street, he was quite prepared to face the prospect that he could not, by the law of the Church, contract another marriage while his wife lived. It did not immediately dawn upon him that he had a very good case for arguing that the necessary intention of indissolubility on the part of both parties had not been present. His petition for an annulment made in 1933 was not granted until 1936, and it was not until 1937 that he made a second and enduring marriage to Laura Laetitia Gwendolen Evelyn (died 1973), a first cousin of his first wife, and youngest of the three daughters of the late Aubrey Nigel Henry Molyneux Herbert, half-brother of the fifth Earl of Carnarvon.

By that time Waugh had consolidated his position as a writer, and had produced what many critics regard as his finest achievement, in which, as he expressed it, he said all he had to say about a society without religion, a work of masterly construction, full of intensely comical situations which nevertheless illustrate a deeply serious theme. This was *A Handful of Dust* which came out in 1934. It was preceded by *Black Mischief* (1932), a high-spirited story made possible by a visit which the author made to Abyssinia in 1930 for the coronation of the Emperor Haile Selassie which he reported for the *Graphic* and as a special correspondent for *The Times*. He went on from Ethiopia to Aden, Zanzibar, Kenya, the Belgian Congo, and Cape Town, recording his travels in *Remote People* (1931). As a war correspondent for the *Daily Mail* he witnessed Mussolini's invasion of Abyssinia in 1935 and returned there in 1936 to complete his account *Waugh in Abyssinia* (1936). These visits gave him material for a second novel with an Abyssinian setting, *Scoop* (1938). Meantime a visit to South America in 1932–3 resulted in another travel book *Ninety-Two Days* (1934).

When war broke out in 1939 Waugh was thoroughly established in the forefront of the younger novelists, with some entertaining travel books to his credit as well. Moreover he had written a biography of Edmund Campion (1935) which had won him the Hawthornden prize. All his profits from this he made over to Campion Hall, Oxford. He had a country house at Stinchcombe in Gloucestershire near the Severn, and a young wife and the beginning of what was to be a family of three sons and three daughters. But being of military age and aware of the dangers of a civilian job to his inventive talent, he immediately began seeking a commission. It was with great difficulty that he secured one in the Royal Marines; he was seconded for service in the Commandos in November 1940, officially transferring to the Royal Horse Guards in 1942. In 1941 he went to the Middle East and served as personal assistant to (Sir) Robert Laycock throughout the battle for Crete. By the end of the year he was back in England and he did not go overseas again until 1944. He was always a problem to his superiors who found his scepticism disruptive and he was never popular with the men under his command. These defects outweighed his marked physical courage and in March 1943 Laycock told him that he was 'so unpopular as to be unemployable'. It was Laycock, nevertheless, who had proposed him for membership of White's where Waugh had many friends.

In the early months of 1944 he was on leave and writing the novel which was to be very much the most successful of all his books in the United States, *Brideshead Revisited* (1945). Before that major undertaking, he had written, with a fluency and speed quite exceptional with him, *Put Out More Flags* (1942), in which in his best comic vein he developed the character of Basil Seal, whom his readers knew well from *Black Mischief*, who was now shown taking full advantage of all the opportunities which the early stages of the war provided for the advancement of his own fortunes. *Brideshead* was altogether more serious, shot through with a religious theme. It divided the critics, many of whom attributed its exceptional appeal to the American public to its detailed depiction of English aristocratic life.

But Waugh's military career was not yet ended. The prime minister's son, Randolph Churchill, was with Brigadier (Sir) Fitzroy Maclean's mission to Tito's Communist partisans in Yugoslavia, and he asked for Waugh for the sake of his company. In July 1944 Waugh joined the mission. Flying from Bari to Topusko the plane in which Churchill and Waugh were travelling caught fire on landing and as a result of their injuries it was not until September that they finally reached partisan headquarters. At close quarters, and with little to occupy him for most of the time, there was plenty of acrimony, sharpened by Waugh's dislike of the whole idea of co-operating to ensure that post-war Yugoslavia would be ruled by the Communists, thus placing the Catholic Croats and Slovenes under intolerant atheist masters. He took considerable risks of being court-martialled by reporting to the Vatican, and by the efforts he made to draw attention to what was happening, reporting on the religious situation to the Foreign Office and instigating questions in Parliament.

After the war ended, Waugh's talent lay fallow, although a short visit to Spain in 1946 with Douglas Woodruff resulted in a light-hearted satire, *Scott-King's Modern Europe* (1947), whose humour was applicable to many other government-sponsored commemorations beside that which was the purpose of this Spanish visit, the fourth centenary of the birth of the Dominican Francisco de Vittoria, who, his fellow countrymen maintained, was the real founder of international law and deserved the credit which the Protestant world had generally accorded to Grotius a generation later.

In 1947 Waugh visited Hollywood to discuss the proposed film of *Brideshead Revisited*. No film was ever made because he refused to alter the story as the producers wished, largely that they might satisfy the standards set by the very powerful Catholic Legion of Decency. But the visit was not barren. With time on his hands he became fascinated with Californian burial practices, and the result was *The Loved One* (1948) which, for all its macabre setting, was a highly successful light novel based on Forest Lawn. He made several further visits to America, went to Goa in 1952 for the four-hundredth anniversary of the death of St Francis Xavier, to Ceylon in 1954, and to Jamaica in 1955.

Meantime in 1950 appeared what was in some ways Waugh's most ambitious work, his only venture into historical fiction, a novel about Saint Helena, the mother of Constantine the Great. He took great pains with this, and the book contains some of his best writing. He used to maintain that it should be read three times because more would be found in it each time.

After a long gestation Waugh's varied war-time experiences came out as a trilogy: in 1952 the first volume, *Men at Arms*, based on his experiences as a Royal Marine, and awarded the James Tait Black memorial prize; in 1955 the second, *Officers and Gentlemen*, drawn from his period with the Commandos and at the Allied reverse in Crete. Then, in 1961 came the final volume, *Unconditional Surrender*, with his experiences in Yugoslavia, the title reflecting the bitter irony that the adventure on which his hero, Guy Crouchback, had set out as on a crusade after kneeling at a crusader's tomb, had ended supporting atheistic Communism. It was only when the trilogy was issued in one volume under the general title of *Sword of Honour* (1962) that its structural unity and irony stood out in their full strength.

The fifties also saw a slight novel called *Love Among the Ruins* (1953); and in 1957 *The Ordeal of Gilbert Pinfold*, remarkable for the self-portrait of the author with which it begins, and for being based on severe hallucinations which had come upon him as a result of taking remedies for insomnia in too large quantities.

Waugh had found the restrictions of postwar Britain irksome and at one time had seriously contemplated moving to Ireland. It was characteristic of him that at a time when most people, if they moved, chose smaller houses, when he finally made his choice in 1956 it was to a house considerably larger and grander than Piers Court. This was Combe Florey House, six miles from Taunton, on high ground, with an imposing gate-house, and large rooms which he decorated in a flamboyant, Victorian manner. He had acquired a large collection of Victorian narrative paintings which could be bought, in the thirties and forties, for a few pounds, and subsequently greatly increased in value. With the proceeds of two lawsuits he arranged with the manufacturers at Wilton for a replica of one of the more startling prizewinning carpets of the Great Exhibition of 1851. Combe Florey was to be his home for the rest of his life, and was a source of great satisfaction to him. He travelled less abroad, but made one further visit with his daughter Margaret in 1961–2 to South America. When he published all that he wished to preserve of his travel books of the thirties it was under the general title *When the Going was Good* (1946).

Before he was sixty Waugh began to feel that he was growing old, and he rather enjoyed exaggerating the degree of deafness which was afflicting him, using his hearing-aid, generally a large, old-fashioned trumpet, in an aggressive manner, putting it down ostentatiously before an unwelcome speaker.

In 1957 Waugh's friend Monsignor Ronald Knox died after a long illness in which Waugh had shown great solicitude. He was Knox's executor and biographer and he immediately set about filling both offices with great thoroughness, even going out to consult Lady Acton in Rhodesia. The biography of Knox appeared in 1959 and was followed by *A Tourist in Africa* (1960), the result of a second visit to Rhodesia, and finally by the first volume of his autobiography. He never succeeded in completing the second volume. His writing life may be said to have ended before he was sixty, although he lived to be sixty-two. His last years were saddened by the course taken by the Second Vatican Council whose changes in the liturgy he hated. He dreaded the prospect of old age with diminishing faculties in an increasingly uncongenial world, but he was spared the ordeal. He died very suddenly on Easter Sunday 10 April 1966, after hearing Mass in the old rite. He was buried in the churchyard adjoining his home at Combe Florey where he had died.

Evelyn Waugh was of less than average height. As a very young man his friend (Sir) Harold Acton described him as faun-like with his reddish hair and light, quick movements; but in middle life he became inclined to portliness, with a reddish face and eyes which seemed to become more protuberant as he glared at the world. His exceptional intelligence brought with it the penalty that he was very easily bored, seeing to the end of situations and conversations before they began, and time hung heavily on his hands. Although he disciplined himself effectively, retiring to Chagford to write his novels, he had few hobbies beyond the collection of Victoriana, did not care for music, and took little interest in public events. But he was continually improvising variants in everyday life, himself writing reports to his children's schools at the end of the holidays as a riposte to the school report, inscribing on his gates 'No admittance on business', and engaging in practical jokes, or behaving quite unpredictably and often very rudely, in an attempt to make everyday life more interesting and amusing. This caused him to be very much discussed by his contemporaries, and gave him some slight relief from his habitual ennui and tendency towards self-hatred. He also did many secret acts of charity and generosity, and when reproached for uncharitableness always replied that without his religion he knew he would be so very much more unpleasant. He told Christopher Sykes that he looked with horror upon Dylan Thomas who in looks, dress, and conversation was in many ways a parody of Waugh: 'He's exactly what I would have been if I had not become a Catholic.' He carried on a large correspondence without employing a secretary, writing everything by hand, and he was as much addicted as Gladstone to the use of postcards which encouraged the economy of language in which he excelled. This was one of the few practical economies in his style of living.

A portrait of Waugh as a young man by Henry Lamb became the possession of Lady Pansy Lamb. A portrait bust by Paravicini is in the possession of the family. Waugh's manuscripts and letters were acquired by the university of Texas where a room has been set apart for them.

[Evelyn Waugh, *A Little Learning*, 1964, *Diaries*, ed. Michael Davie, 1976, and *Letters*, ed. Mark Amory, 1980; Alec Waugh, *My Brother Evelyn and Other Profiles*, 1967; Frances Donaldson, *Portrait of a Country Neighbour*, 1967; *Evelyn Waugh and his World*, ed. D. Pryce-Jones, 1973; Christopher Sykes, *Evelyn Waugh*, 1975; personal knowledge.]

DOUGLAS WOODRUFF

published 1981

WAVELL Archibald Percival

(1883–1950)

First Earl Wavell

Field-marshal, was born 5 May 1883 at Colchester, the only son and second of the three children of Major, afterwards Major-General, Archibald Graham Wavell by his wife, Lillie, daughter of Richard N. Percival, of Springfields, Bradwall, Cheshire. Although the family had for some generations been soldiers (A. J. B. Wavell was his cousin), it derived from a stock of which traces have been found for four or more centuries in and around the city of Winchester.

Wavell received his education at Winchester, where he was in College, and passed fourth into the Royal Military College, Sandhurst, in 1900. After a six-months' course he was gazetted to the Black Watch in time to see service in South Africa. In 1903 he went to India where his early childhood had been spent, and he took part in the Bazar Valley campaign of 1908. At his first attempt he headed the list of entrants to the Staff College and in 1911, on completing his course, he was sent for a year to the Russian Army. When war broke out in 1914, he was in the War Office, but managed to get overseas. At Ypres in June 1915 he had the misfortune to lose an eye, and was awarded the MC. In October 1916 he was sent as liaison officer to the army of the Grand Duke Nicholas, which was fighting in Turkey before Erzerum. In June 1917 he went as liaison officer to Palestine and in March 1918, as a brigadier-general, joined the staff of Sir Edmund (later Viscount) Allenby for whom he conceived a great admiration.

The next ten years were divided between the War Office and the staff. During this period Wavell, already well known within the army, became known outside it as an officer untrammelled by convention; and the general public came to associate him with a phrase he used in a lecture: that his ideal infantryman was a cross between a poacher, a gunman, and a cat-burglar. In 1930 he received command of the 6th brigade at Blackdown which had been chosen for experimental purposes; and five years later, after a short period on half-pay (which he spent in writing a report on the Middle East and in rewriting Field Service Regulations), he was appointed to the command of the 2nd division at Aldershot.

By this time his influence in the army had imperceptibly become considerable. He was recognized as an exceptional trainer of troops. Among the younger generals there was a feeling that the older ones had grown lethargic; public interest in the army was at a low ebb. Wavell's views were sought with respect by both old guard and new. Before he had completed his term with the 2nd division, he was appointed in July 1937 to command in Palestine and Trans-Jordan. Soon after his arrival Arab troubles, which had died down since the outbreak of 1936, broke out with fresh ferocity, and were at their height when he was brought home in April 1938 to take over the Southern Command, one of the two most important commands in the country. He had been there little more than a year when he was sent, at the end of July 1939, to form the new command of the Middle East.

When war broke out in September, the forces at his disposal were small; when Italy came into the war in June 1940 his command had been reinforced by Dominion and Indian troops, but was menaced by superior forces on several fronts. Bold patrolling by light covering troops in the Western Desert imposed upon Graziani's Italians a caution quite out of proportion to the relative strengths of the two armies. Wavell was able also to delay the Italian advances into the Sudan from Ethiopia; but upon the Somaliland front, where the defection of the French in Jibuti prejudiced the defence, the local commander was forced to give ground. During Wavell's temporary absence in London the decision was taken to evacuate the protectorate rather than lose its small but valuable garrison. The prime minister disapproved of this decision, Wavell defended it, and relations between (Sir) Winston Churchill and Wavell were never very happy thereafter. But Wavell's stock never sank either with his troops or with the public, and it rose with the authorities during and after his remarkable run of success in the winter of 1940–1. He had been keeping a careful eye on the gingerly advance of the Italians in the west, and he detected unsoundness in their dispositions. Containing the threat to the Sudan with an elaborate bluff, he switched the 4th Indian division from that front for use in the Western Desert, and caught the Italians napping at Sidi Barrani on 9 and 10 December. The 4th Indian division returned to the Sudan, while the remainder of the Western Desert army swept up Bardia and Tobruk. By mid-February, the whole of Cyrenaica was in British hands, with 130,000 prisoners, more than 800 field guns, and 400 tanks.

Meanwhile (Sir) Alan Gordon Cunningham's army from Kenya and (Sir) William Platt's in the Sudan were forcing the Italians from Ethiopia back into their remotest mountains; they capitulated in the north in May and in the south some weeks later. Elsewhere, however, the odds against Wavell had mounted. He had been urged to send help on a larger scale to Greece, which since the end of October 1940 had been fighting stoutly and successfully against greatly superior Italian forces in Epirus. Hitherto Britain had contributed only air support with ground defence, anti-aircraft, and medical units; but on 9 January 1941 he was told that the support of Greece must now take precedence of all operations in the Middle East. His first reaction was sharply adverse; but throughout January and February mounting pressure was brought to bear on him to reinforce the Greeks with fighting formations and units. After conversations with the Greeks, in which both the Cabinet and the chiefs of staff were represented by (Sir) Anthony Eden and Sir John Dill, and during which various stipulations which he made were accepted by the Greeks, Wavell agreed to intervention at a moment when the enthusiasm of the Cabinet and chiefs of staff was cooling.

In two respects he had been misled: the Greeks had accepted in the conversations that they would withdraw from their exposed positions to a line on the River Aliakmon more in keeping with the weakness of the joint armies; and Wavell's intelligence had assured him that the German ground forces in North Africa, whose arrival was known to be imminent, would not be able to take the field until mid-April at the earliest. But the Greeks did not shorten their line; and the Germans appeared in strength on the frontiers of Cyrenaica before the end of March. By that time a high proportion of Wavell's army, and much of the best of it, was irrevocably committed in Greece; by the middle of April, both Greece and Cyrenaica had been lost, Tobruk was invested, and vast quantities of fighting troops, military technicians, tanks, and material were in enemy hands.

Stout efforts were made to defend Crete, but it was invaded from the air on 20 May and lost after desperate fighting before the month ended. The Royal Navy and the Royal Air Force in the Middle East had both crippled themselves in these operations. New anxieties had developed; Rashid Ali in Iraq had thrown in his lot with the enemy, and Syria, occupied by Vichy forces, was harbouring Germans and seemed likely to follow the example of Iraq. Wavell was urged to undertake three almost simultaneous operations against Iraq, against Syria, and against Rommel in the desert. He protested that he had not the resources for all three, but was overruled. Although the operation against Iraq was successful by early June, a series of operations against Rommel proved a costly failure by 17 June; in Syria, however, the French asked for an armistice early in July. But at the beginning of the month Wavell had been superseded by Sir Claude Auchinleck, whose place he took as commander-in-chief in India.

At first India was by comparison almost a sinecure; but when, in December 1941, Japan came into the war, Wavell, whose reputation stood high in the United States, was nominated supreme commander of the ill-fated command of the South-West Pacific. The speed, preparedness, and overwhelming strength of the Japanese were in inverse ratio to those of the defence. Wavell was criticized for the loss of the British 18th division in Singapore, which was landed only two days before the capitulation; but he still enjoyed the confidence of his troops, and his resilience as a commander was exemplified by the fact that he gave orders for the eventual recapture of Burma to be studied by his planning staff before its evacuation was complete. Policy dictated that the German war should be won before the Japanese, and Wavell had to fight the Burma war with the minimum of help from home. He had little success, and in June 1943 he was appointed viceroy of India in succession to the Marquess of Linlithgow and in July was raised to the peerage as Viscount Wavell, of Cyrenaica and of Winchester. He had been promoted field-marshal in January of that year.

Wavell entered upon his last public service with his usual willingness to shoulder an unpopular task, although, as he wrote to a friend, 'I fear I have no talent for persuasion'. Hindus and Moslems were at loggerheads and had somehow to be reconciled before India might be granted self-government. Wavell's first act was administrative and characteristic. Bengal was in the grip of famine and the new viceroy relieved a critical situation by an immediate personal reconnaissance followed by extensive military aid. Thereafter he was immersed in politics. In the summer of 1945 he took the initiative by releasing the Congress leaders who had been in jail since the rebellion of 1942. He then set to work with limitless patience to seek some way of securing agreement on the future of India. When the first series of talks broke down in July 1945 he issued a public statement taking the blame on himself. His task was not made easier by the fact that after the general election of 1945 the Labour Government, although desiring to endow India with self-government, did not lay down a clear-cut policy. A delegation of three Cabinet ministers conferred with the viceroy and with the party leaders for months in Delhi during 1946, but the parties could not agree. Wavell urged the Government to make up its mind what it would do in the absence of Indian agreement. A definite statement of policy was not made until February 1947, when Wavell's replacement by Lord Mountbatten of Burma was simultaneously announced with some abruptness. Wavell was created an earl with the additional title of Viscount Keren, of Eritrea and Winchester, and returned to London untrammelled by heavy responsibility for the first time for ten years.

The last three years of his life were spent in London and in travel. He was able to indulge at leisure the taste in letters which had long been among his most precious relaxations. He became president of the Royal Society of Literature, and of the Kipling, Browning, Poetry, and Virgil societies; he had been chancellor of Aberdeen University since 1945. He was colonel of the Black Watch; and he steeped himself in regimental matters, visiting its allied regiments in Canada and South Africa. He received honorary degrees from the universities of Aberdeen, St Andrews, Cambridge, London, Oxford, and McGill. He was a commander of the Legion of Honour and received decorations from many countries including Greece, Ethiopia, Poland, Czechoslovakia, Holland, China, Russia, and the United States. He was appointed CMG (1919), CB (1935), KCB (1939), GCB (1941), and GCSI and GCIE in 1943, in which year he was sworn of the Privy Council.

In 1950 Wavell showed signs of illness, culminating in jaundice; in May he underwent a severe operation, from which he seemed to be recovering, when he relapsed and died in London 24 May. His body lay in the chapel of St John at the Tower, of which he had been constable since 1948; on 7 June it was carried up-river in a barge to Westminster, where a service was held; and he was buried that evening by the men of his regiment in the chantry close of his old school at Winchester.

In appearance Wavell was broad and thickset, sturdy and physically tough, with a deep ridge on either side of his mouth. His silences were proverbial, but among intimates he was the most congenial and jovial of company. He delighted in horses and horsemanship, in golf and shooting. He had a prodigious memory and would quote poetry with gusto and at length. His widely popular anthology, *Other Men's Flowers* (1944), consisted entirely of pieces which he had by heart, and showed how catholic was his taste. His *The Palestine Campaigns* (1928) and his biography of his former chief Allenby (produced during years of high pressure and published in two volumes, 1940 and 1943, and in one volume in 1946) were masterly and easy to read. He had delivered the Lees Knowles lectures at Cambridge on 'Generals and Generalship' in 1939; these were published in 1941. He also published essays and lectures on military subjects, which were collected during his lifetime under the title *The Good Soldier* (1948).

As a soldier, for all his misfortunes in the war of 1939–45, his reputation at its end stood as high as those of any of his contemporaries. In none of the eleven campaigns which he fought did he have preponderance in men or in weapons. He left the Middle East, he was relieved of command in Asia, before the arrival of the material and reinforcements with which his successors were to win their country's battles and their own renown. Yet at no time, in public or in private, in print or by the spoken word, did he ever complain or repine.

Wavell married in 1915 Eugénie Marie, daughter of Colonel John Owen Quirk, and had three daughters and one son, Archibald John Arthur (1916–53) who succeeded his father in his titles, which became extinct when he was killed in Kenya, 24 December 1953, in an attack on Mau-Mau terrorists.

A portrait of Wavell by Simon Elwes was in India.

[Lord Wavell, Dispatches from the Somaliland Protectorate, the Western Desert, the Middle East, and the Eastern Theatre based on India (Supplements to the *London Gazette*, 5, 13, 26 June, 3 July, and 18 September 1946); R. J. Collins, *Lord Wavell*, 1947; Winston S. Churchill, *The Second World War*, vols. iii–v, 1950–2; I. S. O. Playfair and others, (Official) *History of the Second World War. The Mediterranean and Middle East*, vols. i and ii, 1954–6; Sir John Kennedy, *The Business of War*, edited by Bernard Fergusson, 1957; V. P. Menon, *The Transfer of Power in India*, 1957; private information; personal knowledge.]

BERNARD FERGUSSON

published 1959

WILLIAMS Raymond Henry

(1921–1988)

Writer and teacher, was born 31 August 1921 in Pandy, near Abergavenny, the only child of Henry Joseph Williams, railway signalman, of Pandy, and his wife (Esther) Gwendolene, daughter of James Bird, farm bailiff. He was educated at King Henry VIII Grammar School in Abergavenny and then went, in 1939 on a state scholarship, to read English at Trinity College, Cambridge. In part i of the tripos (1941) he gained a second class (division II). He was called up in 1941, commissioned in 1942, and fought with No. 21 Anti-Tank Regiment in the Normandy campaign and on to the Kiel canal. He attained the rank of captain.

In October 1945 he returned to Cambridge and took first-class honours in part ii of the tripos in 1946. Although he briefly considered a research degree, Williams entered the world of adult education as a staff tutor of the Oxford University Extra-Mural Delegacy (1946–61). He was based in East Sussex. He had married, in 1942, Joyce ('Joy') Mary (died 1991), daughter of Charles Dalling, coal factor, of Barnstaple. They had met at Cambridge when the London School of Economics was evacuated there during the war. They had two sons and one daughter. Joy Williams was a central influence on her husband's life and work. Later she was concerned with direct research for his books but throughout she was intimately involved with the evolution of his ideas and the publication of his numerous books. It was a deep and formidable partnership.

Although never a pupil of F. R. Leavis, Williams was influenced by Leavis's emphasis on the life-enhancing properties of a close reading of literature. To this end he founded and edited, with Clifford Collins and Leavis's pupil Wolf Mankowitz, *The Critic* and *Politics and Letters* (which absorbed the former) in 1947–8. It was an uneasy marriage of socialist politics with cultural perspectives derived from Leavis. Despite severe disappointments with the wider social impact of any such approach, then and later, Williams consistently returned to the themes and principles of these early years. This firmness of purpose and integrity of behaviour, no less than an attractive diffidence and a generosity of spirit, were commented upon by all who met him throughout his lifetime. The public and private persona were all of a piece.

His first published books were on film and drama, notably *Drama from Ibsen to Eliot* (1952), and heralded a lifelong concern with the manner in which the form of literary works, no less than their content, was directly affected by the material changes wrought by social history. However, the key aspect of his work in the 1950s was his study of the connection between 'culture' and 'society', which was brought to its first conclusion in his path-breaking *Culture and Society* (1958). Its dissection of the meaning that British writers, and a wider society, had given to the word 'culture', since industrialization and under the pressures of democratic changes, had an immediate impact. It can be seen now as the main progenitor of the cultural studies which would flourish from the late 1960s. Williams followed it up with the important, though very different, volumes, *The Long Revolution* (1961), a provocative analysis of the interconnection between institutions, education, and ideas in Britain, and *The Country and the City* (1973), which used wide-ranging literary studies to dispute the notion of accepted boundaries between the rural and urban experience. All his critical writing challenged conventional boundaries of thought and their academic compartmentalization. The techniques of modern technology, advertising, and mass communications were, in a number of suggestive books, analysed as carefully as poems and novels had once been.

In 1961 he moved back to Cambridge as a lecturer in English and a fellow of Jesus College, and, from 1967 to 1974, reader in drama. He received a Cambridge Litt.D. in 1969 and was made the university's first professor of drama in 1974, retiring in 1983. Honours and appointments were many: membership of the Arts Council (1976–8), honorary doctorates from the universities of Wales (1980) and Kent (1984), and from the Open University (1975), and visiting professorships in Europe and the USA. He deeply affected a younger generation through weekly book reviews in the *Guardian* and revealed a keen interest in television, for which he wrote plays and presented documentary films, in a regular column in the *Listener*. His writing had made him a dominant figure, though slightly distanced in some respects, on the so-called 'new left'. In 1967 he largely edited the *May Day Manifesto* (a Pelican Special in 1968), a spirited but doomed attempt to redirect the merely pragmatic stance of the contemporary Labour party by reinvigorating the broader Labour movement with a sense of its socialist traditions and potential. Williams was active for a time in that party but more readily committed himself to wider left causes, such as the Campaign for Nuclear Disarmament. From the 1970s, as in his innovative interview/autobiography, *Politics and Letters* (1979), he called himself a 'Welsh European', a coupling as neat and as provocative as the phrases he used to signify his work, 'cultural materialism' and 'structure of feeling'. The whole corpus had established him, in his own lifetime, as a major socialist thinker. Steadfastly, *Towards 2000* (1983) rebutted nostalgia and defeatism.

He insisted that his fiction and better-known non-fiction writing should be seen as a unity. He had made his impressive début as a novelist with

Border Country (1960); the first of a Welsh trilogy, *Second Generation* (1964); and *The Fight for Manod* (1979), in which his own individual background and general forces external to it, were given shape. *The Volunteers* (1978) was a political thriller of the near future, and *Loyalties* (1985) an indictment of political thrill-seekers of the near past. Two volumes of an incomplete historical novel, about the people of his native Black Mountains from the Ice Age to the present, appeared posthumously in 1989 and 1991. Their startling ability to be both realistic and experimental in tone again broke the mould at the very end of a life that had been heroically dedicated to the proposition that 'culture is ordinary'.

His tall, rather upright figure and long, etched face were instantly recognizable at conferences where, without ever striving for effect, he never failed to hold an audience. He was often said to look 'like a countryman' rather than a don and certainly the pipe, the rather deliberate drawl which was not quite a burr, and an unpretentious manner of dress and bearing all added to the image. Williams died 26 January 1988 at his home in Saffron Walden.

[*Independent*, 28 January 1988; *Guardian*, 27 January 1988; Raymond Williams, *Politics and Letters*, 1979; private information; personal knowledge.]

DAI SMITH

published 1996

WINDSOR (Bessie) Wallis

(1896–1986)

Duchess of Windsor

Wife of the former King Edward VIII, was born 19 June 1896 in Blue Ridge Summit, Pennsylvania, the only child of Teackle Wallis Warfield, an unsuccessful businessman, and his wife, Alice Montague. The Warfields and Montagues were of distinguished Southern stock, but Wallis's parents were poor relations and her father died when she was only five months old. She spent her childhood in cheese-paring poverty, resentfully aware that her friends could afford nicer clothes and more lavish holidays. It seems reasonable to trace to this early deprivation the acquisitive streak which so strongly marked her character.

Though her jaw was too heavy for her to be counted beautiful, her fine violet-blue eyes and petite figure, quick wits, vitality, and capacity for total concentration on her interlocutor ensured that she had many admirers. When only nineteen she fell in love with a naval aviator, Lieutenant Earl

Winfield Spencer (died 1950), son of Earl Winfield Spencer, a member of the Chicago Stock Exchange, and married him on 8 November 1916. It proved a disastrous match. Spencer's promising career disintegrated as he took to drink and Wallis, whose tolerance of weakness was never conspicuous, became increasingly alienated. While they were in Washington in 1922 they decided to separate and when Spencer was given command of a gunboat in the Far East, she remained behind, enjoying a flamboyant liaison with an Argentine diplomat.

In 1924 she joined her husband in China, but the reunion was not a success and they divorced in December 1927. By then she had already won the affections of Ernest Aldrich Simpson, whose own marriage was breaking up, the businessman son of an English father (Ernest Simpson, shipbroker and head of the firm of Simpson, Spence, & Young) and an American mother. She joined him in London, where he was managing the office of his family shipping company, and they married on 2 July 1928. Most of their friends were in the American colony in London; among them Benjamin Thaw of the US embassy, his wife Consuelo, and her younger sister Thelma, Viscountess Furness. Lady Furness was at that time mistress of the prince of Wales, and it was in her house at Melton Mowbray that Mrs Simpson, on 10 January 1931, met the man who was to become her third husband—Edward Albert Christian George Andrew Patrick David, the eldest child of King George V. He was called David by his friends and family.

The precise nature of Mrs Simpson's appeal to the prince of Wales could only be understood by him; probably he hardly understood it himself. It is sufficient to say that by early 1934 the prince had become slavishly dependent on her and was to remain so until he died. The courtiers at first thought that this was just another of his recurrent infatuations, but throughout 1935 they became increasingly alarmed as her role became more prominent and impinged on the performance of his duties. It seems unlikely that Mrs Simpson seriously entertained the possibility that she might become queen; indeed, all the indications are that she enjoyed her role of *maîtresse en titre* and would have been satisfied to retain it. The prince, however, convinced himself that his happiness depended on securing Mrs Simpson as his wife. From his accession to the throne on 20 January 1936 his main preoccupation was to bring this about.

Edward VIII's reign was marked by swelling scandal as his relationship with Mrs Simpson became more widely known. The cruise which the couple undertook in the yacht *Nahlin* around the eastern Mediterranean in September 1936 attracted keen interest everywhere except in the British Isles, where the press maintained a discreet silence. It was, however, the

Simpsons' imminent divorce which convinced the prime minister, Stanley Baldwin (later first Earl Baldwin of Bewdley), that he was faced by a serious constitutional crisis. On 20 October he confronted Edward at the king's country house, Fort Belvedere, but it was only a month later that Edward VIII stated categorically that he intended to marry Mrs Simpson. Baldwin was convinced that this must lead to abdication; the king played with the idea of a morganatic marriage, a solution that would certainly have appealed to Mrs Simpson, but was determined to renounce the throne if that was the price he had to pay.

Once she realized that marriage to her would cost the king his throne, Mrs Simpson tried to change his resolve. Anticipating much hostile publicity when the story broke in the United Kingdom, she retreated first to Fort Belvedere, and then to the South of France. From there, in a series of distraught telephone calls, she tried to persuade Edward not to abdicate, even if this meant giving her up. She accomplished nothing; this was the only subject on which she was unable to dominate her future husband.

On 10 December 1936 Edward VIII abdicated, became duke of Windsor, and went into exile. There followed six months of separation while Mrs Simpson was waiting for her decree absolute (3 May 1937), before, on 3 June 1937, the couple were married at the Château de Candé in Touraine. No member of the royal family was present and the new duchess, on doubtful legal grounds, was denied the title of Her Royal Highness. The refusal of her husband's relations to accept her as part of the family caused embittered and undying resentment in the duchess.

Until the outbreak of war the Windsors lived mainly in Austria and France. The duchess accompanied her husband on his visit to Germany in 1937; it was popularly believed that she had fascist sympathies and it has even been claimed that she worked for German intelligence, but there is no evidence that she held any considered political views, still less indulged in such activities. When war broke out in 1939 she returned with the duke to Britain and then to France. When the Germans overran France in June 1940 the Windsors escaped into Spain and thence to Portugal. From there they left for the Bahamas, where the duke took up the post of governor in August 1940.

The duchess hated their five years in Nassau and made no secret of her views to those close to her, but on the whole she performed the duties of governor's lady conscientiously and well. She entertained stylishly and went through the rituals of opening bazaars and inspecting hospitals with unexpected grace. Her happiest weeks, however, were spent on shopping expeditions in the United States and she was much criticized for irresponsible extravagance at a time when Britain was under assault.

After the war the Windsors settled in France and their life became a dreary—though to her, presumably, satisfying—merry-go-round featuring principally Antibes, Paris, New York, and Palm Beach. The duchess entertained lavishly and was counted among the best dressed and fashionable figures in international society. Some of her friends were raffish, a few even vicious, but it was the sterility of her life that was most remarkable. Though her husband resumed a somewhat cool relationship with his mother and siblings, the duchess was never received by the royal family and remained fiercely hostile to them. In 1956 she published her memoirs, *The Heart Has Its Reasons*, an on the whole good-tempered and balanced book, which was largely ghosted but still reflected fairly her wit and considerable common sense. When the duke died on 28 May 1972 she was invited to Buckingham Palace, but it was too late for the reconciliation to mean much to her. The last fourteen years of her life were spent in increasing decrepitude; during the final five she lived in total seclusion. She died at her home near Paris 24 April 1986 and was buried beside her husband in the royal burial ground at Frogmore.

[Duchess of Windsor, *The Heart Has Its Reasons*, 1956; Michael Bloch, *Wallis and Edward: Letters 1931–1937*, 1986; Ralph G. Martin, *The Woman He Loved*, 1974; private information.]

PHILIP ZIEGLER

published 1996

WINGATE Orde Charles

(1903–1944)

Major-general, was born at Naini Tal, India, 26 February 1903, the third child and eldest son in a family of seven. Both the Bible and the sword were strongly in the family tradition, as also was service in Eastern lands. His grandfather, William Wingate, who came of a Scottish family long settled in Stirlingshire, had been for ten years a missionary to the Jews in Hungary. His father, Colonel George Wingate, who served for more than thirty years in the Indian Army, taking part in three frontier expeditions, had established the Central Asian Mission to the tribes on the North-West Frontier and in Baltistan. His mother, Mary Ethel Stanley, daughter of Captain Charles Orde Browne, Royal Horse Artillery, came of a Gloucestershire family, which had a tradition of military service but had produced also in the preceding generation a distinguished Persian scholar. Her ancestors included Granville Sharp, the philanthropist.

Both Orde Wingate's father and mother were Plymouth Brethren, and he was brought up in a strictly puritan household, which was shown by his deep knowledge and study of the Bible. He was a day boy at Charterhouse, near which his father had settled on retirement. He went on to the Royal Military Academy, Woolwich, and was gazetted to a commission in the Royal Artillery in August 1923. As a boy Wingate had shown proficiency in swimming, boxing, and rifle-shooting rather than in organized games. He was keenly interested in observation of wild birds and beasts, and was fond of music. On joining his battery he became an enthusiastic horseman, riding boldly and well to hounds, and competing with success in point-to-point races and show-jumping. In 1926 he qualified as an instructor in equitation at the army school at Weedon, an exacting test of horsemanship. But he kept his brain active as well as his body, and with the encouragement of his father's cousin, General Sir Reginald Wingate, he began to learn Arabic at the School of Oriental Studies in London. In the autumn of 1927 he went to the Sudan to continue his study of that language. His method of reaching the Sudan was typical. He had practically no means except his pay. He had financed his hunting by his success at races and horse-shows. He now bought a pedal bicycle, rode it to Brindisi, where he sold it and with the proceeds took passage in an Italian boat to Port Sudan. He obtained an appointment in the Sudan Defence Force, in which he spent five years (1928–33) serving mainly on the Abyssinian frontier.

Wingate next made an expedition in the Libyan desert in search of the legendary oasis of Zerzura. He spent five weeks in the desert from the beginning of February 1933 until early in March. Exploration of the desert by motor-car was just beginning at this period, but Wingate went on foot, with camels to carry his gear. His journey produced no results but gave him valuable experience.

During the voyage home Wingate met his future wife, Lorna Elizabeth Margaret, daughter of Walter Moncrieff Paterson, of Tilliefoure, Monymusk, Aberdeenshire, whom he married in January 1935. From 1933 to 1936 he served with artillery units in England. Towards the end of 1936 he applied for and obtained a post on the intelligence staff in Palestine, then in the throes of an Arab rebellion against Jewish immigration. Influenced by the family tradition, Wingate soon became sympathetic to the Jewish cause and he was impressed by the organization and efficiency of the Jewish settlements. He spent his spare time and leave in visiting these settlements and in learning Hebrew, and became a convinced Zionist. He and his wife became friends of the Jewish leader, Chaim Weizmann. The rebellion dragged on; and presently Wingate obtained permission to organize night squads, mainly of youths from the Jewish settlements, to combat Arab sabotage and terrorism. He showed that such work could be more efficiently carried out by local teams than by the orthodox procedure of regular soldiers. The work was exacting and dangerous but productive of results. Wingate's methods had great success and did much to bring the rebellion to an end. He was appointed to the DSO for his services and was wounded in a skirmish in July 1938. His pro-Jewish sympathies and his uncompromising way of expressing his opinions were not always acceptable to some of his superiors and led to controversy with them. Wingate was never an easy subordinate.

The outbreak of war in 1939 found Wingate serving as a brigade-major with an anti-aircraft unit. He was about to attend a course at the Camberley Staff College in 1940, when he was summoned to the Middle East. Sir Archibald (later Earl) Wavell, under whom he had served for some months in Palestine, had asked for him to organize assistance to the rebels in Abyssinia, as a means of embarrassing the Italians, who had now entered the war. Wingate arrived in Khartoum in the late autumn of 1940. He set to work with restless energy and driving power to collect troops, arms, and camels to make an entry into central Abyssinia. One of his first acts was to fly in at great risk to an improvised landing ground and to contact Colonel Daniel Arthur Sandford (a British officer with a long knowledge of Abyssinia who had gone in previously on foot) and some of the principal rebels. In January 1941 Wingate crossed the frontier with the exiled Emperor Haile Selassie, a small mixed force of Sudanese and Ethiopians, and a handful of British officers and NCOs. Less than four months later, on 5 May 1941, he entered Addis Ababa with the Emperor. By a combination of daring and bluff his small force of under 2,000 men had made its way through the rough mountains of western Abyssinia, capturing or putting to flight many Italian garrisons which greatly outnumbered the force. It was a remarkable achievement, the strain of which told on even Wingate's iron nerve and constitution; and he was in hospital in Cairo for some months.

On recovery, Wingate returned home but was soon recalled East again by Wavell, now commander-in-chief in India, to help in stemming the Japanese invasion of Burma. When Wingate arrived the retreat from Burma had been ordered. There was just time before the complete withdrawal for him to visit the front. He quickly grasped the lie of the country and the enemy's tactics and mentality. He put forward proposals for the formation and training of a 'long range penetration group' to operate behind the Japanese lines in the reconquest of Burma. His theory was based on two new factors in war: the power to supply forces for a long period by air, and the use of portable wireless sets to maintain touch between scattered columns. Wingate's ideas were accepted, and in June 1942 he was made a brigadier and given a mixed force of British, Gurkha, and Burmese (Karens, Kachins, and Chins) to organize and train. His preparations were complete by February 1943; and about the middle of that month his eight columns crossed the Chindwin river and struck against the Japanese rear. For some six weeks the force moved and fought behind the enemy front; and although in the end some of the columns had great difficulty in extricating themselves and returning to the base, Wingate's theories had fully justified themselves. He had received a bar to his DSO for his work in Abyssinia and was now given a second bar.

In August 1943 Wingate accompanied (Sir) Winston Churchill to Quebec where he explained his theories to the war leaders, including Roosevelt and Churchill, both of whom he greatly impressed. He was given a force equivalent to a division to train for the operations for the reconquest of Burma under Admiral Lord Louis Mountbatten (later Earl Mountbatten of Burma), and was promoted major-general. The training of the new force was carried out during the winter of 1943–4, and operations began early in March 1944. A new feature of the operations was that the greater part of the force was landed behind the enemy lines by glider and transport aircraft, only one brigade entering on foot. Three weeks after the original landings Wingate's forces commanded a wide area some 200 miles inside the enemy lines. On 24 March during a tropical storm Wingate was flying over the Naga jungles of north Assam in a bomber on a visit to one of his units. From some cause never ascertained the plane crashed into the jungle and all the occupants were killed. He was buried in the Arlington cemetery, United States.

Orde Wingate was cast in the same mould as Thomas Cochrane (Earl of Dundonald), Charles George ('Chinese') Gordon, T. E. Lawrence (with whom on his mother's side he could claim kinship), and others, who have had a genius for novel and unorthodox methods of warfare and the opportunity and energy to put them into practice. Such men are seldom very tractable subordinates, nor are they always easy to serve. Wingate's dynamic personality won acceptance for his ideas. At a time when Japanese tactics of infiltration had produced a feeling of helplessness in some quarters, he showed that similar tactics could be applied even more effectively and on a wider scale against the Japanese themselves. He was no haphazard marauder; his operations were always most carefully planned, his training thorough, and his administrative preparations as complete as possible. He had undoubtedly a high degree of military genius.

Apart from military affairs, Wingate had read widely and thought deeply on many subjects, on which he had very definite views. He could express himself clearly in speech or on paper. He had a strong personal faith in religion and a real belief in prayer.

Wingate had one son, born in 1944 after his father's death.

[*Geographical Journal*, vol. lxxxiii, 1934; private information; personal knowledge.]

WAVELL

published 1959

WODEHOUSE Sir Pelham Grenville

(1881–1975)

Writer, was born 15 October 1881 at 1 Vale Place, Epsom Road, Guildford, the third son of Henry Ernest Wodehouse, a magistrate in Hong Kong, and his wife, Eleanor, daughter of the Revd John Bathurst Deane. She was in England only for the birth of her child and quickly returned to Hong Kong taking him with her. Henry Ernest Wodehouse belonged to a collateral branch of the family of the Earls of Kimberley, being the son of the second son of Sir Armine Wodehouse (fifth baronet), whose descendants were created first Baron Wodehouse in 1797 and first Earl of Kimberley in 1866. His wife belonged to the equally ancient and extremely widespread family of Deane or Adeane.

When their eldest son was six the Wodehouse parents followed the custom of the time in sending him home to England to be educated. For reasons, which are not obvious and which have never been explained, they also sent his younger brothers with him (Pelham then aged two), taking a house in Bath and engaging a Miss Roper to look after them. This regime lasted for three years and then the boys were moved to a dame school in Croydon. Later they were sent to a small public school in Guernsey and finally Armine, the second son, and then Pelham (whose name had been shortened to 'Plum') went to Dulwich College. There were a large number of uncles and aunts on both sides of the family and they were sent to one or other of these in their holidays. Apart from a short period when he was fifteen, and when his parents returned to England and at first took a house near the school (later moving to Shropshire), Armine and Plum boarded at Dulwich.

Deprived so early, not merely of maternal love, but of home life and even a stable background, Wodehouse consoled himself from the youngest age in an imaginary world of his own. He said later in life that he never remembered the time when he did not intend to write and one small story, written when he was seven, remains to prove the skill with which he already handled language. When he went to Dulwich he achieved for the first time in his life some continuity and a stable and ordered life, and, because of the multiplicity of shared interests, he was able to communicate easily with his fellows without any great demands being made upon him. He repaid the happiness he felt there by a lifetime's devotion to the school which sometimes seemed almost obsessive. 'To me', he said in late life, 'the years between 1894 and 1900 were like heaven.'

He was in the school teams for cricket and rugby football and he had the good fortune to be at Dulwich with A. H. Gilkes, a distinguished headmaster and a renowned classicist, whose teaching must have been an important influence. His report for the year 1899 contained the following remarks: 'He has the most distorted ideas about wit and humour; he draws over his books and examination papers in the most distressing way and writes foolish rhymes in other people's books. Notwithstanding he has a genuine interest in literature and can often talk with enthusiasm and good sense about it.'

At first he worked for a scholarship at Oxford, but, when his brother, Armine, succeeded in this ambition (later winning the Newdigate prize), his father told him he could not afford to send them both. When he left school, he therefore went into the Hong Kong and Shanghai Bank. Here he was both unhappy and inefficient and he lived for the end of the day when, in 'horrible lodgings', he could spend his evenings writing. He left the Bank when (Sir) William Beach Thomas, lately a master at Dulwich, offered him a job (at first temporary but later becoming permanent) to write the 'By the Way' column on the *Globe* newspaper. From that time he supported himself by writing and his enormous output (written anonymously, under his own, other people's, and assumed names) included light verse, articles (some of which appeared in *Punch*), and short stories. Chiefly, however, this was the period of the school stories run as serials in the *Public School Magazine* or its rival, *The Captain*. In 1902 his first book, *The Pothunters*, was published by A. & C. Black and this was followed by six other volumes of school stories. *Mike* (1909), the last of these, was distinguished by the entrance of a character called Psmith, an event which Evelyn Waugh said marked the date exactly when Wodehouse was touched by the sacred flame: 'Psmith appears and the light was kindled which has burned with growing brilliance for half a century.'

In 1904 he went for the first time to America, the country which would become his second home, and after that he often travelled backwards and forwards across the Atlantic. He soon began to set some of his novels in the American scene and to use the dialect of the New York gangs. He was in America in 1914 and he stayed there for the duration of the war. He had exceedingly bad eyesight and, although he attempted to register when America came into the war, he was rejected. He could not have served England in any military capacity but, more by his attitudes than by any action, he showed, as he would in the second war, how slight were his hold on reality and his ability to respond to abstractions such as country or tragedy on an impersonal scale.

In 1914 he married Ethel Newton (died 1984), the young widow of Leonard Rowley, of Dee Bank, Cheshire. She had one daughter, Leonora, whom he adopted and to whom he became as devoted as if she had been his own. Leonora later married Peter Cazalet. The Wodehouses were to have no children of their own. From the start Ethel Wodehouse was the dominant partner and she managed all their affairs, leaving him free to write. He had by now begun the extremely successful partnership in musical comedies with Guy Bolton and Jerome Kern, which led to a career in the theatre which seemed at the time as important as his career as a novelist and even more lucrative.

After the war he returned to England, but, although he had a house in London for some years, he still spent much time in America. In 1930 he made the first of two visits to Hollywood, causing a national sensation in 1931 by explaining in an interview that, although he had been paid enormous sums to write films, he had never been asked to do any real work. Finally, in 1934 he and his wife settled in Le Touquet.

In 1939 the Wodehouses remained in Le Touquet, and, when the Germans captured northern France, the writer was interned in Upper Silesia. On being released in 1941, he made five broadcasts to America from Berlin, and, although these were the equivalent of comic articles in his personal vein, and were made with the motive of reassuring all those people who had written to him or sent parcels, this was not understood at the time, particularly as the British propaganda machine was put to work to present him as a man who had served the enemy in return for his release from internment. Although this was proved to be quite untrue, it was held that he might, nevertheless, have committed a technical offence by speaking in wartime on an enemy wavelength, no matter what the content of his speech, and for many years he could not be guaranteed immunity from prosecution if he entered the jurisdiction of his own country. He accordingly went to America and, after settling down there, became an American citizen in 1955.

Because he wrote under other names and often turned novels into plays or plays into novels, it is difficult to be sure of his total output. He published under his own name ninety-seven books (including twenty-one collections of short stories), he wrote the lyrics or some of the lyrics for twenty-eight musical plays, and wrote or collaborated in the writing of sixteen plays. He wrote the scenario for six films and much light verse and innumerable articles. His work was translated into all the major languages of the world and his sales, which ran into many millions, cannot be estimated.

It seems likely that he achieved a permanent place in English literature. He was unique in that, although he wrote primarily for the general public, he had an inspired humour, and a prose style of so much freshness, suppleness, simplicity, and exactitude that, from such early admirers as Asquith, Hilaire Belloc and M. R. James, he has been the delight of generation after generation of writers and intellectuals, his name standing ever higher.

His most famous books are the Jeeves and the Blandings Castle series, and he achieved the ambition of every novelist in that at least two of his characters, Jeeves and Bertie Wooster, and possibly two others, Lord Emsworth and Psmith, have entered what Belloc called 'that long gallery of living figures which make up the glory of English fiction'. He also wrote more amusingly on golf than anyone before or since, *The Clicking of Cuthbert* (1922) and *The Heart of a Goof* (1926) being his masterpieces in this field.

In 1939 the University of Oxford made him an honorary D.Litt. and in 1975 he was created KBE. He died in a Long Island Hospital 14 February 1975, at the age of ninety-three, one of the most admired and probably the most loved of all the writers of his time.

[P. G. Wodehouse, *Performing Flea*, 1953 (autobiography); Richard Usborne, *Wodehouse at Work to the End*, 1977; Benny Green, *P. G. Wodehouse*, 1981; Iain Sproat, *Wodehouse at War*, 1981; James H. Heineman and Donald R. Bensen (eds.), *P. G. Wodehouse, a Centenary Celebration*, 1982; Frances Donaldson, *P. G. Wodehouse*, 1982; David A. Jasen, *P. G. Wodehouse*, 1982; personal knowledge.]

FRANCES DONALDSON

published 1986

WOLFENDEN John Frederick

(1906–1985)

Baron Wolfenden

Schoolmaster and educationist, was born 26 June 1906 at Swindon, the elder son of George Wolfenden, a clerk in the Civil Service, and his wife, Emily Gaukroger, members of large Yorkshire families, who had temporarily emigrated south at the time of their elder son's birth. Two years later they had their second child, also a boy, who died at the age of five, leaving

Jack—as he was universally known—an only child. Educated at Wakefield Grammar School, which had been founded in Elizabethan days, in 1924 he won a scholarship to Queen's College, Oxford, where he fell in love with philosophy and the Greeks, passions which were to endure for the rest of his life, and where he also played hockey for the university. He obtained a second class in classical honour moderations (1926) and a first in *literae humaniores* (1928). After a year at Princeton in the USA, in 1929 he was made fellow and tutor in philosophy at Magdalen College, Oxford. While there he graduated from the university hockey XI to play in goal for England in 1930 and the two following years.

When he was only twenty-seven Wolfenden was made headmaster of Uppingham School in 1934 despite formidable competition from a number of other candidates for the job. He remained there for ten years before moving to Shrewsbury School in 1944, also as headmaster, and after six years there he was appointed vice-chancellor of Reading University in 1950, where he stayed for thirteen years. He proved himself to be a man of so many talents that he was widely in demand to serve on various academic committees, charitable trusts, and governmental bodies of one kind or another. For example, during the war he was director of pre-entry training at the Air Ministry, as well as being chairman of the Youth Advisory Council at the Ministry of Education. Thereafter he chaired the Headmasters' Conference (1945, 1946, 1948, 1949), the Secondary Schools Examinations Board Council (1951–7), the National Council of Social Service (1953–60), and a large number of other bodies for greater or lesser periods of time.

But by far the most celebrated body over which he presided, between 1954 and 1957, was the departmental committee on homosexual offences and prostitution, which eventually issued a report which came to be known as the Wolfenden report. At the time these two subjects were highly contentious, especially homosexuality which was proscribed by law and regarded with a mixture of disgust and unhesitating condemnation by many people. Wolfenden, a heterosexual, knew the risk of public obloquy he would run if he were to accept the home secretary's invitation to chair such a committee, and he knew too that some of the mud, which would probably be thrown at him as a result, might well land on members of his family. It was not until after he had consulted them that he accepted the home secretary's invitation. He chaired that celebrated committee with his accustomed tact, skill, and intellectual incisiveness, and eventually produced a document which was years ahead of its time; it displayed great integrity, honesty, and courage, which must have cost him a great deal, and which was typical of him. The report's recommendations led to the legalization of homosexual activity between consenting adults.

In 1963 he stepped down as vice-chancellor of Reading to become chairman of the University Grants Committee, a post he held for five years before being appointed director and principal librarian of the British Museum for four years before retiring in 1973 at the age of sixty-seven.

Wolfenden was far from idle in retirement. Apart from serving in various capacities in the House of Lords, he presided over a number of academic bodies and committees, the Classical Association, and the National Children's Bureau as well as more than one building society, and he was a regular lecturer on Hellenic cruises, in which capacity he became known to a large number of people for the depth and width of his scholarship and knowledge of the ancient world. However, it is probably true to say that few got to know him well as a man, for he was essentially a very private person, sensitive and vulnerable to criticism, shielding himself from prying eyes behind a screen of courtesy, erudition, wit, and civilized urbanity. Among the recreations he listed over the years in *Who's Who* were: innocent (1966), weeding (1978), waiting to cross the A25 on foot (1980), trying to come to terms with arthritis, bifocals, and dentures (1983), and trying to remember (1984).

He was appointed CBE in 1942, knighted in 1956, and made a life peer in 1974. He had honorary degrees from Reading (1963), Hull (1969), Wales (1971), Manchester (1972), York (1973), and Warwick (1977), as well as American honours.

In 1932 he married Eileen Le Messurier, the second daughter of his old headmaster at Wakefield, Alfred John Spilsbury. They had two daughters and two sons, one of whom died in 1965. Wolfenden died after a short illness in hospital at Guildford 18 January 1985.

[Lord Wolfenden, *Turning Points*, 1976 (memoirs); personal knowledge.]

Antony Bridge

published 1990

WOLFIT Sir Donald

(1902–1968)

Actor-manager, was born 20 April 1902 in New Balderton, near Newark, the fourth of the five children of William Pearce Woolfitt, brewer's clerk, and his wife, Emma Tomlinson. He was educated at Magnus School, Newark. From an early age he wanted passionately to be an actor; after a very short, frustrating burst of schoolmastering, which he disliked almost as much as being at school, in 1920 he managed to join Charles Doran's touring company. From his eighteenth year he had a complete grounding in the plays of Shakespeare and the touring theatre of the time, from the humblest role as assistant stage manager. It proved invaluable. He played walking-on parts and some of the smallest parts in the great plays. He left Doran to play the small part of Armand St Just in the autumn tour of *The Scarlet Pimpernel* with Fred Terry. He had cherished an ambition to appear with this management since he first attended a performance at Nottingham in his early teens, and after several unsuccessful interviews with Terry he achieved it in 1923. The Terrys represented the theatre of which he had dreamed; the splendour of the sets and costumes, the assurance and the style of the actors would be remembered and reproduced when Wolfit himself was to appear as Sir Percy.

Matheson Lang gave Wolfit his first chance to appear in London in *The Wandering Jew* in 1924; nearly thirty years later he recreated the leading part under his own management. After several more years out of London, he was engaged to play good parts at the Old Vic in 1929–30: Touchstone, Cassius, and the King in *Hamlet*. But the season was an unhappy one for him: he never succeeded in disguising his disapproval of actors he did not like personally and in this company he always felt he was on the outside. He was not asked to stay on for another season. In 1930–5 he appeared in plays in the West End and on tour, including for Sir Barry Jackson a tour of Canada in 1931–2, nearly always in good parts in a great variety of plays, among them *She Stoops to Conquer, The Barretts of Wimpole Street*, and new plays. His longest run, over fourteen months, was in the highly successful *Richard of Bordeaux* in which he played Thomas Mowbray to (Sir) John Gielgud's Richard; during this he was able to plan his first managerial venture, the Newark drama week, in his home town in 1934.

Wolfit's two seasons at Stratford in 1936 and 1937 brought him much critical acclaim. It was the first time he had been really stretched as an actor, playing good leading parts, and it made him even more determined to save enough money to go into management to tour the plays of Shakespeare. This he managed to do in 1937, and a nine-week tour followed the end of the Stratford season, with many of the actors who had been with him in the company. He added Shylock and Macbeth to Hamlet and Malvolio which he had already played, and at the end of the tour he was less than £100 out of pocket, which encouraged him enough to plan another for 1938. In January of that year he first appeared as Volpone—one of the parts which suited him best and which he relished playing. For the autumn tour he engaged Rosalinde Fuller as his leading lady, and added *Othello*,

Much Ado about Nothing, and *Romeo and Juliet*, playing all the plays 'in repertoire' so as to mix in the comedy with the dramatic fare. It was during these early seasons that the younger members of his company grew to recognize the effect the parts he was playing had on his backstage personality; full of laughter for Benedick and Touchstone, jokes were in order during the on-stage dances; but they must be a great deal more careful when *Othello* was played, and *Macbeth* night would see them scuttling out of the way of the wrath to come.

During the summer of 1939 Wolfit took a small permanent company to Dublin, and then asked various 'star' names, who were also friends, to go over for special weeks. After the great success of these plays, several in costume but no Shakespeare, he was again planning his autumn tour when war was declared, and although his leading lady, Rosalinde Fuller, was in America, and only after three separate attempts finally reached England, the tour opened in Brighton. On all sides he was told that Shakespeare in wartime, in the blackout, would spell disaster; he approached every theatre in London, until finally his first West End season opened at the Kingsway in 1940. Although fairly short and not a financial success, it did lead to his season of 'Scenes from Shakespeare' being done at the Strand during the lunch hour. It was during this run that all his scenery and costumes, which were in store, were bombed and completely destroyed. He had also joined the Home Guard at Frensham in early 1940 and managed to combine both activities. By 1941, against all the odds, he had formed a company and was on tour again, and for the first time many people who had never dreamt of going to the theatre, especially Shakespeare, were going and finding it exciting. In this year he added a very good Richard III, and returned to the Strand for the winter and spring. Now came his first attempt at King Lear, not yet exactly as he wanted it, but ever since his first season at Stratford (when he played Kent) he was determined to make it his own, and later in his career he called it 'the brightest jewel in my crown'. His season at the Scala theatre in 1944 brought high praise from the critics, not his habitual supporters, and especially from James Agate for his Lear, but it was forced to close prematurely as the 'doodlebug' attacks on London emptied the theatres. Undaunted, he returned to touring, which included a tour to Cairo and Alexandria, for ENSA, where they celebrated VE day.

Immediately after the war Wolfit embarked on his usual tour of the British Isles, and a season at the Winter Garden in London. His life as actor-manager covered more than twenty-five years. Now his leading lady was always Rosalind Iden. He was disappointed that there was no immediate reward for his war service 'Shakespeare for the masses'. He took a highly successful company to Canada in 1947, and followed it with a visit to New York. His postwar career was largely spent touring until, in 1951, he was invited by (Sir) Tyrone Guthrie to appear at the Old Vic in four spectacular leading parts. He opened the autumn season with Marlowe's *Tamburlaine the Great*, directed by Guthrie. It was a tremendous success, and the critics heaped his performance with praise. Sadly from all points of view this state of affairs did not last. During the four weeks he became impossible to act with, resorting to every tiresome trick on-stage, and even sending notes on their performances to his colleagues. After the Old Vic they paid a visit to Stratford, and here it was found necessary to send for Guthrie, unbeknown to Wolfit, for him to see what had happened to his production. He was appalled to see the travesty of what had been a magnificent *tour de force*, and spoke forcefully to his leading man. Soon after, Wolfit claimed breach of contract by the governors, and never returned to the Old Vic.

In 1953, coronation year, he presented an excellent series of classical plays at the King's, Hammersmith, with an unusually strong supporting cast; exceptionally well reviewed were his performances as Oedipus. He finished the year with a splendid Captain Hook in *Peter Pan*. For the next year he did little until he found a play, *The Strong are Lonely*, which suited him, and in 1955 was to be his last major production as actor-manager, in London. The last ten years of his life he really enjoyed away from the theatre and allowed himself, at last, to rest a little, without the urge to drive himself and all those round him, ever more on tour. His last appearance on the stage was as Mr Barrett in *Robert and Elizabeth*, with song, when he took over from (Sir) John Clements in 1966–7.

Wolfit never really enjoyed filming, although he gave some excellent performances towards the end of his career, notably in *Room at the Top*, *Becket*, and just before he died as Dr Fagan in *Decline and Fall*.

He was thrice married: first in 1928 to Chris Frances Castor; they had a daughter, Margaret Wolfit, the actress; secondly, in 1934 to Susan Katherine Anthony; they had a son and a daughter; finally in 1948 and for the rest of his life, to his leading lady of long standing, Rosalind Iden, daughter of Ben Iden Payne.

Wolfit was appointed CBE in 1950 and knighted in 1957, the only actor then living to have been twice honoured. He died in London 17 February 1968.

A portrait by Stanhope Forbes is privately owned; another, by Michael Noakes, hangs in the offices of the Royal General Theatrical Fund.

[Donald Wolfit, *First Interval*, 1954; Ronald Harwood, *Sir Donald Wolfit*, 1971.]

BRIAN MCIRVINE

published 1981

WOOLF (Adeline) Virginia

(1882–1941)

Novelist and critic, was born 25 January 1882 in Kensington, the second daughter of (Sir) Leslie Stephen and his second wife, Julia Prinsep, the widow of Herbert Duckworth. From early childhood, Virginia Stephen was distinguished by two characteristics which were to determine the course of her history: on the one hand a brilliant and imaginative creative intelligence, and on the other a nervous system of extreme fragility, which, under any severe intellectual or emotional strain, was liable to break down and throw her open to fits of suicidal manic depression. Too delicate for the rigours of regular school, she spent her childhood at her family's London house in Hyde Park Gate and country home at St Ives in Cornwall. Her father taught her, talked to her, and gave her the run of his library. By the time she grew up, she was already one of the most richly cultured minds of her day. Her mother died in 1895; after this, she was looked after by her elder half-sister Stella Duckworth. Her half-brother, George Duckworth, attempted to launch her, at the age of nineteen, and her sister Vanessa in formal London society. With small success: although too aesthetically sensitive not to find food for her imagination in the world of fashion, Virginia was at once too intellectual and too unconventional to feel at home there. Meanwhile she had started writing and was soon contributing to the *Times Literary Supplement*. Her father's death in 1904 was followed by her nervous breakdown. After this Virginia, together with her sister Vanessa and her brother Adrian, settled in Gordon Square where they collected round them a group of brilliant young men whom their elder brother Thoby had got to know at Cambridge; notably Roger Fry, J. M. (later Lord) Keynes, Lytton Strachey, Dr Edward Morgan Forster, Mr Leonard Woolf, and Mr Clive Bell. Thus was inaugurated the celebrated Bloomsbury circle, which stood for a point of view combining a rich and refined culture with declared opposition to the religious and moral standards of Victorian orthodoxy. Thoby's death in 1906 came as a blow which threatened Virginia Stephen's mental stability for four years. She continued, however, to live in Bloomsbury, first in Fitzroy Square, and after 1911 in Brunswick Square, devoting herself to the study and perfection of her art.

In 1912 she married Leonard Sidney Woolf with whom she lived partly in London and partly in Sussex. In 1914 she had another serious breakdown, and although after a year she recovered, for the rest of her life her husband saw to it that she lived very quietly. Her condition was never secure: for literary work and the society of her friends, the two things in which she found most satisfaction, were, if over-indulged in, both liable to upset it. Finishing a book, in particular, always left her exhausted. Leonard Woolf's devoted care, however, was successful in preserving her for many years. It was during this period that her chief work was done and her fame established. Of her novels, *Voyage Out* appeared in 1915, *Night and Day* in 1919. They were in a relatively traditional form. *Jacob's Room*, in which Virginia Woolf's characteristic manner first fully revealed itself, came out in 1922, *Mrs. Dalloway* in 1925, *To the Lighthouse* in 1927, *The Waves* in 1931, *The Years* in 1937. She also published two fantasies: *Orlando* (1928) and *Flush* (1933); two books of critical and biographical essays, *The Common Reader* (first series, 1925, second series, 1932); a biography of Roger Fry (1940), and two gracefully written feminist pamphlets, *A Room of One's Own* (1929) and *Three Guineas* (1938). She also took an active part in the management of the Hogarth Press which was founded by her and her husband in 1917. During these years she lived partly in London, in Tavistock Square, and partly at Rodmell in Sussex. In 1939 the Woolfs moved to Mecklenburgh Square where they remained until the bombing of 1940, after which they retired to Rodmell. There in 1941 Virginia Woolf's nervous system suffered its final collapse under the strain of the war, and she drowned herself, 28 March. The following books were published posthumously: *Between the Acts*, a novel (1941); and *A Haunted House*, short stories (1943); four volumes of essays, *The Death of the Moth* (1942), *The Moment* (1947), *The Captain's Death Bed* (1950), and *Granite and Rainbow* (1958); and extracts from her diary, *A Writer's Diary* (1953).

In spite of her disabilities, Virginia Woolf contrived to make a strong and influential personal impression on some of the most distinguished minds of her time. Her closest literary friends were her oldest, notably Dr Forster and Lytton Strachey; but she was also intimate with others, Lady Ottoline Morrell, Miss V. Sackville-West, and in later years Miss Elizabeth Bowen. She was shy in general society; and, even in congenial company, her personality could be formidable from its uncompromising fastidiousness. But it was also fascinating both for her ethereal beauty and for her conversation which combined fresh naturalness and an inexhaustible interest in other people with flights of whimsical fancy and a glinting satirical humour. As a writer she is in the first rank of English women. Her critical essays, at once so charming in form and so just and penetrating in judgement, are perhaps her securest achievement. But her most individual contribution to letters lies in her fiction. This shows the limitations of its author's personality: dramatic force and elemental human sentiment lie outside its scope. But it is distinguished by a subtle power to convey the processes of unspoken thought and feeling; by an extraordinary sensibility to the beautiful in nature and art; and by an original mastery of form that reveals itself alike in the intricate and musical design of her novels and in the shimmering felicities of her style. In Virginia Woolf the English aesthetic movement brought forth its most exquisite flower.

A small sketch in oil of Virginia Woolf by her sister, Vanessa Bell, is in the possession of the artist, who has also a small sketch in oil by Roger Fry, and a portrait and an ink drawing by Duncan Grant. The National Portrait Gallery has a chalk drawing by Francis Dodd and a lead bust by Stephen Tomlin. A portrait by J.-E. Blanche is believed to be in France.

[B. J. Kirkpatrick, *A Bibliography of Virginia Woolf*, 1957; personal knowledge.]

DAVID CECIL

published 1959

WOOLF Leonard Sidney

(1880–1969)

Author, publisher, and political worker, was born 25 November 1880 in Kensington, the second son of Sidney Woolf, QC, and his wife, Marie de Jongh, both members of the Reformed Synagogue. Sidney Woolf died in 1892, leaving a widow, nine children, and just enough money to enable the sons with the help of scholarships to receive a good education. Woolf was a scholar, first at St Paul's, then at Trinity College, Cambridge, where he obtained a first class in part i (1902) and a second in part ii (1903) of the classical tripos. He met and was much influenced by G. E. Moore; Lytton Strachey, Maynard (later Lord) Keynes, and Saxon Sydney-Turner were friends and contemporaries; all of them were Apostles.

Woolf entered the Colonial Service and was posted in 1904 to Ceylon where he very soon showed a capacity for intelligent industry. By 1908 he was assistant government agent in charge of the Hambantota district of the Southern Province and there can be no doubt that he might have risen high in the service. Returning to England on leave in 1911 he found the Cambridge circle of his youth very much extended and already becoming known as 'Bloomsbury'. It included Virginia, a daughter of Sir Leslie Stephen. In 1912 Woolf left the Colonial Service (concerning which he now had political doubts) in order to marry her. At the time of their marriage both Leonard and Virginia Woolf were writing novels. His, *The Village in the Jungle*, was published in 1913; it was followed by *The Wise Virgins* (1914). In 1913 Woolf became a socialist and joined the Fabian Society; he took a special interest in the Co-operative Movement; this led to some political journalism and later to *Co-operation and the Future of Industry* (1919) and *Socialism and Co-operation* (1921). Woolf's political and literary activities were hampered by his wife's precarious mental balance. She had a major breakdown in 1913–14 and again in 1915; in each case recovery was very slow. Until her death her husband did not cease carefully and constantly to act as her monitor and her physician.

Exempted, on medical grounds, from national service, Woolf turned during the war of 1914–18 to the study of international relations and of colonialism. His book *International Government* (1916) formed one of the bases for the British proposals for a League of Nations; in 1920 he published a devastating analysis of imperialist greed: *Empire and Commerce in Africa*. He was editor of the *International Review* in 1919 and of the international section of the *Contemporary Review* in 1920–1. In 1919 he became honorary secretary of the Labour Party's advisory committees on international and imperial affairs; in 1922 he stood unsuccessfully for Parliament as Labour candidate for the Combined Universities.

His wife's health kept Woolf away from London for long periods until 1924. From 1912 he lived at Asham House in Sussex, moving in 1919 to Monks House, Rodmell; but from 1915 until 1924, when they moved to Tavistock Square, they were able to take Hogarth House, Richmond. It was there that the Hogarth Press, beginning in 1917 as a hobby, became one of the most remarkable publishing houses of the time; E. M. Forster, T. S. Eliot, Katherine Mansfield, Freud, Gorki, Maynard Keynes, and the Woolfs themselves were amongst its authors. Woolf spared neither himself nor others in his efforts to make it a success; it became one of the main passions of his life.

Nevertheless he found time to become joint editor of the *Political Quarterly* (1931–59) and literary editor (1959–62). He was also (1923–30) literary editor of the *Nation* and served on the board after it amalgamated with the *New Statesman* in 1931. He wrote *Imperialism and Civilization* (1928), *The Intelligent Man's Way to Prevent War* (1933), *Quack, Quack!* (1935), *Barbarians at the Gate* (1939), and *The War for Peace* (1940). He also attempted a systematic statement of socialism as he understood it in *After the Deluge* (vol. i, 1931, vol. ii, 1939), but these volumes, although they were received with respect, did not excite enthusiasm and, after *Principia Politica* (1953), he made no further attempt to elaborate a complete political philosophy.

The war of 1939–45 was not only the shipwreck of Woolf's hopes for the establishment of international sanity, it also ended his long struggle to preserve his wife from harm; she drowned herself in 1941. He was, however, a man of remarkable physical and moral resilience. He continued to work for the Hogarth Press and for the Labour Party; greatly helped by the sympathy of devoted friends, he rebuilt his life and achieved an extremely happy old age. Living increasingly at Monks House he cultivated his garden and wrote five autobiographical volumes: *Sowing* (1960), *Growing* (1961), *Beginning Again* (1964), *Downhill all the Way* (1967), and *The Journey not the Arrival Matters* (1969). These volumes which, with *The Village in the Jungle*, are likely to prove the most enduring of his works, reveal a very attractive character: highly moral but humorous and tolerant, austerely sceptical but gently humane. Fair, but very forceful in argument he could be convincing when he addressed himself to the intellect rather than to the passions; he exerted considerable influence on others, notably Arthur Henderson, Lord Robert Cecil (Viscount Cecil of Chelwood) and Philip (later Lord) Noel-Baker. Politically he was prescient and acute in his judgements; but his impatience with stupidity or frivolity, together with a fierce honesty of character, made him an indifferent propagandist. He was a superb organizer and had an organizer's love of detail; he was happy to serve his party in ward meetings; he was clerk of his parish; he combined high generosity with scrupulous exactitude in money matters. He declined a CH but accepted an honorary doctorate from the university of Sussex in 1964. He died at Monks House 14 August 1969.

A portrait of Woolf by his sister-in-law, Vanessa Bell, hangs in the National Portrait Gallery, where there is also a bronze head by Charlotte Hewer. There is another portrait by Trekkie Ritchie (coll. the artist) and a bust by Charlotte Evans is at Monks House.

[Duncan Wilson, *Leonard Woolf: A Political Biography*, 1979; Woolf's own writings; Woolf archive, University of Sussex; private information; personal knowledge.]

QUENTIN BELL

published 1981

YOUNG George Malcolm

(1882–1959)

Scholar, was born at Charlton, Kent, 29 April 1882, the only son of George Frederick Young, waterman, later a steamer master, of Greenhithe, and his wife, Rosetta Jane Elizabeth Ross. A scholar of St Paul's, he became captain of the school. A scholar of Balliol, in the year (1900) in which William Temple was elected to an exhibition, Young gained a first in classical honour moderations (1902) and a second in *literae humaniores* (1904), having rowed in the second torpid. He was elected a fellow of All Souls in 1905 and became a tutor at St John's (1906–8). In 1908 he joined the Board of Education, then under the sway of Sir Robert Morant to whom he remained devoted. Young became a junior examiner in the universities branch; then, in 1911, the first secretary of what was to burgeon into the University Grants Committee. In 1916 he joined the newly formed Cabinet Office. Appointed CB in 1917, he was chosen as joint secretary of the new and shortlived Ministry of Reconstruction. He accompanied Arthur Henderson, then a member of the War Cabinet, as secretary on his notorious visit to Russia in 1917 where Young met (Sir) Francis Lindley at that time counsellor in the British Embassy. He went with Lindley to Archangel and later accompanied him to Vienna when Lindley went there as minister. In Vienna, Young was for a time a director of the newly founded Anglo-Austrian Bank: 'a curious anaemic-looking man' not mixing readily but already recognized by his younger British colleagues as 'a great scholar with a wide range of knowledge and a wonderful command of the English language'.

Abandoning the public service in the early post-war disillusion, Young decided to devote himself to writing, but nothing could remove that intense interest in education which shone throughout all his work. He was at heart a born teacher, thirsting to impart the results of his own sharp and constructive thoughts bred of a wide and deep reading in a formidable variety of subjects. Yet he was in no hurry. Although his essay on 'Victorian History' had caught discerning eyes in 1931, it was not until he was fifty that he published his first book, *Gibbon* (1932), a work of pietas but partly too of deliberation to impress upon the new biographers that neither Freud nor Marx had yet explained why there should be great men. And he was to note in Gibbon that 'sense of place' he was himself so compellingly to reveal. He made his home in Wiltshire where at the Old Oxyard at Oare near Marlborough he fell upon the antiquities of Wessex, not forgetting 'Pond Barrows', with far more knowledge and no less eagerness than did his favourite John Aubrey. He shared house with his lifelong friend Mona Wilson, authoress and sister of Sir Arnold Wilson; there she took charge of all those details of everyday life in which Young himself was oddly helpless and dependent. Surrounded in this neighbourhood by many cronies, including a bevy of ex-ambassadors, Young became, alongside Miss Wilson with her short fireside pipe, the centre of intellectual gossip and a dispenser of fascinating talk drawn from the resources of an astonishing memory. Urban in origin and urbane by disposition he was no less at home with countrymen and the railway workers of Swindon. He took pleasure in finding himself a Tory and 'no Tory of whatever rank or class ever thought of a merely moneyed man as his social equal'.

At the perceptive invitation of the Oxford University Press, no doubt at the instigation of (Sir) Humphrey Milford, he edited the two volumes of *Early Victorian England* which appeared in 1934 and to which he himself contributed that final summary chapter which brought his especial quality to the attention of a wider and delighted public, an essay which he developed into *Victorian England, Portrait of an Age* (1936) by which he will be remembered. What was important in history was, in his view, 'not what happened, but what people felt about it when it was happening'. Young had the industry, the learning, the memory, and above all, the penetration to disentangle the main themes from the confused Victorian clamour. His advice to the historian was 'to go on reading until you can hear people talking'. He did not point out that it might still require an interpreter of his talent, erudition, and perception—or with the gifts of his revered F. W. Maitland; and embedded in Young's writing was more food for thought than the common reader had been accustomed to encounter. Nor was his aim objective; even in narrative he would not forgo comment, with an epithet, an adverb, a tone of voice. His Clio was a muse with a sting.

After *Charles I and Cromwell* (1935), an essay in detection published before his developed Victorian masterpiece, came *Daylight and Champaign* (1937), a collection of essays and reviews many of them reprinted from the literary periodicals such as the *Sunday Times* to which Young was by now a valued contributor. There, and in other reprints, which included addresses such as his Romanes lecture on Gladstone in 1944, in his *Today and Yesterday* (1948) and in *Last Essays* (1950) he found elbow-room for good talk, addressed purposely to the middlebrow, about literature, persons, and manners. Unbuttoned, he might be colloquial, give full play to his humour, even show off a little since he was enjoying himself, yet literature remained a very serious matter for him, as were the duties of the clerisy and the continuity of civilization. He was deeply concerned with language as a means of communication; good speech he deemed 'the first political art'. A university he regarded as 'a place where young men and women educate one another by conversation, under the guidance of people a little older, and, more often than they might imagine, somewhat wiser than themselves'.

Young was a trustee of the National Portrait Gallery (from 1937) and of the British Museum (1947–57), a member of the Standing Commission on Museums and Galleries (from 1938), and of the Historical Manuscripts Commission (from 1948); all work lying very close to his being and, until his health began to fail, he gave it much attention and thought. His was a slight figure with a scholarly stoop; he had a longish, inquisitive nose, eyes twinkling well ahead of a coming quip, an unusual manner of clearing his throat, a voice warm and vibrant. He was a shy man and because sensitive, sometimes sharp: an intellectual who lived by his deep if hidden affections. Mona Wilson's death not long after the war, then the sale of the Oxyard were blows from which he never recovered, but he built himself a new existence on his re-election in 1948 to All Souls which provided him with a familiar and congenial refuge. He became a member of the royal commission on the press (1947–9) and he received honorary degrees from Durham (1950) and Cambridge (1953); and what he valued most, Balliol elected him to an honorary fellowship in 1953.

His last book, *Stanley Baldwin* (1952), had been undertaken reluctantly, at Baldwin's own request. As he grew closer to his subject Young was clearly somewhat taken aback by his discoveries and it is not a satisfying book; Young's touch had begun to fail him. In 1956 he published, in collaboration with W. D. Handcock, a volume of *English Historical Documents, 1833–74*, but Young's part in it, undertaken in 1947, was small. An invitation to lecture in Athens, which he had never visited, for a while renewed his flagging spirits, then a cloud descended on him and his death in a nursing-home near Oxford 18 November 1959 was a genuine release.

Young has been called a 'pantomath'; a comment not displeasing to him. If he was not quite that, it was well said of him that few writers have said so many good things upon so many subjects. He lived up to his own definition of the historian as 'one for whom the past keeps something of the familiar triviality of the present, and the present has already some of the shadowy magnificence of the past'. The National Portrait Gallery has a drawing by Henry Lamb.

[*The Times*, 19 and 24 November 1959; R. H. Bruce Lockhart, *Retreat from Glory*, 1934; W. D. Handcock, introduction to *Victorian Essays*, 1962; private information; personal knowledge.]

L. E. Jones
E. T. Williams

published 1971